A
SURVEY OF
THE OLD
TESTAMENT

A
SURVEY OF
THE OLD
TESTAMENT

ANDREW E. HILL
& JOHN H. WALTON

ZondervanPublishingHouse
Academic and Professional Books
Grand Rapids, Michigan

A Division of HarperCollinsPublishers

A SURVEY OF THE OLD TESTAMENT
Copyright © 1991 by Andrew E. Hill and John H. Walton

Requests for information should be addressed to:
Zondervan Publishing House
Academic and Professional Books
Grand Rapids, Michigan 49530

Edited by Leonard G. Goss and James E. Ruark

Library of Congress Cataloging in Publication Data

Hill, Andrew E.
    A survey of the Old Testament / Andrew E. Hill and John H. Walton.
        p. cm.
    Includes bibliographical references and index.
    ISBN 0-310-51600-5 (alk. paper)
1. Bible. O.T.—Introductions. I. Walton, John H., 1952–   . II. Title.
    BS1140.2.H54   1991
    221.6'1—dc20

90-45835
CIP

Printed in the United States of America

    92 93 94 95 96 97 / DH / 10 9 8 7 6 5 4

This edition is printed on acid-free paper and meets the American National Standards Institute Z39.48 standard.

CONTENTS

PART IV: THE POETIC BOOKS

PART V: THE PROPHETS

PART VI: EPILOGUE

MAPS AND ILLUSTRATIONS

The timelines are not listed.

ABBREVIATIONS

AB	*Anchor Bible* Commentary Series
ANET	*Ancient Near Eastern Texts*, 3d ed., ed. J. B. Pritchard (Princeton, 1969)
BA	*Biblical Archaeologist*
BAR	*Biblical Archaeological Review*
BASOR	*Bulletin of the American Schools of Oriental Research*
CAH³	*Cambridge Ancient History* Series, 3d ed. 12 vols., ed. I. E. Edwards et al. (Cambridge, 1981)
CBC	*Cambridge Bible Commentary*
CBQ	*Catholic Biblical Quarterly*
DSB–OT	*Daily Study Bible–Old Testament*
EBC	*Expositor's Bible Commentary*, ed. F. E. Gaebelein
ETSMS	*Evangelical Theological Society Monograph Series*
EvBC	*Everyman's Bible Commentary*
FOTL	*Forms of Old Testament Literature* Series
HER	*Hermeneia* Commentary Series
HSM	*Harvard Semitic Monograph* Series
HTR	*Harvard Theological Review*
ICC	*International Critical Commentary*
IDB	*Interpreter's Dictionary of the Bible*
ISBE	*International Standard Bible Encyclopedia*, rev. ed., ed. G. W. Bromiley
JANES	*Journal of the Ancient Near East Society*
JBL	*Journal of Biblical Literature*
JBLMS	*Journal of Biblical Literature Monograph Series*
JETS	*Journal of the Evangelical Theological Society*
JSOT	*Journal for the Study of the Old Testament*
JSOTSS	*Journal for the Study of the Old Testament Supplement Series*
NCBC	*New Century Bible Commentary*
NICOT	*New International Commentary on the Old Testament*
NIV	*New International Version*
NRSV	*New Revised Standard Version*
OTL	*Old Testament Library* Commentary Series
RB	*Révue Biblique*
SBL	*Society of Biblical Literature*
SBLDS	*Society of Biblical Literature Dissertation Series*
SBT	*Studies in Biblical Theology*
TB	*Tyndale Bulletin*
TIC	*Text and Interpretation Commentary* Series
TOTC	*Tyndale Old Testament Commentary*
VT	*Vetus Testamentum*
WBC	*Word Biblical Commentary*
WEC	*Wycliffe Exegetical Commentary*

PREFACE

Why study the Old Testament? This question has echoed down through the centuries of church history, ever since the New Covenant of Jesus Christ made the Old Covenant obsolete (Heb. 8:13). The apostle Paul faced the question, and he responded that the Old Testament was written for the *instruction and encouragement* of the Christian church (Rom. 15:4; 1 Cor. 10:10).

We have found the study of the Old Testament a truly exciting enterprise, and desire to help you enjoy that same exhilaration of discovery and benefit from divine instruction. In Amos 3:8 the prophet proclaims, "The Sovereign LORD has spoken—who can but prophesy?" Exposed to the revelation of God, Amos felt compelled to respond. Although none of us have the privilege Amos had, to function as God's mouthpiece, our response to God's revelation of himself should be no less compelling.

A proper understanding of the nature of the Old Testament helps us gain that fresh excitement and resolve our questions. In approaching the Old Testament as God's self-revelation, we seek to make the Word come alive. To achieve this we could not be content with literary "anatomy"—history of scholarship and summary of content—as important as that is. We have attempted to go beyond that and capture the living spirit that makes these books more than good literature.

Too often survey books fill their pages with summaries of what the Bible says. Unfortunately this leads many to read the survey instead of the Bible itself. This book is intended to be read *along with* the Bible and not *instead of* it. We have focused on what the Scriptures intend to communicate. *Why* does the Old Testament say what it says? *Why* does it include what it includes? *How* are genealogies and laws, for example, part of God's self-revelation? As we begin to address these questions we can become comfortable poring through previously obscure, difficult, or neglected portions of the Old Testament to discover their meaning and value.

Sometimes we may be surprised at what we find. We should also be encouraged when we occasionally meet the unexpected in Scripture—that is, when the Scriptures convince us of the truth of something that changes our minds or leads us down paths once hidden from view. If we acknowledge the authority of Scripture, we must be willing to submit to it by being open-minded about our opinions. God's Word is the final word.

The authority of God's Word is an essential ingredient to our study. We are committed to it and therefore believe that the content of God's Word is true. God has revealed himself in Scripture, and inspiration guarantees the authority and integrity of that revelation. These convictions define us as evangelicals. And as evangelicals we are heirs to a long legacy of biblical interpretation by those who were similarly committed to the authority of the Bible. In this we are blessed, and we hold in high esteem those who have preceded us. Nonetheless, we must not become confused about the object of our loyalty. In the end, our commitment is to God's Word, not to the traditional interpretations of it by those who have blazed the trail we follow. We must always be ready to to reevaluate our interpretations to ensure that we are attending to the Word rather than being inextricably bound to tradition.

It has been our goal to be objective and to stand by the biblical evidence. At times this has led us to take a more relaxed position on certain issues than our tradition would indicate. In the process of attempting to present some of the directions and insights that have broadened the horizons of interpretation in recent years, we have tried to exercise caution and discretion. A survey cannot offer the documentation or plumb the depths of the evidence that would normally accompany such discussion. Moreover, we have avoided polemical terminology and argumentation. This book is not intended to argue against anyone or defend anything. We simply want to help people understand the message and relevance of the Old Testament and, consequently, to experience the excitement of knowing God.

In its structure and format this textbook is intended to complement *A Survey of the New Testament* by Robert H. Gundry, which was published in a revised edition by Zondervan Publishing House in 1981. Following Gundry's lead, we seek to bring together the most significant data from Old Testament historical and literary backgrounds, critical or technical introduction, biblical commentary, and Old Testament theology. The text offers a 'synthetic' presentation for all of the Hebrew Bible in the order of the English canon. Each book of the Old Testament is treated according to a basic pattern, as follows:

> The Writing of the Book
> The Background
> Outline of the Book
> Purpose and Message
> Structure and Organization
> Major Themes
> Questions for Further Study and Discussion
> For Further Reading

Each chapter draws attention to the way in which the literary structure and organization of a given book contribute to the achievement of the biblical writer's message and purpose. An examination of the key theological themes contained in each book brings perspective to its relationship to the Old Testament as a complete collection of books. In addition, because the Old

Covenant finds its fulfillment in the New, pertinent theological relationships between the Old and New Testaments receive attention in regard to subjects such as the covenant, the presence of God, and Messiah.

Further, this survey introduces the reader to a wide range of topics in Old Testament studies, including hermeneutics (general and special), history (Israelite and ancient Near Eastern), archaeology, canon, geography, Old Testament theology (biblical and systematic), and basic methodologies of higher criticism.

It is our sincere desire that this textbook will prove to be a readable and useful tool, providing basic but thorough coverage of Old Testament survey and challenging the reader to a serious investigation and personal appropriation of God's truth as revealed in the Old Testament. Above all, we hope this text will bring a new vigor and excitement to the study of the Old Testament as readers learn to discover its story for themselves, understand it, and apply it to their lives, reclaiming it as a substantial part of God's revelation of himself to us. Like the psalmist, may we who study the great works of the Lord in the Old Testament truly learn to delight in them (Ps. 111:2).

ACKNOWLEDGMENTS

The publication of this textbook affords me the happy opportunity to credit some of those people who have contributed to the successful completion of the writing project.

I remain indebted to those former teachers whose example both nurtured biblical faith and encouraged scholarly achievement. A special *tōdâ* to Dr. Richard D. Patterson (now Chairman, Department of Biblical Studies, Liberty Baptist Theological Seminary), whose passion for the Hebrew Bible first piqued my own interests in ancient Near Eastern and Old Testament studies back in 1977.

Also, my students have both inspired and shaped this work more than they realize. First, their challenging questions continue to keep my personal studies fresh, while my participation in their joy of discovering the relevance of the Old Testament for life in the contemporary church keeps me enthusiastic about the teaching-learning process. Second, as ruthless critics of a series of Old Testament survey texts I have sampled at their expense—they know what works and what does not! This addition (or edition?) to the "no end of making books" is certainly the better for their input as "textbook consumers." Finally, student research assistants have provided secretarial, bibliographic, and other helps over the past several years and deserve mention—Thomas Cavanaugh, Dennis Fisher, Stephen Getchy, Carol Riebock, Erik Widholm, and Daniel Olson.

I am most grateful to Dr. Stan Gundry, General Manager of Zondervan Publishing House, and Len Goss, Imprint Editor for Zondervan's Academie Books, for the unexpected and unsolicited invitation to participate in the project. Obviously my years of decrying the woeful inadequacies of Old Testament survey textbooks have come full circle! Editors Goss and Jim Ruark are to be commended for melding the disparate writing styles of the co-authors into uniform and highly readable prose. They have succeeded admirably in turning the liability typical of jointly authored books into one of the text's key assets.

To my co-author, colleague, and friend, John Walton, I extend my apologies for having a surname that precedes "W" in the English alphabet. Seriously, I applaud his energy, insight, diligence, and expertise in masterminding and coordinating each phase of our mutual effort. I have benefited both personally and professionally from the experience of our joint enterprise.

Finally, a word of appreciation to my loving wife, Terri, and the three J's in our lives—Jennifer, Jesse, and Jordan—who endured the "backside" of the professor hypnotized by the VDT of his PC without complaint during the fourteen months the manuscript was in process. Psalm 13:5–6!

ANDREW E. HILL

There are many people to thank for a project such as this. The staff at Zondervan, particularly Len Goss and Jim Ruark, have had an immeasurable impact on the shape and quality of the book with their sensitive and discerning editorial work.

The audio-visual department at Moody Bible Institute has aided in the design and production of some of the charts.

My family has exercised patience throughout the process. To my wife, Kim, who read most of the manuscript, and to my own three J's—Jonathan, Joshua, and Jill—I owe a debt of gratitude.

Finally, this book is for students, but it could never have come about without the stimulating input of my students over the years. Many of the ideas that make this book unique are the product of the classroom "laboratory." I therefore want to thank the many students who have challenged me, have asked hard questions, have offered their thoughts and ideas, and have motivated me to communicate in more effective ways.

JOHN H. WALTON

The authors and publishers acknowledge with gratitude those who have provided the charts, maps, and photographs. The sources for charts and photographs are identified where these items appear.

The maps and the timelines are provided by Carta, Jerusalem, which also assisted in the collection of the photographs. Appreciation is expressed to Ms. Barbara Ball of Carta for her diligent attention to details. The timelines and some maps were originally published in the *Zondervan NIV Atlas of the Bible* (1989), of which Carl G. Rasmussen is the author.

PART I

PROLOGUE

Chapter 1

Approaching the Old Testament

Studying the Old Testament is a monumental task, but proper preparation can help the student to reap a rich harvest. The sovereign God who created the universe, who controls history, and who will accomplish his plan in his time has chosen to speak. That in itself is an act of grace, and it behooves us to listen. However, listening may be hindered by many complicating factors. First, God's revelation did not come in the English language or through Western culture. As a result we may have to work harder to receive the message clearly. The more familiar students can become with ancient Near Eastern culture, particularly that of Israel, during the Old Testament period, the more barriers they can eliminate.

A second complicating factor is that even when we are listening, we have a tendency either to be selective about what we hear or to try to make the message conform to what we want to hear. The solution to this is to allow the Bible to speak for itself. We all have presuppositions about the Bible. These need to be constantly evaluated and refined lest they distort the teaching of the Bible. The objectives of the biblical authors must not be subordinated to our own objectives, however worthy the latter may be. There are many valuable things to be learned from the Old Testament, but not all are things that the Old Testament is trying to teach. If students desire to reap authoritative teaching from the text, they must learn to discern what the text is teaching rather than superimposing their own ideas on it. When the Bible is allowed to speak from its own vantage point and with its own agenda, the reader can be more open to learn what it is intending to teach.

Self-Revelation

As God's self-revelation the objective of the Old Testament is that the reader comes to know God better. This process, however, is not intended to be merely cognitive. Instead, knowing God is accomplished by experiencing his attributes. Being able to list God's attributes is insignificant. What must be achieved is that his attributes become the framework of our worldview. By this we mean that our perspective on ourselves, our society, our world, our history, our conduct, our decisions—everything—should be knit together by an informed and integrated view of God. The Old Testament's objective is not transformed lives, though knowing God should transform one's life. The Old Testament's objective is not the adoption of a value system, though a value system would certainly be one outcome of knowing God in a real way. The Old Testament is not a repository of historical role models, dusty hymns, and obscure prophetic sayings, but God's invitation to hear his story.

This story of God begins with creation. The emphasis, however, is not on how the world began, but on how the plan began. Everything was just right for the execution of God's plan. In that sense, creation is simply the introduction to history. God's sovereignty is initially vouchsafed by the fact that he created. While this cannot help but deny any sovereignty to other deities, its intention is not to provide polemic against the pagan polytheism of the day. Rather than taking a negative approach that denounces and refutes other deities, the Old Testament takes the positive approach of telling what the one true God is like and what he has done.

As history begins, it will be observed that the Old Testament is concerned with political or social aspects of history only in a secondary way. The primary interest of this history is how God has revealed himself to people in the past. One reflection of this can be found in the names of God that permeate the pages of Scripture. These names portray him as a God who is holy, almighty, most high, and the one who has caused everything to be. Yet he is also a God who hears, sees, and provides. The habitual rebellion and feeblemindedness of mankind shows him by contrast a God of patience and grace.

Just as creation flows into history, so history flows into prophecy. God's plan was initiated in the beginning, was worked out through history, and will continue until all is accomplished. By seeing God's plan worked out in the past (the Pentateuch and the historical books) and projected into the future (prophetic literature), we can begin to appreciate the unfathomable wisdom of God, who is worthy of praise and worship (Psalms and wisdom literature). The Old Testament, then, should be viewed as a presentation of God's attributes in action. We can know who God is and what he is like by hearing what he has done and intends to do. Once we know who he is and what he is like, the appropriate responses are worship, commitment, and service.

The Covenant

At the core of this self-revelation, delineating the plan of God, is the covenant. Even the English designation "Old Testament" indicates that the covenant is the core concept of this collection of books (testament = covenant). Through the covenant God both reveals what he is like and obliges himself to a particular course of action. His loyalty (ḥesed) to the covenant frequently leads him to acts of grace and mercy, but justice is also built into the covenant to ensure accountability by his people.

Since the covenant is the instrument used by God to effect self-revelation, the Old Testament often appears to be the history of the covenant, or of aspects of it, more than a history of Israel. So Genesis 12–50 is a history of the establishment of the Abrahamic covenant. Exodus–Deuteronomy is a history of the establishment of the covenant at Sinai. Joshua is a record of God's faithfulness to the covenant, while Judges is a record of Israel's unfaithfulness to the covenant. The books of Samuel and Kings are a history of the covenant of kingship (the Davidic covenant). It is the covenant as God's plan that is more in focus than the people who are involved generation after generation.

Several different approaches to the Old Testament are distinguished from one another by the way each understands the covenant idea and the relationship of the covenants to one another. Are there many different covenants that independently govern periods of history, or are there just one or two governing covenants that have other sub-covenants to offer expansion and explanation? Is there a single unconditional covenant that comprises component conditional covenants, or is the whole a conditional covenant?

These are the questions that, answered different ways by different scholars, define the theological controversies about the Old Testament, its relationship to the New Testament, and its relevance to us today. The answers given to these questions, however, do not alter the picture of God that the covenant offers. Only the shape of theology is at stake in this issue, not the nature of God as he is revealed in the Old Testament. Even if one is inclined to draw distinct, separating lines between the covenants, the organic unity of the covenants must not be overlooked.

It is this latter characteristic that helps us to see the plan of God as a consistent, unified entity. In this view, the covenant with Abraham established Israel as the "revelatory" people of God—the people through whom he would reveal himself to the world. The law that is given on Sinai is a major part of the revelation that the covenant was established to provide. At the same time, Leviticus, Deuteronomy, and Joshua contain covenant renewals that reinforce the agreement. The Davidic covenant brings to fulfillment some of the initial promises of God to Abraham (e.g., that kings would come from him) and at the same time expands the agreement to include a dynastic line. The prophets speak of future covenants (cf. Isa. 61:8; Jer. 31:31–34; Ezek. 16:60–63; 34:25–30; 37:19–28; Hos. 2:18–20), and these generally relate to the eventual fulfillment of aspects of the previous covenants that had been unrealized because of the failures of the Israelites.

Each covenant will be discussed more fully in the appropriate places in this survey. At this point it is important for us to recognize the centrality and the organic unity of the covenants in the Old Testament as they relate to God's plan and his self-revelation.

Authority

While it is not improper to study the Bible from a literary perspective and to appreciate it as great literature, we cannot stop there. If the Bible is to be recognized as God's self-revelation, then it must be viewed as representing more than the opinion of godly people. In other words, if God is not understood to be the source of the Old Testament, it cannot serve as a *self*-revelation. If God is the source of the Old Testament, then it can be understood as possessing authority. We study Scripture because we expect to get an authoritative word from God, not the subjective opinions of people, however valuable or true the latter may be. Authority is what makes the Old Testament more than just fine literature. The New Testament therefore refers to the Old Testament as being God-breathed, or "inspired." Inspiration is that quality that designates the source as God and guarantees that the resulting written product has authority (2 Tim. 3:16).

It stands to reason, then, that if we look to the Bible for authoritative revelation from God, the authority must be vested in what it intends to communicate, not in what the reader wants to hear. This is another way in which the Bible is different from other literature. When we read a novel or a poem, the power of the literature can be measured by its ability to evoke a response from the reader and blend that together with the ideas of the writer to create and recreate new "meanings" each time it is read. In this way a poem could mean one thing to one reader and strike an entirely different chord in another reader. Although this dynamic can be an outcome of the application process in reading the Old Testament (see below), the fact that the written word has authority while the reader's response does not should warn against intermingling them. The result is that we cannot be content learning our own lessons from Scripture, as valuable as they may be. We must strive to discover what the author intends to communicate, for that is where authority is vested.

What are the implications of the authority that the text possesses? First is that we accept what it says as truth. If God never made a covenant with Abraham or never spoke to Moses on Sinai; if the conquest is just an imaginary polemic for Israel to defend its territorial expansionism; if the Davidic covenant is nothing more than a political ploy by the Davidites to proclaim divine justification for their dynasty, then it is not God's self-revelation, but simple propaganda and has no relevance to us at all. If there is any sense in which this is God's word, it must be taken as truthful.

A second implication is that we need to respond. If the Bible is truly God's authoritative self-revelation, we cannot afford to ignore or neglect him. He expects not only worship, but obedience, justice, loyalty, faithfulness, holiness, righteousness, and love. In short, he wants us to be like him—that is one of the reasons he reveals what he is like.

How to Study the Old Testament

If we are to respond to the Old Testament, we must know how to interpret it so we know how to respond. Much of the spiritual truth of the Old Testament is evident even through a superficial reading of the text. In-depth study can yield even greater results, but is accompanied by greater difficulties as well. Various principles and methodologies that serve as guides for exegesis and interpretation can only be introduced here, but may provide an introduction for the student.

Aspects of Bible Interpretation

One of the main principles of biblical interpretation has already been mentioned: the Bible must be allowed to speak for itself. This is difficult to attain because every interpreter has presuppositions, that is, preformed ideas about what the Bible is, what it says, and how it fits together. These presuppositions can shape the interpretation of the text and can slant or distort the interpretation. Presuppositions are often subconscious. When they are not subconscious, they are sometimes considered nonnegotiable. Proper interpretation does not require readers to throw away all presuppositions, but insists that readers recognize what presuppositions they hold, constantly reevaluate them for validity, and subordinate them to the text.

The object of this principle is to prevent interpreters from manipulating the text to suit their own agendas. If the text is to speak with authority, it must enjoy a certain amount of autonomy from the interpreter.

In literary circles today there continues to be much discussion about the focus of the interpreter's attention. Traditionally the author and his background and intention (either explicit or inferred) had served as the key to interpretation. More recently literary critics have concluded that the impossibility of achieving any confident identification of what the author intended demands that meaning is the result of the impact of the text (an entity isolated from and independent of its author) on the individual reader. As we have said, however, if the Bible is to be considered uniquely authoritative, it cannot always be treated as just another piece of literature. If the biblical text is accepted as authoritative, the intention of the author (human and divine) must remain the focus of the interpreter's attention. One result of this commitment is that the interpreter should not be searching for hidden meanings or mystical symbolism. Another is that the author's message ought not to be ignored or neglected in favor of how the interpreter wants to use the text (a common practice in Bible study groups and sermons).

Procedures of Interpretation

But how do we try to determine the intention of the author? First, the genre of the literature must be determined. In our contemporary literature, biography will be read differently from mystery, and drama differently from limerick. The type of literature affects how that writing will be approached and interpreted. This applies equally to the Old Testament. Prophecy is a different genre from proverbial literature. To begin with, then, the interpreter must identify the genre of what he or she is trying to interpret and discover as much as possible about that genre. This latter endeavor is approached through a wide variety of critical methodologies, which we will survey below.

Second, it is important to discover all we can about the audience for whom the writing was intended and the circumstances under which it was written. These facts may affect the way certain statements are to be understood.

Third, through an examination of the context, we should try to identify the purpose of the author or editor. This purpose may be addressed explicitly, or it may need to be deduced from observations concerning the author's selection and arrangement of the material.

As interpreters, if we can understand the author, the audience, the situation, and the literary genre as well as possible, we are in a good position to put ourselves in the audience and understand the words and, more important, the message of the section that is being interpreted. Interpretation requires us to become, to the best of our abilities, part of the original audience. The message to them is the same as the message to us.

Approaches to the Bible
(Critical Methodologies)

Most of the critical methodologies have been developed to try to address the question, How should we approach the various literary genres that we find in the Bible? Was each book written at one sitting, or was there a longer process of composition? Could there have been previous editions of some of the books that have gone through stages of editing to reach the form in which we now have them? Do some of the books incorporate texts of one genre into the context of another genre? All these questions are part of an attempt to understand the literary mechanisms as much as possible so that interpretation may proceed.

For much of the twentieth century, biblical scholarship was divided into camps labeled "liberal" and "conservative." While these terms broadly distinguish those who acknowledge less authority in the Bible (liberals) from those who held a more traditional view of biblical authority (conservatives), the absence of a generally recognized benchmark resulted in the use of "liberal" to designate anyone more open-minded than the person applying the label, while "conservative" might be applied to those considered anti-intellectual fanatics. These labels were therefore often used perjoratively to ridicule, caricature, or in other ways depreciate the perspective of the other's position. Recent years have witnessed some relaxation of the tensions and some cross-fertilization of ideas and methods without reducing the ideological chasm that separates the camps.

In this survey, reference will occasionally be made to "critical scholarship." This is neither a derogatory term nor a value judgment. It is a descriptive label that is generally brandished proudly by those to whom it is applied. "Criticism" here refers to the exercise of an expert sense of judgment about the text and should not be confused with "criticism" in the sense of making negative statements. Relative to the old terminology, it must be pointed out that "conservatives" and "liberals" alike use critical methodologies. Their respective presuppositions about the text, however, dictate to what extent and in what ways the various

7

critical methodologies can be used. Contemporary evangelical scholars make extensive use of critical methodologies, but that use can be somewhat restricted by presuppositions about the nature and authority of Scripture.[1] The presuppositions of nonevangelical scholars leave them unfettered by such concerns and often promote, if not demand, dismissal of supernaturalistic claims and reconstruction of biblical history and the text of the Old Testament. When we contrast "critical scholarship" and "evangelical scholarship" therefore, it is not to suggest that evangelical scholarship is uncritical or "pre-critical" in its approach to the Old Testament. Rather, it is a recognition that some scholars use critical methodologies more than others, depending on the nature of their presuppositions.

Some critical methodologies attempt to reconstruct the ways and means by which the text came to be in its present form. These are referred to as "diachronic," for they explore the history of the text and look for meaning in previous forms and settings of portions of the text. Other methodologies recognize that there may well be a history of the text, but seek meaning in the form that the text currently possesses. These approaches view the text as self-sufficient, requiring no outside information for interpretation, and are referred to as "synchronic." Other terminology labels diachronic approaches as "historical-critical" and synchronic approaches as "literary."

Textual Criticism. The aim of textual criticism is to identify errors that may have occurred in the process of copying and recopying the text by hand through the centuries. On one level, textual criticism is necessary when a given manuscript preserves one reading while another manuscript is slightly different. Frequently in Old Testament study, however, suspected transmission (copying)

errors are identified and corrections suggested even when none of the manuscripts contains variant readings. This can be justifiable if the text makes little sense as it stands and a defensible alternative is available. The dearth of Old Testament manuscripts makes this situation much more common than in New Testament textual criticism.

Another feature adding to the complexity is that in the Old Testament, textual criticism often takes place on the basis of Septuagint readings. Because the Septuagint is a Greek translation of the Old Testament that originated no earlier than the third century B.C., it is often difficult to judge whether the variant readings it offers represent an actual alternative in the Hebrew text or just an error on the part of the Greek translators or copyists. The goal of the text critic is to restore the text to its original canonical form.

Source Criticism. No one doubts that sources were used in the compilation of some books of the Old Testament. Chronicles and Kings both name sources that were available to them and from which they drew information. For some two hundred years now, a growing consensus among scholars assumes that many more of the books of the Old Testament were compiled from written or at times oral sources.

Source criticism seeks to identify which sections of a given book belong to each of their hypothetical sources and then to analyze each source. Generally sections are assigned to different sources on the basis of perceived differences in style among parts of the book. Another criterion sometimes is a presupposed theory of theological development. For instance, many source critics would assume that the idea of a centralized place of worship was a relatively late development (perhaps not until the time of Josiah). Other "late" developments would

---

[1]"Evangelical" is a term in vogue to describe those who acknowledge the authority of the Bible. While it is a bit more precise than "conservative," it can represent a range of beliefs.

include several of the festivals, the Aaronic priesthood, monotheism, and the future restoration of Israel.

As a result, any passage from an earlier book that shows concern or understanding about these matters would be assigned to a later source that may have made additions to the earlier work. These hypothetical sources are then analyzed for their style, interests, and theological parameters. This approach tends to fragment the text and has been criticized for being too vulnerable to circular reasoning. The speculative nature of its results has made it less popular in recent years to attach any certainty to its findings, but many persist in believing that most of the books of the Old Testament have resulted from the editing together of various sources, or at least show evidence of additions at the hands of sources other than the writer.

Form Criticism. Form criticism is not so concerned with working with the literary sources that may be behind a certain book as it is with identifying the oral history of the various parts of the text. The assumption is that many sections of any book had functions in society in their oral form that differ from how they are used in their present context. So, for instance, a number of Psalms are sometimes identified as having been used for an annual "enthronement festival" in Israel. In labelling patriarchal narratives "sagas" or the narratives of Joshua "etiologies," form critics exercise great influence on interpretation, for with these identifications comes the implication that these narratives are of less historical value. As with source criticism, the difficulties lie in the speculative nature of the results and the neglect of the final form of the text.

Redaction Criticism. The redaction approach attempts to identify the logic and motivations of the author or, more often, the redactor (editor) who brought the sources together to produce the final form of the text. To a large extent the redaction critic works with the sources identified by the source critic, so this remains a diachronic approach, though it can be seen as providing a transition between diachronic and synchronic approaches. To put this another way, redaction criticism does treat the final form of the text, but it does so by examining how the redactor has reworked, reinterpreted, or in any way reshaped the sources to achieve his purposes.

The success of this method depends on the soundness of the source work and the strength of the evidence for the redactor's role and purpose.

Historical Criticism. The goal of historical criticism is to reconstruct the events that lie behind the biblical narratives. Since the narratives are usually produced with a theological motive or agenda, they may not clearly or completely present the details of the actual event. At other times scholars suspect the narrative of skewing the material, so they offer more substantial reconstructions. Historical critics may therefore offer reconstructions of what "really" happened in the plagues on Egypt or in the crossing of the Reed Sea. Anywhere God's supernatural intervention is portrayed can be subjected to an attempt to offer natural explanations. Likewise, there are sections of the historical literature that some would consider propagandistic or legendary (e.g., David fighting Goliath, the exploits of Samson). The historical critic would seek to identify a "historical kernel" in the account around which the "actual" event might be reconstructed.

There is very little objection to using historical criticism to fill in the gaps of what the Bible leaves unsaid about certain events. There is considerably more skepticism about using historical criticism to discard or discount some of the details given in the text in favor of the critic's reconstructions.

Rhetorical Criticism. In an effort to be more holistic in its approach, rhetorical criticism assumes the unity of form and content. It is interested in discovering how the form of the literature aids the content in communicating the intended message. Literary structures such as chiasmus (a parallel pattern of words, lines, ideas, paragraphs, or rhyming scheme) and inclusio (beginning and ending a section with similar or identical lines) are identified, and even basic distinctions between poetry and prose become significant. Any feature that contributes to the literary art of the author is noted and analyzed. So, for instance, the inclusio in Ecclesiastes (1:2 and 12:8) can be used to identify the major premise of the author and to conclude that 12:9–14 are in some way extraneous to the major part of the book.

Structural Analysis. From a technical standpoint, structural analysis should be defined in relation to a philosophy of linguistics that has been expanded into the field of literary interpretation. In Old Testament studies, however, it has taken on a broader meaning and has come to refer to almost any method that is synchronic in its approach. This type of analysis focuses solely on the literary character and features of the text to derive their meaning. Thus plot, character development, use of motifs, vocabulary, syntax, and other literary elements are explored in depth to the exclusion of historical or archaeological background or the history of the literature.

The Canonical Approach. In the canonical method, prehistory (sources, traditions, previous forms, redactions, etc.) of the text is ignored in favor of understanding the meaning of the final form (canonical form) of the text to the community of faith under whose aegis it took shape. This is a diachronic approach that takes the development of the final canonical form as the starting point for its analysis. It is interested in the history of the text as a composite whole, a piece of Scripture. Furthermore, the canon as a whole can be viewed as a context rather than portions of books or the books themselves being the context.

Application of the Old Testament

When presuppositions have been evaluated and set and methodologies pursued that are consistent with those presuppositions, the goal (to interpret the meaning of the passage) is in sight, but not yet achieved. Interpretation is sterile without application. In application we must not simply ask, "What can I learn?" Application cannot be just an aggregate of impressions gained from reading the text. In reading Joshua 1, for example, we might say that we learned to be more courageous. But that is not what we are looking for in application. More specifically, we must ask, "What can I learn from what the text is teaching?" so that application can be tied effectively to interpretation. If the interpretation identifies the audience as corporate Israel, the promises made may not be applicable to us as individuals, even though they still teach us about God. If the Old Testament is viewed as God's self-revelation, we will expect in most instances to learn first something about God. From that we will then find out what implications that holds for our view of self, others, or the world around us. In this way the message must seep through to our values, conduct, and worldview and affect our decisions and the attitudes we maintain.

If we feed ourselves only on proof texts, role models, types, and "thoughts for the day," we restrict our ability to know God, for only proper interpretation will bring us the full benefit of God's self-revelation. If God has truly spoken, it is incumbent on us as his creatures to get so absorbed in his Word that it becomes second nature to us. It can convict us, challenge us, and confront us as long as we discharge our responsibility to study the Scriptures conscientiously.

Questions for Further Study and Discussion

1. What are some presuppositions commonly held about the Old Testament or about particular books in it? How do such presuppositions affect the critical methodologies?
2. What are some important elements of a "biblical" worldview?
3. What does the Old Testament reveal about God's plan that continues to have relevance today?
4. What are the respective advantages and disadvantages of the synchronic and diachronic approaches?
5. Compare the concepts of inspired editor and inspired author.
6. Discuss the various literary genres of the Old Testament in relation to the proposition that the goal of biblical interpretation is the intended meaning of the author as expressed in the text.
7. If focusing on short, isolated passages of the Old Testament can produce a distorted interpretation, what steps are necessary to safeguard a sound exposition of the text?

For Further Reading

Armerding, Carl E. *The Old Testament and Criticism.* Grand Rapids: Eerdmans, 1983.

Barton, John. *Reading the Old Testament.* Philadelphia: Westminster, 1984.

Carson, D. A., and John Woodbridge. *Hermeneutics, Authority and Canon.* Grand Rapids: Zondervan, 1986.

Conyers, A. J. *How to Read the Bible.* Downers Grove, Ill.: InterVarsity, 1986.

Fee, Gordon, and Douglas Stuart. *How to Read the Bible for All Its Worth.* Grand Rapids: Zondervan, 1982. A helpful discussion of how each literary genre in the Bible ought to be read and interpreted.

Goldingay, John. *Approaches to Old Testament Interpretation.* Downers Grove, Ill.: InterVarsity, 1981.

———. *Theological Diversity and the Authority of the Old Testament.* Grand Rapids: Eerdmans, 1987.

Greidanus, Sidney. *The Modern Preacher and the Ancient Text.* Grand Rapids: Eerdmans, 1988. An excellent treatment of how to incorporate the results of hermeneutically sound exegesis into good sermons.

Hayes, John, and Carl Holladay. *Biblical Exegesis.* Atlanta: John Knox, 1982.

Longman, Tremper, III. *Literary Approaches to Biblical Interpretation.* Grand Rapids: Zondervan, 1987.

McQuilkin, J. Robertson. *Understanding and Applying the Bible.* Chicago: Moody Press, 1983.

Rogerson, John. *Beginning Old Testament Study.* Philadelphia: Westminster, 1982.

Stuart, Douglas. *Old Testament Exegesis.* Philadelphia: Westminster, 1980.

Chapter 2

The Formation of
the Old Testament Scriptures

The Old Testament was composed over a thousand-year period roughly spanning the mid-second to the mid-first millennium B.C. While the New Testament understands God to be the Author of the Old Testament by inspiration of the Holy Spirit (2 Tim. 3:16), at least forty different writers have been identified as human authors. The text of the Old Testament was originally recorded in two languages, classical or biblical Hebrew and imperial Aramaic (Gen. 31:47; Jer. 10:11; Ezra 4:8–6:18; 7:12–26 only). Among the ancient scribes are such well-known biblical personalities as Moses, David, and Solomon. Lesser-known authors include Hebrew women such as Deborah (cf. Judg. 5:1) and Miriam (cf. Exod. 15:20–21) and non-Hebrews such as Agur and Lemuel (cf. Prov. 30:1; 31:1). The Old Testament contains four basic literary genres, or types, including law, historical narrative, poetry, and prophetic utterance.

Text and Transmission

Writing in the Ancient Near East

The earliest systems of human writing predate 3000 B.C. and are attested both in ancient Egypt and in Mesopotamia. The initial stage in the development of writing was the pictogram, in which pictures represented the equivalent material objects (fig. 2.1). Eventually pictograms evolved into ideograms, in which the picture symbols represented ideas also. Over time, the pictograms and ideograms became more abstract (a type of shorthand) and signified both words (logograms) and syllables. The final stage of writing was the shift from the syllabic writing systems to the alphabetic script, in which the characters represent a single letter of the alphabetic writing system.

The Hebrew language of the Old Testament is an alphabetic writing system and is classified as a Northwest Semitic language in contrast to the syllabic writing systems of Assyria and Babylonia in Mesopotamia (fig. 2.2). Hebrew and Phoenician, Moabite, Ammonite, Edomite, and Ugaritic were all alphabetic dialects derived from a common proto-Semitic alphabetic language system (cf. Isa. 19:18, where the prophet identifies the Hebrew language as a Canaanite dialect).

Writing Materials

Various materials were used as writing surfaces by the peoples of the ancient

12

Figure 2.1. Pictograms in Early Civilizations

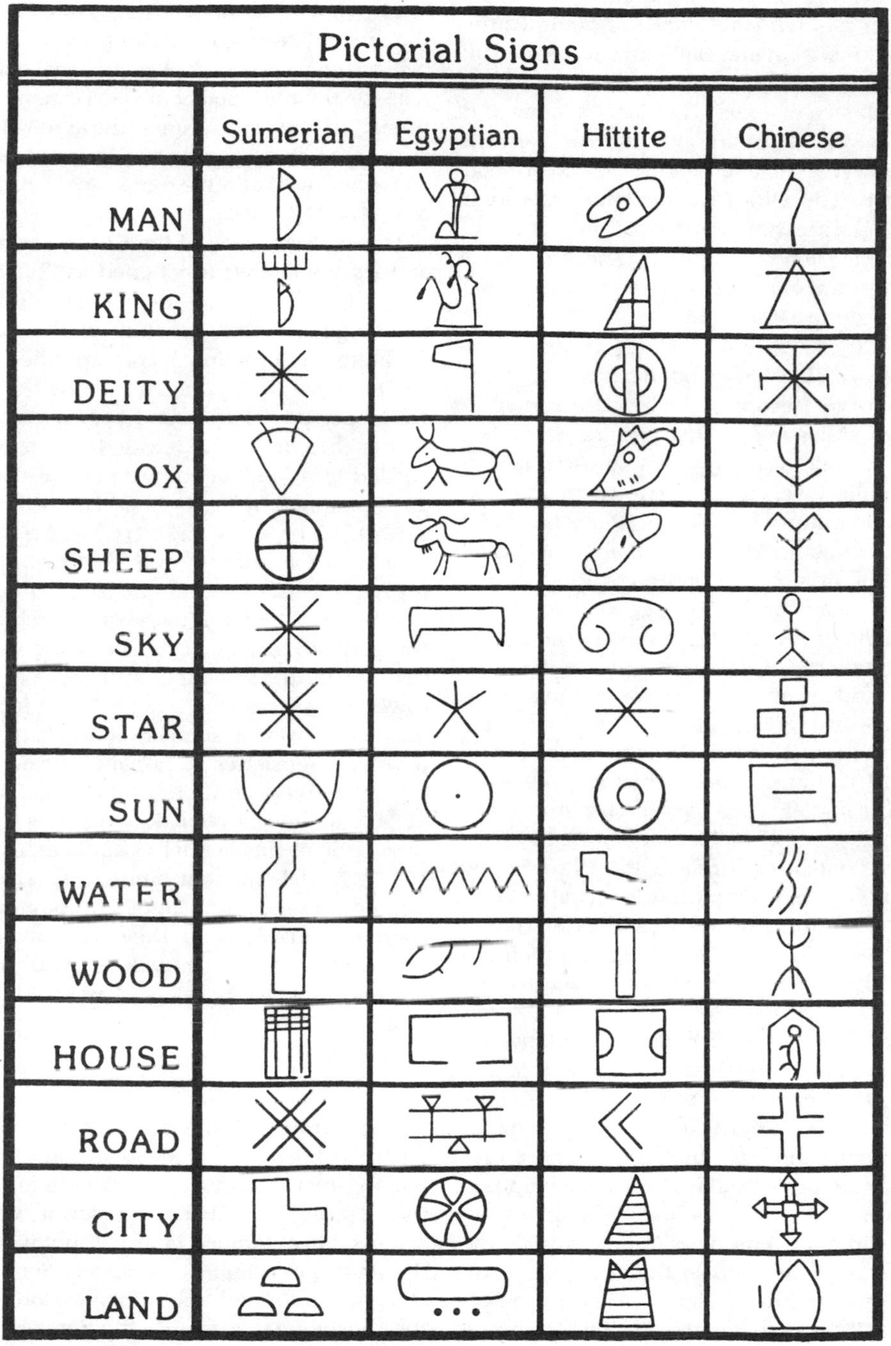

Pictorial Signs				
	Sumerian	Egyptian	Hittite	Chinese
MAN				
KING				
DEITY				
OX				
SHEEP				
SKY				
STAR				
SUN				
WATER				
WOOD				
HOUSE				
ROAD				
CITY				
LAND				

From Martha L. Carter and Keith N. Schoville, eds., *Sign, Symbol, Script* (Madison: Office of the Exhibit, Univ. of Wisconsin, 1984), 3. Used by permission.

Near East. Monumental inscriptions were preserved on rock walls and stone slabs (see list of illustrations). For example, the famous trilingual Behistun inscription of King Darius of Persia was etched in the rock face of a cliff. The Rosetta Stone and the Moabite Stone are other well-known examples of documents carved in solid rock. The Old Testament indicates that the Decalogue was carved in "tables of stone" (Exod. 32:15–16) and that later Joshua wrote a copy of the Law of Moses on stone (Josh. 8:32).

Other ancient writing materials included clay and wooden tablets (predominant in Mesopotamia, but also known in Syro-Palestine at Ebla and Ugarit, cf. Isa. 30:8; Hab. 2:2), papyrus manuscripts and scrolls (used from the third to the first millennium B.C., cf. Job 8:11; Isa. 18:2), and parchment (tanned animal skins). (The scroll of Jeremiah burned by King Jehoiakim may have been papyrus or parchment, cf. Jer. 36:2.) Ostraca (broken pieces of pottery) were commonly used as an abundant and inexpensive writing material throughout the ancient Near East, although they are not mentioned in the Old Testament. Beaten metal scrolls were occasionally used for special purposes. (A copper scroll was found among the writings left in caves along the Dead Sea by the Qumran community; see chapter 5 for a discussion of the Dead Sea Scrolls.)

The Old Testament makes no mention of the ink used for writing on scrolls, but it does list the iron stylus (Job 19:24; Jer. 17:1), reed pen (Jer. 8:8), a penknife for sharpening the pens (Jer. 36:23), and a writing case (Jer. 36:18) as instruments used in writing. The nature of the hand-copying process in the ancient world placed a premium on hearing, memorization, and public reading of documents— hence the emphasis on "hearing" the word of the Lord in the Old Testament. Spreading the written word also prompted the need for servants like message runners, heralds, and scribes (cf. 2 Sam. 18:19–23; Dan. 3:4).

Old Testament Scribes

The development of writing systems in the ancient Near East led to the rise of a professional class of scribes, and this held true for Hebrew society in Old Testament times. In preexilic Israel these official secretaries were key figures in both religious and civil administration (cf. 2 Sam. 8:16–17; 20:23–26).

During the period of the Hebrew monarchies the scribes functioned as "diplomats" in a way, since their expertise in the languages and literature of the day facilitated international correspondence (cf. 2 Kings 18:18–26). The scribes also wrote personal letters and public documents (e.g., Isa. 50:1; Jer. 36:18) and recorded legal, military, and financial data for the monarchy (cf. 1 Kings 4:3; 2 Kings 22:3–4; 2 Chron. 24:11; 26:11). The Levites also served as scribes and recorders for the temple (2 Chron. 34:13, 15).

After the fall of the Hebrew monarchies the scribal class in postexilic Israel was tied solely to the temple and more narrowly focused as to function. These temple scribes were essentially scholars who devoted themselves to copying, preserving, publishing, and interpreting the Law of Moses. Ezra is often identified as the precursor of this scribal class (Ezra 7:1–10). By New Testament times, the scribes formed a powerful religious and political class in Judaism, and they were major opponents of the ministry of Jesus, accusing him of violating Jewish law (cf. Matt. 23:2).

Old Testament Text and Versions

The earliest manuscripts of the Old Testament were composed in the twenty–two consonantal characters of the Hebrew alphabet. The script was arranged in columned lines without word divisions for economy of space. Scribal schools continued the transmission of the consonantal texts until the time of the Masoretes (ca. A.D. 500–900). The Masoretes were Jewish scholars and scribes

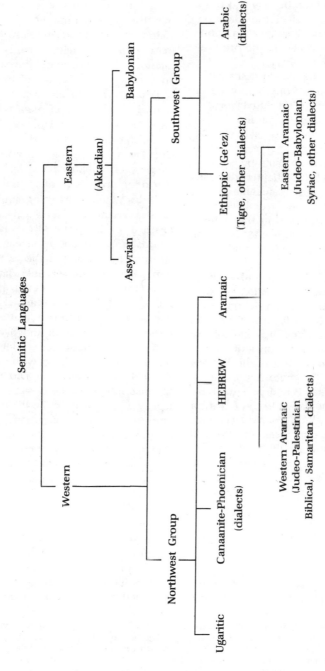

Figure 2.2. The Semitic Languages
(Main Distribution)

From Menahem Mansoor, *Biblical Hebrew Step by Step*, 2d ed. (Grand Rapids: Baker, 1980), 7. Used by permission.

who improved word divisions and added vowel points or signs, punctuation marks, and verse divisions to the Hebrew Old Testament. Today the Hebrew text of the Old Testament is called the Masoretic text (MT), signifying the important contribution of the Masoretes to the preservation of the Hebrew Bible.

In addition to the margin notes left by the Masoretes suggesting improved or corrected readings of individual words or verses, later developments in the Hebrew Bible included the subdivision of Old Testament books into chapters. First introduced in the Latin Bible by Stephen Langdon (1150–1228), chapter divisions were applied to the Hebrew Bible in 1518 (the Bomberg Edition). Numbers were assigned to the chapters in the Hebrew Bible by Arius Montanus (ca. 1571), having already appeared in the Latin Old Testament (ca. 1555).

The changing historical and political fortunes of the Israelite nation necessitated the translation of the Hebrew Bible into other languages (fig. 2.3). Several of these ancient versions are available in manuscript form and represent important witnesses to the text of the Hebrew Old Testament. The more important include the Samaritan Pentateuch (the Bible of the Samaritans dating to the fourth or fifth century B.C.), the Aramaic Targums (pre-Christian paraphrases of the Old Testament in Aramaic, the lingua franca of the Babylonian and early Persian periods, cf. Neh. 8:8), the Greek Septuagint (a by-product of the impact of Hellenism on the Jewish people, ca. 250 B.C.), Jerome's Latin Vulgate (A.D. 382–405), and the Syriac Peshitta (ca. A.D. 400?).[1]

Textual Criticism

The copying and translating of the Hebrew Old Testament over the centuries proliferated the number of manuscripts available so that there are literally thousands of copies extant in different languages from various time periods. Naturally the extended hand-copying process yielded errors of transmission. These human errors of sight, hearing, writing, memory, and judgment are called variants, or variant readings of the text.

Textual criticism, or lower biblical criticism, is the science of manuscript comparison. The goal of textual criticism is to establish or restore the written text of the Old Testament as close to its original reading as humanly possible. The practice or methodology of textual criticism includes gathering, sorting, and evaluating the variant readings of a given verse or passage of Scripture, then rating the manuscript evidence to select the most appropriate reading of the text in question based on the available data (cf. the margin notes in modern English Bibles in 1 Samuel 13:1, where textual criticism has been applied to restore the number indicating the length of King Saul's reign).

A word of caution is in order here, lest we be misled by those who emphasize the textual variants in the Old Testament manuscripts as evidence against the integrity and veracity of the Bible. Given its antiquity, the Old Testament exhibits a remarkable state of preservation. This is due in part to the meticulous copying procedures of the Hebrew and Christian scribes, the early and wide distribution of biblical manuscripts, and the reverence for and commitment to the Bible as "inspired Word of God" by Hebrews and Christians alike through the centuries. Equally important was the work of the Holy Spirit, who inspired the human writers, illumined the readers, and superintended the canonization process.[2]

---

[1]On the text and transmission of the Old Testament Scriptures, see further David Ewert, *A General Introduction to the Bible* (Grand Rapids: Zondervan, 1990), esp. 19–112.

[2]For example, prior to the discovery and subsequent publication of the Dead Sea (or Qumran) Scrolls, the oldest manuscripts dated to around A.D. 900 (i.e., the Cairo Codex of the Former and Latter Prophets, A.D. 815; the Petersburg Codex of the Former and Latter Prophets, A.D. 916; the

Figure 2.3. Old Testament Textual Development

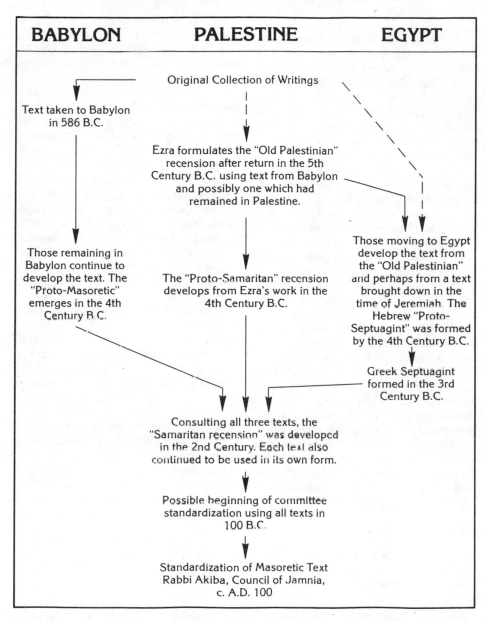

BABYLON	PALESTINE	EGYPT

Original Collection of Writings

Text taken to Babylon
in 586 B.C.

Ezra formulates the "Old Palestinian"
recension after return in the 5th
Century B.C. using text from Babylon
and possibly one which had
remained in Palestine.

Those moving to Egypt
develop the text from
the "Old Palestinian"
and perhaps from a text
brought down in the
time of Jeremiah. The
Hebrew "Proto-
Septuagint" was formed
by the 4th Century B.C.

Those remaining in
Babylon continue to
develop the text. The
"Proto-Masoretic"
emerges in the 4th
Century B.C.

The "Proto-Samaritan" recension
develops from Ezra's work in the
4th Century B.C.

Greek Septuagint
formed in the 3rd
Century B.C.

Consulting all three texts, the
"Samaritan recension" was developed
in the 2nd Century. Each text also
continued to be used in its own form.

Possible beginning of committee
standardization using all texts in
100 B.C.

Standardization of Masoretic Text
Rabbi Akiba, Council of Jamnia,
c. A.D. 100

From John H. Walton, *Chronological Charts of the Old Testament* (Grand Rapids: Zondervan, 1978), 14.

Canon Definition and Formation

Canon Definition

The word "canon" is not found in the Bible, although the root from which it derives occurs in 1 Kings 14:15 and Job 40:21. Originally *qāneh* meant a "reed" or "stalk" of papyrus, oil-grass, or sweet cane. Because reeds were used as measuring rods or ruling sticks for making straight lines, "canon" came to mean "measure" or "measuring reed." The term "canon" was first used as a theological expression in reference to the Holy Scriptures by Athanasius, bishop of Alexandria, in his Easter letter to the churches in which he outlined the contents of the New Testament canon (ca. A.D. 367).

As applied to the Hebrew Scriptures, the idea of canon has both intrinsic and extrinsic connotations. First, canon implies that the individual books of the Old Testament demonstrated the inherent quality of divine inspiration. This self-witness in conjunction with the illumination of the Holy Spirit permitted the recognition of these books as "word of God." Second, canon referred to the list or collection of books comprising the Hebrew Scriptures. This canon of Scripture was deemed supremely authoritative for faith and religious practice by the Hebrew community, and it became the measure or standard by which later books of Hebrew history, tradition, and religious teaching were evaluated.

Canon Formation

Our knowledge of the formation process resulting in a fixed Hebrew canon remains indefinite. Unfortunately we have no ancient documents from the scribes detailing the various steps of the procedure that culminated in a Hebrew Bible. Two things do seem certain. The process was long and involved, and it probably took place in stages over several centuries of Hebrew history. The generic outline of canon formation that follows accommodates the available data on the topic:

Stage 1: "Authoritative utterances." Initially God's revelation to the Hebrew people (and others) was conveyed orally in most cases. (Note the messenger formulas "thus says the Lord of Hosts" and "hear the word of the Lord" in the Old Testament, e.g., Deut. 5:1; Ezek. 5:5.) These authoritative utterances were passed to succeeding generations as the "word of the Lord" in the form of received oral tradition (cf. 48:1–7).

Stage 2: Formal written documents. At some point these divinely inspired words, sayings, and speeches were recorded and preserved for the Hebrew community in written form. On occasion the authoritative utterance and the writing or inscripturating of the pronouncement occurred almost simultaneously (e.g., the Book of the Law in Exodus 24:3—cf. Josh. 1:8—and Jeremiah's oracle to King Jehoiakim, chap. 36). In other instances the documentation of divine revelation took place some time after the historical event or circumstance prompting the word of the Lord. Frequently that event or circumstance is recited as part of the context for God's communication to Israel (e.g., Exod. 15:1; Josh. 8:32; Judg. 5:1).

Stage 3: Collecting written documents. The collecting process was probably both long and comprehensive—that is, long, given the millennium of Hebrew history

---

Aleppo Codex of the entire Old Testament, A.D. 900–950; and the Leningrad Codex of the entire Old Testament, A.D. 1008).

The complete Isaiah scroll found at Qumran dates to about 150 B.C., and analysis of the manuscript has shown the Dead Sea text to be 95 percent identical with the later Masoretic manuscripts. The 5 percent variation consists largely of "slips of the pen and spelling differences" (so Gleason L. Archer, *A Survey of Old Testament Introduction*, rev. ed. [Chicago: Moody, 1974], 25]). On the reliability of the biblical text, cf. James M. Boice, ed., *The Foundations of Biblical Authority* (Grand Rapids: Zondervan, 1978), esp. 85–102.

recorded in the Old Testament (e.g., it is apparent the Psalms came together over a period of five hundred years!), and comprehensive, given the number of ancient sources cited in the Old Testament that remain unknown to modern scholarship (e.g., the Book of the Wars of the Lord, Num. 21:14, and the Book of Jashar, Josh. 10:13). Assembling the written records of the Hebrew experience with Yahweh into anthologies and books was partially a matter of convenience for the Israelite community, since it permitted easy access to and ensured continued preservation of the documents. More important, it signified the value, prominence, and authority of the writings collected for the religious life of the community. These books commanded the special attention of the Hebrew people (e.g., Deut. 31:24).

Stage 4: Sorting written documents and fixing a canon. The procedural details of sorting through the documents are obscure, but we can discern the basic criteria applied to the documents for the purpose of "sorting" and delineating canon. It suffices to say that consensus choices among Hebrew religious leaders guided by the Holy Spirit of God during the course of Israelite history eventually resulted in a Hebrew canon of Scripture.

The Hebrews apparently had a "fixed" or established canon of Scripture well before the time of Jesus Christ. The Prologue to the Apocryphal Wisdom of Jesus ben Sirach, or Ecclesiasticus, makes reference to a threefold collection of "great teaching" including the Law, the Prophets, and the Other Books of Our Fathers (ca. 200 B.C.). Jesus himself appealed to a threefold Hebrew canon consisting of the Law of Moses, the Prophets, and the Psalms (Luke 24:44).

It would seem there were at least four key periods during Old Testament history when the sorting of documents and the fixing of canon would have been crucial for the Hebrew religious community: (a) during the Sinai experience after the Exodus, (b) during the shift from theocracy to monarchy in Israel, (c) at the time of the fall of Jerusalem and subsequent exile in Babylon, and (d) as part of the reforms of Ezra the scribe and Nehemiah the governor in postexilic Jerusalem.

Canon Selection Criteria

Unlike the New Testament, with its primary emphasis on apostolic authorship as the basis for canonicity, there seems to have been several factors or criteria important to the selection process for determining the Old Testament canon.

Foremost was the quality of inherent divine inspiration and authority recognizable to the leaders of the Hebrew religious community through illumination by the Holy Spirit (e.g., the direct manifestation of the Spirit of God in the case of Moses and the seventy prophets in Numbers 11:16–30, and the fulfillment of the divine word, as in Jeremiah 28:9; 44:28). Next, authorship was a key factor in evaluating books for canonicity. By and large the human writers of the books incorporated into the Hebrew canon held divinely appointed offices of leadership such as lawgiver, judge, prophet, priest, and king.

Third, the content of the individual books was examined for internal consistency of teaching and overall unity of theme and message with the covenant experience recorded in the other books recognized as "word of the Lord." Last, the use of particular documents and books by the Hebrew religious community no doubt influenced canon selection. The books read, studied, copied, and obeyed by the Israelites came to be recognized as canon.

In the final analysis we have to assume that the same Holy Spirit who inspired the human authors to write the books also superintended the Hebrew leaders during the process of canon selection.[3]

Canon History and Order

Canon History

The understanding of the Hebrew Scriptures as the "Old Testament" or "Old Covenant" is distinctly a Christian concept, stemming from Jeremiah's reference to the "new covenant" (31:31–36; cf. Matt. 26:17–35) and the comparison made between the "former" and "better" covenant described in the New Testament book of Hebrews (cf. Heb. 9:15–28). In Judaism today, the Hebrew Scriptures are known as the "Tanak," an acronym reflecting the threefold division of the Old Testament: "T" for Torah or Law, "N" for Nebiim or Prophets, and "K" for Ketubim or Writings.

This tripartite division of the Hebrew Scriptures is attested, as we have already noted, as early as the second century B.C. in the Prologue of Ben Sirach and later on by Jesus in Luke 24:44. But it is also affirmed in the Babylonian Talmud (*Baba Bathra* 14b–15a) and by a series of Jewish and Christian figures writing during the first four centuries after Christ (e.g., Philo, Josephus, Melito, Tertullian, Origen, Eusebius, Jerome, and Augustine).

The Hebrews enumerated twenty-four books in their Holy Scriptures. Samuel, Kings, Chronicles, and Ezra–Nehemiah were considered single books, while the twelve Minor Prophets were treated as a unified Book of the Twelve. Hence the Hebrew canon contains fifteen fewer books than our English Old Testament of thirty-nine, although both contain the exact same material. The names or titles for the books of the Hebrew Scriptures were usually taken from the first line or verse of the text, whereas the English titles are derivations from the book headings in the later Greek and Latin versions of the Old Testament.

Canon Order

Apparently the Masoretic scribes established no guidelines for standardizing the order of the Hebrew canon, as early Old Testament manuscripts evidence no uniformity in the arrangement of the books of the Latter Prophets and the Writings. The same holds true for the Septuagint and early Greek texts of the Old Testament. Today's English versions repeat the Old Testament canon order of Jerome's Latin Vulgate, excluding the books of the Apocrypha (fig. 2.4).

"Disputed Books"

Later on, discussion did arise over the inclusion of certain books deemed "canon" by the Hebrew religious community. These disputed books, or *antilegomena* (i.e., "spoken against"), included Esther, because the book nowhere includes the name of God; Proverbs, because the practical nature of the wisdom made the book seem more like "earthly" than divine wisdom—and one need not necessarily "fear the Lord" to gain benefit from the wisdom teachings; Ecclesiastes, due to the pessimistic and hedonistic overtones of the book; Song of Songs, given the erotic nature of the love poetry; and Ezekiel, both for the prophet's bizarre antics and visions and for his teaching on sacrifice that seemingly contradicted the Torah of Moses.

It should be noted that the canonical status of these books was never in doubt. Rather, the questions were related more to the interpretation of the individual books and the scope of their use within the religious community. For example, it was once thought the rabbinic council held at Jamnia or Jabne in or about A.D. 90 fixed the number and order of the

---

[3]On Old Testament canon formation, see further David N. Freedman, "Canon of the Old Testament," in *IDB: Supplementary Volume*, ed. K. Crim (Nashville: Abingdon, 1976), 130–36.

Figure 2.4. Jewish and Christian Canons of the Old Testament

TANAK	ROMAN CATHOLIC AND ORTHODOX	PROTESTANT
Torah	**Pentateuch**	**Pentateuch**
1. Bereshith (Genesis)	1. Genesis	1. Genesis
2. Shemoth (Exodus)	2. Exodus	2. Exodus
3. Wayiqra (Leviticus)	3. Leviticus	3. Leviticus
4. Bemidbar (Numbers)	4. Numbers	4. Numbers
5. Debarim (Deuteronomy)	5. Deuteronomy	5. Deuteronomy
Nevi'im (Former)	**History**	**History**
6. Joshua	6. Joshua	6. Joshua
7. Shofetim (Judges)	7. Judges	7. Judges
8. Samuel	8. Ruth	8. Ruth
9. Melakim (Kings)	9–10. 1 and 2 Samuel	9–10. 1 and 2 Samuel
10. Isaiah	11–12. 1 and 2 Kings	11–12. 1 and 2 Kings
11. Jeremiah	13–14. 1 and 2 Chronicles	13–14. 1 and 2 Chronicles
12. Ezekiel	15–16. Ezra and Nehemiah	15–16. Ezra and Nehemiah
13. TereAsar (The Twelve)	17. Tobit*	17. Esther
Hosea	18. Judith*	
Joel	19. Esther, including The Rest of Esther*	
Amos		
Obadiah	**Poetry and Wisdom**	**Poetry and Wisdom**
Jonah	20. Job	18. Job
Micah	21. Psalms	19. Psalms
Nahum	22. Proverbs	20. Proverbs
Habakkuk	23. Ecclesiastes	21. Ecclesiastes
Zephaniah	24. Song of Solomon	22. Song of Songs
Haggai	25. Wisdom of Solomon*	
Zechariah	26. Ecclesiasticus (Wisdom of	
Malachi	ben Sirach)*	
Kethu'bim	**Prophets**	**Prophets**
14. Tehilim (Psalms)	27. Isaiah	23. Isaiah
15. Job	28. Jeremiah	24. Jeremiah
16. Mishle (Proverbs)	29. Lamentations	25. Lamentations
17. Ruth	30. Baruch, including The	26. Ezekiel
18. Shir Haohirim (Song	Letter of Jeremiah†	27. Daniel
of Songs)	31. Ezekiel	28. Hosea
19. Qoheleth (Ecclesiastes)	32. Daniel, including The Rest of Daniel,* Susanna,* Song of the	
20. Ekah (Lamentations)	Three Holy Children,* Bel and the Dragon*	
21. Esther	33. Hosea	29. Joel
22. Daniel	34. Joel	30. Amos
23. Ezra–Nehemiah	35. Amos	31. Obadiah
24. Dibre Hayamin	36. Obadiah	32. Jonah
(Chronicles)	37. Jonah	33. Micah
	38. Micah	34. Nahum
	39. Nahum	35. Habakkuk
	40. Habakkuk	36. Zephaniah
	41. Zephaniah	37. Haggai
	42. Haggai	38. Zechariah
	43. Zechariah	39. Malachi
	44. Malachi	
	45. 1 Maccabees*	*Apocryphal in Protestant canon
	46. 2 Maccabees†	†Roman Catholic only

From Walter A. Elwell, ed., *Baker Encyclopedia of the Bible* (Grand Rapids: Baker, 1988), 1:301–2.

Hebrew canon. However, it has since been recognized that the Jabne council did not discuss or settle the canon issue; instead it discussed the interpretation of two particular Old Testament books, Song of Songs and Ecclesiastes.[4] The completion of the Jewish Talmud in the fifth or sixth century A.D. essentially ended the discussions over the status of the "disputed books" in the Old Testament canon.

Canon Confirmation

Finally, it is important to understand that the Hebrew canon was established or fixed by the religious leadership of the Hebrew community. Later rabbinic and church councils did not determine canon, but merely affirmed or stamped their approval on the collection of divinely inspired and authoritative books already acknowledged as "word of the Lord" in the Hebrew covenant community.

Old Testament Apocrypha

The word *apocrypha* means "hidden." As applied to the collection of Jewish writings dating from the intertestamental period, the word has two connotations: (1) books that are "hidden away" because of their esoteric nature, or (2) books that are "hidden away" because they deserve to be—in that they were never recognized as canon by the Hebrews.

The Apocrypha is a collection of fourteen (or fifteen, depending on numeration) books composed by pious Jewish writers between 200 B.C. and A.D. 100. These books were originally penned in Hebrew, Greek, and Aramaic and have been preserved in Greek, Latin, Ethiopic, Coptic, Arabic, Syriac, and Armenian. The Apocrypha contains six different genres or literary types, including didactic, religious, romantic, historical, prophetic (epistolary and apocalyptic), and legendary literature (fig. 2.5).

Initially the books of the Apocrypha were added one by one to later editions of the Septuagint, a Greek translation of the Hebrew Old Testament completed about 250 B.C. and made necessary by the impact of Hellenism on Judaism. These books were distinctly separated from the Hebrew Scriptures and were not regarded by the Hebrews as part of the Old Testament canon. However, the Jewish scribes made no notations to this fact, which led to some confusion among the Greek-speaking Christians who adopted the Septuagint as their Bible. This was especially true after about A.D.100, since subsequent copies of the Septuagint were transmitted by Christian scribes.

During the early centuries of Christianity there were conflicting opinions as to the canonicity of the Apocryphal books. For example, Greek and Latin church fathers such as Irenaeus, Tertullian, and Clement of Alexandria quoted the Apocrypha in their writings as "Scripture," and the Synod of Hippo (A.D. 393) authorized the use of the Apocrypha as canon. Yet others like Eusebius and Athanasius distinguished Apocrypha from the Old Testament.

The issue of Apocrypha as Old Testament canon was heightened with the publication of Jerome's Latin Vulgate (A.D. 405). Commissioned by Pope Damasus, this Latin translation of the Old Testament was intended to be the "popular" edition of the Bible for the Holy Roman Church. St. Jerome opposed the recognition of the Apocrypha as Old Testament canon and made careful notations in his Vulgate to that effect. But later recensions of Jerome's Vulgate failed to retain these clear distinctions, and soon most Latin readers understood no difference between the Old Testament and the Apocrypha.

[4]Cf. Walter C. Kaiser, *Toward Rediscovering the Old Testament* (Grand Rapids: Zondervan, 1987), 38–39.

Figure 2.5. The Books of Apocrypha

Type of Book	Revised Standard Version	Catholic Versions
Didactic	1. The Wisdom of Solomon (c. 30 B.C.)	Book of Wisdom
	2. Ecclesiasticus (Sirach) (132 B.C.)	Ecclesiasticus
Religious	3. Tobit (c. 200 B.C.)	Tobias
Romance	4. Judith (c. 150 B.C.)	Judith
Historic	5. 1 Esdras (c. 150–100 B.C.)	3 Esdras* or 1 Esdras‡
	6. 1 Maccabees (c. 110 B.C.)	1 Machabees
	7. 2 Maccabees (c. 110–70 B.C.)	2 Machabees
Prophetic	8. Baruch (c. 150–50 B.C.)	Baruch chaps. 1–5
	9. The Letter of Jeremiah (c. 300–100 B.C.)	Baruch chap. 6
	10. 2 Esdras (c. A.D. 100)	4 Esdras* or 2 Esdras‡
Legendary	11. Additions to Esther (140–130 B.C.)	Esther 10:4–16:24†
	12. The Prayer of Azariah (second or first century B.C.) (Song of Three Young Men)	Daniel 3:24–90†
	13. Susanna (second or first century B.C.)	Daniel 13†
	14. Bel and the Dragon (c. 100 B.C.)	Daniel 14†
	15. The Prayer of Manasseh (second or first century B.C.)	Prayer of Manasseh*

*Books not accepted as canonical at the Council of Trent, A.D. 1546.
†Books not listed in Douay table of contents because they are appended to other books.
‡Numbering depends on whether Ezra and Nehemiah are titled 1 and 2 Esdras or Ezra and Nehemiah.

From David Ewert, *A General Introduction to the Bible* (Grand Rapids: Zondervan, 1990), 75.

The Reformation again brought the issue of Apocrypha as canon to the forefront of church discussion. As the Reformers translated the Old Testament into the language of their constituencies, they discovered that the Hebrew Bible contained no books of the Apocrypha. Thus, in their view these "lesser books" were either excluded from the Old Testament canon or appended as a separate and inferior collection. This discrimination between canon and Apocrypha was anticipated by Wycliffe in his English translation of 1382. The Puritans are credited with the removal of the Apocrypha altogether from the covers of the English Bible. This tradition of excluding the Apocrypha still characterizes the majority of the English versions produced by Protestants.

The Holy Roman Church responded to the Reformers at the Council of Trent (1545–1564). There the fathers reaffirmed the Vulgate as the Bible of the true church and pronounced the Apocrypha equivalent to canonical material (specifically Tobit, Sirach, Wisdom, Judith, 1–2 Maccabees, Baruch, and the Additions to Esther and Daniel). Today this collection is usually called the Deutero-Canon, and it was substantiated as such by the Vatican Council of 1870. The Roman Catholic Church makes some appeal to the Deutero-Canon for doctrine, including the concepts of Purgatory, merit for good works, and the practice of prayers for the dead (cf. Tob. 12:9; 2 Macc. 12:43–45; 2 Esd. 8:33; 13:46; Sir. 3:30).

The Westminster Confession of 1647 rejected the inspiration and authority of the Apocrypha and refused to accept the collection as part of the canon of Scrip-

Figure 2.6. The Standard Collection of the Pseudepigrapha*

Legendary		
	1.	The Book of Jubilee
	2.	The Letter of Aristeas
	3.	The Book of Adam and Eve
	4.	The Martyrdom of Isaiah
Apocalyptic	5.	1 Enoch
	6.	The Testament of the Twelve Patriarchs
	7.	The Sibylline Oracle
	8.	The Assumption of Moses
	9.	2 Enoch, or the Books of the Secrets of Enoch
	10.	2 Baruch, or The Syriac Apocalypse of Baruch†
	11.	3 Baruch, or The Greek Apocalypse of Baruch
Didactical	12.	3 Maccabees
	13.	4 Maccabees
	14.	Pirke Aboth
	15.	The Story of Ahikar
Poetical	16.	The Psalms of Solomon
	17.	Psalm 151
Historical	18.	The Fragment of a Zadokite Work

*Since the discovery of the Dead Sea Scrolls, others have come to light.
†1 Baruch is listed in the Apocrypha.

From David Ewert, *A General Introduction to the Bible* (Grand Rapids: Zondervan, 1990), 81.

ture. The Protestant churches have generally adopted this position regarding the Apocrypha. Although not widely appreciated or observed today, Martin Luther's assessment of the Apocrypha still has merit. He held that the books of the Apocrypha are not equal to the Holy Scriptures, but are profitable to read and valuable for personal edification.

Old Testament Pseudepigrapha

Intertestamental Judaism produced a second body of extracanonical literature distinct from the Apocrypha and known as the Old Testament Pseudepigrapha (or "books written under a pen name"). These eighteen books (fig. 2.6) were composed by pious Jewish writers between 200 B.C. and A.D. 200. They were originally written in Hebrew, Aramaic, and Greek and have been preserved in Greek, Syrian, Ethiopic, Coptic, and Armenian.[5]

Although the collection remained outside the canon recognized in both Judaism and Christianity, the books were circulated and widely read in the early Christian church. In fact, the New Testament letter of Jude (vv. 14–15) quotes 1 Enoch and alludes to the Assumption of Moses (v. 9).

[5]A full discussion of the character and significance of the Old Testament Pseudepigrapha is outside the scope of this survey. See further L. Rost's excellent introduction to the individual books of the Pseudepigrapha, *Judaism Outside the Hebrew Canon*, trans. D. E. Green (Nashville: Abingdon, 1976), 100–190. English translations of the Old Testament Pseudepigrapha include R. H. Charles, ed., *The Apocrypha and Pseudepigrapha in English with Introductions and Critical Notes*, 2 vols. (Oxford: Clarendon, 1913); J. H. Charlesworth, ed., *The Old Testament Pseudepigrapha*, 2 vols. (Garden City, N.Y.: Doubleday, 1983, 1985); and H. F. D. Sparks, *The Apocryphal Old Testament* (Oxford: Clarendon, 1984).

Questions for Further Study and Discussion

1. What does it mean to say that the Hebrew Bible or the Old Testament is "inspired" by God?
2. How did the Hebrew religious community recognize divine inspiration in the books of the Old Testament?
3. Discuss the nature and purpose of textual criticism and its implications for biblical exposition.
4. What is the value of the Apocrypha and Pseudepigrapha for Old Testament study? Why are they largely ignored in Protestant scholarship and preaching?
5. On what basis is the Hebrew Bible or Old Testament considered a "closed" canon?

For Further Reading

Beckwith, R. *The Old Testament Canon of the New Testament Church.* London: SPCK, 1985.

Bruce, F. F. *The Books and the Parchments.* 3d ed. Old Tappan, N.J.: Revell, 1963.

———. *History of the Bible in English.* 3d ed. Oxford: Oxford University Press, 1978.

Ewert, David. *A General Introduction to the Bible.* Grand Rapids: Zondervan, 1990. The most current and readable presentation of general Bible introduction. Comprehensive, systematic, well illustrated. First published in 1983 under the title *From Ancient Tablets to Modern Translations.*

Fisher, M. C. "The Canon of the Old Testament." *EBC.* Grand Rapids: Zondervan, 1979. 1:385–94.

Geisler, Norman L., and W. E. Nix. *A General Introduction to the Bible.* Chicago: Moody Press, 1968.

Harris, R. Laird. *Inspiration and Canonicity of the Bible.* Grand Rapids: Zondervan, 1957.

Harrison, R. K. "The Old Testament Text and Canon." In *Introduction to the Old Testament.* Grand Rapids: Eerdmans, 1969, 260–88. Standard evangelical Old Testament introduction, though now somewhat dated.

Klein, Ralph W. *Textual Criticism of the Old Testament.* Philadelphia: Fortress, 1974.

Kline, Meredith G. *The Structure of Biblical Authority.* Grand Rapids: Eerdmans, 1972. The Old Testament canon characterized as "treaty-canon" originating out of the Old Testament parallels to ancient Near Eastern treaty or covenant literary forms.

Lewis, J. P. *The English Bible: From KJV to NIV.* Grand Rapids: Baker, 1981.

McCarter, P. Kyle, Jr. *Textual Criticism.* Philadelphia: Fortress, 1986.. Helpful introductory chapter on the art and science of textual criticism.

Metzger, Bruce M. *An Introduction to the Apocrypha.* Oxford: Oxford University Press, 1957.

———, ed. *The Oxford Annotated Apocrypha.* New York: Oxford University Press, 1977.

Wurthwein, E. *The Text of the Old Testament.* E. F. Rhodes, trans. Grand Rapids: Eerdmans, 1979. The best treatment of the composition, transmission, primary versions, and textual criticism of the Old Testament.

Chapter 3

Historical Overview of Old Testament Times

Chronology

A few words about chronology are necessary to an overview of the history of the Old Testament period. Readers may well wonder how dates can be assigned to all the events and personages of this ancient period of history when records give, at best, a phrase such as "In the third year of king X." There are many sources from Israel and the ancient Near East that give relative chronology (the third year of one king is the first year of another), and from those data a substantial grid of people and events can be constructed. To establish an absolute chronology (the king began his reign in 465 B.C.), some fixed point must be determined to which the grid of the relative chronology may be attached.

For the ancient Near East, this fixed point is supplied by the Eponym lists of Assyria. The Eponym lists record for each year a designated official who is honored by having the year named after him. In the list his name is given along with one or two of the most significant events of "his" year, usually military campaigns. Fortuitously, in the year of Ishdi-Sagale, governor of Guzana, the list reports that a solar eclipse occurred. Astronomers can

calculate when solar eclipses took place, and therefore the year of Ishdi-Sagale can be identified positively as 763 B.C. This is the primary anchor for the absolute chronology of the ancient Near East, and it is not contested. As a result, it can be determined that the Eponym lists cover the years 893–666 B.C. Since each king of Assyria during this period is (predictably) among those honored, the dates of Assyria can be established for that span of more than two centuries. This is the period of the Neo-Assyrian Empire, so synchronisms of most of the nations of the ancient Near East are made with Assyria for that time. In this way Assyria has become the foundation for the chronology of the ancient Near East.

We should not assume, however, that all chronological problems are thereby solved. Often there are conflicting data with the relative chronology scheme that introduce uncertainties for absolute dating. On other occasions events or people are not related in the textual material to the grid of relative chronology—for instance, the failure of the account of the Exodus to name the pharaoh who was ruling at the time. Still other problems occur when the ancient sources do not

Figure 3.1. The eleventh tablet of the Assyrian version of the Gilgamesh Epic. It records the Babylonian version of the Flood. The twelve tablets in the epic poem were found in the library of King Ashurbanipal. (*Trustees of the British Museum*)

sufficiently record the complexity of a situation—e.g., gaps in chronologies, co-regencies, dynasties or rulers in power simultaneously with other dynasties or rulers in the same country.

Finally, some sources provide information on longer time spans. For example, in the records of Tiglath-Pileser I of Assyria it is stated that the temple built by Shamshi-Adad I had fallen into decay over 641 years; in the prayer of Solomon recorded in 1 Kings 6:1 it is stated that 480 years had passed between the Exodus and the dedication of Solomon's temple. These facts can present problems if they do not mesh with the information supplied by the relative chronology grid.

The result is that there remains a good deal of uncertainty about precise chronology. In the case of the kings of Israel and Judah, the uncertainty is usually only a year or two at most, though at times as many as twelve years divide the various theories from one another. The further back one goes in history, the more uncer-

tainty there will be. The earliest synchronism of the Old Testament with any individual known from the records of the ancient Near East is the raid of Shishak (Sheshonq I) of Egypt on Jerusalem in the fifth year of Rehoboam (925 B.C., 1 Kings 14:25–26). This leaves the judges period and therefore the patriarchal period as well shrouded in chronological mystery and hence the subject of numerous speculative arrangements.

Some believe that the Bible provides the key for unraveling the mysteries of chronology. The text we have cited in 1 Kings 6:1 would appear to date the Exodus to 1446 B.C., while Exodus 12:40 indicates that the stay in Egypt lasted 430 years. Based on these data, Jacob and his family went down to Egypt in 1876 B.C., and the ages given for the patriarchs would then produce a chronological table going back to Abraham. Other scholars, however, find this system unacceptable, because they believe it conflicts with archaeological information that has become available over the last century. Thus the figures in 1 Kings and Exodus are sometimes considered approximations or are understood in nonliteral ways, and chronology remains controversial.

Mesopotamia to the Time of the Patriarchs (2900–2000 B.C.)

The architects for the foundations of Mesopotamian culture were the Sumerians, who were occupying southern Mesopotamia as early as the fourth millennium B.C. The Sumerian Kinglist provides a picture of various city-states having prominence alternatively and at times concurrently. The Sumerian period proper is called the Early Dynastic Period and is divided into three segments, lasting from 2900 until the middle of the twenty-fourth century B.C. During this time there was also a growing Semitic population inhabiting the area. The Sumerians were responsible for many cultural achievements, including the in-

27

vention of writing, and made significant contributions in dozens of fields such as mathematics, architecture, literature, education, law, and medicine. The Early Dynastic Period witnessed major developments in urbanization, kingship, and religious ideas.

The Sumerians were finally overcome by Sargon I, who established the Semitic dynasty of Akkad about 2340 B.C. Sargon is known as the first empire builder of history. He ruled all of southern Mesopotamia and ranged eastward into Elam and northwest to the Mediterranean on campaigns of a military and economic nature. The empire lasted for almost 150 years before being apparently overthrown by the Gutians (a barbaric people from the Zagros Mountains east of the Tigris), though other factors, including internal dissent, may have contributed to the downfall.

Of the next century little is known as more than twenty Gutian kings succeeded one another. Just before 2100, the city of Ur took control of southern Mesopotamia under the kingship of Ur-Nammu, and for the next century there was a Sumerian renaissance in what has been called the Ur III period (fig. 3.2). It is difficult to ascertain the limits of territorial control of the Ur III kings, though the territory does not seem to have been as extensive as that of the dynasty of Akkad. Under Ur-Nammu's son, Shulgi, the region enjoyed almost a half-century of peace. Shulgi exercised absolute rule through provincial governors and distinguished himself in sportsmanship, music, and literature. He himself was reputed to have composed a hymn and was trained in scribal arts. Decline and fall came late in the twenty-first century through the infiltration of the Amorites and the increased aggression of the Elamites to the east, who finally overthrew the city.

It is against this backdrop of history that the Old Testament patriarchs

emerge. Some have pictured Abraham as leaving the sophisticated Ur that was the center of the powerful Ur III period to settle in the unknown wilderness of Canaan, but that involves both chronological and geographical speculation. By the highest chronology Abraham probably would have traveled from Ur to Haran during the reign of Ur-Nammu, but many scholars are inclined to place Abraham in the Isin-Larsa period or even the Old Babylonian period. From a geographical standpoint it is difficult to be sure that the Ur mentioned in the Bible is the famous city in southern Mesopotamia. Reference to it as Ur of the Chaldeans has led some to identify it with a northern city, Ur, mentioned in contemporary sources.[1] All this makes it impossible to give a precise background of Abraham.

The Patriarchal Period (2000–1600)

The Ur III period came to a close in southern Mesopotamia as the last king of Ur, Ibbi-Sin, lost the support of one city after another and was finally overthrown by the Elamites, who dwelt just east of the Tigris. In the ensuing two centuries, power was again returned to city-states that controlled more local areas. Isin, Larsa, Eshnunna, Lagash, Mari, Assur, and Babylon all served as major political centers. Thanks substantially to the royal archives of Mari, the eighteenth century has become thoroughly documented. As the century opened there was an uneasy balance of power among four cities: Larsa ruled by Rim-Sin, Mari ruled by Yaḫdun-Lim (and later, Zimri-Lim), Assur ruled by Shamshi-Adad I, and Babylon ruled by Hammurabi. Through a generation of political intrigue and diplomatic strategy, Hammurabi eventually emerged to establish the prominence of the first dynasty of Babylon.

The Old Babylonian period covers the time from the fall of the Ur III dynasty

---

[1]See Barry Beitzel, *The Moody Atlas of Bible Lands* (Chicago: Moody Press, 1985), 80.

about 2000 B.C. to the fall of the first dynasty of Babylon just after 1600 B.C. The rulers of the first dynasty of Babylon were Amorites. The Amorites had been coming into Mesopotamia as early as the Ur III period, at first being fought as enemies, then gradually taking their place within the society of the Near East. In Hammurabi they reached the height of success. Despite his impressive military accomplishments, Hammurabi is most widely known today for his collection of laws. His was the first major collection uncovered from the ancient Near East and is still the most extensive, with about 250 laws preserved. They predate Moses by at least three hundred years. The first dynasty of Babylon extends for more than a century beyond the time of Hammurabi, though decline began soon after his death and continued unabated, culminating in the Hittite sack of Babylon in 1595. This was nothing more than an incursion on the part of the Hittites, but it dealt the final blow to the Amorite dynasty, opening the doors of power for another group, the Kassites.

The Middle Bronze Age (2000–1550 B.C.)[2] of Canaan that Abraham entered into was dominated by scattered city-states much as Mesopotamia had been, though not as densely populated or as extensively urbanized. The period began about the time of the fall of the dynasty of Akkad in Mesopotamia (ca. 2200) and extended until about 1500 (plus or minus fifty years, depending on the theories followed). In Syria there were power centers at Yamhad, Qatna, Alalakh and Mari, and the coastal centers of Ugarit and Byblos seemed to be already thriving. In Palestine only Hazor is mentioned in prominence. Contemporary records from Palestine are scarce, though the Egyptian story of Sinuhe has Middle Bronze Age Palestine as a backdrop and therefore offers

general information. Lists of cities in Palestine are also given in the Egyptian execration texts. Most are otherwise unknown, though Jerusalem and Shechem are mentioned. As the period progresses there is more and more contact with Egypt and extensive caravan travel between Egypt and Palestine.

Egypt to the Exodus

Roughly concurrent to the Early Dynastic Period in Mesopotamia was the formative Old Kingdom in Egypt that permanently shaped Egypt both politically and culturally. This was the age of the great pyramids. In the Sixth Dynasty, contemporary with the dynasty of Akkad in Mesopotamia, disintegration became evident. From the mid-twenty-second century until about 2000, Egypt was plunged into a dark period known as the First Intermediate Period, which was characterized by disunity and at times practical anarchy. Order was finally restored when Mentuhotep reunited Egypt, and Amenemhet I founded the Twelfth Dynasty, beginning a period of more than two centuries of prosperous growth and development.

The Twelfth Dynasty developed extensive trade relations with Syro-Palestine and is the most likely period for initial contacts between Egypt and the Hebrew patriarchs. By the most conservative estimates, Sesostris III would have been the pharaoh who elevated Joseph to his high administrative post. Others would be more inclined to place the emigration of the Israelites to Egypt during the time of the Hyksos. The Hyksos were Semitic peoples who had begun moving into Egypt (particularly the delta region) as early as the First Intermediate Period. As the Thirteenth Dynasty ushered in a gradual decline, the reins of power even-

---

[2]Archaeologists have developed the terminology "Bronze Age" and "Iron Age" to serve as chronological designations according to technological advance, particularly in time periods when absolute chronology is impossible to establish with confidence.

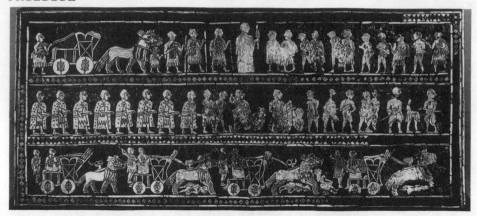

Figure 3.2. "War panel" from a standard found at Ur, depicting the triumph of the king over his enemies. This is a mosaic panel in shell, lapis lazuli, and red limestone dated from the first half of the third millennium B.C. (*Trustees of the British Museum*)

tually fell to the Hyksos (whether by conquest, coup, or consent is still indeterminable), who then controlled Egypt from about the middle of the eighteenth century to the middle of the sixteenth century. It was during this time the Israelites began to prosper and multiply in the delta region, waiting for the covenant promises to be fulfilled.

After nearly two centuries of foreign domination at the hands of the Hyksos, the Egyptians finally set about restoring their nation to their own control. In an explosion of nationalistic fervor, the Hyksos were driven from the land and the Eighteenth Dynasty was established under the Egyptian pharaoh Ahmose. It was perhaps in a reaction against foreigners that the Israelites were reduced to slavery by the newly established regime. It should be noticed that the Egyptians did not fear the military might of the Israelites, but rather were afraid that the Israelites would join forces with the enemy and be driven out (Exod. 1:10). The Egyptians did not want the Israelites to leave, perhaps having become economically dependent on them in some way (see Gen. 47:6).

In the Eighteenth and Nineteenth dynasties Egypt reached the height of its political power, though there were periods of decline. Thutmose III, in the first half of the fifteenth century, extended Egypt's territorial control through Palestine and north as far as Qadesh on the Orontes in Syria. In the south, Egypt pushed up the Nile to include both upper and lower Nubia among its conquests. Thutmose III's son and successor, Amenhotep II, is identified as the pharaoh of the Exodus by those favoring a fifteenth-century date for this event (see chapter 8 for a discussion of the dating of the Exodus).

By the close of the fifteenth century, Egypt had reached the limits of its expansion and had begun a decline fostered by military stagnation and an increased standard of living that reduced concern for maintaining foreign interests. The results of this decline are amply documented in the Amarna archives from the fourteenth century B.C. The central figure of this period and the one blamed for many of Egypt's troubles was the controversial pharaoh Akhenaten. In an attempt to break the power of the priesthood of Amon-Re, Akhenaten deserted the capital at Thebes, where the cult of Amon-Re was centered, and constructed a new capital city about two hundred miles north at modern el-Amarna (Akhetaten), dedicated to the god Aten (the god of the sun disk).

This political strategy was only part of a much larger attempt to establish an almost monotheistic worship of Aten that engulfed art, literature, and nearly every other aspect of Egyptian culture for almost half a century.

The correspondence from the Amarna archives portrays an Egypt that has lost its international respect and is no longer capable of maintaining order among the petty city-states of Palestine, let alone defending its interests against the Hittites in Syria or honoring its treaty with the Mitannian Empire in its death throes in western Mesopotamia. Some holding to a fifteenth-century date for the Exodus contend that the Israelites were making a successful incursion into Canaan at this time, taking advantage of Egyptian neglect of the area. But it is unlikely that the "Ḫabiru" people mentioned as troubling the kings of Palestine should be equated with the "Hebrews." This does not rule out the possibility that the Israelites were among those peoples designated as Habiru who motivated the kings of Canaan to plead with the pharaoh to send auxiliary troops, but usage of the term "Ḫabiru" (or "Ḫapiru") shows it cannot be restricted to an identification of the Israelites.

As the thirteenth century began, Egyptian reputation was restored by the Nineteenth Dynasty, primarily by Rameses II (the Great). Most who maintain that the Exodus occurred in the thirteenth century would view this pharaoh as the one who witnessed the mighty hand of God in delivering the Israelites from Egypt.

The Late Bronze Age (1500–1200)

While Egypt was experiencing the decline of the Eighteenth Dynasty and the Amarna age, the Late Bronze Age began in Syro-Palestine. During this period the Syro-Palestine corridor had a significant role to play. Because this was an age of international trade, control of the trade routes became a great economic advantage. The overland trade routes from Egypt to Anatolia (Asia Minor) and Mesopotamia all passed through Syro-Palestine, and the growing sea trade on the Mediterranean was dependent on the hospitable ports of the Syrian coast (Byblos, Tyre, Sidon, and Ugarit in particular). As a result, each of the military powers desired to expand their control into Syro-Palestine, and many of the great battles of this era took place in Syro-Palestine. According to the earlier chronology, this was the period of the judges of Israel, and the constant burden of foreign oppression described in the book of Judges would fit the profile of this period, though the great political powers are not listed among the oppressors of Israel.

Vying with Egypt for control of Syria at the beginning of this period was the Hurrian kingdom of Mitanni, located along the upper Tigris and Euphrates in northern Mesopotamia, the area the Bible refers to as Aram-Naharaim (Judg. 3:8–10). It was the influence of the Mitannian king Shaustatar that prevented Egypt's Thutmose III from extending his control north of Qadesh. Mitanni was soon overshadowed, however, by the emergence of the Hittites in Anatolia, who were to become the dominant political force in the Near East for the next two and a half centuries. As both Egypt and Mitanni reached periods of decline in the latter part of the fifteenth century, they set aside their differences and made an alliance in order to protect their mutual interests in Syria from the upstart Hittites, but to no avail.

The fourteenth century brought expansion of Hittite influence into Syria under the guidance of Shuppiluliuma I, at the expense of the dormant Egyptians and the floundering Hurrians. With the reestablishment of a strong Assyrian state in 1362, Mitanni came under pressure from both east and west, finally breaking apart about 1350. It is possible that the first oppressors of Israel in the judges period were peoples who had been displaced from Mitanni (Judg. 3:7–11).[3] The Assyrians did not, however, attempt to expand to the west, preferring to exert their influence on Urartu to the north and Babylon to the south. Meanwhile, the cities of Syria had gradually come under the control of the Hittites.

The thirteenth century brought the resurgence of Egypt as the Nineteenth Dynasty began to reverse the devastating policies that had characterized the Amarna period. The capital was moved to the delta region in the north, and control over Palestine was exerted more forcefully. In the mid-thirteenth century Rameses the Great began to challenge the Hittite control of Syria. Both Egyptian and Hittite records preserve accounts of the famous battle of Qadesh, in which Rameses, though surprised by the Hittite forces, managed to avoid humiliation. The resulting occupation of territory suggests that the Hittites retained control of Amurru and Qadesh and perhaps even made gains to the south. Eventually a treaty was made between Hattushili III (Hittites) and Rameses II, probably motivated by renewed interest in Syria on the part of the Assyrian king Shalmaneser I.

The resulting picture of the Late Bronze Age is an ever-shifting stalemate between major political powers, with Syria and, to a lesser extent, Canaan caught in the middle. If the Israelites were in Canaan during this time, they would have been largely unaffected by the international events. Canaan was too far south and too insignificant (compared with Syria) for the northern powers to be interested. The troop movements of the Egyptians during the thirteenth century would have had little effect, for the Israelites were largely settled in the hill country away from the major routes of travel. But the balance of power was about to undergo a drastic change.

Figure 3.3. The great battle of Rameses III against the Sea Peoples (Philistines) as depicted on a relief from the temple of Rameses III at Medinet Habu, Thebes, ca. 1198–1166 B.C. (*Seffie Ben-Yoseph*)

Iron Age I (1200–1000)

The beginning of the Iron Age brought the fall of the Hittite Empire, the destruction of many of the major port cities of Syria including Ugarit, Tyre, and Sidon as well as fortified cities inland such as Megiddo and Ashkelon, a lull in Assyrian power, and substantial decline in Egyptian influence. Much of this political upheaval is blamed on the invasion by a coalition of tribes called the Sea Peoples who appear to have come from the Aegean region by ship as part of a massive population movement). They overthrew the fortified cities, demolished the Hittite Empire, and were repelled by the Egyptians only after massive sea battles exacted heavy casualties (fig. 3.3). One of these tribes, the Philistines, settled on the southwest coast of Canaan. It is from them that the name "Palestine" is derived.

---

[3]Cushan-Rishathaim could represent a Hebrew attempt at rendering a Hurrian name such as * Kuzzarishti. Though this name is not found among known Hurrian names, it is made up of elements frequently attested in Hurrian names.

This period brought the technological development of iron tools and weapons, knowledge of which helped establish Philistine supremacy over Israel (see 1 Sam. 13:19–23).

The resulting situation in the Near East was that international politics was virtually eliminated. With no major powers left to exert control, relatively minor skirmishes in localized areas replaced the massive military campaigns of empires. The resulting power vacuum allowed for the development of empire building on a smaller scale such as that most evident in tenth-century Israel.

The Empire of David and Solomon (1000–900)

Iron Age II extends from 1000 to 586 B.C., but it is preferable to cover this period of history in shorter segments. Toward the end of the judges period the Philistines had been contained by the activities of Samson, though they were in control of Judah (Judg. 15:11). During the time of Samuel they overran the hill country and destroyed Shiloh (1 Sam. 4), but were later driven back (1 Sam. 7). Saul was successful in maintaining the equilibrium throughout most of his reign, but after the battle of Mount Gilboa (in which Saul was killed), the Philistines occupied most of the midsection of Canaan.

When David came to the throne, one of his first tasks was to regain control of Israelite territory. This was accomplished from his newly conquered, fortified base in Jerusalem. After the Philistines were subdued, David's military success continued with the eventual subjugation of most of Syro-Palestine. Some countries were annexed, with military governors ruling in place of native kings (e.g., Ammon); others were conquered but became vassal states (e.g., Moab); some paid tribute and became the site for Israelite garrisons (e.g., Aram-Damascus, Edom); and still others became willing vassals (e.g., Hamath).

As a result of David's successes, Solomon inherited an empire that stretched from the Euphrates in the north to Egypt in the south. Even Egypt entered into a marriage alliance with him (the pharaoh's daughter joined Solomon's harem) as he built a navy and extended his trade to the far reaches of the Mediterranean and south along the full length of the Red Sea. Despite his economic success, Solomon's military capability did not match his father's. Though he fortified strategic cities such as Megiddo, Hazor, and Gezer and built up his cavalry and chariotry, very little military success is recorded for Solomon in the Old Testament (2 Chron. 8:3–6). Though his wisdom was widely recognized and the prosperity of his realm unparalleled, the empire declined under his guardianship and was on the verge of collapse when his son Rehoboam took the throne. Military neglect and a heavy tax burden on the people appear to have been Solomon's most obvious political faults, and the authors of Kings and Chronicles likewise point out his spiritual failures.

Internal unrest and unquenched rebellion among the vassals left Rehoboam little more than the capital city and the wilderness that lay to the south. The kingdom deteriorated even more a few years later when Shishak (known as Sheshonq I in Egyptian records), the pharaoh of Egypt, raided Judah, sacking many of the fortified cities and receiving heavy tribute in return for bypassing Jerusalem.

The Rise of the Aramaeans (950–800)

Even as one of Solomon's officials, Jeroboam, gained control over the northern kingdom of Israel, the reins of political power in the region fell into the hands of the Aramaean states of Syria. The Aramaeans as a people are first mentioned as living along the upper Euphrates toward the end of the Late Bronze

Age. In the wake of the incursion of the Sea Peoples, they began to move into Syria. After gaining independence from Israel in the later years of Solomon, Damascus became the center of a new Aramaean state that had achieved unification by the mid-ninth century. For much of the ninth century Aram was the major political power in the west. It led the western states in coalitions against the developing Assyrian threat and served as a buffer between the Assyrians and Israel for much of the time. There were also numerous battles between the Aramaeans and the northern kingdom of Israel, with Aram maintaining a decisive edge. As the century drew to a close, Hazael, the king of Aram, had successfully overrun and occupied most of Israel.

The First Assyrian Threat and the Resurgence of Israel (850–750)

Nearly concurrent with the rise of the Aramaeans came the resurgence of Assyrian imperialism. This began in the reign of Ashurnasirpal II, who undertook a number of annual campaigns along the upper Euphrates, terrorizing the inhabitants through a policy of ruthless intimidation. This was expanded into a more logical military strategy by his successor, Shalmaneser III, who concentrated on gaining control of the upper Euphrates. Then in 853 Shalmaneser turned his attention to western expansion and launched a campaign into Aram. He was met at Qarqar on the Orontes by a coalition of western states joined by Ben-Hadad of Aram and Ahab, king of Israel. Though Shalmaneser claimed victory, evidence suggests that the coalition had successfully blocked his entry into the west.

Israel and Judah struggled through the ninth century. In the northern kingdom, Israel, Jeroboam was occupied with an enormous task of reorganization in order to achieve complete autonomy from Jerusalem. He attempted to portray himself as a reformer rather than as an innovator, but in so doing enraged those loyal to the temple in Jerusalem and brought a condemnation on his kingdom that is traced methodically through the books of Kings. Jeroboam's son succeeded him, but was assassinated after only two years.

The next dynasty was established by Baasha, who had wiped out Jeroboam's line. It was at this time that the escalation of tensions between Israel and Judah brought the Aramaeans into Israel. His line likewise did not last, but was replaced by the politically successful house of Omri. During the Omride ascendancy the capital of the northern kingdom was moved to Samaria. It was a period of peaceful relations and even included intermarriage with the Davidic line from Jerusalem. Omri's son Ahab was married in political alliance to the Tyrian princess, Jezebel. Though this was a beneficial political arrangement, it proved disastrous for Israel because Jezebel was intent on imposing the worship of her native deity Baal Melqart on the Israelite population. This blatant violation of the covenant was vigorously opposed by the prophet Elijah and led eventually to a public outcry and conservative backlash that brought down the Omride line.

The house of Jehu undertook a bloody purge and also reversed foreign policy. Jehu paid tribute to Shalmaneser III and became a cooperative Assyrian vassal. As Assyrian influence in the west declined toward the end of the century, Jehu's dynasty again became embroiled in skirmishes with the Aramaeans, becoming an occupied Aramaean state by the end of the century.

Judah enjoyed a bit more stability if only because the same dynasty remained in power throughout the century. The line of David, however, failed to maintain an exemplary spiritual posture and remained isolated from international politics. In the first half of the century Asa and his son, Jehoshaphat, attempted some spiritual reform, but much of that was undone by Jehoshaphat's alliance with the house of Ahab, whereby he imported Baalism under Jezebel's influence. Subsequently, when Jehu obliterated the house of Omri in the north, Judah lost a king as well (Jehoshaphat's grandson, Ahaziah), and the Davidic line came within an heir of being wiped out. The infant Joash was rescued and returned to the throne six years later.

Judah was not involved in the conflicts with either the Aramaeans or the Assyrians. The trade routes skirted their country, which was therefore of little value to foreign powers.

The early eighth century witnessed the decline of both Assyria and Aram. Assyria was occupied with internal difficulties and pressure from Urartu. Jeroboam II, the most successful king of Jehu's dynasty, recovered Israelite territory from the Aramaeans and made vassals of Hamath and Damascus. Meanwhile in the south, Azariah (Uzziah) collected tribute from the Ammonites and was successful against the Philistines and Arabians. Between Jeroboam II and Azariah, the territorial control nearly equaled that of David. This was a prosperous time for Israel and Judah, but military success led to decadence and social and spiritual decay. It was this decline that set the stage for the development of classical prophecy, for although Israel and Judah were autonomous and troublefree, a major crisis lay just over the horizon.

The Neo-Assyrian Empire (750–650)

After a lapse of half a century, the Assyrian Empire returned much stronger than before under the capable leadership of Tiglath-Pileser III in 745 (fig. 3.4). This was to become the first "world class" empire known to history, and the first of a line of empires that culminated in the Roman Empire. First on the Assyrian king's agenda was to consolidate control of Syria, which had come under the control of Urartu, and to regain control of

Figure 3.4. Tiglath-Pileser III portrayed on a fragment of gypsum slab from the central palace at Nimrud. (*Trustees of the British Museum*)

the trade routes. Over his first eight to ten years the king accomplished this goal and established a strong military presence in Syria. As part of this process he collected tribute from Menahem, the king of Israel.

While Tiglath-Pileser was pursuing this agenda, however, Rezin, king in Damascus, had his own plan. He had sponsored an upstart, Pekah, from Israel and helped him secure the throne, and together they planned to do the same sort of thing in Judah. Ahaz, the Judacan king, though encouraged by the prophet Isaiah to trust the Lord for deliverance from this threat, chose to summon Tiglath-Pileser to deal with the co-conspirators. The result was the second western campaign in the years 734–732. Pekah was replaced on the throne of Israel by Hoshea, and all but the environs of Samaria were annexed as part of the Assyrian state. Rezin was killed and Damascus destroyed. In the process, Ahaz became an Assyrian vassal.

Tiglath-Pileser was succeeded to the throne by Shalmaneser V, who reigned for only about five years. Very little is known of him, but most significantly, it was during his reign that Hoshea of Israel rebelled against Assyria. Shalmaneser's campaign to the west began a three-year

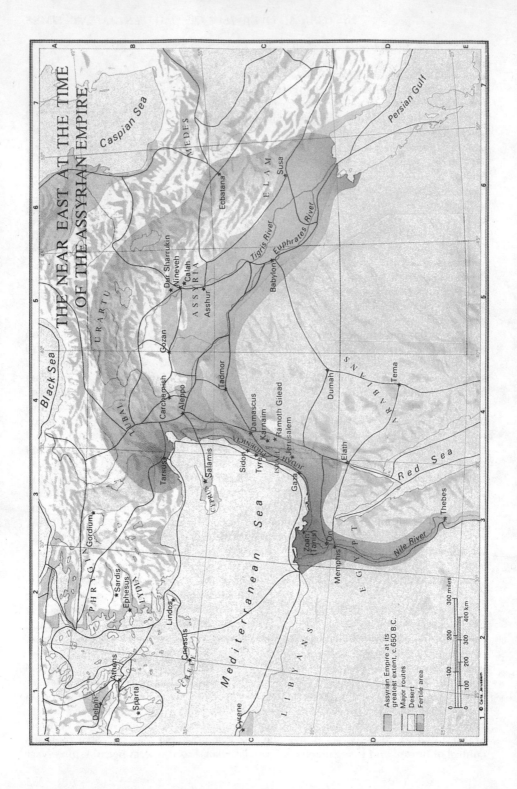

THE NEAR EAST AT THE TIME
OF THE ASSYRIAN EMPIRE

Caspian Sea

MEDES

Black Sea

URARTU

ELAM

Susa

Ecbatana

Persian Gulf

Dur Sharrukin
Nineveh
Calah
Asshur

ASSYRIA

Tigris River

Euphrates River

Babylon

TUBAL

Gozan

Tadmor

ARABIANS

Carchemish
Aleppo

Tema

Dumah

Tarsus

Damascus

Karnaim
Ramoth Gilead

Sidon

PHOENICIA

Tyre

ISRAEL

JUDAH

Jerusalem

Elath

Red Sea

CYPRUS

Salamis

Gaza

Gordium

PHRYGIA

Sardis
Ephesus

LYDIA

Lindos

Delphi

Athens

Sparta

CRETE

Cnossus

Mediterranean Sea

Zoan
(Tanis)

On

Memphis

EGYPT

Nile River

Thebes

LIBYANS

Cyrene

Assyrian Empire at its
greatest extent. c.650 B.C.
Desert
Fertile area

0   100   200   300 miles
0 100 200 300 400 km

© Carta, Jerusalem

siege of Samaria. Upon its fall, the survivors were deported, the city destroyed, and the northern kingdom of Israel annexed entirely to the Assyrian Empire, 722 B.C.

When Sargon II came to the throne, the Assyrian Empire was well established. Most of Sargon's attention was focused on Urartu and Elam, although there were three major western campaigns. Though Hezekiah of Judah was anti-Assyrian, there was little direct action against Judah in these campaigns. That was to change, however, when Sargon's son, Sennacherib, came to the throne in 704.

During the reign of Sargon, Babylon had declared its independence under the leadership of Merodach-baladan. For twelve years Sargon had been unable to deal with this rebel; Merodach-baladan was finally driven from the throne, but escaped. The wily Babylonian had not been idle in the meantime, and when Sennacherib came to power, Merodach-baladan ascended the throne in Babylon and enjoyed the support of concurrent rebellions against Assyria throughout the empire, including one by Hezekiah of Judah. Sennacherib, however, had learned a lesson from his father and went immediately to the source of the trouble. Merodach-baladan became the target of a strategic campaign that quickly subdued Babylon.

Having quenched the uprising in the south, Sennacherib undertook a campaign against the western coalition in 701. He came south along the Phoenician coast and collected tribute from Sidon to Acco. After seizing some cities on the coastal plain, he proceded down into Philistine territory to Ekron. Having cut off the other allies, he was then ready to move against Judah, which was cut off from any potential help. Hezekiah paid tribute at this point, but to no avail. Then, when all seemed lost, Hezekiah trusted the Lord for deliverance and the Assyrian army was mysteriously slaughtered during the night. Sennacherib's account does not report the outcome of the siege.

Hezekiah was succeeded by his son, Manasseh, who adopted a pro-Assyrian position. His long reign spanning the first half of the seventh century came at the height of Assyrian strength and territorial control. Sennacherib's son, Esarhaddon, extended the empire to Egypt and successfully subjugated the north, but it was left to Esarhaddon's son, Ashurbanipal, to capture Thebes in 663. This was the pinnacle of the Assyrian Empire's power, but the cracks of deterioration were already becoming evident.

Empires in Transition (650–600)

Ashurbanipal had inherited an empire at its peak, but decline began in the 650s as Psammetichus gradually cleared the Assyrians out of Egypt. About this time, also, there was civil war in Babylon, led by Ashurbanipal's brother with the support of the Elamites and the Chaldeans. Though this attempt was unsuccessful, the Assyrian king continued to be worn down by revolts. The last several years of his reign are very confused, and it appears that his son assumed kingship before Ashurbanipal died. Shortly after the death of Ashurbanipal in 627, the Babylonians successfully achieved their independence, and the days of Assyrian strength were gone.

In Judah, the decline of Assyria was good news to Josiah, who had ascended the throne at the age of eight just two years after the death of his grandfather, Manasseh. The reform that Josiah undertook in 628 and furthered in 622 took full advantage of the lack of Assyrian presence. At the same time, however, Egypt was strengthening its position in Palestine. Egypt attempted simultaneously to maintain friendly relations with Assyria and to benefit from Assyria's inability to maintain control of the west. As a result, by the 630s the major trade route was controlled by Egypt, and Egypt had a greater presence in Palestine than did Assyria.

The Neo-Babylonian Empire
(600–550)

When the Babylonians declared independence from the Assyrians in 626, it was the Chaldean Nabopolassar who claimed the throne. For the next decade he successfully maintained control of Babylon, but was unable to extend his rule any farther into Assyrian territory. It was clear that Assyria was losing its grasp on the empire, however, and Nabopolassar was not the only one scrambling to take over Assyrian interests. To the east, Cyaxares the Mede was also moving against major Assyrian strongholds. In 614 one of those, the city of Assur, fell to the Medes, and outside the ruins of the city the late-arriving Nabopolassar and the victorious Cyaxares made a pact to join their forces against the floundering Assyrians. Their joint armies were able to bring down the mighty capital of Nineveh just two years later, in 612 B.C. The beleaguered Assyrian government retreated west and regrouped with its headquarters in Haran.

Sinsharishkun had died in the fall of Nineveh, so Ashuruballit assumed the throne, destined to become Assyria's last king. In 610 Haran capitulated, and the Assyrians were forced to retreat another fifty miles west to Carchemish on the west bank of the upper reaches of the Euphrates, just inside modern-day Turkey. Here, though reinforced by the Egyptians under Pharaoh Necho, the Assyrian Empire ended when Nebuchadrezzar,[4] crown prince of Babylon and commander-in-chief of the armies, stormed Carchemish and scattered what was left of the Assyrians, pursuing them as far south as Hamath and claiming Syria for the Babylonian realm. That very year

Nabopolassar died, and Nebuchadrezzar rushed back to Babylon, where he assumed the throne of what had now become the Neo-Babylonian Empire.

Nebuchadrezzar was one of the most successful kings known to history. He ruled from 605 to 562 B.C. and distinguished himself in both military matters and domestic undertakings, foremost of which was the beautification of the city of Babylon. The Assyrian Empire had been divided between the Babylonians and their allies, the Medes. The Babylonians received the Tigris and Euphrates basins from a line just east of the Tigris (approximating the boundary between the modern states of Iraq and Iran) and all of the western states extending as far north as the southeast section of Asia Minor. The Medes ruled the eastern regions (modern-day Iran), Urartu (between the Black and Caspian seas), and the eastern section of Asia Minor. Eventually Nebuchadrezzar was able to extend his domain to include Egypt (568).

The establishment of the Neo-Babylonian Empire had far-reaching effects on Judah. Apparently hoping to contribute to the downfall of Assyria, Josiah attempted to stop the advance of the Egyptian armies hurrying to provide assistance to Ashuruballit at Carchemish. This proved to be a fatal decision, because Josiah, who had accomplished more reform than any of his Davidic predecessors, was killed in the losing effort. He was succeeded to the throne in turn by three sons and a grandson. Jehoahaz, the first son, was taken into exile in Egypt after serving only three months; this occurred upon Necho's return from Syria in 609. Jehoiakim, a second son, was placed on the throne instead. Once Nebuchadrezzar had defeated the Assyrian-Egyptian coalition and claimed control of Syro-Palestine, Jehoiakim became a Babylonian vassal;

---

[4]The forms "Nebuchadrezzar" and "Nebuchadnezzar" both appear in the Hebrew Scriptures, but on the basis of the Akkadian language the authors prefer the form with "r."

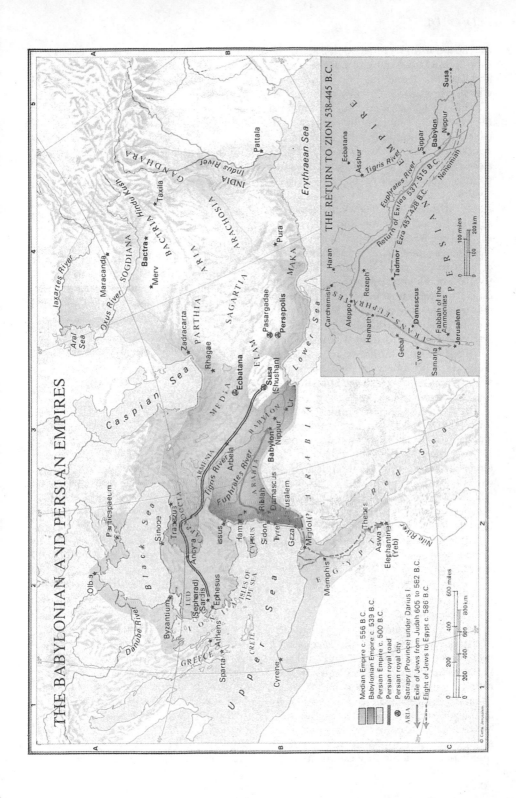

THE BABYLONIAN AND PERSIAN EMPIRES

THE RETURN TO ZION 538-445 B.C.

Median Empire c. 556 B.C.
Babylonian Empire c. 539 B.C.
Persian Empire c. 500 B.C.
Persian royal road
Persian royal city

ARIA — Satrapy (Province) under Darius I

Exile of Jews from Judah 605 to 562 B.C.
Flight of Jews to Egypt c. 586 B.C.

© Carta, Jerusalem

this lasted until he rebelled in 598. By the time Nebuchadrezzar came west, Jehoiakim had died and his son, Jehoiachin, was on the throne. The city of Jerusalem was set under siege and surrendered on March 16, 597. Jehoiachin was taken to exile in Babylon along with many of the people, including the prophet Ezekiel. Nebuchadrezzar set Zedekiah, Josiah's third son, on the throne.

Almost from the start, Zedekiah became involved in seditious schemes against the Babylonians, and finally, with the promise of Egyptian support, he rebelled in 589. The Babylonian army arrived in 588 and blockaded Jerusalem to prevent its stockpiling supplies while other fortified cities were defeated. That summer the siege was lifted briefly, as the Babylonians were diverted to meet an Egyptian force, and then was reinstated. By the following summer, July 587, the walls were breached and Jerusalem was sacked, the temple burned, and the people deported to Babylon.

The Neo-Babylonian Empire did not long survive the death of Nebuchadrezzar. He was succeeded by four relatively obscure and apparently incompetent kings, and one could say the handwriting was on the wall long before that fateful feast of Belshazzar on the eve of the fall of Babylon the Great. In fact, Cyrus had begun moving to consolidate his power within five years of the death of Nebuchadrezzar.

The Medo-Persian Empire
(550–450)

When the Babylonian king Nabonidus negated his treaty with the Medes and realigned himself with Cyrus and the Persians in 556, it gave Cyrus the opportunity he had been waiting for to move against the Medes. He defeated them in 550 and became the ruler of the new Medo-Persian Empire. Over the next decade he was able to defeat the Lydians, a major political force in western Anatolia,

and extend his control in the east as far as the Indus valley. He was now poised to move aginst Babylon. Since numerous segments of the population had good reason to be disgruntled with the policies and prospects of Nabonidus, Cyrus was welcomed into Babylon (October 16, 539 B.C.) as deliverer rather than having to resort to a long siege.

Cyrus was anxious to be recognized as a benevolent liberator rather than as a conquering tyrant, and he set policies toward that end. These policies included granting permits for many of the peoples deported by the Babylonians to return to their homelands and rebuild their temples. The Israelites were among them. Nevertheless, such permission assumed loyalty to the Medo-Persian crown and acceptance of its sovereignty; so although Israel was restored to the land, she was still without a king.

Cambyses, the son of Cyrus, was able to add Egypt to the empire in 526, but he died in an unfortunate accident on the return journey. (According to Herodotus, Cambyses was wounded by his own sword as he attempted to mount his horse and died of the resulting infection.) After some struggle, the throne was secured by Darius the Great, who, because of the difficulties surrounding the succession, was now faced with revolts in every quarter of the empire. By 519, however, he was able to put down the revolts and secure his rule.

By the beginning of the fifth century, the Persians were coming into contact with the Athenians because of some rebellions against Darius in the western cities of Anatolia. This led Darius eventually to attempt an invasion of Greece, which failed miserably when his army was driven into the sea at the Battle of Marathon (490). When Darius died in 486, it was left to his son, Xerxes, to renew the attempt. Disaster followed disaster, however, as the Persians were defeated at Thermopylae and Salamis in Greece and continued to suffer losses as they retreated through Anatolia.

Xerxes was assassinated, and he was succeeded by his son, Artaxerxes I, who officially sponsored the rebuilding of the walls of Jerusalem at the request of his Jewish cupbearer, Nehemiah. War with the Greeks dragged on, yet the Persian Empire remained in power for another century until the lightning conquest by the young warrior, Alexander the Great, in 331.

Questions for Further Study and Discussion

1. Why is chronology important to the study of the Old Testament?
2. What impact did the Late Bronze Age have on the social, cultural, and religious history of the Hebrews?
3. What did technological development during the Iron Age mean for Hebrew history?
4. How do we account for the rise of the Israelite monarchy to empire status under David and Solomon?
5. What is the relationship between the Hebrew prophetic movement and the rise of empire nations in Mesopotamia in the first millennium B.C.?
6. How was Persian military and political policy different from that of Assyria and Babylonia? What did this mean for the Hebrews?
7. How does Old Testament history contribute to the "fullness of time" (Gal. 4:4, NRSV) as understood by the apostle Paul?
8. What did Old Testament history contribute to the understanding of Messiah during the intertestamental period?

For Further Reading

Ackroyd, Peter R. *Israel Under Babylon and Persia.* London: Oxford University Press, 1970.

Bottero, Jean, Elena Cassin, and Jean Vercoutter. *The Near East: The Early Civilizations.* New York: Delacorte, 1967.

Bright, John. *A History of Israel.* 3d ed. Philadelphia: Westminster, 1981. A textbook widely used in colleges and seminaries that is readable and up to date and uses reconstruction moderately.

The Cambridge Ancient History Series. 3d ed. Vols. 1–3. The standard, exhaustive reference work on the history of the ancient Near East.

The Cambridge History of Iran. 4 vols. Cambridge: Cambridge University Press, 1983, 1985. Vols. 2–3.

The Cambridge History of Judaism. D. W. Davies and Louis Finkelstein, eds. Cambridge: Cambridge University Press, 1984. Vol. 1. Introduction: The Persian Period.

Hallo, William. "From Qarqar to Carchemish: Assyria and Israel in the Light of New Discoveries." In *The Biblical Archaeologist Reader 2.* David N. Freedman and E. F. Campbell, eds. 1960; reprint, Missoula, Mont.: Scholars Press, 1975. 152–88.

Hallo, William, and William Simpson. *The Ancient Near East.* New York: Harcourt, Brace, 1971. A good basic introduction to the history of the ancient Near East.

Harrison, R. K. *Old Testament Times.* Grand Rapids: Eerdmans, 1970.

Hayes, John, and J. Maxwell Miller. *Israelite and Judaean History.* Philadelphia: Westminster, 1977. An exploration by a number of contributors of the current state of scholarship on the various periods of Israelite history.

Kramer, Samuel N. *The Sumerians.* Chicago: University of Chicago Press, 1963.

Merrill, Eugene. *Kingdom of Priests.* Grand Rapids: Baker, 1987.

Miller, J. Maxwell, and John Hayes. *A History of Ancient Israel and Judah.* Philadelphia: Westminster, 1986. Probably the most thorough presentation of Israelite history against the background of the ancient Near East, though evangelicals will find it overly reconstructive.

Oates, Joan. *Babylon.* London: Thames & Hudson, 1979.

Pitard, Wayne. *Ancient Damascus.* Winona Lake, Ind.: Eisenbrauns, 1987.

Saggs, H. W. F. *The Greatness That Was Babylon.* New York: Mentor, 1962.

———. *The Might That Was Assyria.* London: Sidgwick & Jackson, 1984. Like the preceding title, an excellent introduction to its subject.

Thiele, Edwin R. *The Mysterious Numbers of the Hebrew Kings.* Rev. ed. Grand Rapids: Zondervan, 1983.

Van Der Woude, A. S. *The World of the Bible.* Grand Rapids: Eerdmans, 1986. An excellent introduction to geography, history, archaeology, and manuscripts.

Wiseman, Donald J. *Peoples of Old Testament Times.* Oxford: Clarendon Press, 1973.

Wood, Leon J. *A Survey of Israel's History.* Rev. ed. Grand Rapids: Zondervan, 1986.

Yamauchi, Edwin M. *Persia and the Bible.* Grand Rapids: Baker, 1989.

Chapter 4

The Geography
of the Old Testament

The history of the Israelite nation developed in a specific geographical context. For this reason the Bible takes geography seriously. It records real events taking place in time and space, not artificial and contrived literary history. However, the Bible is not simply an ancient annal, nor is it intended to be a gazetteer or topographical manual. Like the science of archaeology, geography expands our knowledge of the setting or background of the biblical narratives and thus enriches our understanding of a given Old Testament text.

The physical world of the Old Testament was the ancient Near East, commonly known today as the Middle East. The Old Testament narratives encompass the region of Mesopotamia in the east, Asia Minor or Anatolia in the north, Syro-Palestine and Egypt in the west, and the Arabian peninsula in the south. The modern states of Iraq and Iran occupy most of ancient Mesopotamia, while Asia Minor is now known as Turkey, and Saudi Arabia controls most of the Arabian peninsula. Nearly four-fifths of Old Testament history takes in the area of Syro-Palestine on the eastern Mediterranean coast. This territory now includes the states of Syria, Lebanon, Jordan, and Israel.

The Old Testament World

The Fertile Crescent

The world of the Old Testament is usually identified with the "Fertile Crescent." This area included the Nile River valley and delta, the narrow plains along the Mediterranean coast of Syro-Palestine, and the Tigris and Euphrates river valleys. Adequate rainfall and irrigation along these coastal plains and river valleys permitted agriculture and a settled life, giving rise to the earliest civilizations of the ancient Near East. The first part of this chapter describes the major geographical regions adjoining this fertile crescent and the respective peoples and cultures influencing Hebrew history.

Mesopotamia

The name "Mesopotamia" means "the land between the rivers," namely, the Tigris and Euphrates rivers. The fertile strip of land along the rivers extends some six hundred miles from the mountainous regions on the northern edge of the Fertile Crescent to the expansive alluvial plains at the Persian Gulf. Like Egypt, networks of canals irrigated the flood plain, making lower Mesopotamia

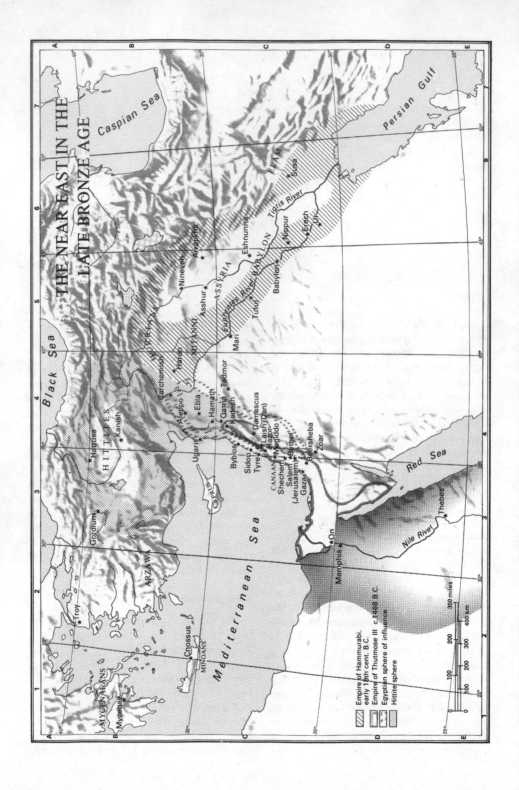

THE NEAR EAST IN THE
LATE BRONZE AGE

Caspian Sea

Persian Gulf

Black Sea

ELAM

Susa

Tigris River

HURRIANS

Nineveh

Arrapha

ASSYRIA

Asshur

Eshnunna

Nippur

Erech

Ur

MITANNI

Euphrates River

Mari

Babylon

Tukulti

BABYLON

Carchemish

Haran

HITTITES

Hattusa

Kanish

Tadmor

Aleppo

Ebla

Hamath

Qatna

Kadesh

Damascus

Laish/Dan

Hazor

Megiddo

Ugarit

Byblos

Sidon

Tyre

Shechem

Salem

(Jerusalem)

Bethel

Gaza

Beersheba

Zoar

CANAAN

CYPRUS

Mediterranean Sea

Red Sea

On

Memphis

Thebes

Nile River

Gordium

ARZAWA

Troy

Cnossus

MINOANS

MYCENAEANS

Mycenae

Empire of Hammurabi,
early 18th cent. B.C.

Empire of Thutmose III c.1468 B.C.

Egyptian sphere of influence

Hittite sphere

300 miles

400 km

100   200   300

0   100   200   300

especially productive agriculturally. Unlike Egypt, Mesopotamia had no natural barriers protecting the region from outside influence and invasion. The city-state cultures of Sumer and Akkad were responsible for spreading early civilization northward along the river basins.

Northern Mesopotamia was the homeland of Israelite origins in that the Hebrew patriarchs lived in the area of Haran in Paddan-Aram between the Tigris and Euphrates. Abraham is identified as an Amorite (Ezek. 16:3), and sometime later Jacob sojourned among Amorite kinfolk in Paddan-Aram (Gen. 28:1–9). Of course, Abraham also migrated from Ur in Mesopotamia (or a "northern Ur" now suggested as an alternative) northward to Haran and finally to Canaan as he followed the revelation and promise of Yahweh.

Later Israelite history is greatly influenced by the empire nations of Mesopotamia, with the Assyrians, the Babylonians, and the Persians all controlling the land of Palestine at some point in their rule of the ancient Near Eastern world. Assyria and Babylonia were also responsible for the destruction of the divided kingdoms of the Hebrews and the deportation of thousands of Hebrews into exile in Mesopotamia. Then, under the enlightened rule of Cyrus and the Persians, these Hebrew exiles were permitted to return to their homeland and rebuild the temple of Yahweh.

Asia Minor/Anatolia

The region of Asia Minor situated northwest of the Fertile Crescent is a rugged, mountainous area. It is a diverse land, with rich soil and Mediterranean climate in the west and south and a dry and barren central plateau and steep mountains in the east toward Armenia. The stores of minerals and metal ores in the central mountain ranges afforded the inhabitants of Anatolia ready resource for commercial trading with the rest of the

ancient Near East for food staples and domestic wares. The peninsula was also the land bridge joining central Asia and southeastern Europe, which meant the area was often subject to invasion and foreign encroachment and influence.

During the second millennium B.C. the central portion of the region was home to the Hittite Empire, a powerful rival to Egypt for control of Syro-Palestine. The Hittites were a military people, hiring out as mercenaries and exporting military technology throughout the ancient Near East. The Hittite treaty form by which Hittite kings subjugated conquered foes became an important literary contribution to the ancient world; it was similar to that used for structuring the writing of the covenant between Yahweh and his people Israel, in both Exodus (19–24) and the book of Deuteronomy. There are also parallels between certain Hittite laws and the Old Testament, and some biblical scholars even find Hittite influence in the form and practice of history writing in Israel.

During the first millennium B.C. the people of Urartu dominated eastern Asia Minor and vied for control of northern Mesopotamia with the Assyrians, while the Lydians controlled western Asia Minor during the Neo-Babylonian period (ca. 885–546 B.C.).

Syro-Palestine

The region of Syro-Palestine constitutes the land bridge between the continents of Africa and Asia. This four-hundred-mile strip of fertile land along the Mediterranean coast was bounded on the west by the Great Sea and in the east by the Arabian desert and the deep gorge of the Jordan cleft. Syro-Phoenicia, or the northern portion of this land bridge, essentially encompasses the modern states of Syria and Lebanon. Palestine, or the southern portion of the land bridge, essentially comprises the modern nations of Israel and part of Jordan. Generally

Mount Hermon marked the boundary between the northern and southern portions of the land bridge. (The physical and geographical features of Syro-Palestine are described later in the chapter.)

The coast of Syro-Phoenicia had the advantage of natural harbors. This gave rise to extensive maritime commerce centered in the region, especially among the Phoenicians and their key ports of Tyre, Sidon, and Byblos. The Phoenicians occupied the northern coast of Palestine from Acco to Ugarit and were merchant traders all along the Mediterranean seaboard for nearly two millennia (cf. Ezek. 27). Both David and Solomon were allied to the Phoenicians, resulting in a Phoenician-designed-and-constructed temple in Jerusalem and a Red Sea port at Elath for Phoenician merchants (1 Kings 7:13–22; 9:26–28). During the period of the divided monarchy, King Ahab of Israel married the Phoenician princess Jezebel, thus importing the religion of Baal Melqart into the political and religious life of the northern kingdom (1 Kings 16:29–34).

The Arameans occupied the inland regions of Syro-Phoenicia during Old Testament times. They were descendants of the Amorites and Hurrians and settled at the large oasis of Damascus in Aram, or Syria. The Arameans shared a border with Israel and were alternately enemies or allies of the Israelites, depending on the menacing power and presence of Assyria.

The region of Palestine, or Canaan, was the land of covenant promise for the Hebrews. However, the presence of the Philistines on the coast and the several Canaanite people groups inland meant that Israel would not possess the land without conflict. The incomplete conquest of Canaan under Joshua left the Hebrews prey to the seductive influence of Canaanite Baalism and its idolatry and immorality (cf. Deut. 7:1–5; Josh. 13:1–7; Judg. 2:11–15). The Philistines controlled the coastal plains and remained a potent enemy of Israel right through the periods of the united and divided monarchies,

until King Uzziah (767–740 B.C.) subdued them (2 Chron. 26:6–15). The Hebrew prophets continued to pronounce judgment on the Philistine cities into the seventh and sixth centuries B.C. (e.g., Jer. 25:20; Zeph. 2:4–7; Zech. 9:5–7).

Egypt

The land of Egypt lay immediately to the southwest of Palestine and has been known since ancient times as "the gift of the Nile." The Nile River was considered a god by the Egyptians because all life was dependent on the flow of this great watercourse. The final 750 miles of the Nile bisected the area known as Egypt in antiquity. The river valley was hemmed in by limestone cliffs on the east and desert on the west. The strip of arable land in the river basin measured from 25 miles to nearly 150 miles in width at the delta. The land of Egypt receives up to eight inches of rainfall annually, with large portions experiencing less than one inch. Agricultural activity was based totally on irrigation of the rich alluvial soil deposited along the river basin as a result of the annual flooding.

Ancient Egypt was divided into an Upper Kingdom (along the narrow strip of river valley in the south) and a Lower Kingdom (essentially the delta area in the north). The predictable flood pattern of the Nile and the great natural barriers of mountains and desert on both the eastern and western borders made for a static Egyptian civilization. Historians often refer to the "splendid isolation" of Egypt, which enabled Egyptian civilization to develop a dependable agriculture-based economy, a stable governmental structure, and an ordered society.

The Early Dynastic and Old Kingdom periods of Egyptian history (ca. 3100–2100 B.C.) witnessed the unification of Upper and Lower Egypt under the pharaoh. This early period was also the time of the building of the great pyramid tombs for the royal family. The Middle

Kingdom (2133–1786 B.C.) and the Second Intermediate Period (1786–1570) would have included Abram's sojourn in Egypt (Gen. 12:10–20), the migration of Jacob and his family to Egypt (Gen. 45:16–47:12), and perhaps the oppression of the Hebrews as slaves (Exod. 1:1–14).

The New Kingdom (1570–1085 B.C.) witnessed the call of Moses as deliverer of the Hebrews and the Exodus from Egyptian captivity (Exod. 3–13). By the end of the Late Bronze Age (ca. 1200 B.C.) Egypt gained control of Palestine under Rameses II, thanks in part to a treaty with the Hittites. Egyptian intervention in Palestine continued with Sheshonk I, who harbored Jeroboam as a political fugitive from Israel (1 Kings 11:40) and who invaded Judah during the reign of Rehoboam (1 Kings 14:25–26). Thereafter Egypt remained an important and necessary ally of both the Hebrew divided kingdoms against the Mesopotamian imperial powers of Assyria and Babylonia.

Later Hebrew history witnessed considerable direct contact with the Egyptians as well. For example, King Solomon married a daughter of the pharaoh as part of a political alliance (1 Kings 3:1–2), and King Josiah of Judah was killed by Pharaoh Neco in battle at Megiddo (2 Kings 23:28–30).

Egyptian influence can be seen elsewhere in the language and literature of the Old Testament. For example, the Old Testament contains nearly fifty Egyptian "loan words," or vocabulary items directly borrowed from the Egyptian language (like 'abrek, "bow the knee," Gen. 41:43 KJV). There are also the long acknowledged parallels between Egyptian and Hebrew wisdom literature and love poetry (see chapter 22).

Hebrew religion may have been compromised on at least two occasions by the pervasive influence of the Apis calf cult of Egypt, namely, the incident of Aaron and the golden calf related in Exodus 32 and Jeroboam's calf worship at Dan and Bethel related in 1 Kings 12. Hebrew statecraft was also influenced by the Egyptians, as the preexilic prophets condemned the Israelites for straying from God and seeking alliances with Egypt (Hos. 7:11). Curiously, Isaiah prophesied that Egypt would one day turn to the Lord and Yahweh would call them his people (Isa. 19:16–25).

The Arabian Peninsula

The Arabian peninsula is a massive, raised plateau, essentially desert, sand dunes, and lava fields surrounded by somewhat fertile coastal fringes. The peninsula is usually divided into three geographical regions: (1) the northwestern area called Arabia of Petra, which includes Petra, Edom, Moab, and the Transjordan, (2) the Arabian Desert in the northern and central areas, and (3) the southern coastal strip called Fortunate Arabia. The extensive desert of the Arabian peninsula formed a major physical boundary between the river valley civilizations of Mesopotamia and Egypt. For this reason, travel from east to west in the ancient Near East moved in a north-south direction along the Tigris and Euphrates rivers to Haran and Damascus.

The Transjordan region of Arabia of Petra was home to several nation-states and semi-nomadic tribes that figured prominently in Israelite history. The Moabites and Ammonites were racially homogenous peoples whose lineage may be traced to Abraham's nephew Lot and his incestuous relationship with his two daughters (Gen. 19:30–38). They were both monarchical nations, organized and governed by a form of tribal kingship.

It was the nations of Moab and Ammon that denied the Hebrews passage through the southern Transjordan on their way from Egypt to Canaan (Deut. 2:9–37). For this reason no Ammonite or Moabite was permitted to enter the assembly of the Lord (Deut. 23:3). Both nations were enemies of Israel during the days of the Judges right through the Hebrew united and divided kingdoms. According to 2 Kings 24 and Jeremiah 37, Moab and Ammon aided the Babylonians in the sack of Jerusalem. Even more troublesome for the Hebrews were the gods of Ammon (Milcom or Molech, 1 Kings 11:7; 2 Kings 23:10) and Moab (Chemosh, 1 Kings 11:7, 33). Perhaps the Moabite best-known to us is the widow Ruth, who pledged allegiance to Yahweh (Ruth 1:16) and eventually found herself in the genealogy of King David (Ruth 4:13–22).

The Edomites lived to the south of Moab from the River Zered to the Gulf of Arabia. Their lineage may be traced to Jacob's older twin, Esau (Gen. 25:19–26). They were a rival nation to the Hebrews from the time of the Exodus to the fall of Jerusalem. The prophets Isaiah, Jeremiah, Ezekiel, Joel, Amos, and Obadiah all pronounced oracles of doom against Edom, "a people always under the wrath of the LORD" (Mal. 1:2–4). (For more on the place of the Edomites in Old Testament history, see chapter 36, "Obadiah.")

Two other groups of people roaming the northern Arabian peninsula bear mention. The first group, the Amalekites—like the Edomites descendants of Esau (Gen. 36:12, 16)—fought with Israel en route from Egypt to Canaan (Exod. 17:8–16) and were part of a coalition of foreign oppressors of Israel during the period of the Judges (e.g., Judg. 6:3; 7:12). Numbers 24:20 and Deuteronomy 25:17–19 predict the utter annihilation of the Amalekites for their unprovoked assault against Israel during the Exodus. The second group, the semi-nomadic Midianites, were descendants of Abraham and lived in northern Arabia (Gen. 25:1–2, 18). In Habakkuk 3:7 the Cushites and Midianites seem to be equated, so these tribes must overlap in some way. Joseph was sold to the Egyptians by Midianite traders (Gen. 37:25–36), and Moses married into the Midianite clan of Jethro while exiled in Sinai (Exod. 2:15–22). During the period of the Judges the Midianites were among the foreign peoples oppressing the Hebrew tribes (Judg. 6:2; 7:2).

The Land of Palestine

The land of Palestine took its name from the Philistines (the Pelishtim in Hebrew) who settled along the Mediterranean coast from Joppa to Gaza about 1300–1200 B.C. According to the Bible, the Philistine people were connected with Caphtor, usually associated with the island of Crete (Jer. 47:4; Amos 9:7). Prior to the Philistine migrations the region was known as Canaan. This term signified a "land of purple" and was probably derived from the purple dye manufactured by the indigenous peoples from the murex shellfish found in abundance along the Mediterranean coast.

Palestine is often referred to as the geographical and theological center of the ancient world. Not only was it located at the crossroads of the important trades routes of antiquity, but it was also in this general area that Judaism, Christianity, and Islam all had their beginnings. The land area measures approximately 150 miles from Dan to Beersheba (north-south) and 100 miles from the Mediterranean Sea to the Jordan River (east-west), or roughly the size of New Jersey. The climate is typical of the Near East, mild to cold winter depending on the altitude, with some snow at the higher elevations. The rainy season lasts from October to April, with hot, dry, cloudless summer months from May through August.

The land is easily divided into four basic longitudinal, or north-south, geographical regions: the coastal plain, the central hill country, the Jordan rift, and the Transjordan plateau. The major latitudinal, or east-west, geographical divisions of Palestine are connected both with the geographical features of the land and the political boundaries of the Israelite divided kingdoms. These divisions included the region of Galilee in the north, Samaria in the north-central area

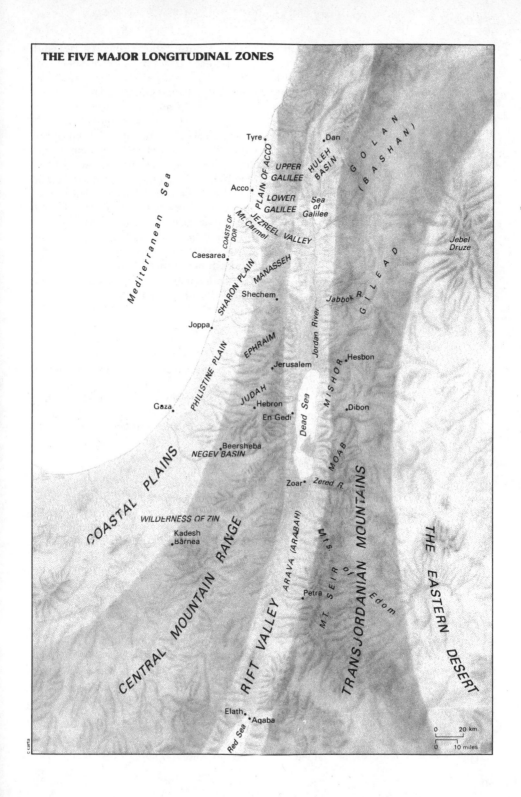

THE FIVE MAJOR LONGITUDINAL ZONES

Mediterranean Sea

Tyre
Dan
PLAIN OF ACCO
UPPER GALILEE
HULEH BASIN
GOLAN (BASHAN)
Acco
LOWER GALILEE
Sea of Galilee
JEZREEL VALLEY
COASTS OF DOR
Mt. Carmel
Jebel Druze
Caesarea
SHARON PLAIN
MANASSEH
GILEAD
Shechem
Jabbok R.
Joppa
EPHRAIM
Jordan River
Jerusalem
Hesbon
MISHOR
Gaza
PHILISTINE PLAIN
JUDAH
Hebron
En Gedi
Dibon
Dead Sea
Beersheba
NEGEV BASIN
MOAB
COASTAL PLAINS
Zoar
Zered R.
WILDERNESS OF ZIN
Kadesh Bärnea
CENTRAL MOUNTAIN RANGE
RIFT VALLEY
ARAVA (ARABAH)
Petra
MT. SEIR
Edom
TRANSJORDANIAN MOUNTAINS
THE EASTERN DESERT
Elath
Aqaba
Red Sea

0 ___ 20 km.
0 ___ 10 miles

C. arta

of Palestine, Judah in the south-central portion of Palestine, the Negev (or "dry" steppe) in the south, and the Sinai peninsula forming a great barrier between Palestine and Egypt (see map and figure 4.1).

The Coastal Plain

The coastal plain gradually widens to distances of ten to twelve miles in southern Palestine. This fertile strip of land receives more than thirty inches of rainfall annually off the Mediterranean Sea. Three distinct plains are identified along the coast: Acre (Acco), extending northward from Mount Carmel (some twenty-five miles long and five to eight miles wide); Sharon, between Mount Carmel and the port city of Joppa (some fifty miles long and ten miles wide); and the plain of the Philistines in the extreme south from Joppa to Gaza. The coastal plain never held primary importance to the Hebrews geographically during Old Testament history. The Phoenicians controlled the northern plain, the Philistines controlled the southern plain, and the plain of Sharon was wasteland, marsh, and dense forest in ancient times.

The Central Hill Country

The region of the central hill country was the most varied geographically and the most important historically in Old Testament times. The majority of Israelite cities were located here, and the territory comprised the bulk of the land area controlled by the Hebrew united and divided monarchies. The mountainous terrain forms the spine, or backbone, of western Palestine and is commonly divided into three major sections: Galilee, Samaria (or Ephraim), and Judah. The slopes reach heights of 3000–3300 feet; the region receives adequate rainfall and was suitable to the Hebrews for agricultural cultivation, including grains, vineyards, and fruit and olive groves.

The principal features of Galilee included Mount Tabor (Judg. 4:6, 12) and the Jezreel valley. The city of Shechem, flanked by mounts Ebal and Gerizim, dominated Samaria (Josh. 8:30–35). Jerusalem was prominently situated at the crossing of the trade routes in Judah (2 Sam. 5:6–12). The strip of land between the coastal plain in the south and the central highlands was known as the Shephelah. This broad and fertile piedmont (or plateau between coast and mountains) was a forested area in Old Testament times and occupied by the Philistines (cf. Judg. 14–15; 1 Sam. 17). During the Judahite monarchy, Beth-Shemesh and Lachish were important fortifications on the southwestern flank of Judah (2 Chron. 25:17–28).

The Jordan Rift

The Jordan River rift, or Jordan cleft, is a great geological depression that begins in Syria in the Lebanon mountains and runs south to the Gulf of Aqabah and the Red Sea. The Jordan River valley that forms the eastern boundary of Palestine is part of this jagged geological trench.

The Jordan River has its origins on the lower slopes of Mount Hermon and rises from three spring-fed rivulets. The Jordan flows southward from Hermon to the Hula Lake and swamp and then drops quickly some 900 feet and empties into the Sea of Galilee. This inland, freshwater lake is 650 feet below sea level and is surrounded by rounded hillocks. The lake itself is some 13 miles wide and 7 miles long. The Jordan River flows south from the Sea of Galilee, winding its way to the great Salt or Dead Sea, nearly 1,300 feet below sea level—the lowest point on the face of the earth.

During antiquity the region around the Sea of Galilee was heavily populated and intensively cultivated by means of irrigation. Further south, the river valley narrowed and was covered with dense jungle-like vegetation, a habitat for wild animals in Old Testament times (cf. Jer.

Figure 4.1. Geological Features of Palestine

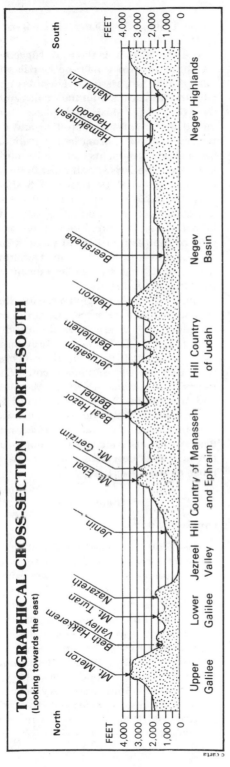

TOPOGRAPHICAL CROSS-SECTION — NORTH-SOUTH
(Looking towards the east)

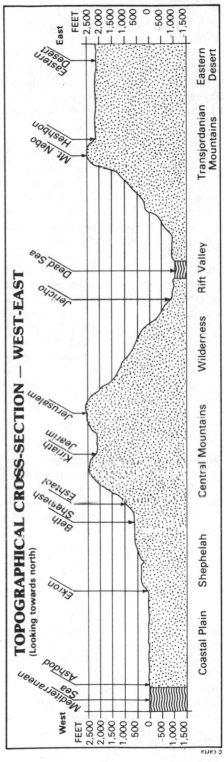

TOPOGRAPHICAL CROSS-SECTION — WEST-EAST
(Looking towards north)

49:19; 50:44; Zech. 11:3). The southern end of the river valley was largely unpopulated, except where the Jabbok River entered the Jordan and at the spring-watered oasis of Jericho. Lined with slippery clay-mud hills and thick vegetation, the Jordan valley still constitutes a natural barrier between Palestine and the Transjordan plateau.

The Dead Sea has no natural outlet, and its mineral rich waters have a salt content of 30 percent. The limestone cliffs lining the western shore of the Dead Sea are pocked with caves that served as hideaways for bandits, political fugitives, and sectarian religious communities. It was here among the caves of this "badlands"-type landscape that the famous Dead Sea or Qumran community scrolls were found. South of the Dead Sea, the Arabah valley stretches some hundred miles to the Gulf of Aqabah. The inhabitants of this desolate and dry desert fringe mined the iron and copper deposits found in the hills bordering the Arabah, or engaged in the caravan trade that transversed the region.

The Transjordan Plateau

Broadly speaking, the Transjordan plateau is an extensive tableland rising some 2000-6000 feet above sea level between the Jordan River and the northernmost reaches of the Arabian desert. The region yields some minerals and is suitable for both agricultural and pastoral lifestyles. Four major wadis or rivers feed the Jordan River and the Dead Sea from the plateau, including the Yarmuk, the Jabbok, the Arnon, and the Zered.

The Transjordan tableland may be subdivided into three main plateaus: the Seir mountain plateau in the south (from the Gulf of Elath to the Zered River), the area of Moab and Gilead in the central Transjordan (extending from the Zered to the Yarmuk rivers), and the Bashan plateau in the north (stretching from the Yarmuk to Dan). The "king's highway" ran the length of the Transjordan plateau from Bozrah to Damascus.

The Seir plateau is the most rugged of the three, with mountain peaks rising to nearly 6000 feet. Here the Edomites and later the Nabateans built their cities amid the rock cliffs. Moab and Gilead contained fertile soil for cultivation and extensive tracts of grazing land for animal herds. Forest remnants can still be found in Gilead. The largest and most fertile of the plateaus was the region of Bashan. Here the tableland sits some 3000-5000 feet above sea level, permitting adequate rainfall for agriculture. The rich volcanic soils of the plain of Bashan made it the best pastureland in the entire Levantine region of the eastern Mediterranean (cf. Ps. 22:12; cf. Amos 4:1).

The Transjordan region was the first area settled by the Hebrews as part of the conquest of Palestine after the Exodus from Egypt (Josh. 13:24−31). Throughout Old Testament history the plateau area was often the site of military conflict as Hebrews, Arameans, Assyrians, Moabites, and Ammonites all vied for control of the trade centers along the King's Highway and of the fruitful land of Gilead and Bashan, a most valuable commodity in the arid and desertlike environment of most of the Near East.

The Trade Routes

Overland Routes

The prophet Ezekiel's description of Phoenician commerce in the first millennium B.C. attests the strategic geographical location of Syro-Palestine (Ezek. 27:12−36). As the land bridge between Africa and Eurasia, Palestine played a prominent role in international trade as early as the third millennium B.C.

There were two major international highways linking Mesopotamia and Egypt via Palestine. Both were very ancient routes, their history traceable to the Early Bronze Age (3000−2100 B.C.). One was known as "the way of the sea" (or Via

Maris in Roman times). The route originated at Qantir (Qantara) in the eastern delta of Lower Egypt, crossed the northern Sinai peninsula, turned north along the coast of the Negev and Judea, and then veered inland through Megiddo to the plain of Beth-Shan. Here the road divided, one artery branching off along the west shoreline of the Sea of Galilee to Dan and Damascus, the other continuing eastward through Bashan to Damascus. At that point the highway turned to the southeast, connecting Babylon and Ur.

The second important trade route was known as "the way of the kings." It too joined Babylon with Egypt, transversing the Sinai desert through Kadesh-Barnea and continuing across the Negev through Edom. The highway then jogged to the north through the Transjordan area of Moab, Ammon, and Gilead to Damascus, and from there into Mesopotamia. King Jehoram identifies the southern portion of this route as the way "through the Desert of Edom" (2 Kings 3:8). Secondary roads branching off "the King's Highway" included a route from Kadesh-Barnea to Elath (perhaps the "way of the Red Sea" in Numbers 14:25) and another route to Elath from Bozrah, mentioned in the battle that the kings of Sodom and Gomorrah waged against Kedorlaomer (Gen. 14:5–6).

A lesser trade route originated at Elath, extending to Babylon via the Arabian desert with stops at Dumah and Tema. There was also a route northward to Damascus from Dumah. In addition, some twenty-three regional or local routes crisscrossed Palestine during biblical times (e.g., "the desert road toward the Red Sea," Exod. 13:18; "the road that goes from Bethel to Shechem," Judg. 21:19; and the "way of the plain," 2 Sam. 18:23).

The Importance of the Trade Routes

Palestine's location as a corridor for commerce between three continents had

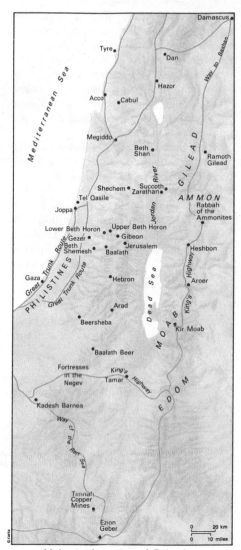

Major trade routes of Palestine

great significance for the Israelites. Politically the location made the Hebrews vulnerable to hostile invasion by foreign powers seeking to control the land bridge for military and economic reasons. This forced Israel to engage in international diplomacy, including forging alliances with surrounding pagan powers. On this account Hosea the prophet rebuked the northern kingdom of Israel (Hos. 7:10–11). In their pride and self-sufficiency the

53

Hebrews sought political treaties with Egypt and Assyria, refusing to seek help from the Lord. Of course, this type of political maneuvering was useless, as the Egyptians, Assyrians, Babylonians, Persians, and later the Greeks and Romans all took their turn overrunning Palestine as part of the military expansion of their empires.

The crucial location of Palestine also had implications for the Israelites socially, economically, and religiously. Trade and commerce fostered the development of a merchant class. Soon the rich were able to gain control of the institutions of society and oppress the poor, breaking down covenant community (and equality before God). Economically the prosperity and wealth associated with those engaged in merchandising sated a segment of the Hebrew people with materialism. This gave rise to pride, arrogance, self-sufficiency, and a false sense of security. Yahweh seemed irrelevant.

The cosmopolitan nature of Syro-Palestine also led to intermarriage between Hebrews and foreign neighbors. This encouraged the syncretism of Hebrew religion with the cults of Baal, Chemosh, Milcom, and so on—not the separation, uniqueness, and holiness God required of his elect. Ultimately it was this "religious pluralism" that led to the overthrow of the Hebrew kingdoms and exile in Assyria and Babylonia (cf. Hos. 4 and Amos 3).

The Theological Significance of the Land

Palestine, or the land of Canaan, is also an important theological symbol in the Old Testament. This real estate was a major component in God's initial covenant promise to Abram (Gen. 12:1–3) and is the goal or focal point of the Pentateuchal narratives. The Exodus from Egypt was divine deliverance for the purpose of bringing the Israelites into "a good and spacious land, . . . flowing with milk and honey" (Exod. 3:8). The land of Canaan

was both the goal of covenant obedience before Yahweh and the reward for maintaining his covenant stipulations.

The Hebrew possession of the land signaled the displacement of the indigenous Canaanites. The conquest under Joshua was a "holy war" against the Canaanites, just punishment meted out by God through theocratic Israel for the gross sin associated with the fertilty cult of Baal and Asherah. The Canaanites had defiled the land, and by purging the land of that presence, the Hebrews themselves were cleansed (Lev. 18:24–30).

Because it was part of God's covenant promise, the land was integrally involved with the Hebrews' covenant relationship with Yahweh. The Ebal ceremony outlined in Deuteronomy 27 and enacted in Joshua 8 formalized the ties between the Hebrews, the Law of Yahweh, and the land of the promise. All three were inextricably bound together under Yahweh's sovereign rule. This meant that God's presence and blessing overshadowed the Israelites as they obeyed the covenant stipulations (Deut. 28:1–14). It also meant that any Israelite trespass of the covenant defiled the land and jeopardized their claim to possess it (Deut. 28:15–68). Practicing the "abominations" of the Canaanites would eventually result in the forfeiture of the land; the land would "vomit" them out as it had the Canaanites (Lev. 18:24–25). Sadly, all this came to pass as a result of the policies and practices instituted by King Manasseh (2 Kings 21:10–15; 24:3). In fact, the length of Israel's exile from the land was directly associated with the concept of sabbatical rest for the covenant land (2 Chron. 36:21; see chap. 9, "Leviticus," in this book).

The Old Testament prophets and poets reminded Israel that possession of the land guaranteed neither God's presence nor his blessing (Jer. 7:1–7). The whole earth belongs to the Lord (Ps. 24:1), and he transcends the "land" in that the earth is but his footstool (Isa. 66:1). By the same token, exile from the land of the promise did not necessarily signify God's abandonment, as Ezekiel's chariot vision testifies (Ezek. 1). The throne of Yahweh is movable, and he is capable of seeing and responding to the needs of Israel in any location.

Nehemiah lamented the hollowness of possessing the land of the promise as slaves to foreign powers because of sin and covenant unfaithfulness (Neh. 9:32–37). He understood that right relationship to the land of covenant promise was rooted in right relationship to God in covenant faithfulness.

Finally, even the language and literary images of the Old Testament were affected by the geography of the land of promise. Psalm 23 abounds with the imagery of the land, and elsewhere the psalmist likened the righteous to trees planted by flowing waters (Ps. 1:3). The premium on water in the arid climate of the Near East conditioned the language of the prophets as well as the psalmists. The rain and dew are often symbols of God's blessing and vindication (e.g., Joel 2:23; 3:18). Likewise, even the epithets for God such as "Rock," "Fortress," and "Refuge" were probably inspired by the rugged and boulder-strewn terrain of the Sinai desert and Judean wilderness (Deut. 32:15). Even the reference to Canaan as a land "flowing with milk and honey" pictured the richness of the land for supporting the lifestyles of both pastoralism (i.e., the "milk" of flocks and herds) and agriculture (i.e., the "honey," or nectar, of crops and produce).

Questions for Further Study and Discussion

1. Why is a knowledge of geography important to the study of the Old Testament?
2. In what ways did the geography of the ancient Near East influence the history of Israel?
3. What was the theological significance of the land of Canaan for the Hebrews?
4. How was life in palestine different for the Hebrews from their life as captives in Egypt?

For Further Reading

Aharoni, Yohanan. *The Land of the Bible: A Historical Geography*. Rev. ed. A. F. Rainey, trans. Philadelphia: Westminster, 1979. Comprehensive and authoritative, an excellent resource.

Aharoni, Yohanan, and Michael Avi-Yonah. *The Macmillan Bible Atlas*. New York: Macmillan, 1968.

Anati, E. *Palestine Before the Hebrews*. New York: Knopf, 1963.

Avi-Yonah, Michael. *The Holy Land: A Historical Geography*. Rev. ed. Grand Rapids: Baker, 1977.

Baly, Denis. *The Geography of the Bible*. Rev. ed. New York: Harper & Row, 1974. The classic, standard work on the topic.

Beitzel, Barry. *The Moody Atlas of Bible Lands*. Chicago: Moody Press, 1985.

Brueggemann, Walter. *The Land: Place as Gift, Promise, and Challenge in Biblical Faith*. Philadelphia: Fortress, 1977. A theological treatment of the "land" as part of Yahweh's covenant promise to Israel and its implications for the Christian church.

Frank, Harry Thomas. *Discovering the Biblical World*. Maplewood, N.J.: Hammond, 1975.

LaSor, William Sanford. "Palestine." *ISBE*. Rev. ed. Grand Rapids: Eerdmans, 1986. 3:632–49. Technical discussions of Palestine's geology, geography, climate, flora, and fauna.

Monson, J. M. *The Land Between*. Jerusalem: Biblical Backgrounds, 1983. A programed text designed to be used with the *Student Map Manual*, introducing Palestinian history and geography.

Pritchard, James B., ed. *The Harper Atlas of the Bible*. New York: Harper & Row, 1987. The most comprehensive Bible atlas available.

Rasmussen, Carl G. *The NIV Atlas of the Bible*. Grand Rapids: Zondervan, 1989. Profusely illustrated, useful for both the specialist and the nonspecialist.

Rogerson, J., and P. Davies. *The Old Testament World*. Englewood Cliffs, N.J.: Prentice-Hall, 1989. Helpful introductory sections on the geography and ecology of ancient Israel.

Simmons, J. *The Geographical and Topographical Texts of the Old Testament*. Leiden: Brill, 1959.

Student Map Manual. Jerusalem: Pictorial Archive, 1979.

Van der Woude, A. S., ed. *The World of the Old Testament*. S. Woudstra, trans. Grand Rapids: Eerdmans, 1986.

Chapter 5

Archaeology and the Old Testament

The purpose of archaeology is to recover the material culture of the peoples of antiquity and, so doing, attempt to reconstruct their history and lifestyles. To achieve this goal requires the cooperation of a large number of technical specialists, first to retrieve information and objects from below the surface of a chosen site and then to evaluate and interpret their significance. Many sites of ancient cities preserve a layer of remains for each of the successive occupations of the settlement through their history. Each layer covers over the remains of the previous habitation. Excavation of these layers is painstakingly tedious, and methods have been designed to uncover one layer at a time to reveal the remains of each successive settlement.

The most common objects found in Near Eastern archaeology are pieces of pottery. These can be classified by their characteristics and are helpful in developing a chronology of the site. Works of art such as statues or reliefs are found much less frequently. Tools and weapons reveal the technologies and skills of the people. Architecture also gets much attention. From the various types of common houses to the most magnificent palaces, architecture can provide archaeologists and historians with an important key to understanding how people lived.

Perhaps the greatest contributions to an archaeologist's task are finds that contain some written record. This would include every form of writing from graffiti on pottery shards to large royal archives. Seals, coins, funerary inscriptions, letters, building inscriptions, jar handles—all sorts of writing help archaeologists fulfill their task.

Near Eastern archaeology has much to contribute to biblical study, for the history and culture that it seeks to reconstruct overlap considerably with the background of the Bible. As a result, scholars and interpreters have often looked to archaeology to provide information that will help them understand the Bible better. Though historically the field of Near Eastern archaeology was developed largely by those who were interested in advancing biblical understanding, that is not a universal goal among scholars today. It must always be remembered that Near Eastern archaeology and biblical studies are independent disciplines, even though they are certainly not unrelated.

57

What Archaeology Can Do
for the Bible

The primary contribution of archaeology to biblical studies is the illumination it provides about life in Bible times. This enlightenment includes (1) the construction of a historical framework that makes use of information given in the Bible and supplements it with the finds of archaeology; (2) the reconstruction of political situations that might supply cause-and-effect explanations for some of the events recounted in the Bible; and (3) the recovery of customs and practices that suggest reasons why people of antiquity acted the way they did. The last category is especially helpful when it sheds light on religious beliefs and practices in the ancient Near East.

A secondary aspect of archaeology's role is authentication. Archaeology occasionally helps those who seek to confirm that names, places, and events of the Bible are authentic and reliably reported. It must be recognized, however, that more often than not, archaeology is unable to provide such confirmation and at such times can make the apologist's task more difficult. Archaeology is capable of providing facts (e.g., Sennacherib was indeed king at the same time as Hezekiah and did conduct a campaign against Jerusalem), but frequently the significance of archaeological data is dependent on one's interpretation of the data, and, as experience has demonstrated, interpretations can change or be incorrect. Sometimes this works to the apologist's advantage, sometimes not; but this factor has to be taken into account when archaeology is used for apologetical purposes.

A third area in which archaeology has made a considerable contribution to biblical studies is linguistics. Through archaeology, the field of comparative Semitics (the study of the group of related languages classified as Semitic) has grown and enriched our understanding of Hebrew, thereby offering exegetical insights that would have been otherwise impossible. Furthermore, understanding the languages of the ancient Near East is one of the best ways to become acquainted with the cultural background of the Old Testament.

What Archaeology Cannot Do
for the Bible

The inherent limitations of archaeology are assessed most clearly in Edwin Yamauchi's compilation of the information "fractions" an archaeologist must live with.

1. Only a fraction of the evidence survives in the ground.
2. Only a fraction of possible sites has been detected.
3. Only a fraction of detected sites has been excavated.
4. Only a fraction of any site is excavated.
5. Only a fraction of what has been excavated has been thoroughly examined and published.
6. Only a fraction of what has been examined and published makes a contribution to biblical studies.[1]

With such restrictions, we must understand that there is much information archaeology could potentially provide that it never actually will. This silence of archaeology often proves to make the interpreter's task more difficult than does the information archaeology discloses.

Another important limitation is that the main point of the biblical writings is beyond archaeology's ability to confirm: the sovereign role of God. The authors of Scripture were not so much interested in how the walls of Jericho fell down as in the fact that the Lord caused them to fall down. Archaeologists could find the walls and maybe even speculate on the scientific cause of their collapse, but they

---

[1]Edwin M. Yamauchi, *The Stones and the Scriptures* (Philadelphia: Lippincott, 1972), 146–62.

cannot address, either to confirm or deny, the role of God in the event. Archaeologists might theoretically find traces of Abraham, but they cannot prove that the Lord made a covenant with him and brought it to pass. Archaeology has information to offer on the fall of Jerusalem and the return from the Babylonian exile, but none of the data could possibly prove that the Lord was controlling those events.

For the authors of Scripture, history is a theological tool by which God reveals himself. Archaeology can authenticate history, but it cannot authenticate theology, and from the biblical perspective, history devoid of theology is meaningless.

What Archaeology Has Done for the Bible

One could page through the Bible enumerating all the archaeological findings pertaining to a particular account or event, but instead this section offers a brief survey of the types of finds that contribute to biblical studies and mentions some key examples of each type. The bibliography at the end of the chapter lists more complete sources.

Archives

More than a dozen major archives (including royal libraries) have been discovered in the ancient Near East, and a number of smaller archives, especially from cities of Assyria and Babylonia. Most of these finds have been royal archives, but some personal archives such as those found at Nuzi have proved very helpful. No Israelite archives have been unearthed, though a few collections of ostraca (pieces of broken pottery that were sometimes written on) have been found, notably at Samaria and Lachish.

A large proportion of many of the archives is made up of economic texts, comprising mostly the documentation of various business transactions (e.g., receipts). While these at times contribute to

biblical studies, much more significance is attached to other classes of literature. Mythological texts, treaties, wisdom literature, epics, historiographical documents (e.g., royal correspondence), and even occasional references to prophecy have all come to light. Religious texts such as omens, incantations, hymns, and prayers are often included among the tablets and provide a background against which the faith of Israel can be examined. Since the archives provide written records and literature, they have more to offer students of the Bible than any other kind of archaeological find.

Ebla. The Italian archaeological team digging at Tel-Mardikh in northern Syria in the mid-1970s determined that they had found the site of the prominent third-millennium city of Ebla. When the royal palace was located and excavated, archaeologists were stunned to discover the archives as well, consisting of thousands of clay tablets. In the years since, many unsubstantiated and now disregarded claims were made about the contents of those tablets, and to this day some of the basic scholarly evaluation is still in process.

The primary significance of the Ebla archive as it has been analyzed thus far is historical. The history of third-millennium Syria was largely unknown prior to the find, and it is now being penciled in as a result of the translation and interpretation of the tablets. The implications of the findings at Ebla for Old Testament studies remain ambiguous and contested.

Mari. The city of Mari was located on the upper Euphrates some three hundred miles northwest of Babylon, just ten miles from the Iraqi border in modern Syria. Mari was a prominent city in the latter part of the third millennium and in the first third of the second millennium. The archives were housed in the palace of Zimri-Lim, one of the most splendid such buildings of ancient times. Covering some eight acres, the palace had more than 260 rooms and courtyards that housed schools, bakeries, wine cellars, and even bathrooms with indoor plumbing.

A major contribution is the data Mari provides for understanding the political situation in the eighteenth century B.C., when Hammurabi of the First Dynasty of Babylon was enlarging his empire. Before the Mari discovery, little more than Hammurabi's own inscriptions attested to the political situation; now a much more balanced view is available. Also of great interest is the largest collection of prophecies extant in the literature of the ancient Near East. This provides comparative material for studying the Israelite institution of the prophets, for in these texts we can discover what prophets of other countries were like and what kinds of prophecies they uttered.

Nuzi. The Nuzi archive is the most important personal library uncovered in the ancient Near East. It dates from the time of the Hurrian empire of Mitanni from 1500 to 1350 B.C. As a personal archive it features a large number of family documents such as marriage contracts, adoption agreements, and land transfers. Consequently the scholars who studied the archive saw the potential for shedding light on the family affairs scattered about the patriarchal narratives of Genesis (even though the patriarchs may have been as much as half a millennium earlier). Though many of the initially suggested parallels have been modified or rejected over time, the archive still offers substantial insight into the family lifestyle of the mid-second millennium B.C. So, for instance, when Abraham and Sarah decide that Sarah's handmaid, Hagar, should be used to produce an heir, they are simply following a common custom that is attested in the marriage contracts of the Nuzi archives.

Amarna. The Amarna archive preserves almost four hundred documents of correspondence that passed between the pharaohs of Egypt and the nations of the Near East in the fourteenth century B.C. These letters document the political complexity of that time, including the loosening of Egypt's iron grip on Syro-Palestine and the corresponding rise of the Neo-Hittite Empire. Especially poignant are the letters from the petty kings of Canaanite city-states that express pleading, cajoling, backbiting, and protesting—at one moment groveling before the mighty pharaoh, at the next admonishing him as one would an incompetent child.

When providing these kinds of data, archaeology is in its glory.

Hattushash. Hattushash (the modern Boghazköy in upper Asia Minor) was the capital of the mighty Hittite Empire that was the dominant force in the ancient Near East throughout most of the Late Bronze Period. Until the discovery of Hattushash and its archives at the turn of the twentieth century, the Hittites were virtually unknown as a people and their political influence was unrecognized. Rarely does archaeology equal the impact of revealing a previously "lost" people of such significance as the Hittites. Besides making the Hittite language and culture accessible to scholars for the first time, the archives provided excellent examples of numerous types of literature. Perhaps the find's greatest impact on biblical studies came from almost three dozen treaties all using a format that has also been recognized in the structure of the book of Deuteronomy and in several of the covenants between the Lord and Israel.

Ugarit. Ugarit was a bustling seaport and city-state in northern Syria in the Late Bronze Age. Until it fell prey to the widespread destruction that came with the incursion of the Sea Peoples at the end of the thirteenth century, this city thrived on the lively sea trade, transporting goods from Mediterranean ships across land to the Euphrates and from there down into Babylonia. Besides political and diplomatic developments of this period, the archives disclosed a new language, Ugaritic, which is very closely related to Canaanite and is among the

Figure 5.1. The well-preserved scroll of Isaiah found in Cave I at Qumran by the Dead Sea in 1946–47. This portion of the twenty-four-foot scroll is opened to Isaiah 49:4–52:12. (*The Shrine of the Book, D. Samuel and Jeane H. Gottesman, Center for Biblical Manuscripts, Israel Museum*)

closest relatives of Hebrew. The mythological texts of Ugarit greatly expanded our knowledge of Canaanite religion in general and the god known as Baal in particular. Most important was a set of six tablets that contain stories of Baal's defeat of the god Yamm (representing chaos), the building of a palace for Baal, and the struggle between Baal and Mot (death) that explains mythologically the cycle of the seasons. The portrayal of Baal and the recounting of his escapades and how he is treated all offer further insight into the Canaanite worship of Baal.

Ashurbanipal's Library at Nineveh. The first of the large archival discoveries, Ashurbanipal's library at Nineveh, is still arguably the richest literary trove in the history of archaeology. It was this archive that first introduced the modern world to ancient classics such as the Gilgamesh Epic, with its startling parallel to the biblical flood account (see fig. 3.1, chap. 3), and Enuma Elish, which discloses some of the Babylonian theology of creation. Other well-known finds include the Epic of Adapa, the Hymn to Shamash, and two wisdom compositions that grapple

with issues similar to those found in the book of Job ("Ludlul bel Nemeqi" and "The Babylonian Theodicy"). This literature has provided the materials necessary to undertake extensive comparative studies between Israelite and Mesopotamian literature that greatly enhance our understanding of the Bible, particularly by elucidating the differences between Israelite and Mesopotamian theology.

The Dead Sea Scrolls

Though the initial discovery of biblical manuscripts in the caves of the Dead Sea region was not made by archaeologists, the Dead Sea Scrolls have pride of place among the most significant contributions of archaeology to biblical studies. The Jewish community that lived in the self-supporting village of Qumran on and off from early in the second century B.C. until the second revolt against Rome in the second century A.D. produced scrolls of many of the Old Testament books as well as other literature (fig. 5.1).

When these scrolls were found, they provided manuscripts of the Old Testament that were a thousand years older than any previously available. They not only increased the credibility of the Masoretic manuscripts that had been the basis of all current English translations, but also provided important information for understanding the transmission of the text of the Old Testament. While the Dead Sea Scrolls remain the oldest manuscript evidence available for much of the Old Testament, an important discovery in 1979 produced the earliest extant fragment of biblical text. In a Jerusalem family tomb from the time of Jeremiah, two small silver scrolls were found that were inscribed with the benediction from Numbers 6:24–26.

Monuments and Inscriptions

Some of the monuments and inscriptions unearthed by archaeologists name kings of Israel or Judah. Others refer to events that are known from the pages of the Old Testament. The examples cited in this section are among the most significant artifacts of this kind.

The Mesha Inscription. When King Mesha of Moab came to the end of his reign, he had a monument inscribed recounting all his accomplishments. Called the Moabite Stone, the inscription includes a report of how Moab had come under the domination of Israel during the reign of Omri, but had regained its independence and recaptured some territory from Israel during the reign of Ahab or Ahaziah (see fig. 17.2, chap. 17). Thus the stone contains some history on which the Bible is silent. It also provides the only extrabiblical reference to the concept of placing things under the ban as Joshua did at Jericho (see Josh. 6:17–19). It is clear, therefore, that this practice was not unique to Israel.

The Stela of Shalmaneser III. The first Assyrian king to have contact with the Israelites was Shalmaneser. Inscriptions speak of his western campaigns against coalitions that include kings Ahab (at the

Battle of Qarqar in 853) and Jehu. The black obelisk that preserves the accounts of Shalmaneser's campaigns from his eighteenth to thirty-first years pictures Jehu—or more likely, his representative—bowing before him with the tribute signifying submission to Assyrian suzerainty (fig. 5.2). This occurred in 841, Jehu's first year on the throne, after the obliteration of the line of Ahab.

Sennacherib's Prism. A notable event during the divided monarchy was the siege of Jerusalem by Sennacherib in the days of Isaiah and Hezekiah, and the subsequent deliverance of the Israelites by the Lord. Theologically the deliverance demonstrated the Lord's power over the mightiest and most feared empire on the face of the earth, and that in response to the trust of King Hezekiah. Politically it marked Judah's success in avoiding the fate of the northern kingdom of Israel; Judah was not destroyed and annexed by Assyria. The Bible reports the details of this classic confrontation in three places—2 Kings 18–19; 2 Chronicles 32; Isaiah 36–37; Sennacherib's account of these campaigns became known with the discovery of an inscribed hexagonal clay cylinder, or prism (see fig. 28.1, chap. 28). Sennacherib details his success against forty-six cities of Judah and his deportation of more than 200,000 Israelites. He also boasts of imprisoning Hezekiah in Jerusalem by subjecting the city to siege.

The prism gives no hint of Sennacherib's suffering a defeat and does not record the outcome of the siege on Jerusalem, but it notes how he received increased tribute from Hezekiah. Thus the inscription confirms the military details as presented in the Bible, but fails to provide any substantiation of the role ascribed to the Lord or the victory claimed in Scripture. Likewise, it says nothing to contradict the version of the events recorded in Scripture.

The Cyrus Cylinder. The deportation programs practiced by Assyria and Babylon were designed to eliminate ethnic

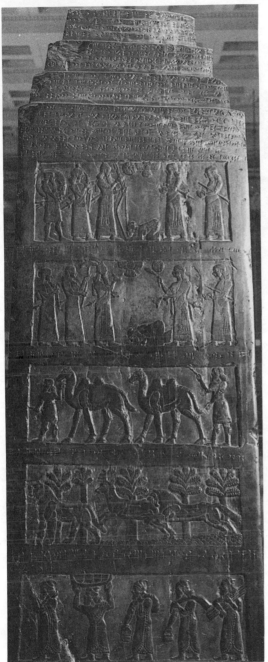

Figure 5.2. The stela of Shalmaneser III, containing twenty panels in sequence, all depicting tribute being brought to the king. The second panel here mentions the tribute paid by "Jehu, Son of Omri." (*Trustees of the British Museum*)

identities of conquered peoples and to assimilate them into a common mixed stock that would foster loyalty to the empire and diminish ethnic and political distinctions. This posed a great threat to the Lord's covenant with Israel as an ethnic and political entity. When the Medo-Persian Empire took over from the Babylonians, Cyrus instituted a new approach to foreign policy. This policy was built on the philosophy that offering increased autonomy to subject peoples would increase loyalty to the empire, not undermine it. That is, if oppression were decreased, the likelihood of revolt was reduced. As a result, many of the subjugated people were allowed to return to their homelands and rebuild their communities and sanctuaries.

The Cyrus Cylinder, a clay cylinder containing the royal decree granting various peoples permission to return, does not mention Judah specifically, but Scripture reports that Judah enjoyed such a benevolence (see fig. 19.1, chap. 19).

Court Chronicles

The official annals and chronicles of the court report on military campaigns and the internal affairs of a kingdom. They provide not only information on events, but also their chronology. The chronicles most significant for biblical studies are the Babylonian Chronicles, for they document Nebuchadrezzar's campaign against Judah in 597 B.C. and King Jehoiachin's capture and exile (fig. 5.3).

Cult Sites

The Old Testament endorses the temple in Jerusalem as the only legitimate cult site in Israel, yet it testifies to the existence of other cult centers. No remains of the Jerusalem temple have been found, but archaeologists have identified nearly a dozen other cult sites that were in operation during Iron Ages I–II in Israel. Most of these are local shrines, but major sanctuaries have been discovered

Figure 5.3. A portion of the Babylonian Chronicles that describes the capture of King Jehoiachin and his being exiled to Babylon around 600 B.C. (*Trustees of the British Museum*)

at Arad and Dan. There is evidence that sacrifices were performed at these two sites, but they do not seem to have featured a statue of the deity. The Arad temple was considered a "House of Yahweh," while the status of the sanctuary at Dan in that regard is less certain.

Biblical References

Beyond these specific types of finds, and often with their help, archaeology has provided valuable insights into people, places, and events referred to in the Bible.

People. Archaeology informs us about biblical figures in several ways. First, some people mentioned in literature, either in the Bible or in tablets, have long been considered by many to be fictional characters. Archaeologists have occasionally been able to dispel these notions by

turning up documents that give these people historical credence. Two notable examples are Belshazzar, the king named in Daniel 5 as the last king of Babylon, and Gilgamesh, the hero of the epic that carries his name; both are now recognized as historical persons rather than literary creations. More recently, texts found at Deir 'Allah (on the east side of the Jordan) have attested to a prophet by the name of Balaam who is now recognized as the person described in Numbers 22–24.

Second, other people have played important roles in history, but have remained somewhat obscure to modern historians until archaeologists lifted the veil of mystery. Some of these such as Sennacherib, Nebuchadrezzar, and Cyrus figured significantly in the biblical drama. Others such as Rameses II are not named in the Bible, but nevertheless had far-reaching influence in certain periods of Israelite history. Archaeology has pieced together the biographies and accomplishments of these people and reclaimed them for modern historians, providing important background information for understanding the Old Testament.

Third, archaeology informs our knowledge of the people of the Old Testament by adding facts and perspectives not derived from Scripture. A good example is the archaeological portrayal of the Israelite kings Omri and his son, Ahab. Omri receives only brief treatment in 1 Kings 16:21–28, but archaeological findings indicate that politically he was probably the most influential king of Israel of the ninth century. His son, Ahab, by contrast, receives extensive treatment from Scriptures that focus on his role as the antagonist of the prophet Elijah and the spineless dupe of his wife, Jezebel, who schemed to convert Israel to Baalism. Archaeology balances this picture with details that suggest that, despite Ahab's failures spiritually and theologically, he had an influential and effective rule in the

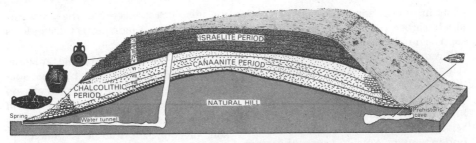

Figure 5.4. Schematic section of a typical tell. (*Carta, Jerusalem*)

international politics of those turbulent times.

Places. Archaeological excavations inform us about biblical places in many of the same ways they inform us about people—that is, largely through written records. Sometimes this information involves cities like Jerusalem, Babylon, and Nineveh that figure prominently in the biblical record. Other cities such as Ur and Hazor play relatively insignificant parts in Scripture, but were important centers and have been excavated to great advantage.

Events. Some events are important to world history, but are passed by without the barest reference in the Bible. This is surely because the human authors of Scripture had a very definite agenda from which they rarely digressed. The famous battle of Qarqar (853 B.C.), mentioned earlier, is the best example of this. The monolith inscription of Shalmeneser III gives a record of this famous military engagement, in which a large coalition of western states, including Ahab of Israel, prevented the Assyrian king from exerting his influence in the west and reducing the Israelites to vassal states.

Still other events mentioned either briefly or at length in the Old Testament are illuminated by archaeology. Annalistic records of the fall of Samaria in 722 and the capitulation of Jerusalem in 597 provide complementary accounts of these significant milestones. Something of only passing interest to the biblical authors such as the fall of Lachish to Sennacherib in 701 is illuminated in reliefs depicting the event on the walls of Sennacherib's palace in Nineveh. The fall of the city to Nebuchadrezzar's forces more than a century later is the background for the Lachish letters, some military correspondence depicting the critical situation on the eve of the collapse of Judah. Both of these destructions are further supported by data gleaned from ongoing excavations at the site.

What Archaeology Has Not Done for the Bible

Despite all the help that archaeology has provided for biblical studies, much remains to be done. There are many pieces of information that archaeology seems capable of supplying, but has not yet delivered. We have already mentioned that there is very little textual evidence for the Old Testament that dates from those times. It is quite possible that an Israelite archive would contain such data, but as yet no such archive has been found.

Another gap in our archaeological information is that no individual Israelite is referred to by name in contemporary literature prior to the ninth century B.C. Omri, king of Israel, is the earliest reference extant. Certainly we would hope that someday archaeology will find inscription references to the kings of the united monarchy. There are likewise personages from later history that have yet to appear in contemporary extrabiblical materials, including Daniel, Esther, and Nehemiah—all of whom held important posts in foreign administrations. From a much earlier period, we could cite Joseph. The most notable foreigner who still remains a mystery to modern historians is Darius the Mede, mentioned in the book of Daniel.

There are some events recorded in the Bible for which archaeological data have served to increase confusion rather than understanding. Notable among these are the Exodus from Egypt and the conquest of the land of Canaan. The excavations at the various cities mentioned in the book of Joshua have produced a number of different reconstructions of the actual course of events. In some cases the archaeological data are interpreted primarily to discredit scriptural accounts. In others the biblical text is accepted as accurate and therefore the archaeological data are viewed and interpreted with considerable skepticism. Between these two poles are numerous theories attempting to reconcile the Bible to archaeology or archaeology to the Bible. Though archaeology has not been able to settle the disputes concerning these events, continuing excavation keeps the windows of hope open.

Finally, there are probable material remains that archaeologists have not succeeded in uncovering. For instance, no trace of the palace or the temple of Solomon has been unearthed. One reason, of course, is that it is difficult to conduct excavations in places still inhabited today.

In conclusion, in reflecting on what archaeology has and has not been able to accomplish, we are reminded that while archaeology is capable of providing much useful information to the study of the Bible, it is also capable of creating confusion. Sound scholarship cannot be so subjective as to rely heavily on archaeology when it supports the favored position, but to reject it outright when it offers contradictory data. A proper use of archaeology requires a consistent approach to its findings and an understanding of its methods and techniques.

Questions for Further Study and Discussion

1. What stance should we take when archaeological data appear to conflict with the biblical record?
2. If an Israelite royal archive were to be discovered, what sorts of documents would we expect to find in it? What areas of biblical study would be potentially influenced, and how?
3. What cautions ought we to exercise in developing parallels between the Old Testament and the ancient Near East?

For Further Reading

Aharoni, Yohanan. *The Archaeology of the Land of Israel.* Philadelphia: Westminster, 1982. A classic by an eminent Israeli archaeologist, presenting the material remains and characterizations of the successive chronological periods.

Avi-Yonah, Michael. *Encyclopedia of Archaeological Excavations in the Holy Land.* Englewood Cliffs, N.J.: Prentice-Hall, 1975. The most important reference resource, giving summary site reports for most of the major excavations in Israel.

Bimson, John J. *Redating the Exodus and the Conquest.* Sheffield, England: JSOT, 1978.

Blaiklock, E. M., and R. K. Harrison. *The New International Dictionary of Biblical Archaeology.* Grand Rapids: Zondervan, 1983.

Campbell, Edward F., and David N. Freedman, eds. *The Biblical Archaeologist Reader 3.* New York: Doubleday, 1970.

Frank, Harry Thomas. *Bible, Archaeology and Faith.* Nashville: Abingdon, 1971.

Freedman, David N., ed. *The Biblical Archaeologist Reader 2.* Missoula, Mont.: Scholars Press, 1975.

Harrison, R. K. *Major Cities of the Biblical World.* Nashville: Thomas Nelson, 1985.

Hoerth, Alfred J. "Archaeology and the Christian Mind" in *Interpreting the Word of God.* S. J. Schultz and M. A. Inch, eds. Chicago: Moody Press, 1976. 31–45.

Kenyon, Kathleen. *Archaeology in the Holy Land.* 4th ed. New York: Norton, 1979.

King, Philip J. *Amos, Hosea, Micah: An Archaeological Commentary.* Philadelphia: Westminster, 1988.

McRay, John. *Archaeology and the New Testament.* Grand Rapids: Baker, 1991.

Matthews, Victor H. *Manners and Customs in the Bible.* Peabody, Mass.: Hendrickson, 1988. Probably the most helpful of the books on manners and customs.

Mazar, Amihai. *The Archaeology of the Land of the Bible.* Garden City, N.Y.: Doubleday, 1990.

Millard, Alan R. *The Bible B.C.: What Can Archaeology Prove?* Phillipsburg, N.J.: Presbyterian and Reformed, 1977. Concise presentation of the role of archaeology from an eminent evangelical Assyriologist.

——— . *Treasures from Bible Times.* San Diego: Lion Publishing, n.d. Beautifully illustrated with very balanced, readable text.

Moorey, Roger. *Excavation in Palestine.* Grand Rapids: Eerdmans, 1981. A good introduction to "dirt" archaeology.

Paul, Shalom, and William Dever. *Biblical Archaeology.* Jerusalem: Keter, 1973.

Pritchard, James B., ed. *The Harper Atlas of the Bible.* New York: Harper & Row, 1987. Profusely illustrated and up-to-date archaeological survey of history.

Schoville, Keith N. *Biblical Archaeology in Focus.* Grand Rapids: Baker, 1978. A fine textbook from a well-established evangelical archaeologist.

Shanks, Hershel, ed. *Recent Archaeology in the Land of Israel.* Washington, D.C.: Biblical Archaeology Society, 1984.

Thomas, D. Winton. *Archaeology and Old Testament Study.* Oxford: Clarendon Press, 1967.

Thompson, J. A. *The Bible and Archaeology.* Rev. ed. Grand Rapids: Eerdmans, 1972.

Walton, John H. *Ancient Israelite Literature in its Cultural Context.* Grand Rapids: Zondervan, 1989. A survey of the parallels between biblical and ancient Near Eastern literature.

Yamauchi, Edwin M. *The Stones and the Scriptures.* Philadelphia: Lippincott, 1972.

PART II

THE PENTATEUCH

Chapter 6

Introduction to the Pentateuch

The term "Pentateuch" is commonly applied to the first five books of the Old Testament: Genesis, Exodus, Leviticus, Numbers, and Deuteronomy. This Greek expression simply means "five scrolls" and was apparently popularized by the hellenized Jews of Alexandria in the first century A.D. The Hebrew-speaking Jewish community traditionally referred to these five books as "The Law" or "Torah," "The Law of Moses," "The Book of the Law of Moses," or "The Book of Moses."

The Pentateuch was the first divinely prompted literary collection acknowledged as Scripture by the Hebrew community. As such, it is the most important division of the Hebrew canon, and it stands first in the threefold Old Testament of Law, Prophets, and Writings. Its supreme rank in the Old Testament canon in respect to authority and holiness is evidenced by its position and separation from the other books in the Septuagint (the Greek translation of the Old Testament). The careful translation of the Hebrew Pentateuch into Greek also attests the Hebrews' high regard for the collection (in contrast to the incomplete and more loosely translated divisions of the Prophets and Writings).

Theme and General Contents

The "five-book" division of the Pentateuch is really a secondary partitioning of what was intended to be a unifed, literary whole. D. J. A. Clines (1979) has cogently argued that the Pentateuch has two basic divisions, Genesis 1–11 and Genesis 12–Deuteronomy 34. In view of the fall of humankind and the broken fellowship between God and humanity, the first division poses the question, "How can that relationship be repaired or restored?" The second division then provides an answer, or at least a partial answer, to the human dilemma depicted in Genesis 1–11. The solution is rooted in the idea of covenant bonding between God and Abram in Genesis 12:1–3. This passage constitutes the focal point of the second division and actually summarizes the key themes of the Pentateuchal narratives: Yahweh's covenant, Abraham's posterity, divine election and blessing, and the grant of a "promised land."

Part 1 explains the origins of the earth and humankind, explains the nature and purpose of man created male and female, records the intrusion of sin into God's good creation, and reveals the character of God who both judges human sin (as

71

Figure 6.1. The Literary Plan of the Pentateuch

Genesis 1–11: Creation, fall, and judgment

Genesis 12–50: Covenant promise, election of Abraham, and providential preservation of his family

Exodus: Miraculous deliverance of Yahweh's people from bondage in Egypt, covenant relationship expanded to Israel as his people at Sinai, and the law given as a theocratic charter for Israel

Leviticus: Expansion of covenant law for the purpose of holiness among the people of Yahweh, since he will dwell in their midst

Numbers: Testing, purging, and purifying of Yahweh's covenant people in the Sinai wilderness wandering, and

Deuteronomy: Covenant renewal and the second law-giving as preparation for entry into the land of the promise by the second generation of Yahweh's people

witnessed in the Flood account) and deals mercifully with fallen creation (as seen in the grace extended to Noah and his family).

Part 2 explains how Israel (through Abraham) became the elect covenant people of Yahweh and God's instrument for revealing himself and restoring the broken and corrupted relationship between the Creator and his creation. The Pentateuchal accounts are significant, both for Israel, due to her unique covenant relationship with Yahweh, and for the nations of the world, since the destiny of humanity is ultimately tied to Israel's covenant with God.

The unifying theological theme of the Pentateuch is Yahweh's covenant promise to Abram in Genesis 12:3. What humankind was unable to do in all its pride and self-sufficiency (epitomized in the Tower of Babel), God initiated in his covenant promise. The literary plan of the Pentateuch is but an expansion of the three-part covenant promise extended to Abram, as outlined in figure 6.1.

The Literature of the Pentateuch

The Pentateuch, or Book of the Law, is a rich collection of literary genres, or types. This diversity of literary types enhances both the artistic nature of the work and the key theological themes unifying the anthology. By the same token, these multiple and complex literary forms have been directly responsible for the ongoing debate over the composition and date of the Pentateuch (see below).

Prose Narrative

Most of the Pentateuchal literature is prose narrative. The narrative is simple, but direct and forceful. The text is largely a third-person account of early Israelite history interspersed with prayers, speeches, and other types of direct discourse (e.g., Abraham's intercessory prayer for Sodom in Genesis 18:22–33; Yahweh's speech to Moses in Exodus 3:7–12; and the exchange between Pharaoh and Moses in Exodus 10:1–21).

The narratives artfully blend historical reporting and theological interpretation, making the Pentateuch more than an ancient annal or a mere register of chronologically ordered events, yet something less than pointed religious propaganda serving to explain or justify certain actions, events, institutions, or theological teachings. Perhaps the best example of this blend of historical reporting and theological interpretation is the providential understanding of Joseph's trials as benefiting all of Jacob's family (Gen. 50:15–21).

The simple and beautiful language of the Pentateuch, its use of anthropomorphic language (i.e., ascribing human qualities to God), and frequent reference to theophany (i.e., a visible and audible manifestation of God to a human being), and the detailed characterizations and repetitious plots in the stories have led some scholars to use terms like "myth" or "saga," "folklore," and "legend" for portions of the Pentateuchal narratives (especially Genesis). Traditionally, evangelical scholars have balked at using such labels for the Pentateuchal narratives because of the ahistorical connotations implied by the terminology. The inability of modern scholarship to define these genres or literary categories clearly has also contributed to this reluctance to use these terms. Once again, presuppositional decisions about the historicity of the Old Testament condition the scholar's willingness to include Genesis (and the rest of the Pentateuch) in these ill-defined genres. This historical aspect of Pentateuchal prose narrative is discussed later on.

Ancient Poetry

The Pentateuch contains some of the earliest examples of Hebrew poetry in all the Old Testament. Careful orthographic (i.e., the spelling of particular words), lexical (i.e., the predilection for certain vocabulary items), and linguistic analysis (especially grammatical forms and syntactical relationships) have demonstrated the antiquity of poetic passages such as Moses' Song of the Sea (Exod. 15), the Balaam Oracles (Num. 23–24), Jacob's Blessing (Gen. 49), and the Song and Blessing of Moses (Deut. 32–33). The dates for the current form of these poetic texts range from the thirteenth to the eleventh centuries B.C. according to this technical analysis.[1]

Specific poetic forms in the Pentateuch include prayers (the Aaronic benediction, Num. 6:22–27), songs of praise (Miriam's song, Exod. 15:21; Israel's song, Num. 21:17–18), victory hymns in epic drama style (Yahweh's triumph over the Egyptians in Moses' Song of the Sea, Exod. 15), blessings on family members by patriarchs (the blessing of Rebekah, Gen. 24:60; Jacob's deathbed blessing of his sons, Gen. 49), prophetic utterances (Yahweh's pronouncement to Rebekah about her twin sons, Gen. 25:23; Balaam's oracles to Israel, Num. 23–24), covenant promises (such as those made to Abram by Yahweh, Gen. 12:1–3; 15:1), and even taunt songs (like Lamech's, Gen. 4:23).

Prophetic Revelation

Prophetic literature in the Old Testament includes both foretelling (or divine revelation) and exposition (or interpretation) of Yahweh's covenant-oriented revelation to Israel. The Pentateuch contains examples of both.

Prophetic revelation in the Law occurs in prose narrative and poetic forms. For example, there is Yahweh's revelation to Abram regarding the oppression and slavery of his descendants (Gen. 15:12–16) or Moses' prosaic forecast about a prophet who will appear in Israel (Deut. 18:17–20; ultimately fulfilled in Jesus of Nazareth, John 1:45). Examples of poetic prophecy in the Pentateuch include Jacob's patriarchal blessing, which connects kingship with the tribe of Judah (Gen. 49:8–12), and Moses' lyrical pronouncements over the tribes of Israel (Deut. 33).

The clearest examples of prophetic-like commentary or interpretation of Yah-

---

[1]Cf. David N. Freedman, "Divine Names and Titles in Early Hebrew Poetry," in *Magnalia Dei: The Mighty Acts of God,* ed. F. M. Cross et al. (Garden City, N.Y.: Doubleday, 1976), 55–107.

weh's divine revelation are Moses' understanding of Israel's earlier covenant history and God's providential guidance and preservation of his people (in the so-called historical prologue of Deuteronomy 1–4) and Moses' pointed exposition of the stipulations by which Yahweh would enforce covenant keeping in Israel by means of blessings and curses. In each case, instruction to the Israelites is followed by admonitions to covenant obedience (Deut. 4:1–10; 29:9).

Law

The idea of law was not unique to the Hebrews in the ancient Near East. Codified law is attested in Mesopotamia as early as 2000 B.C., some five centuries (or more) before the time of Moses. The better known of these legal codexes are the Sumerian Laws of Ur-Nammu (Ur III Dynasty, 2064–2046, or perhaps his son Shulgi, 2046–1999) and Lipit-Ishtar (king of Isin, 1875–1864), and the Old Babylonian Laws of Eshnunna (nineteenth century B.C.), and Hammurabi (king of Babylon, 1792–1750). The influence of the ancient Near Eastern legal tradition on the form and function of Hebrew law is undeniable and widely documented.[2]

Along with this contemporary cultural influence, the Old Testament affirms the divine origin of Hebrew law through Moses as Yahweh's lawgiver. The Pentateuch is most often associated with Law, as many of the Hebrew titles for the five books attest. The English word "law" translates the Hebrew word *torah*, and Old Testament law includes commandments (*miṣwāh*), statutes (*ḥōq*), and ordinances (*mišpāṭ*). More than six hundred laws are contained in the books of Exodus, Leviticus, Numbers, and Deuteronomy. The purpose of the biblical legislation was to order and regulate the civil, religious or ceremonial, and criminal justice life of Israel in accordance with the holiness necessary for maintaining the covenant relationship with Yahweh.

The purpose of Hebrew law also had implications for the literary form of Old Testament legislation. Old Testament law was covenant law; it was contractual law binding and obligating two separate parties. The covenant law paralleled the so-called suzerainty covenants of the ancient world, especially those of the Hittites. Most exemplary are the Covenant Code (Exod. 20–24) and the book of Deuteronomy. The suzerain covenants were granted by independent and powerful overlords to dependent and weaker vassals, guaranteeing them certain benefits including protection. In return, the vassal was obligated to keep specific stipulations certifying loyalty to the suzerain alone.

In general terms, Old Testament law comprised declarative and prescriptive covenant stipulations for the life of the Hebrew people (quite literally in Deuteronomy 30:15–17). The bulk of the Old Testament legal materials are found in Exodus 20–Deuteronomy 33, and they stem from covenant agreement or renewal ceremonies at Mount Sinai and Mount Nebo. Several important subcategories may be identified:

1. Casuistic or case law, usually cast in a conditional "if . . . then" formula, making reference to a specific hypothetical legal situation. For example, "If a man is found sleeping with another man's wife, [then] both the man who slept with her and the woman must die. You must purge the evil from Israel" (Deut 22:22).

---

[2]Though outside the scope of this discussion, the parallels between ancient Near Eastern and Old Testament law have been dealt with at length in John H. Walton, *Ancient Israelite Literature in Its Cultural Context* (Grand Rapids: Zondervan, 1989), 69–94; and H. J. Boecker, *Law and the Administration of Justice in the Old Testament and the Ancient Near East*, trans. J. Moiser (Minneapolis: Augsburg, 1980), 66–176.

2. Apodictic law or direct affirmative and negative commands setting the bounds of appropriate behavior in Hebrew society. For example, "You shall have no other gods before me" (Exod. 20:3) or "Honor your father and your mother, so that you may live long in the land the Lord your God is giving you" (Exod. 20:12).
3. Prohibition or a negative command referring to hypothetical offenses and stating no fixed penalty. For example, "Do not curse the deaf or put a stumbling block in front of the blind, but fear your God. I am the Lord" (Lev. 19:14).
4. Death law, a hybrid of the prohibition that makes a distinct legal statement about specific crimes meriting the death penalty. For example, "Anyone who attacks his father or his mother must be put to death" (Exod. 21:15).
5. The curse, a development from both the prohibition and the death law addressing crimes committed in secret. The curse was designed to protect the covenant community from uncleanness due to violation of covenant stipulation and to bring divine judgment on the perpetrator of the crime. For example, "Cursed is the man who moves his neighbor's boundary stone" (Deut. 27:17) or "Cursed is the man who kills his neighbor secretly" (Deut. 27:24).

The content of ancient Near Eastern law may be summarized under three headings: civil law, ceremonial law, and cultic law. The subdivisions of civil law included marriage and family, inheritance, property, slaves, debt, taxes, and wages. Common subheadings under ceremonial law were murder, adultery and rape, theft, sexual deviation, false witness, assault, and liability. Cultic law organized legislation under four major ideas, including sacrifices, purification, mode or object of worship, and festival observance.

The Composition of the Pentateuch

Both the Old Testament and the New Testament make reference to Mosaic writing activity in connection with the Pentateuch (Exod. 24:4; John 5:46–47), and both covenants assert that Moses was the primary human author of the Pentateuch (Deut. 31:9; Mark 12:19). Until the age of the Enlightenment the large majority of Jews and Christians accepted the divine origin and the Mosaic authorship of the Pentateuch. Although a few dissenting Jewish and Christian scholars challenged the antiquity and integrity of a Mosaic Pentateuch, the scholarship of this period from the early church fathers to the Protestant Reformation was essentially "pre-critical" in respect to the issues of Pentateuchal authorship and date.

However, traditional understanding of the Old Testament (and the New, for that matter) were questioned and overturned during the Age of Reason. This "enlightened" period of Western civilization spawned an era of critical study of the Bible rooted in a humanistic and scientific worldview that continues to shape the landscape of biblical studies. It was presumed that human beings were capable of a reasonable and natural understanding of themselves, the physical world, law, religion, and philosophy. Likewise, external authorities and nonrational assessments of nature, history, religious experience, and science were rejected. This concurrent rise of the scientific method (i.e., empiricism and scientific positivism), deistic theology in religion, and evolutionary theory in respect to origins has thoroughly influenced customary views on Pentateuchal authorship. As a result, several hypotheses or major approaches to Pentateuchal composition have emerged from the past three centuries of scholarly discussion.

One Author Hypothesis

Hebrew, Samaritan, and early Christian tradition all regarded Moses as the author or compiler of the Pentateuch. The one-author view acknowledges that Moses wrote the entire Pentateuch apart from the account of his own death in Deuteronomy 34. Some holding this view allow for the use of pre-existing written sources by Moses, making him the compiler of portions of the Pentateuch.

Evidence adduced for the one-author view include the witness of the Pentateuch (e.g., Num. 33:2); the witness of the rest of the Old Testament and the New Testament to the "Law of Moses" (e.g., Judg. 3:4; John 8:5); the weight of Hebrew, Samaritan, and early Christian tradition; and the burden of material evidence given the eyewitness detail and familiarity with Egyptian language and culture demonstrated by the author.

This approach assumes the divine inspiration and supernatural origin of the (original) written documents through Moses, and the accuracy and reliability of the history as literally reported in the Pentateuch. All numbers are taken at face value (so some 2 million-plus Hebrews left Egypt at the Exodus), and miracles happened as narrated, whether God used natural means or superseded natural law by intervening directly in time and space for the benefit of his people Israel (e.g., the miraculous path through the Sea of Reeds, or Yam Suph, is determined to be more than a mile wide to accommodate the millions of Hebrews passing through the waters).[3]

One Author–Later Editor(s) Hypothesis

The rise of rationalistic biblical criticism during the Enlightenment brought serious challenges against the traditional view of Mosaic authorship of the Pentateuch. The so-called liberal repudiation of the Mosaic authorship view was grounded in part in phenomena within the literature of the Pentateuch itself. This approach constitutes a viable conservative alternative to the multiple-authorship theories characteristic of most modern critical biblical scholarship without rejecting the divine inspiration of the Old Testament Scriptures.[4]

The one author–later editor(s) hypothesis attempts to address honestly the objections to Mosaic authorship raised by the multiple-author hypothesis. These questions were primarily of a literary nature, like the differing style and vocabulary of the Pentateuchal narratives; the so-called literary doublets (i.e., two accounts of the same event, as in the creation versions of Genesis 1:1–2:4a and 2:4b–25); the historical anachronisms (i.e., references to people and places in the Pentateuch from later time periods, such as the mention of the Israelite kings in Genesis 36:31 or of the Philistines in Genesis 21:34); editorial insertions clearly designed to update a later audience (e.g., the reference to Egypt as "the district of Rameses," Gen. 47:11); and even disagreement between narrative accounts (such as the number and kinds of animals on the ark of Noah, Gen. 6:19–20; 7:2, 8–9).

Proponents of this approach respond to these literary difficulties in several ways. They assert that Moses used a variety of literary sources (e.g., Book of the Wars of the Lord, Num. 21:14) and appeal to the ancient Near Eastern literary conventions of repetition, duplication; cite the use of multiple names for deities (e.g., the Canaanite literature of Ras Shamra or Ugarit); recognize the extrabiblical parallels in ancient Near Eastern literature illuminating biblical texts (e.g., Egyptian and Mesopotamian creation and flood stories); cite archaeological evidence sup-

---

[3]This approach is represented by such scholars as Merrill F. Unger, *Introductory Guide to the Old Testament* (Grand Rapids: Zondervan, 1951); Norman L. Geisler, *A Popular Survey of the Old Testament* (Grand Rapids: Baker, 1978); and I. L. Jensen, *Jensen's Survey of the Old Testament* (Chicago: Moody Press, 1978).

[4]Representative evangelical perspectives of the One Author–Later Editor(s) Hypothesis include John W. Wenham, "Moses and the Pentateuch," in *The New Bible Commentary: Revised*, ed. D. Guthrie et al. (Grand Rapids: Eerdmans, 1970), 41–43; and William Sanford LaSor, David A. Hubbard, and Frederick W. Bush, *Old Testament Survey* (Grand Rapids: Eerdmans, 1982), 54–67.

porting the reliability of the Pentateuchal narrative (e.g., the Nuzi Tablet parallels to patriarchal customs described in Genesis); harmonize apparent discrepancies (e.g., understanding Paran in Numbers 13:3 as a general place-name reference and Kadesh-Barnea in Numbers 20:1 as the particular place-name equivalent); and emphasize the important role of later scribes in updating the ancient record, supplementing biblical narratives from parallel accounts, and correcting and clarifying puzzling data (e.g., the clarification of the Hebrew dry measure in Exodus 16:36).

Generally speaking, this approach acknowledges Moses as (1) the compiler of existing written sources into what we now know as Genesis, and (2) the author of the bulk of the other four books of the Pentateuch. In fact, while Moses did not write all the Pentateuch, these sections of the work are directly or indirectly attributed to the writing activity of Moses: Exodus 12, 20–24, 25–32, 34; Leviticus 1– 7, 8, 13, 16, 17–26, 27; Numbers 1, 2, 4, 6, 8, 15, 19, 27–30, 33, 35; and Deuteronomy 1– 33. Although editorial insertions in the Pentateuch are obvious, the greater questions involve the extent of that activity and the time frame in which it was completed. According to this view, the amount of editorial activity was minimal and the Pentateuch may have been completed in its present form as early as the time of the elders of Joshua's day (Josh. 24:26, 31) or as late as the era of Samuel the judge (cf. 1 Sam. 3:20–21).

Multiple Authors and Later Editor(s) Hypothesis

The multiple-authors approach to the composition of the Pentateuch was a response of rationalistic scholarship of the Enlightenment to the difficulties observed in the literature of the Pentateuch itself. For instance, why are there two versions of the creation story (Gen. 1:1– 2:4a and 2:4b–25) or two accounts of the naming of Beersheba (Gen. 21:31; 26:33), or why is there apparent disagreement as to when worship of Yahweh began (cf. Gen. 4:26; Exod. 6:2–3)? Or how does one deal with references to the Israelite kings (Gen. 36:31) and to the Philistines (Gen. 21:34)? And what is meant by phrases such as "to this day" (Gen. 32:32) and "at that time the Canaanites were in the land" (Gen. 12:6)?

These kinds of questions along with obvious differences in literary style and vocabulary gave rise to "source analysis" of the Pentateuch. While biblical scholars had raised questions about Pentateuchal authorship previously, it was the French physician Jean Astruc who initiated modern literary or source analysis of the Old Testament. His commentary on Genesis published in 1753 made the assertion, based on the use of divine names, that Moses used two parallel sources in compiling Genesis. One source identified God as Elohim (E), and the other referred to God as Yahweh (J). Today this source criticism of the Pentateuch is most commonly associated with the Documentary Theory or Hypothesis.[5]

The classical formulation of the multiple-authorship or Documentary Hypothesis was made by the German scholar Julius Wellhausen in 1876–77. Building on the work of earlier scholars such as K. H. Graf, Abraham Kuenen, and Hermann Hupfeld, Wellhausen postulated the view that the Pentateuch is a compilation of at least four major literary documents and that the composition process

---

[5]On the history of the development of Old Testament source analysis, see John Hayes, *An Introduction to Old Testament Study* (Nashville: Abingdon, 1979), 83–120, 155–98. For a concise evangelical response to the Pentateuchal authorship questions raised by source critics, see further Kenneth A. Kitchen, *Ancient Orient and the Old Testament* (London: InterVarsity, 1966), 112–38.

took some four centuries. The standard Graf-Wellhausen Documentary Hypothesis may be outlined as follows:

1. The J or Yahwist document, written by a Judean author during the ninth century B.C. The name "Yahweh" predominates in this source, which is characterized by "epic style and colorful folklore," highlights patriarchal faith, and is given to anthropomorphism (i.e., representing Yahweh in human terms).

2. The E or Elohist document, written by a northern kingdom Israelite in the eighth century B.C. The divine name "Elohim" predominates in this second document, which tends to be moralistic and prophetic. This source praises Jacob and Joseph and emphasizes the northern tribes like Ephraim, Manasseh, and Reuben as well as the northern sanctuaries of Bethel and Shechem.

3. The combination of J and E. The clever interweaving of the two primary sources into a single document sometime after the fall of Samaria to the Assyrians in 722 B.C. was accomplished by a Judean editor (or editors).

4. The D or Deuteronomic source, ascribed to a "school" that produced the book of Deuteronomy and the final edition of the Former Prophets during the reign of King Josiah (ca. 630–600 B.C.). This D source is usually identified with the book of Deuteronomy and is equated with the finding of the "Book of the Law" that prompted Josiah's reform of Judean temple worship (622 B.C.; cf. 2 Kings 22–23). The D source is characterized by distinctive sermonic or hortatory style and covenant-legal vocabulary. Theologically the D source confines the worship of Yahweh to one central shrine (the temple in Jerusalem) and is marked by its strict adherence to a "blessing and curse" interpretation of Israelite history (i.e., "obedience to God brings reward, while disobedience brings punishment").

5. The P or Priestly source, distinguished by its uniform style, orderly arrangement of materials, and repetition of stereotyped phrases (e.g., "these are the generations"). This fourth major document contains liturgical and ritualistic texts, genealogical tables and statistics, laws and prescriptions—all unmistakable interests of the Israelite priesthood. The P source is assumed to be the product of postexilic priests about 500–450 B.C.

6. These four literary sources compiled into a five-volume Pentateuch by a priestly editor (or editors) sometime around 450 B.C., perhaps by Ezra the scribe (cf. Neh. 8:1–12).

Although refinements of the Graf-Wellhausen hypothesis have continued through the century since its introduction (including the further "atomizing" of the Pentateuch into sources like J1 and J2, E1 and E2, P1 and P2, K, L, N, and S), the four-source theory has remained solidified in this basic form (figs. 6.2a, 6.2b, and 6.3).

As a product of Enlightenment scholarship, the Documentary Hypothesis or Source Theory of Pentateuchal authorship was (and remains) rooted in the rationalism and skepticism of the age. The idea of deism ruled theology, so God was not conceived of as free to intervene in his creation. Thus miracles, predictive prophecy, and even divine inspiration were impossible in a universe created by God but closed to his providential participation in human history. Evolutionary theory was applied to the development of Israel's history and religion so that the Hebrews were ever moving from the "primitive toward the complex" (or from polytheism to monotheism). Scientific positivism and the empirical method were also taken over by biblical scholars of the period and applied to the study of Scripture.

In the end, the Old Testament (even the entire Bible) was reduced to a merely human literary product, a sort of Hebrew "religious anthology," and human reason was now elevated above the Scriptures as final authority.

Oral Tradition, Multiple Authors, and Later Editor(s) Hypothesis

The fourth hypothesis assumes that the oral transmission of Israelite histori-

**Figure 6.2a. The Structure of the Pentateuch
According to Source Analysis**

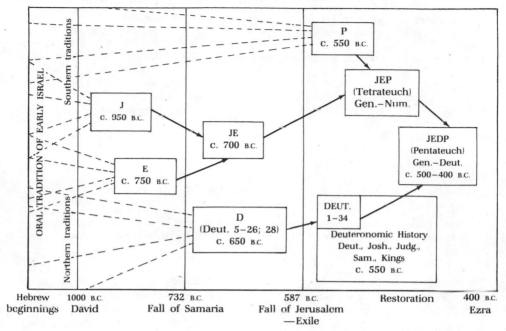

Figure 6.2b. Broad Locations of the JEDP Sources in the Pentateuch

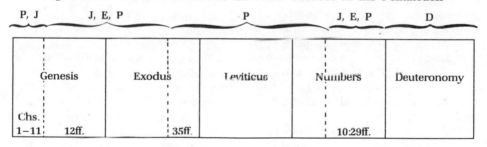

Diagrams adapted from James King West, *Introduction to the Old Testament*, 2d ed. (New York: Macmillan, 1980), 65, 67. Used by permission.

cal traditions and folklore was foundational to the composition of the Pentateuch. By analogy to other ancient cultures and some contemporary societies, proponents of this approach conjecture that oral traditions were eventually written down or "crystallized" in document form. These small literary units were then collected and finally compiled into the five books of the Pentateuch. Many authors and editors were involved in shaping the contents of the literature in the movement from oral tradition to written text. While adherents of this position admit to the antiquity of many of the Old Testament traditions, the written form of

Figure 6.3. Characteristics of Usage in the JEDP Sources

Yahwist (J)	Elohist (E)	Priestly (P)	Deuteronomist (D)
God is Yahweh	God is Elohim	God is Elohim	God is Yahweh
Walks and talks with us	Speaks in dreams, etc.	Cultic approach	Moralistic approach
Stress on blessing	Stress on fear of the Lord	Stress on law obeyed	Stress on Mosaic obedience
Earthy speech	Refined speech	Majestic speech	Speech recalling God's work
Stresses the leaders	Stresses the prophetic	Stresses the cultic	Stresses fidelity to Jerusalem
Narrative and stories	Narrative and warnings	Dry lists and schemata	Long homiletic speeches
Stress on Judah	Stress on northern Israel	Stress on Judah	Stress on whole land of Israel
Uses term "Sinai"	Uses "Horeb"		
Calls natives "Canaanites"	Calls natives "Amorites"		
		Uses genealogy lists	Loves military imagery
			Has many fixed phrases

From Lawrence Boadt, *Reading the Old Testament,* © 1984 by the Missionary Society of St. Paul the Apostle in the State of New York. Used by permission of Paulist Press.

the Pentateuch is usually assigned to the postexilic period of Israelite history.

This authorship hypothesis is often associated with the higher-critical methodology of form criticism. Form criticism attempts to identify the smaller literary units of the Pentateuch, explain their origin and life-setting (*Sitz im Leben*), and delineate the oral traditions that lay behind them. Important to this approach is determining the structure, genre, setting, and intent of each of the smaller literary units identified. The Old Testament narrative genre classifications include myth and folklore, legend and novelette, saga and history.

The efforts to identify the various literary types and forms of the Pentateuchal narratives have proven beneficial in understanding the Pentateuch as a literary composition. However, the approach has eroded the notion of historicity in the Old Testament in general and the Pentateuch in particular. The form critic declares that the Old Testament contains "no history writing" in the modern sense of the term.

Biblical history is usually labeled "popular history," because it is believed the ancient writers indiscriminately drew from reliable historical documents as well as legend, folklore, and saga. The stance of the form critic to Pentateuchal historicity is one of skepticism at best.[6]

Later Editors of Hebrew Traditions Hypothesis

Still another theory contends that a group of editors collected and arranged Hebrew stories, folktales, and other literary materials and traditions (oral and written) into the five books of the Pentateuch during the Babylonian exile and postexilic periods of Hebrew history. The traditions collected are considered largely nonhistorical and shaped by later editors for specific religious and nationalistic purposes. For this reason the modern student of the Bible must approach the Pentateuch with a "certain skepticism," since neither the sources nor the motivations of the editors may be trusted.

[6]On form criticism see further G. M. Tucker, *Form Criticism and the Old Testament* (Philadelphia: Fortress, 1971).

As such, the Pentateuch is a thoroughly late composition in respect to both the time of its writing and the traditions that it preserves. The early history of the Hebrews must be reconstructed largely on the basis of extrabiblical evidence, because the Pentateuchal traditions themselves have been "refashioned" by later editors to serve the purposes of a later generation facing persecution (i.e., those of the Babylonian exile). Especially important to this kind of Pentateuchal analysis is the nature of the community or group shaping the traditions, the geographical location of that community or group, the social and political and religious dynamics affecting the traditions, and the major themes, emphases, or motifs of the traditions.[7]

Pentateuchal Scholarship Today

The extremely hypothetical and subjective nature of Old Testament source analysis (e.g., the use of divine names as criteria for source division and "stylistic" differences), the faulty nature of many of the source analysis assumptions (e.g., the doublets or parallel accounts indicate diverse literary sources), and the inability of source critics to reach any consensus on the problems of Pentateuchal authorship have spawned numerous other approaches attempting to explain the composition of the Pentateuch (e.g., the wide disagreement among the subdividers of the text on the contents of the various sources). Form criticism and tradition history, the historical-archaeological approach, the social-sciences approach, and the canonical approach have emerged as competing alternative theories to traditional source analysis for the modern biblical researcher.[8]

In fact, some biblical scholars have remarked that traditional source analysis is an exercise in "reductionism toward absurdity" and have observed that the multiple approaches to the complexities of Pentateuchal authorship have in effect canceled each other out. One commentator has gone as far as to say that the chaos in liberal scholarship today has put Pentateuchal studies in a most unfavorable position.[9]

So there is a growing movement away from the "microscopic" analysis of source criticism toward the "telescopic" analysis characteristic of literary analysis. This approach focuses attention on the whole picture of the Pentateuch as a literary composition, not on the individual pieces of the jigsaw puzzle. There is an increasing appreciation for the deliberate structuring of the Pentateuchal narratives into a unified composition. This has been due largely to the application of the techniques of literary criticism, especially structural analysis, to the five books of the Pentateuch.

For example, a series of recent books and articles have argued for the integrity of the Pentateuch as a unified composition and without exception have assigned a preexilic date to the work in its completed form. The common denominator of literary analysis characterizing each of those presentations emphasizes repeated words, phrases and motifs in the narratives, artful chiasmus, parallel narrative structure, thematic coherence of larger literary units with smaller sections of the narrative, and the deliberate theological arrangement of literary units for didactic

---

[7]This hypothesis is usually considered part of the "tradition history" approach to Old Testament literature. See further W. E. Rast, *Tradition History and the Old Testament* (Philadelphia: Fortress, 1972); and Walter Brueggemann and H. W. Wolff, *The Vitality of Old Testament Traditions*, 2d ed. (Atlanta: John Knox, 1982).

[8]John Hayes and J. Maxwell Miller. *Israelite and Judean History* (Philadelphia: Westminster, 1977), 64–69.

[9]Cf. E. P. Blair, *The Illustrated Bible Handbook*, rev. ed. (Nashville: Abingdon, 1987), 101.

and mnemonic purposes in understanding the Pentateuch as a literary unity.[10]

Perhaps the current reactions to this new literary criticism and the view of the Pentateuch as a unified literary composition are indicators of future trends in Pentateuchal studies. On the one hand, the results of literary analysis may be presented as a viable alternative on equal standing with source analysis. On the other, it may be rejected (or more likely ignored) by scholars who will continue to look for creative ways to bolster the crumbling source analysis theory.[11] Apart from the literary considerations of Pentateuchal composition, the question of historical reliability remains.

The Pentateuch as History

Historical Background

The five books of the Law narrate a time span from Creation to the death of Moses at Mount Nebo in Moab just prior to the Israelite conquest of Canaan. Obviously it is impossible to ascertain a date for the origin of our earth and its solar system. While estimates for the date of Creation range from tens of thousands to billions of years, it seems best to leave the creation event an "undated mystery."

Roughly speaking, the Pentateuchal narratives from the call of Abram (Gen. 12) to the death of Moses (Deut. 34) may be assigned to the Middle Bronze and Late Bronze ages of ancient Near Eastern history. On a basic chronological continuum this means the patriarchal period extended approximately from 2000 to 1600 B.C., while Moses and the Exodus date to about 1500 to 1200 B.C. (given the early [fifteenth century B.C.] and late date [twelfth century B.C.] options for the Israelite Exodus from Egypt—see below under "Pentateuchal Chronology").

The patriarchs emerged from Mesopotamian culture founded by the Sumerians but reshaped by the Semitic dynasties of Sargon of Akkad that conquered and absorbed the decaying Sumerian civilization about 2400 B.C. The later kingdoms of Sumer and Akkad were in turn influenced by the continuing infiltration of the Amorites from the north and west and the Elamites from the east.

Palestine in the Middle Bronze Age was dominated by scattered Canaanite city-states much like Mesopotamia, though not as densely populated or as urban. According to the Egyptian story of Sinuhe, the fame of Palestine's agricultural abundance was widespread. The Canaanites, Amorites, Jebusites, and non-Semitic Hurrians were among the more important people-groups occupying Syro-Palestine during this period. Later, both the Egyptians and the Hittites influenced Syro-Palestine as they vied for control of this key landbridge (as witnessed by the Amarna tablets and the Boghazköy tablets).

The Egyptians were the most prominent people-group shaping the historical background of Pentateuchal history. Abraham's sporadic contact with the land of Egypt eventually gave way to the migration and settlement of Jacob's entire clan in the region of the Nile Delta. The

---

[10]Cf. Robert Alter, *The Art of Biblical Narrative* (New York: Basic Books, 1981); I. M. Kikawada and A. Quinn, *Before Abraham Was* (Nashville: Abingdon, 1985); Robert Polzin, *The Typology of Biblical Hebrew Prose*, HSM 12 (Missoula, Mont.: Scholars Press, 1976); G. A. Rendsburg, *The Redaction of Genesis* (Winona Lake, Ind.: Eisenbrauns, 1986); Gordon J. Wenham, "The Coherence of the Flood Narrative," *VT* 28 (1977): 336–48; Gordon J. Wenham, "The Date of Deuteronomy: Linch-Pin of Old Testament Criticism," *Themelios* 10, no. 3 (1985): 15–20, and 11, no. 1 (1986): 15–18; R. N. Whybray, *The Making of the Pentateuch: A Methodological Study* (Sheffield, England: JSOT Press, 1987).

[11]As an example of the former, see J. L. Crenshaw, *Story and Faith* (New York: Macmillan, 1986), 60–62; for the latter, see J. H. Tigay, ed., *Empirical Models for Biblical Criticism* (Philadelphia: University of Pennslyvania Press, 1987). One major criticism of source analysis has been its exclusive application to biblical studies. Now source theory methodology has been applied to various ancient Near Eastern documents.

Hebrews then resided in Egypt for several centuries, multiplying into a "great nation" while at the same time being thoroughly acculturated to Egyptian civilization. Examples of this acculturation are that not long after the Exodus the Hebrews lapsed into worship of what may be an Egyptian deity (Exod. 32:1–10); during the desert trek the people clamored to return to Egypt (Num. 11:4–6); and the Pentateuch itself contains some forty-five Egyptian loan words. Ironically, the Exodus narrative pits Moses and Yahweh against the pharaoh and the gods of Egypt, with the central character, Moses, being a former Egyptian courtier. (For more on Egyptian history, see chapter 3.)

Pentateuchal Chronology

Although most of Pentateuchal history may be assigned to the Middle Bronze and Late Bronze ages of ancient Near Eastern history, an exact chronology for the Hebrew patriarchs remains problematic. Some biblical scholars place the patriarchs in a fixed chronological framework, dating Pentateuchal events precisely to the year. For example, Abram was born in 2166 B.C., he began his sojourn in Canaan in 2091, he offered the Mount Moriah sacrifice in 2056, and he died in 1991 B.C. Others place the Hebrew patriarchs on a relative chronological continuum, assigning them broadly to the four centuries between 2000 and 1600 B.C. Given the scanty and sometimes ambiguous biblical data relating to Pentateuchal history and chronology, a relative timeline for the Hebrew patriarchal period is preferable.

However, even a relative chronological continuum for patriarchal history is not without problems, as the comparison chart in figure 6.4 demonstrates.

The discussion centers on two principle issues: the interpretation of biblical numerology and the role of archaeology and comparative historical and literary study in understanding biblical history. Scholars committed to a literal reading of the Old Testament date formulas affirm the historicity of the patriarchal narratives and support an early date for the Exodus from Egypt. Those who interpret the Old Testament date formulas figuratively or symbolically usually hold to a later date of the Exodus, but differ on their understanding of the historicity of the patriarchal narratives. Scholars assuming a skeptical stance toward the Old Testament narratives are regarded as "reconstructionists," because they reject a reading of the text at face value in order to retrieve or establish "real" Old Testament history through the application of historical-critical methodologies to the biblical text.

A second chronological problem arising from the Pentateuchal narratives is the actual date of the Hebrew Exodus from bondage in Egypt. The names of the pharaohs of the Hebrew oppression and Exodus are not mentioned in the biblical text, and as a result of this ambiguity two distinct positions have emerged from scholarly debate. One position interprets the date formulas of Judges 11:26 and 1 Kings 6:1 literally and assigns the Exodus to the fifteenth century B.C. (Early Date). The alternative view reads the same Old Testament date formulas symbolically, places a priority on archaeological data and extrabiblical evidence, and dates the Hebrew Exodus to the thirteenth century B.C. (Late Date). (See further on this in chapter 8.)

Historical Reliability

The source analysis approach that gained prominence during the nineteenth century not only affected the way biblical scholars viewed the Pentateuch as a literary composition, but also had far-reaching implications for the historicity of the patriarchal narratives. Wellhausen, the most influential of the "source critics," asserted that the Pentateuch con-

Figure 6.4. Comparison of Chronological Systems

EARLY EXODUS LONG SOJOURN	EARLY EXODUS SHORT SOJOURN		LATE EXODUS	RECONSTRUCTIONIST
The Patriarchs 2166-1805		21|00		
Migration to Egypt 1876		20|00		
		19	00		
	The Patriarchs 1952-1589	18|00	The Patriarchs 1950-1650	
Egyptian Sojourn 1876-1446	Migration to Egypt 1660	17|00	Migration to Egypt 1650	
Slavery 1730 or 1580		16|00		
	Egyptian Sojourn 1660-1446 Slavery: 1580	15|00	Egyptian Sojourn 1650-1230	The Patriarchs 1500-1300 Gradual migration
		14	00		
Wandering 1446-1406	Wandering: 1446-1406	13|00	Slavery: 1580	Egyptian Sojourn 1350-1230
Conquest and Judges 1406-1050	Conquest and Judges 1406-1050	12|00	Conquest and Judges 1230-1025	Conquest and Judges 1230-1025
		11	00		
United Kingdom 1050-931	United Kingdom 1050-931	10|00	United Kingdom 1025-931	United Kingdom 1025-931
		9	00		
Early date for Exodus and 430-year sojourn in Egypt per Masoretic reading of Exod. 12:40	Early date of Exodus and 215-year sojourn in Egypt per LXX reading of Exod. 12:40		Late date of Exodus and belief in historicity of patriarchal events	Late date of Exodus and reconstruction of biblical history through use of form criticism

From John H. Walton, *Chronological Charts of the Old Testament* (Grand Rapids: Zondervan, 1978), 25.

veys no historicity for the patriarchs, but merely reflects patriarchal stories retold in a later age.

It should be noted that a skeptical stance toward the Old Testament record as history is not peculiar to source analy-sis. Many present-day scholars espousing the unity of the Pentateuch on the basis of literary criticism also deny the essen-tial historicity of the biblical narratives. They speak of "sacred history" and "prose fiction," affirming the theological truth of Scripture but denying that the message reflects historical reality or dismissing the question of historicity as irrelevant.

Three primary reasons have been given for the source critics' skepticism toward historicity: (1) It is assumed that the oral traditions on which the later written documents were based likely suffered from faulty transmission, (2) the historical distance between the actual events of Old Testament history and the documentation of those events seriously undermines the reliability of the written record, and (3) the historical events preserved in these later written documents were no doubt heavily edited by the Hebrew community for theological and political purposes.

Today there are essentially three schools of thought on the historical reliability of the Pentateuchal (and other Old Testament) narratives. One, usually called the orthodox or traditional approach, assumes the supernatural origin of the Old Testament and the complete historical accuracy of the biblical record. The orthodox or conservative scholar appeals to extrabiblical and archaeological resources only to support and elucidate the reliable history of Israel already provided in the Bible.

A second approach, the historical-archaeological, presumes that the Pentateuch (and the Old Testament) are generally reliable. This means the Old Testament in large measure preserved historical traditions rather than creating them. Archaeological data are employed as objective controls to the accounts of biblical history in lieu of the subjective literary and philosophical hypotheses. Those committed to this view believe that ultimately a proper correlation between archaeological data and biblical tradition

will either support the historicity of the Old Testament narratives or permit the proper reconstruction of Israelite history.

The third school of thought is that of the historical reconstructionist. This views takes a skeptical stance toward the biblical narratives on the grounds that they are the work of prescientific ancient and medieval historians. Generally, other ancient extrabiblical sources are considered more reliable than the Old Testament narratives as being older documents and hence closer to the events they report. The historical-critical scholar uses a variety of methodologies including source, literary, form, and "tradition history" criticism to reconstruct the history of Israel in holding that the biblical accounts themselves cannot be taken at face value. Again, it is noteworthy that orthodox or conservative scholars may also use these critical methodologies while presupposing the supernatural origin and the historical reliability of the Old Testament.[12]

So finally, the issue of historical reliability of the Pentateuchal (and other Old Testament) narratives is one of preconvictions about the nature of the biblical text. Proponents of historical reliability are generally committed to the divine inspiration of the biblical narratives assuring an accurate history of Israel. Conversely, proponents of some form of a "reconstructionist" view of Old Testament history generally discount the divine or supernatural origin of the biblical narratives. This preconviction accounts for their critical stance toward the Old Testament as a flawed human and prescientific document and explains the need to reinterpret or recreate Hebrew history in light of extrabiblical literary and archaeological data and contemporary sociopolitical models.

---

[12]See Carl E. Armerding, *The Old Testament and Criticism* (Grand Rapids: Eerdmans, 1983), 1–19.

Interpretation of the Pentateuch

The Old Testament and the Christian Church

Ever since the time of the gnostic heretic Marcion (A.D. second century), the church has been confronted with the problem of determining the rightful place of the Old Testament in the Christian's Bible. Marcion represents one extreme, namely, utter rejection of the Old Testament and its "inferior God." Today the other extreme may be found among those groups who recognize the absolute authoritative nature of the Old Testament writings for the life and practice of the church. More recently this application of the authority of the Old Testament, especially the law, to the life of Christians has witnessed a resurgence in the "theonomics" movement, or Dominion Theology.[13]

The problem of reconciling "law" and "grace" gave rise to multiple methods of interpreting the Old Testament during the Middle Ages. Since it was believed that revelation was both expressed and hidden in the text of the Bible, several hermeneutical or interpretive approaches were used to understand the proper meaning of the Scriptures. Four basic methods emerged: (1) The literal or plain, taking the Bible at face value; (2) the allegorical or hidden meaning, uncovering "buried" meanings for personal faith; (3) the moral or didactic, directing Christian behavior; and (4) the anagogical, focusing on the consummation of faith and the ultimate hope of the Christian.

Since the Reformation, Protestant churches have attempted to resolve the tension between the "law" of the Old Covenant and the "grace" of the New Covenant by one of two basic approaches. The first heightens the discontinuity of the two covenants, in varying degrees, by means of a "dispensational" interpretation that identifies seven self-contained eras, or dispensations, of divine revelation. This approach draws sharp distinctions between Israel and the church and essentially constitutes a messianic suspension of Old Testament law. The second approach, covenant theology, emphasizes the continuity of the "covenant of works" and the "covenant of grace" and underscores their interrelationship.[14]

John Goldingay offers a helpful summary of the contemporary views regarding continuity and discontinuity between the Old and New Testaments. Ironically, his categories largely parallel those of biblical interpretation during the Middle Ages. The first contemporary view, the Old Testament as a "way of life," equates with the moral interpretive method of the Middle Ages, which views the Old Testament as a handbook on personal ethics. The second, the Old Testament as a "witness to Christ," emphasizes allegorical and typological interpretation much like the "hidden meaning" approach. The third, the Old Testament as "salvation history," calls attention to the God who acts redemptively in human history. Like the anagogical approach, this method points to the Christ event as the fundamental link between the Old and New Testaments. Goldingay's final category, the Old Testament as "Scripture," highlights the development of canon as the authoritative voice for belief and practice in the religious community.[15]

According to John Bright, only the approach that takes seriously the Old

---

[13]Greg L. Bahnsen, *Theonomy in Christian Ethics* (Nutley, N.J.: Craig Press, 1979). Bahnsen argues that the predominant character of Old Testament law is moral, hence its content is still binding today. Cf. William S. Barker and W. Robert Godfrey, eds., *Theonomy: A Reformed Critique* (Grand Rapids: Zondervan, 1990).

[14]Cf. D. P. Fuller, *Gospel and Law: Contrast or Continuum?* (Grand Rapids: Eerdmans, 1980), 1–46.

[15]Cf. John Goldingay, *Approaches to Old Testament Interpretation* (Downers Grove, Ill.: InterVarsity, 1981).

Testament as Scripture correctly understands the text and elevates the Old Covenant to its rightful place in the Christian's Bible. There is a sense in which the other three approaches (the Old Testament as a way of life, as a witness to Christ, and as salvation history) reduce the Old Covenant to a second rank in comparison with the New Testament. For Bright, this reading of the Old Testament with "New Testament glasses" robs the former of its authority for the Christian church. Since the Old Testament is intrinsically authoritative by virtue of its canonical status in the Christian community, it too is binding on the church in what it teaches explicitly and affirms implicitly. This canonical status also means the Old Testament is authoritative in its entirety and cannot be appealed to selectively. Only this biblical theological approach preserves the divine authority of the entire Old Testament for the community of the New Testament church, making Paul's statement intelligible: "For everything that was written in the past was written to teach us" (Rom. 15:4; cf. 1 Cor. 10:11).[16]

New Testament Understanding of Old Testament Law

Jesus acknowledged that the law was "legalism" in the sense that it demanded obedience to detailed Old Testament prescriptions and stipulations instituted by Yahweh for Israel (e.g., tithing, Matt. 23:23a). But the true nature of law, according to Jesus, went far beyond the external enactment prescribed by the legal code. Old Testament law comprised essentially justice, mercy, and faithfulness (Matt. 23:23b). Paul affirmed the law as holy, spiritual, righteous, and good (Rom. 7:12–14).

The purpose of the Old Testament law was to point out sin in humanity for what it really was—rebellion and disobedience before God. While demonstrating that sin left all persons without excuse before the holy God, the law exposed the human need for divine redemption. It was intended to tutor Israel and thus prepare them (and the world) for the revelation of Jesus of Nazareth as the Christ (Gal. 3:24). Ultimately the sacrificial and ethical demands of Old Testament law foreshadowed the New Testament gospel: justification by faith in Jesus Christ.

In one sense, the divinely revealed legal tradition of the Hebrews represents a continuum between the Old and New Covenants. Jesus fulfilled all the law in his very person and his special ministry as God's Messiah (Matt. 5:17). By his teaching, Jesus not only certified the continuing authority of Old Testament law, but also clarified and illuminated what had been implicit regarding human intent and motives. Biblical law was indeed more than external acts and rituals; it embodied the thoughts of the mind and the intents of the heart (e.g., Jesus' teaching on anger and adultery, Matt. 5:21–32). That Old Testament law was "internal" every bit as much as it was "external" is seen in Jesus' summary of the commandments: "Love the Lord your God with all your heart. . . . Love your neighbor as yourself" (Matt. 22:37, 39; cf. Deut. 30:1–10). Finally, this love for God that prompts obedience to his commandments marks the true child of God (1 John 5:1–5).

The continuity between the covenants is also demonstrated by the New Testament understanding of Old Testament Law. Three specific interpretive approaches may be identified, including the typological (i.e., Old Testament persons, events, and things "foreshadow" the corresponding New Testament entities), allegorical (i.e., the biblical text is understood

---

[16]Cf. John Bright, *The Authority of the Old Testament* (Reprint, Grand Rapids: Baker, 1975), esp. 151–60, containing examples of the Old Testament's authority in its biblical theology by implicit principle even in those texts superseded by the teachings of the New Testament.

figuratively or symbolically), and the didactic (i.e., the instructional value of the Old Testament for today's readers). For example, the book of Hebrews outlines the typological relationship of Old Testament levitical law to the priesthood of Jesus Christ (Heb. 7–9). Paul allegorically interprets Deuteronomy 25:4 in defending apostolic privilege to earn a living by preaching the gospel (1 Cor. 9:8–11). Elsewhere Paul underscores the didactic value of the Old Testament Scriptures (including the law) for the life of the believer and the Christian church (Rom. 15:4; 1 Cor. 10:11).

Yet we must recognize the contrast or discontinuity between the Old and New Testaments. Their understanding of God, faith, and even law are not identical.[17] Jesus specifically abrogated the ceremonial food laws of Leviticus 11 and Deuteronomy 14 in his teaching that all foods are "clean" (Mark 7:14–23; cf. Peter's vision in Acts 10:9–23). Of even greater significance, the levitical legislation related to the office of priest and the institution of animal sacrifice is superseded in the person and work of Jesus Christ as the greater high priest and the "once-for-all" atoning sacrifice for human sin (Heb. 7:15–28; 9:11–14).

However, the undergirding theological principles of Old Testament law remain intact apart from the functional abrogation of aspects of the civil and ceremonial law by New Testament teaching. As "God-breathed" revelation (2 Tim. 3:16), the Old Testament Scriptures are inherently authoritative, whether in explicit teaching or in implicit theological idea. So while Jesus Christ is the Passover Lamb, rendering all further animal sacrifices obsolete and unnecessary (1 Cor. 5:7), the New Testament still admonishes all believers in Christ to present themselves as "living sacrifices" unto God (Rom. 12:1–2). Likewise, all believers are obligated to be holy even as God is holy (1 Peter 1:16) because they now constitute a royal priesthood in Christ Jesus (1 Peter 2:9).

Questions for Further Study and Discussion

1. What is the significance of the similarities and differences between the legal literature of the Hebrew Pentateuch and that of the rest of the ancient Near East?
2. Trace the development of the concept of "covenant" in the Pentateuch.
3. How are the five books of the Pentateuch related literarily and theologically?
4. Define theophany. What is the significance of theophany in the Pentateuchal narratives?
5. How is patriarchal "religion" similar to Mosaic "religion" in the Pentateuch? How is it different?

For Further Reading

Aalders, G. C. A Short Introduction to the Pentateuch. London: Tyndale, 1949.
Bright, John. A History of Israel. 3d ed. Philadelphia: Westminster, 1981. Esp. 69–110. Informative section in support of patriarchal historicity.
Carpenter, E. E. "Pentateuch." ISBE. Rev. ed. Grand Rapids: Eerdmans, 1986. 3:740–53.
Clines, D. J. A. The Theme of the Pentateuch. JSOTSS 10. Sheffield, England: JSOT Press,

---

[17]For a concise statement on differences between Old Testament and New Testament faith, see Goldingay, Approaches to Old Testament Interpretation, 29–37.

1979. Classic monograph tracing the covenant theme unifying the literature and theology of Pentateuchal narratives.

Dyrness, William A. *Themes in Old Testament Theology.* Downers Grove, Ill.: InterVarsity, 1979. Esp. 113–42.

Expositor's Bible Commentary. Vol. 2: Genesis–Numbers. Grand Rapids: Zondervan, 1990. Thoroughly evangelical analysis, including helpful bibliographies.

Hamilton, Victor P. *Handbook on the Pentateuch.* Grand Rapids: Baker, 1982. Practical exposition of Pentateuchal content, excluding discussion of issues related to critical study of the Old Testament, but including extensive bibliographies.

Harrison, R. K. *Introduction to the Old Testament.* Grand Rapids: Eerdmans, 1969. Esp. 493–662. Now dated, but still the most comprehensive evangelical review of Old Testament studies, with exhaustive section on the Pentateuch.

———. *Old Testament Times.* Grand Rapids: Eerdmans, 1970.

Hayes, John. *An Introduction to Old Testament Study.* Nashville: Abingdon, 1979. Esp. 83–198. A useful survey of the historical-critical study of the Old Testament, but giving scant attention to evangelical concerns and responses.

Hayes, John, and J. Maxwell Miller. *Israelite and Judean History.* Philadelphia: Westminster, 1977. Esp. 70–212.

Knight, D. A., and G. M. Tucker, eds. *The Hebrew Bible and Its Modern Interpreters.* Philadelphia: Fortress, 1985.

Livingston, G. H. *The Pentateuch in Its Cultural Environment.* Grand Rapids: Baker, 1974. Well-researched introduction to the history and culture of ancient Israel prior to the conquest, with comparative study in ancient nonbiblical religious literature.

Martens, E. A. *God's Design: A Focus on Old Testament Theology.* Grand Rapids: Baker, 1981.

Millard, Alan R., and Donald J. Wiseman, eds. *Essays on the Patriarchal Narratives.* Winona Lake, Ind.: Eisenbrauns, 1983. Evangelical reexamination of the historical reliability and theological teaching of the Old Testament patriarchal narratives in light of recent research.

Patrick, D. *Old Testament Law.* Atlanta: John Knox, 1985.

Schultz, Samuel J. *The Gospel of Moses.* New York: Harper & Row, 1974.

Walton, John H. *Ancient Israelite Literature in Its Cultural Context.* Grand Rapids: Zondervan, 1989. A survey of the parallels between the various literary genres common to the Bible and the literature of the ancient Near East.

Wiseman, Donald J. *People of Old Testament Times.* Oxford: Clarendon, 1973. Standard reference on the history and impact of ancient Near Eastern peoples and cultures on the Hebrews

Chapter 7

Genesis

Genesis is the book of beginnings and contains the foundations for much of the theology of the Old Testament. An understanding of the book's content and message is essential to the study of the rest of the Bible. It is not a book of science, though scientists are right to investigate its claims. It is not a book of biographies, though much can be learned from the lives of men and women portrayed in its pages. It is not a book of history, though history is the path it follows. It is a book of theology, though its task is not accomplished systematically.

The Writing of the Book

The book of Genesis does not identify its author in its pages, nor does any other book of the Bible explicitly name the author of Genesis. Traditionally it has been attributed to Moses, and not without good reason. The other books of the Torah connect Moses to their writing, and most of the biblical literature treats the Torah as a unit. It is therefore understandable that Moses came to be consid-

ered the author of the whole. As has been often noted in the past, who better to put together the book of beginnings?

Logic and tradition aside, however, it is difficult to produce much evidence to connect Moses to the writing of the book. As noted in the previous chapter, much of the scholarship of the last century has been inclined to divide the book between sources dating largely to the late preexilic and early postexilic periods. Specific challenges to this critical perspective on the composition of Genesis have come from computer analysis that contests the criteria by which the various sources are isolated[1], as well as from alternative critical schools such as redaction criticism.[2] There truly is no end to theories concerning the authorship of this book.

Whoever put Genesis together—whether it was Moses (as we are inclined to think) or someone in the time of David and Solomon or the time of Josiah or the time of Ezra—the book clearly has one outstanding compositional feature: it is organized around eleven sections with each governed by a *toledoth* formula. The

---

[1]Y. T. Radday and H. Shore, *Genesis: An Authorship Study* (Rome: Biblical Institute Press, 1985).
[2]Gary Rendsburg, *The Redaction of Genesis* (Winona Lake, Ind.: Eisenbrauns, 1986).

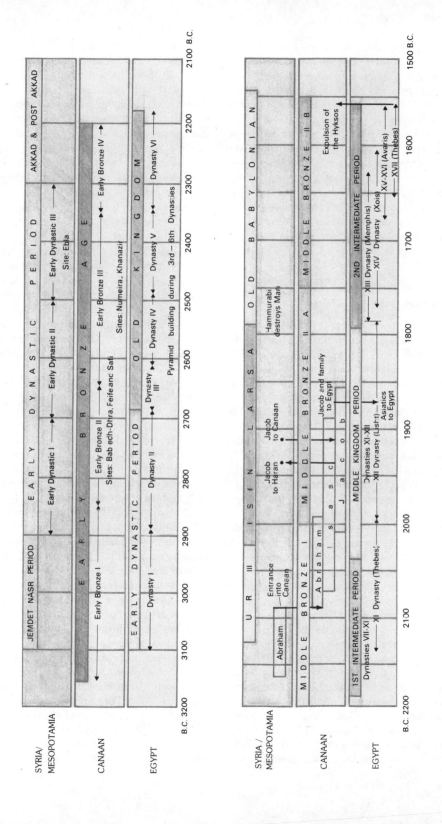

first of these formulas comes in 2:4: "This is the account [*toledoth*] of the heavens and earth when they were created." The other ten are connected to individuals (Adam, Noah, Shem, etc.). This suggests that either a compiler used these formulas to indicate the documents that served as his sources, or the author used them to organize his material. Since there is no reason to doubt that some of the material of Genesis was in written form even prior to the time of Moses, we would view someone like Moses as doing mostly the work of an editor rather than the work of an author.

The Background

Primeval History (Gen. 1–11)

The account of the primeval history in Genesis has been found to have some parallels in the literature of the ancient Near East, particularly that of Mesopotamia. The Atra-Ḫasis Epic contains an account of creation, growing population, and a destructive flood with similarities to some of the details of Genesis 2–9. The flood story of Atra-Ḫasis, with some modifications, is also found in the eleventh tablet of the famous Epic of Gilgamesh. Further information about Mesopotamian concepts of creation have been found in a number of Sumerian myths as well as in the work entitled Enuma Elish, which is a hymnic account of the rise of the god Marduk to the head of the Babylonian pantheon.

It has been common in some scholarly circles to view Genesis as containing adapted versions of Babylonian mythology. Since Mesopotamia holds pride of place as the cradle of ancient Near Eastern culture, and since the Babylonian literature is older than the generally accepted dates for the book of Genesis, it has been assumed that the similarities demonstrate biblical dependence on the Babylonian material. This has been affirmed in the minds of these interpreters by the fact that Israel's ethnic roots are traced to Mesopotamia, even by the Bible's own account (Abraham was originally from Mesopotamia).

According to this theory, Israelites borrowed the basic mythological concepts from the Babylonian material, but over the centuries adapted them to their distinctive monotheistic outlook. A major difficulty in all this is that it implies that the primeval history is actually only primeval mythology. If Genesis 1–11 is only a revamped mythology, then one does not need to believe that people named Adam, Eve, Cain, Noah, or Shem ever really existed. A mythological perspective usually does not affirm the reality of the garden of Eden or the ark of Noah, though it depends on how one defines myth. By any definition it is widely acknowledged that the function of Genesis 1–11 in Israel is very similar to the function of myth in the ancient Near East.

How, then, should we approach comparative studies? Though much is at stake, we cannot afford to ignore the similarities between biblical and ancient Near Eastern literature and hope they will go away. Rather, the ancient Near Eastern material needs to be used to help us gain an appropriate perspective on the Israelite literature preserved for us in the pages of Scripture. The Bible affirms the Mesopotamian roots of the Israelites, and the fact that God chose to use human authors to write the Bible should lead us to expect that there will be some similarities to contemporary literature. However, we cannot stop there. Comparative studies demand that we examine both the similarities and the differences.

When we undertake this type of analysis with the primeval history, we find that differences outnumber similarities and that the similarities can be explained more easily in other ways than by resorting to theories of literary borrowing. As an example, the flood story found in Mesopotamia follows a story line similar to that found in Genesis. A person is warned by deity to build a boat so that he can be spared from an impending flood intended to wipe out the human population. The boat is built, the storm comes, and after the waters subside, the boat comes to rest atop a mountain. Birds are sent out to determine when the inhabitants of the boat may safely disembark. The account ends with the offer of a sacrifice and a blessing bestowed on the survivors.

But the differences must also be considered. Among these are the type of boat, the length of the flood, the people who were saved, the landing place of the boat, the outcome for the hero, and most important, the role of the gods. Many who have done thorough linguistic and literary analysis (e.g., A. Heidel, A. R. Millard, D. Damrosch) conclude that literary dependence cannot be demonstrated. Here, as in most of the parallels in the primeval history, it is considered more likely that Mesopotamian and biblical traditions are based on a common source. Some understand this common source to be a piece of more ancient literature, while others consider it the actual event. In either case, the Mesopotamian literature provides a background for understanding some of the concerns of the primeval history of Genesis in contradistinction to the theology of the ancient Near East.

*The Patriarchal Narratives
(Gen. 12–50)*

In general, the patriarchal narratives ought to be viewed against the background of the archaeological periods designated Middle Bronze I (ca. 2000–1900 B.C.) and Middle Bronze IIA (ca. 1850–1750). During this time Mesopotamia made the transition from the highly successful Sumerian renaissance of the Ur III period to the Amorite domination of the Old Babylonian period. There is little in this background, however, that gives us great insight into the book of Genesis or the lives of the patriarchs. The only passage of Genesis that offers correlation

with events in world history is chapter 14, which remains an enigma.

It does seem clear from the archaeological data that through these periods there was a general trend in the social structure of Palestine from a semi-sedentary character to more of an urban character with fortified cities eventually springing up toward the end of Middle Bronze IIA. The Bible's description of the sparsely populated land of Abraham's travels is supported by archaeological analysis. Likewise, the general lifestyle and culture of the patriarchs has been authenticated by archaeological findings.

Though numerous scholars have contested the historicity of the patriarchs, neither the genre of the literature nor the nature of the events related in the accounts nor the cultural or geographical setting offers any reason to doubt that what these narratives preserve is realistic and true. Only presuppositions that rule out God's involvement with humankind can sustain the contention that these are merely legends devised to explain Israelite origins.

Outline of the Book

I. Creation (1:1–2:3)
II. Before the patriarchs: The need for a covenant people
  A. *Toledoth* of heavens and earth (2:4–4:26)
  B. *Toledoth* of Adam (5:1–6:8)
  C. *Toledoth* of Noah (6:9–9:29)
  D. *Toledoth* of Shem, Ham and Japheth (10:1–11:9)
  E. *Toledoth* of Shem (11:10–26)
III. The patriarchs in Palestine: The establishment of a covenant people
  A. *Toledoth* of Terah (11:27–25:11)
  B. *Toledoth* of Ishmael (25:12–18)
  C. *Toledoth* of Isaac (25:19–35:29)
  D. *Toledoth* of Esau (36:1–8)
  E. *Toledoth* of Esau (36:9–37:1)

Figure 7.1. Beni Hasan Tableau depicting an Asiatic caravan coming to Egypt, derived from a wall painting found in a tomb from about 1900 B.C.

IV. The patriarchs in Egypt:
Incubation for the covenant
people
   A. *Toledoth* of Jacob (37:2–50:26)

Purpose and Message

The purpose of the book of Genesis is to recount how and why Yahweh came to choose Abraham's family and make a covenant with them. The covenant is the foundation of Israelite theology and identity, and its history is therefore of understandable significance. The book continues the tale of how the covenant was established by detailing the various stumbling blocks and threats to the covenant. Finally, we discover how the Israelites ventured to Egypt, thus setting the scene for the Exodus.

The message of the book has several aspects. First of all, it provides an appropriate introduction to the Israelite God, Yahweh. We find that he is the sovereign creator of a world made especially for human habitation. Already in this we can identify an intentional contrast to Mesopotamian theology developing. In Mesopotamian thinking, creation was given two emphases. On the one hand, creation of cosmic forces and elements was generally described by the birth of the deity that had jurisdiction of that area. So, for example, the creation of the sea would be described as the birth of the goddess of the sea. There is typically no creator god

directing this process; creation is accomplished through divine procreation. On the other hand, there is a clear emphasis on organization of the cosmos rather than on the creation of it. In the hymn to Marduk called Enuma Elish, Marduk is elevated to the head of the pantheon and immediately acts to bring organization to the cosmos.

In contrast to the Mesopotamian view, Genesis insists that Yahweh is the creator, not just the organizer (though he is also responsible for giving order to the cosmos). Furthermore, procreation of gods is not used to explain the origin of the cosmic elements. Creation proceeds from the mouth of God.

A second aspect of the message of Genesis concerns the role of people in the newly created world, and again a contrast to Mesopotamian thinking is present. A key message of Genesis is that humans were created in the image of God. The world was created for them and with them in mind. When the first human pair are created they are accorded dignity and entrusted with responsibility. Genesis insists that all this was the design and intention of God. This is a stark contrast to the Mesopotamian mythology that understands humanity as an afterthought of the gods. In Atra-Ḥasis, for instance, people are created to take over the labor that the gods have tired of doing. There is no sense that all creation was undertaken with people in mind, and there was little dignity to offer when slave labor was the only motivation.

Amid this contrast with Mesopotamian theology, it is not the intent of Genesis simply to debate. The point of the Genesis narrative is to establish that Yahweh was sovereignly pursuing a plan of history. People were created with every advantage and were placed lovingly by God in an ideal situation. This is important, for it moves us to the next point of the message of the book. It was this man and woman, not God, who disturbed the equilibrium and brought about the lamentable state of our present existence.

It was the continuing failure of humanity as a whole that led Yahweh to send the Flood, scatter the people from the plain of Shinar, and eventually work through one man and his family, Abraham. The message of the book is to offer this as the explanation of why Yahweh has chosen to work through a chosen people. This is his plan of revelation of himself. Furthermore, it is demonstrated that it was not because of any merit on the part of Abraham that God chose him. Rather, it was an act of God's sovereignty. To Abraham's credit, he responded in obedience and exercised faith that Yahweh would honor his promises.

The message of the patriarchal narratives is that through many difficult situations the patriarchs and, more so, the Lord persevered to result in the establishment of Abraham's family. The text does not hesitate to show the shortcomings of Abraham and his family, but God is faithful and consistently, in his providence, brought good out of intended evil (cf. 50:20).

This is the theological message of the book. There are also other levels on which Genesis has a message. From a geographical standpoint, the book establishes that Abraham and his family were native to Mesopotamia (not Egypt), but spent three generations in Canaan before going down to Egypt. This is significant for their ethnic as well as theological identity.

Finally, Genesis seeks also to explain how Israel came to be organized the way that it was. The message clarifies some of the relationships of the twelve tribes to one another and accounts for the prominence of some and the obscurity of others. The geographical message, the sociological message, and the polemical message should be understood as subjects the compiler intended to address. But all these should be viewed as subordinate to the theological message, in which the covenant and Yahweh are central.

Structure and Organization

Creation (1:1–2:3)

The creation account is a highly structured literary composition. Using a framework of formulas (e.g., "it was so" and "God saw that it was good"), it presents God as the one who takes what was "without form and empty" and then forms and fills it. The first three days are occupied with forming, while in the next three God fills what he has formed. The focus of the composition is that everything is formed and filled so as to be perfectly suited for people to inhabit. This serves as an apt introduction to who God is and what he has made man and woman to be.

Before the Patriarchs:
Primeval History (2:4–11:26)

The primeval history has a universal focus with all humanity as the subject of discussion. In the previous section people were seen in relation to the rest of God's creation. This section begins with people seen in terms of the contrast between their high status and function as originally established on the one hand, and the situation that they brought on themselves by disobedience on the other. The initial disobedience by Adam and Eve brought expulsion from the garden, separation from God, and eventual death. Cain's murder of his brother Abel demonstrated that the new order of things had only become more deeply entrenched.

The passage of time conveyed by the genealogies only made matters worse. Beyond the offenses by Adam, Eve, and Cain, Lamech's attitude showed a boastful glee about his violence. By the time of Noah, violence had become a way of life. The selection of material by the compiler is intended to document in the most graphic terms the moral disintegration that occurred from the Fall to the Flood.

The Flood represented God's punishment on the world, but also his grace. Noah and his family were spared to make a new beginning. Again, some contrast to the Mesopotamian view is evident. There the gods had not planned to spare anyone. Rather, it was an act of betrayal by one of the gods that informed Atra-Ḥasis of the impending disaster. Moreover, while in Genesis it was humankind that was saved by sparing Noah and his family, Atra-Ḥasis saved civilization by including among his passengers artisans of the various craft guilds. The contrast is that in Genesis, God had no intention of saving society; in some ways, it was society that needed destroying.

After the Flood, the blessing was renewed, but degeneration occurred rapidly. The compiler continues to build his case for the insidious effect of man's fallen nature, seen even in Noah's own sons. God's eventual response to this occurred when people were no longer scheming to make themselves like God, but when they began to distort God so as to make him more like themselves. We believe this to be the threshold that was crossed when the ziggurat (the Tower of Babel) was constructed on the plain of Shinar (11:6). God then placed limitations on people's ability to unite in rebellion by means of geographical dispersion and linguistic differentiation. This not only restricted human ability to act in solidarity, but also set the scene for God's change of strategy. God's grace now became evident in his determination to reveal himself to humanity through one man and his family.

The Patriarchs in Palestine: Patriarchal Narratives (11:27–37:1)

While genealogical continuity is established from Noah to Abraham, there is no attempt to establish a faith continuity. Abraham is not introduced as a righteous man, nor is he identified in any way as contrasting to the world around him. Other Scripture makes it clear that Abraham's family did not worship Yahweh (cf. Josh. 24:2). So in a real sense, the Lord came to Abraham "out of the blue." The first contact is described in 12:1–3, where Abraham was instructed to take drastic action to separate himself from his roots so that a new beginning can take place. Yahweh asked Abraham to leave his land, his family, and his inheritance (father's household) and promised him in return his own land, his own family, and his own inheritance (blessing). They did not actually enter into a covenant agreement on this occasion, but the offer was made to do so once the conditions were met.

Chapters 12–22 present the checkered history of the establishment of the covenant between Abraham and the Lord. Once Abraham left his home behind, the next forty or fifty years provided continual suspense concerning how the promises of God would be fulfilled to Abraham. The narrative is very artistically executed so as to keep the reader guessing how things might turn out.

The primary approach of the narrator is to introduce various elements that place the covenant promises in jeopardy. As each obstacle is surmounted, a successive step is introduced toward the fulfillment of the covenant promises. Obstacles variously take the form of alternate heirs or the form of threatening situations for the primary characters.[3]

The first threat came when Abraham and Sarah went down to Egypt to escape the famine in the land of Canaan. The danger was that the pharaoh might take Sarah into his harem, or that a child born to Sarah may not be Abraham's. The threat was eliminated when Abraham and Sarah were escorted out of Egypt.

The first obstacle to overcome regarding an heir was the presence of Abraham's nephew, Lot. Since Abraham and Sarah had no children, Lot was the heir apparent. His presence with Abraham also could arguably have given him a claim to the land. The obstacle was removed in chapter 13 when Lot chose the plain toward Sodom for his claim, taking him out of the land. This led to the promise to Abraham that all the land would now belong to him and his descendants (13:14–17).

At this point in the text an appendix to the Lot narrative was included recounting how Abraham rescued Lot and many others from an invading army. The reason for including this may be to show that Abraham derived none of his wealth from the Canaanite population (14:21–24), though it is difficult to be certain.

The narrative continues in chapter 15 with the introduction of a second alternate heir, Eliezer, the head of Abraham's household. The Lord indicated, however, that Abraham's heir would be his own child, so another obstacle was removed.

The end of chapter 15 recounts the actual ratification of the covenant between the Lord and Abraham. Again the land was guaranteed to Abraham, but he was also given the information that the land would not actually come into the possession of his family for another four hundred years.

In chapter 16 a third alternate heir came on the scene. In this episode, Sarah suggested that since she had been unable to have children, Abraham should follow customary procedure whereby a slave in the household serves as a substitute wife in order for the line to be continued. In this manner Ishmael was born, a full and legitimate son of Abraham by the customs of the day.

Thirteen years went by, during which time, we assume, Abraham considered Ishmael his heir. In the midst of receiving instructions for the sign of circumcision and receiving affirmation from the Lord that he would become a great nation (chap. 17), Abraham was shocked to hear that the promised heir had not yet been born, but would be the natural child of Sarah (vv. 15–21). This message was reconfirmed (chap. 18) by the visit of three men to Abraham's tent.

The narrator now keeps us in suspense by relating two significant events that transpired prior to the actual arrival of Isaac. The first was the destruction of the cities of the plain, from which Lot and his daughters were delivered. This raised the possibility of Lot's reentering the picture, but the threat was quickly eliminated when he chose to live in the hills.

The second threat was much more serious. Chapter 20 relates an incident in which Sarah was about to be taken into a foreign king's harem, a scene reminiscent of the incident recorded in chapter 12. This time the king was Abimelech of Gerar. This threat was so alarming because Isaac was supposed to be born within the year. If Sarah were taken into Abimelech's harem even briefly, questions would arise as to whether or not Isaac was actually the son of Abraham. Again the problem was averted when the Lord alerted Abimelech in a dream that Sarah was Abraham's wife and must be restored to him.

Finally, the long-awaited child, Isaac, was born (chap. 21), and the reader is

---

[3]L. Helyer, "The Separation of Abram and Lot: Its Significance in the Patriarchal Narratives," *JSOT* 26 (1983): 77-88.

inclined to breathe a sigh of relief that everything has worked out well in the end. But the suspense is not over yet. We find out quickly that Ishmael was not to be so easily dismissed from contention. Nevertheless, even that last obstacle to heirship was removed.

And yet, as we would expect from a skillful narrator, just when it seems that all is well, the largest and most difficult problem imaginable looms over the horizon.

In the account of God's asking Abraham to go and sacrifice his son Isaac (chap. 22), we sense that the narrator has brought us to the climax of the narrative. The Lord had promised Abraham that Isaac specifically was the son through whom the covenant promises would be fulfilled, and so the covenant was again in great jeopardy. All the previous obstacles and threats came from human error or decision. This one came from deity. As the text relates (v. 12), the function of this test was to provide Abraham with the opportunity to demonstrate that he feared God. To be sure, Abraham had been characterized as obedient and full of faith throughout the narrative, but it is much easier to obey when one stands to profit from one's actions. Here Abraham could demonstrate to the Lord that his obedience was motivated by fear of the Lord, not by what he would gain by obeying. Once the threat was resolved, the promises were reiterated to Abraham (vv. 16–18).

The remaining sections of the *toledoth* of Terah continue to offer events pertaining to the establishment of the covenant, though the suspense has been broken. Chapter 23, while recalling the death of Sarah, apparently is included because this relates the only time when Abraham purchased land in Canaan. Since the acquisition of the land was part of the covenant promise, it is important to tell of this first instance.

For Abraham to have a big family, not only must there have been a son, but a son who would marry and have sons of his own. The obstacle to this (chap. 24) was to acquire a wife for Isaac in a way that would neither lead to assimilation with the people of Canaan nor require Isaac to leave the land. This was accomplished by Abraham's having his servant fetch a bride for Isaac from Abraham's extended family.

Finally, the account of Terah's family ends with the identification of Abraham's other children—again, these were potential heirs, so the text shows how they were cared for in the inheritance—and Abraham's death. Amid many obstacles, therefore, the covenant became established.

In keeping with the practice of the narrator, the noncovenant line is traced before the story returns to the main character. So the account of Ishmael precedes that of Isaac, and the account of Esau precedes that of Jacob.

Most of the account of Isaac concerns the conflict between Jacob and Esau and its eventual resolution. The conflict itself was a threat to the covenant, because it was serious enough that it could lead to murder and the extinction of Abraham's family (see 27:45). Beyond that, Jacob's leaving the land for some twenty years also threatened to undo the covenant by opening the possibility that the family of Abraham would simply return to Mesopotamia. From a theological standpoint, it is also clear that Jacob was not the man of faith that Abraham became. This leads the reader to wonder whether this might just turn out to be another failed experiment. It is these conflicts that give structure to this section. The covenant is still the main focus.

While most of the account of Isaac is therefore understandable as continuing coverage of the covenant struggle, the narratives that frame the Jacob-Esau conflict prove a bit more difficult to understand. Chapters 26 and 34 appear to be interludes of sorts, since they have little direct relation to the covenant. Like chapters 14 and 23, however, they relate incidents in which agreements were made with people of the land of Canaan. So they have covenant significance, for they concern the land and the ethnic distinctiveness of Abraham's family.

The Patriarchs in Egypt:
The Joseph Story (37:2–50:26)

The Joseph story is a cohesive narrative with the exception of chapter 38. Like the other interlude chapters, this one concerns an occasion when there was a relationship formed between Abraham's family and the people of the land of Canaan. The episode may also be intended to contribute to the emerging profile of Judah, who had great significance for the later tribal history.

Judah's role in chapter 38 is parallel to Jacob's in chapter 37. Like his father (37:32–33), Judah was deceived and asked to recognize a piece of evidence concerning identity (38:25–26). In this way Judah's actions against Jacob and Joseph were already coming back to haunt him. The end of chapter 38 also shows a younger son forcing his way out just when all seemed lost (vv. 27–30), thus making a "breach" (KJV). This was exactly what Joseph proceeded to do when his story resumes again in chapter 39.[4]

The main intent of the Joseph story appears to be to recount how the family of Abraham ended up in Egypt. In this way it is preparatory for the Exodus narratives. Though the covenant is barely mentioned, God's providential care of Joseph and sovereign control of history are evident as the plot develops and is resolved.

Major Themes

The Covenant and Election

The book of Genesis makes it clear that the Lord did not choose Abraham and his family because they were more righteous, more faithful, more pious, or more deserving than any other family. His electing them was an act of grace. Furthermore, while the covenant could not be ratified until Abraham left his family, no clear conditions were placed on the covenant itself. To be sure, the benefits of the covenant could be lost for periods of time, but no mention is made of the possibility of abrogation. The family of Abraham, for good or ill, constituted God's chosen people.

In Christianity, when we speak of the church as God's people, we refer to those who have accepted salvation through faith, specifically faith in Jesus Christ. The church could therefore be identified as the people of God in a soteriological—i.e., salvational—sense. Undoubtedly many Israelites of the Old Testament could be identified as God's people soteriologically by virtue of their faith in Yahweh; but their divine election and the divine covenant made the Israelites the people of God only in a revelatory sense. By this we mean that God chose them as his instrument of revelation. God revealed himself to the world through Israel—through the law he gave to them, through their history (which demonstrates his benevolence, grace, faithfulness, and sovereignty), through the writing of the Bible, and most of all, through the birth, life, death, and resurrection of Jesus Christ.

God's revelation of himself came through Israel.

The covenant thus became the centerpiece of Israelite theology. It speaks of God's intentions to bless them and honor them as channels of God's revelation. Throughout the Old Testament we learn most about the nature of God by seeing him act in accordance with his covenant promises and by sharing in the benefits of his revelation to and through Israel.

---

[4]See especially U. Cassuto, "The Story of Tamar and Judah," *Biblical and Oriental Studies*, vol. 1 (Jerusalem: Magnus, 1973), 29–40 (a reprint of a 1929 article); and Judah Goldin, "The Youngest Son: or, Where Does Genesis 38 Belong?" *JBL* 96 (1977): 27–44.

Monotheism

Generally speaking, monotheism is the worship of one God. There are, however, several levels of monotheism, ranging from preference for one deity, to worship of one deity, to believing that only one deity exists. Even the Ten Commandments insist only on a practical monotheism (exclusive worship of one deity) rather than a philosophical monotheism (only one God exists). This leads us to inquire whether the patriarchs were monotheists. Abraham's relatives apparently practiced the popular polytheistic paganism that was current in Mesopotamia (Josh. 24:2, 14), and the Bible nowhere attributes monotheism to Abraham. Nevertheless, though Abraham is never seen condemning the worship of other gods, there is never a hint that any other god has a place in Abraham's worship. This evidence would lead us to the conclusion that Abraham was at least a practical monotheist.

Also to be considered, however, is the question, "Which God did Abraham worship?" Though the personal name "Yahweh" occurs frequently in Genesis, a problem arises when we read the opening chapters of Exodus. In Exodus 6:2–3 God says to Moses, "I am Yahweh; and I appeared to Abraham, Isaac and Jacob as El Shaddai, but by my name, Yahweh, I did not make myself known to them." Though some scholars have suggested that Yahweh and Shaddai were two originally independent deities that became merged, the biblical texts unanimously accept them as alternative names for the same deity.

It seems most likely, from current research, that the patriarchs would have identified their God as "El," with both "Shaddai" and "Yahweh" serving as epithets to describe certain aspects of El's activity. Exodus 6:3 would then be understood as explaining that El-Shaddai was the epithet most appropriately connected with how God interacted with the patriarchs and what he accomplished for them. They did not experience firsthand the significance of the epithet Yahweh. It was Moses' generation who would come to know (experience) God as Yahweh.

The book of Genesis helps us see this distinction between Shaddai and Yahweh in the theophanies attributed to each (fig. 7.2). A theophany is a visible and audible manifestation of God as a human being, a phenomenon distinctive to the Old Testament. Both Abraham and Jacob experienced one "Shaddai theophany" and one "Yahweh theophany." For both, the Yahweh theophany came first and at the initiation of the agreement between God and the patriarch. The emphasis of the Yahweh theophany was on the land that would be given to the patriarch (15:7–17; 28:13–15).

In contrast, the El Shaddai theophanies came when the patriarchs accepted participation in the covenant. In the case of Abraham especially, the actual fulfillment was about to take place. The emphasis was on the element that began to find fulfillment in the patriarchs' lifetimes: descendants. Even in usage apart from the theophanies, the name El Shaddai is most closely connected with descendants (28:3; 43:14; 48:3). Both Shaddai theophanies feature a name change for the patriarch, showing that each considered himself in allegiance with El Shaddai (17:1–8; 35:11–12).

The conclusions to be drawn from this differentiation are that the epithet Yahweh was connected to the longer-term promises of God to the patriarchs—specifically the land, which even Abraham was told would be a long time coming. The patriarchs could truly be considered then not to have "known" God by his name Yahweh, for the promises that he had been most closely associated with had not yet come to pass. Yet it was now Yahweh who was being sent by Moses to take the Israelites to the land that had been promised to them in the covenant. Our conclusion, then, is that Abraham

Figure 7.2. Theophanies in Genesis

"I am Yahweh"	"I am El Shaddai"
Initiation of agreement	Initiation of fulfillment

Abraham

Genesis 15:7–17	Genesis 17:1–8
1. Occasion: Ratification of covenant	1. Occasion: Indication of acceptance of covenant (circumcision)
2. Emphasis: Giving of land	2. Accepts name change; Isaac promised within year
	3. Emphasis: Many descendants, nations, kings will come from you

Jacob

Genesis 28:13–15	Genesis 35:10–12
1. Occasion: First promise of covenant blessings to Jacob	1. Occasion: Indication of acceptance of covenant (destruction of foreign gods, pillar set up)
2. Emphasis: Bringing him back to land and giving it to him	2. Accepts name change
	3. Emphasis: Many descendants, nations, kings will come from you

was a practical monotheist worshiping El, who had revealed himself to Abraham through several epithets. Though the patriarchs were aware of the name Yahweh, the epithet most appropriate to Abraham was El Shaddai. However, it was the epithet Yahweh that eventually came to be understood as the primary name of Israel's covenant God.

Sin

One of the key themes of Genesis is the introduction of sin into the world and the impact it has had on human history. When Adam and Eve were created, immortality was within their grasp, for the tree of life was in the garden and available for their use. When they succumbed to temptation, they were cast from the garden and were denied access to that tree. The desire to be like God that led to their disobedience included a desire for autonomy, just as children long to gain autonomy from their parents and make their own decisions.

The punishment was suitable and logical. Autonomy often brings separation, and so it was with Adam and Eve's relationship to God. Also, as children find out when they become adults, autonomy is not the same as independence. The pronouncement of Genesis 3:16–19 delineates a different sort of dependence. This was the beginning of several cycles of sin and punishment that constitute the primeval history. For Adam and Eve and Cain and Abel the sin was individual in nature. In Lamech's actions (4:23–24) and in the behavior of the "sons of God" (6:1–

4) we can identify expansion into the institutions of society (the family and kingship). By the time of Noah, sin completely infiltrated every corner of humanity. The destruction by flood did not eliminate sin, as it progressed again from individual sin (9:20–23) to coordinated acts of rebellion (11:1–9).

The election of Abraham did not put an end to sin. We are particularly struck by Jacob's acts of deception. Again, however, God suited the punishment to the crime. Jacob procured the blessing for himself by disguising himself as Esau (chap. 27). He became the victim of deceit when he married Leah, who was disguised as Rachel. Even more poignant was the deceit of his sons, who produced a bloodied coat to convince Jacob that his son Joseph was dead. In this theme of sin and punishment, we see God's mercy as well as his justice.

Origins

Although, as we have noted, the book of Genesis is not a book of science, it does purport to say something about origins and therefore has traditionally been of some interest to scientists. Those who believe in the trustworthiness of the Bible often find themselves today in the awkward position of trying to reconcile what the Bible says about origins to what scientific theory tells us about origins. It is important, therefore, to establish precisely what the Bible says about origins.

God created. This is the most basic affirmation of Genesis. Even though Genesis does not recount creation of everything (for example, it does not relate the creation of angels), there is no room given for any other creative power. It is possible, depending on how one translates Genesis 1:1, that the raw material of earth was already in existence when the narrative of the book begins. But one could not infer from this that God was not its creator.

How did God create? The text emphasizes the spoken word of God, but some have felt this does not rule out the possibilty that God could have set in motion an evolutionary sequence. Those who reject this possibility contend that God's function as Creator must be intended, if nothing else, to emphasize his sovereign control. They see this control threatened by the random, arbitrary, and chance nature of the processes included in evolutionary theory. Nevertheless, one could likewise argue that the weather is random, arbitrary, and subject to chance, yet that is not thought of as undermining God's sovereign control of his creation. To the extent to which evolution is defined in exclusively naturalistic ways, it is unacceptable to the theology of Genesis, because creation, by the insistence of Scripture, is supernaturalistic.

When did God create? The seven-day structure of Genesis 1 has long created controversy even among conservative interpreters. While some have used it as the basis for a scientific defense of a "young" earth, others have felt that the word "day" was sufficiently flexible to accommodate the long ages proposed by geologists. Still others have contended that the seven-day structure is intended as a literary device rather than a chronological guide. All these positions can garner an impressive amount of supporting evidence that can be baffling to the person trying to decide between them.

The difficulty comes in part because we are asking questions that Scripture never intended to address. The point of the text is not to satisfy our curiosity about scientific matters, but to reveal to us the nature of God. Science attempts to explain origins without God; Scripture insists that the most important aspect of origins to understand is that God created. These two philosophies cannot really coexist. Attempts to reconcile the biblical perspective to the scientific perspective are acceptable only as long as they do not compromise the biblical affirmations.

Questions for Further Study and Discussion

1. How do comparative studies contribute to an understanding of the Old Testament? What dangers do they represent?
2. What would the Israelites have considered the primary impact of the Fall?
3. What approach should we take when challenged to reconcile the book of Genesis with modern science?
4. Why would God use multiple names in Genesis and elsewhere in the Old Testament in his revelation of himself?
5. Discuss and contrast the terms "revelatory people of God" and "soteriological people of God" (assisted by the subject index).

For Further Reading

Baldwin, Joyce. *The Message of Genesis 12–50.* Downers Grove, Ill.: InterVarsity, 1986.

Blocher, Henri. *In the Beginning.* Downers Grove, Ill.: InterVarsity, 1984. Evangelical approach to philosophical and exegetical problems encountered in Genesis 1–3.

Damrosch, David. *The Narrative Covenant.* San Francisco: Harper & Row, 1987. Analysis of relationship between biblical and ancient Near Eastern literature in terms of genre transformation. Particularly interesting section on Gilgamesh and Genesis.

Fields, Weston. *Unformed and Unfilled.* Nutley, N.J.: Presbyterian and Reformed, 1976. A well-written critique of the "Gap theory" that includes discussions of most of the terms of theological significance in Genesis 1–2.

Fokkelman, J. P. *Narrative Art in Genesis.* Amsterdam: Van Gorcum, Assen, 1975.

Garrett, Duane A. *Rethinking Genesis.* Grand Rapids: Baker, 1991.

Hamilton, Victor. *The Book of Genesis 1–17.* Grand Rapids: Eerdmans, 1990.

Heidel, Alexander. *The Gilgamesh Epic and Old Testament Parallels.* Chicago: University of Chicago Press, 1946. Translation of the Gilgamesh Epic and detailed comparison of it to the pertinent sections of Genesis.

———. *The Babylonian Genesis.* Chicago: University of Chicago Press, 1951. Translation of Enuma Elish and analysis of similarities and differences with the book of Genesis.

Kikawada, Isaac, and Arthur Quinn. *Before Abraham Was.* Nashville: Abingdon, 1985. A view of the structure of the book of Genesis that rejects the usual division into sources.

Millard, Alan R. "A New Babylonian 'Genesis' Story." *TB* 18 (1967): 3–18.

Millard, Alan R., and Donald J. Wiseman, *Essays in the Patriarchal Narratives.* Winona Lake, Ind.: Eisenbrauns, 1983.

Miller, Patrick. *Genesis 1–11: Studies in Structure and Theme.* Sheffield, England: JSOT Press, 1978.

Rendsburg, G. *The Redaction of Genesis.* Winona Lake, Ind.: Eisenbrauns, 1986.

Ross, Allen. *Creation and Blessing.* Grand Rapids: Baker, 1988. An evangelical treatment using the literary approach to the text.

Sailhamer, John. "Genesis." *EBC.* Vol. 2. Grand Rapids: Zondervan, 1990.

VanGemeren, Willem. *The Progress of Redemption.* Grand Rapids: Zondervan, 1988. A biblical theology that presents Genesis in its theological context within the Bible.

Walton, John H. *Ancient Israelite Literature in its Cultural Context.* Grand Rapids: Zondervan, 1989. A survey of the comparisons between Genesis and the ancient Near Eastern texts.

Wenham, Gordon J. *Genesis 1–15.* WBC. Vol. 1. Waco, Tex.: Word Books, 1987. A sound presentation of modern evangelical interpretation of Genesis.

Westermann, Claus. *Genesis 1–11*. Minneapolis: Augsburg, 1984. Translation of German commentary first published in 1974, containing the most thorough presentation of critical scholarship on the book of Genesis.

Youngblood, Ronald. *The Genesis Debate*. Nashville: Thomas Nelson, 1986. Discussion of the issues of Genesis 1–9 reflecting differing evangelical opinions.

Chapter 8

Exodus

The English name for this second book of the Pentateuch, or Law of Moses, comes from the Greek Old Testament title *Exodus,* meaning a "going out" or "departure' (19:1). The title is a logical one in that Israel's Exodus from Egypt is the dominant theme of the book. But the Hebrews gave a different title to the book, "these are the names," derived—in keeping with ancient custom—from the first two words of the opening verse (1:1).

The book of Exodus continues the record of the early history of the Hebrews in Egypt following Jacob's migration (cf. 1:1–7) through the chartering of Israel as the people of God at Sinai (chaps. 19–24).

Although Moses is the primary human character of the Exodus narratives, the real story is the redemptive work of Yahweh in delivering Israel from slavery in Egypt and establishing a unique covenant relationship with the nation. These acts of God signaled his good intentions to keep the promises made generations ago to Abraham and the patriarchs (cf. 3:7–16). Israel's Exodus from Egypt is the redemptive model of the Old Testament, and along with the covenant ceremony at Sinai, it constitutes the highwater mark of Old Testament salvation history.

The Writing of the Book

According to Jewish and Christian tradition, Moses wrote the book of Exodus at the command of God in connection with Israel's covenant experience with Yahweh at Sinai (cf. 17:14; 24:4; 34:27). Some scholars consider Moses to have written major portions of Exodus with certain additions made by later editors (e.g., the genealogy in 6:14–27). Still others regard Exodus as the literary product of Moses' successor, Joshua, or of Eleazar the priest, based on oral tradition received from Moses and Aaron. Regardless, all these views acknowledge Moses as the source for the origin of the written document recording the Exodus from Egypt.

Scholars who accept Mosaic authorship for all or part of Exodus assign the work to the fifteenth or thirteenth century B.C., depending on the view taken for the dating of the Exodus event.

Biblical scholars who are committed to some form of multiple authorship associated with the documentary hypothesis for the composition of the Pentateuch divide Exodus into three major sources: the J (or Yahwist), the E (or Elohist), and the P (or Priestly) documents. Chapters 1–34 are generally considered a "splic-

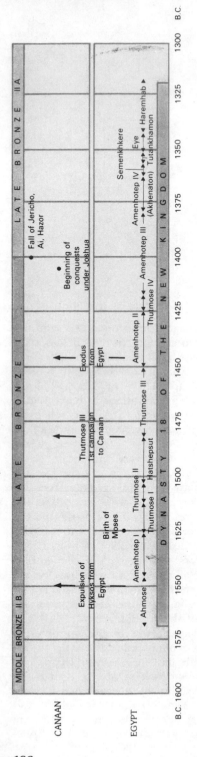

ing" of J and E and P, while chapters 35–40 are considered Priestly material (P). Traditional source analysis attributes the final "weaving" of the literary sources in Exodus into a complete text or book to unknown Priestly authors-editors of the exilic or postexilic period (ca. 600–400 B.C.).

According to this hypothesis, the oral traditions on which the book of Exodus was based underwent considerable expansion, revision, and rewriting over the course of several centuries (i.e., the ninth to the fifth centuries B.C.). For this reason, critical Old Testament scholarship maintains a stance of suspicion toward the book's literary integrity and skepticism toward its historicity.

An examination of the text of Exodus confirms Mosaic authorship for at least four sections of the book. These four literary units were apparently written in association with the events they record and include the "memorial" of the war with the Amalekites (17:8–16; esp. v. 14), the covenant code (19:1–24:18; cf. 24:4; 34:27), the Song of the Sea (15:1–21), and the additional covenant stipulations (34:1–28; esp. v. 27).

The extensive third-person narratives of the book (including the passage lauding Moses, 11:3) along with the parenthetical insertions intended to bring a later audience up to date (e.g., 16:31–36) suggest someone other than Moses compiled Exodus in its present form. It seems reasonable to assume that the four passages cited as composed by Moses were collected and arranged by a contemporary, perhaps even his protégé Joshua. The book of Exodus stands substantially as the literary product of Moses. Any later editorial activity is largely limited to the modernization of archaic or technical terminology and geographical place names (e.g., 15:23). Whether the rest of the narrative and legislation of the book was composed by Moses or dictated to scribes remains unspecified (cf. 25:1; 30:11, 17). Exodus and the rest of the Pentateuch were probably cast in the form of a unified, five-volume book sometime between the days of Joshua and the elders of Israel (Josh. 24:31) and the era of Samuel (1 Sam. 3:19–21).

The Background

The Date of the Exodus

The book records events from the birth of Moses to the completion and dedication of the tabernacle at Sinai in the first month of the second year after the Exodus from Egypt (cf. 1:1; 2:1–14; 19:1; 40:17). Thus the actual history of the book covers a span of about eighty-five years.

The main problem for scholars has been determining the century in which the events associated with the departure from Egypt actually took place. Pinpointing the date of the Exodus constitutes one of the major chronological problems of Old Testament study, and the complex issue remains a topic of debate. Two basic positions have emerged from the discussions, the so-called Early Date and Late Date views. The chronology of the Exodus is further complicated because the migration of Jacob's family to Egypt due to famine in Palestine cannot be precisely calculated either. In an attempt to account for the biblical and extrabiblical chronological and geographical data, four chronological systems have been developed (see fig. 6.4, chap. 6).

Since only two pharaohs of Egypt ruled for more than forty years (the length of Moses' exile in the wilderness during the Hebrew oppression), their reigns have become the focal points of discussion for dating the Exodus. The Early Date view identifies Thutmose III (1504–1450) as the pharaoh of the oppression and Amenophis II (1450–1425) as the pharaoh of the

Exodus. Both reigned during the Eighteenth Dynasty of the period of Egyptian history known as the New Kingdom era and date to the Late Bronze Age of ancient Near Eastern history.

The Late Date position identifies Rameses I (1320–1318) and Seti I (1318–1304) as the pharaohs of the Hebrew oppression and Rameses II (1304–1237) as the pharaoh of the Exodus. All were kings of the Nineteenth Dynasty of the Egyptian New Kingdom era and are dated to the century of transition between the Late Bronze and Early Iron ages of ancient Near Eastern history.

(The arguments for the two positions are summarized in figures 8.1a and 8.1b.)

At issue in the controversy over the date of the Exodus is the interpretation of the biblical and extrabiblical data. Proponents of the Early Date position emphasize the literal interpretation of the biblical numbers recorded in Exodus 12:40, Judges 11:26, and 1 Kings 6:1 and selectively appeal to archaeology for support (e.g., both camps cite archaeological evidence from Jericho and Hazor in support of their postions). Those holding to the Late Date view understand the biblical numbers symbolically and place priority on the extrabiblical historical information and archaeological evidence. The approach adopted in this volume assumes the historical validity of the biblical numbers while recognizing the "slippery" nature of the evidence garnered by both camps from the selective appeal to extrabiblical and archaeological data.[1]

The Route of the Exodus

Our understanding of the Hebrew Exodus is further complicated by geographical considerations, as the exact route of

[1]For example, the Late Date view of the Exodus identifies the Arad of Numbers 21:1 with the modern Tell Arad because it is an Iron Age settlement and lacks both Middle Bronze and Late Bronze Age occupation levels. By contrast, the Early Date proponents suggest that Arad should be identified with Tell el–Milh some eight miles southwest of Tell Arad, since it exhibits Middle Bronze Age fortifications.

Figure 8.1a. Early Dating of the Exodus

Suggested early dates:	Date B.C.	Reigning pharaoh
	1446	Amenophis II (1450–25)
	1440	Amenophis II (1450–25)
	1437	Amenophis II (1450–25)

Arguments for the early date

1. 1 Kings 6:1 indicates the Exodus occurred 480 years prior to the 4th year of Solomon's reign. His 4th year is variously dated at 966/960/957 B.C., placing the Exodus at 1446/1440/1437.

2. According to Judg. 11:26, Israel had occupied Canaan for 300 years before the judgship of Jephthah, which is dated between 1100 and 1050. This dates Joshua's conquest between 1400 and 1350. Adding Israel's 40 years in the desert puts the Exodus between 1440 and 1390.

3. Moses lived in exile in Midian 40 years (Acts 7:3; cf. Exod. 2:23) while the pharaoh of the oppression was still alive. The only pharaohs who ruled 40 years or more were Thutmose III (1504–1450) and Rameses II (1290–1224).

4. The Merneptah Stela (ca. 1220) indicates Israel was already an established nation at this time.

5. The Amarna tablets (ca. 1400) speak of a period of chaos caused by the "Ḫabiru," very likely the Hebrews.

6. The early date allows for the length of time assigned to the period of the judges (at least 250 years). The late date allows only 180 years.

7. The Dream Stela of Thutmose IV indicates he was not the legal heir to the throne (i.e., the legal heir would have died in the tenth plague).

8. Archaeological evidence from Jericho, Hazor, etc., supports a 15th-century date for the Exodus.

9. Exod. 12:40 dates the entrance of Jacob into Egypt during the reign of Sesostris/Senusert III (1878–43) rather than during the Hyksos period (1674–1567).

Adapted from Andrew E. Hill, *Baker's Handbook of Bible Lists* (Grand Rapids: Baker, 1981), 70–71. Used by permission.

the Hebrew desert trek and the location of Mount Sinai remain uncertain. Three alternatives have been advanced for the Exodus route taken by the Hebrews: the extreme northern Sinai route theory, the central Sinai route theory, and the traditional southern Sinai route theory.

Arguments lending support to the northern route theory include the tentative identification of Baal-Zephon with Ras Kasrun in the northwestern area of the Sinai. Also, the northern route fits Moses' request to Pharaoh for three days to journey to worship Yahweh (Exod. 3:18), and the route marks the shortest distance to Kadesh-Barnea, the immediate objective of the Hebrews. Yet the northern route is the least likely option of the three, since it keeps the Israelites so close to Egyptian territory. Further, this view discounts the biblical texts indicating that Mount Sinai was an eleven-day journey from Kadesh (Deut. 1:2) and that God deliberately maneuvered the Hebrews away from the occupied areas along the coast (cf. Exod. 13:17).

The central route theory locates Mount Sinai in northwest Arabia, beyond Aqabah, partly on the grounds that the Exodus narrative of the covenant experience describes an active volcano (19:16–25) and partly because the same region is traditionally connected with the homeland of the Midianites (cf. Exod. 3:1; 18:1). Today the central route alternative has been largely discounted by biblical scholars

Figure 8.1b. Late Dating of the Exodus

Suggested late dates:	Date B.C.	Reigning pharaoh
	1350	Tutankhamen (1361–52)
	1290	Rameses II (1304–1237)
	1280	Rameses II (1304–1237)
	1275	Rameses II (1304–1237)
	1225	Rameses II (1304–1237)

Arguments for the late date

1. The 480 years of 1 Kings 6:1 is a symbolic figure for 12 generations. Because a generation is about 25 years, the actual figure should be 300 years, placing the Exodus around 1266/1260 B.C..

2. The 300-year figure cited by Jephthah is merely an exaggerated generalization, since he had no access to historical records.

3. The 40 years Moses spent with the Midianites is not a chronological figure, but a symbolic figure indicating a long period of time.

4. The Merneptah Stela (ca. 1220) indicates Israel was in the land of Palestine by this date. The name "Israel" does not occur in any other historical records or documents before 1220. This would be unlikely had Israel begun occupation of the land 200 years earlier, in 1400.

5. The "Habiru" of the Amarna tablets cannot be identified with the Hebrews. The "Habiru" were a diverse people, native Canaanites. They are attested from the 18th to the 12th centuries B.C.

6. With the overlapping of judgships and the use of symbolic numbers (e.g., 40 years), the period of the judges need not span more than 150 years.

7. That Thutmose IV was not the legal heir to the Egyptian throne in no way proves the legal heir died in the tenth plague.

8. Archaeological evidence from Lachish, Jericho, Bethel, Hazor, Debir, etc., supports a 13th-century date for the Exodus.

9. The 430 years of Exod. 12:40 from the late date for the Exodus places Jacob's entrance into Egypt during the Hyksos period (1730–1570). This period of foreign domination in Egypt is a more likely time period for Israel's entrance into Egypt.

10. The civilizations of Edom, Ammon, and Moab were not in existence in the 15th century, thus it would have been impossible for Israel to have had contact with these nations if the Exodus occurred in that century. Since Israel did have such contact, the Exodus must be dated to the 13th century.

11. The Old Testament does not mention the Palestinian invasions of Seti I or Rameses II, very likely because Israel was not yet in the land of Palestine.

12. The Israelites were building Pithom and Raamses (Exod. 1:11), cities of the delta region. Raamses was founded by Seti I (1318–1304) and completed by Rameses II (1304–1237).

13. Thutmose III was not noted as a great builder.

Adapted from Andrew E. Hill, *Baker's Handbook of Bible Lists* (Grand Rapids: Baker, 1981), 71–72. Used by permission.

due to the strength of counterarguments made in separate studies. First, it has been demonstrated that the Sinai theophany is typical of other recorded ancient Near Eastern divine manifestations that do not presuppose an active volcano; there is therefore no need to place Sinai in Arabia, the nearest site for volcanic activity. Second, Moses is identified as being related to the Kenites as well as to the Midianites, and it is believed the Kenites were a nomadic Midianite clan whose presence in the Sinai region is well attested (cf. Judg. 1:16; 4:11); so there is no need to place Moses in Arabia.

The traditional southern route theory of the Exodus still accommodates all the known biblical and geographical information most convincingly. It seems likely that the crossing of "the Sea of Reeds" took place somewhere in the salt marshes and lakes between the Mediterranean Sea and the Gulf of Suez. Lakes Menzaleh, Balah, and Timsah along with the Great Bitter Lakes have been suggested as possible candidates for the Reed Sea of the Hebrew Exodus. The northerly jog in the route is best accounted for by the "wall" of the canal of Shur recently discovered in the eastern Nile delta. Certainly the escaped Hebrew slaves would have avoided this Egyptian fortification. Finally, Jebel Musa, or Mount Horeb, in the southern Sinai peninsula has been identified as the Mount Sinai of Moses' revelation by Christian tradition dating to the fourth century A.D.

Outline of the Book

I. Israel in Egypt
  A. Slavery in Egypt (1)
  B. Birth, early life, and call of Moses (2–4)
  C. Pharaoh's oppression of Israel (5:1–6:13)
  D. Genealogies (6:14–27)
  E. The plagues and the Passover (6:28–12:36)
II. The journey from Egypt to Sinai
  A. The Exodus from Egypt (12:37–14:31)
  B. The song of Moses (15:1–21)
  C. The wilderness of Shur (15:22–27)
  D. The wilderness of Sin (16)
  E. The rock at Rephidim (17)
  F. Jethro and Moses (18)
III. Covenant and law at Sinai
  A. Preparations for covenant (19)

  B. The Decalogue (20:1–17)
  C. The covenant code (20:18–23:33)
  D. Ratification of covenant (24)
  E. The tabernacle (25–40)
    1. Specifications (25–27)
    2. The priests (28–29)
    3. The furniture (30)
    4. The craftsmen (31:1–11)
    5. The Sabbath (31:12–18)
    6. Israel's breach of covenant with the golden calf (32)
    7. Yahweh and Moses (33)
    8. Covenant renewal (34)
    9. Construction of the tabernacle (35–38)
    10. The priestly garments (39)
    11. Completion and dedication of the tabernacle (40)

Purpose and Message

The message of Exodus is summarized in two passages: the commission of Moses (6:2–9) and the preface to the covenant ceremony at Sinai (19:1–6). The three basic components of the message include (1) the judgment of the oppressor nation Egypt, (2) the deliverance of Israel from slavery in Egypt by the "mighty arm" of Yahweh, and (3) the establishment of Israel as God's special possession among all peoples.

Several themes or emphases unify the Exodus narratives. Judgment and deliverance figure prominently in chapters 1–12, and Yahweh's paternal guidance in the wilderness and the promise of settlement in Canaan follow in chapters 13–18. Theocratic covenant and law combine to form Israel's charter as the people of Yahweh (19–24), and the book concludes with preparations for worship of the Holy One of Israel (25–40).

The historical purpose of Exodus was the preservation of accounts explaining how the Israelites came to be slaves in Egypt, their deliverance, and their presence in the wilderness of Sinai. The

SUGGESTED ROUTES OF THE EXODUS
and the Conquest of Canaan

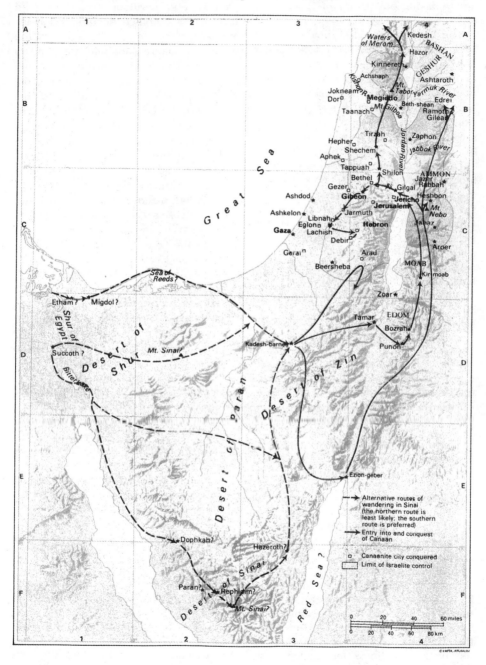

Alternative routes of wandering in Sinai (the northern route is least likely; the southern route is preferred)

Entry into and conquest of Canaan

☐ Canaanite city conquered

☐ Limit of Israelite control

0   20   40   60 miles
0   20 40 60 80 km

C.CARTA, JERUSALEM

Exodus narrative forms a bridge between the patriarchal stories and the theocratic nation taking possession of Canaan (cf. 6:4).

The basic theological purpose of the book is divine self-disclosure. God has not only remembered his covenant promises to the Hebrew patriarchs, but has also now revealed himself to Israel as Yahweh (6:2–3). Although this revelation of Yahweh occurs in a variety of manifestations, the end result is that he will take Israel for his people and will be their God (6:7).

Last, the didactic purpose of the book includes instruction on the importance of maintaining covenant relationship with Yahweh and the importance of his law as an instrument for shaping and preserving Israel's identity as Yahweh's people (23:20–23). Only through obedience to the covenant stipulations can Israel be a kingdom of priests to Yahweh and a holy nation, fulfilling her divine destiny among all the nations (19:5–6).

Structure and Organization

The book of Exodus is easily arranged into three large blocks of narrative material based on the sequence of geographical locations for Israel as they journeyed from Egypt to Mount Sinai:

1. Israel in Egypt (1:1–13:16)
2. Israel's wilderness trek (13:17–18:27)
3. Israel at Sinai (19:1–40:38)

Thematically Yahweh's deliverance of the Hebrews from bondage in Egypt as told in Exodus connects the deliverance of Jacob's clan by Joseph (Gen. 46–50) and the deliverance of the Israelite nation by Moses to the threshold of the land of promise (Numbers and Deuteronomy). Exodus as the book of Yahweh's redemption of his covenant people complements Genesis as the book of the inauguration of the covenant and anticipates Leviticus as the book of holiness for the covenant people.

The language and content of Exodus also bear deliberate marks of transitions indicating that the narratives of Genesis, Exodus, and Leviticus are to be read together as a unified document. For example, the repetition in Exodus 1 of the names of Jacob's sons who migrated to Egypt ties the Exodus accounts with the story of Jacob's sojourn in Egypt (Gen. 46–50). Likewise, the concluding passage of Exodus describing the glory of Yahweh's filling the tabernacle (40:34–38) anticipates the departure of Israel from Sinai led by the cloud of guidance (Num. 10:11–35). Last, as in the books of Leviticus and Numbers, the divine oracle formula is found repeatedly in Exodus (i.e., "and the LORD said to Moses," 19:21; 25:1; etc.), while the introductory phrase "this is what the LORD has commanded" connects the legislation of Exodus and Leviticus (e.g., Exod. 35:4; Lev. 8:5; 17:2).

Section 1 relates the judgment of Egypt and the deliverance of Israel from slavery. First Moses is introduced as God's instrument for securing the release of the Hebrews, and then he is commissioned and equipped to accomplish the task. God's long-suffering and the preeminence of obedience to his commands are underscored in the passage, as Yahweh bestows confirming signs on Moses, appoints Aaron as his spokesman, and affirms the success of the mission by revealing himself as Yahweh—an inexhaustible resource for the task of bringing out the Hebrews. However, before Moses can deliver Israel from Egypt to covenant ratification with Yahweh at Sinai, he must first obey the stipulations of God's earlier covenant terms within his own family (cf. 4:18–26).

God's method for delivering Israel by means of a series of plagues was designed to bring divine judgment on the Egyptian nation (12:12). The institution of the Passover Feast was a teaching memorial for future generations of Israelites. As a reminder of Yahweh's mighty act in history it was intended to inspire reverence and prompt worship among the Hebrews (12:14–27)

Section 2 explains how Yahweh turned a mob of former slaves into a "special possession" as his covenant people, by means of a covenant agreement at Sinai (19:1–6). It is now widely accepted that the Hebrew covenant with Yahweh parallels the literary form of the Hittite suzerain treaty of the Late Bronze Age. The treaty form was a common way for a ruling lord to exact obedience from vassal states in binding the servant through carefully prescribed covenant stipulations. Consider some specific elements of the treaty form in the covenant code of Exodus:

Preamble: 20:2a

Historical prologue: 20:2b

Stipulations: 20:3–17 (= Decalogue); 20:21–23:19

Deposit and Public Reading: 24:7

List of Witnesses: 24:1–11

Blessings and Curses: 23:20–33 (delineated more formally in Leviticus 26)

The final section gives details of the tabernacle of Yahweh and its furnishings. The very presence of God would be established in the midst of Israel through this Tent of Meeting (25:8). The ordination of Aaron and his sons as priests for the sanctuary helps explain the inclusion of the genealogy (chap. 6), which legitimized the Aaronic priesthood. The idolatry and rebellion of Egypt judged by Yahweh in the Exodus had their parallel in the golden calf episode that occurred when Israel was encamped at Sinai (cf. 32:1–10). The wrath of Yahweh was stayed by the intercessory prayer of Moses for Israel, and the mercy of God made covenant renewal possible (cf. 32:11–34:17). Given Israel's penchant for rebellion and waywardness from God, this pattern characterized much of her history in the Old Testament. Small wonder the new covenant will be one written on the heart, not on tablets of stone (cf. Jer. 31:31–34).

Major Themes

Yahweh

The revelation of the name "Yahweh" (or Jehovah) to Moses as the divinely appointed deliverer of Israel marked a new stage in God's progressive self-disclosure to the Hebrew people. The name is usually translated "I AM" and connotes the personal, eternal, and all-sufficient aspects of God's nature and character.

At issue is the occurrence of "Yahweh" in the Genesis records. Some biblical scholars have assumed the Hebrew patriarchs did not know the name Yahweh for God. They argue the name was written into the text of Genesis anachronistically (i.e., after the fact) or else the book is a compilation of later writings that included the divine name. In contrast, biblical scholars who are committed to the antiquity and integrity of the Pentateuch have asserted it is more reasonable to assume that the patriarchs knew the name Yahweh, but were unfamiliar with the radical new dimension of theological meaning for the name that stemmed from Israel's Exodus experience.

The unveiling of the divine name Yahweh was not the only way in which God revealed himself to Israel during the Exodus experience (see pp. 100–101). Several other types of theophanies are reported in the Pentateuchal narratives. For example, Yahweh revealed his nature and person as well as his will and divine purposes for Israel by means of the angel of the Lord (Exod. 3:2; 14:19) and other angelic agents (23:20; 33:2), miraculous event (8:16–19), a flame in a bush (3:2), fire, smoke, thunder, and lightning at Sinai (19:18–20), vision and dream (cf. Num. 12:6–8), voice and direct communication (Exod. 24:1), the cloud of glory (16:10), the cloud of guidance and pillar of fire (40:34–38), and even "face to face" with Moses (33:11; cf. vv. 20–23).

More important than the variety of divine manifestations to the Hebrews was the content they disclosed about this covenant God, Yahweh. He was a God who remembered his previous covenant obligations (Exod. 2:24), a God of judgment and deliverance (12:27), transcendent yet immanent (19:10–15; 25:1–9), who rules the nations for the providential benefit of his elect, Israel (15:4–6, 13–18), a unique and holy God far above and more powerful than the gods of the nations (15:11; 18:10–12), and a gracious, merciful God who relents of anger and responds favorably to intercessory prayer and repentance (32:11–14).

The Ten Plagues

The text of Exodus declares that the confrontation between Moses and Pharaoh is actually a cosmic struggle between the true God, Yahweh, and the false gods of the Egyptian religion (cf. Exod 12:12; 15:11; 18:11). This is why Yahweh must elevate Moses to a position "as God" so he can oppose Pharaoh as an equal, since the office of the pharaoh was the physical expression of the sun-god Aten, or Ra (cf. 7:1).

Although many biblical scholars attempt to identify a particular deity as the object of each of the ten plagues, it seems better to understand the plagues collectively as judgment against the whole pantheon of Egyptian gods. However, the final two plagues do appear to be aimed at the primary Egyptian deity and his earthly representative, the pharaoh. By blotting out the sun in Egypt and permitting daylight in Goshen, and by interrupting the pharaonic cycle of deity in the death plague, Yahweh showed himself Lord to the Egyptians.

The "miraculous" nature of the signs and wonders brought by Yahweh against Egypt continues to generate discussion among biblical scholars, given the prominence of anti-supernaturalist assump-

tions in our post–Enlightenment era. The terms "signs" and "wonders" (Exod. 7:3) express the idea of a miracle demonstrating one's power. The word "miracle" may be understood as either the intensification of natural law or phenomena or the superseding of natural law or phenomena.

Today the ten plagues are often interpreted as a sequence of natural cause-effect phenomena associated with the regular flood cycle of the Nile River. This is the case not only among scholars committed to anti-supernatural presuppositions, but also among certain evangelical traditions predisposed toward a "literary" understanding of the Exodus narrative.[2] Here the "miraculous" is seen in the providential timing of the events, the severity of the natural disasters, and the fact that Moses had foreknowledge of each plague in its sequence. Moreover, the phenomenological character of the plague narrative is attributed to the "pre-scientific" worldview of the Hebrew writer. According to this view, the ancient Hebrews did not understand the natural world as a closed system governed by the laws of physics, but as a completely and constantly open system in which Yahweh was free to intervene according to his divine purposes. In general, scholars holding to a naturalistic interpretation today view the plague narration as embellished literary and liturgical tradition.

By contrast, biblical scholars committed to the plague narrative literally and historically as Yahweh's supernatural intervention into the created order are quick to note the instantaneous aspects of the plague sequence rendered at the command of Moses and Aaron (e.g., Exod. 8:16–17). Also, the response of the magicians (7:22; 8:18–19) is difficult to understand if the plagues were merely "intensification" of a natural sequence of events

---

[2]For example, J. K. West, *Introduction to the Old Testament*, 2d ed. (New York: Macmillan, 1981), 161–64; and William Sanford LaSor, David A. Hubbard, and Frederick W. Bush, *Old Testament Survey* (Grand Rapids: Eerdmans, 1982), 137–40.

to which the Egyptians were accustomed. Finally, the isolation of the Hebrews in Goshen from the nine plagues and the death of the firstborn are inexplicable apart from supernatural activity and purpose.

How did the Egyptian magicians perform counter-miracles against Aaron (7:8–13) and duplicate the effects of the first two plagues (7:14–8:15)? These diviners of Pharaoh's were a powerful and revered priestly class in Egyptian society. They were devotees of the moon-god Thoth, who was also the god of magic and divination. According to the teaching of both the Old and New Testaments, these kinds of idolatrous religious systems are energized by demonic powers (cf. Deut. 32:16–17; Ps. 106:36–37; Acts 16:16–18; 1 Cor. 10:20; 2 Thess. 2:8–12).

How do we explain the "hardening of Pharaoh's heart"? First, God was already aware of Pharaoh's stubbornness (Exod. 3:19–20). The series of signs and wonders (i.e., the plagues) were used to confirm Pharaoh in his sinful rebellion against Yahweh in oppressing the Israelites and refusing to release them to worship God (7:3–4). Pharaoh continued to harden his heart through the two miracles of Moses and Aaron and the first five plagues (7:8–8:32). Even his own magicians admitted the limitations of their power before Yahweh (8:19), yet Pharaoh steeled his resistance to the truth that Yahweh is Lord (cf.7:5).

After the sixth plague, we are told, the Lord himself hardened Pharaoh's heart (Exod. 9:8–12). It would seem that Pharaoh no longer had an option to relent and obey the command of Yahweh. God's course of judgment for Egypt became irrevocable. God had given Pharaoh over to the sinfulness of his own heart, confirming him in his rebellion through the signs and wonders (cf. Rom. 1:24, 26, 28). Henceforth he and the Egyptians were without excuse before God and deserved the death penalty (or death plague; cf. Rom. 1:20, 32).

It is possible that the pharaoh's hardening his heart against God is akin to the sin of blasphemy of the Holy Spirit condemned by Jesus in the New Testament (cf. Mark 3:28–30). Even as Jesus' enemies attributed the miraculous works of God to Satan, so Pharaoh in his rejection of God's signs and wonders had willfully denied God's activity in human history. Implicitly he attributed the divine works to the demonic by not acknowledging Yahweh (Exod. 5:2), by calling for counterfeit signs from his magicians (7:11), and by ignoring their discernment of the "finger of God" intervening in Egyptian history (8:19).

The Passover

The historical context of the original Passover event (Exod. 12) was the last plague against Pharaoh, the Egyptians, and the Egyptian gods. This death plague precipitated the Hebrew flight from oppression and bondage (vv. 21–27). Future generations were commanded to observe the Passover as a feast commemorating the Hebrew deliverance accomplished by the mighty arm of Yahweh (contra the "mighty arm of Pharaoh," cf. 13:14).

The Feast of Unleavened Bread accompanied the Passover memorial as a reminder of the great haste in which the Israelites left Egypt (12:11). Later on, the ordinance for the dedication of the firstborn to the Lord with statutory offerings was designed as a perpetual reminder of the mercy of Yahweh in sparing all those firstborn from the "destroyer" in the Israelite homes that had been sprinkled with the Passover blood (Exod. 12:23; 13:2; 22:29–30; Num. 3:13, 40–51).

As a memorial feast the Passover ceremony had important didactic implications for the Hebrew family. The actual instruction took the form of query and response. The meaning of the Passover for the Hebrews was summarized in the formal answer of the father to his son's question, "What does this service mean?" The father responded, "It is the sacrifice of the Lord's Passover, for he passed over the houses of the people of Israel in Egypt, when he slew the Egyptians but spared our houses" (cf. 12:24–27).

The New Testament writers understood the Old Testament Passover typologically as a precursor of Jesus' dying sacrificially as the Lamb of God who takes away the sin of the world (cf. John 1:29). The parallels between the Passover ceremony and the death of Christ are significant in number and in kind (e.g., cf. Exod. 12:46 and Num. 9:12 with John 19:36).

The institution of the Lord's Supper, or Eucharist, is rooted in the Passover rite, both from the standpoint of a memorial feast (cf. Luke 22:7–30) and in the atoning deliverance of the Paschal Lamb of God (cf. Rev. 5:6–14).

The Ten Commandments

Also known as the Decalogue or "Ten Words," the Ten Commandments are recorded in Exodus 20:1–17 and repeated in Deuteronomy 5:6–21. In contrast to the rest of the divinely revealed legislation of the Pentateuch, Moses is not cited as the mediator of these injunctions. Instead, God himself writes the commandments on tablets and speaks directly to all the Hebrews (20:1; 32:16). Interestingly, Yahweh indicates he spoke to the people from heaven, not from Mount Sinai, after delivering the Ten Words to the Israelites (20:22; cf. Lev. 25:1)—perhaps denoting the perfect and eternal character of the Decalogue.

Only two of the statutes are cast in the form of positive imperatives: the fourth, "Remember the Sabbath day . . . ," and the fifth, "Honor your father and mother . . ." (Exod. 20:8–12). Eight of the ten laws are apodictic prohibitions (i.e., they take the form "you shall not . . ."). The particular grammatical construction used

shows that these commands were to have binding authority for that contemporary generation and for all future generations of the Hebrews. The harsh tone of the Decalogue created by the repetition of the most severe negation possible in the Hebrew language served to underscore the absolute nature and permanent character of this divine law.

The Ten Commandments are patterned after the literary format of the Hittite suzerain-vassal treaty with a preamble, historical prologue, and a list of basic stipulations (see "Structure and Organization"). The first four statutes circumscribe the relationship of the vassal (Israel) to the suzerain (Yahweh), while the last six commandments order human relationships within the vassal (Israelite) community. Ultimately the Decalogue was an extension of Yahweh's grace to Israel already demonstrated in the Exodus from Egypt. The Ten Commandments brought a sense of righteousness to Israel's religion and social life. Israel's covenant obedience was but a response of gratitude to the grace of God, not a burdensome duty by which they earned or merited God's favor and redemption.

(The variations in the Deuteronomy 5 rendering of the Decalogue are accounted for by the covenant renewal procedure, in which the basic covenant stipulations were modifed or adapted to accommodate changing historical and sociological circumstances.)

According to G. E. Mendenhall, the purpose of covenant is to create new relationships, whereas the purpose of law is to regulate existing relationships by ordering means. The explicit purpose of the Decalogue is stated in Exodus 20:20: ". . . that the fear of God will be with you to keep you from sinning." The Ten Commandments express the eternally perfect moral character of Yahweh, and as such they constituted the basic principles governing (or "ordering the means") of the life of faith for the Hebrews.[3]

As law, the Decalogue is connected with covenant in that these regulations summarize the covenant stipulations requisite for maintaining the agreement between Yahweh and Israel. The Decalogue probably also functioned as a general statement of criminal law for Israelite society, delineating "serious crime" in relation to covenant with Yahweh. This was essential to the well-being of the nation, because an offense against Yahweh's covenant jeopardized the entire covenant community.

In the New Testament, Jesus summarized the vertical and horizontal dimensions of the covenant stipulations in the Decalogue in two commandments (Matt. 22:36–39; cf. Deut. 6:5) and emphasized that the essence of the Old Testament law is justice, mercy, and faith (cf. Matt. 23:23).

The Presence of God

One important outcome of the covenant agreement between Yahweh and Israel was the very presence of God accompanying the Hebrews on their journey from Egypt to the plains of Moab via Mount Sinai. Although this mysterious presence of God was made manifest to Israel in alternative forms—a cloud and a pillar of fire—the essential point of the Pentateuchal narrative is the "Lord dwelling in the midst of his people" (cf. Exod. 25:8).

The tabernacle structure described in Exodus 25–40 was designed to symbolize the active presence of the Lord among the Hebrews (see fig. 10.4 in chap. 10). The tabernacle was also called the Tent of Meeting, because there God convened his assemblies with Israel, with the holy priesthood ordained to represent the Hebrew people before Yahweh (cf. Lev. 1:1). In part, the presence of God associated with the tabernacle restored the intimate fellowship enjoyed by God and man and woman in the garden experience before the Fall (Gen. 3:8).

The New Testament renews this theme of God's presence among humankind with the announcement found in John's gospel that "the Word became flesh and lived [or 'tabernacled'] among us" (1:14; cf. Isa. 7:14). Perhaps this return of the "divine presence" to Israel fulfilled Haggai's prophecy about the latter glory of the temple being far greater than the glory of the former (i.e., Solomon's) temple (Hag. 2:9; cf. Luke 2).

Questions for Further Study and Discussion

1. What is the significance of the name "Yahweh" for our understanding of the book of Exodus?
2. How do we explain Yahweh's hardening of Pharaoh's heart? What does this disclose about God's dealing with nations?
3. How is God portrayed in the Song of Moses and Miriam in Exodus 15? How does this compare with the way he is depicted elsewhere in the book?
4. What is the relationship between covenant and law?
5. Is one's understanding of the message of the book affected by one's position regarding the route and date of the Exodus from Egypt? Explain.

[3]Cf. G. E. Mendenhall, *The Tenth Generation* (Baltimore: Johns Hopkins University Press, 1973), 198–214, esp. 200.

For Further Reading

Beegle, D. M. *Moses, The Servant of Yahweh.* Ann Arbor: Pryor Pettengill, 1979.

Bimson, John J. *Redating the Exodus and Conquest.* JSOTSS 5. Sheffield, England: Almond Press, 1981.

Brisco, T. V. "Exodus, Route of the." *ISBE.* Rev. ed. Grand Rapids: Eerdmans, 1982. 2:238–41.

Cassuto, U. *A Commentary on the Book of Exodus.* I. Abrahams, trans. Jerusalem: Magnes Press, 1967. Classic Jewish commentary, sensitive to the book as literature and rejecting the conclusions of source criticism. Excellent discussion of the book's message.

Childs, Brevard S. *The Book of Exodus.* OTL. Philadelphia: Westminster, 1974. Detailed and technical study of Exodus' place in the Old Testament canon, with thought-provoking theological discussion.

Clements, R. E. *Exodus.* CBC. Cambridge: Cambridge University Press, 1972.

Cole, R. A. *Exodus: An Introduction and Commentary.* TOTC. London: Tyndale, 1973. Brief, but well-researched and readable. Thoroughly evangelical in perspective. Helpful introductory sections of the historical background and theology of Exodus.

Davis, J. J. *Moses and the Gods of Egypt.* Grand Rapids: Baker, 1971.

Durham, J. I. *Exodus.* WBC. Vol. 3. Waco, Tex.: Word Books, 1987. Extensive bibliography, but a disappointing assessment of the historicity of the Exodus narratives. Blindly committed to source analysis.

Ellison, H. L. *Exodus.* DSB–OT. Philadelphia: Westminster, 1982. Insightful contemporary application of the book's message to Christians corporately and individually.

Hoffmeier, J. K. "Moses." *ISBE.* Rev. ed. Grand Rapids: Eerdmans, 1983. 3:415–25.

Hyatt, J. P. *Exodus.* NCBC. London: Marshall, Morgan, & Scott, 1971.

Kaiser, Walter C. "Exodus." *EBC.* Vol. 2. Grand Rapids: Zondervan, 1990. 287–497.

––––––. *Toward Old Testament Ethics.* Grand Rapids: Zondervan, 1983. Esp. 81–111. Lucid exposition of the legislation of the Decalogue and covenant code.

Miller, P. D. *The Divine Warrior in Early Israel.* Cambridge: Harvard University Press, 1973.

Shea, W. H. "Exodus, Date of the." *ISBE.* Rev. ed. Grand Rapids: Eerdmans, 1982. 2:230–38.

Wright, C. J. H. "Ten Commandments." *ISBE.* Rev. ed. Grand Rapids: Eerdmans, 1988. 4:786–90.

––––––. *God's People in God's Land.* Grand Rapids: Eerdmans, 1990. Exegesis and interpretation of Old Testament law as it applies to family, land, and property, with insightful application to Christian social ethics.

Chapter 9

Leviticus

Leviticus, the third book of the Pentateuch, is a manual of priestly regulations and duties and a handbook of instructions prescribing practical "holy living" for the Israelite covenant community. The Hebrew title of the book, "And he called," is taken from the opening verse of the text, "And the Lord called unto Moses" (KJV). The English name "Leviticus" derives from the Greek title *Leuitikon*, given in the Septuagint and meaning "pertaining to the Levites."

The Writing of the Book

The human author of Leviticus is not mentioned in the book. Yet the phrase "the Lord said to Moses" occurs more than twenty-five times in the text (at least once in every chapter except 2, 3, 9, 10, and 26). Orthodox Jewish and Christian scholars have traditionally attributed the book to Moses, the lawgiver of Israel. Although no divine commandment is given for the recording of this legislation delivered to Moses, it is assumed by analogy to the book of Exodus that Moses wrote down the words spoken to him by the Lord (cf. Exod. 17:14; 24:4; 34:27).

As to the date of writing of Leviticus, two options are set forth by scholars holding to the traditional Mosaic or single-author view: (1) those committed to an early date for the Israelite Exodus from Egypt place the work to the first half of the Late Bronze Age (ca. 1400 B.C.), while (2) those inclined toward a late date for the Hebrew Exodus set the writing in the early Iron Age (ca. 1200 B.C.).

Biblical scholars who hold to some form of multiple authorship or Documentary Hypothesis for the composition of the Pentateuch assign the whole of Leviticus to the Priestly (P) source. This Pentateuchal literary strand is distinguished by the unmistakable priestly and liturgical interests of the levitical order such as rituals, purity laws, and genealogies. According to this theory, the P document was composed by one or more unknown levitical priests between 550 and 450 B.C. When the Priestly contributions were then added to the other documents or strands of written tradition about 400 B.C., the result was the complete Pentateuch as we know it today.

A third position on the authorship of Leviticus mediates between the traditional Mosaic view and the Documentary approach. This view maintains that the P source is preexilic in date, but not Mosaic in origin. Arguments supporting this alternative are grounded in the similarities between the teachings of Leviticus and the books of Judges and Samuel on topics like personal holiness, war, and blood sacrifice (e.g., Lev. 17:10–16 and 1 Sam. 14:33–34) and the quotations of Leviticus that appear in Old Testament books that are clearly preexilic or exilic (e.g., Deut. 26:14; Ezek. 18:13; 20:9).

When all the available evidence is taken into account, there are no compelling reasons for denying the antiquity and authenticity of the book of Leviticus. Moses is explicitly and repeatedly cited as the recipient of Yahweh's commandments, and everywhere the book assumes a desert context. The numerous Mesopotamian legal parallels to Leviticus support an early date for the book (at least as far back as the united monarchy), while Ezekiel's extensive appeal to the legislation of Leviticus shows that the work at least predates the Babylonian exile. On a more practical note, careful examination of Leviticus reveals that much of the legislation is ill-suited for the civil and ceremonial context of the postexilic Hebrew community. Finally, linguistic analysis of the so-called P source exhibits considerable discontinuity with other biblical Hebrew texts from identifiable, later time periods.[1]

Whether Moses compiled the materials of Leviticus himself or dictated the revelation to scribes remains unclear. However, it seems likely that the content and arrangement of the legal materials were standardized very early in the Hebrew covenant experience, since they constituted a handbook for priestly procedure and function.

The Background

Chronology

The book of Leviticus originates in the revelation of Yahweh given to Moses from "the tent of meeting" (1:1) and at Mount Sinai (25:1) during Israel's eleven-month sojourn at Sinai after the Exodus from Egypt (cf. Exod. 19:1; 40:17; Num. 10:11). (For the historical background of Leviticus, see the previous chapter.)

Given an early date for the Hebrew Exodus (i.e., the fifteenth century B.C.), Moses or his scribes recorded the legislation of Leviticus during the first half of the period known as the Late Bronze Age (1550–1200 B.C.). In ancient Near Eastern chronology, this corresponds to the Eighteenth Dynasty of the New Kingdom in Egypt, with Thutmose III (1504–1450) the pharaoh of the Hebrew oppression and Amenophis II (1450–1425) the likely pharaoh of the Exodus.

Given a late date for the Hebrew Exodus (i.e., the thirteenth century B.C.), Moses transcribed or dictated the legislation of Leviticus during the transition from the Late Bronze Age to the Early Iron Age (1200–900). This corresponds with the Nineteenth Dynasty of the New Kingdom in Egypt, with Rameses II (1304–1237) the likely pharaoh of the Exodus.

Cultural Background

The Hebrews were not alone in the ancient Near East in the practice of ritual purification and animal sacrifice. Highly structured priestly classes in charge of sanctuaries or temples are known in virtually all the religious traditions concurrent with Hebrew faith as recounted

---

[1]E. G. R. Polzin, *Late Biblical Hebrew: Toward an Historical Typology of Biblical Hebrew Prose,* HSM 12 (Missoula, Mont.: Scholars Press, 1976). Cf. Y. T. Radday et al., "Genesis, Wellhausen and the Computer," *Zeitschrift für die alttestamentliche Wissenschaft* 94 (1982): 467–81. This study notes considerable similarities between the so-called J and P sources in sections of Genesis and suggests that stylistic differences in biblical texts are determined more by the distinctiveness of literary genres than by assuming multiple authorship and the evolutionary development of the written sources.

Figure 9.1. Small four-horned, limestone altar from the Iron Age, found at Megiddo. (*Israel Antiquities Authority*)

in the Old Testament. Ceremonial washing and anointing or purification rites before worship or service before the gods were common to both Mesopotamian and Egyptian religion.

Canaanite religions included "peace offerings" and "whole" or "burnt" offerings similar to those of Hebrew practices (fig. 9.1).

Despite these similarities in priestly office and form of ritual, the Hebrew religion remained distinct from other ancient Near Eastern religions in several ways. The differences include the idea of direct divine revelation and theophany, the concept of strict monotheism, the understanding of human sin, the highly

ethical and moral nature of Hebrew religion in contrast to the Canaanite fertility cult, and the holy and righteous character of Yahweh in contrast to the capricious behavior of the pagan deities. Moreover, many of the other religions practiced human sacrifice.[2]

Outline of the Book

I. Approaching a holy God
  A. Laws about sacrifice (1–7)
    1. Burnt offering (1:1–17)
    2. Grain offering (2)
    3. Peace offering (3)
    4. Sin offering (4:1–5:13)
    5. Guilt offering (5:14–6:7)
    6. Instructions for priests (6:8–7:38)
  B. Laws about the consecration of priests (8–10)
    1. Anointing of Aaron and his sons (8)
    2. Aaron's sacrifice (9)
    3. Death of Nadab and Abihu (10)
II. Living in the presence of a holy God
  A. Laws about "clean" and "unclean" things (11–15)
    1. Food (11)
    2. Childbirth (12)
    3. Leprosy and skin diseases (13–14)
    4. Discharges and secretions (15)
  B. Laws about holiness (16–25)
    1. The Day of Atonement (16)
    2. Taboo on eating and drinking blood (17)
    3. Laws about sexuality (18)
    4. Civil and ceremonial laws (19)

---

[2]For discussions of similarities and differences between Israelite and ancient Near Eastern religion and religious literature, see G. H. Livingston, *The Pentateuch in Its Cultural Environment* (Grand Rapids: Baker, 1974); H. Ringgren, *Religions of the Ancient Near East*, trans. J. Sturdy (Philadelphia: Westminster, 1973), 124–76; J. Finegan, *Myth and Mystery* (Grand Rapids: Baker, 1989), 119–54.

5. Various laws and punishments (20)
6. Laws for priests (21–22)
7. Feasts and calendar (23–25)
III. Covenant blessings and curses (26)
IV. Appendix: Laws about vows and gifts (27)

Purpose and Message

The central teaching of the book is summarized in the command to "consecrate yourselves and be holy, for I am holy . . ." (Lev. 11:44–45). The first part of Leviticus outlines the requirements for worshiping Yahweh (chaps. 1–10), and the second section prescribes how the covenant people of God are to translate the idea of holiness into daily living (chaps. 11–27).

Leviticus is basically a manual or handbook on holiness designed to instruct the covenant community in holy worship and holy living so that they might enjoy the presence and blessing of God (cf. Lev. 26:1–13). The laws and instructions were to transform the former Hebrew slaves into "a kingdom of priests and a holy nation" (cf. Exod. 19:6).

Structure and Organization

Leviticus is a natural extension of the narrative found in Exodus 25–40. The Exodus account concludes with the assembly and dedication of the tabernacle, and Leviticus begins with God's addressing Moses from "the tent of meeting" about the prescriptions for the worship and service to take place there. The use of the simple conjunction "and" in Leviticus 1:1 (omitted in the NIV) indicates the two books are to be read as one continuous record. Finally, the distribution of the divine oracle introductory formula "the LORD said to Moses" (e.g., Exod. 31:1; 33:1; 34:1; 40:1; Lev. 1:1; 4:1; 6:1) and the concluding formula "Moses did as the LORD commanded" supports the interrela-

tedness of Exodus and Leviticus (e.g., Exod. 40:16; Lev. 8:13; 16:34).

The laws of Leviticus have affinity with the larger block of Pentateuchal legal material. First, like Exodus and Deuteronomy, the legislation of Leviticus is cast in the framework of historical narrative (e.g., chaps. 8–10; 24). Second, the divine oracle formula is repeated consistently throughout Leviticus (in which the phrase begins twenty of the twenty-seven chapters) and the Pentateuch as a whole. Third, the repetition of key words and the opening and closing formulae are used to mark literary units or related units of legislation. (For example, the phrase "this is the law" or "this is the thing" identifies chapters 6–17 as a literary unit [6:8; 7:1; 11:1; 17:2], and the recurring "I am the LORD your God" is a standard refrain in chapters 18–26). And the formulation of legislation to meet specific needs of the Hebrew community remains a constant in Leviticus (e.g., 24:10–23; cf. Exod. 18:13–27; Num. 15:16).

The presentation of the legislation in Leviticus is logically ordered in connection with the construction and dedication of the tabernacle in Exodus 40:1–33. A "tent of meeting" for Yahweh presumes religious activity of some sort and authoritative personnel to conduct such activity. Leviticus documents the nature and purpose of Hebrew liturgy for the tabernacle, including the various sacrifices (chaps. 1–7) and the requirements for the priesthood in charge of the worship.

The remainder of the book contains laws regulating the life of the Hebrew people so they might reflect God's holiness as his people in the routine of daily living (cf. Exod. 19:6). Chapters 11–16 address various impurities inhibiting proper worship and community relationships, while chapters 17–25 constitute practical guidelines for holy living so that Israel's religious and "secular" life might not be mutually exclusive.

The last two chapters of the book (26–27) reinforce the covenantal context of the

Figure 9.2. The Cycle of Sanctification

levitical legislation. The basic purpose of the book is delineated in chapter 26, including the recitation of the covenant blessings and curses. This chapter also connects the legislation with the covenant-making process at Sinai so that Israel might be his people and Yahweh might be their God (26:45–46). The concluding chapter appears to be an appendix, attached because covenant relationship is really "oath taking" before Yahweh (cf. the similarity in the concluding formulas in 26:46 and 27:34). The laws involving vows and gifts further instruct the people on the solemn and sacred nature of their vows before God.

Major Themes

Holiness

The central teaching of Leviticus is summarized in the command "consecrate yourselves and be holy, for I am holy" (Lev. 11:44–45). The first part of the book gives the procedures for approaching the Holy One of Israel in worship (chaps. 1–10); the second prescribes how those joined covenantally to God translate the idea of Yahweh's holiness to the sphere of daily living (chaps. 11–27). The basic purpose of Leviticus, then, was to provide instruction for the Hebrew community in "holy worship" and "holy living," so that as the covenant people they might enjoy the blessing of Yahweh's presence (cf. 26:1–13).

The Old Testament word "holiness" essentially conveys the notion of "separation" from the mundane for service and/or worship to Yahweh, who himself is wholly separate from his creation. The legislative holiness of Leviticus could prove effective only as Israel practically implemented the ideal of "the holy" into everyday human experience. At issue was discernment between the holy and the common and between the clean and the unclean (10:10–11).

Applying the concepts of the holy, common, clean, and unclean to the physical, moral, and spiritual realms of life was basic to the ancient Hebrew worldview. The distinctions allowed the people to order their relationship to the natural world in such a way that they might indeed "be holy" as the Creator is holy.

On the basis of this levitical law, everything in life was either holy or common for the Hebrews. Those things determined common were subdivided into categories of clean and unclean. Clean things might become holy through sanctification or unclean through pollution. Holy things could be profaned and become common or even unclean. Unclean things could be cleansed and then consecrated or sanctified to be made holy. The relationship of these concepts is illustrated in figure 9.2.[3]

Common (i.e., clean) things or persons devoted to God became holy through the mutual efforts of human activity in sanctifying (or consecrating) and the Lord as the sanctifier (cf. Lev. 21:8). Uncleanness may be caused by disease, contamination, infection, or sin; it could be cleansed only by ritual washing and sacrifice. Hence the importance of the instructions regarding

---

[3]Cf. Gordon J. Wenham, *The Book of Leviticus*, NICOT (Grand Rapids: Eerdmans, 1979), 18–29.

sacrifices in the book of Leviticus. The presence of the holy God resided in the Israelite camp within the tabernacle, and therefore it was imperative to prevent the unclean from coming into contact with the holy (7:20–21; 22:3; cf. Num. 5:2–3). Failure to prevent contamination resulted in death (Num. 19:13, 20; cf. Num. 15:32–36; Josh. 7).

The apostle Paul understood the atonement in the age of the new covenant in a similar way. All human beings are unclean because of inherited sin due to the fall of Adam (Rom. 5:6–14). The redemptive work of Jesus Christ washes (elevates to cleanness) and sanctifies (makes holy) the repentant sinner (1 Cor. 6:9–11). The exhortation to practical holiness (e.g., Matt. 5:48; 1 Peter 1:16) can be realized only as the believer in Christ yields to the Spirit of God in obedience to the teachings of righteousness found in Scripture (Rom. 6:15–23; 8:12–17).

Sacrifice

The ritual sacrifice was but one way the Hebrew people might gain access to their God Yahweh, the Holy One of Israel (in addition to prayer, Jer. 29:12; repentance and contrition, Isa. 66:2; etc.). The idea of sacrifice was not unique to the Hebrews in the ancient world, as animal, grain, and drink offerings to deities were common to the religious cults of Mesopotamia and Syro-Palestine. While the parallels between Israelite and ancient Near Eastern sacrificial practices attest the universal need for humanity to placate the gods, the Hebrew sacrificial system was distinctive in that it was divinely revealed and was directed toward the goal of personal and community holiness (fig. 9.3).

Five basic types of sacrifices, or offerings, were instituted as part of formal, corporate worship and personal celebration in Hebrew religious expression: cereal or grain, fellowship or peace, burnt, sin, and guilt or trespass offerings. These sacrifices, described in Leviticus, fell into two categories: (1) those offered spontaneously to God in praise and thanksgiving for blessings received or favors granted (e.g., the cereal or grain offering and the three types of peace offerings, Lev. 2:1–16; 3:1–17), and (2) those demanded by Yahweh on the occasion of sin in the Hebrew community (e.g., the burnt, sin, and trespass or guilt offerings, Lev. 1:3–17; 4:1–5:13; 5:14–6:7). The former were grateful responses to the goodness of God, while the latter were necessary to atone for or "cover" the sin committed, accomplish reconciliation with Yahweh, and restore the penitent sinner to fellowship with other persons and God.

According to Leviticus 17:11, the principle of life is represented in the blood. Thus blood on the altar was necessary for the symbolic cleansing of sinful human beings (cf. Heb. 9:22). The word "atonement" used here is part of the word group related to the Hebrew term *KPR*. This root word conveys the idea of appeasement and reconciliation in contexts related to animal sacrifice (e.g., Exod. 32:30) and ransom or atonement money in connection with the sanctuary tax as part of Moses' census of Israel (Exod. 30:12–16); it was also used to describe the gold cover of the ark of the covenant (i.e., the "mercy seat," Exod. 25:17). Elsewhere the term was applied to the great Day of Atonement ritual of Leviticus 16, known today as Yom Kippur (fig. 9.4).

The teaching in both Old Testament and New Testament clearly indicates that animal sacrifices were not salvific or efficacious in any way for individual or corporate Hebrew redemption. The believer under the old covenant was made righteous by faith in the promise of Yahweh demonstrated through obedience to his covenant stipulations (e.g., Gen. 15:6; Hab. 2:4). The external act of ritual sacrifice was symbolic and representative of the internal attitude and disposition of the heart. Psalmist, sage, and prophet all reiterated the truth that

Figure 9.3. The Sacrificial System

Name	Portion burnt	Other portions	Animals	Occasion or reason	Reference
Burnt offering	All	None	Male without blemish; animal according to wealth	Propitiation for general sin, demonstrating dedication	Lev. 1
Meal offering or tribute offering	Token portion	Eaten by priest	Unleavened cakes or grains, must be salted	General thankfulness for first fruits	Lev. 2
Peace offering a. Thank offering b. Vow offering c. Freewill offering	Fat portions	Shared in fellowship meal by priest and offerer	Male or female without blemish according to wealth; freewill; slight blemish allowed	Fellowship a. For an unexpected blessing b. For deliverance when a vow was made on that condition c. For general thankfulness	Lev. 3 Lev. 22:18–30
Sin offering	Fat portions	Eaten by priest	Priest or congregation: bull; king: he-goat; individual: she-goat	Applies basically to situation in which purification is needed	Lev. 4
Guilt offering	Fat portions	Eaten by priest	Ram without blemish	Applies to situation in which there has been desecration or de-sacrilization of something holy or there has been objective guilt	Lev. 5:1–6:7

From John H. Walton, *Chronological Charts of the Old Testament* (Grand Rapids: Zondervan, 1978), 45.

God does not desire sacrifice, but repentance leading to obedience (cf. 1 Sam. 15:22–23; Ps. 51:16–17; Prov. 21:3; Isa. 1:12–17; Jer. 7:21–23; Hos. 6:6; Amos 5:21–24; Mic. 6:6–8).

In his lovingkindness God granted forgiveness to anyone manifesting "the broken and contrite heart" of sincere repentance (e.g., 2 Sam. 12:13; Ps. 51:1, 16–17). The effectual removal of guilt and atoning for sin were accomplished through confession and the petition and intercession of prayer to the gracious and merciful Lord (e.g., Exod. 32:11–13, 30–35; Isa. 6:5–7). Ultimately the purpose of Hebrew sacrifice was didactic in that the enactment of the ritual of atonement was designed to instruct the Israelites in the principles of God's holiness, human sinfulness, substitutionary death to cover human transgression, and the need for repentance leading to cleansing and renewed fellowship within the community and with Yahweh.

More important, the New Testament understands the sacrifices of the Old Testament as theological "types" or illustrations pointing to the redemptive work of Jesus of Nazareth as the Messiah. John the Baptist recognized and proclaimed Jesus as the Lamb of God who takes away the sin of the world (John 1:29–34). Jesus himself understood his role as the good shepherd who lays down his life for his sheep (John 10:1–21). Elsewhere New Testament writers interpreted the crucifixion of Jesus Christ as the "once for all" sacrifice for the sins of humanity (e.g., Rom. 5:6–11; Heb. 10:10, 12). The writer to the Hebrews in fact connected the Day of Atonement ceremony with the death of Jesus Christ, which became an atoning sacrifice through the offering of his body (Heb. 9–10; cf. Lev. 16).

Finally, the New Testament writers found the new covenant equivalent of ritual sacrifice in "spiritual sacrifices" offered by Christians to God through Christ Jesus (1 Peter 2:5). These spiritual sacrifices include generous and cheerful giving (Phil. 4:18), worship—especially praise and thanksgiving—(Heb. 13:15–16; cf. Ps. 50:13–14), prayer (Rev. 5:8; 8:3–4), evangelism (Rom. 15:16–17; cf. Isa. 66:20), and selfless service to Christ—even to death (Rom. 12:1–2; Phil. 2:17; 2 Tim. 4:6; Rev. 6:9).

Interestingly, all the expiatory or atoning sacrifices were for "unwitting" covenant violations. There was no specific sacrifice for premediated and malicious covenant transgression or rebellion.

Sabbath Rest and Sabbatical Year

The levitical prescriptions for holiness in Hebrew life extended even to the calendar. The great religious festivals were ordered according to the agricultural calendar of Palestine so that the Israelites might acknowledge Yahweh as their provider and sustainer (Lev. 23:4–44). The command to observe one day in seven as a Sabbath rest to God prefaced this religious calendar (23:1–3).

The Sabbath ordinance reminded Israel that Yahweh was the Creator (cf. Exod. 20:8–11). It also brought a sense of "timelessness" to the worship of Yahweh and a sense of "holiness" to the human idea of time. Keeping one day holy to God certainly meant rest and refreshment for humankind and animals, but more important, it sanctified the human endeavor so that in the other six days of the week man might truly "eat, drink, and find enjoyment in his labor" as a gift from God (cf. Eccl. 2:24–26; 5:18–20).

In the book of Exodus, the Sabbath was a covenant sign between Yahweh and Israel denoting Israel's special relationship with God and testifying that her holiness was rooted in the Holy One, not in law and ritual (Exod. 31:12–17; cf. Lev. 26:2). By the time of Jesus, the practical and humanitarian benefits of the Sabbath had been obscured if not forfeited by the legalism of Judaism (cf. Matt. 12:1–4; Mark 7:1–13).

The Hebrew religious calendar provid-

Figure 9.4. Jewish Special Days

Special days	Hebrew name	Day	Reference	Reading (Megilloth)	Commemoration
Passover (Feast of Unleavened Bread)	Pesach	14 Nisan	Exod. 12 (Lev. 23:4–8)	Song of Solomon	Deliverance from Egypt
Pentecost	Shavuoth	6 Swan	Deut. 16:9–12 (Lev. 23:9–14)	Ruth	Celebration of the harvest
9th of Ab	Tish'ah be'ab	9 Ab	No direct reference	Lamentations	Destruction of temple 586 B.C. and A.D. 70
Day of Atonement	Yom Kippur	10 Tishri	Lev. 16 (23:26–32)		Sacrifices for sins of the nation
Feast of Tabernacles	Succoth	15–21 Tishri	Neh. 8 (Lev. 23:33–36)	Ecclesiastes	Wanderings in the wilderness
Dedication	Chanukah	25 Kislev	John 10:22		Restoration of temple in 164 B.C.
Lots	Purim	13–14 Adar	Esth. 9	Esther	Failure of plot against Jews by Haman

From John H. Walton, *Chronological Charts of the Old Testament* (Grand Rapids: Zondervan, 1978), 18.

ed for a "sabbath" of rest for the land of the promise as well. After six years of sowing, cultivating, and harvesting, the land was to lie fallow in the seventh year (Lev. 25:1–7). Practically speaking, the poor and socially disadvantaged were the beneficiaries of the sabbatical year, as they could glean the produce of the fallow land (Exod. 23:11). The laws of Deuteronomy expanded the sabbatical program to include the cancellation of debts, generous relief for the poor, and the release of Hebrew slaves (Deut. 15:2–18). The sabbatical cycle culminated in the Jubilee, or year of emancipation (Lev. 25:8–24). After seven sabbatical-year cycles, the land was "sanctified" in the fiftieth year. Along with the sabbatical year sanctions, property reverted to the families of its original owners.

The Sabbath and sabbatical-year ordinances were designed to foster social and economic equality and inculcate important covenant community principles in Hebrew society, including (1) thanksgiving for past provision and faith in God's continued sustenance during the fallow year, (2) forgiveness in the remission of debts, (3) respect of persons created in the image of God in the manumission of slaves, and (4) the practice of generosity and the idea of stewardship in the redistribution of the covenant land.[4]

According to the prophet Jeremiah, it was the neglect of the sabbatical laws and the consequent rejection of the covenant instruction inherent in the commands that was responsible for the fall of Jerusalem and the Hebrew exile to Babylon (cf. Jer. 25:8–14; 2 Chron. 36:17–21).

Questions for Further Study and Discussion

1. What does the legislation of Leviticus reveal about "Yahweh"?
2. How were the Hebrew sacrifices different from the pagan offerings made to pagan deities? How were they the same? Is the concept of sacrifice "bargaining" with God? Explain your answer.
3. Does the legal code of Leviticus motivate covenant obedience by works of the law or by divine grace? Explain.
4. How do the levitical laws compare in severity with other legal codes of the ancient Near East? What purpose did the stringent penalties for violation of levitical law serve for the Israelite community?
5. Why did God seek to order Hebrew life with a ceremonial, or liturgical, calendar? Discuss the value of a liturgical calendar for the church today.

For Further Reading

Carpenter, E. E. "Sacrifices and Offerings in the Old Testament." ISBE. Rev. ed. Grand Rapids: Eerdmans, 1988. 4:260–73.

de Vaux, Roland. Ancient Israel: Its Life and Institutions. Vol. 2. J. McHugh, trans. New York: McGraw-Hill, 1961.

Gammie, John. Holiness in Israel. Minneapolis: Augsburg Fortress, 1989.

Hamilton, Victor P. Handbook on the Pentateuch. Grand Rapids: Baker, 1982. 245–311.

Harris, R. Laird. "Leviticus." EBC. Vol. 2. Grand Rapids: Zondervan, 1990. 501–654.

Harrison, R. K. Leviticus: An Introduction and Commentary. TOTC. Downers Grove, Ill.: InterVarsity, 1980. Somewhat brief, but a most readable commentary with useful

[4]Cf. John H. Yoder, The Politics of Jesus (Grand Rapids: Eerdmans, 1972), 64–77.

introductory sections. Thoroughly evangelical in its stance, with concern for contemporary application.

Noth, Martin. *Leviticus: A Commentary.* OTL. J. E. Anderson, trans. Philadelphia: Westminster, 1965.

Porter, J. R. *Leviticus.* CBC. Cambridge: Cambridge University Press, 1976.

Ringgren, H. *Religions of the Ancient Near East.* J. Sturdy, trans. Philadelphia: Westminster, 1973.

Snaith, N. H., ed. *Leviticus and Numbers.* CB. London: Nelson, 1967.

Wenham, Gordon J. *The Book of Leviticus.* NICOT. Grand Rapids: Eerdmans, 1979. Best commentary in English on the topic. Clear exposition with appreciation for ancient Near Eastern backgrounds to Old Testament sacrifice and ritual. Complete discussion of Old Testament relationships to New Testament and the theological significance of the book.

Chapter 10

Numbers

The book of Numbers, the fourth book of the Pentateuch, continues the story of the Israelite Exodus from Egypt, the covenant ceremony at Mount Sinai, and the journey to Canaan. The book highlights the wilderness testing and rebellion of the covenant people during the formative period of the Hebrew nation's relationship with Yahweh.

The Hebrew title of the book, "in the wilderness," is taken from the opening verse. The name is appropriate, because Numbers records the significant events associated with the period of "desert wandering" prior to the death of Moses and the Hebrew occupation of Canaan. The English title "Numbers" is a translation of the Greek Old Testament name for the book, *Arithmoi*, reflecting the two census takings of the Hebrews related in chapters 1 and 26.

The Writing of the Book

Traditionally, Jewish and Christian scholars have credited the writing of Numbers to Moses, the Hebrew lawgiver. Yet the book itself contains only one reference to Moses as an author of the material, and that is specifically limited to the itinerary of the Israelites in their desert trek from Egypt to Moab (Num. 33:2). Elsewhere the text implies that priests were also recording and preserving the divine instructions and regulations, especially those pertinent to their duties associated with the tabernacle (cf. 5:23).

As with Leviticus, the introductory formula "and the Lord said to Moses" pervades every chapter of the book. Until more solid evidence surfaces to the contrary, it may be assumed by analogy to the book of Exodus that the bulk of the text in Numbers is the literary product of Moses, stemming from the fifteenth or thirteenth century B.C. (depending on the date of the Hebrew Exodus).

However, the references to Moses in the third person in the narrative (e.g., Num. 12:3; 15:22–23) and the sporadic editorial insertions designed to inform a later audience (e.g., 13:11, 22; 27:14; 31:53) suggest that the book took its final form sometime after the death of Moses. It seems correct to assume that the substantial portions of the history and legislation of Numbers originated with Moses during the thirty-eight years of desert wandering that the book recounts (cf. Num. 33:38; Deut. 1:3). Whether he transcribed the words of Yahweh himself or dictated them to a scribe is unclear. But Numbers and the rest of the Pentateuch were cast in the form of a unified, five-volume book sometime between the days of Joshua and the elders of Israel (Josh. 24:31) and the era of Samuel (cf. 1 Sam. 3:19–21).

Biblical scholars holding to some form of the Documentary Hypothesis for the composition of the Pentateuch regard the book as a patchwork of four (or more) literary sources (see chap. 6). Essentially Numbers 1–10 is assigned to the block of Priestly (P) materials extending from Exodus 35 through Numbers 10. Chapters 11–36 of Numbers are considered a composite of the Yahwist (J) and Elohist (E) sources and two different P traditions (with portions of 11–14, 16, and 20–25 assigned to J and E; portions of 13–17, 20, and all of 25–36 assigned to P). According to this source analysis, Numbers underwent expansion, revision, and rewriting until the book took its final form at the hands of Priestly editors in the fifth century B.C.

Mounting evidence against the late date for the Priestly source has spurred growing appreciation for the antiquity of many of the traditions preserved in Numbers, even among those holding to a multiple-authorship view. Recently Gordon Wenham has argued that the great familiarity of Deuteronomy with Numbers suggests that all of Numbers predates Deuteronomy. Assuming the seventh-century B.C. date for Deuteronomy commonly accepted by critical scholars, the Priestly source is apparently centuries older than generally understood by adherents to the Documentary Hypothesis. This leads Wenham to conclude that if J, E, and P are legitimate Pentateuchal sources, they can no longer be regarded as originating in widely different periods of history.[1]

The Background

According to the date formulas given in the Pentateuch, the book of Numbers covers a span of some thirty-eight years and nine months, the period of early Hebrew history commonly known as the wilderness or desert wanderings. The events associated with the desert trek of the first generation of Hebrews after the Exodus from Egypt are narrated in three distinct stages: (1) a twenty-day period at Mount Sinai from the completion of the tabernacle to the taking up of the cloud of guidance (1:1–10:11), (2) the thirty-eight-year "sentence" of wilderness wandering from Sinai to Kadesh, for the first generation of Hebrews who came out of Egypt, due to their unbelief and rebellion (10:11–20:13; cf. 33:38), and (3) a six-month duration at the end of the thirty-eight years when the second generation after the Exodus journeyed from Kadesh to the plains of Moab (20:14–36:13; cf. 33:38 and Deut. 1:3).

The complete log of key date formulas found in the Pentateuch for marking the development of Hebrew history after the Exodus is shown in figure 10.1.

The precise dating of these "years" after the Exodus from Egypt is unknown. The relative dating of the events is entirely dependent on one's view of the date of the Exodus. An early date for the Exodus places the events of Numbers around 1400 B.C., while the late date pushes the narrative nearer 1200 B.C. (see chap. 6, esp. fig. 6.4).

The narrative of Numbers contains numerous references to ancient regions and cities on the periphery of Palestine. The biblical record also indicates that organized kingdoms were firmly established in these border regions. For example, early opposition to the Hebrews during their wilderness wanderings came from Canaanites and Edomites in the

---

[1]Gordon J. Wenham, *Numbers: An Introduction and Commentary*, TOTC (Downers Grove, Ill.: InterVarsity, 1981), 23.

Negeb and from the Moabites, Ammonites, and Midianites in the Transjordan (cf. Num. 21 and 31).

Critical scholars have challenged the historicity of these narratives relating Hebrew encounters with foreign nations and peoples for lack of supporting archaeological evidence. The archaeological picture of the Transjordan is incomplete, and disagreement over site identification and selective appeal to available archaeological data further confuse the issue. Yet experience has shown that calling into question the historicity of the biblical text for lack of evidence is unwarranted, because subsequent archaeological discoveries tend to confirm Scripture (as in the case of the Nabonidus Chronicle and the book of Daniel).[2]

Outline of the Book

I. Preparations for departure from Sinai
   A. Numbering and organization of the tribes (1–4)
   B. Special legislation (5–6)
   C. Tribal offerings for the tabernacle (7)
   D. Purification of the Levites (8)
   E. Passover (9:1–14)
   F. The cloud of guidance and the silver trumpets (9:15–10:10)
II. From Sinai to Kadesh
   A. Arrangement of the tribes marching (10:11–36)
   B. Grumbling and unrest (11:1–15)
   C. God's provision of food (11:16–35)
   D. Insubordination of Aaron and Miriam (12)
   E. The twelve spies (13–14)
   F. Supplemental laws (15)
   G. Rebellion of Korah and others (16–17)
   H. Duties of priests and Levites (18)
   I. Purification ritual for the unclean (19)
   J. Miriam's death and Moses' sin (20:1–21)
III. From Kadesh to the plains of Moab
   A. Aaron's death (20:22–29)
   B. Defeat of Arad, Sihon, and Og (21)
   C. Balak and Balaam (22–24)
   D. Israel's idolatry and immorality at Baal-Peor (25)
   E. Second numbering of Israel (26)
   F. Inheritance case of Zelophehad's daughters, part 1 (27:1–11)
   G. Selection of Joshua as Moses' successor (27:12–23)
   H. Additional legislation on offerings and vows (28–30)
   I. War against Midian (31)
   J. The Transjordan tribes (32)
   K. Itinerary of Israel's journey from Egypt to Canaan (33:1–49)
   L. Allotment of Transjordan lands (33:50–34:29)
   M. Levitical cities and cities of refuge (35)
   N. Inheritance case of Zelophehad's daughters, part 2 (36)

Purpose and Message

The book of Numbers in literary terms is a diary of Israel's early days of covenant relationship with Yahweh (cf. Deut. 8:1–10). Israel experienced firsthand the tragic consequences of disobedience to the covenant stipulations (e.g., Num. 16:25–50; 25:1–18). Its message is, first, one of God's patience and faithfulness in the face of Israel's continual grumbling and rebel-

[2]Cf. Wenham's discussion of recent archaeological investigation related to sites associated with Numbers 21, 31, and 32 in *Numbers: An Introduction and Commentary*, 154–63, 209–216.

Figure 10.1. Timetable After the Exodus

Exodus from Egypt	15th day of 1st month	Exod. 12:2, 5; Num. 33:3
Arrival at Mount Sinai	1st day of 3d month	Exod. 19:1
Yahweh reveals himself at Sinai	3d day of 3d month	Exod. 19:16
Completion of tabernacle	1st day of 1st month of 2d year	Exod. 40:1, 16
Command to number Israel	1st day of 2d month of 2d year	Num. 1:1
Departure from Sinai	20th day of 2d month of 2d year	Num. 10:11
Arrival at Kadesh	1st month of 40th year?	Num. 20:1
Death of Miriam	1st month of 40th year?	Num. 20:1
Death of Aaron and thirty days of mourning	1st day of 5th month of 40th year	Num. 20:29
Departure for Moab	1st day of 6th month of 40th year?	Num. 20:22; 21:4
Moses addresses Israel in Moab	1st day of 11th month of 40th year	Deut. 1:2–3
Death of Moses and thirty days of mourning	?	Deut. 34:8
Joshua and Israel enter Canaan	10th day of 1st month of 41st year	Josh. 1:19

lion, and second, one of further disclosure of the nature and character of Israel's covenant God, Yahweh. The austere holiness of Yahweh remains constant throughout, but other facets of God's person are revealed during this developmental stage of Israel's covenant relationship with the Lord. The desert experience gave Israel glimpses of Yahweh as a patient and faithful provider, a sovereign and providential intervener, a compassionate responder to intercessory prayer, and a jealous and just God.

The book of Numbers serves an important historical purpose in its cataloging of early Hebrew history. The record of Israel's journey from Sinai to the plains of Moab continues the narratives of Exodus and Leviticus and helps explain the Hebrew presence in the land of Canaan. Numbers everywhere anticipates the occupation of the land of the covenant promise, thus bridging the legislation of Sinai and the conquest of Palestine. (For example, the section 33:50–36:13 is devoted to the possession, distribution, holiness, and inheritance rights of the land of Canaan—cf. 26:52–56; 33:51–53; 35:31–34; 36:9).

Theologically, the purpose of Numbers was to preserve the accounts of the initial phases of the practical outworking of God's recently established covenant with Israel. The book emphasizes the holiness of God, the sinfulness of humanity, the necessity of obedience to Yahweh, the tragedy of disobedience to Yahweh's commands, and the utter faithfulness of God to his covenant agreement.

Pragmatically, part of the purpose of Numbers was to order and organize the former Hebrew slaves into a unified community of God prepared to fulfill their covenant obligations. The legislation, instructions, census takings, tribal marching and camping arrangements, priestly ordinances, cloud of guidance, and laws related to the allotment and inheritance of the land were intended to transform an oppressed people into a kingdom of priests and a holy nation.

Finally, the tragic examples of covenant disobedience preserved in Numbers were a stern warning to future generations of the Hebrew nation. Moses understood the didactic value of these historical object lessons for covenant obedience, hence his departing reminder to Israel to "take heed" to the works of the Lord accomplished during the desert wandering (Deut. 4:9; cf. Pss. 78:40–55; 95:9–11). The New Testament echoes this truth, acknowledging that the record of the Old Testament was inscripturated for a warning to the Hebrews and for the instruction of the church of Jesus Christ (cf. Rom. 15:4; 1 Cor. 10:11).

Structure and Organization

The book of Numbers almost defies dissection into logical literary units, making it perhaps the most difficult Old Testament book in which to identify order and structure. Rather than despairing, several Old Testament commentators have suggested that the complexity of the book's literary structure only attests the integrity of the biblical accounts and the honesty of the Hebrew scribes responsible for preserving the record. Instead of forcing the material into an artificial structure for the sake of the reader, these scribes faithfully reproduced the written tradition they had received.

Some general observations may be made in respect to the overall structure of the book, however. Roughly speaking, the book is ordered in chronological sequence according to the date formulas contained in the text. This may help account for the seemingly disjointed nature of the composition, as portions were simply recorded and added to the growing history as the events occurred. Also, Numbers 1–10 is part of the larger block of material originating with Israel's sojourn at Sinai. Key themes unifying that extensive literary unit (Exod. 19–Num. 10) include the founding of the tabernacle,

the formation of the covenant community, and the anticipation of possessing Canaan as the land of the promise.

Numbers conveniently divides into three chronological periods of events and revelation bridged by narrative accounts of the intervening journeys of the Israelites. This schema may be outlined as follows:

1:1–10:10	Israel encamped at Sinai
10:11–13:25	Journey from Sinai to Kadesh (first post-Exodus generation of Hebrews)
13:26–20:21	Israel encamped at Kadesh
20:22–21:35	Journey from Kadesh to Moab (second generation)
22:1–36:13	Israel encamped on the plains of Moab

All five sections reinforce the basic messages of Numbers—the faithfulness of Yahweh in the face of Israel's rebellion, and the dire consequences attached to covenant disobedience. The numbering of the tribes and additional covenant legislation serve to affirm God's providential keeping of Israel while she was captive in Egypt and his fulfillment of promises made to Abraham about "a great nation" (Gen. 12:2; 17:5–6). The trek from Sinai to Kadesh and the events associated with that journey also underscore Yahweh's faithfulness (e.g., the provision of manna and quail, Num. 11:4–15) and the folly of rebelling against God (e.g., Korah's story, Num. 16).

In a touch of irony the meek and faithful character of Moses becomes a foil for the pride, selfishness, disobedience, and rebellion of Aaron, Miriam, and others. Yet even Moses fails God miserably at Meribah and becomes a foil for the unchanging faithfulness of Yahweh.[3]

---

[3]It must be remembered that Moses' sin went beyond simple disobedience to God's command to speak instead of striking the rock. Moses' anger and self-promoting statements are tantamount to insubordination as he and Aaron usurp Yahweh's preeminent place before the people of Israel (Num. 20:2–13; esp. v. 10). The severity of Moses' punishment (i.e., denial of entry into Canaan) seems justified, given the nature of responsibility associated with those exercising leadership gifts in the Old Testament and given Yahweh's consistently harsh judgment of rebellion elsewhere in Numbers.

Figure 10.2. Arrangement of the Twelve Tribes Around the Tabernacle

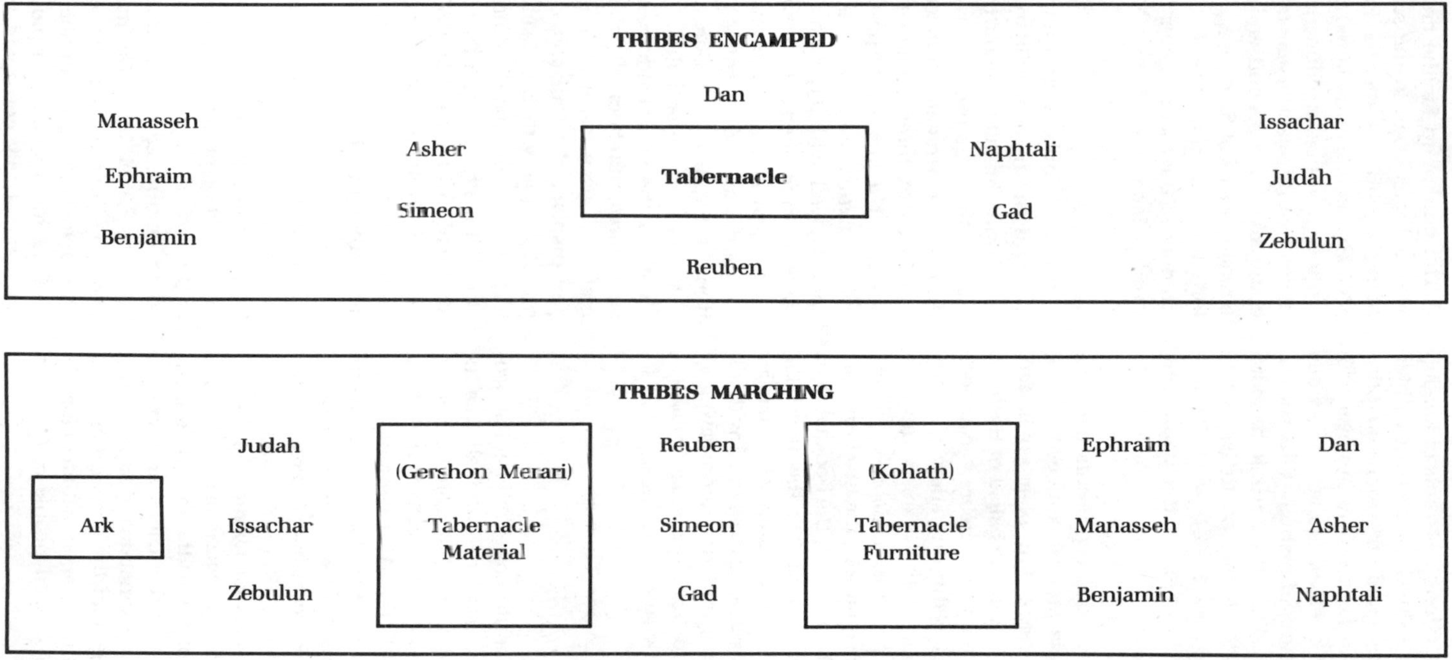

TRIBES ENCAMPED

	Issachar
Dan	Judah
Naphtali	Zebulun

Manasseh		
Ephraim	Asher	Naphtali
Benjamin	Simeon	Gad

Tabernacle

Dan

Reuben

TRIBES MARCHING

	Dan
Ephraim	Asher
Manasseh	Naphtali
Benjamin	

(Kohath)
Tabernacle
Furniture

| Reuben |
| Simeon |
| Gad |

(Gershon Merari)
Tabernacle
Material

| Judah |
| Issachar |
| Zebulun |

Ark

The last sections of Numbers tangibly demonstrate Yahweh's covenant faithfulness and his good intentions to bring them into the land of the promise with the defeat of enemies along the way and the appointment of Joshua as the successor to Moses. Even the Aaronic benediction of chapter 6 returns to Israel full-circle in chapters 22–24, when Yahweh overturns the curses of the pagan seer Balaam so that he pronounces blessings on the people of God.

Finally, the book represents a collection of diverse literary sources and features, including the four poems of Balaam (chaps. 22–24) and the ballad of Heshbon (21:27–30)—both non-Hebrew compositions originally; the quotation of poetry from the Book of the Wars of the Lord (21:14–18)—perhaps a Hebrew military document of some sort; the two formulaic census lists from which the book takes its name (chaps. 1 and 26); the travel log composed by Moses (chap. 33); extensive historical narrative interspersed with direct discourse; and the interweaving of narrative and legal materials (including both apodictic and case law).

Major Themes

The Census Numbers

The enumeration or enrollment of peoples (whether local or national) was an administrative procedure common to the ancient Near East. The census had three primary functions: (1) ascertaining and recruiting manpower for war (cf. Num. 1:3), (2) allotment of work assignments in the corvée—forced labor gangs—and the religious cult (e.g., Num. 3:4), and (3) establishing a basis for taxation (cf. Moses' census for a sanctuary tax in Exodus 30:11–16). Along with the instructions for ordering the Hebrew tribes in marching and camping formations (chap. 2), the census takings had the practical effect of contributing to the organization of former slaves into a unified people of God (fig. 10.2).

The command for the first enlistment of Israel was given in the second month of the second year after the Exodus (Num. 1:1). This census numbered the first generation of post-Exodus Israelites, all males twenty years of age and older. The command for a second enlistment of all Israelite males of fighting age came in the fortieth year after the Exodus, and it numbered the second generation of post-Exodus Israelites (cf. 20:1, 22–29; 33:38). The census figures are compared in figure 10.3.

If these numbers are understood literally and the men of military age constitute approximately one-fourth of the population, then the projections for the total number of Israelites ranges anywhere from two to three million people. Supporters of a literal interpretation of the census figures note that this view corresponds well with Pharaoh's fear of the rapidly multiplying Hebrews' overrunning Egypt and with the promises made to Abraham about becoming a great nation (cf. Exod. 1:7–12; Gen. 12:2; 17:5–6).

Yet critics contend that, given the inability of the Sinai wilderness to sustain such large numbers of people and animals and given Israel's failure to subdue and displace the Canaanites, such rapid population growth is unlikely and therefore the the numbers cannot be understood literally. These difficulties associated with a literal reading of the census figures in Numbers have prompted alternative approaches to interpreting these and other numbers in the Pentateuch.

It has been suggested, though not widely accepted, that the census totals in Numbers are "misplaced" census lists from the era of David's monarchy. Other biblical scholars view the numbers as part of the writer's "epic prose" style, intended to emphasize the cumulative wholeness of Israel and the magnitude of Yahweh's miraculous deliverance. Still others discount the numbers as either artificial literary fiction or pious exaggerations hopelessly corrupted by centuries

Figure 10.3. Census Figures in Numbers 1 and 26

Tribe	Reference	Figures	Reference	Figures
Reuben	1:20–21	46,500	26:5–11	43,730
Simeon	1:22-23	59,300	26:12–14	22,200
Gad	1:24–25	45,650	26:15–18	40,500
Judah	1:26–27	74,600	26:19–22	76,500
Issachar	1:28–29	54,400	26:23–25	64,300
Zebulun	1:30–31	57,400	26:26–27	60,500
Ephraim	1:32–33	40,500	26:35–37	32,500
Manasseh	1:34–35	32,200	26:28–34	52,700
Benjamin	1:36–37	35,400	26:38–41	45,600
Dan	1:38–39	62,700	26:42–43	64,400
Asher	1:40–41	41,500	26:44–47	53,400
Naphtali	1:42–43	53,400	26:48–50	45,400
Totals		603,550		601,730
Average		50,296		50,144
High		74,600		76,500
Low		32,200		22,200

Greatest increase: Manasseh (20,500)
Greatest decrease: Simeon (37,100)

Adapted from William Sanford LaSor, David A. Hubbard, and Frederick W. Bush, *Old Testament Survey* (Grand Rapids: Eerdmans, 1982), 167. Used by permission.

of rewriting and revising the Pentateuchal sources.

The most widely accepted alternative approach contends that the Hebrew word for "thousand" has been mistranslated due to confusion arising from the lack of vowel markings in earlier Hebrew manuscripts. This means that the same cluster of consonants could be read as "clan," "tribe," or even "unit" (e.g., Judg. 6:15; Zech. 9:7) or even "chieftain" or "armed warrior" (e.g., Gen. 36:15). Hence the census lists of Numbers record either military "units" of an unspecified number of warriors or individual (armed) fighting men. Such accounting lowers the Israelite army to a figure somewhere between 18,000 and 100,000 men, with the total Hebrew population numbering between 72,000 and 400,000 people.

It is argued that these drastically reduced figures are more consistent with available historical and archaeological data regarding population patterns dur-

ing the period of the Hebrew Exodus. This approach also corroborates the biblical affirmations about the size of Israel when compared with surrounding nations (cf. Deut. 7:1–7; Exod. 23:29). Yet it must be emphasized that none of the interpretive options for the Numbers census figures is without problems or inconsistencies. Generally speaking, one's view of Scripture determines a person's stance on the biblical numbers, with one end of the spectrum inclined toward literalness, the other end skeptical about their historicity and reliability, and between them a moderate view of openness toward alternative readings.

The Testing by Yahweh

Probationary experience or testing is a repeated theme in the Pentateuch, and it becomes a major theme in the book of Numbers. The Genesis narrative records early humankind's probationary experience in the Garden of God (2:15–17).

Moreover, the presence of a "tempter" in the Garden coupled with the New Testament expression "elect angels" suggests that even the angelic hosts were subjected to some kind of testing or probationary experience (cf. 1 Tim. 5:21). Elsewhere God tested Abraham's faith in calling for the sacrifice of Isaac (Gen. 22:1–14), and Joseph was divinely motivated to test the loyalty of his brothers (Gen. 44:1–17).

Moses described Israel's forty-year sojourn in the wilderness as a test of faith in Yahweh and covenant loyalty (Deut. 8:1–2). The purpose of Yahweh's testing was to humble the Israelites so they might learn total dependence upon him, teach obedience to his commandments, and show them the true condition of their "hearts." The New Testament commentary on this episode of Israelite history is found in Stephen's speech before the Sanhedrin (Acts 7:39; cf. Heb. 3:16–4:4); he indicated that the Hebrews failed because they never came out of Egypt in their hearts.

The Old Testament accounts of Abraham (Gen. 22), David (Pss. 17:3; 26:2), Job (23:10), and many others suggest that testing by Yahweh is common to the experience of God's elect. The Chronicler and the prophet Jeremiah both understand Yahweh as a God who tests the heart and mind (1 Chron. 29:17; Jer. 11:20). In fact, David invited the testing because he knew it was beneficial in keeping the faithful of God on the way everlasting (Ps. 139:23). Ultimately the testing of God diagnoses the root of human motive and attitude, thus preventing the holy name of Yahweh from being profaned (Isa. 48:10–11). This testing exposes and condemns unbelief and rebellion, leaving human beings without excuse before God.

By the same token, human beings are not to put God to the test (Deut. 6:16). The prophet Malachi helps illuminate this prohibition in his careful instructions to postexilic Israel. On the one hand, he commends putting God to the test from the standpoint of obedience and faith (3:10); on the other, he discourages putting God to the test from the standpoint of disobedience and unbelief (3:15). The word found in Malachi 3:15 also appears in the Old Testament texts describing Israel's testing of God during the desert sojourn (Exod. 17:2; Pss. 66:10; 78:18, 41; 95:9). Those who "tested" God out of unbelief and disobedience erred in their hearts, had no regard for the ways of God, and were punished accordingly (cf. Ps. 95:9–11). By contrast, the word for testing in Malachi 3:10 is the same one found in Job 23:10 and Psalms 17:3; 26:2; 139:23. There it connotes the purification and strengthening of faith for those who put God to the test from a position of trust and obedience to his commandments.

The New Testament agrees with the Old Testament understanding of God's testing humankind. Even Jesus was tested in every respect as we are so that he might be our sympathetic High Priest (Matt. 4:1–11; Heb. 4:14–16). The use of two different words for testing in the book of James conforms to the Old Testament language pattern and substantiates Old Testament teaching. God tests human beings with a view toward approving faith and developing godly character traits (James 1:2–4), but he does not tempt individuals with the purpose of inciting evil or disapproving faith (1:12–15). That is the work of Satan as the enemy of the righteous. Finally, like King David before him, the apostle Paul recognized the "redemptive" benefits of divine testing (Rom. 5:1–11).

The Revelation of God in Human Culture

The book of Numbers illustrates both the supra- and the intra-cultural dimensions of Yahweh's revelation to Israel in the context of ancient Near Eastern history. For example, the freedom of God to work outside ancient Near Eastern cultural norms is demonstrated in the Mosa-

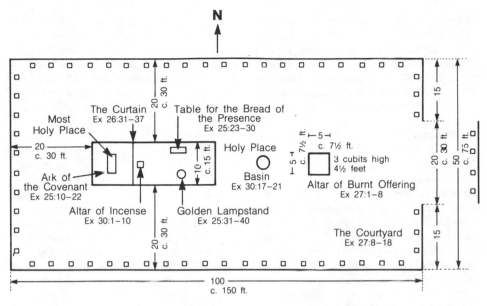

N

Figure 10.4. Floor plan of the tabernacle. (From *Expositor's Bible Commentary*, vol. 2 [Grand Rapids: Zondervan, 1990], 301)

ic legislation establishing "cities of refuge" for those guilty of the crimes of involuntary or accidental manslaughter (Num. 35:9–28; cf. Deut. 4:41–43; 19:1–13; Josh. 20–21). The concept of a haven for the protection of the "manslayer" was designed to short-circuit the ancient Near Eastern custom of blood vengeance, in which the near kinsman of the victim was obligated to avenge the death of his deceased relative by killing the manslayer. The institution of the cities of refuge was unique in the ancient world and elevated Hebrew social and moral life to a higher plane than the surrounding nations.

The landmark decision of Moses in the inheritance case of Zelophehad's daughters constitutes another example of Yahweh's overturning ancient Near Eastern legal customs in his dealings with the Hebrews as his special people (Num. 27:1–11; 36:1–13). In Mesopotamian law, daughters did not normally inherit shares in the family estate, and this apparently became the practice among the Hebrews as well (cf. Deut. 21:15–17). But the legis-

lation in Numbers elevates the status of women in Hebrew society in contrast to the neighboring peoples and also indicates Yahweh's intention to fulfill his promises regarding the covenant land (Num. 33:50–36:1; cf. Gen. 12:1; 17:8).

Yet God also chose to accommodate aspects of his revelation to the cultural conventions of the ancient Near East. Examples of this include the use of human language and human agents to convey divine truth (e.g, Num. 33:2), the command for the census taking (Num. 1:2), and the legislation regarding Nazirite vows (Num. 6:1–21)—all reflecting practices common to ancient Near Eastern civilizations. An interesting illustration of this cultural conformity in divine revelation entails the laws protecting against jealousy for a woman suspected of adultery (Num. 5:11–31). In Mesopotamian law, the accused party took an oath before the gods (e.g., the River God, Id) and then plunged (or was thrown) into the river. The gods would see that justice prevailed, determined by whether the defendant was spared (denoting innocence) or was caused to drown (denoting guilt). Although the procedure for the Hebrew "adultery test" was more enlightened than the Mesopotamian "river ordeal," it was still a male-dominant legal tradition in that the test was given only to a female.

Of course, the intent of Yahweh was to establish holiness among the people of Israel and prevent criminal violation of the covenant stipulations, whether his revelation took conventional social and legal forms or totally superseded them. Looking at Yahweh's revelation in the context of human culture yields two important principles: (1) God demonstrates his respect and appreciation for human culture by working through it, rather than above or outside it, and (2) the higher goals of covenant obedience and personal and corporate holiness may require supra-cultural approaches to relational ministry carried out in the name of Yahweh.

The Balaam Oracles

The antiquity of Balaam's poetic utterances as preserved in Numbers 22–24 has long been recognized. They constitute an important contribution to the early Israelite poetry comprising the so-called Primary History of the Hebrew Bible.[4]

Undoubtedly the poetry is more widely known for the humorous misadventures of a pagan prophet hired by the Moabite Balak to curse Israel and thus assist Moab in defeating them in battle (Num. 22:1–6). At first the Lord commands Balaam not to go with Balak, then he relents and lets the

seer follow Balak to the Israelite camp. A verbal exchange with the Angel of the Lord and Balaam's own donkey ensues, apparently due to divine detection of Balaam's impure motives (cf. 22:32). Ironically Balaam pronounces only blessings upon the people of Israel and only curses upon the nations of Moab, Edom, and Amalek (24:15–24).

The inclusion of the Balaam oracles in the Numbers narrative enhances the basic message of Yahweh's covenant faithfulness to Israel by reminding them that they are a "blessed" people (22:12), nurtured and protected by Yahweh's very presence (23:21–22). The poetry also serves to encourage Israel as she journeys toward the land of the promise by demonstrating Yahweh's sovereign control over the nations in the region. Moreover, it extends the promise of future messianic kingship in the prophecy of the star and scepter (24:17; cf. Gen. 49:10).

Later Balaam joined with the Midianites and indirectly succeeded in cursing Israel by inciting them to participate in the idolatry and immorality of the Baal cult of Peor (25:1–3; cf. 31:8–16). In the New Testament, Balaam is cited as an example of a false prophet corrupted by greed and the desire for personal gain (Jude 11).

A fragmentary inscription written in Aramaic on a plastered wall at Deir 'Allah in Jordan recounts another story of a seer named Balaam conveying the message of the gods to a disobedient nation. If this is indeed the Balaam of Numbers 22–24, the text gives evidence of the prophet's lasting and widespread renown as a "diviner."[5]

---

[4]Cf. William F. Albright, "The Oracles of Balaam," *JBL* 63 (1944), 207–53; and David N. Freedman, *Pottery, Poetry, and Prophecy: Studies in Early Hebrew Poetry* (Winona Lake, Ind.: Eisenbrauns, 1980), 77–178. Freedman's corpus of early Hebrew poetry constituting the "Primary History" includes The Testament of Jacob (Gen. 49), The Song of the Sea (Exod. 15), The Oracles of Balaam (Num. 23–24), The Testament of Moses (Deut. 33), The Song of Deborah (Judg. 5), and several poetic fragments (Exod. 17:16; Num. 6:24–26; 10:35–36; 12:6–8; 21:17–18, 27–30; Deut. 34:7; Josh. 10:12–13).

[5]A translation and discussion of the text, along with its implications for Old Testament study, is published in J. Hoftijzer and G. van der Kooij, *Aramaic Texts from Deir 'Allah* (Leiden: Brill, 1976).

Questions for Further Study and Discussion

1. How does the book of Numbers portray Moses? How does it portray Yahweh?
2. Why does the writer of Numbers give such a prominent place to the complaints, unbelief, rebellion, and punishment of the Hebrew people?
3. What does Numbers teach about Yahweh and his revelation in relationship to human culture?
4. How does the purpose of the cities of refuge described in Numbers 35:6–34 relate to Yahweh's covenant with Israel?
5. What do the portraits of women in the book of Numbers suggest about the role of women in ancient Hebrew society?
6. How are we to understand Yahweh's command to Israel to "take vengeance" on the Midianites (31:1–2)?
7. What does Yahweh's interaction with a pagan prophet like Balaam tell us about his intervention in history?

For Further Reading

Allen, Ronald B. "Numbers." *EBC*. Vol. 2. Grand Rapids: Zondervan, 1990. 657–1008.

Budd, P. J. *Numbers*. WBC. Vol. 5. Waco, Tex.: Word Books, 1984. Helpful bibliographies.

Harrison, R. K. *Numbers*. WEC. Chicago: Moody Press, 1990.

Maarsingh, B. *Numbers: A Practical Commentary*. TIC. J. Vriend, trans. Grand Rapids: Eerdmans, 1987.

Noth, Martin. *Numbers*. OTL. J. D. Martin, trans. Philadelphia: Westminster, 1968.

Riggans, W. *Numbers*. DSB–OT. Philadelphia: Westminster, 1983. Useful parallels between the teaching of Numbers and the ministry of Jesus Christ.

Snaith, N. H. *Leviticus and Numbers*. NCBC. London: Nelson, 1967.

Sturdy, J. *Numbers*. CBC. Cambridge: Cambridge University Press, 1976.

Wenham, Gordon J. *Numbers: An Introduction and Commentary*. TOTC. Downers Grove, Ill.: InterVarsity, 1981. Easily the best commentary on the topic. Readable, thoroughly researched, solidly evangelical, with insightful exposition and thoughtful contemporary application.

Chapter 11

Deuteronomy

The book of Deuteronomy does not give a "second law" as the name suggests, but rather provides an important summary of the history of the wilderness period and organization of the legal material. Framed in the words of Moses shortly before his death, the book tries to give the Israelites a broad perspective on the events of the previous generation as it affords the opportunity for the renewal of the covenant.

The Writing of the Book

As we have seen, the dating of Deuteronomy has served as the basis for two popular critical theories of modern times: the Documentary Hypothesis of the Pentateuch, and the theory of the Deuteronomistic History. Both models date Deuteronomy to the latter part of the seventh century B.C. and view it as the foundation document for the reforms of King Josiah in 622. While its function in Josiah's reform is unquestioned, there is a growing opinion that Deuteronomy contains much material that must be viewed as considerably earlier than the seventh century. As a result, studies on the nature, content, and origin of the earliest form of Deuteronomy abound.

One reason scholars have for not retaining Moses' association with the book is that Deuteronomy teaches that worship should be centralized at one temple (Deut. 12). It is maintained that such centralization could not have been an issue before the temple was built in Jerusalem. Furthermore, there is no historical evidence for true concern about centralization until the time of Josiah, or perhaps a bit earlier, in the reign of Hezekiah. Also, these scholars contend that the warning about kingship (chap. 17) must have originated after the founding of the monarchy.

These objections beg the question to the extent that they deny the possibility of Moses' logically anticipating the issues that would need to be addressed. We see no reason to deny that the book is indeed an accurate record of the words of Moses. It is not necessary that Moses committed them to writing, but the nature of the book and its unity suggest that it was written down quite close to the time when the speeches were given. A few sections, such as chapter 34, might be better understood as having been appended at a later time.

The unity of the book is evidenced by

Figure 11.1. Treaty Format and Biblical Covenants

Order of sections in Hittite treaties (2d millennium)	Description	Exod.–Lev.	Deut.	Josh. 24
Introduction of speaker	Identifying author and his right to proclaim treaty	Exod. 20:1	1:1–5	Vv. 1–2
Historical prologue	Survey of past relationship between parties	20:2	1:6–3:29	Vv. 2–13
Stipulations	Listing of obligations	Decalogue 20:1–17 Covenant code 20:22–23:19 Ritual 34:10–26 Lev. 1–25	Chs. 4–26	Vv. 14–25
Statement concerning document	Storage and public reading instructions	Exod. 25:16?	27:2–3	V. 26
Witnesses	Usually identifying the gods who are called to witness the oath	None	Chs. 31–32	Vv. 22, 27
Curses and blessings	How deity will respond to adherence to or violation of treaty	Lev. 26:1–33	Ch. 28	V. 20

the fact that it takes the structure of an ancient Near Eastern vassal treaty. More than fifity such treaties have been discovered in the ancient Near East ranging in time from the mid-third millennium to the mid-first millennium B.C. Almost half of them are from the archives of the Neo-Hittite Empire in the mid second millennium.

Studies have shown that each general time period tends to have its own characteristic outlines for setting forth the terms of the treaty. It has been argued that Deuteronomy follows the form of the mid-second millennium treaties as compared with those of other time periods, therefore demonstrating that the book can be dated with confidence to the time

of Moses.[1] Others have attempted to prove that there is more similarity to the Neo-Assyrian treaties of Esarhaddon in the seventh century.[2]

While Deuteronomy appears to be closer in form to the Neo-Hittite treaties than to any other attested treaties, there is not absolute conformity. Also, the lack of wide geographical representation in first-millennium treaties unfortunately makes it difficult to rule out the possibility that the Neo-Hittite form may have been used well into the first millennium in some geographical areas. Nevertheless, the fact that Deuteronomy most closely resembles the Hittite treaty form certainly gives some credibility to the dating of the book in the second millennium (fig. 11.1).

[1]See Kenneth Kitchen, *Ancient Orient and Old Testament* (Downers Grove, Ill. InterVarsity, 1966), 90–102.

[2]M. Weinfeld, *Deuteronomy and the Deuteronomic School* (New York: Oxford University Press, 1972), 59–157.

The Background

The ancient Near Eastern vassal treaties give us a literary background for understanding the book of Deuteronomy. The standard treaty included (1) a preamble introducing the speaker, usually the suzerain, the author of the treaty; (2) a historical prologue emphasizing the suzerain's benevolence and authority; (3) stipulations detailing what is expected of the vassal; (4) a statement regarding the document's display, storage, or terms for its periodic recital; (5) a list of witnesses, usually deities; and (6) curses or blessings to be effected by the gods according to the performance of the stipulations.

In Deuteronomy the Lord is introduced as the suzerain and author of the covenant. The historical prologue recounts how the Lord brought the Israelites out of Egypt, revealed himself at Sinai, and brought them to the land he had promised to their father Abraham. Stipulations comprise the bulk of the book. The most likely document clause in Deuteronomy is the command that when the people arrive in the promised land they are to set up stones there and write the law on them (27:2–3; cf. Josh. 8:30–32). Chapters 31–32 provide the witness section. Moses is instructed to compose a song to serve as a witness (31:19–22; cf. 32:39–43, where the song includes an oath by the Lord); the Book of the Law as well as the heavens and earth are also called to witness (31:26–28). Blessings and curses are found in chapter 28.

While Deuteronomy can therefore be seen to include each of the sections that make up the ancient Near Eastern treaties, it should be noted that the order shows some variation in that the witness section comes after the blessings and curses. This comparison helps us to understand Deuteronomy as an official document ratifying a formal relationship between the Lord and Israel, with the Lord as suzerain and Israel as vassal.

Outline of the Book

I. First speech of Moses
  A. Preamble (1:1–5)
  B. Historical prologue (1:6–3:29)
  C. Introduction to stipulations: Exhortation to obey the law (4:1–43)
II. Second speech of Moses
  A. Introduction to speech (4:44–5:5)
  B. Stipulations (5:6–26:19)
    1. The Decalogue (5:6–21)
    2. Response of the people (5:22–33)
    3. Elaboration of the Decalogue (6:1–26:15)
      i. Commandment 1 (6–11)
      ii. Commandment 2 (12)
      iii. Commandment 3 (13:1–14:21)
      iv. Commandment 4 (14:22–16:17)
      v. Commandment 5 (16:18–18:22)
      vi. Commandment 6 (19–21)
      vii. Commandment 7 (22:1–23:14)
      viii. Commandment 8 (23:15–24:7)
      ix. Commandment 9 (24:8–16)
      x. Commandment 10 (24:17–26:15)
    4. Concluding exhortation (26:16–19)
  C. Document clause (27:1–10)

D. Curses and blessings (27:11–28:68)

III. Third speech of Moses: Final charge (29–30)

IV. Last words of Moses
   A. Miscellaneous matters (31)
   B. Song of Moses (32)
   C. Blessing of Moses (33)
   D. Death of Moses, transition to Joshua (34)

Purpose and Message

Deuteronomy is intended to formalize and in so doing to urge adherence to and give broader understanding of the covenant that Israel entered into with the Lord at Sinai. It is the charter document of the Sinai covenant, offering the second generation of the Exodus an opportunity to renew the covenant in preparation for entering the land. In relation to the covenant promises made to the patriarchs, Deuteronomy gives most emphasis to the element of the land. More specifically, the purpose of the stipulations section is to address the spirit of the law. This is accomplished by developing a legislative portfolio for each of the ten commandments in order to discuss their implications, nuances, and broader ramifications.

The message of the book is the message of the law and the message of the covenant. It has long been identified by the Jews with the famous *Shema* ("Hear"—the first Hebrew word in this section) found in 6:4–9, but is even more succinctly summarized in 10:12–13:

And now, O Israel, what does the LORD your God ask of you but to fear the LORD your God, to walk in all his ways, to love him, to serve the LORD your God with all your heart and with all your soul, and to observe the LORD's commands and decrees that I am giving you today for your own good?

Structure and Organization

As we have seen, the book of Deuteronomy is largely structured in accordance with the ancient Near Eastern treaties. The sections of the treaty are divided among three addresses given by Moses, as indicated in the outline. The four chapters that follow these addresses record some other words of Moses and complete the transition of leadership from Moses to Joshua.

Most important to understanding the structure of the book is the logic of organization of the stipulations section. Over the centuries scholars have struggled to identify principles of organization that would give some order or logic to chapters 6–26, but they have generally experienced only frustration in the attempt. In 1979 a breakthrough came in the landmark article of Stephen Kaufman suggesting that chapters 12–26 could be divided to correlate with the Ten Commandments.[3] Subsequently the correlation was expanded to include chapters 6–11 and viewed not just as a literary framework, but as an intent to address the spirit of the law.[4] This approach offers the long-sought explanation of the choice and arrangement of the legal material.

Though the commandments are addressed in order from 1 to 10, the grouping of the legal material suggests four general topical issues: authority, dignity, commitment, and rights and privileges. Commandments 1–4 address these four issues as they pertain to relationship with God; commandments 5–10 address these same four issues as they pertain to relationship among human beings.

Commandment 1: Divine Authority (Deut. 6–11)

"You shall have no other gods before me."

[3]S. Kaufman, "The Structure of the Deuteronomic Law," *Maarav* 1, 2 (1978–79): 105–58.
[4]John Walton, "Deuteronomy: An Exposition of the Spirit of the Law," *Grace Theological Journal* 8 (1987): 213–25.

Figure 11.2. The Decalogue and Deuteronomy

	Divine	Main Issues	Human	
1 Deut. 5 6,7 / Ex. 20: 2-3	God should be our top priority and final authority. We owe Him preference and obedience. Deut. 6-11	Authority	Human authority must not sidetrack God's authority. Deut. 16:18-18:22	**5** Ex. 20: 12 / Deut. 5: 16
2 Deut.5: 8-10 / Ex. 20: 4-6	Worship must reflect a proper view of God. It cannot be manipulative or self-serving. It cannot accomodate to the world's standards. Deut. 12	Dignity	The dignity of man must be preserved – involves his life, his family and his status. Deut. 19:1-21:23 Deut. 22:1-23:14 Deut. 23:15-24:7	**6-7-8** Ex. 20: 13-14-15 / Deut. 5: 17-18-19
3 Deut. 5:11 / Ex. 20:7	Must take our commitment to God seriously by remaining above reproach and avoiding anything that will lead astray. Deut. 13:1-14:21	Commitment	Must take our commitments to fellow man seriously. Deut. 24:8-24:16	**9** Ex. 20: 16 / Deut. 5: 20
4 Deut. 5: 12-15 / Ex. 20: 8-11	God has a right to our gratitude shown by dedicating things to Him; and a right to ask compassion in His name. Deut. 14:22-16:17	Rights & Privileges	Must understand the limits to our rights and must not violate the rights of others. Deut. 24:17-26:15	**10** Ex. 20: 17 / Deut. 5: 21

These chapters differ from chapters 12–26 in that they do not comprise individual laws. Instead they present examples of how to adhere to the first commandment. The section exhorts love and obedience to God and warns against testing him. The fact that God has elected Israel and has loved her show that he is worthy of the respect and status he demands. He has kept his promises and will continue to do so. Besides all this there are two statements of God's authority (6:4; 10:17) and numerous warnings against worshiping other gods. The overall message of these chapters is that God should be the Israelites' first priority and final authority. That is what the first commandment is all about.

Commandment 2: Divine Dignity
(Deut. 12)

"You shall not make for yourself an idol."

This section concerns how God is to be treated. The significance of the central sanctuary in this context is that it is intended to prevent the Israelites from simply taking over Canaanite sanctuaries and converting them to sanctuaries for Yahweh. Such conversions would make Israel too vulnerable to syncretism, while the use of one central sanctuary would preserve homogeneity.

The main concern lies in how the ritual aspect of worship takes place. The Lord is not to be treated the way the Canaanites treated their gods, nor worshiped that way (12:4, 30–31). Canaanite ritual was manipulative and self-serving. In contrast, Israelite ritual was expected to acknowledge the true and unique nature of the Lord as sovereign and autonomous. Anything less jeopardizes his dignity. Ritual may never accommodate pagan standards, and it must not be an end in itself. True worship must give God his proper place and cannot be manipulative or self-serving. Thus the second commandment is seen to go far beyond a prohibition against the use of idols.

Commandment 3: Commitment to Deity (Deut. 13:1–14:21)

"You shall not misuse the name of the LORD your God."

Commitment to God ought to be reflected in one's conduct. Chapter 13 introduces a hypothetical example of the most basic and blatant offense—enticement to worship other gods. Whether the offense is committed by a highly respected religious authority, a good friend, or a large group of people, the wickedness must be purged. God does not hold guiltless those who do not take him seriously, and neither should the Israelites hold such people guiltless. While seriousness about God requires severe action in blatant cases, it requires a response that is above reproach in the more subtle areas of conduct. So chapter 14 uses the dietary laws as an example.

The truly committed person would demonstrate that devotion in diet.

Commandment 4: Rights and Privileges of Deity (Deut. 14:22–16:17)

"Observe the Sabbath day by keeping it holy."

God has a right to receive honor from Israel in remembrance for his work in creation (Exod. 20:11) and in gratitude for his delivering her from Egypt (Deut. 5:15). But that is not the limit of God's prerogatives. Because he is the source of their goods and the source of their freedom, it is appropriate for the Israelites to dedicate goods to him and to offer goods and freedom to others in his name. All the legislation of this section suggests ways that this can be done, thus moving beyond the issue of the Sabbath, which is only one example of the honor that is God's right and his people's privilege.

Commandment 5: Human Authority (Deut. 16:18–18:22)

"Honor your father and your mother."

The text now considers the realm of human relationships. When Deuteronomy addresses human authority, we find it is not really concerned about how we respond to human authority, as might have been inferred from this commandment. Rather, it seeks to establish human authority as important for making sure that the covenant is preserved. Parents' being honored by children is at the core of this, for it is in the home that instruction in the covenant took place (6:6–9). This explains the connection of the phrase "that you may live long and that it may go well with you in the land" (5:16).

Other forms of authority have a role to play in the chain of instruction in society, including judges, the king, priests, and prophets. The biblical author moves backward through the line of authority. God communicates his instructions through the prophets; the priests instruct the people in the Word of God; kings are responsible for setting up a system based on the instructions of God; and judges must enforce the system that has been set up. These human authorities need to be honored, for each has a significant role to play in communicating God's instructions. It is likewise essential that these officials not jeopardize the covenant by failing to carry out their responsibilities.

Commandments 6–8: Human Dignity (Deut. 19–21; 22:1–23:14; 23:15–24:7)

"You shall not murder.
"You shall not commit adultery.
"You shall not steal."

Human dignity is addressed on three fronts: the dignity of existence, the dignity derived from homogeneity of a corporate group, the dignity of personhood. There is much potential overlap here and also among this section and the following sections. Distinguishing the sections from one another becomes more theoretical at this point, and various alternatives are possible. Nevertheless, the general ideas are evident enough in the verses that are at the core of each section.

The Dignity of Existence. This section deals mostly with cases in which life may be taken without violating the sixth commandment. Chapter 19 discusses the judicial taking of life, thereby suggesting that the Bible does not consider capital punishment to be a violation of the sixth commandment. Chapter 20 discusses rules for warfare. This again gives insight for today, for the Bible apparently does not consider killing in the context of war a violation of the commandment.

The Dignity of Homogeneity in a Corporate Group. The difficulty in relating all the legal issues treated in this section is reflected in the vagueness of the heading we give it. One way to understand the diverse laws of 22:1–12 is to see them in light of things that belong together and things that do not. Two kinds of seed or two kinds of thread do not belong to-

gether. A neighbor's animal does not belong away from its place, etc. This is how adultery is viewed as well: One person should not be intruding into the marriage of another; the integrity of the family is sacrosanct. So 22:12–30 treats different categories of adultery. Chapter 23 moves to corporate Israel and situations that can threaten the group's homogeneity. The dignity of the group is threatened when it is infiltrated by persons who do not belong.

The Dignity of Personhood. Often people who have been robbed express the feeling that they have been violated and their privacy invaded, and they feel vulnerable. Deuteronomy implies that such a phenomenon is not limited to circumstances when tangible things are stolen, but is also characteristic when intangibles are involved. Stealing someone's freedom or self-respect by ill treatment is just as serious and threatening as stealing one's possessions. Even when kidnapping is discussed (24:7), the emphasis is placed on how the victim was treated, showing again that the dignity of the individual is at stake. It is clear, then, that the prohibition of commandment 8 is not intended to be limited to taking something that doesn't belong to you, but is viewed in the larger context of any invasion of privacy. Such actions have the effect of dehumanizing and threatening the dignity of personhood.

Commandment 9: Commitment to Humankind (Deut. 24:8–16)

"You shall not give false testimony against your neighbor."

A primary commitment toward our neighbors is to deal truthfully with them. This involves both what we say to them and what we say about them. The result of taking commitments seriously is the development of mutual trust, and that is the common denominator in this section.

148

Commandment 10: Human Rights and Privileges (Deut. 24:17–26:15)

"You shall not covet . . . anything that belongs to your neighbor."

Coveting is desiring to have something that is possessed by another. The legislation surrounding this commandment suggests that the rights of individuals need to be protected. These include the right to justice, the right to subsistence, the right to bear children, the right to fair treatment, and the right to a fair wage. Furthermore, it urges that rights we enjoy ought not be taken for granted.

Summary

The importance of Deuteronomy is that it makes clear that the law was never intended to be a mechanical list of wooden rules. Rather, it provides entry into the whole matter of true piety and true morality. It promulgates a worldview encompassing what is entailed in an appropriate approach to God and what is entailed in an appropriate treatment of and relationship to one's neighbor. It is easy to see why Jesus endorsed the summary of the law offered by the Jewish lawyer: "Love the Lord your God with all your heart and with all your soul and with all your strength and with all your mind, and, love your neighbor as yourself" (Luke 10:27).

Major Themes

The Law

We are used to drawing a sharp contrast between law and grace. This would have puzzled the ancient Israelite, for whom there was hardly any greater display of God's grace than that demonstrated in his giving of the law. In the ancient Near East, gods were not known for their consistency. Worshipers were left to guess what might please their god or displease him, and this could change from day to day. That doubt and uncertainty led to constant confusion, and one could only surmise whether he or she was in favor or out of favor by evaluating one's daily fortune.

The law changed all that for the Israelites. Their God had chosen to reveal himself and to tell them plainly what he expected of them. Though many of the laws in the Bible have some similarity to laws in the ancient Near East, there are striking contrasts between them. In the ancient Near East the law was the tool of society to govern itself; in Israel it was God's revelation. In the ancient Near East, a violation of law was an offense against society; in Israel it was an offense against God. The law in the ancient Near East emphasized order in society; the law in Israel emphasized right behavior in the eyes of God.

One result of this perspective is that in the Old Testament the Israelites are not heard complaining about the burdensomeness of the law. It was a great example of God's love for them that he would communicate to them in this way. They considered themselves fortunate to be able to know what God required of them. The law was viewed as a delight rather than drudgery, as freedom of revelation rather than fetters of restriction. There is no place where this positive perspective on the spirit of the law is as evident as in the book of Deuteronomy.

In the New Testament, if Paul conveyed any disenchantment with the law (e.g., Gal. 3), it is only in the sense that the Jews of his time had attempted to make the law a vehicle of salvation rather than only a vehicle of God's revelation. That the law is not an example of the gracious provision of salvation does not mean it should not be considered an act of grace. Just as the people of God can be understood in terms of either salvation or revelation, so the grace of God is evident in providing salvation as well as revelation. The two ought not be confused.

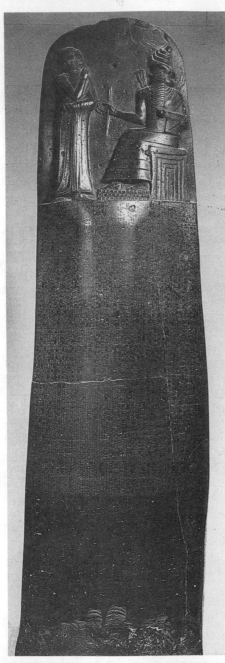

Figure 11.3. The stele, engraved in Old Babylonian cuneiform, that contains 282 laws from the Code of Hammurabi, a legal collection dating from the eighteenth century B.C. (*Réunion des Musées Nationaux*)

The Central Sanctuary

The idea of one sanctuary in Israel was symbolically related to the concept of one God. In the ancient Near East different cities had different patron deities with temples constructed in their honor. Therefore it was proper for Israel, who had just one God, to have just one legitimate temple. However, one could find numerous temples to the same deity in the ancient Near East. But the theology of God's continual special presence in the temple in Jerusalem made it impossible for more than one shrine to be maintained. God's presence could not be represented by idols as it was in other religions, and the rituals had to be performed in God's presence. Centralization was therefore important for reasons of theology as well as for safeguarding orthodox religious practice. It was the failure to accomplish centralization that perpetuated many of the religious problems occurring before the Exile.

History as Theology

In Israel, history was not viewed as the simple sequence of events evaluated in terms of cause and effect, but it was God in action. History is the evidence of Israel's election—the working out of the details represented in the statement "I will be your God and you will be my people." History does not flow at random. It was not coincidence or human endeavor that brought Israel out of Egypt after four hundred years and led them to the land promised to Abraham. History is revelation and requires response; that is why it was crucial to the covenant.

The fact that God had acted in history on their behalf served as the clarion call for the Israelites to accept the Lord's benevolent rule. It was insisted (Deut. 4) that the Israelites should learn the lessons of history; this exhortation was repeated in the New Testament concerning the revelation in history of who God is (Rom. 15:4; 1 Cor. 10:1–13). While God's hand may be seen in all of history and lessons can be learned from any segment of world history, the history of Israel is unique as a specially designed vehicle of God's self-revelation.

The Retribution Principle

Conforming to God's expectations is rewarded, and violating God's commands brings punishment. That is how God operates with nations. This also came to be understood as the way God deals with individuals, a concept disclosed in the context of poetry and the wisdom literature. God's expectations of Israel were delineated in the law and recorded as stipulations of the covenant. The blessings of the covenant would be forfeited if its conditions were not met, though this does not mean that the covenant would become entirely null and void. The curses attached to the covenant figured prominently later on in the indictment brought by the classical, preexilic prophets.

Questions for Further Study and Discussion

1. What significance can be attached to Deuteronomy's having a standard treaty format? What does that add to our understanding of the book?
2. How is our understanding of the theological concept of law enhanced by interpreting Deuteronomy as an exposition of the Decalogue?
3. What are the strengths and weaknesses of the theory that Deuteronomy 6–26 expounds the spirit of the Ten Commandments?
4. Is history still revelation? Suggest a contemporary theology of history.
5. Some consider Deuteronomy to contain the most significant theology of the Old Testament. In what ways can this view be supported?

For Further Reading

Craigie, P. C. *The Book of Deuteronomy*. Grand Rapids: Eerdmans, 1976. Probably the best of the conservative commentaries, though it was published prior to Stephen Kaufman's seminal article on Deuteronomy and the Decalogue.

Driver, S. R. *A Critical and Exegetical Commentary on Deuteronomy*. Edinburgh: T. & T. Clark, 1895. Classical presentation of the critical understanding of the book.

Kaufman, Stephen A. "The Structure of the Deuteronomic Law." *Maarav* 1, 2 (1978–79): 105–58.

Kline, Meredith G. *The Treaty of the Great King*. Grand Rapids: Eerdmans, 1963. Evangelical exposition of the treaty format of Deuteronomy and its implications.

McCarthy, Dennis J. *Treaty and Covenant*. Rome: Biblical Institute Press, 1978. The most thorough study of the formal aspects of treaties of the ancient Near East and the biblical covenant.

Mendenhall, George E. *Law and Covenant in Israel and the Ancient Near East*. Pittsburgh: Biblical Colloquium, 1955. The first major presentation in English of the comparison between treaty and covenant.

Nicholson, E. W. *Deuteronomy and Tradition*. Philadelphia: Fortress, 1967.

Thompson, John A. *Deuteronomy*. Downers Grove, Ill. InterVarsity, 1974. Brief but solid evangelical commentary.

Walton, John H. "Deuteronomy: An Exposition of the Spirit of the Law." *Grace Theological Journal* 8 (1987): 213–25.

Weinfeld, Moshe. *Deuteronomy and the Deuteronomic School*. New York: Oxford University Press, 1972.

PART III

THE HISTORICAL BOOKS

Chapter 12

Introduction to the Historical Books

The English arrangement of the historical books of the Old Testament include Joshua, Judges, Ruth, 1 and 2 Samuel, 1 and 2 Kings, 1 and 2 Chronicles, Ezra, Nehemiah and Esther. In the Hebrew arrangement, Joshua, Judges, and the books of Samuel and Kings constitute a group referred to as "the Former Prophets." Labeling them as prophetic rather than historical suggests that these books are primarily theological in nature rather than annalistic. The prophets play a prominent role in most of these books; but more important, the books share a prophetic view of history in which cause and effect are tied to the blessings and curses of the covenant.

The remainder of the books—Ruth, Chronicles, Ezra, Nehemiah, and Esther—form part of the section of the Hebrew canon called "the Writings."

The Deuteronomistic History

Theory

In the first half of the twentieth century it was common for source critics to subject the books of Joshua–Kings to the same kind of analysis used on the Pentateuch, identifying identical sources (i.e.,

Jahwist, Elohist, Deuteronomist, Priestly). At the same time, a growing number of scholars were denying the presence of the Pentateuchal sources in the early historical books, suggesting instead that they were made up of small, originally independent literary units woven together by an editor or series of editors. The latter view was adopted and defended in detail in 1943 by Martin Noth, who was a longtime professor of Old Testament at the University of Bonn.

The theory presented by Noth maintains that Deuteronomy–2 Kings was a unified work written substantially during the exilic period. Noth called this "the Deuteronomistic History," because he believed it was designed to show how the theology of Deuteronomy was reflected in the history of Israel. This theory still provides the framework for most of the research on the historical books.

Composition

Despite the wide acceptance of the concept of a Deuteronomistic History comprising Deuteronomy–2 Kings, a number of different theories have arisen as to when and how the work came together. The most common view today is

155

that the initial editing of the work took place as early as the time of Hezekiah at the end of the eighth century, but that the first edition was largely the product of the time of Josiah's reform toward the end of the seventh century. A subsequent edition was considered to have been compiled with certain sections added during the Exile, with the work being virtually complete by about 550 B.C. Variations in theories of composition focus largely on the questions of date and the number of editions.

Characteristics

The Deuteronomistic History shares with the book of Deuteronomy a common perspective on history and theology. Israel's history is viewed in terms of her loyalty to the covenant. Obedience to the law and faith in the Lord bring the blessings and prosperity of the covenant (Deut. 28), while disobedience and apostasy bring the curses listed there. Dependence on formulaic phrases (e.g., "the Israelites did evil in the eyes of the Lord" in Judges; "walked in the ways of Jeroboam" as the common indictment of the northern kings in the books of Kings) and the rhetorical use of speeches to recapitulate at important junctures (cf. Deut. 4; Josh. 23; Judg. 2:11–23; 1 Sam. 12; 2 Sam. 7; 1 Kings 8; 2 Kings 17:7–23) are among the stylistic similarities.

Message

The message of the Deuteronomist is brought out by repetition. Recurring formulas identify the author's primary concerns. For example, failure to depart from the sins of Jeroboam is the condemnation of each of the kings of the northern kingdom—even Zimri, who reigned for only seven turbulent days and would have found it difficult to initiate a programmatic reform during that time had he been so inclined. For the kings of the Davidic dynasty in Judah, the primary standard of evaluation was how they measured up to David for faithfulness and how successful they were in carrying out reform toward centralized worship in Jerusalem and extermination of apostasy. These are typically considered the themes of the preexilic edition of the book assigned to the time of Josiah.

The so-called exilic edition is thought to be more concerned to develop the theme of sin and punishment. In pursuit of the answer to the exiles' question "Where did things go wrong?" the suggestion is made that things went wrong right from the start and that the pattern continued virtually unabated throughout the long history of the monarchy. The constant presence of the prophetic word to kings during this period confirmed that the Lord gave plenty of warning and ample opportunity to respond. God's patience and faithfulness to the covenant were totally vindicated. It can be seen, then, that the message of these books was tied closely to the covenant.

Though it is common to hear sermons built on the role models (good or bad) offered by the various people who cross these pages, it should be evident that God is the main character. This is not revelation of Joshua, Samson, David, Elijah, or Josiah. It is revelation of God.

Critique

While many commendable insights have resulted from this Deuteronomistic approach over the years, some aspects warrant reconsideration. There should be no objection to the fact that Joshua–2 Kings has the perspective of Deuteronomy as its foundation. However, the many scholars who view Deuteronomy as compiled to promote the reform of Josiah are thereby forced to date the Deuteronomistic History no earlier than that.

Scholars with more conservative presuppositions, by contrast, have not on the whole been convinced of this late date of Deuteronomy. They are inclined to accept the book as largely the work of

Moses, in accordance with the book's own claim. The result is that there are far fewer restrictions concerning the compilation date of the historical material. The text of Scripture does not designate a single author for this historical material, so we are not compelled to support a single-authorship model. The books of Kings mention sources used in the writing process, so it seems likely that editorial activity was involved. This does not require abandoning a conservative view of inspiration, for editors can be inspired as well as authors.

Another important observation is that while the books included in the Deuteronomistic History share a common perspective, it must also be recognized that each book has a distinctive literary style. The cycles of Judges differ considerably from the programmatic overview of Kings, though they both emphasize God's patience despite the unfaithfulness of Israel. Joshua concerns the fulfillment of the covenant promise of the land, while Samuel addresses the establishment of the covenant of kingship. The former features an annalistic style using reports and lists, and the latter is more anecdotal. As a result, each of the books must be recognized as autonomous from a literary standpoint, though there are editorial techniques that draw them together also.

If one is inclined, as we are, to assign Deuteronomy to an earlier date, it would not be unreasonable to view Joshua and Judges as independent products of the united monarchy period, with Samuel written during the divided monarchy (though possibly as early as Solomon) and Kings completed and combined with the others by means of light editing during the exilic period. There would be no objection to referring to this final product as a Deuteronomistic History.

Concept of History in Israel and the Ancient Near East

When historians study the records of a civilization, they are interested in identifying what model of history is assumed by those documents. As an example, it is said that present Western civilization has adopted a linear model. In this, history is seen as a straight line moving from point A, the beginning, to point Z, the end along the continuum of time. Cause and effect are viewed in strictly naturalistic terms as opposed to supernatural.

By contrast, cause and effect in the world of the ancient Near East is viewed almost entirely in supernatural terms. Even when natural cause and effect was evident or obvious, it was judged insignificant compared with the supernatural aspect. Time appears to be of much less importance, evidenced by the lack of any system of absolute chronology. It has been suggested that rather than a linear view of history, there was a cyclic view that was built on the paradigm of the regular cycle of the seasons. In this view there is a fixed sequence of several stages through which history passes, returning eventually to an original point.

The cyclic view can be subsumed under a more comprehensive model called "recurrence." This takes into account both biblical and Near Eastern approaches to history and places the greater emphasis on recurring patterns of history rather than on the mythical focus of the cycles. Some of this perspective is retained in the modern adage that those who do not learn from the errors of history are doomed to repeat them.

In the ancient Near East, the key to the patterns of historical recurrence was sought out by use of omens. It was believed that the action of deity had innumerable related effects throughout the natural world in addition to influencing history. As a result, if one could record unusual occurrences in nature that happened around the time of a particular event, it would be possible to use those data to know when a similar event would recur. For example, observations of the alignment or motion of heavenly bodies, the activity of animals, the flight of birds, or the configurations of the entrails of sacrificed animals would regularly be compared with past observations of the same phenomena in order to discover whether they boded well or ill. If the omens suggested that catastrophic events were about to recur, attempts would be made to dodge destiny through recitation of the appropriate incantations. History and theology merged because belief in supernatural cause and effect in history prompted ritual activity.

The fact that deity was believed to play such a central role in the historical events of the ancient Near East, combined with the arbitrary and capricious nature of deity, made the omen system necessary. In contrast, the monotheism of the Israelites greatly simplified the matter, for they did not have to concern themselves with dozens of deities who might influence history with no discernible rhyme or reason. Furthermore, divination, omens, and incantations were prohibited to Israelites by the law; therefore, given the recurrence worldview, they saw the need to conform to the covenant and keep the law (rather than relying on certain rituals) in order to exert some control over history. Yahweh was defined by his attributes, which were constant, and he had committed himself to specific obligations through the covenants.

As a result, theology and history merged in Israel, not through ritual, but through the covenant. The actions of deity could not be predicted, altered, or in any way manipulated by ritual. Rather, whenever Israel was unfaithful to the covenant, the Lord could be expected to punish in accordance with the covenant. Human activity and decisions fall into particular patterns, and to the same extent, God's cause-and-effect activity in history follows corresponding patterns. Both the cycles of the book of Judges and the litany of apostasy in the books of Kings bear witness to the principle of recurrence. It is the foundation of Deuteronomic theology. The ancient concept of history can therefore be described as theological in contrast to the Western view, which is entirely secular.

Purpose of History Writing in Israel and the Ancient Near East

As would be expected, one's concept of history is reflected in the purpose for recording history. In Western societies there are numerous reasons why history might be written. In a textbook, history is written for purposes of teaching about events or perhaps so that lessons might be learned from the experience of others. Journalists record history for information's sake, but often attempt to identify and analyze elements of cause and effect. These genres of historiography are largely driven by a desire to record what actually happened. The print media may also have other agendas such as defending certain principles or advocating certain opinions. Different historical media or genres may have different purposes, and it is important for the readers of that history to know what the purposes were.

In the ancient Near East there were various genres of history writing as well. Studies have suggested that the historiography of the ancient Near East was rarely intended to present an objective view of what actually happened. More often, propaganda was clothed in historical attire with the purpose of benefiting those in power. Royal inscriptions were often self-serving documents whereby a king could boast of his accomplishments, embellishing the positive, ignoring the negative, and at times taking credit for the achievements of his predecessor. When the purpose is self-aggrandizement and the rewards are power and prestige, accuracy becomes of little concern. As a result, historiographical documents of the ancient Near East have to be interpreted very carefully if an accurate account of the events is to be reconstructed.

Some interpreters of the past have contended that Israel's historiography likewise reflected a propagandistic agenda. So, for instance, the fact that the Davidic dynasty received divine legitimation through the covenant recorded in 2 Samuel 7 has fostered suspicion concerning its authenticity. Yet it must be admitted that there is actually very little that the Deuteronomist has to say about the Davidic dynasty that is positive. Even David himself is portrayed in such a way that his faults are as evident as his achievements. The book of 2 Samuel would make very ineffective propaganda.

While the historiography of the ancient Near East focuses generally on the king and his military and domestic achievements, it is clear that Israel's historiography is motivated by theological concerns. The purpose of the historical literature of the Bible is to show the ways in which the Lord has acted in history to fulfill his covenant promises and to carry out his agenda. One could call it didactic (giving instruction) in the sense that it is revelation of who God is by recording what he has done. To the extent that the covenant affirms special status for Israel, this emphasis could be viewed as having propagandistic value; but such a purpose for the literature is negated by the continual emphasis on the failures and unfaithfulness of Israel. Both didactic literature and propagandistic literature will be selective about the events and details recorded. The selection of the propagandist will be motivated by what will portray the subject in the desired light. The selection of the didactic author will be motivated by a desire to focus on the lesson in view.

Deity is seen as the central cause of the events of history in the ancient Near East as a whole, but nothing in the historiographical literature functions specifically to reveal God. There is likewise no historiographical work that treats the kind of large time span covered by the Deuteronomistic History. Israel's God is revealed as One who has a plan for history and who intervenes to ensure that the plan is executed. While Israel's neighbors believed that their gods at times intervened in history, the intervention was generally done to maintain a status quo. The God of Israel, however, intervened at times to work toward a goal that had never yet been achieved. He also intervened to punish his own people when necessary. All God's intervention is focused toward a single goal: the execution of his plan.

Understanding Historical Literature

The historical literature needs to be understood within the frame of reference that it is a strategic part of God's self-revelation. As we noted earlier, a modern tendency is to regard the message of the historical literature as being the role models offered by the persons who cross its pages. In contrast, as God's self-revelation, its intention is to convey instruction about and knowledge of God. This message is conveyed not so much by individual narratives, but by the patterns and cycles of history portrayed generation after generation.

Some readers are inclined to look for new insights and lessons in each account. But rather than our seeking out "lessons from the life of Asa" or "lessons from the life of Saul," the text continually points us to patterns, themes, and motifs that we ought to see as weaving the historical tapestry into a picture of the sovereign God of the covenant. The significance of each thread is the contribution it makes to the tapestry; by itself the thread has little to offer. The quality of its color has no intrinsic value, but its function in the tapestry helps to create dimension and hue. So the narratives must be approached through their context, and God must be seen as the focus. This tapestry will be unveiled as each biblical book is studied in its turn.

Questions for Further Study and Discussion

1. How can we accommodate both the supernaturalistic view of Old Testament story and the current trend toward analyzing human-natural cause and effect behind historical events?
2. Why was divination forbidden to Israel?
3. Why is history an important part of God's self-revelation?
4. If an account of history is selective, is truth compromised? Explain. What are the implications of selectivity for biblical inerrancy?

For Further Reading

Albrektson, Bertil. *History and the Gods.* Uppsala: Lund, 1967. A stimulating study comparing the Israelite and ancient Near Eastern views of history.

Alter, Robert. *The Art of Biblical Narrative.* New York: Basic Books, 1981.

Fretheim, Terence. *Deuteronomic History.* Nashville: Abingdon, 1983.

Gese, Hartmut. "The Idea of History in the Ancient Near East and the Old Testament." *Journal for Theology and the Church* (1965): 49–64.

Long, Burke O. *First Kings: With an Introduction to Historical Literature.* Grand Rapids: Eerdmans, 1984.

Noth, Martin. *The Deuteronomistic History.* Reprint. Sheffield, England: JSOT, 1981.

Polzin, Robert. *Moses and the Deuteronomist.* San Francisco: Harper & Row, 1980.

———. *Samuel and the Deuteronomist.* San Francisco: Harper & Row, 1989.

Tadmor, Hayim, and Moshe Weinfeld. *History, Historiography and Interpretation.* Jerusalem: Magnes, 1984.

Trompf, G. W. *Notions of Historical Recurrence in Classical Hebrew Historiography.* VT Supplement 30 (1979). 213–29.

Van Seters, John. *In Search of History.* New Haven: Yale University Press, 1983.

Walton, John H. *Ancient Israelite Literature in its Cultural Context.* Grand Rapids: Zondervan, 1989.

Weinfeld, Moshe. *Deuteronomy and the Deuteronomic School.* New York: Oxford University Press, 1972.

Chapter 13

Joshua

Joshua was one of the outstanding persons of the Old Testament: assistant to Moses (Exod. 24:13; 32:17; 33:11), one of the twelve spies (Num. 14), successful general (Exod. 17). Courageous and godly, he served as God's instrument for bringing the people of Israel into the Promised Land. The book rightly bears his name, but in the end it must be realized that the book is not about Joshua—it is about God.

The Writing of the Book

The critical study of the book of Joshua has focused on two separate yet related issues: composition and historicity.

Composition

Early in the twentieth century it was not unusual to see references to the "hexateuch," a group that contained six books—the Pentateuch plus the book of Joshua. Though some still maintain that approach, it is much more common today to find Joshua included in the work referred to as the Deuteronomistic History.

The view that Joshua was part of a "hexateuch" was based on the assump-tion that the Pentateuchal sources (see chap. 6) are traceable into Joshua. This has been largely rejected in favor of the theory that a Deuteronomistic School was responsible for the composition of the historical group of books from Joshua through 2 Kings.

If Joshua is included in the work of the Deuteronomistic historian, the date set for the writing of the book will be dictated by one's theory regarding the Deuteronomistic School. Scholars who attribute the foundation of the school to a book of Deuteronomy first compiled in the late seventh century and accepted by Josiah as the basis of his reform must of necessity date most of the history writing to Josiah's time or later. Scholars who are open to an earlier date for Deuteronomy, however, are at liberty to consider a much wider range for the composition of the historical books.

A number of elements in the book of Joshua suggest an early date for its composition. Among the most convincing, Joshua 16:10 mentions that the Canaanites were not driven out of Gezer and lived there "to this day." First Kings 9:16 reports that Pharaoh conquered Gezer and killed all the Canaanites living there;

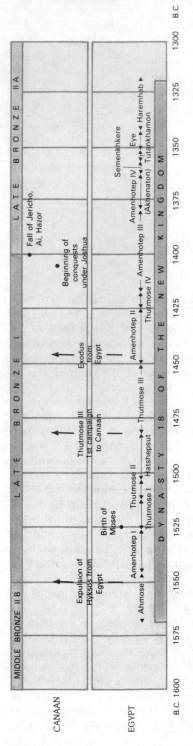

this suggests that Joshua was written before the time of Solomon. Other examples include Joshua 15:63, which records that the Jebusites still inhabited Jerusalem, and 13:6, which emphasizes the Sidonians rather than the city of Tyre, which had become dominant by the time of David.

For those who accept the Mosaic authorship of Deuteronomy, there are no restrictions as to how soon after Joshua's lifetime the book could have been written. On the one hand, Joshua 8:32 gives an indication that there was scribal activity among the Israelites during that lifetime, so there is no reason to rule out the possibility that this is a contemporary record. On the other hand, there is no reason to demand that it was given its final form by Joshua himself. Joshua is not identified as the author of the book. The time of Samuel is one possibility. The frequent reference to phenomena observable "to this day" may well suggest that some time had passed between the events related and the composition of the book.

Historicity

Some scholars are inclined to see the book of Joshua as an unrealistic portrayal of the conquest. In place of the large-scale invasion recorded in Joshua that subdued the native peoples within a relatively short period, they hold that a localized, gradual, piecemeal conquest (supposedly described in Judges 1) is more likely. Their consensus on Joshua is that it is composed of etiological legends (fictional stories contrived to give some explanation for an observed phenomenon or situation), a theory they support by pointing to the recurring comment "until this day" (4:9; 5:9; 7:26; 8:28–29; 9:27; 10:27; 13:13; 14:14; 15:63; 16:10).

Others have found no persuasive reasons to reject the biblical account as presented. First, they see no contradiction entailed between the accounts of the conquest in Joshua and Judges 1. While some verses in Joshua seem to suggest that the entire land was conquered (e.g., 11:23; 21:43–45), these must be balanced against other statements in the book that clearly indicate there was much still to be done (e.g., 13:1–6; 17:12–13; 18:2–3; 23:4–5, 13). It is the latter situation that is in view in Judges 1. The former condition is not contradictory to this, but represents a theological assertion to the effect that God had fulfilled his promises in putting the entire land under the Israelites' control. The major powers of the area had been defeated by Joshua, so by default the territory that they had controlled now belonged to Israel. Israel's control, however, was neither accepted nor enforced. This accounts for the apparent discrepancy.

Second, there is still much discussion concerning the genre of etiological legend. Depending on one's definition, it is possible to consider some of the elements in Joshua etiological in nature (e.g., the naming of the Valley of Achor in 7:26). The more important issue is whether the explanation given for the phenomenon can be considered historical or not. If one insists that the label "etiological" implies that the explanation is fictional or legendary, then such a label must be discarded. Brevard Childs, however, has demonstrated that such a narrow view of the genre is not sustainable.[1] As a result, even if these narratives should be considered etiological, there is no reason to deny a factual basis to the account.

Beyond this, however, it must be seriously questioned whether these narratives can be relegated to the category of etiology. The purpose of etiological narrative is to give explanation of and assign cause to situations or phenomena. Is that the purpose of the biblical author in introducing these accounts to the reader? While it may be admitted that etiological information is given, to ascribe an etiological purpose to the author is to trivialize the theological cohesiveness that is evident in the selection and arrangement of the material.

Another challenge to the historical authenticity of the book of Joshua comes, not from literary analysis, but from the archaeological record. One would expect that archaeology had great potential for confirming the destruction of Canaanite cities and the repopulation of the land by the Israelites. These are events that excavation should be able to detect and provide details for. Yet the nature of the data leaves the picture controversial and unclear.

Theoretically, what is needed is to find a period of time when each of the cities mentioned in Joshua 1–12 shows evidence of being occupied and when three of them—Jericho, Ai, and Hazor—show signs of being destroyed.[2] When clear-cut answers are not forthcoming, some reject the biblical record, others reject the archaeological results, and still others seek to harmonize the two by making adjustments to one or the other or both.

The date of the conquest most naturally suggested by the text of Scripture, about 1400 B.C., has frequently been rejected by archaeologists because destruction and occupation levels of the relevant cities did not correlate to this time period. Those who used the archaeological record to identify a more suitable date concluded that the end of the thirteenth century provided the closest correlations to the biblical account. As more and more

---

[1]Brevard S. Childs, "A Study of the Formula 'Until This Day,' " *JBL* 82 (1963): 279–92; and "The Etiological Tale Re-examined," *VT* 24 (1974): 387–97.

[2]Jericho was destroyed at the end of Middle Bronze Age II, traditionally about 1550 B.C., and not occupied again until about 1400. There was a subsequent destruction in the fourteenth century. The site traditionally identified as Ai was unoccupied between 2400 and 1200 B.C. Hazor also shows a destruction level at the end of Middle Bronze Age II and another in the thirteenth century, which is thought to coincide with the incident reported in Judges 4–5.

Figure 13.1. Two views of Tel Hazor, north of the Sea of Galilee, which is regarded as the site of a Canaanite city-state defeated by the armies of Joshua. (*From the Yigael Yadin Collection. Courtesy Israel Exploration Society*)

difficulties arose with this date, many rejected the biblical picture of a conquest altogether in favor of a view that Israel gained control of Canaan over a long period of time by means of peaceful infiltration by independent nomadic groups that eventually banded together and became "Israel." Because this model depends on increasingly suspect sociological concepts (especially with regard to nomadism and tribal organizations), it gave way to a model portraying the "conquest" as a peasant revolt instigated by a group from Egypt but carried out primarily by disenchanted internal factions. This model suffers from a total lack of biblical support and represents something of a modern Marxism superimposed on ancient cultures with little sociological evidence.

More recently, John Bimson has put forth a theory that seeks to deal with the problem in a totally different way. Many of the cities listed in the conquest narratives of Joshua show evidence of their city walls having been destroyed at the end of the period that archaeologists have designated Middle Bronze II. This era has traditionally been considered to have ended about 1550, and the destruction of cities in Canaan was attributed to the Hyksos or to the Egyptians who were chasing the Hyksos out of Egypt.

Bimson has garnered evidence to suggest that the end of Middle Bronze II should be revised to about 1420 and that the destructions should be seen as having been wrought by the Israelites under Joshua. Jericho and Hazor (fig. 13.1) both saw substantial city walls destroyed at the end of Middle Bronze II. Ai is more problematic, for there is some dispute about whether the site has been identified properly. Bimson argues for identifying Ai with Khirbet Nisya rather than the traditional identification with Khirbet et-Tell. The latter was not occupied between 2400 and 1200 B.C., so it did not make a very good candidate.[3]

The Background

As we have seen, the dates of the Exodus and the conquest are matters of ongoing dispute that will not be resolved here. However, whether the events of Joshua took place at the end of the fifteenth century or sometime in the thirteenth, they occur after the expulsion of the Hyksos from Egypt in the mid-sixteenth century and before the invasion of the Sea Peoples about 1200 B.C.

The expulsion of the Hyksos brought the powerful Eighteenth Dynasty to the throne of Egypt. By the mid-fifteenth century the dynasty was firmly established and at the peak of its strength. At this same time (about 1460) the Neo-Hittite Empire also took shape, and over the next two centuries the Egyptians and the Hittites competed for control of the trade routes and ports of Syro-Palestine. During most of this period, a third power center was located in northern Mesopotamia. Until about 1350 this was the Hurrian Empire of Mitanni along the upper Euphrates. When the Hittites overthrew the Hurrian capital, the power void was filled by the Assyrians, who dominated the east for most of the thirteenth century. The result of this triad of competing political powers was a stalemate, with continual adjustments and shifts of advantage based on the skillfulness of the respective kings and armies and the effectiveness of their diplomatic strategies.

At stake in this international game of intrigue was control of the busy seaports

---

[3]For a summary of Bimson's position see "Redating the Exodus," *BAR* 14 (1987): 40–52; for a full treatment see his book *Redating the Exodus and the Conquest*, 3d ed. (Sheffield, England: n.p., 1988). Though Bimson's position is controversial and may still undergo some adjustment, it offers a very sound approach to interpreting the archaeological data with integrity while respecting the authority of the biblical text.

of the Syrian coast—Byblos, Ugarit, and Sidon being among the most prosperous—and the overland trade routes, particularly the Great Trunk Road that guided caravans and troops from Egypt through major cities in Palestine, through Damascus, Hamath, and Aleppo, and finally east to the Euphrates and down through the heartland of Mesopotamia to the Kassites, who controlled Babylonia.

Palestine and Syria at this time were checkered with independent or loosely confederated city-states, each anxious to benefit from the economic opportunities its location provided. Letters found at the ancient Egyptian capital Tell el-Amarna, written from petty kings of Canaanite city-states to the Egyptian court in the fourteenth century, provide reliable information about this situation. The fourteenth century saw a decline in the power of Egypt through the Eighteenth Dynasty before the final glory days of the Nineteenth. The city-state kings who wrote the letters sought military assistance from the dormant Egyptians. It is clear from the correspondence that Egyptian control of Palestine had diminished and the Canaanite kings were shuffling for political power. The lack of Egyptian control had caused two problems: (1) some city-states were taking advantage of Egyptian absence to enlarge their territories, and (2) groups of displaced peoples posed a threat in attempting to carve out a new home by driving out the current inhabitants. The Amarna letters refer to these people as "the Ḫabiru."

Some scholars have wondered whether the Habiru might refer to the Hebrews, for given an early date of the Exodus, the timing would be about right. Further study, however, has shown that while the Israelites could have been included, the term "Ḫabiru" refers to a much broader range of peoples.

As the Nineteenth Dynasty came to power in Egypt and began its ascent, the tension between the Egyptians and the Hittites increased. The first half of the thirteenth century saw a major confrontation between their two armies at Qadesh on the Orontes River in Syria. Fighting to a stalemate, Rameses II of Egypt was unable to wrest control of Amurru and Qadesh from the Hittites. By mid-century, peace was established between the two powers, with Egypt retaining control of Palestine and the port cities of Syria as far north as Ugarit. The Hittites would rule the Orontes and inland territory in Syria.

The resulting picture in Palestine during the conquest (at whichever date) is that Egypt had at least nominal control of the area, but locally a network of city-states governed. Egypt's primary interest was securing the trade routes and maintaining her garrisons. Even in the times of greatest strength, Egypt probably would have intervened in Palestine only when her own interests were threatened. During periods of Egyptian weakness, the people of Palestine were on their own.

Outline of the Book

Figure 13.2. Theological Purpose in the Book of Joshua

God instructs the Israelites to enter the land	1:1−9
God has gone before them to terrify the occupants of the land	2:9−11
God brings them across the Jordan	3−4
Circumcision required for rededication	5:1−12
The commander of the Lord's army	5:13−15
God-given strategies	6:2−5; 8:2
God-given victories	6:16; 8:7; 10:42
Defeat when God's instructions had been violated	7:5−12

    1. Reuben, Gad, and half-Manasseh in Transjordan (13)
    2. Caleb (14)
    3. Judah (15)
    4. Manasseh and Ephraim (16−17)
  B. Remainder of tribes (18−19)
  C. Cities of refuge established (20)
  D. Levitical cities allocated (21)
IV. Covenant matters
  A. Potential violation in altar building (22)
  B. Covenant exhortations to tribal leaders (23)
  C. Covenant renewal at Shechem (24)

Purpose and Message

There are two popular misconceptions about the book of Joshua. One is that it is just the story of a courageous and godly person; the other, it is a military record of the conquest. Both must be passed over in identifying the reason why the book was written. Regarding the first, the lack of biographical details and a dearth of expressions of approval or disapproval of Joshua's actions suggest that Joshua is not really the focus of the material, though he certainly plays a central role in the events of the book. As to the second, a close examination reveals that there is actually very little given of the details of military strategy and achievement—only the barest sketch of an outline.

Furthermore, neither biography nor military history explains the land allotment segment in chapters 13−19. Any identification of the purpose of the author must include all sections of the book.

These misconceptions dispelled, we see that when military strategies are described in the text, they are God's strategies, not Joshua's. In each battle narrative, only enough information is given to convey that (1) God was the one who engineered the victory, and (2) God's instructions were carried out in placing the defeated cities under the ban.

The orientation of the texts toward the role of God is evident in several places. The incidents identified in figure 13.2 show that this is not simply military history. Rather, a theological point is being made even though military records are used to get the point across.

Based on this orientation toward the role of God, on including every segment of the writing, and on the comments made by the narrator, it is evident that the purpose of the book is to convey how God kept his covenant promise to bring the Israelites into the land he had showed to Abraham. The faithfulness of God in carrying out his end of the covenant is important to affirm. It explains why there is frequent reference to the Lord's giving the land to the people and why his role gets so much attention.

The message is that God keeps his promises, no matter how impossible they may seem. God's covenant with Abraham is something that he took very seriously and intended to fulfill. God was deter-

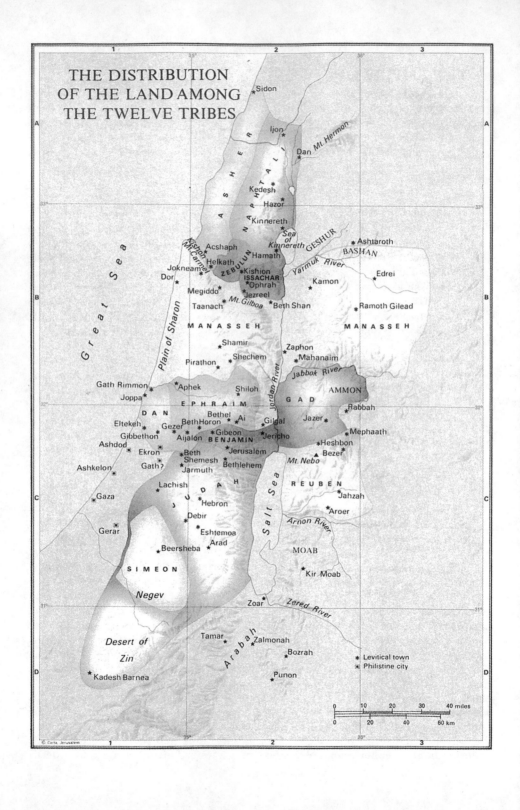

THE DISTRIBUTION
OF THE LAND AMONG
THE TWELVE TRIBES

* Sidon

Ijon

Dan Mt. Hermon

A S H E R

N A P H T A L I

Kedesh

Hazor

Kinnereth

Sea
of
Kimnereth G E S H U R

* Ashtaroth

Kishon
Mt. Carmel Acshaph

Helkath Hamath

Jokneam ZEBULUN Kishion

Dor ISSACHAR Ophrah

Megiddo Jezreel

Taanach Mt. Gilboa Beth Shan

B A S H A N

Yarmuk River

Edrei

Kamon

Ramoth Gilead

M A N A S S E H

M A N A S S E H

Shamir Zaphon

Shechem Mahanaim

Pirathon Jabbok River

Gath Rimmon Aphek Shiloh G A D A M M O N

Joppa Rabbah

D A N E P H R A I M

Bethel Ai Jazer

Eltekeh Gezer BethHoron Gilgal Mephaath

Gibbethon Aijalon Gibeon Jericho Heshbon

Ashdod Ekron BENJAMIN Bezer

Gath? Beth Jerusalem Mt. Nebo

Ashkelon Shemesh Bethlehem

Jarmuth R E U B E N

Gaza Lachish J U D A H Jahzah

Gerar Hebron Aroer

Debir Arnon River

Eshtemoa Arad M O A B

Beersheba

S I M E O N Kir Moab

Negev

Zoar Zered River

Desert of Tamar Zalmonah

Zin Bozrah

Kadesh Barnea Punon

* Levitical town
▣ Philistine city

G r e a t   S e a

Plain of Sharon

Jordan River

Salt Sea

A r a b a h

0   10   20   30   40 miles
0   20   40   60 km

© Carta, Jerusalem

mined to carry it out and is capable of carrying it out.

Structure and Organization

The first section of the book (1–5) gives some details concerning the Israelites' entering the land. From the start, the text focuses on the covenant, expressing God's intention to bring them into the land that he promised to Abraham (1:2–6) and exhorting them to keep the law (1:7–8). It is clear from the text that God gave the instructions to enter the land. The story of the spies in Jericho is told at length, not because of the military strategy it discloses, but because of the information gained by the spies. The inhabitants of the land were all fearful because they had heard what the Lord had done for Israel. The conclusion in 2:24 is that "the LORD has surely given the whole land into our hands."

The crossing of the Jordan was accomplished with the help of a miracle from God, and a memorial was built to acknowledge that fact. The narrative includes a consecration to the Lord (3:5) and prominently features the ark of the covenant (e.g., 3:8). Again, the conclusion emphasizes the work of God (4:23–24). The renewal of the rite of circumcision (chap. 5) also serves as a rededication to the covenant in preparation for God's fulfillment of his promises.

The second section of the book is the most familiar to Christians in general. In the important introduction (5:13–15) Joshua is confronted by one who identifies himself as the commander of the Lord's army. This event has some parallel to the episode of the burning bush in the life of Moses, but its greatest significance is that it again demonstrates that the Lord is the one who will do the fighting and will enable the Israelites to possess the land. It is the Lord's army who will conquer.

The actual conquest narratives begin with the famous battle of Jericho. The emphasis on carrying out the ban (6:17–21) and the fact that the instructions they received resemble a ritual more than a battle plan set the tone for the narratives as conveying the covenantal aspects rather than the military aspects of the conquest, though military records would have been used as sources.

Chapter 7 provides one of the most detailed accounts of the conquest narratives, and it concerns not a military encounter, but a covenant issue: the violation of the ban. The defeat at Ai (7:2–5) showed again that the Lord was the one granting victory or defeat. The discovery of the violator, Achan, and the appropriate punishment of the crime cleared the way for subsequent victory (chap. 8). This event was followed by the building of an altar and the reading of the law on mounts Ebal and Gerizim to give recognition to the Lord for giving the people this first foothold in the land.

Chapter 9 functions, first, to give background for the conflict related in chapter 10 and, second, to explain why an action that was ostensibly a covenant violation (making a treaty with inhabitants of the land) was tolerated by the Lord. The reason is that the Gibeonites' deception of Joshua exonerated the Israelites from punishment.

The account of the battle of Gibeon in chapter 10 also serves to point out the Lord's part in bringing the victory. God miraculously intervened both in honoring Joshua's request about the sun and moon (10:12–15) and in sending hail to batter the enemy (10:10–11). (The ancient book of Jashar, which has not been preserved, is referred to as confirming these events.) The mopping-up operation (10:16–43) showed Joshua's faithfulness in following God's instructions regarding "the ban" (see below).

The northern coalition was the next army to confront the Israelites. But since there is no mention of a specific, miraculous divine intervention, the narrative has nothing to report about the battle. It tells only who was involved and reports that the Lord delivered the enemy into the Israelites' hands (11:8). Chapter 12 concludes this section by listing the kings who were defeated.

Section three gives detailed descriptions of the boundaries of the territory allotted to each tribe and in so doing helps us to identify the purpose of the book of Joshua. If God was enabling Israel to possess the land, he would also supervise their disposition of it. This constituted the fulfillment of God's promise. The narrative makes this point explicit in the conclusion of this section: "So the LORD gave Israel all the land, . . . and they took possession of it and settled there. The LORD gave them rest on every side. . . . The LORD handed all their enemies over to them. Not one of all the LORD's good promises to the house of Israel failed; every one was fulfilled" (21:43–45). That is what the Book of Joshua is all about.

Chapters 22–24 concern Israel's response to the occupation and focus on the covenant. Especially important is the covenant renewal at Shechem containing a restatement of what God had done and what the Israelites agreed to do.

Major Themes

Covenant and Land

In Israel's perception of herself as the covenant people of God, nothing is more central than the land. God had promised Abraham a land, though it was not to belong to his family for some four centuries (Gen. 15:13–21). The delivery of that land into the hands of Israel is the focus of the book of Joshua. Forever after, the land is viewed in the history and literature of Israel as evidence of God's having chosen her as his covenant people and bestowing his favor on them. When Israel's offenses against the Lord required judgment, the worst sentence that the prophets could deliver was the threat of

banishment from the land. In the same manner, the hope of restoration and a future kingdom were both rooted in the promise that the Lord would regather Israel to the land.

The book of Joshua, then, has great theological significance, for its narratives demonstrate, more than anything else could, that the Lord was keeping the covenant promises he had made to Abraham. Just as Israel did not come out of Egypt by its own power, so the land was not taken by Israel's military might or by Joshua's strategies.

The Ban

A prominent theme of Joshua is found in the instructions regarding how the conquered cities of Palestine were to be treated. Legislation on the ban—"destroy them totally; . . . show them no mercy"— is found in Deuteronomy 7:1–11 and 20:10–18, and the promulgation of it is made in Joshua 6:17–19. The term "ban" is inadequate to convey the meaning of the concept, but it is widely used for lack of suitable alternatives. The verb has recently been defined as follows: "consecrate something or someone as a permanent and definitive offering for the sanctuary; in war, consecrate a city and its inhabitants to destruction; carry out this destruction; totally annihilate a population in war; kill."[4] The concept is not unique to Israel, for it occurs also in the ninth-century inscription of Mesha, king of Moab.

Yet the question often arises, Why the ban? Why did God command the complete annihilation of the occupants of the land? Ethicists and philosophers over the centuries have debated this, and various explanations have been offered. Scripture suggests that the Canaanites brought this destruction on themselves by their own wickedness (Deut. 9:5), reflected not only in their abhorrent practices (e.g., fertility

[4]*TDOT*, V:188.

rites and child sacrifice), but also in their resistance to the action of the Lord (cf. Josh. 9:1–4; 10:1–5; 11:1–5).[5]

The Divine Warrior

The Lord is frequently described, from the time of Samuel, as "YHWH of armies." But he is seen earlier, in the book of Joshua (10:14), as engaging in combat on behalf of the Israelites as a divine warrior. In the Old Testament this motif is related to Yahweh as Creator (Isa. 45:12–13) and describes his role in the Exodus (Exod. 15; Deut. 33:2–3) and in the return from the Exile as related in the prophetic literature (e.g., Isa. 51:9–11; 52:7–12). When the Israelites set out from Sinai with the ark in the lead, the formula recited by Moses addressed Yahweh as One going forth in battle (Num. 10:35).

The significance of this theology is laid out succinctly in Proverbs 21:31: "The horse is made ready for the day of battle, but victory rests with the LORD."

Sovereign Intervention

It seems clear that the miraculous element cannot be removed from the book of Joshua without severely damaging its theological intent. The book is insistent that the Lord sovereignly intervenes in history in order to execute his plan and carry out his promise. This is not portrayed as haphazard intervention like that evidenced in the polytheistic theology of the ancient Near East. Rather, it is part of the ongoing, consistent plan of God that is delineated by the historical literature, projected further by the prophetic literature, and brought to a climax in the birth, life, and death of Jesus the Christ.

The Exodus and the conquest represent the first great demonstration of the sovereignty of God in the history of Israel. What he had promised to an undistinguished emigrant from Mesopotamia who traveled to Canaan and raised a small family, which left the land two generations later, came true. Though more than four hundred years had gone by, the land of Canaan again belonged to the family of Abraham.

Corporate Solidarity

In Joshua 7, the consequences of Achan's sin first fell on all Israel as she lost a battle against Ai (with thirty-six Israelite casualties), and then the punishment fell on Achan's family, who were all stoned to death. In the individualistic orientation of our culture, it seems grossly unfair that so many should suffer for one person's offense. It even seems contrary to the dictates of the law (Deut. 24:16), though other passages warn us against reading that law too simplistically (Exod. 20:5–6).

The sense of national or ethnic identity was much stronger for Israel than it is in today's Western societies, though corporate identity still survives in areas where teamwork is necessary and "team spirit" is valued (e.g., small companies or organized sports). This solidarity was reflected positively in the laws of levirate marriage and land redemption, which provided that family members come to the aid of a disadvantaged member of the clan. Negatively, all could suffer for the sake of one.

Besides the account of Achan, we see evidence of this practice in the destruction of the families of Korah, Dathan, and Abiram (Num. 16:27–33). In these cases innocent parties shared in the punishment of an individual, not because they shared his guilt, but because they had a share in his identity. Achan's violation of the ban resulted in his being included in the ban. By bringing himself under the ban, he doomed his family, for the function of the ban was to obliterate all lines of continuity.

[5]This observation comes from Lawson Stone.

Questions for Further Study and Discussion

1. If the book of Joshua is intended to be read as theology rather than biography or military history, how should we approach the book in Bible study and exposition?
2. How is corporate identity a factor in our understanding of God's action in history?
3. Compare Joshua and Moses religiously, militarily, and politically.
4. How does the story of Rahab function in the book of Joshua?

For Further Reading

Bartlett, John. *Jericho*. Grand Rapids: Eerdmans, 1983.

Bimson, John J. *Redating the Exodus and the Conquest*. Sheffield, England: n.p., 1988. A technical presentation of his theory for revising the date of the end of Middle Bronze Age II and correlating it with the conquest under Joshua.

_____. "Redating the Exodus." *BAR* 14 (1987): 40–52. A popular presentation of his theory for redating Middle Bronze Age II.

Boling, Robert. *Joshua*. Garden City, N.Y.: Doubleday, 1982. A good historical and archaeological treatment with helpful, though not evangelical, exegetical notes.

Childs, Brevard S. "A Study of the Formula 'Until This Day.'" *JBL* 82 (1963): 279–92.

_____. "The Etiological Tale Re-examined." *VT* 24 (1974): 387–97.

Craigie, Peter C. *The Problem of War in the Old Testament*. Grand Rapids: Eerdmans, 1978. A thorough study of the concept of war from both textual and ethical perspectives.

Kaufmann, Yehezkel. *The Biblical Account of the Conquest of Palestine*. Jerusalem: Magnes, 1953.

Kitchen, Kenneth A. *Ramesses II: Pharaoh Triumphant*. London: Aris and Phillips, 1982. A superb historical account drawing heavily on the inscriptional material, yet very readable.

Longman, Tremper, III, and Dan Reid. *Yahweh as the Divine Warrior*. Grand Rapids: Zondervan, forthcoming.

Miller, J. Maxwell. "Archaeology and the Israelite Conquest of Canaan: Some Methodological Considerations." *Palestine Exploration Quarterly* 109 (1977): 87–93.

Wiseman, Donald J. *Peoples of Old Testament Times*. Oxford: Oxford University Press, 1973. Summary of the history of many of Israel's neighbors during the Old Testament period.

Woudstra, Marten. *The Book of Joshua*. Grand Rapids: Eerdmans, 1981. A good commentary from an evangelical perspective emphasizing the book's theology.

Younger, Lawson. *Ancient Conquest Accounts*. JSOTS 98. Sheffield, England: JSOT Press, 1990.

Chapter 14

Judges

When Joshua renewed the covenant with the people at Shechem, the Israelites insisted they would never forsake the Lord for other gods after all he had done for them. Joshua responded that they were incapable of serving the Lord, would be unfaithful, and would bring disaster on themselves (Josh. 24:16–20). For several centuries, as Joshua's apprehensions proved well founded, the Lord periodically provided leaders to come to the aid of Israel just when she seemed to be on the brink of extinction. These leaders were called "deliverers," or "ones bringing justice"—the "judges" for whom the book is named.

The Writing of the Book

There is no indication anywhere in Scripture as to the identity of the author or the compiler of the book. Jewish tradition identifies Samuel as the author, though no evidence is available to support such a claim. Recent scholarship has generally included the book within the Deuteronomistic History, as discussed earlier.

The consensus today is that the book comprises narratives that may have been composed nearly contemporary with the events and put in a theological-literary setting by a compiler at a later date. So, for instance, the Song of Deborah (Judg. 5) is frequently dated to the pre-monarchical period, while the narrator's refrain, "In those days Israel had no king" (e.g., 17:6; 18:1), gives clear evidence that at the time he was writing the nation had a king. From such indications we understand that the book's composition involved a process that may have consumed several centuries. This does not pose a threat to those holding a traditional view of inspiration, for other books of the Bible were clearly compiled over centuries by numerous hands (e.g., Psalms).

The Background

Chronology

The dating of the period of the judges depends, of course, on one's view of the date of the Exodus and the Conquest. Given a thirteenth-century date for the Exodus, the judges period would cover most of the eleventh and twelfth centuries B.C., which corresponds roughly to what archaeologists have called Iron Age I. The earlier, fifteenth-century date of the Exodus would yield a judges period twice

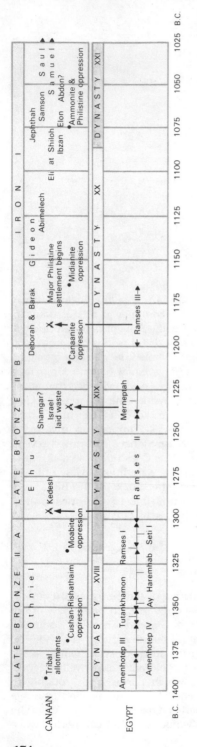

as long, extending from the fourteenth century through the eleventh and including both Iron Age I and the period referred to as the Late Bronze Age II.

Some internal evidence for the dating of the book exists, but it is not conclusive. Adding up the years of each oppression and the years of rest noted at the end of each cycle yields a total of 410 years, but this is too many to fit even the longer period. Some discrepancy has been accounted for by assuming that numbers are rounded off, but it is likewise probable that at least some of the oppressions and judges are more local rather than national and coincide (cf. Judg. 10:7). As a result, we cannot date the judges period precisely with confidence. It does appear, however, that the period cannot be limited to Iron Age I, for Judges 11:26 affirms without dispute that at the time of Jephthah, Israel had already been in the land for 300 years. The longer period also seems to correlate more easily with the information given in 1 Kings 6:1, where 480 years are said to have transpired between the Exodus and the dedication of the temple by Solomon.

Historical Background

The Late Bronze Age II witnessed empires struggling in a virtual stalemate with the advantage constantly shifting from one power to another. As the Egyptians and Hittites vied for control of the lucrative trade routes and seaports of Syro-Palestine, the Mitannian Empire and later the Assyrians provided a third political center whose allegiance could shift the balance of power from one side to the other. Though some of the most powerful and distinguished kings in history reigned during this time (e.g., Rameses the Great), the book of Judges offers no acknowledgment of them. Since the territory occupied by the Israelites was primarily confined to the hill country and away from the major trade routes, the struggles of the empires may have had little impact on them. More important, however, the narrator of Judges seems more interested in the theological implications of history, allowing him to ignore important international events as being superfluous to his purpose.

When the Sea Peoples invaded the ancient Near East from the Mediterranean at the end of the thirteenth century B.C., the stalemate ended. The Hittite Empire fell, the Egyptians relapsed into internal struggles, and the trade that the empires had sought to control by their military expansion was devastated in the destruction of a number of the prosperous seaports. The result was a political vacuum in which there were no international powers threatening the peoples of Palestine. This opened the way for the growing influence of the Philistines (one of the groups of the Sea Peoples who settled on the southern coast of Palestine) and the infiltration of the Aramaean tribes who were to become a dominant political force during the time of the Israelite monarchy.

Cultural Background

When the Israelites came into Canaan, they found not a unified country, but numerous city-states with separate governments. At times these city-states were loosely confederated as allies, and more frequently they were aligned with major powers, especially Egypt, that often dominated the region. The correspondence from some of these cities found in the Amarna letters shows that they did not always receive the help from Egypt that they expected or needed, and also that they were not above implicating one another in conspiracies against the pharaohs. Yet the narratives of the book of Joshua show that they could work together against a common enemy when the need arose.

In contrast, Israel was organized politically by a tribal structure. Each clan descended from Jacob's sons had its own

leaders. Some have suggested that the organization of twelve tribes united by a central sanctuary had parallels in the Greek amphictyonies such as that centered on the sanctuary of Apollo at Delphi. In an amphictyony, various neighboring states or tribes banded together to defend a common religious center; the central sanctuary was the setting not only for religious festivals, but for tribal councils convened to discuss military or diplomatic action to be taken in concert. The details of the theory developed by Martin Noth have almost all been contested to the extent that a sociological parallel between amphictyonies and the Israelites is now nearly universally rejected. The idea that the tribes of Israel were intended to be united by their distinctive relationship to Yahweh allows comparison with amphictyony, but in reality, any unity maintained by Israel during this period probably had more to do with ethnic ties than with loyalty to a central sanctuary.

Outline of the Book

I. Background: Failure to drive out the Canaanites (1:1–2:5)
II. Introduction: Cycle of apostasy (2:6–3:6)
III. Cycles: "The Israelites did evil in the eyes of the Lord"
   A. Othniel (3:7–11)
   B. Ehud (3:12–31)
   C. Deborah (4–5)
   D. Gideon (6–8)
      1. Abimelech (9)
      2. Tola and Jair (10:1–5)
   E. Jephthah (10:6–12:7)
      1. Ibzan (12:8–10)
      2. Elon (12:11–12)
      3. Abdon (12:13–15)
   F. Samson (13–16)
IV. Tribal depravity: "Everyone did as he saw fit"
   A. Danites (17–18)
   B. Benjaminites (19–21)

Purpose and Message

The purpose of the book of Judges is to explore what happened theologically during the years between Joshua and David. The Lord had given the Israelites the land, and they had formalized their commitment to remain faithful to him by covenant at Shechem (Josh. 24). But there ensued centuries of failure, finally brought to an end by the Lord's formal installation of kingship by covenant (2 Sam. 7). How was God working between these covenants, and why were the Israelites not enjoying the blessings of the covenant?

The message of the book is that the problem was not the Lord's fault, but was created and sustained by Israel's continued disobedience. The judges period was characterized by acts of depravity, not just individually, but on the tribal level. This is conveyed by the two sets of refrains that recur in their respective sections of the book. Each cycle in chapters 3–16 is introduced by the observation that "the Israelites did evil in the eyes of the LORD" (2:11; 3:7, 12; 4:1; 6:1; 10:6; 13:1), indicating the tendency toward theological apostasy. The second refrain serves as an inclusio by appearing at the beginning and end of chapters 17–21 (17:6; 21:25): "In those days there was no king in Israel; everyone did as he saw fit." The first half of the phrase is used in two other places as well to sustain the narrative in between (18:1; 19:1).

This second section is not so distinctly covenant oriented as the first section, though covenant violations abound. It rather shows that injustice was the natural by-product of the Israelites' apostasy. Since the refrain appears to blame the conditions on the lack of kingship, some have seen this section as an apologetic for monarchy. Though this seems to us doubtful, the refrain shows that tribal leadership was ineffective in maintaining conformity to covenanted theocracy.

In these refrains can be seen an obvious contrast to David, who "had done what was right in the eyes of the LORD" (1 Kings 15:5), but the books of Kings show that the monarchy was also unsuccessful in keeping people faithful to the covenant. Yet in all these times, though apostasy and injustice brought punishment, the mercy of the Lord was also evident. In the books of Kings God's mercy is evident in his raising up of prophets to warn the people; in Judges it is evident in his raising up judges to deliver the people. The message emphasized Yahweh's long-suffering grace in the face of continual and rampant apostasy and injustice among his people. Covenant failures of the people were met by covenant faithfulness from the Lord.

Structure and Organization

The first section of the book establishes the failure of Israel to carry out the directions of the Lord to purge the land of the Canaanites. The result was that, although the land had been formally given into the control of the Israelites by virtue of the Conquest, it was neither possessed nor controlled by them. This failure to rid the land of Canaanites led in turn to the apostasy of Israel that characterized the judges period. The book of Joshua has made it clear that there was no possibility of blaming the Lord for doing only a partial job. Judges 1 likewise discounts this possibility. The Lord's refusal to drive out the inhabitants of the land was a direct result of the people's disobedience—a point made in the speech of "the angel of the Lord" at the end of the first section (2:1–5).

The next part (2:6–3:6) introduces the cycles that constitute the theological framework of the period. Formulas are used through most of the cycles to demonstrate that the pattern is typical. First the people did evil in the eyes of the Lord—usually described in broad terms indicating the practice of worshiping Canaanite deities. The typical response was

Figure 14.1. The large granite stele discovered at the temple tomb of the pharaoh Merneptah in Egypt, significant because it contains one of the rare references to Israel in ancient nonbiblical documents and complements the history of the days of the judges. (*Encyclopaedia Judaica*)

for the Lord to punish them, doing so by sending foreign oppressors. It is noteworthy that on only one occasion were the Canaanites the oppressors (chap. 4).

As might be expected, the people would eventually cry out to the Lord to deliver them. Yet neither in the introduction to this section (chap. 2) nor in the actual cycles (chaps. 3–16) do we read that the people offered repentance. They cried for help, but with the exception of

10:10–16 there is no indication that repentance or reform accompanied that cry. Nevertheless, the Lord would raise up a deliverer as an act of compassion, and this deliverer would bring liberation during his lifetime, only to have the cycle begin all over again once he died.

This is the cycle of apostasy introduced in chapter 2 and then followed through six full repetitions in chapters 3–16. The major intrusion into this is chapter 9, which recounts an occasion when Abimelech, one of the sons of Gideon, tried to make himself king. This aborted attempt served as an early warning to the Israelites that monarchies are only as successful as the king who sits on the throne.

Chapters 17–21 show that the Israelites, despite this cycle of human apostasy and divine deliverance, failed to establish a just and righteous social order. There was no consistent basis for ethics and morality. The book thus ends in a scene of gloom and depression. Kingship was a logical and moral option to pursue. But the reason why a king was needed, as inferred from Judges, was to help the people do what was right in the eyes of the Lord, so that oppression would not come. Merely to have someone in charge who would go out and fight their battles for them (1 Sam. 8:20) missed the point of the Judges narrator entirely.

Major Themes

The Nature of Charismatic Leadership

The office of judge in this period of Israelite history is not easy to define. The judges were not elected, nor did they inherit their office. They were not appointed in any official way, nor were they anointed. They are referred to as charismatic leaders, because they spontaneously took leadership roles when the need arose. Thus it can be affirmed that God raised them up to deliver Israel.

Though a similar term to that rendered "judge" is used to describe tribal leaders in the Mari texts and magistrates in Phoenician and Punic literature, the function of the judge in Israel can best be determined by developing a profile from the book of Judges. The most prominent tasks undertaken by the judges were military in nature. In this sense the judge was establishing justice for the Israelites who were oppressed by other peoples. There is very little civil function mentioned for the judges, though it is generally assumed that disputes would have been brought to these persons for resolution.

There is even less information given for any sort of spiritual function. The situation of Deborah does not clarify the matter, for she is identified as a prophetess. The judges had no relation to the tabernacle or to the ark of the covenant, and they did not call the people back to Yahweh. Though the Lord is identified by the narrator as the One who raised up the judges, there is little evidence to conclude that they were chosen on the basis of their spirituality. Gideon, Jephthah, and Samson all acknowledged the Lord in their speech and acted in his name, but—typical of the times—had major blemishes on the record: Gideon was blamed for improper worship involving the ephod he made (8:27), Jephthah performed child sacrifice (11:30–40), and Samson habitually cavorted with Philistine women, thereby undermining his ability to accomplish his task (chaps. 14–16).

We must conclude, therefore, that the judges were not intended to be spiritual role models, nor was their spirituality necessarily a criterion for God's raising them up. Indeed, the text never implies that it was. This is not to suggest that the judges did not act in faith; rather, it warns us not to place them on too high a pedestal. There were unquestionably some unethical things done by certain judges (e.g., 3:20; 15:4–5). The Bible does not express approval even though it acknowledges that deliverance was still possible nevertheless.

The task of the judge was to be a deliverer—in fact, the Lord's instrument for providing deliverance. In 2 Kings 13:5 the same term, "deliverer," is used and probably refers to a foreign king. It could thus be concluded that the person might at times be unaware that he was functioning as a deliverer and did not necessarily intend to be so. The fact that deliverance was accomplished does not imply approval of the means used. Of Samson it is noted that the Lord was using even his bad choices to accomplish his purposes (14:4). Acting as deliverer was part of the larger role of being responsible for maintaining justice for the people. This was the basic job description of the kings of the ancient world, and it would seem that functionally the office of judge was not greatly different from king. They differed primarily in the way one came to the office and in the fact that there was no political machinery to support the office of judge.

It is very possible that many of the judges exercised only local jurisdiction, but this is a difficult point to prove. A distinction is often made today between "major" and "minor" judges, though this reflects their treatment in the book more than their historical importance or the extent of their influence or jurisdiction. The designation "major" is used for those judges who are directly connected to the cycles of the book (Othniel, Ehud, Deborah, Gideon, Jephthah, and Samson). These are also the ones apparently raised up by God for a specific task. These judges had experiences with prophets (Deborah, herself a prophetess, was used by the Lord to raise up Barak); angels (Gideon, Samson's parents), and the Spirit of the Lord (Othniel, Gideon, Jephthah, Samson). These experiences were the evidence of the Lord's role in directing and empowering the charismatic leaders of Israel.

The Spirit of the Lord

The Spirit of the Lord plays a prominent role in the book of Judges. It was under his power that several of the judges accomplished their tasks, and this therefore demonstrated that the Lord was at work and ultimately responsible for the deliverance brought by a judge. Much correlation can be drawn between the Spirit of the Lord in the Old Testament and the Holy Spirit in the New Testament, but there are also points of discontinuity that need to be recognized.

Our current understanding of the Trinity and the place of the Holy Spirit in it is the result of progressive revelation and should not be imputed to the Israelites. It is very likely that the Spirit of the Lord was understood by the Israelites, not as a separate entity, but as an extension of Yahweh's power and authority. In this sense it was viewed as something like "the hand of the LORD" (2 Kings 3:15; Ezek. 1:3; 3:14, 22, etc.; cf. 1 Kings 18:46, KJV). This discontinuity, however, concerns only perception, not reality. That is, we need not doubt that the Spirit of the Lord in the Old Testament was actually a manifestation of the Holy Spirit. Only we cannot assume that the Israelites thought in those terms.

Another point of discontinuity is the understanding that the Spirit of the Lord did not explicitly indwell believers in Old Testament times as the Holy Spirit did after Pentecost. The text speaks of the Spirit's empowering individuals. This empowerment was not the same as the baptism of the Holy Spirit and need not imply spiritual regeneration. The empowerment function did carry over to the New Testament as we understand the Holy Spirit to empower people to holy living and to bestow spiritual gifts. And in both the Old and New Testaments, the Spirit gave people the ability or authority to do what they normally could not have done. As a result, the Old Testament most frequently refers to the Spirit of the Lord

as empowering and authorizing the prophets (e.g., Num. 11:25–29; 1 Sam. 19:20; Ezek. 3:24; 11:5). The Spirit also gave Bezalel his artisan skills (Exod. 31:3; 35:30–31) and David and Saul their authority to rule (1 Sam. 16:13–14).

None of these instances, however, offer a suitable definition of the role of the Spirit of the Lord with regard to the judges. In most cases the Spirit is mentioned in relation to military ventures of the judges, with Samson's experiences being the prominent exception. The text explicitly states that on three occasions Samson was endowed with the Spirit of the Lord (14:6, 19; 15:14). In each case, along with the time when he prayed for strength to pull down the temple at his death, it was an event in which Samson took life. This seems to be the only common denominator among these instances, perhaps suggesting that Samson had been granted authority to take life in the larger scheme of God's deliverance.

By contrast, with Gideon (6:34), Jephthah (11:29), and later on, King Saul (1 Sam. 11:6), the Spirit of the Lord is mentioned just before the troops were mustered. (Othniel may fall into this category [3:10], but his account is too brief for us to be certain.) This suggests that the Spirit was viewed as granting these persons the authority necessary to gain the cooperation of other tribes. Since there was no central human authority in Israel, no one had the right or authority to summon another tribe to battle. But it was the prerogative of the Lord in the theocracy to call the armies together. Therefore, when someone successfully mustered the troops it was evident to all that the Lord was empowering that person.

Israel's Apostasy

Reading the book of Judges, one wonders how the Israelites could have gone so wrong. The Lord prepared their escape from Egypt by means of the plagues,

Figure 14.2. A relief of Baal, the Canaanite storm-god, found at Ugarit (Ras Shamra) on the Syrian coast. This most powerful god in the Canaanite pantheon is depicted with a club in his raised right hand and a lance connoting lightning in his left. (*Réunion des Musées Nationaux*)

parted the sea before them, gave them his law at Sinai, sustained them in the wilderness, and brought them into the land of Canaan and settled them there. How

could they just turn their backs on all that and worship other gods?

To understand this we must, first, recall that Israel's legacy included only a very tentative monotheism. Though Yahweh was presumably recognized as their chief patron, there was no command prior to Sinai that the people were to worship only him. The prophets inform us that even in the wilderness the Israelites worshiped other gods (Amos 5:25–26; Jer. 7:25), and we have no reason to assume that monotheism was practiced during the four hundred years in Egypt. As a result, it is evident that Sinai presented Israel with an entirely new concept: exclusive worship of one deity.

Second, we must recognize that the difference between the monotheism commanded at Sinai and the polytheism of the ancient Near East involved much more than the number of deities. Monotheism offered a whole new perspective on deity. In this system God is the ultimate power in the universe. He is not subordinate to anyone or anything. He does not manifest himself in natural phenomena, though he controls all of nature. He is moral and consistent and expects behavior that is moral and just. He is autonomous and therefore cannot be manipulated by cultic ritual.

In contrast, the Israelites were still steeped in the old pagan concepts. The Canaanite religion is observable in tablets found in the port city of Ugarit from the time of the judges. Each god had its respective sphere of influence and was subject to the decrees of the assembly of the high gods. There likewise existed a power above the gods that could be appropriated by the gods and, to a lesser extent, by men and women through divination. These gods were often connected with and manifested through the forces of nature (fig. 14.2). They were capricious and unpredictable and not particularly prone to moral behavior. Their demands were largely ritual in nature, and it was thought that the temple and sacrifice satisfied their needs. And since they had needs that they were dependent on humans to provide, the gods could be manipulated.

These two views of deity—Israelite monotheism and Canaanite polytheism—were mutually exclusive. The monotheistic view that was accepted in theory at Sinai involved sophisticated philosophical adjustments that most of the people simply never made. Once the Israelites had arrived in the land and had scattered to their respective territories, the ever-present Canaanite religion influenced the way they thought about God. Not only did they worship the Canaanite gods, but as even the prophets indicated at a much later date, they treated the Lord as if he were one of the pagan deities.

If the first few generations failed to remain theologically distinct, it is no surprise that the problem lasted a long time, for the system had been set up so that the law would be transmitted within the family (Deut. 6:4–9). Though it is clear that Israel remembered her history during the judges period (6:13; 11:14–27), there is little to suggest that the law was known to them. The priesthood was most to blame for this lapse (for example, see Judg. 17–21; 1 Sam. 2–4), and their failure may have precipitated the decline of priestly influence.

Questions for Further Study and Discussion

1. How does the book of Judges illustrate the need to distinguish between the plan of God and the will of God? How can God's plan be carried out by people who are not self-consciously seeking to do God's will? (Consider the book of Habakkuk and Genesis 50:20 in your answer.)
2. What validity was there in Gideon's oracle of the fleece and in Jephthah's vow? Would these be legitimate methods to use today, and if so, under what conditions or restrictions?
3. Can someone who is empowered by the Spirit of the Lord do things contrary to God's will? Explain your answer.
4. What theological conclusions can be drawn from the continuity and discontinuity observable between the Old Testament and New Testament roles of the Spirit?

For Further Reading

Boling, Robert. *Judges*. Garden City, N.Y.: Doubleday, 1975. Helpful archaeological and historical information. Exegetically good, though not evangelical.

Burney, C. F. *Judges and Kings*. 1903; reprint, New York: Ktav, 1970. Though out of date in many respects, still a helpful source of textual observations.

Cundall, Arthur, and Leon Morris. *Judges and Ruth*. TOTC. Downers Grove, Ill.: InterVarsity, 1968.

de Geus, C. H. J. *The Tribes of Israel*. Assen, the Netherlands: Van Gorcum, 1976. A rebuttal to Martin Noth's amphictyony model of the judges period.

de Vaux, Roland. *The Early History of Israel*. Philadelphia: Westminster, 1978. A comprehensive treatment of scholarly reconstructions of the literature and history of this era.

Gottwald, Norman. *The Tribes of Yahweh*. New York: Orbis, 1979. The most thorough treatment of the various models of the conquest and a defense of the peasant revolt theory.

Gray, John. *Joshua, Judges, Ruth.* NCBC. Grand Rapids: Eerdmans, 1986.

Kitchen, Kenneth A. *Pharaoh Triumphant: The Life and Times of Rameses II.* London: Aris and Phillips, 1982. A very thorough and delightful reconstruction of the life and accomplishments of Rameses the Great, drawing heavily on the inscriptional data.

Soggin, J. A. *Judges.* Philadelphia: Westminster, 1981. Heavy on literary and reconstructive analysis, light on exegetical.

Weippert, M. *The Settlement of the Israelite Tribes in Palestine.* Naperville, Ill.: Allenson, 1971. A survey of the scholarly debates concerning the conquest and settlement of the Promised Land.

Wood, Leon J. *The Distressing Days of the Judges.* Grand Rapids: Zondervan, 1975. A good summary of the biblical data presented from an evangelical perspective.

Yadin, Yigael. *The Art of Warfare in Biblical Lands.* London: Weidenfeld and Nicolson, 1963. A compendium of information about weapons, armaments, defenses, fortifications, and strategies used in the various periods of Old Testament history.

Chapter 15

Ruth

The touching story of Ruth introduces the reader of the Old Testament to one of the quiet heroines of the faith. As a record of an incident that occurred during the judges period, it offers a stark contrast to the negative perspective of Israelite faith offered there. Rather than Israelites abandoning their loyalty and deserting the worship of Yahweh for other gods, the story portrays Ruth acting out of loyalty and embracing Yahweh, denouncing other gods.

The Writing of the Book

No author is named for the book, so it remains anonymous. Though it is placed after Judges in the English Bible, following the lead of the Septuagint and Vulgate, the Jewish ordering counts it among the third division of the canon, the Writings. As a result, the book is not considered to be part of the Deuteronomistic History.

The opening verse implies that the judges period is past, and the closing genealogy suggests that the audience would have been familiar with David. If the genealogy is not a later addition, the book is a product of the monarchy period at the earliest. Other factors such as the language and customs (e.g., levirate marriage) have been used by some to support a preexilic date, by others to defend a postexilic date. There is no consensus on the matter, although a preexilic date is gaining support and seems to us to be favored by the evidence.

The Background

Historical Background

Little can be offered to place this story with any confidence in a particular part of the judges period. The Moabites oppressed Israel early in the period and were driven out by Ehud (Judg. 3), so we would not expect that the story occurred then. If the genealogy at the end of the book is complete, the events would most logically be placed toward the end of the twelfth century B.C., roughly contemporary with Jephthah.

Not much is known about Ruth's people, the Moabites, during the judges period aside from the brief oppression at the time of Ehud. The Moabites were a kindred people to the Israelites, descended from Abraham's nephew Lot (Gen. 19:37). They occupied the territory across the Dead Sea from Judah. They had been antagonistic toward the Israelites at the time of Moses (Num. 21–25), but were sympathetic to David's cause when he was a fugitive from Saul (1 Sam. 22:3–4). Later they were subjugated by David (2 Sam. 8:2).

Literary Background

Rich in dialogue, the book of Ruth has all the literary trappings of a dramatic play in four scenes. This has contributed to a growing number of scholars' treating the book as folklore. Its literary qualities have long been appreciated, from its succinct prose to its skillful character development. Its pastoral setting, portrayal of common people, and lack of a villain qualify it as an idyll, though idylls are usually fictional. Robert Hubbard has built a case for the classification "short story," which would not preclude historical accuracy.[1]

Outline of the Book

I. Flight and tragedy of Elimelech's family (1:1–5)
II. Naomi and Ruth return to Bethlehem (1:6–22)
III. Ruth meets Boaz (2)
IV. Naomi's plan and its success (3)
V. The marriage of Ruth and Boaz, and birth of a son (4:1–17)
VI. The genealogy of Perez (4:18–22)

Purpose and Message

Because the book ends with David, many have seen in it a message concerning the king. The question is, what point is the book making about him? Is it an attempt to explain and excuse his foreign ancestry? Does it intend to show divine providence at work in preserving the line to which he was heir? Others, seeing the book's connection to David as secondary,

have seen a polemical purpose intended to urge conversion of the foreign peoples or to discourage Israelite intermarriage with them. Both ideas are difficult to support, because of the turn of events traced in the book and because of its gentle, nonpolemical tone.

Although David should not be ignored in determining the intent of the author, the actual purpose of the narrative may supersede a narrow focus on David alone. The judges period that provided the setting was notorious for its apostasy and covenantal ignorance and offense; faith was at a premium. How did the faith of Israel survive? We suggest that it survived in the families of common folk such as Elimelech and Naomi. The overall picture was glum, but there were faithful individuals. This issue is not without significance for the reader's understanding of David. As the historical narratives move from the judges period to the monarchy, David can be viewed with great incredulity. How could faith like this still exist after four hundred years of conditions such as those described in the book of Judges? The story of Ruth, drawn from David's ancestry, offers an explanation of the survival of faith.

The message is that God preserved families of faith and that from one such family King David came. As Hubbard has pointed out, the preservation of this family shares many motifs with God's preservation of the patriarchs.[2] Thus it provides another example of God's covenant loyalty and the faith it engenders.

Major Themes

The Kinsman-Redeemer

The levirate system is expounded in the legal literature of Israel in Deuteronomy 25:5–10. Under this law, if a man died without having a son, his brother

---

[1]Robert L. Hubbard, *The Book of Ruth* (Grand Rapids: Eerdmans, 1988), 47–48. As is common with short stories, the book of Ruth can entertain as well as instruct.
[2]Ibid., 40–42.

was obligated to bear a son by his widow. That son would thereafter be considered the heir to the dead brother's household. In this way families could not easily die out.

An expanded interpretation of this custom of levirate marriage is combined with land redemption rights to provide the legal setting for the book of Ruth. The term *gō'ēl* (kinsman-redeemer) is taken from the land redemption law (Lev. 25:25–31, 47–55). According to this law, land sold by a person could be bought back by a relative so as to keep the land in the family. Both the land law and levirate marriage were intended to preserve family and land—covenant matters of the first degree. They were social provisions by which God's covenant promises could continue to be realized even for families in crisis. The *gō'ēl* provided the means by which jeopardized covenant blessings could be regained and thus served as an appropriate metaphor for God's grace. Yahweh constantly acted as *gō'ēl* for Israel, and the New Testament was quick to apply that concept to the role of Christ.

Hesed

Related most frequently to covenant loyalty, the term *hesed* envelops all the far-reaching implications of Yahweh's loyalty to his covenant. The King James Version frequently translates the term "mercy," while the New American Standard Bible chooses the compound term "lovingkindness." These only begin to introduce all the varied ways whereby God demonstrates his covenant loyalty, and this variety is reflected in the decision by the translators of the New International Version to use an array of terms: kindness, love, loyalty, and more.

Ruth is a book of *hesed* on both the human and the divine levels. The most explicit statement of this is found in Ruth's stirring expression of commitment to Naomi (1:16–17). It is this quality that gains her Boaz's favor (2:12). Boaz is likewise praised for the *hesed* he shows to Naomi (2:20, where the subject is most likely Boaz [so the NIV] rather than Yahweh). The issue of *hesed* serves as the premise for the discussion between Boaz and Ruth as negotiations are made (3:9–13). The Lord's *hesed* is introduced in 1:8–9 as the factor that will eventually lead to the successful remarriage of Naomi's daughters-in-law, so that it cannot help but be recognized in the provision of a *gō'ēl* for Ruth (cf. 4:14).

All this demonstrates that *hesed* to one another is among the most fitting vehicles God can use to display his own *hesed*. This again provides a contrast to the book of Judges, in which loyalty within the bounds of the covenant is scarce.

Questions for Further Study and Discussion

1. What are the various ways in which *hesed* is expressed in the book?
2. What significance would the Israelites attach to the fact that Ruth was from Moab?
3. What did the principle of levirate marriage imply regarding the family culture of ancient Israel?
4. Why did the book of Ruth become associated with the Feast of Pentecost in later Judaism?

For Further Reading

Atkinson, David. *The Wings of Refuge*. Downers Grove, Ill.: InterVarsity, 1983.
Campbell, Edward F. *Ruth*. Garden City, N.Y.: Doubleday, 1975. Straightforward and helpful, though not evangelical.

Cundall, Arthur, and Leon Morris. *Judges and Ruth*. TOTC. Downers Grove, Ill.: InterVarsity, 1968.

Gray, John. *Joshua, Judges, Ruth*. NCBC. Grand Rapids: Eerdmans, 1986.

Hubbard, Robert L. *The Book of Ruth*. Grand Rapids: Eerdmans, 1988. The best of the commentaries on Ruth: evangelical, thorough, insightful, and readable.

Sasson, Jack M. *Ruth*. Baltimore: Johns Hopkins University Press, 1979. A sociological approach that offers many stimulating and some radical suggestions.

Chapter 16

1-2 Samuel

The books of 1 and 2 Samuel fall together naturally as a unit and originally constituted a single book. Together they cover the period of the transition from the judges through the establishment of the monarchy, including the reigns of Saul and David. Although the Septuagint combines the books of Samuel with the books of Kings under the title "Kingdoms," the Hebrew text traditionally has referred to these books as the books of Samuel in recognition of the significant role of Samuel in the establishment of the monarchy.

The Writing of the Book

The events of the book took place in the last half of the eleventh century and the early part of the tenth century B.C., but it is difficult to determine when the events were recorded. There are no particularly persuasive reasons to date the sources used by the compiler later than the events themselves, and good reason to believe that contemporary records were kept (cf. 2 Sam. 20:24–25). If the books are part of a larger "Deuteronomistic" work, the compiler would have worked late in the period of the divided monarchy.

The Background

Sources for this period of history are scarce. Neither Egypt nor Mesopotamia was in any position to look beyond her borders, so smaller nations of Syro-Palestine were left to squabble among themselves. Threats to Israel posed especially by the Philistines necessitated a greater amount of cooperation among the tribes than was the case previously, and these are directly responsible for the decision to switch to a monarchic form of government. Saul had occasional victories over the Philistines, but he died in the battle at Mount Gilboa and the Philistines overran at least the central portion of Palestine. It was left to David, therefore, to drive out the Philistines. David was also successful in extending Israelite control over most of Syro-Palestine through a series of conquests and treaties.

Outline of the Books

I. The Shiloh traditions (1 Sam. 1:1–4:1a)

II. The ark narrative (1 Sam. 4:1b–7:1)

III. The institution of the monarchy (1 Sam. 7:2–12:25)

IV. The reign of Saul (1 Sam. 13–15)
V. David's rise to power (1 Sam. 16:1–2 Sam. 5:10)
VI. David's successes (2 Sam. 5:11 – 9:13)
VII. David's Failures
   A. Men acting against him: The succession narrative (2 Sam. 10–20)
   B. God acting against him: Appendix (2 Sam. 21–24)

Purpose and Message

As we noted in the introduction to historical literature, these books do not have a strictly historical purpose. That is, this is not history for history's sake. Neither are these books biographical in intent, though certainly some biographical data are included. The major purpose is theological. As Genesis gives us the history of the establishment of the Abrahamic covenant, so Samuel gives us the history of the establishment of the Davidic covenant. The emphasis in these books and ultimately in the covenant itself is the development of the proper concept of divine authority.[1]

The message has several aspects to it. The primary message is that the Davidic covenant was established by God. People may choose kings, as they did Saul, but God chooses dynasties. Even though the people chose the first king and God did not approve of either their motivation for or their concept of kingship, the institution of a monarchy was in God's plan for Israel (Deut. 17:14–20).

Surely another concern of the narrator was to demonstrate to the reader that David was not a usurper of the throne, but painstakingly avoided taking any action against the house of Saul. This concern is pursued to make it clear that God placed David on the throne, lest anyone think of David as a renegade who plotted to seize the throne, assassinated the king and his rightful heirs, and then attempted to excuse his atrocities by claiming divine legitimation. However, this is not a whitewash of David. The narrative portrays David in all his humanity and refuses to obscure in any way his weaknesses or the punishments he received at the hand of God. The second half of 2 Samuel then turns to problems within David's family and kingdom with the message that David's own failures were magnified in his children to the extent that the covenant was put in jeopardy, with the story to be continued into the books of Kings.

Structure and Organization

The Shiloh traditions introduce us to Samuel and give us the information that even from birth, there was something unique about him. This is appropriate, for he was the one who was going to serve the important transitionary function between the period of the judges and the monarchy. After relating the circumstances surrounding his birth and arrival at the temple, the narrative draws a contrast between Samuel and Eli and Eli's rebellious sons. The prophetic word of the demise of the house of Eli came to Samuel and established his reputation as a man of God. He also wore the linen ephod of the priest. The wretched condition of the priesthood is exemplified in Eli's house and demonstrates the extent of the apostasy of the judges period.

The judges period ended in exile—a self-imposed exile of the Lord represented in the ark of the covenant's being captured by the Philistines and taken out of the land of Israel. Usually the victory of one army over another was thought to signal the victory of the gods of that nation over the gods of the defeated nation. The fact that the ark had been captured would have naturally led to the

---

[1]W. J. Dumbrell, "The Content and Significance of the Books of Samuel: Their Place and Purpose Within the Former Prophets," *JETS* 33 (1990): 50.

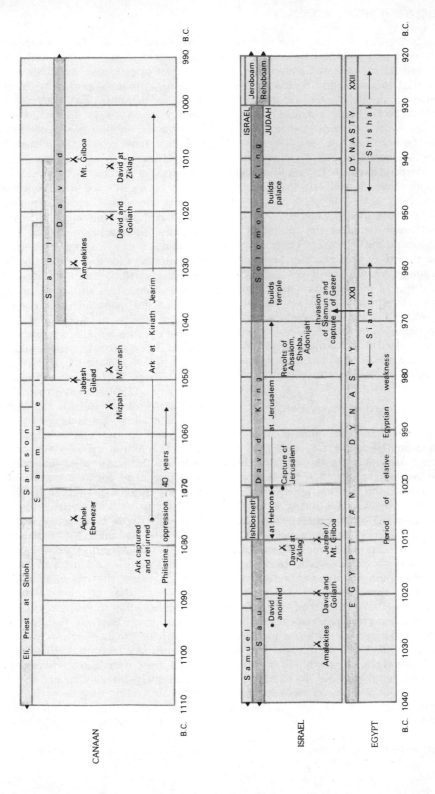

conclusion that the Philistine god, Dagon, was more powerful than the Israelite God, Yahweh. The events in chapters 5–6 are reported to dispel any such idea. With Yahweh's demonstration of his power over the idol of Dagon and also his plague on the Philistine people, it became clear that the Lord had not been overpowered, but had rejected and therefore abandoned the Israelites. The motif of divine abandonment is well-known in the ancient Near East.

This self-imposed exile marked a distinct break between the period of the judges and the monarchy. The account of the return of the ark from exile uses language that is reminiscent of the Exodus.[2] It is of theological interest that the ark's temporary housing continued through all of Saul's reign and that the ark was not officially brought back into prominence until David brought it to Jerusalem (2 Sam. 6). This suggests that both Samuel and Saul were transitional figures.

The Institution of the Monarchy

A section on the institution of the monarchy begins at 1 Samuel 7. At the outset, Samuel is functioning not only as prophet and priest, but also as judge. Despite all the political power vested in Samuel, he was still not a king. That condition led to the request by the people that Samuel preside over a change in the form of government, from judges to kings. This was not supposed to be as big a change as the people imagined it would be. Both systems ought to have been theocratic in nature. Even when there was a human king, he was supposed to be only the representative of the divine King. The fact that the people had not understood this is reflected in the Lord's analysis that the people had rejected him, not Samuel. If the Lord was not king, a human king would not meet their expectations.

Mention of Samuel's disappointment may suggest that he considered himself the most appropriate candidate for the position. This is supported by the references to Samuel's age and his sons' waywardness (8:4–5). In fact, the NIV confirms this in the translation, "It is not you they have rejected, but they have rejected me as their king" (8:7).

Chapter 9 introduces both Saul and a literary device into the text. The format of the text regarding the united monarchy (Saul, David, and Solomon) is to relate the appointment of a king, describe his potential and successes, and finally recount his failures and the results of those failures (fig. 16.1). Saul's installation included several steps showing Samuel, the Lord, and the people all having distinctive roles to play in his appointment. It is notable that the terminology used by the Lord in describing Saul's appointed function (9:16–17) and the incident at Jabesh Gilead (chap. 11) both seem to portray Saul more as a judge than a king. Also, as with many of the judges, Saul seemed well-intentioned, but lacking in spiritual depth and a sound knowledge of the Lord. This is not unexpected, since he came on the scene after four hundred years of general apostasy that characterized the judges period. A judge was expected to be a deliverer, and that is what the people expected of a king as well. At the beginning, Saul succeeded in doing this, fulfilling his potential. But God expected more of a king, and Saul was unable to meet the requirements.

The conclusion of this section (chap. 12) indicates that the people's insistence on having a king was really a willful rejection of the Lord's rule over them. Their primary error was that they assumed they were being oppressed because they had no king to lead them into battle; in reality they were being oppressed for their sin. Kingship would not cure this problem; it would make it

[2]A. F. Campbell, *The Ark Narrative* (Missoula, Mont.: Scholars Press, 1975), 203ff.

Figure 16.1. Narrative Emphasis in the History of the United Monarchy

	Saul	David	Solomon
Appointment	1. By Samuel 2. Public process 3. Activated by the Spirit	1. By Samuel 2. Long process 3. By people	1. By David 2. By Zadok and Nathan
Successes and	Victory over Ammonites	1. Taking of Jerusalem 2. Defeat of Philistines 3. Bringing ark back 4. Covenant 5. Expansion of empire	1. Dream and request for wisdom 2. Wisdom and administration of empire 3. Building of temple
potential failures	1. Impatient offering 2. Placing people under improper oath 3. Disobeying instructions in Amalekite war	1. Adultery with Bathsheba and murder of Uriah 2. Wrongful taking of census	1. Foreign wives' religious practices accommodated 2. Labor and tax on people
Results of failures	Bad judgment, incompetence, and jealousy	1. Bloodshed within family (Amnon, Absalom, Adonijah) 2. Rebellion in kingdom (Absalom, Sheba)	1. Military problems 2. Division of kingdom

worse. Therefore chapter 12 also established the continuing importance of the prophetic office to provide God's guidance to the king.

One might ask, why did God appoint Saul if he knew the king would fail? But that is the wrong question. God used Saul to bring temporary deliverance for Israel—in the same way he had used Gideon, Samson, and other judges. They all had their failures, yet God accomplished his will despite them. Saul had the potential to succeed, but he did not develop into a man who knew God. His naïveté becomes clear as the text recounts his failures.

The Vindication of David

Chapters 13–15 concern the failures of Saul. It is significant that although chapters 19–28 appear to have enough damaging information about Saul to convince readers that he was unsuitable for the throne, there is some concern to show the failures of Saul independent from and antedating his relationship with David. The point is that David did not cause Saul's failure; rather, Saul had disqualified himself before David ever came on the scene.

It is difficult to dissect Saul's offense of offering the sacrifice for the consecration of the soldiers prior to battle (chap. 13). Saul was in an awkward position. Samuel had not come to offer the sacrifice in preparation for battle, and Saul dared not go into battle without it—yet the opportunity for attack was passing quickly and the army was beginning to desert. What would be the most appropriate course of action? Saul acted in his best judgment and reluctantly offered the sacrifice. In doing so, he followed a Canaanite model of kingship, in which the king had certain priestly prerogatives. When Samuel arrived and learned what Saul had done, he was absolutely livid. This is an example of Saul's inability to make wise decisions. The wisdom that was the natural endowment of a true king had escaped Saul; he

neither possessed it nor requested it. One could not succeed as king on good intentions.

Chapters 14 and 15 continue to show how Saul's lack of wisdom surfaced in consistently bad decisions. His leadership ability gradually eroded to the point that he gave in easily to the people's demands on him (14:45; 15:15, 24). This was the legacy of Saul, and it led the Lord to direct Samuel to anoint Saul's successor.

Although the history of David's rise continues to reveal the shortcomings of Saul, the narrative is arranged around David and tells his story. From his anointing in 1 Samuel 16 to his enthronement in 2 Samuel 5, the text is oriented toward David. As previously mentioned, the concern of the narrator here was to demonstrate that even though David was destined by the Lord to rule Israel, he did not usurp the throne of Saul.

There are three major points supporting the narrator's contention. The first is Saul's animosity. There is a firm case built in these narratives that Saul was consistently the initiator of the antagonism that grew up between him and David. It was Saul who threw spears at David, who sent men to arrest David during the night, and who pursued David around the wilderness of Judah. This point is also made by the narrator's clear statements of Saul's motivation in various situations when David was sent against Philistines (1 Sam. 18:17–25).

The second and most extensive proof is David's nonaggression. This is demonstrated in his friendship and covenant with Jonathan, Saul's son and heir to the throne (18:1–4; 19:1–7; 20:1–42). Similarly, David's marriage to Michal, Saul's daughter, even though he considered himself unworthy to marry into Saul's family, shows David's benevolent attitude toward them (18:17–29). The major evidence, however, in the narrator's case is the two occasions on which David could have killed Saul—and was urged to do so, but refused (1 Sam. 24 and 26).

Furthermore, a number of narratives strive to demonstrate that David was not involved in actions taken against Saul and his house.[3] He was not in the battle in which Saul was killed, so he could not be blamed for assassination under the cover of battle (1 Sam. 28–29). The text goes to great lengths to describe David's activities with the Philistines and how he was dismissed from taking part in the battle—all to vindicate David on this point.

After Saul's death, the kingdom fell to his son, Ish-Bosheth, but Abner, who had been Saul's commander-in-chief, seemed to have been in charge. When he and Ish-Bosheth had a falling out, Abner determined to deliver the kingdom to David. Unfortunately, while he was on his mission to David, Abner was assassinated. The narrator was careful to establish that there were hard feelings between Abner and Joab (2 Sam. 2) so that the reader can understand that when Joab killed Abner, he did so for personal reasons rather than at David's command (2 Sam. 3:28–39). Likewise, the narrator wanted to establish that David neither killed nor ordered the killing of Ish-Bosheth (2 Sam. 4).

Another sign of the text's vindicating David of action against Saul's house lies in the treatment of David's wife Michal. Through most of his reign she was out of favor, but this had nothing to do with her being Saul's daughter. The narrator told the story of Michal's ridicule of David that led to her fall from favor (2 Sam. 6:16–23). Then there was the case of Shimei— a descendant of Saul who was put to death by Solomon on David's instruction. As the text relates, however, this execution was not without good reason (2 Sam. 16:5–13; 19:16–23; 1 Kings 2:36–46) and was not motivated by Shimei's relationship to Saul.

A final case is presented in the appendix of Samuel, and this was perhaps the most suspicious to observers of the royal house. Seven members of the house of Saul were executed because of their lineage (2 Sam. 21). Again, however, it is explained that David did not instigate this action, and the circumstances are used to suggest that it was done at the Lord's bidding (vv. 1, 14).

Part of the stated evidence of David's innocence in these acts of aggression is the severe action that he took against those who were responsible. He executed the Amalekite who claimed to have killed Saul (2 Sam. 1:1–16) as well as those who killed Ish-Bosheth (2 Sam. 4). He even censured and eventually doomed Joab for the assassination of Abner (2 Sam. 3:28–39; 1 Kings 2:28–34). Also to be noticed are the lament taken up for Saul (2 Sam. 1:17–27) and the preservation of Jonathan's son Mephibosheth in keeping with David's covenant with Jonathan (2 Sam. 9). All this was used by the narrator to demonstrate David's nonaggression toward the house of Saul.

The third point supporting the contention of the narrator is his interest in presenting statements affirming David's innocence or destiny. Such statements were made by Samuel when David was anointed (1 Sam. 16:12–13) and by Samuel's spirit (1 Sam. 28:16–18). The story of Nabal and Abigail may have been related for the very purpose of recording Abigail's testimony that David represented the voice of the people (1 Sam. 25:30). Most significant are the statements by Jonathan (1 Sam. 19:4–5; 20:14–15; 22:16–18) and by Saul himself (1 Sam. 20:31; 24:16–22; 26:21–25).

It is alleged by some that all this represents no more than a propaganda campaign aimed at legitimizing David's claim to the throne. There can be no doubt that the narrator was presenting evidence by which he intended to legitimize David's claim to the throne. Furthermore, there can be no doubt that this material had propagandistic value. The most serious question, however, is

---

[3]For further discussion see P. Kyle McCarter, "The Apology of David," *JBL* 99 (1980): 489–504.

whether or not there was propagandistic disinformation given to hide the facts. On the one hand, our high view of Scripture prohibits such a view of the text. On the other hand, we find it difficult to substantiate that disinformation was involved here, because David is not treated very well by the text overall. Incidents of deception, poor judgment, and even murder of civilians permeate the narratives from 1 Samuel 21–2 Samuel 3. There is therefore no reason to suspect that the narrator construed the text to favor David. Rather, the narrator was demonstrating that David was legitimately appointed to the throne by the Lord, leading inexorably to the establishment of the Davidic covenant.

David's successes as king are presented in 2 Samuel 5–9. They include his conquests and his establishment of Jerusalem as the new capital city. This was crowned by bringing the ark of the covenant out of exile and placing it back in operation. It should not be thought coincidental that this was followed immediately by the formation of the Davidic covenant, which stood as the charter for the new era. Thus, in chapter 6 David reestablished the throne of Yahweh (i.e., the ark), while in chapter 7 Yahweh established the throne of David.

The Davidic covenant was the centerpiece of the narrator's agenda. Everything in the narrative up to this point had been moving in this direction. From here on in the narrative, everything is to be understood in light of this covenant.

The Succession Narrative has as its main focus the family of David. The foundation of this section is David's adultery with Bathsheba and his subsequent arrangement for the death of her husband, Uriah. (Some would contend that the Succession Narrative begins with chapter 9, and that is possible. In our opinion, however, the story of David's kindness to Mephibosheth is better suit-

ed to the section on David's rise and successes, for it brought to conclusion his obligation to the house of Saul through his covenant with Jonathan.) Chapter 10 relates how the Israelites got into war with the Ammonites. Chapter 11 gives the details of the actual crimes, and chapter 12 recounts how David was confronted with his sin by Nathan the prophet and records the announcement of the punishment. The case that Nathan presented to David was designed to have David pass judgment on himself. Though the legal situation was different (adultery and murder vs. theft), the common ground was that both David and the rich man of the parable acted treacherously with no compassion or pity (12:6). The judgment passed on David's house became the litany of his family history (12:10–12).

It may not be coincidental that David decreed a fourfold restitution (12:6) and that the ensuing narratives eventually record the loss of four heirs to the throne of David (the child by Bathsheba, 2 Sam. 12; Amnon, 2 Sam. 13; Absalom, 2 Sam. 18; and Adonijah, 1 Kings 2),[4] but we can be certain of the legacy of sexual misconduct and violence that overshadowed David's family. In either case, the purpose of the narrator was to trace the effects of David's conduct (as epitomized in the Bathsheba affair) in the conduct of his children. This does not reflect a didactic concern for showing how sons tend to walk in their father's footsteps. Rather, there was a theological agenda designed to document how human sin and bad judgment jeopardized the Davidic covenant as far back as David himself. We have already seen how covenant jeopardy was a theme in the patriarchal narratives of Genesis. Here, as there, the covenant jeopardy brought into sharp focus the sovereignty and grace of God.

So the narratives of 2 Samuel 13–20 tell of how Amnon's incest led to his murder by Absalom and how Absalom

---

[4]This observation comes from H. C. Brichto.

successfully dethroned his father David, but was killed in the ensuing battle against David's forces. In both cases sexual misconduct and murder are reminiscent of David's crimes. Though chapter 20 does not involve a son of David, it has significance here because it shows that tension was already building that threatened to rend the kingdom. The point is made: the result of the unrest in David's house was that the unity of the kingdom and, therefore, the covenant was in jeopardy. The text is careful to note, however, that though there was failure and jeopardy, the Lord still supported David and was faithful to him, despite these acts of others against him. This is most evident in the fact that the rebellions of Absalom and Sheba were unsuccessful.

Though the Succession Narrative picks up again in 1 Kings, the book of 2 Samuel comes to a close with an appendix that reflects on events in David's life that could be inferred to be failures because of apparent action of God against him. Chapters 13–20 had focused on human action against David. Chapters 21 and 24, which frame this section, both relate cases of God's taking action against David—namely, through famine and plague. This circumstance is balanced by the central sections, which report some successful exploits of David, but above all insist that the Lord supported him in giving him victory over his enemies (chap. 22) and making the covenant with him (23:1–7).

Major Themes

The Ark of the Covenant

The ark of the covenant was the most important religious artifact in Israel. Built at Sinai under the supervision of Moses, it represented Yahweh's presence in their midst. Occupying the place in the temple that was given over to the idol of the deity in most of the religions of the ancient Near East, the ark was nevertheless considered only the footstool of Yahweh's throne.

One reason why idols were prohibited in Israelite religious practice is that they were commonly used in rituals to obligate or force the deity to act in the way desired by the worshipers. Unfortunately the ark was at times subject to this same abuse. The foremost example of this, recorded in 1 Samuel 4, occurred when the sons of Eli decided to take the ark into battle in an attempt to assure their victory over the Philistines. The theory was that a deity would not allow himself to be captured. But the Lord was not going to allow such manipulation. It was the Lord himself who directed the comings and goings of the ark. The ark was not taken captive, but instead departed from Israel (1 Sam. 4:21).

Likewise, when the time came, the ark returned to Israel on a cart without a driver (1 Sam. 6:10–16). There was even an abortive reinstallation attempt when the ark was not handled properly (2 Sam. 6:1–11), leaving David to wonder how the ark could come to him (v. 9). All of this demonstrated the autonomy of the ark; it operated only at the initiative of the Lord.

From the havoc wreaked in Philistia by the presence of the ark (1 Sam. 5), to the destruction in Israelite Beth Shemesh for profaning the ark when it returned from Philistia (1 Sam. 6:19–20), to the punishment of Uzzah when David was trying to bring the ark to Jerusalem (2 Sam. 6), the ark is seen to be much more than a relic. There was no other physical object that had the endowment of Yahweh's presence as the ark did. We can therefore see that the successful installation of the ark in Jerusalem at the beginning of David's reign was not simply a ritual, but designated the Lord's approval of the new era

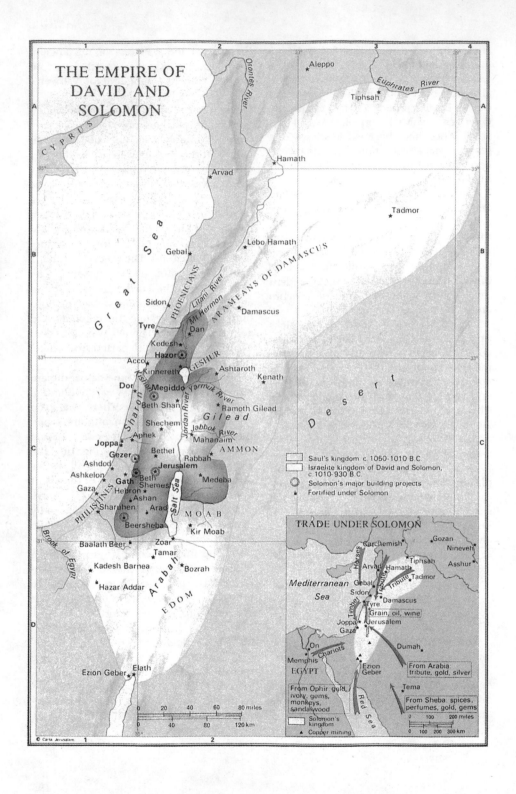

THE EMPIRE OF DAVID AND SOLOMON

Aleppo

Euphrates River

Tiphsah

Orontes River

CYPRUS

Hamath

Arvad

Tadmor

Great Sea

Lebo Hamath

Gebal

ARAMEANS OF DAMASCUS

Litani River

Sidon

PHOENICIANS

Mt Hermon

Damascus

Tyre

Dan

Kedesh

Hazor

Acco

Kinnereth

GESHUR

Ashtaroth

Kenath

Dor

Megiddo

Kishon River

Yarmuk River

Beth Shan

Gilead

Sharon

Shechem

Ramoth Gilead

Aphek

Jordan River

Jabbok River

Mahanaim

Joppa

Bethel

AMMON

Gezer

Rabbah

Ashdod

Jerusalem

Ashkelon

Beth Shemesh

Gath

Medeba

Gaza

Hebron

Ashan

PHILISTINES

Sharuhen

Arad

Salt Sea

M O A B

Beersheba

Kir Moab

Brook of Egypt

Baalath Beer

Zoar

Tamar

Arabah

Kadesh Barnea

Bozrah

Hazar Addar

E D O M

Ezion Geber

Elath

D e s e r t

☐ Saul's kingdom c. 1050-1010 B.C.
☐ Israelite kingdom of David and Solomon, c. 1010-930 B.C.
◎ Solomon's major building projects
• Fortified under Solomon

0   20   40   60   80 miles
0   40   80   120 km

© Carta, Jerusalem

TRADE UNDER SOLOMON

Carchemish

Gozan

Nineveh

Horses

Arvad

Hamath

Tiphsah

Asshur

Mediterranean Sea

Gebal

Tribute

Sidon

Tadmor

Timber

Tyre

Damascus

Joppa

Grain, oil, wine

Gaza

Jerusalem

Dumah

On

Chariots

Memphis

Ezion Geber

From Arabia: tribute, gold, silver

EGYPT

Tema

From Ophir: gold, ivory, gems, monkeys, sandalwood

Red Sea

From Sheba: spices, perfumes, gold, gems

☐ Solomon's kingdom
▲ Copper mining

0   100   200 miles
0 100 200 300 km

and his favor on David. This theology of the ark is supported in Psalm 78:54–72.[5]

Kingship

From a biblical standpoint, kingship over Israel was the prerogative of Yahweh (Judg. 8:23; 1 Sam. 8:7; 12:12). The function of the king was to maintain justice, both in a domestic sense in society and in an international sense by means of an effective military force. In the judges period the Lord raised up and empowered individuals to accomplish this purpose. The people of Samuel's day viewed kingship as a more permanent office that would eliminate the need to wait for the Lord to raise up a deliverer.

It was this perspective on kingship that caused the Lord to be angry. There was nothing intrinsically wrong with a monarchic form of government. We should remember that even as early as the Abrahamic covenant it was promised that kings would come from Abraham's family (Gen. 17:6). Likewise, the appointment of a king was anticipated in the book of Deuteronomy (17:14–20). The crime of the people, then, was not their request for a king, but their expectation that a human king could succeed where they believed that the Lord had failed.

Saul was chosen as the one who would "go out before us and fight our battles" (1 Sam. 8:20). That this view was ultimately flawed is shown in 1 Samuel 17 There we learn that Saul was unwilling to fight the Israelites' battles for them, so he offered a reward to anyone who would go out and fight Goliath.[6] In contrast, the true king—David—fully realized that it was the Lord who fought their battles for them (1 Sam. 17:37, 46). A proper monarchy still had to function as a theocracy rather than replace it. The king was to be viewed as the earthly head of God's theocratic kingdom.

The Davidic Covenant

As the central focus of the books of Samuel and a significant aspect of Old Testament theology in general, the covenant made with David merits some close examination. Several points require discussion: (1) What did the Lord promise David? (2) was the covenant conditional or unconditional? and (3) what impact did the covenant have on the rest of Israelite history?

What Did the Lord Promise David? First, the Lord promised to make David's name great (2 Sam. 7:9). This was similar to the promise made to Abraham (Gen. 12:2), so immediately a parallel is seen between these two great covenants. Second, the Lord promised a place in which he would plant Israel (2 Sam. 7:10), and again a parallel can be seen in the promise of land to Abraham. The further promise to make the land a place of security (2 Sam. 7:10–11) is reminiscent of the Lord's promise that he would curse those who cursed Abraham (Gen. 12:3). We conclude, therefore, that the first part of the Davidic covenant merely positions David in the line of Abraham and shows the subordination of that covenant to the Abrahamic covenant.

The departure from the Abrahamic covenant begins in 2 Samuel 7:12. There it is promised that David's descendant would be established on the throne after him. Though this was similar to the Abrahamic covenant in that it dealt with descendants, it was clearly a new development. David's successor would construct the temple that David had so much wanted to build (2 Sam. 7:1–7). The Lord would have a parental relationship with him that evokes discipline rather than rejection (2 Sam. 7:14). Furthermore, this successor would also have the opportunity to extend the terms of the covenant to his successor and so on.

---

[5]This section draws heavily on Campbell, *The Ark Narrative*, 199–210.
[6]This observation comes from Matt Condron.

The terminology used indicates that this covenant would better be described as open-ended rather than eternal. The word translated "forever" (*'olam*) in verses 13 and 16 is the same word used with regard to the covenant with Eli and his house in 1 Samuel 2:30. (For other important occurrences of this word, see 1 Samuel 1:22; Deuteronomy 15:17; and Jeremiah 17:4). Yet it is clear that that covenant could be cut off by the Lord in the case of insubordination. In fact, the Lord had done exactly that.

With this understood as an open-ended covenant, what was guaranteed to David was that his son would succeed him and would not be rejected (as Saul had been). The potential existed for continuance beyond that point, but there were no guarantees. That David understood the terms is indicated in 2 Samuel 7:29, when he prayed that the Lord might be pleased to extend the blessings continuously to his line.

Was the Covenant Conditional or Unconditional? It has often been noted that there are no conditions set on the covenant in 2 Samuel 7. This only means that the promises made to David were unconditional. However, as we have seen, the covenant was subject to periodic renewal, so we would expect that there must have been criteria by which it was decided whether or not the covenant would be renewed to the next generation. Indeed, such conditions became clearly evident when the covenant was discussed with Solomon. In 1 Kings 2:4, David instructed Solomon about the covenant; in 1 Kings 6:12 and 9:4–5, the Lord spoke to Solomon about it; and in 1 Kings 8:25, Solomon reported his understanding of the covenant in his prayer of dedication for the temple.

Conditions are clearly stated in each of these passages: "If you walk before me in integrity of heart and uprightness, as your father David did, and do all I command and observe my decrees and laws, I will establish your royal throne over Israel forever [i.e., indefinitely], as I promised David your father when I said, 'You shall never fail to have a man on the throne of Israel'" (1 Kings 9:4–5). The Bible states clearly, then, that David was promised unconditionally that his son would succeed him and serve a full term, but the terms beyond that were conditional on the conduct of his son. The potential existed for unlimited continuity. We suggest that there were no conditions placed on David because he had already met the conditions.

What Impact Did the Covenant Have on the Rest of Israelite History? When Solomon failed to meet the conditions of the covenant, did it become null and void? This issue is addressed in 1 Kings 11:32–39. Verses 34–35 imply that allowing Solomon to remain on the throne for all his days fulfilled the promise made to David. The Lord was free to take the kingdom from him and give it to someone else (see also 11:12–13). However, as an act of grace, not of obligation, the Lord promised to leave one tribe under the control of David's line (11:36). This was not required by the covenant arrangements in 2 Samuel 7, but was done for the sake of David. Although a new arrangement, somewhat similar to the one made with David, was made with Jeroboam (11:38), the promise of a continued "lamp" and the understanding that reduced control was only temporary (11:39) sustained the hope of the Davidic line through the ensuing centuries (2 Chron. 21:7; cf. Ps. 89).

The hope that someday a Davidic king would come who would meet the conditions and bring the restoration of the full Davidic covenant was the foundation for the messianic theology as we see it in the prophets. Jeremiah 33:14–22 may be the clearest statement of this, presenting a renewal of the Davidic covenant through an ideal Davidic king. Rather than a new David, this individual could be construed as a new Solomon, a shoot growing out of a cut-off stump (Isa. 11:1).

This view of the Davidic covenant helps us to understand the long history from the fall of Jerusalem even to the present, during which time there has been no Davidic king on the throne. The New Testament came to recognize Jesus as the one who would bring the renewal of the Davidic covenant. By meeting the conditions, the way was cleared for a truly eternal kingdom.

Assessment of Saul

Saul has often been viewed as a man tormented by jealousy and paranoia, and one can easily see how such an impression could be formed by reading the narratives of 1 Samuel 18–30. But Saul certainly had not always been so. In the earlier section of Samuel, Saul is portrayed as a shy, sincere, and likable sort. He is presented as just the kind of individual whom people would naturally choose as king. What brought the change? Why did Saul fail?

One factor identified by the narrative was the Spirit of the Lord. The Spirit came upon Saul (1 Sam. 10:10), empowering him for the task of kingship. Then this Spirit was replaced by an evil spirit from the Lord (1 Sam. 16:14). From that point on, Saul lost the empowering from God that was essential to be a successful king. Saul did not make good decisions, nor did he maintain justice.

But even before this time there were indications that all was not well. Saul's failure seemed to be fueled by his lack of spiritual sensibility. He was sincere but superficial. This was evident early on when Saul appeared totally unaware of Samuel's identity or function (1 Sam. 9:10–15), even though Samuel's home was barely five miles from Saul's. Further evidence is found in Saul's inability to recognize that a serious offense had been committed when he offered the sacrifice before battle (13:8–12) and when he failed to execute Agag (15:13–35). Even Jona-

than, his son, condemned Saul's lack of good sense (14:29).

An episode near the end of Saul's life—when he decided to use divination to gain information (1 Sam. 28)—suggests that he never quite understood some of the basic tenets of orthodox Israelite theology. It is true and to his credit that he did not worship other gods, but it is likely he failed to see how Yahweh was different from them. Since he was an Israelite of the eleventh century B.C., Saul's shortcoming is understandable and puts him in no different category from most of the populace or even the judges who had served Israel over the previous centuries. But that is exactly the point. A king had to be in a different category. Saul neither had nor acquired the theological sophistication to see and perform his role in proper perspective or to function in it successfully.

Assessment of David

Just as Saul has tended to be despised by ancient and modern readers of the Bible, so David has frequently been put high on the pedestal of a spiritual giant. Yet again we must be careful to offer a textually informed appraisal. In contrast to Saul, there can be no doubt of David's heart for God, spiritual sensitivity, and theological sophistication.

Yet David committed a number of serious errors. These came, not from ignorance of what is right, but from being impulsively driven by the need of the moment without reflecting on the consequences. His lies cost people their lives (1 Sam. 21); his temper jeopardized his royal destiny (1 Sam. 25); his duplicity led him to execute civilians (1 Sam. 27); his lust entangled him in a murderous plot (2 Sam. 11); his unwillingness to take firm disciplinary action contributed to the bloodshed within his family (2 Sam. 13–14); and his pride brought a pestilence that devastated the land (2 Sam. 24). Yet God chose David and affirmed that he walked in accordance to his law. David was loyal to the Lord and recognized when he had committed sin. A balanced view of David recognizes his godliness, but realizes that, like any of us, he was not immune to lapses in judgment.

Questions for Further Study and Discussion

1. What is the theological significance of viewing Samuel and Saul as transitional figures?
2. If Saul was not God's choice, how ought we to understand 1 Samuel 9–10?
3. How can a monarchic government function also as a theocracy? What might the resulting theology of kingship look like?
4. What are the significant points of continuity and discontinuity between the Abrahamic and Davidic covenants?
5. What is the contribution of Psalm 89 to our understanding of the Davidic covenant?

For Further Reading

Anderson, Arnold. *2 Samuel.* WBC. Vol. 11. Waco, Tex.: Word Books, 1989.

Baldwin, Joyce G. *1 and 2 Samuel.* TOTC. Downers Grove, Ill.: InterVarsity, 1988. Brief but insightful evangelical treatment.

Birch, B. *The Rise of the Israelite Monarchy.* Missoula, Mont.: Scholars Press, 1976.

Carlson, R. A. *David: The Chosen King.* Uppsala: Almqvist & Wiksell, 1964.

Dothan, Trude. *The Philistines and Their Material Culture.* New Haven: Yale University Press, 1982.

Driver, S. R. *Notes on the Hebrew Text and the Topography of the Books of Samuel.* Oxford: Clarendon Press, 1913.

Dumbrell, W. J. "The Content and Significance of the Books of Samuel: Their Place and Purpose Within the Former Prophets." *JETS* 33 (1990): 49–62. An excellent treatment of the purpose and themes of the books.

Fokkelman, J. P. *Narrative Art and Poetry in the Books of Samuel.* Assen, the Netherlands: Van Gorcum, 1986. Extremely detailed analysis of the narrative from a literary perspective.

Gordon, Robert P. *I and II Samuel: A Commentary.* Grand Rapids: Zondervan, 1986. Highly recommended evangelical treatment.

Gunn, David. *The Fate of King Saul.* Sheffield, England: JSOT Press, 1980.

——. *The Story of David.* Sheffield, England: JSOT Press, 1982.

Hertzberg, H. W. *1 and 2 Samuel.* Philadelphia: Westminster, 1964.

Ishida, T. *Studies in the Period of David and Solomon.* Winona Lake, Ind.: Eisenbrauns, 1983.

Klein, Ralph W. *1 Samuel.* WBC. Vol. 10. Waco, Tex.: Word Books, 1983.

Long, V. Phillips. *The Reign and Rejection of King Saul.* Atlanta: SBLDS 118 (1989).

McCarter, P. Kyle. *1 Samuel.* Garden City, N.Y.: Doubleday, 1980.

——. *2 Samuel.* Garden City, N.Y.: Doubleday, 1984. The best and most up-to-date commentaries on these books.

——. "The Apology of David." *JBL* 99 (1980): 489–504.

Miller, Patrick, and J. J.M . Roberts. *The Hand of the Lord.* Baltimore: Johns Hopkins University Press, 1977.

Whybray, R. N. *The Succession Narrative.* London: n.p., 1968.

Chapter 17

1–2 Kings

The books of Kings conclude the history of Israel from its origins in the clan of Abraham, as recorded in Genesis, to the fall of Jerusalem that ended Hebrew national independence. The two books are in the section of the Hebrew Bible designated "the Former Prophets" (Joshua, Judges, Samuel, and Kings), which comprises Israelite annals presenting a theological interpretation of Hebrew history in view of the covenant relationship with Yahweh and the attendant national blessings and curses conditioned by obedience to his covenant stipulations. The two books document the covenant history of Israel from King David's death and Solomon's succession to the throne through the demise of the divided kingdoms of Israel and Judah.

The separation of Kings from Samuel is somewhat artificial, as early Greek manuscripts of the Old Testament classify Samuel and Kings as *Basileiai* ("reigns, kingdoms") in four volumes: Samuel = First and Second Books of "Kingdoms," Kings = Third and Fourth Books of "Kingdoms." The division of Kings from one book in the Hebrew Old Testament into two books in the Greek Old Testament was simply a matter of convenience due to the length of the record. English Bibles have adopted the fourfold division of the history books in the manner of the Septuagint, but retained the Hebrew titles of Samuel and Kings.

The Writing of the Book

Like most of the Old Testament historical books, the authors of the Kings annals remain unknown. The Jewish tradition preserved in the Babylonian Talmud (*Baba Bathra* 15a) attributes the books of Kings to Jeremiah the prophet. This association may have been based on the similarities between Jeremiah 52 and 2 Kings 24–25. It has also been noted that the history recorded in Kings gives a prominent place to the lives of the Old Testament prophets and the accuracy of the prophetic word in relation to the Israelite and Judean monarchies. However, there is little concrete evidence for identifying the writer on the basis of context, theological theme, and purpose of writing.

Two distinct theories of the authorship and unity of the Kings history prevail among biblical scholars. The traditional view accepts Jewish lore and identifies the prophet Jeremiah as the compiler of

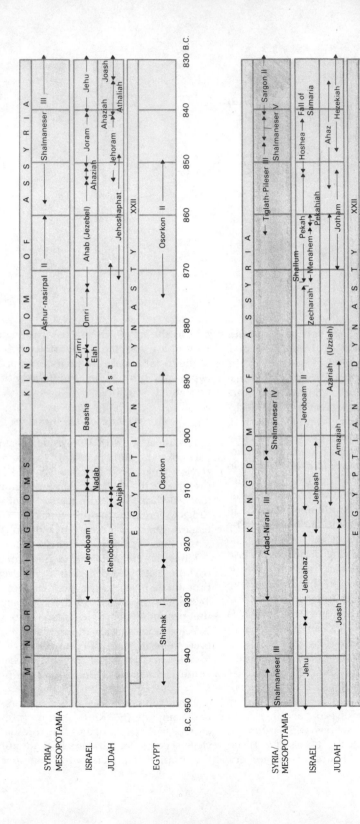

the books. Those who discount this tradition nonetheless argue that the books of Kings bear the mark of a single author or compiler who was an eyewitness of the fall of Jerusalem. It is suggested that this writer skillfully spliced many historical sources into a unified script to portray the two kingdoms' "covenant failure" and the divine rationale for foreign exile. Most supporters of this view of authorship admit that the two historical abstracts appended to 2 Kings (25:22–26, 27–30) are later additions to the book.

The alternative view generally understands 1–2 Kings to be the product of the so-called Deuteronomistic School. According to this view, this scribal school began sometime in the late eighth or early seventh century B.C. and was closely aligned with the southern monarchy. The literary activity of these "Deuteronomistic editors" was motivated by specific theological interests, namely, the purity of temple worship and the centrality of the temple cult in Jerusalem, the fulfillment of previous prophetic revelation related to Hebrew kingship, and the reality of the blessings-and-curses formulas of the book of Deuteronomy for the history of the Israelite monarchies.

According to this theory, Kings was composed in two redactions, or editorial stages: the first, labeled the preexilic stage of writing, was associated with the reforms of King Josiah in Judah around 600 B.C., the second, the exilic stage, was prompted by the release of King Jehoiachin from prison in Babylonian captivity and dated near 550 B.C. The first stage presumably explains the clear pro-Judahite bias in the Kings history.

Opponents of this view are quick to point out that actual evidence for the Deuteronomistic History hypothesis is scant. No consensus exists among its advocates as to the origin and extent of the History. The basic theological concerns identified with the Deuteronomistic School are in fact tenets of covenant teaching central to Hebrew theology from the time of Moses. Notable variances between Deuteronomy and Kings on points of thematic emphasis and style abound (e.g., Deuteronomy is hortatory or sermonic narrative and prescriptive whereas Kings is formulaic historical narrative and evaluative). Even more problematic is the widely acknowledged similarity between Deuteronomy's structure and the Hittite suzerain treaty of the second millennium B.C. All this makes the idea of a Deuteronomistic School in the time of Josiah most tenuous (see chap. 12).[1]

The unknown compiler of Kings makes reference to three specific sources used in assembling the "covenant history" of Israel's monarchies. The "Book of the Acts of Solomon" (1 Kings 11:41), the "Book of the Chronicles of the Kings of Israel" (mentioned seventeen times, e.g., 1 Kings 14:19), and the "Book of the Chronicles of the Kings of Judah" (mentioned fifteen times, e.g., 1 Kings 15:23) are all named as resources the reader might consult for verification or further information. These documents were probably official court histories kept by royal scribes (cf. 2 Sam. 8:16; 20:24–25) and very likely parallel the royal annals of the Mesopotamian civilizations of Assyria and Babylonia.

Biblical scholars have proposed that there are some other sources for Kings, though none are cited in the text:

---

[1]For a nontechnical discussion of the standard Deuteronomistic History and the "Deuteronomic Reformation," see B. W. Anderson, *Understanding the Old Testament*, 4th ed. (Englewood Cliffs, N.J.: Prentice–Hall, 1986). Recent studies on the antiquity and unity of Deuteronomy include R. Polzin, *Moses and the Deuteronomist* (New York: Harper & Row, 1980), and *Samuel and the Deuteronomist*. (New York: Harper & Row, 1989); and Gordon Wenham, "The Date of Deuteronomy: Linch-Pin of Old Testament Criticism." *Themelios* 10, no. 3 (1985): 15–20, and 11, no. 1 (1986): 15–18.

1. The "Succession Narrative" or "Court History of David" (a united monarchy narrative comprising 2 Samuel 9–20, with 1 Kings 1–2 usually associated with the present books of Samuel)

2. A conjectured "Dynasty of Ahab" record (perhaps contained within 1 Kings 16— 2 Kings 12)

3. The Elijah–Elisha prophetic cycle (contained within 1 Kings 17–19, 21; 2 Kings 1–13)

4. An Isaiah source (since Isaiah 36:1–39:8 is almost identical with 2 Kings 18:13– 20:19)

5. An independent prophetic source that contained biographies of Old Testament prophets associated with the Israelite monarchies (e.g., Ahijah, 1 Kings 11:29– 33 and 14:1–16; Micaiah, 1 Kings 21:13– 28; and certain unnamed prophets, 1 Kings 12–13 and 20:35–43).

Although hypothetical, these proposed contributions do fit the context of the Kings history, and they have gained widespread acceptance among biblical scholars as probable sources underlying the composition of Kings.

Given the available evidence, we do best to assign the books of Kings to an anonymous compiler-author of the sixth century B.C. Whether he was a prophet or not is uncertain, but he understood the covenantal nature of Israel's relationship to Yahweh and its implications for Hebrew history. The book was probably composed in Palestine sometime between the fall of Jerusalem (587/586 B.C.) and the decree of King Cyrus of Persia that permitted the Hebrews to return to their homeland (539 B.C.). It is possible that the book was composed in two stages. Most of the history of Hebrew kingship could have been completed between the fall of Jerusalem and the Babylonian reprisal for the assassination of the governor Gedaliah (a third deportation in 582 or 581 B.C., which was described in the first historical appendix, 2 Kings 25:22– 26 and Jer. 52:30). The final edition of the work may have been published sometime after the release of King Jehoiachin from

prison in Babylon by Nebuchadrezzar's successor, Evil-Merodach (ca. 562/561 B.C., reported in the second historical appendix, 2 Kings 25:27–30). A date of 550 B.C. appears reasonable for the completed Kings record.

Historical Background

The books of Kings represent a selective history of Israel from the closing days of King David's reign until the Babylonian conquest of Jerusalem. By way of chronology, 1–2 Kings documents the political history of Israel during the united monarchy, beginning about 970 B.C., through the Assyrian exile of the northern kingdom of Israel (722 B.C.) and the Babylonian exile of the southern kingdom of Judah (587/586 B.C.).

Two historical footnotes are attached to the end of 2 Kings. The first (25:22–26) recounts King Nebuchadrezzar's appointment of Gedaliah as the governor of Judah and Gedaliah's assassination by a group of Jewish conspirators led by one Ishmael sometime between 586 and 582 B.C. The second (25:27–30) records the release of King Jehoiachin from prison in Babylon after the death of King Nebuchadrezzar (March 562 or 561 B.C.).

The Kings history surveys the Israelite "golden age" of united empire under King Solomon, the split of the monarchy during the reign of Rehoboam, and the ebb and flow of the political and religious fortunes of the divided kingdoms of Israel and Judah until their collapse. Israelite interaction with the surrounding foreign powers is also integrated into the Kings account (fig. 17.1).

Archaeology has made significant contributions to the illumination and substantiation of the biblical record in 1–2 Kings. Specific discoveries include the unearthing of sites associated with the periods of both the united and the divided Hebrew monarchies (e.g., Megiddo, Hazor, Gezer, Samaria, Beersheba, Arad, Lachish, and Dan). Extrabiblical

Figure 17.1. Foreign Powers Mentioned in the Books of Kings

Egyptians	An unnamed pharaoh	1 Kings 3:1
	Shishak [945–924]	1 Kings 11:40
	So or Osorkon [726–715]	2 Kings 17:4
	Necho [609–594]	2 Kings 23:29–35
Aramaeans	Rezon [940–915]	1 Kings 11:23–25; 15:18
	Tabrimmon [915–900]	1 Kings 15:18
	Ben-Hadad I [900–860]	1 Kings 15:18, 20
	Ben-Hadad II[860–841]	1 Kings 20
	Hazael [841–806]	2 Kings 8:15
	Ben-Hadad III [806–770]	2 Kings 13:3
	Rezin [750–732]	2 Kings 15:37
Phoenicians	Ethbaal [874–853]	1 Kings 16:31
Edomites	Hadad [?]	1 Kings 11:14–22
Moabites	Mesha [853–841]	2 Kings 3:4ff.
Assyrians	Tiglath-Pileser III [745–727]	2 Kings 15:19–22
	Shalmaneser V [727–722]	2 Kings 17:3–6
	Sargon II [721–705]	Isaiah 20:1; 2 Kings 18:17
	Sennacherib [704–681]	2 Kings 18–19
Babylonians	Merodach-Baladan II [703]	2 Kings 20:12–13
	Nebuchadrezzar [604–562]	2 Kings 24–25
	Evil-Merodach [562–560]	2 Kings 25:27–30

inscriptional evidence from Assyria, Babylonia, and Syro-Palestine has greatly supplemented our understanding of the classical Hebrew language, both Hebrew and ancient Near Eastern chronology, and Hebrew political history, religious experience, social customs, and daily life. All this is disclosed in the context of ancient Near Eastern culture—e.g., the Moabite or Mesha Stone, the Black Obelisk of Shalmaneser III, the Sennacherib Prism, the Assyrian Annals, the Babylonian Chronicle, and the Lachish Letters (see fig. 17.2).

Two of the most outstanding archaeological finds related to the Kings account are the famous Siloam Inscription commemorating the completion of Hezekiah's water tunnel (cf. 2 Kings 20:20; 2 Chron. 32:2–4) and the Babylonian "prison-ration" tablets, dated to 595 and 570 B.C., which mention daily foodstuff allotments for exiled King Jehoiachin of Judah and his entourage (cf. 2 Kings 25:27).

Chronology of the Books

The United Monarchy

The Dynasty of Saul
Saul (?–1011)
Ish-Bosheth (1011–1009)

The Dynasty of David
David (1011–971)
Solomon (971–931)

Fixing a date for the beginning of kingship in Israel is complicated by the loss of a phrase during the process of manuscript transmission in 1 Samuel 13:1, which capsulizes the reign of Saul. The figures for both Saul's age at his ascension to the throne and the length of his reign have dropped out of the Hebrew text. The Septuagint inserts the number "thirty" and gives thirty-two years as the length of Saul's reign. Other Bible versions understand the length of Saul's reign as forty-two years, based on the apostle Paul's speech in Pisidian Antioch (cf. Acts 13:21).

Ish-Bosheth, or Esh-baal, Saul's fourth son, attempted to perpetuate the Saulide dynasty and waged civil war with David for two years as king of Israel (2 Sam. 2:1–11; 4:1–12; 1 Chron. 8:33; 9:39).

David's forty-year tenure as king of Israel may be divided into two phases. The first, his rival kingship over Judah, was centered in Hebron and lasted for seven years and six months (2 Sam. 2:11). The second began sometime after the assassination of Ish-Bosheth when David was installed as king of all Israel and reigned in Jerusalem for thirty-three years (2 Sam. 5:1–5).

Solomon's forty-year reign is usually touted as Israel's "golden age." After his death the monarchy split into the kingdoms of Israel and Judah (figs. 17.3a and 17.3b).

The Divided Kingdom

The Israelite (northern) kingdom was less stable politically than the Judahite (southern). Both its shorter duration as an independent nation (some 209 years) and the violence associated with succession to the throne attest this fact. The Kings historian characterized all nineteen—or twenty, if one includes Omri's rival Tibni (1 Kings 16:21)—rulers of Israel as "evil" because they perpetuated the "golden calf" cult of Jeroboam. An average reign for an Israelite monarch was but ten years, with nine different ruling families laying claim to the throne. Charisma was as useful as ancestry for ascending the throne, but it was no guarantee of preservation; seven kings were assassinated, one committed suicide, one was stricken by God, and one was deposed to Assyria.

The southern kingdom persisted about a century and a half longer (some 345 years). In contrast to Israel, the reigns of Judah's nineteen kings and one queen averaged more than seventeen years per monarch. The dynasty of David was sole claimant to the southern throne, enhancing political stability. Queen Athaliah's

Figure 17.2. The Moabite Stone (or Mesha Stele), discovered in Transjordan, that recounts military exploits during the reigns of kings Omri and Ahab and praises the Moabite god Chemosh. (*Carta, Jerusalem*)

reign of terror was the only interruption to Davidic succession. Yet Judah had its share of political intrigue, as five kings were assassinated, two were stricken by God, and three were exiled to foreign lands. The Kings historian reported that eight of Judah's rulers were "good" because they followed the example of David and obeyed Yahweh (i.e., Asa, Jehosaphat, Joash [Jehoash], Amaziah, Azariah [Uzziah], Jotham, Hezekiah, and Josiah).

The prophets and prophetesses of Yahweh served as the "conscience" of the king during the monarchical era. The prophetic voices influencing the throne as recorded in the books of Kings are arranged chronologically in figure 17.4.

Outline of the Books

I. King Solomon (1 Kings)
   A. His succession (1–2)
   B. His wisdom (3)
   C. His reign (4–11)
II. King Rehoboam (12:1–22)
III. Kingdoms of *Israel* and Judah from 931 to 853 B.C.
   A. *Jeroboam I* (12:22–14:20)
   B. Rehoboam (14:21–33)
   C. Abijah (15:1–8)
   D. Asa (15:9–24)
   E. *Nadab* (15:25–32)
   F. *Baasha* (15:33–16:7)
   G. *Elah* (16:8–14)
   H. *Zimri* (16:15–20)
   I. *Omri* (16:21–28)
   J. *Ahab* (16:29–34)
IV. Prophetic ministries of Elijah and Elisha
   A. Elijah and *King Ahab* (1 Kings 17:1–22:40)
   B. King Jehoshaphat (1 Kings 22:41–50)
   C. *King Ahaziah* (1 Kings 22:51–2 Kings 1:18)
   D. Elisha and *King Jehoram* (2 Kings 2:19–8:15)
V. Kingdoms of *Israel* and Judah from 852 to 722 B.C.
   A. Jehoram (8:16–24)
   B. Ahaziah (8:25–29)
   C. Jehu (9–10)
   D. Athaliah and Joash (11–12)
   E. Jehoahaz (13:1–9)
   F. Jehoash (13:10–25)
   G. Amaziah (14:1–22)
   H. *Jeroboam II* (14:23–29)
   I. Azariah (15:1–7)
   J. *Zechariah* (15:8–12)
   K. *Shallum* (15:13–16)
   L. *Menahem* (15:17–22)
   M. *Pekahiah* (15:23–26)
   N. *Pekah*/Assyrian campaign against Israel (15:27–31)
   O. Jotham (15:32–38)
   P. Ahaz (16)
   Q. *Hoshea* (17:1–6)
   R. Fall of Samaria to Assyria (17:4–41)
VI. Kingdom of Judah from 729 to 587/586 B.C.
   A. Hezekiah/Assyrian campaign against Judah (18–20)
   B. Manasseh (21:1–18)
   C. Amon (21:19–26)
   D. Josiah (22:1–23:30)
   E. Jehoahaz (23:31–35)
   F. Jehoiakim/First Babylonian invasion (23:36–24:7)
   G. Jehoiachin/Second Babylonian invasion (24:8–17)
   H. Zedekiah (24:18–20)
VII. Fall of Jerusalem to Babylonia (25:1–21)
VIII. Historical appendix A: Governor Gedaliah (25:22–26)
IX. Historical appendix B: Jehoiachin in exile (25:27–30)

Purpose and Message

The books of Kings relate the history of the Hebrew united and divided monarchies in their "covenant failure." The narrative focuses on the figures primarily responsible for covenant keeping in Israel—the kings and the prophets. The prophetic voice has a prominent place in the story of kingship because those divinely appointed messengers functioned as the conscience of the monarchies.

The history of the Hebrew nation is told through the lives of the Israelite and Judean kings as representatives of the nation, because the fortunes of the king and the plight of the people were entwined. Rebellion and disobedience in the form of idolatry and social injustice on the part of the king brought divine retribution on the nation in several forms, including oppression by the surrounding hostile powers, overthrow of the royal dynasties, and ultimately exile into foreign lands. Conversely, the blessing of Yahweh's favor in the form of peace, security, prosperity, and deliverance from foes rested upon the people of God when

Figure 17.3a. The Kings of Israel (Northern Kingdom)

	Hayes and Hooker	Thiele	Bright	Cogan and Tadmor
Jeroboam	927–906	931–910	922–901	928–907
Nadab	905–904	910–909	901–900	907–906
Baasha	903–882 [880]	909–886	900–877	906–883
Elah	881–880	886–885	877–876	883–882
Zimri	7 days	885	876	882
Omri	879–869	885–874	876–869	882–871
Ahab	868–854	874–853	869–850	873–852
Ahaziah	853–852	853–852	850–849	852–851
Jehoram (Joram)	851–840	852–841	849–843/2	851–842
Jehu	839–822	841–814	843/2–815	842–814
Jehoahaz	821–805	814–798	815–802	817–800
Jehoash (Joash)	804–789	798–782	802–786	800–784
Jeroboam II	788–748	793–753	786–746	789–748
Zechariah	6 months	753–752	746–745	748–747
Shallum	1 month	752	745	747
Menahem	746–737	752–742	745–737	747–737
Pekahiah	736–735	742–740	737–736	737–735
Pekah	734–731	752–732	736–732	735–732
Hoshea	730–722	732–722	732–724	732–724

Figure 17.3b. The Kings of Judah (Southern Kingdom)

Rehoboam	926–910	931–913	922–915	928–911
Abijah	909–907	913–911	915–913	911–908
Asa	906–878 [866]	911–870	913–873	908–867
Jehoshaphat	877–853	872–848	873–849	870–846
Jehoram	852–841	853–841	849–843	851–843
Ahaziah	840	841	843/2	843–842
Athaliah	839–833	841–835	842–837	842–836
Joash (Jehoash)	832–803 [793]	835–796	837–800	836–798
Amaziah	802–786 [774]	796–767	800–783	798–769
Azariah (Uzziah)	785–760 [734]	792–740	783–742	785–733
Jotham	759–744	750–732	750–735	758–743
Ahaz	743–728	735–716	735–715	743–727
Hezekiah	727–699	716–687	715–687/6	727–698
Manasseh	698–644	697–643	687/6–642	698–642
Amon	643–642	643–641	642–640	641–640
Josiah	641–610	641–609	640–609	639–609
Jehoahaz	3 months	609	609	609
Jehoiakim	608–598	609–598	609–598	608–598
Jehoiachin	3 months	598–597	598/7	597
Zedekiah	596–586	597–586	597–587	596–586

Chronologies for the Hebrew monarchies will vary between one and ten years depending on the source consulted. The sources cited are J. H. Hayes and P. K. Hooker, *A New Chronology for the Kings of Israel and Judah* (Atlanta: John Knox, 1988); E. R. Thiele, *The Mysterious Numbers of the Hebrew Kings*, rev. ed. (Grand Rapids: Zondervan, 1983); J. Bright, *A History of Israel*, 3d ed. (Philadelphia: Westminster, 1981); and M. Cogan and H. Tadmor, *Second Kings*, in AB, vol. 11 (Garden City, N.Y.: Doubleday, 1988). In addition, see J. Finegan, *Handbook of Biblical Chronology* (Princeton: Princeton Univ. Press, 1964); and W. R. Wifall, "The Chronology of the Divided Monarchy of Israel," *Zeitschrift für die Alttestamentliche Wissenschaft* 80 (1968): 319–37.

the king was obedient to the law of Moses (or instituted religious and social reforms after repentance and revival).

The accounts of the rival Hebrew monarchies in Kings also convey the story of alternative modes of kingship competing in Israel and Judah. Indeed, part of the purpose of the Kings history is the legitimization of the Davidic dynasty through the agency of the prophetic office, because the kingship covenant previously announced by Nathan sanctioned the tribe of Judah and the family of David as rightful heirs to the Hebrew throne (cf. 2 Sam. 7:1–17).

The most obvious purpose of the Kings narrative is to complete the written history of Hebrew kingship as a sequel to the books of Samuel. The record of Hebrew monarchies implicitly balances the notion of God's sovereign hand in Israel's covenant history and the reality of human freedom and accountability for those joined to him in covenant relationship. This prophetic view of Israelite history served both to admonish the king and people for past breaches in covenant keeping and to warn them of the grave consequences attached to continued disobedience to Yahweh's covenant stipulations. By the same token, 1–2 Kings contained a word of exhortation and offered a word of hope to Israel and Judah. God still ruled human history and remained faithful to his agreement with the Hebrews as his "elect" (cf. Ps. 115:5–6). The repeated references to fulfilled prophecy and the two historical appendices especially called to mind the Davidic covenant and God's promise to establish kingship forever in Israel.

Structure and Organization

The historical record of Hebrew kingship in 1–2 Kings is ordered chronologically from the accession of Solomon to the fall of Jerusalem, with some exceptions, given the writer's thematic interests. For instance, the summary account of Solomon's administration (1 Kings 4) appended to the narrative describing his great wisdom (1 Kings 3), the overview of Solomon's architectural achievements (1 Kings 5:1–7:12) prior to the dedication of the temple (1 Kings 8:62–66), certain events related to the reigns of Jeroboam I and Hezekiah (cf. 1 Kings 13 and 14:1–20; 2 Kings 18:7–19:37 and 20), and the condensed version of the prophetic ministries of Elijah and Elisha—all are thematically arranged.

The histories of the two monarchies are recounted simultaneously through the interweaving of concurrent kingships in the northern and southern kingdoms. Variations from this basic pattern include the cycle of Elijah and Elisha narratives that interrupt the chronicle of the Omri-Ahab and Jehoram dynasties (see the outline above).

The accounts of the ministries of Elijah and Elisha are important not only as representative biographies of the nonliterary prophetic movement, but also as tracts of faith commemorating key figures in a religious drama with cosmic implications. After his marriage to the Phoenician princess Jezebel, King Ahab installed Baalism as the official religion of the northern kingdom (1 Kings 21:25–26). In contrast, the biographies of Elijah and Elisha stand as monuments to uncompromised faith in Yahweh as the God of the Israelites (cf. 1 Kings 18:16–18). They served as living testimonies of God's covenant faithfulness to Israel and his supremacy over the Canaanite storm-god, Baal. Figure 17.5 shows how the ministries of Elijah and Elisha refuted popular understanding of Baal's basic character and power.

The Kings history is similar to other ancient annals in that it is a terse and formulaic reporting of the key political and military events of a given king's reign. The characteristic formula framing Judahite kingship includes (1) introduction of the king by name, the name of his father, and his accession (usually syn-

Figure 17.4. Prophets in the Monarchical Era

Prophets	Kings	Reference
Nathan	David, Solomon	1 Kings 1
Ahijah	Solomon, Jeroboam, Abijah	1 Kings 11:26–40; 14:1–16
"Man of God"	Jeroboam	1 Kings 13:1–10, 20–32
"Lying prophet"	Jeroboam	1 Kings 13:11–19
Jehu	Baasha, Elah	1 Kings 16:1–4, 12–13
Elijah	Ahab, Ahaziah, Jehoram	1 Kings 16:29–19:21; 2 Kings 1:1–2:12
Elisha	Ahaziah, Jehoram, Jehu, Jehoahaz, Jehoash	2 Kings 2:13–8:15; 13:14–21
Zedekiah and other "lying prophets"	Jehoshaphat, Ahab	1 Kings 22:5–12
Micaiah	Jehoshaphat, Ahab	1 Kings 22:13–28
Jonah	Jeroboam II	2 Kings 14:25
Isaiah	Hezekiah	2 Kings 19–20
Huldah	Josiah	2 Kings 22:14–20

chronized with the reign of his Israelite counterpart); (2) among the biographical details recited, the king's age at accession, the length of his reign, the name of the queen mother, Jerusalem as the capital city of the king, and an evaluation of the king's moral character and spiritual leadership; and (3) identification of additional sources documenting facts about the king's reign, a death and burial statement, and an announcement of his successor.

The biographical sketch for the Israelite kings typically contained the same information, except for the name of the royal city (usually Samaria) and the name of the queen mother (usually omitted).

Sandwiched into this selective rehearsing of a king's reign were prophetic speeches (1 Kings 18:20–29), direct discourse (2 Kings 18:19–27), wisdom sayings (1 Kings 20:11; 2 Kings 14:9), and poetic materials (1 Kings 22:17; 2 Kings 19:21–28).

Major Themes

Assessment of King Solomon

The reign of Solomon ushered in the "golden age" of Hebrew history. As king he was "loved by Yahweh" (the meaning of the name Jedidiah, cf. 2 Sam. 12:24–25), was divinely endowed with the gift of wisdom (1 Kings 3), brought unprecedented peace, wealth and prosperity, glory and splendor to Israel during his tenure on the throne (1 Kings 10:14–29), achieved international fame as a master builder (1 Kings 6:1–7:12) and sage (1 Kings 10:23), and was an ardent student of the "arts and sciences" (1 Kings 4:29–34).

Yet the latter years of Solomon's rule were marked by steady political decline and religious and moral decay. Ironically King Solomon fell prey to the seductions of the foreign women within the royal harem (1 Kings 11:1–3). Consumed by sensuality and materialism, he was unable to avoid the "snare" about which he had repeatedly warned others (e.g., Prov. 5:1–14; 7:6–27).

The Kings historian rightly attributes the division of Israel's united monarchy to Solomon's sin of idolatry (cf. 1 Kings 11:33, perhaps foreshadowed in 3:3). However, the collapse of the empire was merely the regrettable by-product of years of gross mismanagement of the affairs of state by Solomon.

The policies and programs instituted by Solomon contributing to the eventual split of the kingdom included (1) political alliance to foreign nations by marriage (1 Kings 3:1–2), (2) tendencies toward

Figure 17.5. Baal (of the Canaanites) vs. Elijah and Elisha (of Yahweh)

Baal, as storm-god, controls the rains.	Elijah commands drought (1 Kings 17:1).
Baal ensures agricultural fertility and bountiful harvests.	Israel experiences famine and drought, yet Elijah and Elisha provide grain and oil miraculously (2 Kings 4:1–7, 42–44).
Baal controls lightning and fire.	Elijah commands fire from heaven in the name of Yahweh (1 Kings 18:38; 2 Kings 1:10–12; 2:11).
Baal controls life and death.	Elijah and Elisha heal and raise the dead in the name of Yahweh (1 Kings 17:7–24; 2 Kings 4:8–37; 5:1–20).

From L. Bronner, *The Stories of Elijah and Elisha* (Leiden: Brill, 1968).

religious syncretism in an effort to appease both the Canaanite and the Hebrew populations in Palestine (i.e., participation in both the Hebrew religion associated with Yahweh and the Canaanite cults of Baal and other deities, 1 Kings 11:1–8), (3) the geographical realignment of Israel into twelve administrative districts in an attempt to erase old tribal boundaries and loyalties (a practice similar to "gerrymandering" in modern politics, cf. 1 Kings 4:7–19), (4) the proliferation of state bureaucracy (1 Kings 4:22–28), (5) lavish building projects that required slave labor, among both the non-Hebrew and the Hebrew residents of Israel (1 Kings 9:15–22; cf. 5:13–18 and 12:9–11), (6) the influx of pagan political and religious ideology in Jerusalem as a result of international trade and commerce (cf. 1 Kings 9:26–28; 10:22–29), and (7) the revolt of satellite states as Solomon's military power waned (with the ensuing loss of foreign tribute as revenue, offset by increased taxation of the Israelites, 1 Kings 11:9–25).

It is small wonder that when the split of the kingdom came at Rehoboam's accession, the rallying cry of the seceding ten northern tribes became "Now look after your own house, David" (1 Kings 12:16). The old tribal loyalties had resurfaced, and Israel was now a house divided.

Pre-Classical and Classical Prophecy

The development of Hebrew kingship prompted the emergence of parallel nonwriting (or pre-classical) and writing (or classical) prophetic movements in Israel. In the Elijah–Elisha cycle the Kings historian freely weaves a representative biography of the personalities and ministry of the nonwriting prophets to the Hebrew kingship.

Although somewhat artificial, some general distinctions have been made between the pre-classical and classical prophets. The former slightly predate the latter. The records of the the nonwriting prophets tend to be preserved in story form, including accounts of their miraculous signs confirming divine authority in their message. The ministry of the nonwriting prophets was essentially to the royal family, and their message was one of judgment and national destruction for covenant violation.

By contrast, the message of the classical (or writing) prophets (e.g., Hosea, Amos, Isaiah) was generally preserved in oracle form and was often underscored with symbolic behavior rather than a miraculous event. The prophets took their message to the political and religious leaders of the monarchies as well as to the populace. In some cases their prophetic ministry was even expanded to the surrounding nations (see chap. 27).

Dynastic Succession and Charismatic Leadership

The type of kingship associated with Judah is usually called the "dynastic succession" model of royal rule. In this, one family claimed (or in David's case is divinely granted, cf. 2 Samuel 7) royal authority in perpetuity. At a monarch's death the throne passed to his eldest son, thus establishing a sequence of kings from the same ruling family in dynastic succession for generations. Often the aging king appointed his successor or arranged a tenure of co-regency for his successor in order to guarantee the smooth transition of power.

By contrast, the northern kingdom of Israel combined the dynastic succession model of kingship with the charismatic leadership model typical of the era of the Hebrew judges. In this case God raised up a gifted and able male or female leader for Israel to respond to political and religious crises (e.g., Gideon in Judges 6–7). This leader was empowered by the Holy Spirit—an anointing often manifested by extraordinary physical strength, courage, and spiritual zeal. Charismatic leadership was not handed down from one generation to the next. Rather, God commissioned deliverers from different Hebrew tribes and families on the basis of inherent abilities, covenant faith, and historical circumstances. This random and sporadic investiture of charismatic leaders was no doubt designed to instill faith in Yahweh as the ultimate sovereign in Israel.

Unlike Judah, dynastic succession in Israel was conditional. The ruling family's claim to the throne was contingent on the king's obedience to the statutes of God, according to Ahijah's prophecy to Jeroboam (1 Kings 11:37–38). Failure to obey the commands of Yahweh brought a pronouncement of disaster on the royal household from the prophet of God (1 Kings 14:10–11). Often this prophetic curse included the charge to the succeeding king to systematically execute the family of his predecessor (sometimes resulting in little more than a "bloody coup" in later Israelite history, cf. 1 Kings 16:3–4, 11–12). God then appointed a new king "up from the dust" to lead the people of Israel through the word of his messenger (1 Kings 16:2).

The Golden Calf Cult

The Hebrew term for "calf" is a flexible word connoting any male or female animal of the bovine family. The New English Bible translates the word "bull-calf," and this is probably the best approximation of the identity of the molten gold symbols of a young bull worshiped by Israel during the wilderness wanderings (Exodus 32) and later in the northern kingdom of Israel under Jeroboam I (1 Kings 12).

All evidence seems to indicate that the Hebrews borrowed the bull-god symbol from the Egyptians, probably the Apis cult of Memphis. Apis was the sacred bull later known as the incarnation of the son of Osiris. This sacred bull was a fertility deity who gave life, health, and strength to the king and agricultural and reproductive fertility to the kingdom. It seems very likely that Jeroboam brought the bull-god symbol to Israel upon his return from exile in Egypt during the reign of Solomon (1 Kings 11:40).

Upon returning to Israel, Jeroboam possibly also combined elements of the Canaanite bull-god worship once he assumed the throne. This would explain the presence of both Canaanite and Egyptian motifs characteristic of the Israelite "calf cult."

The bull-gods that Jeroboam erected at the shrines of Dan and Bethel were not originally intended to represent idols of a foreign religious cult. Jeroboam's religious reforms were designed to win the allegiance of the Yahwists in the northern kingdom and thus prevent them from making the three annual pilgrimages to the temple in Jerusalem that was controlled by the southern kingdom. It is conjectured that these bull-calves of Jeroboam were intended to be symbols representing Yahweh in some way, perhaps as pedestals for his throne or platforms for his very presence. Thus the bulls, like the fortification of Shechem and the border cities near Judah, were a political stratagem used by Jeroboam to consolidate his power and authority in Israel.

Whatever the intital intentions of Jeroboam, it is clear that the golden bull-gods soon became identified with religious ideology and practice much different from Yahwism. Ahijah acknowledged the images as "other gods" (1 Kings 14:9), and by the time of Hosea the bull-gods were repudiated by the prophet as "idols, not God" (Hos. 8:4–5). By that time the golden bull became associated with the Canaanite fertility cult deities. The worship of the calf-god was thoroughly entwined with the rituals of Baalism (Hos. 10:5; 11:1–2; 13:1–2). The progression from false idols to fertility cult, astral worship, and human sacrifice in Israel is outlined in 2 Kings 17:15–17.

This breach of covenant not only brought an end to the dynasty of Jeroboam, but ultimately led to the dissolution of the nation of Israel by Yahweh in his anger (2 Kings 17:18).

Questions for Further Study and Discussion

1. What is the relationship between prophecy and kingship in 1–2 Kings?
2. What was the political and religious significance of the "bloody coups" for the northern kingdom of Israel?
3. What purpose do the accounts of Elijah and Elisha serve in the Kings' history?
4. How is Solomon's request for wisdom an example of "dramatic irony" on the part of the Kings historian?
5. In light of George E. Mendenhall's article on "The Monarchy," discuss the problem of mixing politics and religion in the Hebrew monarchy.
6. Examine 1–2 Kings for instances when the Old Testament historian recorded Yahweh's intervention in human history. How does this compare with the nature and frequency of divine interventions in Joshua, Judges, and Samuel?
7. Discuss whether the Solomon narrative (1 Kings 1–11) is the Hebrew equivalent of the literary form known as "epic drama" (cf. Leland Ryken, *How to Read the Bible as Literature* [Grand Rapids: Zondervan, 1984], 78–81).

For Further Reading

Albright, William F. *The Biblical Period from Abraham to Ezra.* New York: Harper & Row, 1963.

Bright, John. *A History of Israel*. 3d ed. Philadelphia: Westminster, 1981. The definitive sourcebook for the history of Israel from the patriarchal to the Maccabean periods.

Cogan, M. *Imperialism and Religion: Assyria, Judah and Israel in the Eighth and Seventh Centuries B.C.E.* Missoula, Mont.: Scholars Press, 1974.

Cogan, M., and Hayim Tadmor. *Second Kings*. AB. Vol. 11. Garden City, N.Y.: Doubleday, 1988.

de Vaux, Roland. *Ancient Israel*. New York: McGraw-Hill, 1961. Valuable discussions on the civil institutions of ancient Israel (e.g., the Israelite concept of the state, kingship, royal officials, administration of the kingdom).

De Vries, S. J. *First Kings*. WBC. Vol. 12. Waco, Tex.: Word Books, 1985. Extensive bibliographies. View of 1 Kings as the product of the Deuteronomistic School.

Gray, J. *First and Second Kings*. 2d ed. OTL. Philadelphia: Westminster, 1970. An indispensable commentary for its treatment of the Hebrew text, historical background, and annalistic sources of Kings, though his reconstructionist Hebrew history is not always agreeable to evangelicals.

Hayes, John H., and J. Maxwell Miller. *Israelite and Judean History*. Philadelphia: Westminster, 1977.

Hobbs, T. R. *Second Kings*. WBC. Vol. 13. Waco, Tex.: Word Books, 1985. Extensive bibliographies. View of 2 Kings as "tragic drama" from a single author interpreting Israelite and Judean covenant failure.

Holladay, J. "Assyrian Statecraft and the Prophets of Israel." *HTR* 63 (1970): 29–51.

Jones, G. H. *First and Second Kings*. NCBC. Grand Rapids: Eerdmans, 1984.

Malamat, M. "Origins of Statecraft in the Israelite Monarchy." *BA* 28 (1965): 34–65.

_____. "The Last Kings of Judah and the Fall of Jerusalem." *Israel Exploration Journal* 18 (1968): 137–56.

Mendenhall, George E. "The Monarchy." *Interpretation* 29 (1975): 155–70. A provocative socioeconomic analysis of Hebrew kingship during the united monarchy, addressing the problems of political and religious syncretism in Israelite society.

Merrill, E. H. *Kingdom of Priests: A History of Old Testament Israel*. Grand Rapids: Baker, 1987. Comprehensive history of Israel from an evangelical perspective, weak on the literary nature of Hebrew historiography, with spare bibliography.

Newsome, J. D., ed. *A Synoptic Harmony of Samuel, Kings, and Chronicles*. Grand Rapids: Baker, 1986.

Patterson, R. D., and H. J. Austel. "First and Second Kings." *EBC*. Grand Rapids: Zondervan, 1988. 4:3–300. Largely descriptive commentary with theological emphasis, containing useful historical information in the "Notes" sections.

Payne, David F. *Kingdoms of the Lord*. Grand Rapids: Eerdmans, 1981.

Porten, B. "The Structure and Theme of the Solomon Narrative." *Hebrew Union College Annual* (1967): 93–128.

Thomas, D. W., ed. *Documents from Old Testament Times*. New York: Harper & Row, 1961.

Walton, John H. *Ancient Israelite Literature in Its Cultural Context*. Grand Rapids: Zondervan, 1989.

Wiseman, Donald J. *Chronicles of the Chaldean Kings*. London: British Museum, 1956.

_____, ed. *Peoples of Old Testament Times*. Oxford: Clarendon, 1973.

Wood, Leon J. *A Survey of Israel's History*. Rev. ed. David O'Brien, ed. Grand Rapids: Zondervan, 1986.

_____. *Israel's United Monarchy*. Grand Rapids: Baker, 1979. Detailed study of the Hebrew united monarchy, including in-depth discussions of the reigns and personalities of Saul, David, and Solomon.

Yamauchi, Edwin M. *Foes from the Northern Frontier*. Grand Rapids: Baker, 1982.

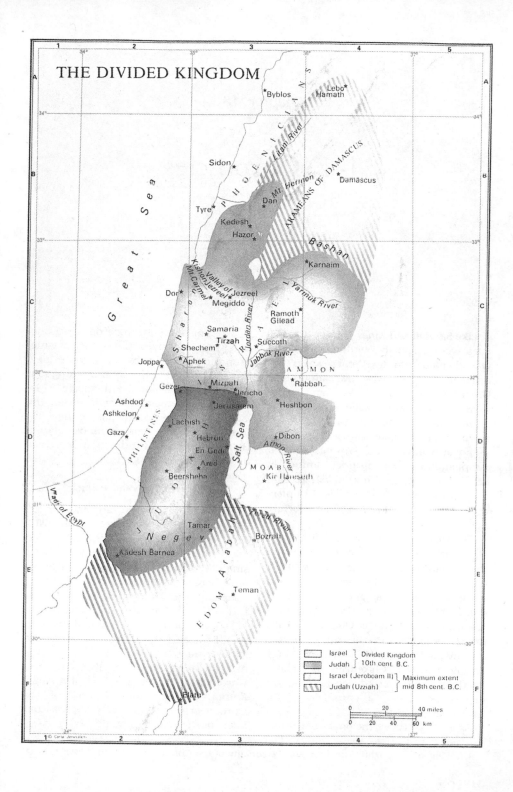

THE DIVIDED KINGDOM

Byblos

Lebo
Hamath

PHOENICIANS

Litani River

Sidon

Mt. Hermon

Damascus

Tyre

Dan

ARAMEANS OF DAMASCUS

Kedesh

Hazor

Bashan

Great Sea

Karnaim

Valley of Jezreel

Kishon River

Mt. Carmel

Dor

Jezreel

Yarmuk River

Megiddo

ISRAEL

Ramoth
Gilead

Jordan River

Samaria

Tirzah

Succoth

Shechem

Jabbok River

Joppa

Aphek

AMMON

Gezer

Mizpah

Rabbah

Jericho

Ashdod

Jerusalem

Heshbon

Ashkelon

Lachish

PHILISTINES

Hebron

Dibon

Gaza

En Gedi

Arad

Salt Sea

Arnon River

JUDAH

MOAB

Beersheba

Kir Hareseth

Wadi of Egypt

Tamar

Zered River

Negev

Bozrah

Kadesh Barnea

EDOM

Arabah

Teman

Elath

Israel	Divided Kingdom
Judah	10th cent. B.C.
Israel (Jeroboam II)	Maximum extent
Judah (Uzziah)	mid 8th cent. B.C.

0   20   40 miles

0   20   40   60 km

© Carta, Jerusalem

Chapter 18

1–2 Chronicles

Like Samuel and Kings, 1 and 2 Chronicles were originally one book. The text was divided into two books when the original Hebrew was translated into Greek. Chronicles follows Ezra–Nehemiah in the Hebrew Bible, suggesting it either was accepted into the Old Testament canon at a later date or was viewed as an appendix to the Writings since it supplemented the histories found in Samuel and Kings. The English version follows the Greek Old Testament in placing Chronicles after Kings and before Ezra–Nehemiah.

The Hebrew title of the book is literally "the words of the days," or "the events" of the monarchies. While the Hebrew title is characteristically taken from the first verse, here the title phrase is actually found in 1 Chronicles 27:24. The books are called "The Things Omitted" in the Greek Septuagint, that is, things passed over by the histories of Samuel and Kings. The English title "Chronicles" is a shortened form of Jerome's suggestion that the history be called "a chronicle of the whole divine history."

As literary history, the books of Chronicles supplement the records of Samuel and Kings, rehearsing the history of Israel from the patriarchs (by way of genealogy) through the fall of the southern kingdom of Judah to Babylon. As theological history, the Chronicles concentrate on the legitimization of priestly and levitical authority and the contributions of the Hebrew united and Judahite monarchies to the religious life of Israel.

The Writing of the Book

The Chronicles are an anonymous composition. The stylistic and linguistic similarities with Ezra–Nehemiah have led many biblical scholars to conclude that a single "Chronicler" was responsible for all four books. Based on Jewish tradition assigning the Chronicles to Ezra the scribe (Babylonian Talmud: *Baba Bathra* 15a), W. F. Albright championed the view that Ezra and the Chronicler were the same person.[1] At one time there was overwhelming consensus that Ezra and Chronicles were the product of a single author, but the identification of the Chronicler with Ezra the scribe has not been universally accepted.

[1] Cf. William F. Albright, "The Date and Personality of the Chronicler," *JBL* 40 (1921): 104–14.

Furthermore, during the last two decades biblical researchers have questioned the literary ties between Chronicles and Ezra–Nehemiah. Today most Old Testament scholars recognize the unity of the two books of Chronicles but separate them from the books of Ezra and Nehemiah, citing thematic differences such as the lack of Davidic messianism, "second exodus" overtones, and the "pan–Israelite" emphasis in the latter. At present it seems best to recognize the books of Chronicles as a unified composition written by an unknown chronicler. Given the writer's pointed interests in the temple and its priestly and levitical personnel, it is likely that he was a priest or Levite employed in the service of the temple. The exact relationship of the Chronicler's writings to the books of Ezra–Nehemiah remains an open question.

The Chronicles are, with Ezra–Nehemiah, probably the latest books of the Old Testament in respect to the date of composition. The date of their writing has been placed anywhere from the reforms of the prophets Haggai and Zechariah (ca. 515 B.C.) to well into the Greek period (with dates ranging from 300 to 160 B.C.). The last dated event in Chronicles is the record of Cyrus' decree permitting the Hebrews to return to Palestine from the exile in Babylonia (ca. 538 B.C.; cf. 2 Chron. 36:22–23). However, if Zerubbabel's genealogy in 1 Chronicles 3:17–21 is ordered in a chronological sequence, this internal evidence moves the date of Chronicles nearer 400 B.C. than 500 B.C. The widely acknowledged associations between Chronicles and Ezra–Nehemiah (whether or not Ezra is identified as the Chronicler) also suggest a date near 400 B.C. (see chap. 19).

Considerable attention has been given to the numerous sources used by the Chronicler in compiling his history of Israel. In addition to extensive appeal to canonical sources such as the Pentateuch and Samuel–Kings, the Chronicler explicitly cites noncanonical records and

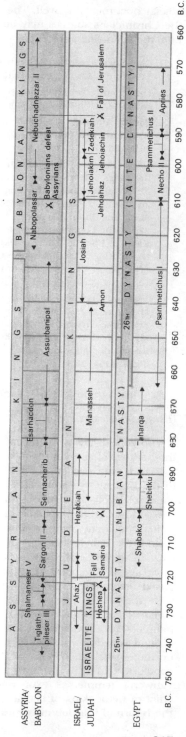

official documents as well. The array of the Chronicler's sources may be divided into the following categories:

1. Genealogical records (1 Chron. 4:33; 5:17; 7:9, 40; 9:1, 22; 2 Chron. 12:15)

2. Letters and official documents (1 Chron. 28:11–12; 2 Chron. 32:17–20; 36:22–23)

3. Poems, prayers, speeches, and songs (1 Chron. 16:8–36; 29:10–22; 2 Chron. 29:30; 35:25)

4. Other histories, including the Book of the Kings of Israel and Judah (2 Chron. 27:7; 36:8), the Book of the Kings of Judah and Israel (2 Chron. 16:11; 25:26; 28:26; 32:32), the Chronicles of David (1 Chron. 27:24), the Commentary on the Book of Kings (2 Chron. 24:27), the Directions of David, King of Israel, and the Directions of Solomon His Son (2 Chron. 35:4)

5. Prophetic writings, including the Chronicles of Samuel, Nathan, and Gad (1 Chron. 29:29), the Prophecy of Ahijah and the Visions of Iddo the Seer (2 Chron. 9:29), and the Records of Shemaiah, Jehu and Isaiah (2 Chron. 12:15; 20:34; 32:32).

Background to the Book

Historical Background

The genealogies of 1 Chronicles trace the heritage of covenant faith from Adam to David, with particular attention given to the Hebrew patriarchs and the twelve sons of Jacob. The actual history addressed in Chronicles spans the Hebrew united monarchy from the close of Saul's reign to the Babylonian captivity of Judah (ca. 1020–586 B.C.). The accounts of David's and Solomon's kingships are focused on events and figures associated with the ark of the covenant and the construction and dedication of Yahweh's temple. The Chronicler's history of the divided kingdoms virtually ignores the northern side. The books of Chronicles conclude with this same emphasis on Yahweh's temple, as expressed in the edict of Cyrus, king of Persia, permitting the return of the Hebrew exiles to Pales-

tine to rebuild the edifice (ca. 538 B.C.; cf. 2 Chron. 36:22–23).

The backdrop for the writing of Chronicles was the postexilic period of Hebrew history. Whether the books are assigned to 500, 400, or 300 B.C., the conditions in postexilic Jerusalem were essentially the same. Judah remained an insignificant and struggling backwater province throughout the entire Persian period and into the Greek period. Hebrew national and political life was overshadowed by the pagan "super empires" of Persia and Greece, and Hebrew religion was challenged by the rival temple and worship of the Samaritans, the great cult of Ahura Mazda, and the Greek mystery religions.

The despair over the apparent failure of Zerubbabel and others to inaugurate the messianic kingdom in Judah as predicted by Haggai and Zechariah, coupled with the disappointment of the seemingly shallow and short-lived religious reforms carried out by Ezra and Nehemiah, engendered the Chronicler's "theology of hope," couched in the annals of Israelite history. The present distress would one day give way to the restoration of Israel, according to the theocratic ideal expressed in Chronicles. The second exodus envisioned by Zechariah was delayed, but not canceled. The kingdom of God would eventually break into human history, and Jerusalem would indeed be established as the political and religious focal point of the nations (cf. Zech. 8:1–8; 14:9–21).

Historical Reliability

The Chronicler exercised considerable freedom in selecting, arranging, and modifying the extensive source material from which he composed his history. This condition has led many biblical scholars to disparage the integrity and historical reliability of the Chronicler's record. In fact, the accuracy of the book of Chronicles has been called into question more than any other book of the Old Testament except Genesis.

Specific accusations leveled against the validity of the Chronicler's history include the bias shown in omitting material from Kings related to the northern kingdom; the neglect of the sins of David and the apostasy of Solomon and the overemphasis on the favorable character traits and deeds of the Hebrew kings; the tendency to modify material from Samuel and Kings in moralizing and theologizing terms (e.g., 2 Sam. 24:1 compared with 1 Chron. 21:1); the addition (or fabrication?) of historical material not found in Samuel–Kings (e.g., 2 Chron. 33:18–20); and the inclination to enlarge (or exaggerate?) the numbers reported in the parallel accounts of Samuel–Kings (e.g., 2 Sam. 23:8 compared with 1 Chron. 11:11).

Scholars who are committed to the trustworthiness of the books of Chronicles as a historical document have responded to these charges with a variety of arguments. For example, the Chronicler's omission of materials from Samuel–Kings should not be construed as intentional deception. Rather, the writer assumed the reader's working knowledge of the earlier Hebrew histories. This allowed the compiler carefully and deliberately to select only those excerpts that had direct bearing on the religious life of the Israelite community or promoted the theology of hope the Chronicles were intended to convey.

Likewise, the skeptical stance toward the historical accuracy of the Chronicler's "additions" to the history of the Hebrew kings is unwarranted, given his wide appeal to sources outside the Samuel–Kings narrative. Many of these sources are identified by name and may actually represent older traditions than those underlying the Samuel–Kings narratives. More important, archaeological data and extrabiblical historical materials have cor-

roborated the Chronicler's record in those instances where the different sources converge or overlap.[2]

Several explanations have been adduced for the Chronicler's "embellishment" of the numbers and statistics taken from the parallel Samuel–Kings narrative (fig. 18.1). Clearly, some of the numerical discrepancies can be attributed to scribal error (e.g., 2 Kings 24:8; 2 Chron. 36:9), while others reflect a rounding off of totals rather than exact readings. It is even suggested that the Chronicler may have introduced the ancient equivalent of allowing for inflation in his numerology (since he was writing some five hundred years after the time of David). Last, it is possible that portions of the books of Chronicles may have been based on older (and perhaps more reliable?) Hebrew texts and manuscripts than the Samuel–Kings accounts.

The Chronicler's modification of the historical narratives of Samuel–Kings proves more difficult to assess. Here the concept of Yahweh's continuing and progressive revelation in Hebrew history and the consequent development of Hebrew theology aids our understanding of the Chronicler's use of the ancient sources. For instance, 2 Samuel 24:1 states that the Lord incited David to take a census, whereas the parallel account in 1 Chronicles 21:1 attributes the instigation to Satan. This seems an unmistakable example of later development of Hebrew theology regarding "the agency of Satan" in Yahweh's sovereign design to test motive and punish sin among humanity (cf. Job 1–2 and Daniel's expansion of Hebrew understanding of resurrection from the dead, in 12:2 based on Isaiah 26:19).

Another category of conflicting reports in the Samuel–Kings and Chronicles parallels finds its solution by analogy to the New Testament quotation of Old Testament passages. Even as the New Testa-

---

[2]Cf. J. M. Myers, *First Chronicles*, in AB, vol. 12 (Garden City, N.Y.: Doubleday, 1965), 240; and S. Japhet, "The Historical Reliability of Chronicles," *JSOT* 33 (1985): 83–107.

Figure 18.1. Numbers in Chronicles That Disagree with Old Testament Parallels

	Higher	Lower		Parallel passage	Evaluation of Chronicles
a)		1 Chron. 11:11	300 slain by Jashobeam, not 800	2 Sam. 23:8	Scribal error
b)	18:4		Hadadezer's 1000 chariots and 7000 horsemen, not 1000 chariots and 700 horsemen	8:4	Correct
c)	19:18a		7000 Syrian charioteers slain, not 700	10:18a	Correct
d)		19:18b	and 40,000 foot soldiers, not horsemen	10:18b	Correct
e)	21:5a		Israel's 1,100,000 troops, not 800,000	24:9a	Different objects
f)		21:5b	Judah's 470,000 troops, not 500,000	24:9b	More precise
g)		21:12	Three years of famine, not seven	24:13	Correct
h)	21:25		Oran paid 600 gold shekels, not 50 silver	24:24	Different objects
i, j)	2 Chron 2:2, 18		3,600 to supervise temple construction, not 3,300	1 Kings 5:16	Different method of reckoning
k)	2:10		20,000 baths of oil to Hiram's woodmen, not 20 kors (= 200 baths)	5:11	Different objects
l)	3:15		Temple pillars 35 cubits, not 18	7:15	Scribal error
m)	4:5		Sea holding 3000 baths, not 2000	7:26	Scribal error
n)		8:10	250 chief officers for building temple, not 550	9:23	Different method of reckoning
o)	8:18		450 gold talents from Ophir, not 420	9:28	Correct or scribal error
p)		9:16 (Chron. is same)	300 gold bekas per shield, not 3 minas	10:17	Different method of reckoning
q)	9:25		4000 stalls for horses, not 40,000	4:26	Correct
r)	22:2		Ahaziah king at age 42 years, not 22	2 Kings 8:26	Scribal error
s)	36:9		Jehoiachin king at age 8, not 18	2 Kings 24:8	Scribal error

Compared with its parallels, Chronicles is the same once, higher 10 times, and lower 7 times.

Total disagreements: 19 (j repeats i) out of 213 parallel numbers.

From J. Barton Payne, "1, 2 Chronicles," *EBC*, vol. 4 (Grand Rapids: Zondervan, 1988), 561.

ment writers both quoted and interpreted Old Testament texts for specific theological purposes, so also the Old Testament writers, in a similar vein under the inspiration of the Holy Spirit, made appeal to earlier documents at their disposal. This kind of interpretive quotation has sometimes been labeled "inspired exposition." Apparently God is free to interpret his own record![3]

Outline of the Books

Purpose and Message

The Chronicler's message centers on the Israelite united monarchy and the crucial roles played by David and Solomon in establishing and maintaining the temple of Yahweh in Jerusalem. The Chronicler highlighted David's kingship to communicate the centrality of the temple, while Solomon's success was directly tied to the proper worship of Yahweh. The new exodus and restoration of the Hebrew community predicted by the prophets could only have been realized as postexilic Jerusalem imitated the model of past faithfulness and obedience in worship and service to the Lord of Hosts.

For postexilic Jerusalem, the Chronicler's message concerned Yahweh's elec-

---

[3]Cf. S. Lewis Johnson, *The Old Testament in the New* (Grand Rapids: Zondervan, 1980), 39–51. For a discussion of variant readings in the Samuel–Kings and Chronicles parallels, see J. Barton Payne, "Validity of Numbers in Chronicles," *Near East Archaeological Society Bulletin* 11 (1978): 5–58, and the pertinent sections of his commentary, "1, 2 Chronicles," in *EBC* (Grand Rapids: Zondervan, 1988), 4:302–562. For a more strained approach harmonizing these variant readings, see Gleason L. Archer, *Encyclopedia of Bible Difficulties* (Grand Rapids: Zondervan, 1982).

tion of Israel (which was implicit in the extensive genealogical catalogs at the beginning of the work) and the providential activity of Yahweh in Israel's history (as seen in the accounts of David's and Solomon's reigns, e.g., 1 Chronicles 18–20). The rehearsal of Israel's past became a guarantee of God's continued intervention to accomplish his covenant purposes for the Hebrews as his special possession (e.g., 1 Chron. 17:16–27).

The historical review of Judah (the southern kingdom) underscored another key message for postexilic Jerusalem, namely, the divine retribution associated with the blessings and curses conditioning Yahweh's covenant with Israel. Respect for divinely appointed authority figures and obedience to the covenant stipulations were absolutely essential for the success of the postexilic community.

The Chronicler conveyed several important purposes in his reassessment of Israelite history. First, his emphasis on Davidic and Solomonic kingship was intended to demonstrate the continuity between preexilic and postexilic Hebrew history. More important, the kingdom of Judah was set forth as the rightful heir of the covenant promises made by Yahweh to the "true Israel." The incorporation of the genealogies of Jacob's descendants reminded Israel of her former tribal unity and called the whole people once again to band together in covenant unity before Yahweh. Only by faithful adherence to Yahweh's covenant stipulations could Israel recapture the glory days of the past delineated by the Chronicler.

The Chronicler's fixation with the Davidic and Solomonic kingdoms was more than a plea for the return of "the good old days" of Israel's history. Those kingships served as models of an "ideal" Israel under theocratic rule for the present community. The centrality of the temple, the proper worship of Yahweh, and the authoritative role of the priests and Levites in the temple service demonstrated the supremacy of the Hebrew God and the superiority of Hebrew religion in the face of encroaching paganism.

Finally, the Chronicler's history engendered hope in postexilic Jerusalem by assuring the present community that the sovereign Lord of Hosts, having been active during the reigns of David and Solomon, would continue providentially to intervene in Hebrew history to accomplish the prophetic vision of Zion as the political and religious center of the nations (cf. Zech. 14:12–21).

Structure and Organization

The Chronicler was a theologian and religious teacher as well as a historian. His interpretive and apologetic history of Israel was specifically designed to awaken covenant faith and evoke hope in the midst of the beleagered postexilic Hebrew community. The macro-structure of Chronicles highlights this hopefulness in that the first book opens with the building of the first temple (with Gentile help) and the second book closes with the edict of a Gentile king commanding the building of the second temple (cf. 2 Chron. 36:22–23). An expanded version of this so-called Cyrus colophon in 2 Chronicles appears in Ezra 1:1–3, thus bridging the history of the Chronicler and the books of Ezra–Nehemiah. The connection of the Ezra–Nehemiah reforms with Israel's "temple history" reinforces the Chronicler's theocratic ideal and the expectation of a "new exodus."

It is assumed that the historical materials of Chronicles were spliced in at least two distinct stages. The original work comprising 1 Chronicles 10–2 Chronicles 34 was probably compiled in conjunction with the prophetic ministries of Haggai and Zechariah about 500 B.C. The second stage of the history saw the addition of 1 Chronicles 1–9 and 2 Chronicles 35–36 in association with the reforms of Ezra and Nehemiah (ca. 450–400 B.C.).

The genealogies of 1 Chronicles 1–9

preface the review of the Davidic and Solomonic monarchies (1 Chron. 10–2 Chron. 9). Unfortunately the Chronicler's catalog of obscure (and unpronounceable!) Hebrew names is better known as antidote for insomnia than for its literary merit. Yet the section does make important contributions to the overall plan and purpose of the book. While the genealogies call attention to the unity of "all Israel" (a necessary theme after the fall of the divided monarchies), the particular focus rests on Judah and Levi—the tribes of kingship and priesthood in Israel. There is also a sense in which the recitation of the Hebrew lineages confirmed Yahweh's election of Israel and legitimized the royal and priestly leadership of the nation, since they are carefully traced to Abraham, the patriarch chosen by Yahweh, the covenant-making God.

The section outlining the reigns of Saul and David presents a study of contrasts. Saul's disobedience, failures, and neglect of the ark of the covenant serve as a foil for David's faithfulness, triumphs, and careful attention to the ark of God (1 Chron. 10–29). In keeping with the Chronicler's interest in the "theocratic ideal," David's return of the ark to Jerusalem, his preparations for building the temple, and his arrangements for the temple service take center stage in the narrative (chaps. 13–17, 21–29).

The history of Judah, the southern kingdom and successor to the Davidic covenant, concludes the Chronicler's narrative (2 Chron. 10–36). Special attention is given to the "good" kings of Judah, exalting those whose reforms directly affected Yahweh's temple and Hebrew worship. In fact, even as David is cast as a "second Moses" and Solomon a "second Joshua," so kings Hezekiah and Josiah are idealized as Davidic and Solomonic type figures because of their cleansing of the temple and restoration of proper worship in Jerusalem. This concluding section also emphasizes the importance of the prophetic word for maintaining covenant

relationship with Yahweh and the reality of divine retribution in light of the blessings and curses appended to the covenant code (cf. 2 Chron. 36:17–21).

Rebellion before God and disobedience to his covenant jeopardized not only Hebrew kingship, but also the temple of Yahweh. King Nebuchadrezzar of Babylon taught Judah this dreadful and costly lesson when he terminated Davidic kingship, deported the Hebrews to Babylonia from the land of covenant promise, and laid waste the temple of the Lord of Hosts—the very symbol of Yahweh's theocratic presence and rule among the Israelites. And yet, just as the word of the Lord was fulfilled in Judah's defeat and exile, so it was fulfilled in the promise of return and restoration under King Cyrus (cf. 2 Chron. 36:21–22).

Major Themes

Worship in the Old Testament

The worship of Yahweh was an integral part of the Chronicler's theocratic ideal for postexilic Jerusalem. The accounts of Hebrew worship in the Chronicles are representative of the wide range of Israelite religious experiences and are useful as a summary statement of Old Testament worship in general.

Although the Chronicler emphasized the former, he clearly understood the importance of both corporate and individual worship (1 Chron. 15:29; 2 Chron. 31:20–21). The Chronicler also offered examples of ordered and priestly led worship in keeping with the liturgical calendar (2 Chron. 35:1–19) and the spontaneous response to Yahweh's steadfast lovingkindness (1 Chron. 16:28–34; cf. Hezekiah's celebration of two Passovers in one year!—2 Chron. 30:13–22). The private aspect of worship is more implicit in Chronicles (e.g., 1 Chron. 16:23–27), but gatherings for public worship abound in the two books (1 Chron. 16:36; 29:9; 2 Chron. 5:2–14; 6:3–11). More important, the Chronicler recognized that unfeigned worship of Yahweh was motivated both by the fear of the Lord (2 Chron. 6:31, 33) and out of love for God with a whole heart (1 Chron. 28:9; 2 Chron. 19:9).

That the Chronicler valued worship as an attitude, a condition of human heart and mind, is demonstrated in the discussion that follows (cf. 1 Chron. 16:10–11; 28:9; 2 Chron. 15:12, 15). In addition, worship for the Hebrews was an active experience before God, not passive. Acknowledging the worth of God and giving him the reverence and adoration due his name through gestures, acts, and movements included drink offerings and libations, the presentation of sacrifices and burnt offerings, bowing down, burning incense, giving thank offerings and votive gifts, prayer in various postures, fasting, ritual washing and cleansing, dancing, tearing of the clothes (in repentance), feasting, and observing the great religious festivals (cf. 2 Chron. 29:12–19, 31–36; 32:13–27; 34:12, 22–28).

Of special importance to the Chronicler was the significance of worship as word. There was the word of oath taking, of praise and thanksgiving, of prayer, joyful song, confession, and liturgical responses by the Hebrew congregation (cf. 1 Chron. 15:29; 16:4, 9, 23, 36, 40; 17:16–27; 2 Chron. 15:15). Of course, preeminent in the Chronicler's theocratic ideal was worship as a place, namely, the temple of Yahweh (cf. 2 Chron. 5:2–7:10). Yet he also acknowledged that true worship of the Lord God of Israel is not limited by the bounds of time or the confines of a "sacred place" (cf. 2 Chron. 6:12–23).

Finally, some mention of the personnel directing Hebrew worship is pertinent, because the Chronicler devotes large sections of his record to the role of the priests and Levites in the religious life of the nation. The priests and Levites were the Old Testament equivalent of a professional clergy, since they were supported by the offerings and votive gifts of the people. They were consecrated solely to the service of God through the institution of Yahweh's sanctuary.

Basically the priests were the descendants of Aaron, Israel's first high priest, and they were responsible for guiding and representing the Hebrews in the sacrificial and festival worship. The rest of the Levites (i.e., the other male members of the tribe of Levi) were assigned to specific tasks related to the maintenance and services of the Lord's sanctuary.

The Chronicler gave special attention to the role of the priests and Levites for several reasons. The building of the temple and a permanent home for the ark of the covenant meant that the Levites no longer had to serve as porters for the sanctuary (cf. Num. 4:1–49). In the Chronicles the Levites were assigned, by royal decree, to service guilds such as singer, musician, gatekeeper, and teacher of the law and judge (cf. 1 Chron. 24–26; 2 Chron. 17:7–9; 19:11).

This centralization of responsibility for official religion in the office of the Hebrew king sanctioned priestly and levitical authority, and when kingship ceased in Israel they became the heirs of divine administration. The Chronicler assumed that the priests and Levites would bring in the new order and reestablish theocracy in Israel. However, Malachi and others censured the priesthood and the Levites for their failure to keep their sacred trust before God (e.g., Mal. 1:6–2:9). According to the New Testament and a Christian perspective of Hebrew history, this only served to heighten the priesthood of Jesus, the surety of a better covenant (Heb. 7:20–22).

The Chronicler's Vocabulary

The Chronicler's repeated use of standard expressions related to the attitude and intent of the heart of individual and corporate Israel indicate that he understood divine retribution as more than the mere mechanical cause-and-effect concept of "sowing and reaping."[4]

First, the emphasis on "repentance" in Chronicles reveals that the compiler knew the mercy of Yahweh and his gracious capacity for turning from wrath in the face of genuine repentance by his people (e.g., 2 Chron. 12:6–12; cf. Exod. 32:11–14). Illustrations of past repentance are recited as concrete examples assuring God's continued response of merciful forgiveness to those who return to him (2 Chron. 15:4; 32:26). The enduring lovingkindness of Yahweh is exhibited in his willingness to receive those from the apostate northern kingdom who turn to him (2 Chron. 30:6–9), and even the wicked Manasseh experienced Yahweh's mercy (2 Chron. 33:12–14).

Other stock phrases giving evidence of the Chronicler's awareness of the need to balance the "inner" and "outer" factors of true religion include his attention to "rejoicing and serving God with a pure heart" (e.g., 1 Chron. 28:9; 29:9, 19; 2 Chron. 16:9), "generous giving and faithfulness" (e.g., 1 Chron. 29:1–9, 14, 17; 2 Chron. 19:9), and "thankful and joyful celebration and worship" (e.g., 1 Chron. 16:4, 7; 23:30; 29:13).

Typology

Formal typology is one aspect of biblical hermeneutics or interpretation. Typology is a method of exegesis that establishes historical correspondence between Old Testament events, persons, or objects and ideas and similar New Testament events, persons, or objects and ideas by way of foreshadowing or prototype. Usually the Old Testament correspondent is identified as the "type"; the New Testament correspondent expressing the Old Testament truth in a greater way is regarded as the "antetype." For example, the writer of the epistle to the Hebrews understands the priesthood of Melchizedek in the Old Testament (Gen. 14:17–24; Ps. 110:4) as the prototype of the superior priesthood of Jesus Christ (Heb. 7:1–22). In the same manner, the tabernacle (and later the temple) were symbols or types of the new covenant, foreshadowing Christ's eternal sacrifice (Heb. 9:6–14).

In describing the preparations for and construction of the temple of Yahweh, the Chronicler portrayed David as a "second" Moses and Solomon as a "second" Joshua.[5] Specifically, David was prohibited from completing the temple even as Moses was denied the privilege of leading the Hebrews into the land of covenant promise (cf. Num. 20:2–11; 1 Chron. 22:8).

Likewise, Solomon exemplified Joshua in that both were chosen as successors privately and given public acclaim, both received popular support without political or military resistance, both were exalted by God, and both led the Hebrew people into an era of "rest" and "blessing." Finally, both Joshua and Solomon were given the same charge in assuming their leadership roles, a charge "to be strong and courageous" (Deut. 31:6; cf. 1 Chron. 22:13), because "the LORD goes before you" (Deut. 31:6, 8, 23; Josh. 1:5, 9; cf. 1 Chron. 22:11, 16), and "he will never leave you nor forsake you" (Deut. 31:6, 8; Josh 1:5, 9; cf. 1 Chron. 28:20).

---

[4]Often the Chronicler used the repetition of key vocabulary items to logically connect a variety of literary sources. Cf. Andrew E. Hill, "Patchwork Poetry or Reasoned Verse: Connective Structure in 1 Chronicles xvi," *VT* 33 (1983): 97–101.

[5]Cf. R. B. Dillard, "The Chronicler's Solomon," *Westminster Theological Journal* 43 (1981): 207–18; and H. G. M. Williamson, "The Accession of Solomon in the Book of Chronicles," *VT* 26 (1976): 351–61.

Questions for Further Study and Discussion

1. Why is King David the "ideal" king for the Chronicler?
2. What are the strengths and weaknesses of typology as a method of biblical interpretation?
3. How are we to explain the variant readings between the parallel passages of Samuel–Kings and Chronicles? What does this mean for the doctrine of biblical inspiration?
4. What significance does the Chronicler's rehearsal of Israelite history have for individual and corporate Christianity today?

For Further Reading

Ackroyd, P. R. "History and Theology in the Writings of the Chronicler." *Concordia Theological Monthly* 38 (1967): 501–15.

———. *Israel Under Babylonia and Persia*. Oxford: Clarendon Press, 1970.

———. "The Chronicler as Exegete." *JSOT* 2 (1977): 2–32.

Braun, R. "Chronicles, Ezra and Nehemiah: Theology and Literary History." In *Studies in the Historical Books of the Old Testament*. J. A. Emerton, ed. *VT Supplement* 30. Leiden: Brill, 1979. 52–64.

———. *1 Chronicles*. WBC. Vol. 14. Waco, Tex.: Word Books, 1986. Useful discussion of theological themes, with extensive bibliographies.

Bright, John. *A History of Israel*. 3d ed. Philadelphia: Westminster, 1981.

Coggins, R. J. *The First and Second Books of Chronicles*. CBC. Cambridge: Cambridge University Press, 1976.

DeVries, S. J. *1–2 Chronicles*. FOTL. Vol. 11. Grand Rapids: Eerdmans, 1989. Helpful analysis of each literary unit in Chronicles by structure, genre, setting, and intention according to form criticism, but undermines historical integrity of the books.

Dillard, R. B. *2 Chronicles*. WBC. Vol. 15. Waco, Tex.: Word Books, 1987. Extensive bibliographies.

Dumbrell, W. J. "The Purpose of the Books of Chronicles." *JETS* 27 (1984): 257–66. Concise statement of theological and historical purposes in Chronicles.

Fishbane, M. *Biblical Interpretation in Ancient Israel*. Oxford: Clarendon Press, 1985. 385–407. Penetrating discussion of historical exegesis in the Chronicler.

Freedman, David N. "The Chronicler's Purpose." *CBQ* 23 (1961). 436–42.

Goldingay, John. "The Chronicler as Theologian." *Biblical Theology Bulletin* 5 (1975): 99–121.

Japhet, S. "The Historical Reliability of Chronicles." *JSOT* 33 (1985): 83–107.

McConville, J. G. *I and II Chronicles*. DSB–OT. Philadelphia: Westminster, 1984. Insightful contemporary application of the Chronicler's message.

Myers, J. *First Chronicles*. AB. Vol. 12. Garden City, N.Y.: Doubleday, 1965.

———. *Second Chronicles*. AB. Vol. 13. Garden City, N.Y.: Doubleday, 1965.

Newsome, J. D. "Toward a New Understanding of the Chronicler and His Purposes." *JBL* 94 (1975): 204–17.

———. *A Synoptic Harmony of Samuel, Kings, and Chronicles*. Grand Rapids: Baker, 1987.

Payne, J. Barton. "1, 2 Chronicles." *EBC*. Vol. 4. Grand Rapids: Zondervan, 1988. Helpful discussions of the variant readings between the parallels of Samuel–Kings and Chronicles.

Sailhamer, John. *First and Second Chronicles*. EvBC. Chicago: Moody Press, 1983.

Wilcock, M. *The Message of Chronicles.* Downers Grove, Ill.: InterVarsity, 1987.

Williamson, H. G. M. *I and II Chronicles.* NCB. Grand Rapids: Eerdmans, 1982. Informative introductory section on the Chronicler and his sources.

_____. *Israel and the Book of Chronicles.* Cambridge: Cambridge University Press, 1977.

Wilson, R. R. "Between 'Azel' and 'Azel': Interpreting the Biblical Genealogies." *BA* 42 (1979): 11–22.

_____. *Genealogy and History in the Biblical World.* New Haven: Yale University Press, 1977.

Chapter 19

Ezra–Nehemiah

Ezra and Nehemiah were contemporaneous reformers of the postexilic period. Like their earlier compatriots, Haggai and Zechariah, they had complementary ministries in Jerusalem of both a physical and spiritual nature. Ezra, a priest and scribe who was skilled in the law of Moses, is best remembered for his reading of the Torah to the postexilic community and the consequent religious revival it inspired (cf. Neh. 8:1–12). Nehemiah is well known for the administrative skill he demonstrated in organizing the restoration community to repair and rebuild a large section of the wall of Jerusalem destroyed by the Babylonians in 587 B.C.

Both men came to Jerusalem from Susa in Persia during the reign of Artaxerxes I (464–424 B.C.), and both were members of some standing in Persian royal circles. By virtue of his levitical pedigree, it is suggested that Ezra held a position akin to secretary or counsel for Jewish affairs in the royal cabinet (cf. Ezra 7:1–6), while Nehemiah was a cupbearer to King Artaxerxes (Neh. 1:11; 2:1–2). Prayerful zeal for the plight of the restoration community in Jerusalem motivated both men to journey to Palestine from Persia. Their efforts to reform the religious, social, and economic life of the Hebrew city were rooted in a nationalistic sense of pride for the tradition of the Hebrew forefathers (e.g., Neh. 2:3) and a genuine concern for the reputation of the name of Yahweh in the midst of pagan opposition (cf. Ezra 9:1–15; Neh.. 1:4–11).

Ezra and Nehemiah form a single book in the Hebrew Old Testament. Along with other historical books like Samuel, Kings, and Chronicles, it was divided into two books in the Septuagint. Ezra and Nehemiah actually comprise the second volume of a two-part work by the Chronicler that presents a theological interpretation of Hebrew history. The two parts of Chronicles constitute the first volume of that history. The books of Ezra and Nehemiah are placed after 1–2 Chronicles in the Greek, Latin, and English Bibles. The reverse order in the Hebrew Old Testament may indicate the order of acceptance of the books into the canon.

Two books in the Old Testament Apocrypha are titled "Esdras," the Greek equivalent of the name Ezra. The apocryphal 2 Esdras is an apocalyptic work of the late first century A.D. and has no connection with the historical Ezra. The apocryphal 1 Esdras dates to the second century B.C.

and includes material from 2 Chronicles 35:1 through the end of the Old Testament book of Ezra, with Nehemiah 7:73–8:12 forming an appendix to the text. Though the book of 1 Esdras has some value for comparative analysis with the biblical texts of Chronicles, Ezra, and Nehemiah, the book is generally considered inferior both historically and theologically to the Old Testament book of Ezra (e.g., 1 Esd. 5:70–73).

The Writing of the Book

The majority view among biblical scholars today, regardless of theological persuasion, attributes the combined books of Ezra–Nehemiah to the postexilic Chronicler. It is assumed that this compiler of the books of Chronicles also edited the book of Ezra–Nehemiah, because 2 Chronicles 36:22–23 constitutes a colophon, or closing inscription, presupposing the introductory verses of Ezra 1:1–2. Jewish tradition identified Ezra the scribe as the Chronicler of the postexilic history narrated in 1–2 Chronicles and Ezra–Nehemiah (so Babylonian Talmud: *Baba Bathra* 15a). Although this idea remains a possibility, most interpreters regard the Chronicler as an anonymous compiler of Hebrew historical sources.

The actual composition of the books of Ezra–Nehemiah occurred in stages and was probably completed around 400 B.C. The sequence of writing and compiling may be outlined as follows: (1) Ezra and Nehemiah draft individual memoirs (ca. 440–420 B.C.); (2) the Chronicler combines the Ezra and Nehemiah memoir sources, deliberately interweaving the materials; (3) the Chronicler adds the Sheshbazzar/Zerubbabel narrative to form a prologue, or introduction, to the Ezra and Nehemiah autobiographies.

The intentional interweaving of memoir materials from Ezra and Nehemiah has raised some suspicion among certain biblical scholars as to the integrity of the compiler and the historical accuracy of

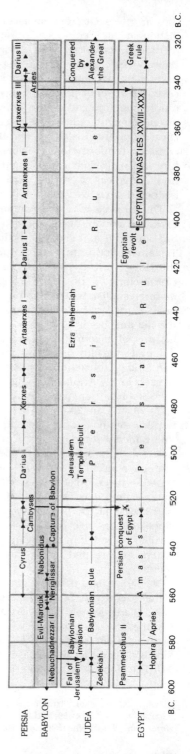

the narratives. Far from being confused or dishonest, the compiler artfully documented a very pragmatic history of the Hebrew restoration period, emphasizing particular religious themes (including covenant keeping, purity of religion, separation from foreigners, etc.). This practice of conveying a religious message in the context of the historical narrative is a common tendency in Old Testament history writing (see chap. 18). The phenomenon is typical of ancient Near Eastern historical texts as well.[1]

This approach to the composition of Ezra–Nehemiah need not compromise the biblical teaching of the writing of Old Testament Scripture by the inspiration of the Holy Spirit (2 Tim. 3:16), in that the Chronicler was no doubt inspired in a manner similar to Luke as he compiled early Christian historical sources about the life and teaching of Jesus Christ into his gospel account (cf. Luke 1:1–4).

Ezra is one of two Old Testament books containing substantial sections of text written in the Aramaic language and not the Hebrew language (Ezra 4:8–6:18; 7:12–26; cf. Dan. 2:4–7:28). By the Persian period, Aramaic was the language of international trade, making it difficult to determine the place of writing for the memoir sources of Ezra and Nehemiah. Whether he completed his work in Persia or Palestine, it is certain the Chronicler had access to the Persian state archives, since the Aramaic passages of Ezra appear to be verbatim quotations of official letters and related governmental documents.

It is possible, therefore, that Ezra or Nehemiah wrote the Sheshbazzar/Zerubbabel narrative or that they aided the Chronicler's effort in some way by virtue of their good standing with the Persian king Artaxerxes (cf. Ezra 7:1–10; Neh. 1:1–11). The Hebrew adaptation of the Cyrus edict (Ezra 1:2–4) and the Artaxerxes letter (Ezra 7:12–26) suggest that the final compilation of the books of Ezra–Nehemiah occurred in Palestine.

It is widely recognized that the Chronicler's compilation of Ezra and Nehemiah was motivated by keen theological interests. The more important themes identified as shaping the careful construction of the literature include covenant renewal in the restoration community (e.g., Neh. 8–10), the rebuilding and dedication of the wall of Jerusalem as a physical demonstration of God's fulfillment of earlier promises to restore the remnant of Israel (cf. Zeph. 3:19–20; Hag. 2:1–9), the historical and theological continuity between preexilic and postexilic Israel (e.g., the institution of the temple, installation of officers like the priests and temple servants, and the importance of the Torah of Moses as the guide for Hebrew religious and social life), and the legitimacy of the restoration community's religious, political, economic, and social agenda as God's elect (cf. Neh. 9:32–37).

The Background

The Jerusalem of Ezra and Nehemiah was little different from the Jerusalem to which Haggai and Zechariah had prophesied some sixty years earlier (ca. 520–518 B.C.; cf. Ezra 5:1–2). The reconstructed second temple was a mere shadow of the magnificent edifice erected by Solomon (cf. Ezra 3:12). Rather than inspiring the hope of covenant restoration in the community, the building served only as a monument to remind the people of messianic expectations dashed by the reality of Medo-Persian domination. Indeed, the promise of Yahweh to make Jerusalem an ensign among the nations was all but forgotten as postexilic Judah subsisted on the remote fringes of a pagan empire that

[1]Cf. S. Mowinckel, "Israelite Historiography," *Annual of the Swedish Theological Institute in Jerusalem* 2 (1963): 4–26; and J. J. Finkelstein, "Mesopotamian Historiography," *Proceedings of the American Philosophical Society* 107 (1963): 461–72.

and Nehemiah arrived on the scene in the mid-fifth century B.C. Nehemiah's initiative to repair the walls of Jerusalem was undertaken against considerable resistance offered by a coalition of local alien enemies, including Sanballat (the Samaritan governor in control of the province of Judah), Tobiah (called "the Ammonite" and an influential member of the Jerusalem aristocracy by marriage), Geshem (an Arab official), and the Arabs, Ammonites, and citizens of Ashdod (Neh. 4:1–9).

The earlier call to religious and social reform by the prophets Haggai and Zechariah had seemingly little impact. Only a generation later, the prophet Malachi (ca. 500–475 B.C.) rebuked the people for breaking faith with Yahweh and called them to repentance and covenant renewal. Now, two generations after Malachi's preaching, Ezra and Nehemiah encountered similar religious apathy and social decay. In fact, the reforms instituted by Ezra and Nehemiah were directed against many of the very same covenant violations decried by the postexilic prophets, including spiritual apathy and improper worship, social injustice, divorce, intermarriage with foreign women, neglect of the tithe, moral laxity, and abuse of authority on the part of the priests.

The exact date of Ezra's arrival in Jerusalem remains a disputed issue among biblical scholars. Three options for the chronology of Ezra's ministry in Jerusalem have emerged from the discussion. According to the traditional view, Ezra arrived in Jerusalem during the seventh year of King Artaxerxes I, or 458 B.C. (cf. Ezra 7:8).

The second view is established on the assumption that the text of Ezra 7:8 has been corrupted through the course of manuscript transmission and should read the "thirty-seventh" year of Artaxerxes I, instead of the "seventh." This would place Ezra in Jerusalem in 428 B.C. during Nehemiah's second term as governor of the community. This view is the

Figure 19.1. The Cylinder of Cyrus, a clay cylinder giving the royal decree that allowed conquered peoples (such as the Hebrews, although they are not specifically mentioned) to return to their homelands. (*Trustees of the British Museum*)

was at that time controlling most of the known world (cf. Hag. 2:20–23).

In fact, the very existence of the Hebrew postexilic community appeared threatened by the opposition of hostile enemies surrounding Jerusalem during the governorship of Zerubbabel (ca. 520 B.C.; cf. Ezra 4:1–5; 5:1–7). This situation had not really changed by the time Ezra weakest of the three, because the hypothesis of a textual error in Ezra 7:8 has absolutely no supporting textual-critical evidence.

The third view argues that Ezra ministered in Jerusalem during the seventh year of the reign of King Artaxerxes II, or 398 B.C. This chronology for Ezra's arrival presumes that the priest Johanan mentioned in Nehemiah 12:22 and the high priest Johanan named in the late fifth-century Elephantine papyri are to be identified as the same person.

Despite the problems encountered in reconciling the relationship of Ezra and Nehemiah as co-reformers in Jerusalem, the traditional view continues to provide the most satisfactory explanation of all the evidence. A date of 458 B.C. for Ezra's arrival in Jerusalem is preferred. The date for Nehemiah's arrival in the postexilic community is firmly fixed during the twentieth year of the reign of King Artaxerxes I, or 445 B.C.

The following chronology of the later postexilic period of Hebrew history supplements the timeline on page 229:

Xerxes, king of Persia, 485–465 B.C.
Esther (1:1), ?
Artaxerxes I, king of Persia, 464–424 B.C.
Return of Ezra (Ezra 7:7–8), 458 B.C.
Return of Nehemiah (Neh. 2:1–2), 445 B.C.
Nehemiah governor of Judah for twelve years (Neh. 13:6), 445–433 B.C.
Nehemiah's second governorship (Neh. 13:7), after 433 B.C. to ?[2]
Darius II, king of Persia, 423–405 B.C.
Artaxerxes II Mnemon, king of Persia, 404–359 B.C.
Chronicler compiles 1–2 Chronicles and Ezra–Nehemiah, ca. 400–380 B.C.

Outline of the Books

I. Sheshbazzar and Zerubbabel narrative (Ezra)
A. Decree of Cyrus (1:1–4)

B. Return under Sheshbazzar (1:5–11)
C. Return under Zerubbabel (2)
D. Rebuilding the altar and temple (3–6)
II. Ezra's memoirs: Part 1 (Ezra)
A. Ezra's arrival (7–8)
B. Ezra's religious and social reforms (9–10)
III. Nehemiah's memoirs: Part 1 (Nehemiah)
A. Nehemiah's arrival (1–2)
B. Rebuilding the wall of Jerusalem despite opposition (3–4)
C. Nehemiah's economic and social reforms (5:1–7:73a)
IV. Ezra's memoirs: Part 2 (Nehemiah)
A. Reading of the law (7:73b–8:12)
B. Worship and confession (8:13–9:37)
C. Covenant renewal (9:38–10:39)
V. Nehemiah's memoirs: Part 2 (Nehemiah)
A. Repopulation of Jerusalem (11:1–12:26)
B. Dedication of the wall of Jerusalem (12:27–13:3)
C. Further social and religious reforms of Nehemiah (13:4–31)

Purpose and Message

Historical

The books of Ezra and Nehemiah report a significant portion of the history of Israel during the postexilic, or Persian, period. The highly stylized account documents key events roughly from the edict of Cyrus in 538 B.C. to Nehemiah's second governorship in Jerusalem (sometime after 433 B.C.). This record of restoration history is contained in three distinct literary sources, as explained earlier. The essential content of the three sources

---

[2]Nehemiah's second governorship must have ended by 407 B.C., since the Egyptian Elephantine papyri of the fifth century B.C. mention a certain Bagoas as governor of Judah.

may be summarized as follows: (1) the Hebrew return to Jerusalem from Babylonian exile, including the rebuilding of the altar and temple; (2) the arrival and ministry of Ezra, including the religious reform of of the community based on the law of Moses; and (3) the arrival and ministry of Nehemiah, including the repair of the Jerusalem wall and continued social and economic reform in the restoration community.

The purpose of the books is historiographic, given the need to preserve the record of the return to Jerusalem from Babylonia by the former Hebrew exiles. As such, the accounts highlighted Yahweh's faithfulness and thereby instilled hope in postexilic Israel by demonstrating God's providential working among human kings and governments. Theologically the narrative recounting the ministries of Ezra and Nehemiah in restoring Jerusalem physically and spiritually affirmed Yahweh's promises to renew the remnant of Israel. Pragmatically speaking, the history probably stems from the obligation placed on Ezra and Nehemiah to chronicle their experiences for the sake of reporting to the king of Persia. The covenant renewal ideas discussed below reinforce this understanding of the basic purpose of the two books.

Theological

The dominant theological idea of the memoir material of both Ezra and Nehemiah is covenant renewal in the postexilic community. The call to spiritual renewal and social justice by the two reformers was aimed at correcting abuses and gross misconduct among the returned remnant, and instilling hope and boosting the morale of the people. It was important for the community despairing over God's apparent neglect to recognize that obedience to covenant stipulations was a mandatory prerequisite for Yahweh's blessing and restoration of Israel as his special possession. While Ezra and Nehemiah no doubt recorded their memoirs simply to preserve a small piece of history for posterity, the more profound message of God's providential rule of human activity for the ultimate benefit of his "elect" was most welcome news (e.g., note how "the hand of God" was upon Ezra [7:9] and Nehemiah [2:8], and the repetition of epitaphs like "the God of heaven" [Ezra 7:11–28; Neh. 2:1–8]).

The theme of covenant renewal is also part of the Chronicler's theological agenda in the arrangement of the historical sources of Ezra and Nehemiah. For the Chronicler, the return from exile in Babylon was a new exodus for Israel. He understood the covenant relationship between Yahweh and the Hebrew people as an important link bridging historical and religious continuity from the preexilic to the postexilic periods of Israelite history.

Although subservience to the Persian overlord prohibited the reestablishment of Israel as a nation-state ruled by a "Davidic" king, the covenant renewal event served to legitimize the postexilic community as the "heir" of that tradition and the people of the restoration as the "covenant people" of God. The particular emphasis on religious purity and social exclusiveness in the community now helped maintain Hebrew identity as a "separate people," since the vibrant nationalism associated with the political independence of the preexilic period was but a memory.

Finally, the Chronicler reaffirmed and expanded the notion of God's sovereign rule of human history. The inclusion of the Sheshbazzar/Zerubbabel narrative as a prologue to the Ezra and Nehemiah memoirs underscored God's involvement in the restoration of Israel by revealing Yahweh's role in prompting Persian kings to permit Israel to return to her land and rebuild the temple. Two additional theological truths of great importance for the restoration community are implicit in the careful splicing of the historical and memoir sources: (1) the people may have hope in the present because the work of God on behalf of Israel in the past stands as the model for Yahweh's participation in the future of the community; and (2) the ministry of Ezra and Nehemiah in restoring Jerusalem attested God's ability to continue to raise up his servants to accomplish his purposes and fulfill his promises to Israel.

Structure and Organization

The book of Ezra opens with a recitation of Cyrus's proclamation for the restoration of Jerusalem (Ezra 1:1–4), and the book of Nehemiah concludes with the reforms of Nehemiah implemented during his second stint as the Persian-appointed governor of Jerusalem (Neh. 13:6–30). Generally speaking, the books recount postexilic history from about 538 B.C. to sometime after 433 B.C.—a span of some hundred years.

These overlapping accounts of the ministries of Ezra and Nehemiah in postexilic Jerusalem give evidence of careful literary construction. The author-editor used a variety of written sources of several different literary types, or genres. Three large units of material may be readily distinguished: the Sheshbazzar/Zerubbabel narrative (Ezra 1–6), the Ezra autobiography (Ezra 7–10; Neh. 7:73–10:39), and the Nehemiah autobiography (Neh. 1:1–7:73; 11–13).

The outline of the complete composition reveals the deliberate weaving or interleaving of the literary units by the compiler:

Sheshbazzar/Zerubbabel Narrative (Ezra 1–6)

Ezra's Memoirs: Part 1 (Ezra 7–10)

Nehemiah's Memoirs: Part 1 (Neh. 1:11–7:73a)

Ezra's Memoirs: Part 2 (Neh. 7:73b–10:39)

Nehemiah's Memoirs: Part 2 (Neh. 11–13)

These sections of the two books are logically arranged according to the compiler's theological purposes related to Yahweh's reaffirmation of covenant relationship with Israel. The literary units work together to describe the sequence of Hebrew migrations back to Palestine and the physical rebuilding and spiritual renewal of Jerusalem.

The variety of literary types within these larger units includes first-person memoir material from the autobiographies of Ezra and Nehemiah, third-person narrative materials (e.g., Ezra 8:35–36), historical documents and official correspondence (e.g., the Cyrus edict in Aramaic, Ezra 6:3–5, and the communication between Tattenai and Darius, Ezra 5:7–17), speeches and prayers (e.g., Neh. 9:5–37), songs (e.g., Ezra 3:11), numerous catalogs and census records of individuals and families who participated in the return to Jerusalem from exile (e.g., Ezra 2:2–70), and even an inventory list of temple vessels returned to Jerusalem (Ezra 1:9–11).

The historical reliability of Ezra and Nehemiah has been confirmed by continuing archaeological discoveries. Extrabiblical evidence garnered from inscriptions on papyri, official seals, and commemorative vessels substantiates the biblical account at several points, including the names of significant characters in the biblical narrative (e.g., Sanballat, Neh. 2:10, and Judahite priests like Jehoiada and Johana, Neh. 12:22; 13:28), the Hebrew understanding of postexilic chronology (e.g., the placement of Geshem the Arab in the first half of the fifth century B.C., Neh. 6:1–6), and the illumination of particular events in postexilic Hebrew history (e.g., Nehemiah's expulsion of Jehoiada's son, Neh. 13:28).[3]

The exact nature of the relationship between the ministries and reforms of Ezra and Nehemiah proves more difficult

[3]Cf. Edwin M. Yamauchi, "The Archaeological Background of Ezra" and "The Archaeological Background of Nehemiah," *Bibliotheca Sacra* 137 (1980): 195–211, 291–309.

to assess. Neither Ezra nor Nehemiah mentions the other in his memoirs, and apart from one reference in Nehemiah 8:9, they do not appear together as co-workers in the text. Yet this is hardly sufficient reason for doubting the contemporaneous aspects of their ministries. Neither Haggai nor Zechariah mentions the other, and they prophesied in Jerusalem during the same two-year period. It may well be that the compiler juxtaposed the memoirs of Ezra and Nehemiah to emphasize the complementary ministry of the two, based on the earlier pattern of Haggai and Zechariah.

Major Themes

Yahweh as Covenant Keeper

The labors of Ezra and Nehemiah to rebuild and reform postexilic Jerusalem were largely inspired by the theological truth of Yahweh as covenant keeper (cf. Neh. 9:32). God's faithfulness to his word as a keeper of covenant oath meant "there is still hope for Israel" (Ezra 10:2). It was the certainty of this teaching that energized the postexilic prophets to announce messages of hope and encouragement to the restoration community as well (cf. Zech. 1:3; Mal. 1:2). Perhaps more important was the faith of these postexilic servants who trusted God for accomplishing feats that served as concrete manifestations of his covenant-keeping ability (e.g., the reconstruction of the second temple and the repair of the Jerusalem city wall).

Yahweh's willingness to return to those who returned to him assured the postexilic community of his desire to bless and restore the covenant people (Hag. 2:4–9; Zech. 1:16–17; Mal. 3:6–7). As a covenant-keeping God, Yahweh heard and responded to the petitions of Israel and declared them "his people" (Ezra 7:9–10, 27–28). Indeed, the very presence of a remnant of Israel in the land of Palestine was a gracious token of God's covenant-keeping nature (cf. Ps. 111:4–5, 9).

Restoration Period Reforms and the Seeds of Pharisaism

The reordering of Hebrew society under Ezra and Nehemiah had both immediate and far-reaching implications. Two primary concerns shaped the reform of the restoration community. The first was the prevention of another Hebrew exile, since the loss of the land of covenant promise was unthinkable. The second was the preservation of the ethnic identity of the Israelite people while they languished beneath the Persian yoke in a fringe province surrounded by hostile foreign nations.

Specific measures taken by Ezra and Nehemiah to ensure Hebrew possession of the land of the promise included the covenant renewal ceremony (cf. Neh. 9:38–10:27), the rehabilitation of the priesthood (e.g., Ezra 10:18–44), the reinstitution of temple ritual and Sabbath observance (Neh. 8:13–18; 13:15–22), and the introduction of the law of Moses as the rule of community life (Neh. 8:1–12). Attempts to maintain ethnic purity of the Israelite community included social and economic reforms based on covenant principles (e.g., Neh. 11:1–2), renewed emphasis on the ceremonial purity of the entire populace of Jerusalem (cf. Neh. 10:38–39), and the divorce and expulsion of foreigners from the assembly of God (Ezra 10:1–8, Neh. 9:1–5; 13:1–3).

The immediate consequences of these reforms had a considerable impact on the nature and structure of postexilic Hebrew society. Israel's identity as the people of God took on a new dimension as temple and priest replaced state and king as the stabilizing institutions of the Hebrew community. The law of Moses became the charter or constitution by which society was reorganized into a priestly "temple-state." Religious, social, and economic policy was now determined by the Torah, bringing a new emphasis on Hebrew "exclusiveness" and "separation" from the Gentiles and their polluted world order.

Perhaps more significant was the metamorphosis that took place in the offices of priest and scribe. In the preexilic period a scribe was a high-ranking cabinet member of the state bureaucracy (e.g., 2 Sam. 20:24–25; 2 Kings 18:18) who never functioned as a priest. The role of the scribe was redefined with the arrival of Ezra. As a priest-scribe he became the model for a later class of religious professionals whose sole task was the study and exposition of Scripture (cf. Ezra 7:10).

The long-term ramifications of this restructuring of Hebrew society emerged in the attitudes and teachings of later Judaism. Unfortunately the consequences for Hebrew religion were mostly negative. Yet the historical and theological developments traced from the postexilic period through the intertestamental period contribute greatly to the understanding of New Testament backgrounds, especially Jesus' encounters with the religious elite of Palestine in the first century A.D.

For example, the zealous but misguided appeal to Mosaic law for community rule eventually led to a pharisaical legalism that tithed "pepper seeds" with ruthless calculation, but ignored the very essence of Torah—faith, justice, and mercy (Matt. 23:23). To increase community obedience to covenant stipulations related to personal purity, the Mosaic code was "fenced in" or supplemented by a legal hedge called the oral law, or "tradition of the elders" (cf. Matt. 15:1–9). Gradually the supplemental code displaced the primary code of Moses, prompting Jesus to decry a religion that neglected the law of God to cling to the traditions of men (cf. Mark 7:1–9).

The idea of Hebrew exclusiveness fostered by Ezra slowly degenerated into an unhealthy preoccupation with separation from the "unclean" lifestyle of the Gentiles. As a result, the majority of the Jews were blinded to their divine commission as a light to the nations (Isa. 42:6; Luke 2:32) and desensitized to their own spiritual bankruptcy (Luke 5:27–31; 10:25–37).

Finally, the study and teaching of the law of Moses continued to be divorced from the priesthood. For their part, the priests were more concerned about political and economic issues due to the influence of Hellenism on the ruling aristocracy of Jerusalem. By New Testament times, however, a professional class of scribes or "lawyers" had usurped the priestly role as spiritual leaders of the people. Jesus condemned them as little more than "blind guides" and "whitewashed tombs" (Matt. 23:16, 27). Small wonder the multitudes were astounded at the teaching of Jesus as one who spoke with authority (cf. Mark 1:22)!

Questions for Further Study and Discussion

1. How were Ezra and Nehemiah complementary reformers?
2. What was the significance of the reading of the law of Moses by Ezra (Neh. 8) for postexilic Israelite history?
3. How were the migrations of the Hebrew exiles from Babylonia to Palestine a "new exodus"?
4. How does the response of Ezra and Nehemiah to the sins of the Hebrews align with the rest of the teaching of the Bible on the attitude of the righteous to sin?
5. How is Nehemiah a good example of doing the work of God from an administrative perspective?
6. How are we to understand the Hebrew separation from "all foreigners" in Nehemiah 9? Is this a form of racism?

7. How are we to understand the marriage reforms recorded in Ezra 9–10 and Nehemiah 13? What are the ethical implications of this mass divorce legislated by Ezra and Nehemiah? How do these accounts of mandatory divorce compare with other teachings of Scripture on divorce?

For Further Reading

Ackroyd, P. R. *Exile and Restoration.* Philadelphia: Westminster, 1968.

––––––. *Israel Under Babylon and Persia.* London: Oxford University Press, 1970. A standard work on the historical background of the postexilic period by the acknowledged expert on the topic.

Bickerman, E. *From Ezra to the Last of the Maccabees.* New York: Schocken, 1962.

Bright, John. *A History of Israel.* 3d ed. Philadelphia: Westminster, 1981. The standard history of Israel in English.

Clines, D. A. *Ezra, Nehemiah, Esther.* NCBC. Grand Rapids: Eerdmans, 1984.

Cross, Frank M. "A Reconstruction of the Judean Restoration." *JBL* 94 (1975): 4–18. A careful study of the problems of postexilic chronology, supporting the traditional view of Ezra's arriving in Jerusalem in 458 B.C.

Eskenazi, T. C. "The Structure of Ezra–Nehemiah and the Integrity of the Book." *JBL* 107 (1988): 641–56.

Fensham, F. C. *The Books of Ezra and Nehemiah.* NICOT. Grand Rapids: Eerdmans, 1982. Thorough, conservative, well-researched, and well-organized. Most readable, with useful application of the books' message to the contemporary situation. Probably the best evangelical commentary currently available.

Kidner, Derek. *Ezra and Nehemiah.* TOTC. Downers Grove, Ill.: InterVarsity, 1979.

Myers, J. M. *Ezra–Nehemiah.* AB. Vol. 14. New York: Doubleday, 1965.

––––––. *The World of the Restoration.* Englewood Cliffs, N.J.: Prentice-Hall, 1968.

––––––. *I and II Esdras.* AB. New York: Doubleday, 1974.

Williamson, H. G. M. *Ezra, Nehemiah.* WBC. Vol. 16. Waco, Tex.: Word Books, 1985. Detailed historical and linguistic analysis, careful exegesis, insightful exposition and application. Less useful than it might be due to awkward format.

Yamauchi, Edwin M. "Ezra and Nehemiah." *EBC.* Grand Rapids: Zondervan, 1988. 4:565–771. Informative discussion on the contributions of Persian history, language, and biblical archaeology to the understanding of the life, times, and message of Ezra and Nehemiah.

––––––. *Persia and the Bible.* Grand Rapids. Baker, 1990

Chapter 20

Esther

It would be difficult to find a more riveting, dramatic, and suspense-filled plot in the pre-Hellenistic world than the book of Esther. Although the book is in the center of a number of swirling controversies, they all fade into the background as we are introduced to the pretentious and impressionable Xerxes/Ahasueras, who plays the foil to his irrepressible and obstreperous Queen Vashti and the rest of the cast, with the beautiful, wise, and courageous Esther at center stage.

The Writing of the Book

There is no indication that the story was intended to be performed as a stage play, but it could be easily adapted to such a medium. Despite the fine literary characteristics, the vindictive nature of some of the action in the book and, more particularly, the absence of any mention of God have occasionally brought objections regarding its inclusion in Scripture. Furthermore, though actual events can appear more contrived than fictitious ones, modern interpreters have often considered the plot too artificial to stake a claim to historical accuracy. This has prompted the search for a consensus concerning the genre of the book.

The book gives no indication as to its author, and though some have speculated that Mordecai may be a candidate, there is little evidence available to promote any theories. So we must consider the author anonymous. Whoever it was, he or she shows great skill as a narrator and had access to court records (cf. 10:2). The author demonstrates a breadth of knowledge about the operation of the Persian court and appears to possess information that would have only been known to Mordecai and Esther.

The setting of the book is the Persian Empire of the early to mid-fifth century B.C., so obviously it must have been written after that time. Though there are no Hebrew manuscripts of the book that date earlier than the eleventh century A.D., analysis of the Hebrew language used in the book indicates that it is older than the second century B.C. It is most likely that the book was written down in the fourth or even the late fifth century B.C.

In the Greek translation, the book has over a hundred additional verses. This longer version was available as early as Jerome in the fourth century A.D. and already had a long tradition by then. In this expanded form the story included such passages as a dream of Mordecai that reveals to him the plot against the king, letters from Mordecai and Xerxes, and prayers of Mordecai and Esther. These additions served the function of inserting God more obviously into the plot, but they have no claim to authenticity.

The Background

By the early part of the fifth century, the Achaemenid rulers of Persia were secure enough in the East to attempt expansion across the Mediterranean at the expense of the Greeks. Though this expansion was decidedly unsuccessful, the Persian Empire controlled the Near East longer than the Neo-Assyrian and Neo-Babylonian empires combined, and it ruled much more territory than any of its predecessors.

Xerxes I is identified with Ahasueras (KJV) and reigned from 486 to 465 B.C. He was the son of the eminently successful Darius the Great, who had annexed parts of India and Eastern Europe into his burgeoning empire. Darius's confrontations with the Greeks, however, did not have so favorable an outcome, as the rout at Marathon (490 B.C.) attested. Though Xerxes was able to crush rebellions in Egypt and Babylon, the humiliation of the Persians at the hand of the Greeks continued in the defeats suffered at Salamis and Mycale and in the embarrassing loss of the entire Persian fleet at Eurymedon. The primary source for this period is the earliest of the Greek historians, Herodotus, a contemporary of Xerxes and his son, Artaxerxes.

Though the details offered in Esther give it a ring of authenticity and suggest a realistic historical setting for the book, many have drawn the conclusion that this book is not intended as an accurate chronicling of events. This opens up the question of literary genre: Is this history? Is it a historical novel? Is it parable or allegory? Belief in the authority of Scrip-

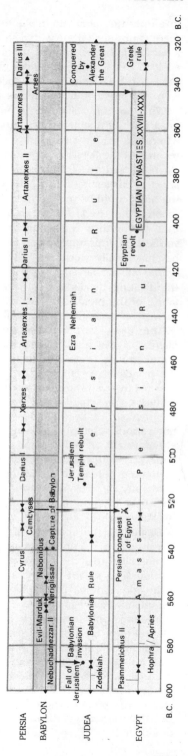

ture does not eliminate this question, for there is nothing wrong with a story being a parable if that is what its author intended it to be. As interpreters we would be remiss to treat something as factual if it were not intended by the author to be so.

What are the claims of the book? The most forthright statement occurs in 10:2, where the reader is referred to the court records of the Persian Empire to verify at least the stature of Mordecai. This falls short of suggesting that all the events of the book could be verified from the court records, but it does give an indication that the author was concerned about verification, thus implying an intention to be historically accurate. Though this would be further supported by the authenticating details woven through the fabric of the plot, historical fiction often thrives on authenticating details.

The most serious objection to the claims of the book is the inability of contemporary sources to identify most of the principle players, notably Vashti, Esther, Mordecai, and Haman. Herodotus includes somewhat lengthy discussion of the exploits of Xerxes' queen Amestris, but various attempts to identify her as either Vashti or Esther have not gained widespread support. While this is problematic and potentially threatening to the credibility of the narrative, it is not sufficient to outweigh the book's own insistence on its accuracy.

Defending the accuracy of the book, however, does not obligate the interpreter to postulate that the book's primary intention is to record history. The literary style and features of the book do not commend it as belonging to a genre that is intended only to chronicle history. On the contrary, it possesses many of the characteristics of the modern short story, with fast-paced action, narrative tension, irony, and reversal. The blend of these literary features with a historical setting and a theological purpose, however, suggest that the genre of the Book of Esther is unique to itself. There is nothing like it in

ancient literature, and in the Bible, only the story of Joseph comes close.

Outline

I. Esther's rise to power (1–2)
II. Mordecai's refusal to bow
   A. Haman's anger: Mordecai's jeopardy (3:1–6)
   B. Xerxes' decree: Israel's jeopardy (3:7–15)
III. Plan for deliverance: Esther's jeopardy (4–5)
IV. Esther's first banquet
   A. Xerxes' insomnia: Mordecai remembered (6:1–5)
   B. Haman's humiliation: Mordecai honored (6:6–13)
V. Esther's second banquet
   A. Xerxes' anger: Haman exposed and doomed (7)
   B. Xerxes' decree: Israel given right to defend itself (8)
VI. Israel's enemies destroyed (9:1–19)
VII. Purim observed (9:20–32)
VIII. Resulting stature of Mordecai (10:1–3)

Purpose and Message

The book of Esther has very particular points to make about the saving acts of the Lord. Israel's history was replete with the marvelous interventions of the Lord on behalf of his covenant people. The mighty plagues, the deliverance from Egypt, the parting of the sea, and the crumbling of the walls of Jericho were classic examples of Yahweh's miraculous deliverance of Israel. More recently, the return of the exiles from their Babylonian captivity was evidence of God's continuing ability to accomplish the impossible.

But God is not so visible in the book of Esther. Where others may see coincidences, Israel saw the Lord at work. A king's insomnia could just as easily bring deliverance as receding waters. In the course of this book it therefore becomes evident that the well-known themes of

Figure 20.1. A view of ruins at Persepolis in southern Persia (southcentral Iran), which was the capital city of Darius the Great and was noted for its architecture, promoted by Darius and Xerxes. (*B. Brandl*)

prophecy and wisdom were still viable expressions of God's intentions even though Israel was scattered among the nations. The prophetic theme of God's protection of Israel and the judgment of her enemies (e.g., Zech. 1:21) was operating as the plot unfolded. Even more evident is the wisdom theme that God would prosper the righteous and bring to naught the schemes of the wicked (cf. Ps. 37:12–15).

The message comes through clearly: God's methods may vary, but his purposes do not. His workings may be obscured to skeptics by the disguise of coincidence, but the people of God recognize his sovereign hand in the ebb and flow of history. His name is not mentioned, but his influence is unmistakable.

Structure and Organization

There is a growing consensus among those analyzing Esther that the plot is built and the message is conveyed through the technique of reversal. This occurs when the current state of affairs is turned around or when the plot develops in a way that is opposite or contrary to what one would expect. Among the most

notable examples of this phenomenon are the elevation of Mordecai, the downfall of Haman, and the Jews' destroying their enemies rather than being destroyed by them.

The effect of reversal is heightened by the use of irony throughout the narrative. Irony occurs when the reader has information that the characters do not. Perhaps the most poignant example of this occurs when Haman comes into the court to ask permission to execute Mordecai, and before he can ask, the king requests Haman's opinion concerning how to bestow a great honor. The irony is heightened when Haman assumes that the king means to honor him and reaches a climax when Haman is then forced to personally bestow the honor on Mordecai whom he sought to kill.

Haman is the main foil for the irony of the text. He thinks he is being honored by being invited to Esther's banquets when in actuality he is being set up. He seeks to destroy the Jews and then is reduced to begging for his life from a Jewess. Not least of all, he is hung on his own gallows. All these turns make him almost a comic figure whom the narrative cannot resist humiliating time and again.

The significance of the irony is that it demonstrates that there is always more going on than meets the eye, and more possibilities available than any single person understands or is aware of. God's control cannot be calculated, God's solution cannot be anticipated, and God's plan cannot be thwarted, because no one has all the necessary information. It is the effective use of irony and reversal that serve throughout the plot to make the message plain. The narrative tension created by the crisis into which Mordecai and the Jews are thrown headlong is resolved through an apparently circumstantial chain of events that could not have been guided by anyone but a sovereign God.

The basic flow of the plot is evident as one reads through the narrative. As can be seen from the outline, the first five chapters set up the situation, moving Esther into the palace and establishing the feud between Mordecai and Haman that escalates into an attempt by Haman to exterminate the Jews. The major turn takes place in chapter 6, between the two banquets, just before Esther exposes Haman. From that point the prediction of Haman's wife becomes nearly self-fulfilling as Haman is executed and his genocidal plot is reversed. Mordecai and Esther gain high positions and the favor of the king, and the Jews are saved from their enemies.

Major Themes

Purim

The book of Esther is read annually at the Jewish celebration of the feast of Purim ("lots"). The festival commemorates the deliverance reported in the book and, likewise, the book establishes the celebration of the festival. A number of interpreters have concluded that the book itself is an etiology devised to provide an explanation for the celebration of the feast. Others have seen chapter 9 as a later addition to the narrative that seeks to legitimize a non-Israelite festival. Neither explanation is necessary or persuasive. If the events recorded in the book actually took place (as we would affirm), it is logical and understandable that a feast would be established to commemorate the occasion. The name "Purim" is entirely appropriate, for God's deliverance does not come by the angel of the Lord slaying the enemy in the night, but by means that others would view as chance. The theology of Purim affirms that God is no less at work in the latter than in the former (cf. Prov. 16:33).

The People of God

We recall from the chapter on Genesis that God chose Abraham and his family to become the people of God in the sense that his revelation would come through them. They were to be the "revelatory" people of God. Upon reaching the book of Esther, the reader has been brought through a 1,500-year story of God's self-disclosure through his people Israel despite themselves. Now Esther perhaps implies that a shift took place in the postexilic period. The deliverance of Israel recorded in this book was not done in such a way that it bore witness to the world of God's power. Rather it was accomplished so as to confirm the believer in his faith in a sovereign God, while the skeptic might easily dismiss it as coincidence.

Certainly it was always God's desire that the people through whom he was revealing himself would be in a proper relationship with him (i.e., the revelatory people of God would also be the soteriological people of God). But in the postexilic period, the spiritual condition of the people moved to the top of the agenda, and the revelatory function seems at best to be have been put on hold until the righteous remnant would emerge (cf. Dan. 9:24). The book of Esther exemplifies this shift. The comment of Haman's wife demonstrates that, to a large extent, the revelatory purpose of God was achieved: "Since Mordecai, before whom your downfall has started, is of Jewish origin, you cannot stand against him—you will surely come to ruin" (6:13). This was the same woman who earlier had urged Haman to build the gallows on which to hang Mordecai (5:14). But in this change of heart she recognized that the Jews were a people specially blessed and protected, and thus attested indirectly to the sovereignty of their God.

Questions for Further Study and Discussion

1. If God has shifted to using more subtle methods of deliverance, is it still appropriate to speak of the existence of a "revelatory" people of God?
2. Of what importance for the message and purpose of the book of Esther is the question of its historicity?
3. How does the book of Esther in the Old Testament compare with the Additions to Esther in the Old Testament Apocrypha?
4. What does the character of Esther contribute to our understanding of the role of women in the Old Testament?
5. How does the literary device of "reversal" help to unify the book of Esther?

For Further Reading

Baldwin, Joyce G. *Esther*. TOTC. Downers Grove, Ill.: InterVarsity, 1984. Excellent, though brief, evangelical treatment.

Berg, Sandra Beth. *The Book of Esther*. Missoula, Mont.: Scholars Press, 1979. A dissertation, but very readable and informative.

Clines, David J. A. *Ezra, Nehemiah, Esther*. Grand Rapids: Eerdmans, 1984. A well-done, though brief commentary.

Fox, Michael. "The Structure of the Book of Esther." In Alexander Rofé, ed., *Safer Isaac L. Seeligmann*. Jerusalem: Rubenstein, 1983. 291–301.

Gordis, R. "Religion, Wisdom and History in the Book of Esther: A New Solution to an Ancient Crux." *JBL* 100 (1981): 359–88.

Huey, F. B. "Esther." *EDC*. Vol. 4. Grand Rapids: Zondervan, 1988.

Moore, Carey. *Esther*. New York: Doubleday, 1971. Probably the best of the liberal commentaries.

———. *Studies in the Book of Esther*. New York: Ktav, 1982. A collection of several dozen of the most significant articles on the book of Esther, with about a hundred pages of introduction by Moore.

Talmon, S. "Wisdom in the Book of Esther." *VT* 13 (1963): 419–55.

Wright, J. Stafford. "The Historicity of the Book of Esther." In *New Perspectives on the Old Testament*. J. Barton Payne, ed. Waco, Tex.: Word Books, 1970. 37–47.

PART IV

THE POETIC BOOKS

Chapter 21

Hebrew Poetic and Wisdom Literature

Introduction

The boundaries of poetic literature in the Old Testament are not easy to delimit, since little is known about the exact nature of biblical Hebrew poetry. Unlike its classical and modern counterparts, ancient Hebrew poetry has no distinctive scheme of accentuation, meter, or rhythm to differentiate it from prose. Only within the past two centuries has this fact been fully appreciated in biblical scholarship.

The most significant early contribution to the study of Hebrew poetry was made by Bishop Robert Lowth in the mid-eighteenth century. He noted parallelism, or the counterbalancing of ideas in phrases, as a fundamental feature distinguishing Hebrew poetry from prose. His delineation of the various types of parallelism remains basic to the understanding of Old Testament poetic structure.

J. Hoftijzer in 1965 published an analytical method for identifying Hebrew poetry based on the distribution of the marker for the direct object in Old Testament texts (i.e., 'et syntagmemes, or the direct object particle 'et and the word or group of words following it). F. I. Andersen and David N. Freedman refined this approach for separating Hebrew poetry from prose through a "prose particle" counting method. In this the total occurrences of the grammatical particles for the direct object marker, the relative pronoun, and the definite article are apportioned to the total number of words per chapter in a given text (those particles generally being typical of prose and atypical of poetry).

Old Testament texts exhibiting prose-particle densities of 15 percent or more are considered prose in nature, while those demonstrating prose-particle densities of 5 percent or less are regarded as poetic. Old Testament prophetic literature yielding densities between 5 and 15 percent is labeled "oracular prose," connoting its poetic tendencies.

The most recent development in the study of Old Testament poetry is the application of modern linguistic terminology and methodology to the Hebrew text.[1] Here the assumption is that biblical Hebrew is not unique as a language and

[1]For example, Michael O'Connor, *Hebrew Verse Structure* (Winona Lake, Ind.: Eisenbrauns, 1980).

consequently can best be analyzed by the same procedures contemporary linguists use on other languages. This has led to a greater appreciation of Old Testament poetry as literature and has in some instances enhanced our understanding of the meaning of biblical texts. No doubt the traditional descriptions and analytical methods applied to Hebrew poetry will continue to undergo change as modern linguistic and literary research influences biblical studies.

Today biblical scholars acknowledge that poetry comprises about one third of the Hebrew Old Testament. This poetry ranges from brief extracts (Gen. 4:23–24; Num. 21:18; 1 Sam. 18:7) to complete compositions like songs, hymns, and oracles (Gen. 49:2–27; Exod. 15:1–18; 1 Sam. 2:1–10) in the Pentateuch and historical books, to the long and ornate poetic works of Job and the Psalms, to the bold and vivid oracular prose of Isaiah 40–66, Nahum, and Habakkuk.

Psalms, Proverbs, Song of Songs, and Lamentations are entirely poetic in form. Most of Job and portions of Ecclesiastes are poetic, while the prose narratives in the books of Genesis, Exodus, Numbers, Deuteronomy, Judges, and 1–2 Samuel contain substantial poetic sections. The prophetic books of Obadiah, Micah, Nahum, Habbakuk, and Zephaniah are composed completely in oracular prose (with the exception of the superscriptions or title verses). This is also true for major portions of Isaiah, Jeremiah, Ezekiel, Daniel, Hosea, Joel, and Amos. In the Old Testament only Leviticus, Ruth, Ezra, Nehemiah, Esther, Haggai, and Malachi contain little or no poetic material.

Although the Old Testament wisdom books are usually poetic in form, they are classified as wisdom literature for other reasons. To the Hebrews, "wisdom" constituted "skill in living" that combined the powers of observation, the capacities of human intellect, and the application of

knowledge and experience to daily life. Wisdom literature may be didactic or instructional in nature, or argumentative in a reflective or speculative sense. Wisdom sought to teach practical moral principles for behavior or prompted the reader rationally to investigate the many problems associated with human existence—all from a viewpoint firmly rooted in "the fear of the Lord."

The wisdom literature of the Old Testament includes the instructional books of Proverbs and Song of Songs and the speculative books of Job and Ecclesiastes, along with select wisdom psalms (e.g., 1, 37, 49, 112) and portions of the prophetic books employing wisdom terminology or themes (e.g., Isa. 40:12–17, 21–26; Amos 3:10; 5:4, 6, 14).

Poetry and Wisdom in the Ancient Near East

Poetry in the Ancient Near East

Israel was the beneficiary of a long and well-developed literary tradition in the ancient Near East. While the earliest Hebrew poetry extant dates to the thirteenth or twelfth centuries B.C., the rudiments of Egyptian poetry can be traced to a triumph hymn for the pharaoh dated near 3200 B.C. Poetic couplets occur in the famous Pyramid Texts of the Fifth Dynasty (ca. 2350 B.C.), and matching couplets appear as early as 2300 B.C. in the victory hymn for Pepi I:

This army returned in safety,
After it had hacked up the land of the
[Sand] Dwellers.
This army returned in safety,
After it had crushed the land of the
Sand Dwellers.[2]

Scholars have long recognized the similarities between Psalm 104 and the sun hymn of Akhenaten. For example, compare the excerpt from the Aten Hymn with Psalm 104:25–26 (fig. 21.1a). The

²ANET, 228.

Figure 21.1a. Similarities in Poetry: 1

Aten Hymn

The ships are sailing north and south as well,
For every way is open at thy appearance.
Thus fish in the river dart before thy face,
Thy rays are in the midst of the great green sea.†

Psalm 104:25-26

There is the sea, vast and spacious,
teeming with creatures beyond number—
living things both large and small.
There the ships go to and fro,
and the leviathan, which you formed
to frolic there.

Figure 21.1b. Similarities in Poetry: 2

Egyptian Love Song 31

One, the lady love without a duplicate,
more perfect than the world,
see, she is like the star rising
at the start of an auspicious year.
She whose excellence shines, whose body glistens,
glorious her eyes when she stares,
sweet her lips when she converses,
she says not a word too much.
High her neck and glistening her nipples,
of true lapis her hair,
her arms finer than gold,
her fingers like lotus flowers unfolding.
Her buttocks droop when her waist is girt,
her legs reveal her perfection;
her steps are pleasing when she walks the earth,
she takes my heart in her embrace.
When she comes forth, anyone can see
that there is none like that One.‡

Song of Songs 4:1-7

How beautiful you are, my darling!
Oh, how beautiful!
Your eyes behind your veil are doves.
Your hair is like a flock of goats
descending from Mount Gilead.
Your teeth are like a flock of sheep just shorn,
coming up from the washing.
Each has its twin;
not one of them is alone.
Your lips are like a scarlet ribbon;
your mouth is lovely.
Your temples behind your veil
are like the halves of a pomegranate.
Your neck is like the tower of David,
built with elegance;
on it hang a thousand shields,
all of them shields of warriors.
Your breasts are like two fawns,
like twin fawns of a gazelle that browse
among the lilies.
Until the day breaks
and the shadows flee,
I will go to the mountain of myrrh
and to the hill of incense.
All beautiful you are, my darling;
there is no flaw in you.

---

†From *ANET*, 3d ed. (Princeton: Princeton Univ. Press, 1969), 370.

‡From W. K. Simpson, ed., *The Literature of Ancient Egypt*, rev. ed. (New Haven: Yale Univ. Press, 1973), 315–16.

same holds true for the Egyptian Love Songs of the New Kingdom (ca. 1570–1085 B.C.) and the biblical Song of Songs. Note the affinities between Song 31 from Egypt and the Song of Songs 4:1–7 (fig. 21.1b).

These same kinds of poetic traditions developed concurrently in ancient Mesopotamia. Parallel couplets occur already in the building inscription of Gudea, prince of Lagash (ca. 1900–1800 B.C.). Old Babylonian kingdoms (ca. 1900–1600 B.C.) canonized earlier Sumerian literature, including poetic hymns and prayers like the "Prayer to Any God":

In ignorance I have eaten that forbidden of my god,

In ignorance I have set foot on that
protected by my goddess.[5]

This period also saw the composition
of Neo-Sumerian prayers and hymns
such as the long "Hymn to Shamash":

At thy rising the gods of the land
assemble;
By thy frightful brilliance the land is
overwhelmed.
Of all countries (even) those different in
languages,
Thou knowest their plans; thou art
observant of their course.
All mankind rejoices in thee;
O Shamash, all the world longs for thy
light.[6]

Probably the most notable Old Babylonian poetic literary works are the Gilgamesh Epic (containing the Babylonian
flood story) and the Enuma Elish (the
Babylonian creation epic). An excerpt
from the Enuma Elish follows:

When on high the heaven had not been
named,
Firm ground below had not been called
by name,
Naught but primordial Apsu, their beget-
ter,
(And) Mummu-Tiamat, she who bore
them all,
Their waters commingling as a single
body;
No reed hut had been matted, no
marsh land had appeared,
When no gods whatever had been
brought into being,
Uncalled by name, their destinies unde-
termined—
Then it was that the gods were formed
within them.[7]

Though Egyptian and Mesopotamian
culture influenced Syro-Palestine, equally
important are the ancient Near Eastern
parallels to biblical poetry found in the
Canaanite literature discovered at Ras

Shamra, or Ugarit. The written poetry of
Ugarit dates to approximately 1400–1200
B.C., but these were probably preceded by
at least two centuries of oral recitations.

Ugaritic poetry is similar to its Hebrew
counterpart in vocabulary and style. For
example, the identification of hundreds of
parallel (or A/B) word pairs that also
occur in Hebrew poetry indicate that the
Old Testament poets used a common
parallelistic poetic tradition. The Ugaritic
epics of Baal, Ahqat, and Keret also contain poetic features like chiasmus, numerical climax, and synonymous and synthetic parallelism. Note the parallelism
and chiasmus in this sample text from
the Baal Epic:

I tell thee, O Prince Baal,
I declare, O Rider of the Clouds.
Now thine enemy, O Baal,
Now thine enemy wilt thou smite,
Now wilt thou cut off thine adversary.
Thou'lt take thine eternal kingdom,
Thine everlasting dominion.[8]

Like the Hebrew psalter, some Ugaritic
texts include superscriptions, subheadings, colophons, and on occasion even
musical notations. These striking similarities between Ugaritic and Hebrew poetry
point to a common West Semitic linguistic and literary heritage.

Wisdom in the Ancient Near East

Biblical wisdom literature, like Hebrew
poetry, must be understood in an international context. The Bible touts the
sapiential tradition of the Egyptians (e.g.,
Exod. 7:22; 1 Kings 4:30), of the Edomites
and Arabians (e.g., Jer. 49:7; Obad. 8), and
the Babylonians (e.g., Isa. 47:10; Dan. 1:4).

Surviving Egyptian wisdom literature
consists of two basic types, or genres:
instructions and discussions. The instructions, or teachings, are largely the

[5]*ANET*, 391.
[6]Ibid., 388.
[7]Ibid., 60–61.
[8]Ibid., 130–31.

product of the pharonic court as the king prepared his son to assume the administration of the monarchy. The examples of speculative wisdom include political satire and skeptical treatises on the ironies of life. The essence or governing principle of Egyptian wisdom was the concept of *maat*, the embodiment of truth, justice, and order.

Both types of Egyptian wisdom literature contain striking parallels to the Hebrew wisdom of the Old Testament. For example, portions of the "Teachings of Amenemope," an Egyptian sage writing near 1200 B.C., exhibit remarkable similarities in language and theme with the "Sayings of the Wise" in Proverbs (22:17–24:23). Note the associations between Amenemope,

> Guard yourself from robbing the poor, from being violent to the weak. Do not associate with the rash man nor approach him in conversation.[9]

and Proverbs 22:22–23,

> Do not exploit the poor because they are poor
> and do not crush the needy in court,
> . . .
> Do not make friends with a hot-tempered man,
> do not associate with one easily angered.

The discussion literature of Egyptian wisdom includes works like "The Dispute Over Suicide," "The Tale of the Eloquent Peasant," and "The Song of the Harper." These writings are contemplative, analytical, even pessimistic in tone and mood and are reminiscent of the wisdom assembled by the Preacher (or Qoheleth) in Ecclesiastes. The discussions address topics such as finding meaning and joy in life, social injustice, the problem of evil,

and the reality of pain and death in a fashion akin to the biblical books of Job and Ecclesiastes. Note, for example, the similarities on the topic of enjoyment in life between the Harper Song,

> Let not thy heart flag.
> Follow thy desire and thy good.
> Fulfill thy needs upon earth, after the command of thy heart.
> Until there come for thee that day of mourning.[10]

and Ecclesiastes 8:15,

> So I commend the enjoyment of life, because nothing is better for a man under the sun than to eat and drink and be glad. Then joy will accompany him in his work all the days of the life God has given him under the sun.

Although the Bible attests to a significant wisdom tradition among the Edomites, little written evidence remains that might indicate the extent or content of Edom's wisdom. The book of Job probably preserves remnants of the influence of Edomite wisdom tradition on the Hebrew sages, in that the name Job is a shortened form of Jobab (an Edomite king mentioned in Genesis 36:34, not to be identified with Job). One of Job's friends is from an Edomite clan (Eliphaz the Temanite, Job 2:11), and the land of Uz was apparently located in Edom (cf. Lam. 4:21).

If "Massa" is a proper name in Proverbs 30:1 and 31:1 (so RSV; elsewhere translated "oracle"), then the words of Agur son of Jakeh (30:1–33) and King Lemuel (31:1–9) may reflect the influence of Arabian wisdom on the developing Hebrew wisdom tradition. Massa has been identified with the tribes settled in northwestern Arabia near Teman (cf. Gen. 25:14; 1 Chron. 1:30).

Mesopotamian wisdom literature also

---

[9]John H. Walton, *Ancient Israelite Literature in Its Cultural Context* (Grand Rapids: Zondervan, 1989), 192: quoting from translation by John Ruffle, "The Teaching of Amenemope and Its Connection with the Book of Proverbs," *TB* 28 (1977).

[10]*ANET*, 467.

contains instructions in the form of proverbs and fables along with discussions related to theodicy (i.e., the vindication of divine attributes like holiness and justice in respect to the existence of evil). One text, "A Man and His God," is known as the Sumerian Job. Note the similarity between the lament in that writing,

Never has a sinless child been born to its mother, . . .
a sinless workman has not existed from of old.[11]

and Job 15:14–16,

"What is man, that he could be pure, or one born of woman, that he could be righteous?
If God places no trust in his holy ones, if even the heavens are not pure in his eyes,
how much less man, who is vile and corrupt, who drinks up evil like water!"

Yet another Mesopotamian text, "The Babylonian Theodicy," has friends making speeches to a tormented man whose gods have forsaken him. Still another, "The Dialogue of Pessimism," reflects on the emptiness and irony of human existence from the perspectives of indulgence and abstinence in a similar vein to the Preacher's contrasts of excess and asceticism (Eccl. 7:14).

While the many similarities between ancient Near Eastern wisdom literature and the Hebrew wisdom of the Old Testament are certainly not just coincidental, the resemblances are as much the product of the universal nature of attempts to cope with the problems associated with human existence as they are a result of any cultural or literary borrowing. The search for meaning and purpose in life, the mystery of life and death, the reality of suffering, pain, injustice, and the relationship of the divine to the problem of evil are questions common to the human experience—whether Egyptian, Babylonian, or Hebrew.

Moreover, despite the special thematic and literary relationships that may be demonstrated between ancient Near Eastern and Hebrew wisdom, one fundamental difference remains. Unlike the other ancients who paid homage to assorted pantheons of deities, the Israelite wisdom of the Old Testament acknowledged only one God, Yahweh (Prov. 22:17–19). Thus the Hebrews denied materialism (since matter was created by God), pantheism (because Yahweh as Creator was above all creation), and dualism (since creation was originally made "good" by God). Ideologically this meant that the Hebrews owed allegiance to Yahweh alone and had neither room nor time for these false deities and competing religious systems. Practically speaking, however, the facts of Hebrew history indicate that this was not always the case.

Literary Character of Hebrew Poetry

The two distinctive features of Hebrew poetry (including the poetic wisdom books) are rhythm of sound and rhythm of thought. Rhythm of sound is the regular pattern of stressed or unstressed syllables in lines (or stichs) of Hebrew poetry; it may also be the repetition of sounds through devices like alliteration or assonance. Rhythm of thought or sense is the balancing of ideas in a structured or systematic form. The primary vehicle for conveying rhythm of thought in biblical poetry is a feature described as "parallelism of members." A pervasive mode of thought in ancient Near Eastern literary circles, this parallelism was elevated with exceptional artistry by the Hebrew poets. Although Hebrew parallelism is beyond absolute and rigid categorization, it can be understood by biblical examples.

[11]*ANET*, 590.

Rhythm of Thought

1. Antithetic parallelism balances the thoughts or ideas within the line pairs (or distichs) of poetry by stating the truth of the first line in an opposing or negative way or by introducing a contrast.

> For the LORD watches over the way of the righteous, / but the way of the wicked will perish (Ps. 1:6).

2. Chiastic or inverted parallelism contraposes or alternates the words or phrases in consecutive lines.

> For I know my transgression, / and my sin is always before me (Ps. 51:3).

> Ephraim will not be jealous of Judah, nor Judah hostile toward Ephraim (Isa. 11:13).

3. Emblematic parallelism uses simile or metaphor to convey poetic meaning. One line expresses a thought in a literal manner, while the other line repeats or builds on it in figurative terms.

> As a father has compassion on his children, / so the LORD has compassion on those who fear him (Ps. 103:13).

> Like a partridge that hatches eggs it did not lay / is the man who gains riches by unjust means (Jer. 17:11).

4. Synonymous parallelism, sometimes called identical or complete parallelism, is the exact balancing of thoughts or meanings in two lines of poetry. Essentially the poet says the same thing twice with the same grammatical structure by composing lines of poetry with similar meanings but different words.

> Hear this, all you peoples; / listen, all who live in this world (Ps. 49:1).

5. Synthetic or climactic parallelism contains a second line that adds to or completes the thought of the first line. Occasionally this kind of parallelism consists of a tiered structure in which each line begins from the same point but ascends beyond the preceding thought by recapitulation and extension. Compare the following:

> Above all else, guard your heart, / for it is the wellspring of life (Prov. 4:23).

> Ascribe to the LORD , O mighty ones, / ascribe to the LORD glory and strength.
> Ascribe to the LORD the glory due his name; / worship the LORD in the splendor of his holiness (Ps. 29:1–2).

Rhythm of Sound

The second distinctive feature of Hebrew poetry, rhythm of sound, is demonstrated through a variety of techniques used by the ancient poet.

1. Acrostic Poem. An acrostic is verse in which the initial letters of consecutive lines of a stanza form an alphabet, word, or phrase. The Old Testament contains thirteen complete alphabetic acrostic poems (Pss. 9 and 10, 25, 34, 37, 111, 112, 119, 145; Prov. 31:10–31; Lam. 1, 2, 3, 4) and perhaps one incomplete alphabetic acrostic (Nah. 1:2–10). More than a matter of personal style, the acrostic poem was a mnemonic tool, or memory device, in the ancient scribal schools. Although it was somewhat artificial, as a literary feature it conveyed ideas of order, progression, and completeness within the poetic message. Unfortunately this aspect of Hebrew poetry cannot be appreciated fully in translation (though the acrostics are often identified in the margins or in footnotes in many English versions).

A sample of the Hebrew alphabetic acrostic is offered in English translation (fig. 21.2). Psalm 112 contains twenty-two lines, one for each letter of the Hebrew alphabet. The first six lines of the psalm have been translated to form an acrostic. Note that the English rendering is somewhat strained.

2. Alliteration. A common feature in Old Testament poetry is alliteration, the consonance of sounds at the beginning of

Figure 21.2. Acrostic Structure

aleph	(a)	Ah, the happiness of the one who fears the Lord,
beth	(b)	because of his commandments he delights exceedingly!
gimel	(g)	Great on the earth will be his "seed";
daleth	(d)	descendants of the upright will be blessed.
heh	(h)	Honor and riches are in his house;
waw	(w)	without end his righteousness endures.

words or syllables. Again, the English translation is inadequate to represent the resonant cadence of the Hebrew *š* (sh) and *l* (l) in Psalm 122:6:

Transliteration: *ša'lû š'lôm y'rûšalaim*

Translation: "Pray for the peace of Jerusalem."

3. Assonance. Assonance is the rhythm of sound using the correspondence of vowel sounds, often at the end of words. Like alliteration, assonance may serve as a literary ploy to emphasize an idea or theme or to set a certain tone for the poem. An example of this feature appears in Psalm 119:29, with the *e* class vowels Seghol and Sere and the *i* class Hiriq.

Transliteration: *derek–šeqer hāsēr mimmenî / w'tôrāt'ka hānnēnî*

Translation: Keep me from deceitful ways, / be gracious to me through your law.

4. Paronomasia. The Hebrew poets and especially the prophets often incorporated paronomasia, or word play, into their poems and oracles. This word play consisted of the repetition of words similar in sound, but not necessarily in meaning, to heighten the intended impact of the message. The prophet Amos saw a basket of summer fruit (*qayiṣ*) and announced the end (*qēṣ*) of the nation of Israel (Amos 8:2). On his deathbed Jacob predicted Judah (*y'hûdâ*) would be praised (*yôdûkā*) by his brothers (Gen. 49:8). And the prophet Isaiah ended his Song of the Vineyard with this masterful stroke (5:7b):

And he looked for justice [*mišpāṭ*],
    but saw bloodshed [*mišpāḥ*];
for righteousness [*ṣedāqâ*],

but heard cries of distress [*ṣe'āqâ*]!

5. Onomatopoeia. The use of words that sound like what they describe was another feature conditioned by the orality of Hebrew poetry. The Israelite poets enhanced the vividness of their description of the reality around them by dipping into the rich cache of onomatopoeic words in the Hebrew vocabulary. Samples of onomatopoeia in the Old Testament include the simple interjection "woe" (*'ôy*) as in Isaiah 24:16, the "thunder" (*ra'am*) in Psalm 81:7, even the quaking of the earth (*rā'aš*) in Psalm 68:8, and the hoofbeats of horses (*dah'rôtdah'rôt*) in Judges 5:22.

6. Ellipsis. The omission of a word or words that would complete a given parallel construction is common in Hebrew poetry and has been marked as one of the criteria for distinguishing poetry from prose. An example is found in Psalm 115, where "their idols" in verse 4 is understood in verses 5–7.

7. Inclusio. The inclusio is a special form of the repetition common to Hebrew poetry. The device is sometimes called an envelope figure, since by repeating keywords and phrases the poet returns to the point from which he began. For example, Psalm 118 begins (v. 1) and ends (v. 29) with the lines:

Give thanks to the LORD, for he is good; / his love endures forever.

Rhythm of Form

1. Meter. Meter has been assumed in Hebrew poetry on the basis of analogy with other kinds of poetry. Recent studies have challenged this assumption (e.g.,

James Kugel and Michael O'Connor). The exact nature of meter remains a topic of discussion because the formal characteristics constituting Hebrew poetry are still ill-defined.

The two common methods of gauging Hebrew meter are counting the stressed or accented syllables in line pairs (or distichs) of poetry and counting the total number of syllables in the two lines of poetry. For example, the normal pattern is a three-stress first line followed by a two-stress second line (3 + 2, the so-called *qinah*, or dirge meter, of Lamentations). Other common patterns include three-stress couplets (3 + 3) and two- and four-stress lines (2 + 2 and 4 + 4). These approaches do not describe meter so much as they provide a guide to its structure. The concept of syllable counting as a reflection of Hebrew poetic meter continues to be a topic of debate among biblical scholars. Recent research that connects syntactical and statistical analysis with modern linguistic methodology and comparative poetics offers the most promise for unraveling the complexities related to understanding meter in Hebrew poetry.

2. *Strophe.* Strophic patterns, the grouping of lines into larger units, are not readily discernible in most Hebrew poetry. While certain acrostic poems exhibit an alphabetic strophic structure (e.g., Ps. 119; Lam. 1, 2, and 4), most attempts to isolate these larger units of biblical poetry remain unconvincing.

On occasion, Old Testament poems contain refrains or repeated lines of text that may indicate strophic structure (e.g., Pss 42:5,11; 43:5; 107:8, 15, 21, 31; or 136), but more often there are no formal markers of stanzas in the poem. Thus, while greater structures of symmetry are assumed to exist in Hebrew poetry, there is at present no methodology that will demonstrate these strophic patterns with consistency and certainty.

Life Situation and Genre

Like all other poetry, that in the Bible is an expression of human creative energy filtering and responding to all facets of reality comprising the experiences of life in a language of images (e.g., birth, Gen. 25:23; life, Eccl. 3:1–9; death, 2 Sam. 1:17–27; blood revenge, Gen. 4:23–24; war, Josh. 10:12–13; and marriage, Gen. 24:60). Israel's poetry was shaped further by an intense faith in the God Yahweh, because he had acted in history on behalf of his people (cf. Exod. 15:1–18, 21; Judg. 5:1–31), and by an inherent desire to celebrate the worth and meaning of human existence (cf. Pss. 92, 112, 127, 128; Eccl. 5:18–20). It is for these reasons that Old Testament poetry transcends the historical setting of ancient Israel and informs the very fabric of modern culture (perhaps explaining why the Psalms remain the most popular literature in all the Bible).

The poetry of the Old Testament was also musical in nature. It was usually intended to be sung or chanted to the accompaniment of musical instruments (e.g., Deut. 31:30–32:44; Pss. 5, 6). The musicality of Hebrew poetry aggrandized the artistry of the literary form, added an important liturgical dimension, and aided the oral transmission of the poetry. Although the "orchestral scores" for Old Testament poetry are now lost, vestiges of its musicality remain, particularly in the Psalms. This Israelite hymnbook retains superscriptions denoting the specific accompanying instruments (e.g., Pss. 54, 55, 67, 150), the composer or recipient (Pss. 70, 72, 73, 77, 81), the occasion prompting the composition (Pss. 45, 70, 92, 100), and the musical tune or arrangement to which the poem was (played and) sung (Pss. 12, 22, 39, 57, 58, 80).

A general thesis regarding the types of Hebrew poetry has emerged by scholarly consensus. Early poetry was brief and limited to one situation or event; mixing types and greater length began during the era of the Conquest, accelerated under the united monarchy, and reached its zenith during the Exile and shortly thereafter.

Several basic poetic types, or genres, have been identified: the no longer extant historical anthologies (e.g., Num. 21:14; Josh. 10:13), victory songs (Exod. 15:1–18; Judg. 5:1–31), curses (Num. 21:27–30), taunt songs (Isa. 14:1–27; 47:1–15), funeral dirges and eulogies (2 Sam. 1:17–27; Jer. 9:17–22), wisdom songs (Pss. 1, 37), royal songs (Pss. 20, 21, 45), hymns (Pss. 8, 29), songs of trust (Pss. 11, 62), thanksgiving poems (Pss. 18, 30, 65), laments (Pss. 27, 28) and penitential poems (Pss. 32, 38), songs of litigation (Isa. 45:20–21; Mic. 1:1–7), love poems (Song 4:1–7), wedding songs (Ps. 45), and predictive poetry (Gen. 49:1–27; Num. 23:8–10, 19–24).

The Idea of Wisdom

Terms and Definitions

The idea of wisdom stems from the need for people to cope with the reality of human existence for sheer survival. This desire to gain mastery over life through the powers of reason marks one of the universal phenomena of ancient and modern societies.

Another pervasive aspect of the human wisdom tradition is the belief that the accumulated knowledge of experience and observation can be taught to the succeeding generation. For this reason, much of the literature published by the sages or keepers of the wisdom traditions takes the form of instructions designed to "steer" one safely and successfully through the course of life.

The concept of "the fear of the Lord" distinguished Hebrew wisdom from its ancient Near Eastern counterparts. For Israel, wisdom and the knowledge of God were inseparable because God was the source and dispenser of insight and understanding (cf. Job 12:13; Prov. 2:5–6; Isa. 31:1–2). This "Yahweh orientation" of Hebrew wisdom meant that the knowl-edge of God had implications for Israel's emotional and spiritual life (as expressed in Old Testament poetry) and for her physical and experiential life (as reflected in Old Testament wisdom).

The word for "wisdom" originally denoted some kind of technical skill, aptitude, or ability like that necessary for crafting wood and metal, artistic design and architecture, sea navigation, and even politics. The most common word for wisdom, *ḥokmâ*, reflected this practical aspect of the term in several different Old Testament contexts. For example, Bezalel and Oholiab were given special "wisdom" in artistic design and craftsmanship for their work in the construction of articles and utensils for the tabernacle (Exod. 31:1–11). In another time and place, Solomon's architectural genius demonstrated in the planning and building of the temple in Jerusalem was attributed to this same expertise, or "wisdom" (1 Kings 5:9–18). Elsewhere, the word was applied to the handiwork of artisans (cf. 1 Kings 7:14; Isa. 44:9–17).

Equally important are the philosophical and intellectual connotations of this term. The word also means "superior mental ability." So the translation "intelligence" is appropriate in Job 38:36 and 39:17. The same expression is applied to the intellectual brilliance and vast knowledge of Solomon as the writer of songs and proverbs (1 Kings 4:29–34). The term itself is morally neutral, so "wisdom" may also include the devious conniving of Jonadab and Absalom (2 Sam. 13) and the clever scheming of Joab and the wise women of Abel and Tekoa amid difficult circumstances (2 Sam. 14; 20:16–22).

In respect to wisdom proper, this same Hebrew word has acquired a derived meaning equivalent to "experience" or even "good common sense" (cf. Job 32:7; Prov. 1:7). Essentially the wisdom mentioned in these texts connotes the judicious or skilled application of the powers of human reason to the issues of life. Other Old Testament wisdom terminology includes a series of related words usually translated in the following manner: "understanding, knowledge" or even "discernment" (Prov. 1:5; 3:5; 4:1), "insight, sensibility, intelligent, clever, have success" (Prov. 12:8; 16:20; 19:14; 21:11), "aptitude" or "skill" (Prov. 10:23; 11:12), and "prudence, success, good results" (Prov. 3:21; Isa. 28:29).

In the Old Testament, then, wisdom is basically the very practical art of being prudent, sensible, and skillfully insightful so that one might prosper and have good success in life. Wisdom is also disciplined and proper behavior, learning how to do what is right and just and fair (Prov. 3:1–5). Wisdom taps the life experience of accumulated years and harnesses that knowledge and understanding for the purpose of safety, long life, right behavior, sound moral character, happiness, material prosperity, and integrity (cf. Prov. 1:33; 2:8–9; 3:1–2). Ultimately wisdom is learning how to steer through life in a way that wins favor and a good name in the sight of both humanity and God (Prov. 3:4).

The Form of Wisdom

The sage, or wise man, was an important figure in Israelite society from the earliest days of the monarchy. He is cited, along with the priest and the prophet, as one of the three sources of authoritative guidance for the community of God (cf. Jer. 18:18; Ezek. 7:26). It appears that royal counselors were part of the corps of professional officers comprising the cabinet in the courts of David and Solomon (2 Sam. 8:16–18; 20:23–26; 1 Kings 4:1–6).

Hence the setting of wisdom as a professional circle of wise men played a significant role in the royal court of the united monarchy and King Solomon (1 Kings 4:32–33; Prov. 25:1). In fact, biblical scholars suggest that the wisdom of Proverbs was in effect a school textbook for the royal family and the elite of society. They were trained in the ways of wisdom so that in the future they might be wise and productive leaders of the next generation of Israelites (cf. the "my son" formula in Prov. 1:8; 2:1; 3:1; 4:1, etc.).

There are essentially two genres of wisdom literature in the Old Testament. The first and most prevalent type is didactic or practical wisdom. The book of Proverbs is the most representative example of this practical instruction. Didactic wisdom consists of wise sayings or popular proverbs that advocate all sorts of prudential habits, skills, and virtues (e.g., Prov. 21:23; 22:3; 23:22). These utilitarian lessons were aimed at developing moral character, personal success and happiness, safety, and well-being. In one sense, didactic wisdom was a practical exposition of and ethical commentary on the law of Moses.

The second type of Old Testament wisdom is that found in Ecclesiastes, or Qoheleth, and to some extent Job. The genre is usually categorized as philosophical, speculative, or even pessimistic wisdom. This strand of wisdom tradition is critical, reflective, and questioning as it delves into the deeper and more vexing issues confronting humankind. The skepticism characteristic of this speculative and philosophical literature portrays most vividly the emptiness and folly of the search for insight and understanding apart from God (Eccl. 1:1–18; 12:12–14).

Hebrew wisdom is like a mountain full of precious gemstones that must be carefully mined out of sediment and rock formations one by one. The basic unit of Hebrew wisdom is the proverb. The proverb is merely an analogy attempting to uncover basic truth about life by means of comparison. Characteristically the proverb is a popular saying expressing in pithy terms certain observed regularities in the external world of nature or in human behavior. There are several other types or patterns of the proverbial speech form, as shown in figure 21.3.

Hebrew wisdom literature is a composite of several wisdom speech forms like the parable. In Proverbs the parable is

Figure 21.3. Proverbial Speech Forms

1. The proverb: "Before his downfall a man's heart is proud, / but humility comes before honor" (Prov. 18:12).

2. The folk saying: "The laborer's appetite works for him; / his hunger drives him on" (Prov. 16:26).

3. The paradoxical: "He who is full loathes honey, / but to the hungry even what is bitter tastes sweet" (Prov. 27:7).

4. The analogous: "Like cold water to a weary soul / is good news from a distant land" (Prov. 25:25).

5. The absurd: "Of what use is money in the hand of a fool, / since he has no desire to get wisdom" (Prov. 17:16).

6. The classification: "If a man is lazy, the rafters sag; / if his hands are idle, the house leaks" (Eccl. 10:18).

7. The proportional or relative value: "Better a meal of vegetables where there is love than a fattened calf with hatred" (Prov. 15:17).

8. The cause and effect or consequential: "Wealth is worthless in the day of wrath, / but righteousness delivers from death" (Prov. 11:4).

usually understood as a "warning speech" (e.g., the warning against adultery in 6:20–35). The precept is an authoritative instruction or regulation for behavior based on the rules and values and religious tenets of society. The ethical aspects of this literary form connect Hebrew wisdom with the moral codes of Hebrew law (e.g., "Do not withhold good from those who deserve it, / when it is in your power to act," Prov. 3:27). The riddle is a puzzling question stated as a problem calling for mental acumen to solve it (e.g., Samson's riddle, "Out of the eater, something to eat; / out of the strong, something sweet," Judg. 14:14). The fable is a brief tale embracing a moral truth using people, animals, or inanimate objects as characters (cf. Jotham's fable about the trees choosing a king, Judg. 9:7–20).

Other literary categories and devices used by biblical wisdom writers include the wise saying (a generalization about the way of wisdom based on the insight of experience or a folk expression of plain common sense (e.g., Prov. 18:18; 20:19), the numerical proverb (which takes the form of culminating numerical progression—Prov. 6:16–19; 30:18–31), the rhetorical question (Prov. 5:16; 8:1), allegory (the personification of wisdom in Proverbs 8–9 and the "old age" poem in Ecclesiastes 12:1–8), and satire and irony (Prov. 11:22; Eccl. 5:13–17).

The Practice of Wisdom

The Bible knows only two "paths" of life. Either one follows the way of the righteous, or one walks in the way of the wicked (Ps. 1). In the New Testament, Jesus affirmed this basic description of the course of life as a choice between "the narrow way" and "the broad way" (Matt. 7:13; 12:30). In Proverbs those who walk the narrow path of righteousness are called "wise" (10:8, 14), "upright" (11:3, 6), and "righteous" (10:16, 20); those who carelessly speed down the broad road are labeled "fools" (10:1, 8, 14), "wicked" (10:3, 6, 7), and "unfaithful ones" (11:3).

Of singular importance here is the notion that "the way of wisdom" is not so much knowledge and intellect as it is behavior and character. More than pithy sayings and clever maxims, true wisdom is a lifestyle. Biblical wisdom is a code of ethics rooted in the legal tradition of the law of Moses. Its purpose is to school one's attitude, character, and behavior in the fear of the Lord so he or she might walk in the way of goodness and keep to the paths of righteousness (Prov. 2:20).

The antithesis of the wise man in wisdom literature is the fool. Various terms are used to caricature the fool in the Old Testament wisdom, including the naïve youth who is untutored and easily deceived (*peṭî*, Prov. 14:15), the person who is stupid in practical affairs and shameless in religious affairs (*keşîl*, Prov. 1:1), the one whose obstinance leads into folly (*ʾĕwîl*, Prov. 1:7), those who are crude and dull like beasts (*baʿar*, Prov. 12:1), the brutal and the godless (*nābāl*, Prov. 17:7), the babbler and scoffer (*lēṣ*, Prov. 1:22), and the deluded, mad, and irrational (*hōlēl*, Prov. 28:4). All these foolish ones are characterized by disdain for wisdom and instruction, the rejection of discipline and correction, and insolence and irreverence before the Lord God.

The New Testament confirms this understanding of the way of wisdom as divine instruction that prompts the practical outworking of godliness in human behavior. According to the book of James, those who are truly wise demonstrate their insight by a "good life" and works done in "meekness of wisdom." Unlike earthly wisdom, godly wisdom is pure, peaceable, loving, gentle, open to reason, submissive, full of mercy and good works, impartial, and sincere (3:13–18).

The Person of Wisdom

The ancient Hebrews recognized that wisdom was more than mere teachings of the sage or the accumulation of experience over the years of life. The basic goal of Hebrew wisdom was a proper relationship to Yahweh, the very God of Wisdom (Job 12:13; Isa. 31:1–2). This "Lord who is wise" has revealed his knowledge and understanding in creation, and he continues to display his wisdom in his providential rule of the nations (e.g., Ps. 104:24; Prov. 3:19; Isa. 10:13). As the God of wisdom he also grants this gift to humanity, to those searching for it like hidden

treasure (Prov. 2:4; 1 Kings 3:28; Dan. 2:21).

The Old Testament expression "the fear of the Lord" best conveys this relational dimension of Hebrew wisdom (Ps. 111:10; Prov. 1:7). The fear of the Lord was the source of Hebrew wisdom and actually connoted a complex of interrelated attitudes and actions:

1. The desire to get understanding that arises from a choice grounded in the human will (Prov. 1:29; 2:5)
2. Awe and reverence for the God of creation and redemption that elicits genuine worship and willing obedience to his commands (Prov. 24:21)
3. Dread at God's holiness and trepidation of his divine judgment (Eccl. 12:13–14)
4. Faith and trust in God's plan for human life, and a rejection of self-reliance (Ps. 115:11; Prov. 3:5–6)
5. Hating and avoiding evil, and refusing to envy sinners (Prov. 3:7; 9:13; 16:6; 23:17)
6. Generally the reward of prosperity and long life to the prudent (Prov. 10:27; 14:27; 19:23)
7. Disciplined instruction that instills wisdom, humility, and honor (Prov. 15:33; 22:4)

The personification of wisdom in the book of Proverbs also illustrates the personal aspects of the fear of the Lord. Wisdom is portrayed both as an itinerant female pedagogue seeking students at the city gates (Prov. 8:1–12) and as a preexistent master architect participating in God's creative works (Prov. 8:22–31). In each case, emphasis is placed on the experience of a relationship with the "person of wisdom."

The New Testament further develops this concept of the person of wisdom by identifying Jesus Christ as "the master architect" of creation (Col. 1:15–17). Elsewhere the apostle Paul indicates that the Christian's walk in the way of wisdom begins when he or she acknowledges that God is the source of life in Jesus Christ and that God made this Jesus our wisdom, righteousness, holiness, and redemption (1 Cor. 1:30).

The Content of Wisdom

Theodicy

The topics addressed in Old Testament wisdom literature are as numerous and varied as the human experience, yet there are recurring themes in the speculative and instructional wisdom writings.

The philosophical discussions of Job and Ecclesiastes focus on questions related to the notion of theodicy (i.e., the reality of pain, suffering, and death in the world in relationship to God's holiness and justice). Specific issues addressed in the discussions of speculative Old Testament wisdom include human suffering, poverty, and social injustice (e.g., Job 21:7–26), the "crookedness" of life (especially the prosperity of the wicked—Eccl. 8:14–15; 9:11–12), the fact of evil and death (Eccl. 9:1–6), the afterlife (Eccl. 3:16–22), and purpose and meaning in this life (Eccl. 4:1–3).

The Retribution Principle

The idea of divine retribution based on the merits (or demerits) of human behavior is a common theme in the poetic and wisdom literature of the Old Testament. The retribution principle is rooted in the blessings and curses of the Mosaic covenant (Deut. 28). The rewards or punishments appended to the legislation of Yahweh's pact with Israel stipulate that obedience to the commands of God will bring divine blessing, whereas disobedience to the Lord's statutes will send the curses of Yahweh upon the Hebrews. This fundamental teaching of Old Testament theology is examined from four complementary perspectives in the following chapters (Job, Psalms, Proverbs, and Ecclesiastes).

Instruction

Didactic wisdom literature is essentially practical social commentary based on the ethical demands of Hebrew law. Hence the instructions and warnings of the sayings in the book of Proverbs aimed at regulating daily life cover a diversity of topics, including familial relationships (23:22–25), retribution and discipline (3:12; 28:10), friendship (17:17), control of the tongue (26:18–28), marriage and adultery (5:1–23), the poor and the needy (14:21, 31), the wise contrasted with the foolish (18:1–16), the industrious contrasted with the sluggardly (26:13–16), drunkenness (23:29–35), life and death (13:14), anger (29:22), kingship (20:28), etiquette (25:2–7), indebtedness (11:15), wisdom (1:7), and the fear of the Lord (2:5–6).

Questions for Further Study and Discussion

1. How do we account for the similarities between the poetry and wisdom literature of the Hebrews and that of the rest of the ancient Near East?
2. What is the relationship between Old Testament wisdom literature and the so-called prosperity gospel espoused in some sectors of the Christian church today?
3. How do the apocryphal wisdom of Sirach (Ecclesiasticus) and the Wisdom of Solomon compare with the canonical Old Testament wisdom in style and theme?
4. What is the relationship of wisdom literature to the ethical teachings of the Prophets?
5. Select a psalm and try to identify examples of the various types of parallelism that characterize Hebrew poetry.

6. What role should wisdom literature have in the teaching of the contemporary Christian church? Is there a place for the "sage" in today's church?
7. How does our understanding of the life situation of the Hebrew poet aid in the interpretation of biblical poetry?

For Further Reading

Alter, Robert. *The Art of Biblical Poetry.* New York: Basic Books, 1985.

Andersen, F. I., and David N. Freedman. *Hosea.* AB. Vol. 24. Garden City, N.Y.: Doubleday, 1980.

Bullock, C. Hassell. *An Introduction to the Old Testament Poetic Books.* Rev. ed. Chicago: Moody Press, 1988.

Crenshaw, J. L. *Old Testament Wisdom: An Introduction.* Atlanta: John Knox, 1981. A comprehensive introduction to the idea of wisdom and wisdom literature in the Bible and the ancient Near East.

———, ed. *Studies in Ancient Israelite Wisdom.* New York: Ktav, 1976.

Freedman, David N. *Pottery, Poetry and Prophecy.* Winona Lake, Ind.: Eisenbrauns, 1982.

Gammie, John, and Leo G. Perdue, *The Sage in Israel and the Ancient Near East.* Winona Lake, Ind.: Eisenbrauns, 1990.

Gordis, R. *Poets, Prophets, and Sages.* Bloomington: Indiana University Press, 1971.

Gray, G. B. *The Forms of Hebrew Poetry.* Reprint. New York: Ktav, 1972.

Hoftijzer, J. "Remarks Concerning the Use of the Particle *'t* in Classical Hebrew." *Oudtestamentische Studien* 14. 1–99.

Kidner, Derek. *The Wisdom of Proverbs, Job and Ecclesiastes: An Introduction to Wisdom Literature.* Downers Grove, Ill.: InterVarsity, 1985.

Knight, D. A., and G. A. Tucker, eds. *The Hebrew Bible and Its Modern Interpreters.* Chico, Calif.: Scholars Press, 1985.

Kugel, James. *The Idea of Biblical Poetry: Parallelism and Its History.* New Haven: Yale University Press, 1983. Arguments against the ideas of parallelism and meter in Hebrew poetry and for Hebrew poetry as essentially synthetic.

Longman, Tremper, III. *How to Read the Psalms.* Downers Grove, Ill.: InterVarsity Press, 1988.

Lowth, Robert. *Lectures on the Sacred Poetry of the Hebrews.* Boston: Crocker & Brewster, 1829. Reprint.

Murphy, R. E. *The Tree of Life.* Garden City, N.Y.: Doubleday, 1990.

———. *Wisdom Literature and Psalms.* Nashville: Abingdon, 1983.

———. *Wisdom Literature.* FOTL 13. Grand Rapids: Eerdmans, 1982. Classification and analysis of individual units of wisdom literature according to genre.

Noth, Martin, and D. W. Thomas, eds. *Wisdom in Israel and in the Ancient Near East.* VT Supplement 3 (1955). Rowley Festschrift.

O'Connor, Michael. *Hebrew Verse Structure.* Winona Lake, Ind.: Eisenbrauns, 1980. An attempt to move the study of Hebrew poetry away from the emphasis on parallelism and meter by shifting the focus to Hebrew syntax through the application of modern linguistic techniques.

Pritchard, J. B., ed. *ANET.* 3d ed. Princeton: Princeton University Press, 1969.

von Rad, Gerhard. *Wisdom in Israel.* J. D. Martin, trans. Nashville: Abingdon, 1972.

Ryken, Leland. *How to Read the Bible as Literature.* Grand Rapids: Zondervan, 1984.

Scott, R. B. Y. *The Way of Wisdom.* New York: Macmillan, 1971. A popular introduction to canonical and extracanonical wisdom literature, including historical background, literary forms, and contemporary significance.

Simpson, W. K., ed. *The Literature of Ancient Egypt.* Rev. ed. New Haven: Yale University Press, 1973.

Walton, John H. *Ancient Israelite Literature in Its Cultural Context.* Grand Rapids: Zondervan, 1989. Useful survey and discussion of the parallels between Old Testament and ancient Near Eastern literature according to genre. Extensive bibliographies.

Chapter 22

Job

The book of Job leads us to consider one of the basic philosophical questions of human existence. It has been found to be a very practical book because the questions have not changed much over the last five thousand years of history. We still seek reasons for personal and corporate suffering and wonder what logic can suffice to defend its seeming arbitrariness. The book of Job undertakes such a defense and offers a biblical perspective on suffering.

The Writing of the Book

There can be little doubt that the form of Job we now possess has the unified structure of a literary composition. Much speculation, however, has been given as to what process may have been involved in the production of the work. Literary critics have not been reticent to identify particular sections as later additions. Prominent among these would be the Elihu speeches (chaps. 32–37), the Hymn to Wisdom (chap. 28), the second speech of Yahweh (40:6–41:34), and the prose prologue and epilogue, which are often presented as adopted from an ancient Epic of Job.

The most contested section is that containing the speeches of Elihu. Some scholars note that Elihu is not mentioned among the friends in either the prologue or the epilogue, and they contend that he does not really add anything new to the debate. The latter objection will be addressed in the discussion on the structure of the book. As to the former, there is good reason for Elihu to be omitted in the narrative portions of the book. In the prologue he would not be mentioned because of his lack of status. His introduction of himself in chapter 32 makes it plain that he was not one of the recognized wise men; he was rather like a graduate student daring to reprimand his professors for their lack of insight. That Elihu is not mentioned in the epilogue can be explained in that he had not committed offense in his response to Job. The other friends advised Job in effect to confess to unknown or unreal sins to appease an angry deity. Elihu did not so misconstrue God and was not called to account. There is therefore no reason to consider Elihu's speeches as secondary additions.

Once it is recognized that Job is part of the corpus of wisdom literature, it is possible to accept, as most scholars do, that the dialogue presented is not offered as a reporter's transcript quoting the precise words of each person involved. A high view of biblical inspiration requires one to take into consideration the literary genre of a book in order to understand how it ought to be interpreted.

The result of this is that the composition of the book of Job may not have occurred until centuries after the experiences of the man. While this would allow more room for the possibility of sections being added to the core of the work, the evidence that such a process actually took place is vague, and we see no need for such a theory of composition. The unified structure argues for the integrity of each section, and we believe that each section makes a unique contribution to the purpose of the whole. To put it another way, the book would fall short of accomplishing its purpose if any of the sections were deleted.

The individual named Job shows no indication of being an Israelite. The place names rather suggest that he was Edomite. Consequently there is no mention of the covenant or the law, and God is rarely identified as Yahweh. Since the book is a work of Wisdom, there is little information of a historical nature in its content to help us to date either its events or its composition. Traditionally the events of the book have been dated roughly to the patriarchal era because the lifestyle and longevity of Job are most similar to those found in Genesis. It is further pointed out that the existence of roving bands of Sabaeans and Chaldeans (Job 1:15, 17) suits best the early second millennium B.C. There are no real problems with this view, though it must be recognized that the evidence is scant.

In contrast, it is not considered likely that the book was composed that early. While some have attempted to make connections to the Persian period, the orthography of the book appears to be preexilic, and many scholars now hold to a date during the divided monarchy.

Evidence is extremely difficult to establish, and in any case, the timeless nature of the message makes the dating of the book a moot point.

The Background

While ascertaining historical background is neither possible nor pertinent, it is necessary to discuss the literary background of a book such as Job. The book contains a variety of literary genres, including dialogue (chaps. 4–27), soliloquy (e.g., chap. 3), discourse (e.g., chaps. 29–41), narrative (chs. 1–2), and hymn (chap. 28). These literary genres are common to wisdom literature, but are rarely mixed in so sophisticated and skillful a manner as found in Job.

Wisdom literature of the ancient Near East features a few compositions that address the same general philosophical questions. A Sumerian work entitled "Man and His God" (Ur III period, about 2000 B.C.) is a monologue by a person who does not understand why he is suffering. At the end he is shown what his sin was and therefore concludes that there is no such thing as undeserved suffering.

In an Akkadian monologue, "Ludlul bel Nemeqi" (I will praise the lord of wisdom), dating to the latter half of the second millennium B.C., a man who considers himself in favor with Marduk, the chief god of the Babylonians, wonders why he is suffering. In the end his sins are forgiven, so again the solution is that there is no such thing as a righteous sufferer (fig. 22.1).

A third piece, "The Babylonian Theodicy" (about 1000 B.C.), takes the form of a dialogue between a sufferer and his friend. The friend offers the standard lines of advice and explanation only to find each refuted by the sufferer. The conclusion finally reached is that the gods are inscrutable—whatever evil men do is done because the gods made them that way (fig. 22.2).

Although the literature from Mesopota-

Figure 22.1. Excerpt from Mesopotamian Wisdom: 1

My lofty head is bowed down to the ground,
Dread had enfeebled my robust heart.
A novice has turned back my broad chest.
My arms, though once strong, are both paralysed.
I, who strode along as a noble, have learned to slip by unnoticed.
Though a dignitary, I have become a slave.
To my many relations I am like a recluse.
My family treats me as an alien.
The pit awaits anyone who speaks well of me,
While he who utters defamation of me is promoted.
My slanderer slanders with god's help;
I have no one to go by my side, nor have I found a helper.
What strange conditions everywhere!
When I look behind, there is persecution, trouble.
Like one who has not made libations to his god,
Nor invoked his goddess at table,
For myself, I gave attention to supplication and prayer:
To me prayer was discretion, sacrifice my rule.
The day for reverencing the god was a joy to my heart;
The day of the goddess's procession was profit and gain to me.
The king's prayer—that was my joy,
And the accompanying music became a delight for me.
I instructed my hand to keep the god's rites,
And provoked the people to value the goddess's name.
I made praise for the king like a god's,
And taught the populace reverence for the palace.
I wish I knew that these things were pleasing to one's god!
What is proper to oneself is an offence to one's god,
What in one's own heart seems despicable is proper to one's god.
Who knows the will of the gods in heaven?
Who understands the plans of the underworld god?
He who was alive yesterday is dead today.
For a minute he was dejected, suddenly he is exuberant.
One moment the people are singing in exaltation,
Another they groan like professional mourners.
My god has not come to the rescue in taking me by the hand,
Nor has my goddess shown pity on me by going at my side.
Then the Lord took hold of me,
The Lord set me on my feet,
The Lord gave me life,
The Babylonians saw how Marduk restores to life,
And all quarters extolled his greatness:
'Who thought that he would see his Sun?
Who imagined that he would walk along his street?
Who but Marduk restores his dead to life?
Apart from Sarpanitum which goddess grants life?

From "Ludlul bel Nemeqi," in *Babylonian Wisdom Literature*, trans. W. G. Lambert (New York: Oxford Univ. Press, 1960): I:73–79, 92–95, 98; II:10–13, 23–42, 112–20; IV:2–4, 29–36.1.

Figure 22.2. Excerpt from Mesopotamian Wisdom: 2

Sufferer III

23 My friend, your mind is a river whose spring never fails,
24 The accumulated mass of the sea, which knows no decrease.
25 I will ask you a question; listen to what I say.
26 Pay attention for a moment; hear my words.
27 My body is a wreck, emaciation darkens [me,]
28 My success has vanished, my *stability* has gone.
29 My strength is enfeebled, my prosperity has ended,
30 Moaning and grief have blackened my features.
31 The corn of my fields is far from satisfying [me,]
32 My wine, the life of mankind, is too little for satiety.
33 Can a life of bliss be assured? I wish I knew how!

Friend VI

56 O palm, tree of wealth, my precious brother,
57 Endowed with all wisdom, jewel of [gold,]
58 You are as stable as the earth, but the plan of the gods is
       remote.
59 Look at the superb wild ass on the [plain;]
60 The arrow will follow the gorer who trampled down the fields.
61 Come, consider the lion you mentioned, the enemy of cattle.
62 For the crime which the lion committed the pit awaits him.
63 The opulent nouveau riches who heaps up goods
64 Will be burnt at the stake by the king before his time.
65 Do you wish to go the way these have gone?
66 Rather seek the lasting reward of (your) god!

Sufferer VII

67 Your mind is a north wind, a pleasant breeze for the peoples.
68 Choice friend, your advice is fine.
69 Just one word would I put before you.
70 Those who neglect the god go the way of prosperity,
71 While those who pray to the goddess are impoverished and dis-
       possessed.
72 In my youth I sought the will of my god;
73 With prostration and prayer I followed my goddess.
74 But I was bearing a profitless corvée as a yoke.
75 My god decreed instead of wealth destitution.
76 A cripple is my superior, a lunatic outstrips me.
77 The rogue has been promoted, but I have been brought low.

Friend XXIV

254 O wise one, O savant, who masters knowledge,
255 In your anguish you blaspheme the god.
256 The divine mind, like the centre of the heavens, is remote;
257 Knowledge of it is difficult; the masses do not know it.
258 Among all the creatures whom Aruru formed
259 The prime offspring is altogether . . .
260 In the case of a cow, the first calf is lowly,
261 The later offspring is twice as big.

262 A first child is born a weakling,
263 But the second is called an heroic warrior.
264 Though a man may observe what the will of the god is, the
      masses do not know it.

Sufferer XXVII

287 You are kind, my friend; behold my grief.
288 Help me; look on my distress; know it.
289 I, though humble, wise, and a suppliant,
290 Have not seen help and succour for one moment.
291 I have trodden the square of my city unobtrusively,
292 My voice was not raised, my speech was kept low.
293 I did not raise my head, but looked at the ground,
294 I did not worship even as a slave in the company of my asso-
      ciates.
295 May the god who has thrown me off give help,
296 May the goddess who has [abandoned me] show mercy,
297 For the shepherd Šamaš guides the peoples like a god.

Excerpts from "The Babylonian Theodicy," in *Babylonian Wisdom Literature*, trans. W. G. Lambert (New York: Oxford Univ. Press, 1960).

mia shows some general similarities in form and content to the book of Job, the latter has a much higher level of sophistication both in literary form and in philosophical depth and integrity.

If the genre of Job is to be identified based on a correlation with these Mesopotamian pieces, an argument could be made against those who view the book as a stage play, though certainly it could be adapted to that use. Likewise, because wisdom literature by definition makes frequent use of hypothetical situations and dialogue, there is no reason to over-emphasize the historicity of the conversation. Equally, there is no reason to doubt that the narrative is based on the experiences of real people.

Outline of the Book

I. Prologue (1–2)
II. Dialogues
  A. Job's opening lament (3)
  B. Cycle 1: Consolation
    1. Eliphaz (4–5)
    2. Job (6–7)
    3. Bildad (8)
    4. Job (9–10)
    5. Zophar (11)
    6. Job (12–14)
  C. Cycle 2: The fate of the wicked
    1. Eliphaz (15)
    2. Job (16–17)
    3. Bildad (18)
    4. Job (19)
    5. Zophar (20)
    6. Job (21)
  D. Cycle 3: Specific accusations
    1. Eliphaz (22)
    2. Job (23–24)
    3. Bildad (25)
    4. Job (26–27)
III. Interlude: Hymn to Wisdom (28)
IV. Discourses
  A. Discourse 1: Job
    1. Reminiscence (29)
    2. Affliction (30)
    3. Oath (31)
  B. Discourse 2: Elihu
    1. Introduction and theory (32–33)
    2. Verdict on Job (34)
    3. Offense of Job (35)
    4. Closing statement of summary (36–37)
  C. Discourse 3: God
    1. Speech 1 (38–39)

Purpose and Message

The purpose of the book of Job is to explore the justice of God's treatment of the righteous. This investigation takes two major directions. First, the satan implies in 1:9–11 that God's policy of blessing the righteous is counterproductive to the development of true righteousness. Blessing induces people to be righteous for what they stand to gain from it. He suggests that his claim can be demonstrated by cutting off Job's blessings. The satan's contention is that disinterested righteousness does not exist and, indeed, cannot exist in the system that God operates. God's policies are placed on trial here, not Job. Second, Job wonders how God can possibly allow the righteous person to suffer. Again, it is God's policies that are on trial.

In carrying out this purpose, the book refuses to take any shortcuts. The narrator goes to great pains to establish Job's impeccable reputation. The easy solutions of the ancient Near East are thereby discounted from the start as well as rejected in the shallow philosophy of Job's friends. In the end, it is not important to the purpose of the book that God vindicated Job. The audience knew of Job's innocence from the start. What is essential to the development of the book's purpose is that Job vindicates God by maintaining his integrity even when he is not being blessed for it.

The message of the book in regard to the satan's concern is that God's practice of blessing the righteous is not a hindrance to the development of true righteousness. In regard to Job's situation, the message is that God is not always under obligation to make sure that the righteous receive blessing and *only* blessing. The world is more complex than that. In both cases God's justice is inferred from his wisdom. Though we cannot get enough information to vindicate God's justice, we do have enough information to be convinced of his benevolent wisdom. God's self-defense, if it can be called that, is conducted by establishing that his wisdom exceeds all human wisdom.

While this purpose and message offer an understanding of the book on the level of its plot, some have wondered what might have given the Israelites an interest in this piece of literature that seems to have originated outside their society. A common answer has been that the book of Job may have become of interest to the Israelites who were experiencing the Babylonian exile and trying to reconcile that event with their view of God.

Although the book unquestionably contains discussion and information that would be invaluable to the exiles (especially the idea that God's wisdom is the basis on which his justice may be vindicated), the scenario in Job seems too unlike Israel of the sixth century to invite too close a correlation. Most obviously, the book is insistent on Job's absolute innocence and vindicates him in the end. Such could hardly be said of Israel. Undoubtedly, however, the minority who were righteous in Israel may well have taken solace and found comfort in the teachings of the book of Job.

Structure and Organization

The prologue of Job functions in several ways. First, it introduces the characters and sets up the conditions under which the drama unfolds. It does this in such a way that the audience is made aware of certain details that the characters themselves do not know (for instance, Job and his friends do not know of the discussion that took place between the Lord and the satan). The result is that the audience is put in a position to see readily that the friends are wrong in their remarks to Job.

Second, the prologue introduces one of the philosophical concerns of the book in the satan's challenge to God. The two scenes in the prologue lead to the ruin of Job's family and possessions and then to the collapse of Job's health.

Excursus: Satan

There is a reason why we have referred to "the satan" throughout this chapter, rather than the more common personal name "Satan." Our purpose is to reflect the Hebrew text more accurately. In the book of Job, "Satan" is not a personal name, but the description of a function. The function described by the Hebrew word *satan* can be performed either by human beings (1 Sam. 29:4; 2 Sam. 19:17–24; 1 Kings 5:16–20; 11:14–23; Ps. 109:6) or by supernatural beings (Num. 22:22; 1 Chron. 21:1; Zech. 3:1–2). In each case the being functions as an adversary. The adversarial role is not necessarily an evil one as can be seen from Numbers 22, where "the angel of the Lord" is so designated.

While there is no reason to deny that the satan in the book of Job actually is the being we designate by the name "Satan," it must be recognized that the Israelites of the Old Testament period may not have known of the existence of a chief of demons, a satan par excellence. The only place where the noun occurs without a definite article ("the") is in 1 Chronicles 21:1, one of the last books of the Old Testament canon to be written. In this context it may be a personal name (Satan) or it may just be indefinite (a satan). Since the angel of the Lord is in view in Numbers 22, we cannot insist that the function is always performed by the same individual. Nevertheless, the book of Job is an important resource for tracing the development of the understanding of Satan in the history of theological thought.

Structure

Job's lament in chapter 3 introduces the three cycles of dialogues that occupy chapters 4–27. In the dialogue section, the friends become more and more antagonistic, while Job increasingly isolates himself and directs his statements to God. It is difficult to find anything wrong with the theology of the friends, though their role as comforters leaves much to be desired. The friends affirm traditional theology: The righteous will prosper and the wicked will suffer. This is known as "the retribution principle" and is affirmed in general in the books of Psalms and Proverbs. The friends also affirm a deduced corollary: Those who prosper must be righteous and those who suffer must be wicked. Although this idea is never presented as truth by Scripture, it is clear that the Israelites largely believed it to be true. This corollary becomes the basis of the friends' accusations against Job. If the retribution principle and its corollary are true, and if God is just, then Job must be guilty of some heinous crime.

As the dialogue section proceeds, Job generally affirms both the retribution principle and its corollary. (Chapter 21 appears to be an exception to this at first, but what Job is doing there is observing that if there can be exceptions to the retribution principle in the occasional prosperity of a wicked person, then there could as easily be an occasional exception in the suffering of a righteous person.) However, since he is insistent that he has done nothing to deserve such suffering, Job is forced to look upon God's justice with some suspicion. The major part of Job's speeches is taken up with rejection of his friends' conclusions and wisdom on the one hand and increasing demands of God for a court hearing on the other.

Job desires to have his case tried in court. With his complaint against God, he seeks to position himself as accuser and God as defendant. God's practices ought to be called to account. Of course, Job is unaware that it is God's being called to account (by the satan) that led to his predicament in the first place.

The remarks by Job's friends serve the purpose of offering some of the philosophical answers of that day to the problem of suffering. These answers are the ones that we have already seen in the Mesopotamian material. The Mesopotamian response was to give up on ever making sense of life. Confession of unknown or uncommitted crimes was used as a means of appeasing a largely irrational deity. This is what Job's friends wanted him to do. Job's last speech in the dialogue section (27:1–6) shows that it is precisely in his refusal to respond in this way that he has maintained his integrity. Though Job has had serious doubts about God's justice, and though his self-righteousness at times sounds presumptuous, he has refused to treat God as one would treat one of the irrational pagan deities (cf. 42:7). The fact that Job is not willing to confess falsely as an act of appeasement so that he can be restored to favor and blessing is the demonstration that his righteousness is true, disinterested righteousness.

This first section of the book has given an answer to the challenge posed by the satan. Yes, there is disinterested righteousness, and Job is an outstanding example of that fact. But Job's problem remains: How can a just God allow the righteous to suffer? The placement of the Hymn to Wisdom in chapter 28, at the conclusion of the dialogue section, suggests that true wisdom has not yet had its say. The traditional wisdom of the wise has been insufficient to meet the challenge of the complexity of Job's situation. This hymn portrays God as the founder of wisdom and as the possessor of wisdom that dwarfs the relatively insignificant wisdom of mankind. Human wisdom, puny as it is, can only come through the fear of the Lord—trusting in his wisdom rather than our own. This leads then to

the discourse section and hints already at the direction the resolution will take.

The first discourse contains the final case made by Job. He recalls his past high position (chap. 29), laments his current distress (chap. 30), and most significantly takes an oath of innocence (chap. 31). This oath is intended to force God to act. If Job is guilty of any of the offenses included in the oath, God would be expected to enact the appropriate curses. Continued silence by God would then serve as a vindication of sorts.

The second discourse comprises the speeches of Elihu. It fulfills a narrative function in keeping the reader in suspense about how God will respond to Job's oath. It serves a philosophical function of offering a more sophisticated response to Job's problem than that suggested by the other friends. Elihu first insists that God governs justly. This is in agreement with the other advisers, but is a refutation to Job, who has been expressing his doubts. Then Elihu affirms the retribution principle, but rejects the corollary. In his view, suffering may be preventative as well as punitive. That is, Job need not have committed any horrible crimes; the suffering he is experiencing may be God's way of turning him away from a wrong course. As a result, suffering can just as easily become an expression of God's mercy.

Elihu's perspective is difficult to contest and seems to be affirmed at least partially in God's statements about Job (40:8). However, since we have the prologue, we know that Elihu has not offered an accurate identification of the cause of Job's suffering.

When we finally arrive at the third discourse—God's speeches—we expect to find a resolution of some sort to the problem of the book. We can observe several things. First, God's reply totally ignores Job's complaint and likewise avoids responding to the oath of innocence. Second, while God does not identify any actual offense committed by

Job, neither does he indicate the cause of Job's suffering. Rather, the whole discussion is turned from consideration of God's justice to consideration of his wisdom. The string of unanswerable rhetorical questions shows that Job is no match for God in a dispute. God's wisdom is put on display in manifesting him as Creator and Lord. He is responsible for the created structure of the world as well as for its sovereign maintenance.

God implies that the natural order was not established with the retribution principle as an operational foundation (38:26). When the retribution principle operates, it gives evidence of God's sovereign intervention; but nature does not automatically enforce the retribution principle. God even challenges Job to devise a system with the retribution principle built into it (40:10–14).

The resolution offered by the speeches of God is that his justice must be deduced from his wisdom. Causes of suffering cannot be consistently or accurately deduced, and no one has sufficient wisdom to call God's justice into question. In Job's brief responses he is at first speechless (40:3–5) and then finally retracts his challenge (42:1–6). Eliphaz had urged Job to repent (*shub*) of his sin (22:23); God leads him to recant (*naham*) what he had said about him (42:6). Though Job has maintained his integrity and is vindicated as a righteous man, he was not without offense. His pride and self-righteousness served as a platform for questioning God's justice.

The epilogue ties some loose ends together. The report of Job's renewed prosperity is not gratuitous. Though the satan does not appear in the epilogue, the prosperity poured out on Job is the answer to the satan: God will continue his policy of intervening to bless the righteous. Job's friends are rebuked, not for accusing Job, but rather because they did not speak properly of God (42:7–8).

Though Job is vindicated, he is never given an explanation of his suffering. This is not a problem for the book, for the question was not really *why* Job was suffering, but the more general concern of the propriety of God's actions and conduct. There was never any suspense for the audience regarding Job's righteousness or how his particular suffering came about. By maintaining his integrity Job vindicated God's practice of prospering the righteous. God vindicated Job in the eyes of his friends. God's justice is vindicated, not by identifyng a "legitimate" cause for suffering, but by demonstrating his great wisdom.

Major Themes

The Retribution Principle: Part 1

The retribution principle provides a framework for the philosophical discussion presented in the book of Job. As we have seen, the principle is stated by means of conditional clauses: If a person is righteous, he will prosper; if a person is wicked, he will suffer. The corollary was deduced from the principle on the assumption that the principle is always true. One could then believe that if a person prospered, he must be righteous; and if a person suffered, he must be wicked. The principle serves as a popular explanation of changes in the daily fortune or misfortune of individuals or nations.

Though the principle was widely believed to be true by the Israelites and their neighbors, it is clear from the Psalms (cf. 37) that theory and experience did not always mesh. In Israel the gap between theory and experience created an especially poignant problem because of the Hebrews' view of God. Since there was only one sovereign God, suffering could not come from any other source. Because this one God was believed to be absolutely just, suffering must have a logical explanation. Furthermore, if God was really just, suffering must be in proportion to wickedness and prosperity must be in proportion to righteousness.

In the book of Job everyone assumes that the retribution principle is true. The central questions concern the relationship of the principle with the justice of God, particularly calling the corollary into question. In the end, the book affirms God's intention of operating by the retribution principle, but implies that we cannot predict how or when it is going to operate. Since the principle is not always observably true, the corollary must be rejected.

The retribution principle should be accepted as an explanation of what God is like. He delights in prospering the righteous and guarantees that the wicked will be punished. This is consistently affirmed in Old Testament theology as true of individuals as well as nations. The principle cannot be used, however, to demand action from God or to deduce what a person is really like. It cannot provide consistent explanations for any particular person's prosperity or adversity. It is not intended to address issues of causation. We often cannot know what causes our suffering, but we can take comfort that all is in the hand of an infinitely wise and sovereign God.

The Wisdom, Justice, and Sovereignty of God

The divine attributes of wisdom, justice, and sovereignty are emphasized in the book of Job and in the wisdom literature generally. We can appreciate these themes best in comparison to other emphases. For instance, in the covenant emphasis of Israelite theology, it is common to see loyalty (ḥesed), compassion (raḥûm) and graciousness (ḥanûn) mentioned prominently (cf. Exod. 34:6; Joel 2:13; Jonah 4:2; Neh. 9:17; Pss. 86:15; 103:8; 145:8).

An interesting contrast of focus can also be seen in modern lists of God's attributes. They often emphasize omni-science (knowing everything) instead of infinite wisdom. They tend to focus on omnipotence (all-powerful) perhaps at the expense of sovereignty (control and maintenance). Christians tend to think of justice as something that they fortunately did not receive, for all have sinned and fall short of the glory of God; therefore God's judgment is feared. Yet Job's greatest desire was that God judge his case. C. S. Lewis has clarified this last contrast by observing that the Christian views judgment as a criminal case with himself as defendant; he seeks mercy, not justice. The Israelite views judgment as a civil case with himself as plaintiff; he seeks justice in place of injustice.[1]

In this situation we see the broader categories of God's attributes. Omniscience is only one small and relatively insignificant part of God's infinite wisdom. Omnipotence is likewise only one aspect of God's sovereignty. Similarly, mercy is sometimes a more personalized reflection of God's justice. The broader categories help us focus more on who God is instead of on what he can do for a particular person.

Mediator

The question of whether Job could or would be aided by a mediator (referred to by a variety of Hebrew terms) arises several times in the book (5:1; 9:33; 16:18–22; 19:25–27; 33:23). Job pleads for the intercession of a mediator and appears convinced that such a one will arise (19:25–27), though the exact nature of his expectation is a matter of continuing controversy. Some see in Job's affirmations a belief in the resurrection of the body, while others translate and interpret the text to convey only his confidence that he will be vindicated and restored before his death.

Regardless of Job's position on the timing of his vindication, the role of the

[1] C. S. Lewis, *Reflections on the Psalms* (New York: Harcourt, 1958), 9–19.

mediator is clear. He is an individual (most would agree that it is God himself whom Job expects) who would serve as defense attorney in court to afford Job a fair hearing and a just verdict. Additionally, some of the terminology used to describe the mediator portrays him as a near relative (kinsman-redeemer; see chap. 15, "Ruth") who would appear at the height of the crisis to bring relief by providing a dignified resolution.

It is important that though the mediator issue dominates the dialogue section, it fades into the background as the book reaches its conclusions. In the end, no mediator is necessary and none appears. Job's claim of having been treated unjustly dissipates in the face of God's challenges, and his need for a kinsman-redeemer is eliminated by his restoration.

Questions for Further Study and Discussion

1. How can the information gleaned from the book of Job be used to comfort someone who is suffering?
2. What does the book offer as an appropriate response to suffering?
3. Does God operate by means of the retribution principle today? Explain your answer.
4. Is there any observable connection between the retribution principle and the Pharisees' view of the law? Explain.

For Further Reading

Andersen, Francis I. *Job*. TOTC. Downers Grove, Ill.: InterVarsity, 1976. Excellent treatment by a renowned evangelical linguist.

Blackwood, Andrew W., Jr. *Out of the Whirlwind*. Grand Rapids: Baker, 1959.

Clines, D. J. A. *Job 1–20*. WBC. Vol. 17. Waco, Tex.: Word Books, 1989.

Gordis, Robert. *The Book of God and Man*. Chicago: University of Chicago Press, 1965. Thematic treatment from a Jewish background.

Hartley, John. *The Book of Job*. Grand Rapids, Eerdmans: 1988. Recent, conversant with scholarship, evangelical (though not always in a traditional sense), thought-provoking, thorough, and arguably the best.

Pope, Marvin. *Job*. New York: Anchor: 1965. Good treatment from an ancient Near Eastern backdrop in particular.

Tsevat, Matitiahu. "The Meaning of the Book of Job." In *The Meaning of the Book of Job and Other Biblical Studies*. New York: Ktav, 1980. A seminal article, originally published in 1966, on the book of Job and the retribution principle.

Westermann, Claus. *The Structure of the Book of Job*. Philadelphia: Fortress, 1981. A helpful form-critical study.

Chapter 23

Psalms

The book of Psalms is one of the best-loved and most-used books of the Old Testament, yet at the same time it is one of the most problematic in the canon. Questions surrounding authorship, composition, theology, interpretation, application, and function all contribute to the book's complexity. The fact that many believers through the ages have found comfort from its pages in time of need, never once considering any of those questions, stands as testimony to the power of God to minister through the books of Scripture.

The Writing of the Book

Two aspects of the writing need to be considered: the authorship of individual psalms, and the composition of the psalter as a whole. Since some of the psalms purport to have been written in the mid-second millennium B.C., while others are clearly postexilic (i.e., after 539 B.C.), we know that (1) the composition of the whole did not take place until sometime after the Exile, and (2) thus the editor (the person or persons responsible for collecting and organizing the psalms) is to be differentiated from the author (who composed the individual psalm). We will use the terms "author" and "editor" to distinguish these functions.

Authorship

The main source of information for the authorship of the psalms comes from the psalm titles. Of the 150 psalms, all but 34 have titles of some sort. Of the 116 titles, 100 indicate an author (and often other information as well, such as musical style or directions for performance), and of those 100, 73 are attributed to David. Other authors identified are Moses (90), Solomon (72, 127), Asaph (50, 73–83), Heman (88), Ethan (89), and the group called the Sons of Korah (42, 44–49, 84–85, 87). There has been some question as to whether the persons named in the titles are being designated as authors or as dedicatees. For instance, Psalm 72 seems to be a blessing on Solomon (by David) rather than a psalm that Solomon would have written.

Others have wondered about the reliability of the titles. Would we consider them inspired? Even the oldest manuscripts of the Old Testament contain the titles, though they are not part of the composition proper. If they are later additions by an editor, they are still very ancient and therefore have a claim to authenticity. It is difficult to prove that they are inspired, but most conservative interpreters treat them as accurate.

Composition

The book of Psalms is divided into five books as follows:

Book I: 1–41
Book II: 42–72
Book III: 73–89
Book IV: 90–106
Book V: 107–50

This division is older than our oldest manuscripts, but until recently, interpreters had few clues as to its significance. Some headway has been made in the recognition that smaller collections exist within the larger whole. Among collections that have been identified:

Davidic Group I: 3–41
Sons of Korah Group I: 42–49
Davidic Group II: 51–65
Asaph Group: 73–83
Sons of Korah Group II: 84–88 (exc. 86)
Congregational Praise Group I: 95–100
Halleluyah Group: 111–17
Songs of Ascent to Jerusalem: 120–34
Davidic Group III: 138–45
Congregational Praise Group II: 146–50

The editor has woven these smaller collections together into the five-book structure to produce the larger composition that we call the book of Psalms. What purpose guided the editor as individual psalms and collections of psalms were set in their places?

One helpful suggestion is that the editor's purpose is discernible from the "seam" psalms. These are the psalms that come at the end of each of the first four books (i.e., 41, 72, 89, and 106). The theory speculates that these have been used by the editor to mark transitions from one book to the next, so that by examining them carefully we may be able to distinguish the primary topic of each book. These data would be supplemented by other evidences of editorial activity such as the comment in Psalm 72:20, which notes the end of the prayers of David even though many Davidic psalms appear later in the psalter.

The most significant evidence of the editor's work and purpose is thought to be represented in Psalms 1 and 2, which many consider an introduction to the whole book.

The point to note here is that these observations combine to suggest there is a definitive, purposeful arrangement of the psalms that offers a message that transcends what any individual psalm has to offer. In the same way that the writers of the historical literature took narratives from various sources and edited them into a unified composition with a particular theological agenda in mind, so it may be with the editor of Psalms. Just as some historical literature (especially Kings) was compiled in stages, so, it is likely, was the book of Psalms.

Evidence that the five books of Psalms were not initially compiled all at one time comes from the psalm manuscripts found among the Dead Sea Scrolls. These manuscripts date to the last century and a half B.C. Among the thirty-odd manuscripts available, the psalms of books I–III are almost always in the same order as they are in the Bible. The order of the psalms in books IV and V, however, frequently varies from that found in the Old Testament. This seems to suggest that books I–III had already attained final form by the second century B.C., whereas books IV–V may still have been under development. It is possible, then, that the editorial arrangement was not fixed until just before the time of Christ.

Thus the book of Psalms is made up of individual poetic compositions written during a thousand-year period by several persons. These compositions were at various times gathered into small collections, which in turn were arranged in stages into a larger work edited with a particular theological agenda in mind.

The Background

It is more appropriate to speak of the literary background of the book of Psalms than of a historical background. Study of the Mesopotamian and Egyptian hymns and prayers has provided much information by which we can better understand the Psalms. In a comparative study like this, it is necessary to consider both similarities and differences to gain a balanced picture. Aspects of both form and content can contribute to the analysis (fig. 23.1).

Form

The psalms of the Bible can be classified into three general categories—praise, lament, and wisdom—with a number of subcategories as well. For the most part, each psalm falls into only one of the classifications—one exception being Psalm 22, in which verses 1–21 are a lament psalm and verses 22–31 comprise a praise psalm. Both the praise and lament psalms have typical characteristics that make them easily identifiable. For instance, the lament psalms generally contain a vocative in the first line (e.g., "O Lord"; cf. Pss. 3–7), and congregational praise psalms almost always start with an imperative (e.g., "Sing to the Lord"; cf. Pss. 96, 98).

Additionally, each psalm type follows a fairly consistent format. Lament psalms regularly include elements such as complaint, petition, confession of trust, and vow of praise.

The psalms of Mesopotamia do not contain distinctly lament compositions. Instead, lament and praise are characteristically combined into single entities. In this we can see both similarity and difference with the Psalms. The difference lies in the Babylonians' combining praise and lament; the commonality is that Israelites and Babylonians use generally the same forms of lament when they are complaining against deity and similar forms of praise when they are praising deity.

One type of praise, however, is common in the Bible but does not occur in Mesopotamian literature. Israelite psalms manifest both "descriptive praise" and "declarative praise," but only the former appears in Mesopotamia. Descriptive praise extols God for who he is; it focuses on the attributes of God. Declarative praise is usually the praise of a person thanking God for answering his prayer about a specific instance in the past.

Content

In reading the psalms and prayers of the Babylonians, someone who was familiar with the Bible would surely recognize a general similarity in the matters of praise and in the situations that brought complaints to God. Petitions are also similar. Yet many differences would also be immediately apparent. Descriptive praise is of a different nature in the Babylonian materials, where there is a tendency simply to list attributes and epithets (titles) of deities. There is very little of the Israelite imperative approach to praise, in which the hymn requests the worshiper to join in praise to God.

Several differences are also observable in lament psalms. Most obvious is the fact that most of the laments of Mesopotamia are used in conjunction with magical rituals and incantations intended to coerce the deity to comply with the petition. In these rites the Mesopotamian worshiper accepts the idea that the deity considers him or her guilty of offense, though the person has no idea what the offense might be. He or she does not assume that the god is consistent or just; the worshiper merely seeks to appease him by performing the appropriate ritual.

The case in Israel is far different. In the laments in the book of Psalms, the worshiper most frequently considers himself innocent and therefore seeks vindication. There is no hint of magic, incantation, appeasement, or manipulation. When the Israelite author does consider himself

Figure 23.1. Excerpt from a Mesopotamian Psalm

Prayer to the Moon-God

O Sin, O Nannar, glorified one . . . ,
Sin, unique one, who makes bright . . . ,
Who furnishes light for the people . . . ,
To guide the dark-headed people aright . . . ,
Bright is thy light in heaven. . . .
Brilliant is thy torch like fire. . . .
Thy brightness has filled the broad land.
The people are radiant; they take courage at seeing thee.
O Anu of heaven whose designs no one can conceive,
Surpassing is thy light like Shamash thy first-born.
Bowed down in thy presence are the great gods; the decisions of the
    land are laid before thee;
When the great gods inquire of thee thou dost give counsel.
They sit (in) their assembly (and) debate under thee;
O Sin, shining one of Ekur, when they ask thee thou dost give the oracle
    of the gods.
On account of the evil of an eclipse of the moon which took place in
    such and such a month, on such and such a day,
On account of the evil of bad and unfavorable portents and signs which
    have happened in my palace and my country,
In the dark of the moon, the time of thy oracle, the mystery of the great
    gods,
On the thirtieth day, thy festival, the day of delight of thy divinity,
O Namrasit, unequaled in power, whose designs no one can conceive,
I have spread out for thee a pure incense-offering of the night; I have
    poured out for thee the best sweet drink.
I am kneeling; I tarry (thus); I seek after thee.
Bring upon me wishes for well-being and justice.
Make my god and my goddess, who for many days have been angry
    with me,
In truth and justice be favorable to me; may my road be propitious; may
    my path be straight.
After he has sent Zaqar, the god of dreams,
During the night may I hear the undoing of my sins; let my guilt be
    poured out;
(And) forever let me devotedly serve thee.

From "Sumero-Akkadian Hymns and Prayers," in *ANET*, 3d ed. (Princeton:
Princeton Univ. Press, 1969), 386.

guilty (e.g., Ps. 51), the offense is typically of an ethical or moral sort, whereas the offense in the Mesopotamian laments would more likely be cultic (e.g., the failure to offer appropriate sacrifice).

In conclusion, many of the similarities have to do with general content or literary style. The differences are more substantial and most frequently are related directly or indirectly to the contrasting views of God and how he is worshiped. This shows us that from a literary standpoint, the psalms do not represent too great a departure from what can be found throughout the ancient Near East. The uniqueness of the Psalms is found in the way they reflect the theological distinctiveness of Israel.

Outline

This outline is based on the view that an editor's agenda is behind the arrangement of the psalms. It must be remembered that this approach is still speculative. The table in figure 23.2 helps to explain the outline.

  I. Introduction (1–2)
  II. David's conflict with Saul (3–41)
  III. David's kingship (42–72)
  IV. The Assyrian crisis (73–89)
  V. Introspection about the destruction of the temple and the Exile (90–106)
  VI. Praise and reflection on the Return and the new era (107–45)
  VII. Concluding praise (146–150)

Purpose and Message

Since we have identified two levels of composer—author and editor—we must also address two levels of purpose.

Author

Very little can be said about purpose at the level of the author. Each author would have had a specific purpose for each composition. Older commentaries have offered suggestions for the historical situation that lay behind each psalm, but this practice was highly speculative and did not produce satisfying results. By contrast, it is probable that many of the compositions were written to meet liturgical needs. More recently some scholars have been inclined to identify festivals or rituals behind each psalm. Unfortunately, to substantiate this theory they must assume that Babylonian festivals (such as the enthronement festival), otherwise unknown in Israel, were adopted, regularly observed, and had a well-developed liturgy. Evidence for this remains very tentative.

In the end we must be willing to consider the whole range of possible situations. Some of the psalms would have been motivated by a particular historical occurrence. (For instance, thirteen of them cite historical instances in their titles: 3, 7, 18, 34, 51, 52, 54, 56, 57, 59, 60, 63, 142. All are Davidic, and all but one are in books I or II.) Others would have been written for various liturgical occasions. Still others may have been private devotional thoughts. The point is that there is no unified purpose or message to be identified at the authors' level.

Editor

We have already suggested that Psalms 1 and 2 serve as an introduction to the book as a whole and that the "seam" psalms are instrumental in helping us to discern the editor's agenda. What conclusions can be drawn from these about the editor's purpose and message?

Psalm 1 draws a brief but sharp distinction between the conduct of the righteous person and that of the wicked person. It also addresses their respective destinies. We find that this accurately introduces one of the major themes of Psalms: concern for the ultimate vindication of the righteous and the ultimate punishment of the wicked.

Psalm 2 presents the idea that God has chosen the Israelite king and will defend him against the conspiracies of the nations. This provides a national aspect to parallel the individual aspect of Psalm 1.

These two levels of message (individual and national) come together in David. He stands as the righteous person who is in need of vindication from God and also the king of Israel par excellence who represents not only the nation of Israel, but also all the successive kings of his line. His heart for God led God to choose him as king and to make a covenant of kingship with him.

The seam psalms, then, help us to see how these two aspects of the editor's message are going to be addressed. With Psalm 72, the seam between books II and III, we see a transition from David to Solomon. This psalm includes elements

Figure 23.2. A Cantata About the Davidic Covenant

Introduction   Ps. 1. Ultimate vindication of the righteous
Psalms 1–2   Ps. 2. God's choice and defense of Israelite king

Book	Seam	Theme	Content
Book 1	41	David's conflict with Saul	Many individual laments; most psalms mention enemies
Book 2	72	David's kingship	Key psalms: 45, 48, 51; 54–64 mostly laments and "enemy" psalms
Book 3	89	Eighth-century Assyrian crisis	Asaph and Sons of Korah collections; key psalm: 78
Book 4	106	Introspection about destruction of temple and exile	Praise collection: 95–100; key psalms: 90, 103–105
Book 5	145	Praise/reflection on return from Exile and beginning of new era	Halleluyah collection: 111–117; Songs of Ascent: 120–134; Davidic reprise: 138–145; key psalms: 107, 110, 119

Conclusion   Climactic praise to God
146–150

of both covenanted kingship and righteous rule. Reverting to the seam between books I and II, we can discern a transition from the monarchy of Saul, when David was hunted and persecuted, to David's vindication in coming to the throne after the death of Saul. Psalm 89, the seam between books III and IV, shows a covenant in disarray and a people confused and under siege. This would bring to mind the preexilic monarchy perhaps from Solomon to the fall of Jerusalem as the focus of book III, though it may have more specific reference to the eighth-century Assyrian crisis. The last seam, Psalm 106, is a litany of the failures of Israel and a plea to regather the people from exile, clearly suggesting an exilic context for book IV.

This analysis of Psalms 1 and 2 and the seam psalms has led to the conclusion that the five books of the psalter are intended to trace the history of Israel, particularly with regard to the Davidic covenant, which is the covenant of king-

ship. Intertwined with this is consideration of the righteous man and his response. The "righteous man" potentially refers to any righteous person in Israel who seeks to understand the national dilemma and cope with the national failures. How does the godly person view the demands on conduct when the nation is going astray and God's actions are not always comprehensible? These are presented as poetic reflections intended to convey the consistency of God's justice and faithfulness to the covenant and the righteous.

David is the quintessential example of the righteous man vindicated. He was vindicated vis-à-vis Saul, vindicated vis-à-vis Absalom, and ultimately vindicated on a national and eschatological scale in the development of the Davidic covenant. This shows us a "wisdom" aspect to the editor's message (the righteous will be vindicated) as it addresses the individual and an "eschatological" aspect (God's commitment to Davidic kingship) addressing the nation.

Structure and Organization

Just as Kings and Chronicles contain theological reflection about God through a recitation of history, so Psalms may use the arrangement of liturgical compositions to reflect on the nature of God and the response of the individual. In many ways, therefore, the Psalms would resemble a cantata. The arrangement is not based on the circumstances or dates when the psalms were composed, but on other factors. For instance, Psalms 138–145 are in the so-designated postexilic section, yet they are Davidic psalms. Why would the author place them there? This is the kind of question we need to address.

We have seen that the seam psalms and introductory psalms appear to indicate a general agenda, but the question has been raised whether individual psalms or even collections of psalms were set in an order to suit that agenda. Some psalms certainly seem to be placed specifically with the intention of fulfilling the editor's agenda as we have identified it. Among the most persuasive are these:

- 45 Coronation Hymn for David
- 48 Correlation to the conquest of Jerusalem by David
- 51 Repentance concerning sin with Bathsheba
- 78 Reflection on the fall of Samaria and the northern kingdom
- 90 Moses' anticipation of exile beginning the exilic section
- 103 Critical discussion of God's forgiving the sins of the nation
- 110 The return of victorious kingship with theocratic and eschatological focus
- 119 Correlation to the establishment of the law as the focus of the postexilic community

These psalms are all placed exactly where one would expect them to be in a presentation of the sort we have been discussing. There are many more individual psalms for which a rationale of placement can be identified, suggesting that the editor's work did involve such arranging.

There are also cases in which entire collections seem to have been set in place. We would not expect that all the Asaph psalms were placed together where they are by mere coincidence. It is more logical to assume that the editor used the tone of the Asaph collection or something that stood out in the collection to decide where it would best fit in his cantata.

The best examples of this kind of thematic placement appear in book V. The Halleluyah collection (111–117) appropriately follows Psalm 110 with its recurring themes of God's faithfulness, deliverance, and theocracy. The "Songs of Ascent" (120–134) were originally composed for the pilgrimage feasts for which thousands of Israelites journeyed to Jerusalem. In this new context they would reflect on *the* return to Jerusalem after decades of exile. The themes of deliverance and trust in God are also quite fitting. Finally, the last Davidic collection (138–145) functions to give David the "last word" before the grand finale. The closing psalm in the group, 145, is particularly well-suited to this purpose.

Much has yet to be done in identifying the rationale of each psalm or collection, but enough is evident to conclude that an editorial intention did exist and that the editorial purpose is discernible at least in its broad strokes.

Book I contains mostly laments, and many of the psalms make some mention of the psalmist's enemies. As the writer cries out to God for vindication and deliverance, we can easily see the correlation of this book to the time David spent in the wilderness fleeing from Saul. Psalms 3–13 would parallel 1 Samuel 19–23, the beginning of David's troubles with Saul. Psalm 18 reports deliverance from enemies and could correlate to 1 Samuel 24, where David spares Saul's life and Saul stops the chase. Psalms 23–24 appear strikingly appropriate to 1 Samuel 25, when God provides for David's needs through the wisdom of Abigail. Parallels to David's second sparing of Saul's life can be seen in Psalms 27–30. In general the tone of the psalms in the first book fits well with this period in David's life.

We have already mentioned some of the individual psalms in book II (45, 48, 51). As a whole the psalms can be correlated with the events of David's reign as recorded in 2 Samuel. Another major section of laments in Psalms 54–64 would parallel the crisis represented in Absalom's rebellion, with David being driven from the throne by his own son (note esp. 55:12–14, 21).

Book III is more difficult to assess than the other books. This is because it is composed of two collections that, we assume, have been placed according to collection. Psalm 78 appears to offer the most insight to its orientation, with a possible correlation to the fall of the northern kingdom. Because the seam psalm (89) offers a crisis and, apparently, a resolution of the crisis, the book may be limited to the Assyrian crisis in the latter half of the eighth century B.C., though it could refer to the entire period from Solomon to the fall of Jerusalem.

Book IV begins with a psalm of Moses and ends with a recapitulation of a history of rebellion, leading to a hope and a plea for restoration. Along the way it includes a small collection of praise psalms (95–100) that appropriately presents the affirmations of hope and faith sustained in the Exile. Themes in this small collection include the Lord as King, a new song, deliverance, idol worshipers put to shame, Yahweh above all

gods, judgment on the nations, and the continuing faithfulness of the Lord. Psalm 102 is a fitting plea for the Lord to have compassion on Zion. The book concludes with a series (104–106) surveying the mighty and gracious deeds of the Lord, from creation and sovereignty, to election and covenant, to the rebellion and failures of the people.

Finally, book V begins with Psalm 107, the Israelites' thankfulness to God for regathering them. The roles of Psalm 110, of Psalm 119, and of the three collections in this book have already been discussed. Psalm 145 provides a conclusion to book V, while Psalms 146–150 serve as the finale to the entire cantata.

Major Themes

Two of the major themes in the book of Psalms are those introduced in Psalms 1 and 2: the retribution principle and kingship.

The Retribution Principle: Part 2

The retribution principle can be summed up in two two-part affirmations: (1) The righteous will prosper and the wicked will suffer, and (2) those who prosper are righteous, while those who suffer are wicked. The first of these affirmations is generally supported in Psalms and throughout Scripture (cf. Ps. 1). It was acknowledged, however, that exceptions existed (compare the English proverb "crime doesn't pay"). The second affirmation, although it is not given the support of Scripture, was clearly believed by many Israelites. This is obvious from the actions and concerns of Job's friends, as related in the book of Job, and also from the statements in many of the psalms (e.g., Ps. 37).

For the Israelites, this principle was a theological issue: If God is a just God, how can the righteous suffer or the wicked prosper? Though this question still perplexes even at times today, the situation was much worse for the ancient

Israelites. The reason is that today we find consolation in the belief that even if the righteous person does not prosper here on earth, he has the expectation of heaven. Likewise, we are assured that the wicked will face the judgment of God for eternity rather than escape unscathed. Because of these assurances, the justice of God is not so seriously questioned, although we continue to struggle with theology as we try to cope with our circumstances.

The ancient Israelites did not have the advantage of these assurances. God had not yet revealed to them the fact that judgment of the righteous and wicked would take place after death with each kind receiving just rewards. All that the Israelites knew of God's justice was its execution in this life (cf. Pss. 27:13; 91:5–8). This made the retribution principle a much more serious matter for them than for us.

The lament psalms reflect this concern the most. The psalmist complains to the Lord because enemies have gained the upper hand even though the psalmist is the righteous one. He pleads for God to intervene and put his enemies to shame and in so doing vindicate him. The psalmist does not consider himself absolutely righteous, but he is more righteous than his enemy, and he feels he certainly does not deserve the degree of persecution that has come his way.

The degree of persecution or suffering is important, because if God is just, the wicked person should suffer in proportion to his wickedness and the righteous person should prosper in proportion to his righteousness. It is not just for a very wicked person to be punished in a very small way.

This observation can help us understand what is often considered one of the most difficult problems in the book of Psalms. Several of the lament psalms include a curse or imprecation on the writer's enemies—sometimes of a general sort (28:4), sometimes more specific

(137:9). Some whole psalms are devoted to this type of expression (58; 109). Once we understand the need for the retribution principle to be carried out proportionately, we can see that these imprecations are simply an outgrowth of theology. Desperately wicked people had to be punished by God in drastic ways if his justice was to be upheld. The specific call for drastic punishment was the psalmist's way of asserting how wicked his enemy was, emphasizing the need for God to exercise his justice by righteous judgment.

Psalms as a book confirms that it is legitimate for righteous people to expect God to prosper them for their righteousness and for God to bring the destruction of the wicked. It is never promised, however, that there will be no exceptions to that general rule. David is held up as an example of a righteous man who was vindicated, and it is in the nature of God to work in that way. But life is not always that simple, and Scripture does not offer a firm rule that will hold in every case. The book of Job has already shown us that answers to the hard situations in life are not always forthcoming. Psalms also teaches us that trust in the sovereign will of God is proper, whatever one's circumstances.

Kingship

There are nine psalms scattered through the psalter that specifically concern the king: 2, 18, 21, 45, 72, 89, 110, 132, 144. Of these, four are attributed to David (18, 21, 110, 144), and three have important editorial functions (2, 72, 89). They are at times considered messianic psalms, and in terms of the continuum that exists from David through his dynasty to the eventual ideal Davidic king (Messiah), that is accurate. Nevertheless, in most cases it is inappropriate to see these psalms as dealing specifically and exclusively with the ideal Davidic king. More often than not, they are more generic and could be applied to any Davidic monarch.

Psalm 2 sets the tone with the affirmation of the Lord's choice and protection of the king. Psalm 18 praises God for delivering the king from his enemies (vv. 37–50). Many of the psalms in this set either ask for deliverance, victory, or blessing for the king or discuss the covenant that established kingship. It is affirmed that God promised victorious kingship to the kings who trust in him and that he is fully able to carry out that promise. This is best viewed as relating to the future ideal king, for there was not an abundance of kings in David's line who trusted the Lord. In contrast, the coming, ideal king would exercise perfect trust and would therefore enjoy all the blessings of God on his reign.

Nature and Creation

Several praise psalms focus on God's relationship to nature. This was an important matter to address for several reasons. Israel was an agricultural community, which means that the people were dependent on the climate for their livelihood and even their survival. God's favor or disfavor was most easily inferred from the bounty of the harvest. The blessings and curses connected to the covenant were tied to the produce of the land.

Another reason for this emphasis is that much popular theology of the day concerned the world around them. The gods the Canaanites most highly esteemed were fertility gods, and most of the pagan gods were intertwined with the forces of nature. It was important, then, for the God of the Israelites to be distinguished from these pagan gods; he is not bound by nature or identified with the forces of nature in the same way.

In the psalms addressing God and his creation (8, 19, 29, 65, 104) several important points are established. God is the Creator and maintains and orders all of creation (104). Creation and nature reveal the glory of God (19). Humankind has been placed at the head of creation (8). The forces of nature are instruments of his power and blessing (29, 65). God is thereby elevated above nature in a way that was not possible in the polytheistic systems of the ancient Near East.

Excursus: Devotional Use of the Psalms

The book of Psalms uses the praise, complaint, and exhortation of God's people to reveal the character of God. As readers to whom the authority of God's Word is important, our task is to submit ourselves to the God who is here revealed. Praise psalms extol the attributes and actions of God and compel us to kneel before him. Wisdom psalms explore theological axioms for means to comprehend God's ways. Lament psalms help us to see God through the emotional struggles of a believer in crisis who is thrown to dependence on him.

The historical books help us learn more about God by telling us his stories. The Psalms give us a different perspective by helping us come into contact with God through our daily experiences and the questions that arise from them. When journalists want to find out about a person, they don't just read the biography, but they interview the people who knew him or her best. When someone applies for a job, the employer doesn't stop with reading the applicant's résumé, but also checks the references. These analogies show the difference in how the historical literature and the psalms reveal God to us. Unquestionably, an interview or references are more likely to be subjective than a biography or résumé. But the subjective aspect can be just as important a guide to knowing the individual.

When we relate to God day by day, it is usually this subjective aspect that poses the hard questions. We often grapple with affirming God's attributes, not because we have philosophical reservations, but because our experience leads us to question his attributes. The true affirmation of his attributes comes through acknowledging them even when our life experiences do not seem to support them. That is the long-term effect that Psalms should have on us. Affirmation of God's attributes is the goal of our devotional reading. This process prepares us for or sustains us through trial and loss. It likewise keeps God in focus and everything in perspective when life goes smoothly.

Even in our devotional use of psalms, however, we must be careful to interpret properly. We cannot allow our picture of God or our expectations of him to be distorted by twisting or manipulating the information given about him to our own advantage. The fact that God prospered or delivered someone in a particular situation is testimony to what God can do, not a promise that he will always do so for us. Each psalm and the book of Psalms as a whole contribute to our understanding of God. Though this composite picture of God may serve to satisfy our emotional vicissitudes, it still must be exegetically derived. We cannot afford a distorted picture of God derived from an uninformed handling of the text, for especially in times of crisis we must avoid misleading ourselves with false hopes dependent on misconstrued promises.

Questions for Further Study and Discussion

1. How can the reader of Psalms find a balance between the message of each psalm as an individual composition and the message of each psalm as a part of the larger whole? Is either aspect more important than the other?
2. What is the significance of the psalm types for interpreting the book of Psalms?
3. How does the retribution principle apply today?
4. Suppose you were pulled over and ticketed for driving 60 m.p.h. in a 55 m.p.h. zone while everyone else was going 70–75 m.p.h. Reflect on your response in relation to the lament psalms.
5. How do we strike a balance between the contextual view of the royal psalms and the messianic view? How does a passage such as Luke 20:41–44 affect our view?
6. How should our understanding of the form, content, purpose, and message of the book affect our devotional use of psalms?

For Further Reading

Allen, Leslie. *Psalms 101–150*. WBC. Waco, Tex.: Word Books, 1983.

Anderson, B. W. *Out of the Depths*. Philadelphia: Westminster, 1983.

Craigie, Peter. *Psalms 1–50*. WBC. Waco, Tex.: Word Books, 1983. The best evangelical commentary on Psalms.

Hayes, John H. *Understanding the Psalms*. Valley Forge, Pa.: Judson, 1976.

Kraus, Hans-J. *Theology of the Psalms*. Translated by Keith Crim. Minneapolis: Augsburg, 1986.

_____ . *Psalms 1–59*. Minneapolis: Augsburg, 1988. Most helpful commentary from a nonevangelical perspective.

_____ . *Psalms 60–150*. Minneapolis: Augsburg, 1989.

Lewis, C. S. *Reflections on the Psalms*. New York: Harcourt, 1958.

Longman, Tremper, III. *How to Read the Psalms.* Downers Grove, Ill.: InterVarsity, 1988. An excellent introduction to the book.

Miller, Patrick. *Interpreting the Psalms.* Philadelphia: Fortress, 1986.

Walton, John H. "The Psalms: A Cantata About the Davidic Covenant." *JETS* 34 (1991): 21–31.

Westermann, Claus. *Praise and Lament in the Psalms.* 1965. Reprint. Atlanta: John Knox, 1981. The forerunner for treatment of the psalm types.

Wilson, Gerald. "The Qumran Psalms Manuscripts and the Consecutive Arrangement of Psalms in the Hebrew Psalter." *CBQ* 45 (1983): 377–88.

_____. "Evidence of Editorial Divisions in the Hebrew Psalter." *VT* 34 (1984): 337–52.

_____. "The Function of Untitled Psalms in the Hebrew Psalter." *Zeitschrift für die alttestamentliche Wissenschaft* 97 (1985).

_____. "The Use of Royal Psalms at the 'Seams' of the Hebrew Psalter." *JSOT* 35 (1986): 85–94.

Chapter 24

Proverbs

The book of Proverbs represents the literary legacy of the Hebrew sages, or wise men. With the priests, prophets, and kings the sages rounded out the four basic leadership classes of Israelite society (cf. Jer. 18:18; Ezek. 7:26–27).

The "wise men," or "counselors," generally were associated with the royal court, as reflected in Proverbs and Ecclesiastes. They were "compilers" and "assemblers" of wisdom literature, both of the Hebrews and of foreign nations. As teachers of the wisdom tradition, their goal was to "weigh, study, and arrange proverbs" and "teach the people knowledge" (especially the next generation of Hebrew leaders, Eccl. 12:9).

The Hebrew word for "proverb" conveys a wide range of meanings, including the idea of comparison, a code of behavior, and the discovery of hidden truth. Essentially the book of Proverbs is a collection of comparisons based on observation and reflection that seeks to instruct people in "right behavior." As such it is practical or utilitarian wisdom rooted in the experiences of life common to human culture. This quality explains the enduring value of Proverbs for both religious and secular audiences through the centuries.

The Writing of the Book

The book of Proverbs contains a preface (1:1–7) and eight collections of wise sayings, five of which include brief introductions or superscriptions identifying the author-compiler of the proverbial wisdom. The eight collections are evident in the outline given on page 288.

King Solomon's sagacity, scientific interests, encyclopedic knowledge, and literary skills are well attested in the Old Testament. According to 1 Kings 4:29–34, Solomon's knowledge and understanding surpassed that of all the other sages in the academies of the ancient Near Eastern world. Solomon is credited with uttering some 3000 proverbs (hundreds of which are preserved in the book of Proverbs) and 1005 songs (e.g., Pss. 72, 127). Clearly King Solomon stands as the "patron of the arts" in ancient Israel. Not only did he popularize the wisdom tradition of the Hebrews, but also his example as sage and scholar served as the model for future generations.

Nothing is known of Agur and Lemuel of Massa. It seems likely they were members of the northern Arabian tribe of Massa, one of the sons of Ishmael (Gen. 25:14; 1 Chron. 1:30). The records of their "counsel" are further examples of the universality of wisdom traditions in the ancient world. They also give evidence of the international character of Israelite wisdom. The Hebrew sage and scribe sought pleasing and truthful words of practical instruction, whether of Hebrew, Edomite (e.g., Job), or Arabian origin (e.g., Agur and Lemuel).

The reference to the editorial work of Hezekiah's scribes in compiling at least one of the wisdom collections in Proverbs indicates the book could not have been completed before his reign over Judah ended (end of eighth century; cf. Prov 25:1). The Solomonic collections of 10:1–22:16 and chapters 25–29 are regarded as the oldest material in the book, dating to the tenth century B.C. Chapters 1–9 probably combine Solomonic sayings with later wisdom teachings from anonymous sages. The placement of the two collections of anonymous sayings (22:17–24:22 and 24:23–34) suggests that they come from the period between Solomon's reign and the activity of Hezekiah's scribes. The appendices (chaps. 30–31) may have been added as late as the time of the Hebrew exile.

This means that the wisdom literature of Proverbs dates anywhere from the tenth century to the sixth century B.C., the latter being the most likely time for the final composition of the book.[1]

The Background

The actual events of Hebrew history play almost no role in the book of Proverbs. This only serves to underscore the universal nature and value of practical wisdom. The same holds true for the instruction literature of the Egyptians and Mesopotamians. Wisdom literature was outside history in the sense that its purpose was to instruct people in the principles of right conduct. Instructional wisdom was centered in three institutions, the family or clan, the royal court, and the scribal schools. The collection and "canonization" of instructional literature was largely the responsibility of the royal courts in Israel and elsewhere in the Near East, since the wisdom tradition was crucial to the training of young men employed in governmental service.

The historical context for the development of the Hebrew wisdom tradition included the united monarchy under Solomon and the Judahite part of the divided monarchy under Hezekiah. The association of the Hebrew sages with the royal court followed the pattern established in the wisdom circles throughout the ancient world (cf. 1 Kings 4:30–31). Israel's successful participation in the international community as God's "light" to the nations depended on sound and godly leadership. The wise men were charged with the responsibility to instruct royal officals in the way of wisdom so they might be effective administrators and leaders modeling godly character and behavior.

The influence of wisdom was also important to Hebrew kingship for bringing a sense of balance and perspective to the economic structure of Hebrew society, protecting the rights of the poor and needy (Prov. 31:8–9). It is even possible that the instruction of the wisdom literature was used to supplement the religious reforms of the godly kings of Judah (cf. 2 Kings 18:1–6; 2 Chron. 29–31).

The practice of wisdom held reciprocal benefits for both Hebrew kingship and

---

[1]According to the comparative literary analysis of William F. Albright, Proverbs must predate the Aramaic sayings of Ahiqar (ca. seventh century B.C.). Cf. "Canaanite–Phoenician Sources of Hebrew Wisdom," in *Wisdom in Israel and the Ancient Near East*, festschrift for H. H. Rowley, ed. Martin Noth and D. W. Thomas, *VT* Supplement 3 (Leiden: Brill, 1955), 1–15. The comparative analysis of Kenneth A. Kitchen also supports a preexilic date for Proverbs (at least chapters 1–24); see "Proverbs and Wisdom Books of the Ancient Near East: The Factual History of a Literary Form," *TB* 28 (1972): 69–114.

Hebrew society. The rule of the king was made more secure by the instruction, instilling respect for parental and royal authority, while the quality of life for Hebrew citizens was improved as the king enacted principles of righteousness and justice (Prov. 20:28; 24:21; 25:2–7).

Outline of the Book

I. Title and purpose (1:1–7)
II. A father's reflections on the way of wisdom
   A. Discourses on wisdom (1:8–4:27)
   B. Instructions on marriage and warnings against adultery (5–7)
   C. Wisdom personified (8–9)
III. Proverbs of Solomon (10:1–22:16)
IV. Anonymous wise sayings (22:17–24:22)
V. More anonymous wise sayings (24:23–34)
VI. More proverbs of Solomon (25–29)
VII. Appendices
   A. Sayings of Agur (30)
   B. Sayings of King Lemuel (31:1–9)
   C. Anonymous acrostic poem on the ideal wife (31:10–31)

Purpose and Message

The message of Proverbs hinges on the belief that wisdom can be taught and can be passed on from one generation to the next (4:1–9). Since knowledge and understanding are heirlooms more precious than jewels, gold, and silver, it is imperative for young people to listen, receive, and obey the teachings of the elders, the sages, and especially their parents (1:8–9). The heart of Old Testament wisdom instruction is desiring and choosing to learn and apply "the fear of the Lord" to daily life (2:1–6). This means forsaking the way of darkness, evil, and death (2:11–15) and walking in the path of integrity,

righteousness, justice, and life (2:1–10). This is the way of wisdom.

The purposes of the book of Proverbs are stated in the prologue to the wisdom collections (1:2–7). They include

—To know wisdom and instruction (1:2; cf. 3:21–26)
—To receive teaching in wise dealing, righteousness, justice and equity (1:3; cf. 2:9)
—To help the simple gain prudence and the youth to gain knowledge and discretion (1:4; cf. 2:20–23)
—To increase learning and to acquire skill in understanding (1:5; cf. 9:9)
—To understand proverbs, parables, wise sayings, and riddles (1:6; cf. 4:10, 20)
—To learn the fear of the Lord (1:7; cf. 2:5–6)

The practical benefits of the way of wisdom are numerous for those disciplined enough to walk in the path of knowledge and understanding. The way of wisdom results in understanding the fear of the Lord and finding the knowledge of God, thus fostering covenant relationship with him (2:5, 17). Essentially, then, the fear of the Lord is a worshiping, reverent submission to the God of the covenant. The fear of the Lord is a right relationship to God, one of obedience to his covenant stipulations that prompts right method in thought and right behavior in action.

So the way of wisdom promotes the understanding of righteousness, justice, equity, and every good path (2:9). This preserves the wise from evil and delivers them from ruin and death (2:12). Conversely, the way of wisdom tends to safety, health, abundant welfare, peace and long life, prosperity and integrity, and righteousness (1:33; 2:7; 3:2, 8). Finally, those who walk in the way of wisdom find favor and a good reputation in the sight of God and humankind (3:4).

By analogy to the wisdom traditions of the ancient Near Eastern societies, the book of Proverbs was very likely a "school textbook" and an important part of the curriculum in the education of Hebrew youth. This practice continued into the early centuries of the Christian church as portions of the biblical Proverbs and the apocryphal book of Sirach (or Ecclesiasticus) were incorporated into the catechism designed to train the Christian youth in godliness.

Structure and Organization

Three major divisions in the literature of Proverbs are easily identified: the discourse material (1–9), the collections of proverbs (10–29), and the Massaite appendices (30–31). However, because the book is a collection of collections compiled over at least three centuries, systematic arrangement of the writings is largely lacking. Only general observations on the basic relationships of the various collections are suggested here.

The wisdom prologue of 1:1–7 serves as an introduction to the entire corpus of literature. It sets the general historical context for the instruction in wisdom, outlines the purposes and goals of the teachings contained in the collections of wise sayings and provides certain interpretive principles, and introduces the major theme of biblical wisdom literature.

The series of discourses in chapters 1:8–9:18 are generally understood to post-date the proverbial collections of 10:1–29:27. The speeches of instruction and exhortation, warning and admonition in this section elaborate on the theme of wisdom presented in the prologue. True wisdom comes from God, and those who would gain understanding must learn the fear of the Lord. Implicitly the fear of the Lord is rooted in and conditioned by the directives of Yahweh's covenant with Israel (e.g., 6:16–19). These discourses illustrate the fear of the Lord by contrasting the behavior of the wise and righteous with the foolish and wicked (e.g., 4:10–19).

Overt references to Israel's religion are less prominent in the proverbial collections of 10:1–29:27 than in the discourses, yet they are not absent entirely (e.g., the issue of sacrifice and prayer is raised in 15:3, 8–9). This section reinforces the teaching of the discourses by specifying how the fear of the Lord pragmatically shapes the behavior of the righteous or wise. The proverbial instruction of the sages constitutes a practical exposition of the moral law of the Torah designed to aid the "seekers" in applying wisdom principles to the daily routine of life.

The appendices (30–31) rehearse themes previously discussed in the proverbial sections, especially the control of the tongue, sensual indulgence, and drunkenness. Appropriately, the acrostic poem in praise of the virtuous woman concluding the book serves as a "case study" highlighting the preferred outcomes of the way of wisdom.

The appendices also affirm the divine authority inherent in the Hebrew wisdom tradition (30:5–6), perhaps even holding canonical significance for the entire collection of wisdom. Lastly, the Massaite additions to the book recapitulate the importance of the "horizontal" or social aspects of the way of wisdom promoted in the proverbial sections—maintaining the rights of the poor and needy (31:8–9).

The several collections of the literature contained in Proverbs incorporate a variety of wisdom speech forms, including the two- and four-line proverb (with the antithetic and comparative types predominant in 10:1–22:16), the extended wisdom discourse (especially in 1:8–9:18), numerical sayings (30:18–19, 21–28), and the alphabetic acrostic poem (31:10–31).

Major Themes

The Fear of the Lord

The Egyptian instructions of Amenemope give credence to the god of magic and wisdom, Thoth, or other gods of Egypt such as Aten and Khnum. The Babylonian proverbs and fables make appeal to the gods Shamash, Anu, or other deities like Humma, Shaham, and

Nisaba. However, the wisdom literature of the Old Testament acknowledges only one God, Yahweh (e.g., Prov. 22:17–19).

The book of Proverbs equates the fear of the Lord with the knowledge of God (2:5–6). In the Old Testament, the knowledge of God is associated with the experience of covenant relationship with Yahweh (so Hosea 6:1–3). Since God alone possesses wisdom and dispenses understanding to humanity, only those who know God through the experience of covenant loyalty will find wisdom's hidden treasures.

The concept of the fear of the Lord bridges the human subject with the divine king in such a way that God's storehouse of wisdom may be appropriated by his saints (2:7–10). The fear of the Lord in Proverbs is a composite response of attitude and will shaping human behavior in conformity with the commandments of God. (See "The Person of Wisdom" in chapter 21.)

Finally, the idea of the fear of the Lord prevents proverbial wisdom from degenerating into a rigid and mechanistic system of cause and effect that oversimplifies the complexities of life and offers pat answers to hard questions. The fear of the Lord preserves the inscrutable nature of God and maintains the profound mystery of life. This aspect helps us explain the tension between the two strands of Hebrew wisdom—the instructions for the ideal life and the discussions about the consuming issues of real life.

The Retribution Principle: Part 3

The retribution principle expressed in the blessings and curses of the Pentateuchal covenant formulas resurfaces in the wisdom literature of the Old Testament. The expectation of reward for the nation's conformity to the law of God is logically applied to the individual Hebrew "Godfearer" in the proverbial wisdom.

The tangible benefits of walking in the way of wisdom are conditioned by two important assumptions of the sages. First, proverbial wisdom presumes that the "vertical" dimension of covenant relationship with Yahweh has been a firmly established pattern of life. The practice of covenant loyalty and faithfulness is presupposed as part of a godly lifestyle. Second, the "blessings" of the path of wisdom are contingent on the premise that the "horizontal" dimensions of covenant relationship with Yahweh have been demonstrated practically in doing what is "right and just and fair" (Prov 2:9).

More important, the "ideal" paradigm of obedience—an adherence to the way of wisdom that naturally yields the "profits" of prosperity, peace, health, and long life—is qualified by the reality of human sin and the "crookedness" of a fallen world. So the Preacher reminds us that the race is not always won by the swift, nor the battle by the strong, but "time and chance happen to them all" (Eccl. 9:11–12).

The truisms of Proverbs are not absolute promises, but general principles based on careful observation of the human experience. The psalmist recognized the inherent flaw of mechanically ascribing the corporate blessings and curses of covenant law to the individual situation (e.g., Ps. 73). Here the writer questions his life of integrity in the face of the apparent ease and success of the wicked. Not until he entered the Lord's sanctuary did he gain perspective on the incongruities of life. Even Job's rebuttal to the "counsel" of his friends mocked a rigid interpretation of the retribution principle, as he satirically noted "the tents of marauders are undisturbed" (Job 12:1–6).

Finally, equal attention must be given to character development as part of the benefits of walking in the way of wisdom. More than material prosperity, the better fruits of understanding are the qualities of personal character such as discretion, prudence, wise dealing, righteous behavior, justice, and integrity. In fact, the words translated "prosperity" in Proverbs

13:21 and 21:21 (NIV) are better rendered "well-being" and "righteousness" respectively. Ultimately the way of wisdom is keeping to the path of righteousness, because only men and women of integrity will remain in the land (2:20–21).

Human Speech

The book of Proverbs has much to say about the use and abuse of the "tongue." In fact, three of the abominations in the warning against the seven sins God hates are directly related to human speech. Wisdom teaching on human speech in Proverbs can be summarized as follows.[2]

First, words have great power, for even death and life are in the power of the tongue (18:21). They may be used to wound or heal one's spirit (12:18; 15:4), shape attitudes and perceptions (18:8; 29:5), and form beliefs and convictions (10:21; 11:9). But the mouths of the wicked spread discord and strife like a "scorching fire" (16:27–28), in contrast to the mouth of the righteous, which is like a fountain or tree of life dispensing truth and knowledge (10:11; 15:2, 4, 7).

Second, words are sometimes futile as well. Human speech cannot serve as a substitute for concerted action (14:23), nor can it change the facts or conceal hidden motives or disguise one's inner character (24:12; 26:23–28).

Finally, Proverbs gives instructions on human speech at its best. The words of the wise spring from righteous character and reflective deliberation (12:17; 14:5). The words of the wise are marked by the qualities of honesty (16:13), brevity (10:14), serenity (15:1), and aptness (15:23).

Human Sexuality

The wisdom of Proverbs extols the virtue of (monogamous) marriage and

warns against the folly of sexual license. The insights of the Hebrew sages on the intricacies of the male-female relationship remain a valid resource for addressing the problems associated with human sexuality in the modern era. The biblical affirmations, admonitions, and guidelines for this aspect of human life include

— The value of wisdom instruction as an antidote for sexual sin (2:16)
— The sanctity of marriage and the appropriateness of erotic (heterosexual) love within marital bonds (5:15–23; 18:22)
— The need to guard and discipline the "eyes" and "mouth" as these are the primary gates for the temptations that lead to unchastity (5:1–6; 7:21–23; cf. Job 31:1)
— Being aware of the destructiveness of jealousy stemming from adultery (6:20–35)
— Being aware of the dangers spawned by "idleness" (7:6–9)
— The importance of the family unit in teaching and enforcing sexual mores (7:1–5, 24–27)
— Being aware of the subtlety of sexual sins (23:26–28)
— The easy manner in which sexual sins are rationalized, thus hardening the heart to godly moral principles (7:14–20; 30:20)
— The need to evaluate and choose a marriage partner based on internal standards related to character, not external standards related to physical attraction and "sex appeal" (31:10–31; cf. 1 Peter 3:1–6)
— The necessity for mates to avoid quarreling and maintain open channels of communication (19:13; 27:15)

In many respects, the instructions of Proverbs on human sexuality and marriage constitute a practical commentary on the Genesis account of the creation of man and woman and their union as one flesh (Gen. 2:18–25).

---

[2]This is a summary of Derek Kidner's excellent essay on the theme "Words." See *The Proverbs: An Introduction and Commentary*, TOTC (London: Tyndale, 1964), 46–49.

Questions for Further Study and Discussion

1. What is "the fear of the Lord"? How does this idea relate to the teachings of the law of Moses?
2. What does Proverbs 31:10–31 suggest about the role of some women in ancient Israel?
3. How is the content of the New Testament book of James similar to the wisdom of Proverbs?

For Further Reading

Kidner, Derek. *The Proverbs: An Introduction and Commentary.* TOTC. London: Tyndale, 1964. Useful introductory section on the themes of Proverbs.

McKane, W. *Proverbs: A New Approach.* OTL. Philadelphia: Westminster, 1970. Highly specialized and technical study, somewhat ponderous; demanding but rewarding reading.

Mouser, W. E. *Walking in Wisdom: Studying the Proverbs of Solomon.* Downers Grove, Ill.: InterVarsity, 1983. A most readable introductory guide to the literary forms of Proverbs, with emphasis on interpreting biblical wisdom and its contemporary application.

Scott, R. B. Y. *Proverbs, Ecclesiastes.* AB. Vol. 18. Garden City, N.Y.: Doubleday, 1965. A good introduction to wisdom literature in general.

Thompson, J. M. *The Form and Function of Proverbs in Israel.* The Hague: Mouton, 1974.

Waltke, Bruce K. "The Book of Proverbs and Old Testament Theology." *Bibliotheca Sacra* 136 (1979): 302–17.

Whybray, R. N. *The Book of Proverbs.* CBC. Cambridge: Cambridge University Press, 1972.

_____ . *Wisdom in Proverbs.* SBT. Vol. 45. Naperville, Ill.: Allenson, 1965.

Williams, J. C. *Those Who Ponder Proverbs: Aphoristic Thinking and Biblical Literature.* Sheffield, England: Almond Press, 1981. An analysis of wisdom literature in the Old and New Testaments in light of contemporary linguistic theory.

Chapter 25

Ecclesiastes

The book of Ecclesiastes has often been avoided by people who feel overwhelmed by the view of life offered in its pages. Like the book of Job, it refuses to dodge the hard questions of life and does not allow easy solutions. Interpreters of the book have struggled with the issues it raises, leading some to question the orthodoxy of the author or whether the book even belongs in the Old Testament canon.

The Writing of the Book

The wisdom of Ecclesiastes comes from one who is identified as "Qoheleth." It is not certain whether this is a personal name, some sort of pseudonym, or the title of an office. Judging from the meaning of the related verb, it would seem that the word means "convener" or "assembler"—thus the common English translations "Teacher" (NIV) or "Preacher."

Traditionally Qoheleth has been identified as Solomon because of the information given in the first two verses of the book. It is argued that no one else was "son of David, king in Jerusalem." Yet it must be admitted that the designation "son of David" could be used to refer to anyone in the line of David. It is likewise enigmatic why Solomon would hide behind a pseudonym. The Solomonic flavor of sections like 2:1–11 leave no doubt that the author intended that the reader think of Solomon's experiences. But the claim in 1:16 and 2:9 that he surpassed all who were before him in Jerusalem would mean little if his father were his only predecessor. It is further noted that the language of the book differs in a number of ways from that found in Solomon's other writings. In conclusion, it is not impossible that Solomon was Qoheleth, but evidence to the contrary is sufficient to make it doubtful. Since Scripture is silent on the matter, we cannot be confident in identifying Qoheleth.

Not only is Qoheleth's identity concealed, but it seems that though his wisdom is presented in the book, he was not the author. Rather, he is initially introduced in the third person, and even when first person is used, it is sometimes presented as quoted material (7:27). This suggests that an unnamed author was presenting the wisdom of Qoheleth, a famed assembler of wisdom, for our consideration. The book ends by giving some biographical facts about Qoheleth and a summary of his message.

The result is that even if Qoheleth was

**Figure 25.1. Excerpt from the Harper's Song
from the Tomb of King Intef**

Hence rejoice in your heart!
Forgetfulness profits you,
Follow your heart as long as you live!
Put myrrh on your head,
Dress in fine linen,
Anoint yourself with oils fit for a god.
Heap up your joys,
Let not your heart sink!
Follow your heart and your happiness,
Do your things on earth as your heart commands!

From *Ancient Egyptian Literature*, vol. 1, trans. Miriam Lichtheim
(Berkeley: Univ. of California Press, 1976), 196–97.

Solomon, the author may have lived at a later time. Some have dated the book in the third or fourth century B.C., claiming that the Hebrew of the book has characteristics of postbiblical Hebrew and that there is discernible influence from Greek philosophy. This view, while popular among some scholars, must treat the book as a royal fiction, a genre well-known in both Mesopotamia and Egypt. The presence of a few Persian loanwords and the identification of some Aramaic influence have been used to bolster this position.

More common among conservative interpreters is the view that the distinctive Hebrew is dialectical and therefore cannot give much help in dating the book. Those who do not date the book to the time of Solomon have been most inclined to place it sometime in the eighth or seventh centuries B.C., but one can not really be more precise. Fortunately the timeless nature of the wisdom of the book makes it unnecessary to link it to any particular time period.

From the middle of the second century A.D., some have questioned the authority of the book and therefore also its canonical status. Initial objections from the rabbinic school of Shammai and others are cited in the Talmud, but were never sufficient to cause serious doubt.

The Background

Like several of the other poetic books, Ecclesiastes contains a number of literary genres. It makes use of allegories, sayings, metaphors, proverbs, and other forms. Beyond genre identifications there are a number of literary works known from the ancient Near East that address situations in which conventional wisdom is viewed as incongruent with reality or experience. Certainly this was the case in Job and its ancient Near Eastern counterparts. While this literature does not reject wisdom, it shows its limitations and insufficiency.

In Mesopotamian literature an example would be the work known as the Dialogue of Pessimism. This is a rather satirical piece in which a man suggests various courses of action that are affirmed by his slave's wisdom-style observations. In each case the man then changes his mind and decides not to pursue the stated course of action. This decision is likewise affirmed in each case by the slave with a wisdom-style observation. The conclusion one would draw is that wisdom sayings can be used to rationalize any given course of action.

In Egyptian literature there is a piece in which a man considering suicide discusses various frustrations of life and his failure to find satisfaction. In this respect it has some similarity to Ecclesiastes.

Likewise similar in content are the Harper's Songs, which encourage enjoying life because one cannot know what will come after (fig. 25.1). These, however, seem to suggest a life of pleasure that is rejected by Qoheleth (2:1–2).

Outline of the Book

I. Introduction (1:1–11)
II. Fulfillment: Problem and solution
  A. Problem: Fulfillment not to be found
    1. Not found in Wisdom (1:12–18)
    2. Not found in escapism (2:1–11)
    3. Not found in legacy (2:12–23)
  B. Solution: Fulfillment not to be sought
    1. Enjoy life as from the hand of God (2:24–26)
    2. God has ordained life's vicissitudes (3:1–8)
    3. Desire to find meaning should lead us to God (3:9–15)
III. Frustrations: Problem and solution
  A. Problem: Frustrations unavoidable
    1. Life is unfair and then you die (3:16–22)
    2. Frustration of being a victim
      a. Victim of oppression with no defender (4:1–3)
      b. Victim of your own envy (4:4–6)
      c. Victim of isolation (4:7–12)
      d. Victim of fickleness (4:13–16)
      e. Don't look for relief through vows (5:1–7)
    3. Frustration of graft
      a. Victim of political injustice (5:8–9)
      b. Don't look to wealth for relief (5:10–6:9)
    4. No prospects that anything can or will change (6:10–12)
  B. The solution: Frustrations not to be avoided
    1. Learn lessons from the hard experiences of life (7:1–12)
    2. Accept prosperity and adversity as from the hand of God (7:13–18)
    3. Don't expect to find righteousness or wisdom in a fallen world (7:19–29)
IV. Guidelines for plotting a course through life
  A. Live under authority, but don't expect government to solve your problems (8:1–9)
  B. Live as if the retribution principle were true, but don't expect to see it operating in your experience (8:10–14)
  C. Don't expect to know all the answers (8:15–17)
  D. It's a fallen world, and death is all it has to offer (9:1–6)
  E. Enjoy the life God has given (9:7–10)
  F. Expect the unexpected (9:11–12)
  G. Wisdom is better than strength
    1. Much wisdom can be undone by a little folly (9:13–10:1)
    2. Results and conduct of folly (10:2–20)
  H. Be cautious and prepared, but not to the extent of paralysis (11:1–6)
  I. Enjoy life, but remember that you are accountable for what you do (11:7–10)
  J. Don't wait till you are old to get the right perspective on life (12:1–8)
V. Colophon (12:9–14)

Purpose and Message

The outline has been given in greater detail so as to convey the purpose and message of the book. The purpose of Qoheleth was to contend that there is nothing "under the sun" that is capable of giving meaning to life. Even if some level of fulfillment or self-satisfaction were achieved, death is waiting at the end. Frustration and adversity are unavoidable, and answers to the hard questions of life are not forthcoming. On these terms the book confronts the crookedness and uncertainty of life and shows, probably unconsciously, the need for a concept of resurrection to bring harmony out of the discord of reality.

The message of Ecclesiastes is that the course of life to be pursued is a God-centered life. The pleasures of life are not intrinsically fulfilling and cannot offer lasting satisfaction, but they can be enjoyed as gifts from God. Life offers good times and bad and follows no pattern such as that proposed by the retribution principle. But all comes from the hand of God (7:14). Adversity may not be enjoyable, but it can help make us the people of faith we ought to be.

It is clear by now that we believe the book to have a positive and orthodox message. This is a matter of some controversy among the interpreters of Ecclesiastes, because many scholars have found in its pages only pessimism or cynicism. An early Jewish view still widely held today is that Qoheleth's unsound theology is given as an example of incorrect thinking and is corrected only in the last chapter. As we look at the colophon, however, the summary offered in verses 13–14 is simply a restatement of what Qoheleth is saying all through the book.

Structure and Organization

We should not look for principles of organization such as might be found in philosophical treatises of Western civilization. The inclusio of 1:2 and 12:8 and the recurring refrain—"There is nothing better for a man than to . . ." (cf. 2:24–26; 3:12–13, 22; 5:18–20; 8:15; 9:7–9)—show us that this is a unified work, but the author proceeds by introducing various pertinent topics for discussion. It is helpful to keep in mind that wisdom literature often tries to convey *how* to think rather than *what* to think.

After the introduction to the problem in 1:1–11, Qoheleth's own experience is used to suggest that nothing "under the sun" is able to give life meaning. In life "under the sun," God is far removed and not a factor. Once Qoheleth has considered the potential sources of fulfillment and has rejected them, he offers an alternate perspective on life. In 2:28–3:15 he advises a moderate course of action. Though nothing can offer fulfillment, one need not adopt a pessimistic, cynical, or fatalistic view toward life. Enjoy life for what it is: a gift from the hand of God. If God is in the center of one's worldview, the pursuits of life can be put in their proper place, not offering meaning for life, but offering enjoyment.

Using pairs of antitheses in 3:1–8, Qoheleth begins to address why it is that God needs to be in the center of our worldview. We are not in control of the "times" of life, and many of the times of life can be difficult. Stability can only be found in a God-centered approach. God has imposed these limitations on us, but has put "eternity in our hearts" so that we might seek him out.

The basic worldview of Qoheleth having been set forth, the next sections address the application of that worldview to the situations of life. It is not difficult to apply it when life is going smoothly, but how does it stand up when adversity comes? That is the concern of 3:16–7:29. Qoheleth considers various situations in life that produce adversity. It is of interest that he focuses on the daily, routine frustrations that are all too frequently our common lot. If the book of Job were to be criticized, one might complain that the scenario is too artificial. No one we know is the kind of person Job was, and very likely no one we know suffered to the extent Job did. In that book it was important for theory's sake to consider the most contradictory situation imaginable. But Qoheleth makes sure that we can identify with the examples he offers. The end result is that frustrations and adversity cannot be avoided. So what does his worldview offer?

The solution suggested in chapter 7 is that we should not try to avoid frustration and adversity. A God-centered worldview is willing to accept both prosperity and adversity as coming from the divine hand. Here Qoheleth deals not with cause (that is, that God causes our frustrations), but with the idea that adversity serves a useful purpose in shaping us as individuals and particularly as people of faith. This is precisely the attitude Job took in the face of his troubles (Job 1:21).

Qoheleth's solution leads to the last section of the book, where the writer offers guidelines for plotting a course through life. Much of chapters 8–9 concerns adjusting our expectations of this world. That is followed by warnings in chapter 10 about the power and effects of foolish behavior. Chapter 11 urges a cautious, but not too-cautious approach to life and reminds us that we are accountable for how we live and for the decisions we make. Finally, chapter 12 uses a flow of diverse images and allegories to encourage the reader to act now. As the old adage goes, "You can't learn any younger."

Following the inclusio line of verse 8 comes what we call a colophon. This was used in ancient Near Eastern literature to identify the author further and to epitomize what was written in the manuscript or tablet. As mentioned earlier, there is nothing here that reverses or negates the message of the book or offers a corrective to its teaching.

Major Themes

The Retribution Principle: Part 4

The primary sections of Ecclesiastes that address the retribution principle are 3:16–22 and 8:10–14, though it is also involved in the statements of 7:15–17 and 9:1–6. The position Qoheleth comes to is an acceptance of the retribution principle in theory, but a denial of its ability to predict how one might fare in life or to explain any person's current situation. In this sense Qoheleth is in agreement with the book of Job. Both view the retribution principle as conveying something about God rather than offering guarantees in life. Time and chance are too great a factor in this life (9:11).

Even though it is clear from the book that Qoheleth had no revelation concerning God's eventual judgment of the righteous and the wicked in the afterlife, his seemingly inconsistent position concerning the retribution principle can be vindicated by the progress of revelation. The fact that God will reward the righteous and punish the wicked in eternity is consistent with Qoheleth's belief that the retribution principle is true, but cannot be applied solely to this life. As in Job, this constitutes a denial of the corollary that suggests that one who prospers must be righteous and one who suffers must therefore be wicked.

Experience vs. Revelation

The approach of Qoheleth is one that is not uncommon in evidential apologetics even today. If someone is unwilling to acknowledge that God has spoken in the Bible, it is useless to use the Bible to support one's case. Qoheleth built his case without any presupposition about revelation. He made no reference to the Law or the Prophets, and nothing was said about Israel's place in God's plan or the covenant. His approach was philosophical and based on experience and wisdom. The absence of the standard

Israelite elements of theology does not suggest ignorance or rejection of them by Qoheleth, but may reflect an attempt to address a wider audience.

Epicureanism vs. Piety

Some have worried about Qoheleth's "enjoy life" philosophy. It has seemed perhaps too close to the Epicurean dictum "Eat, drink, and be merry, for tomorrow we die." Moreover, he said little about a life of piety, faith, or even good works. What of discipline, virtue, and morality? Where is repentance or a sense of sinfulness? We must recognize that the book of Ecclesiastes is not intended to be a systematic theology. Qoheleth's primary purpose was to establish that life "under the sun" cannot offer fulfillment and to offer an alternate worldview. The philosophy expressed is not simply "enjoy life," but "enjoy life and fear God." This is not abandonment of all for a life of pleasure; it is a responsible, optimistic integration of life and faith. The result is that few books of the Bible offer as clear a challenge to our contemporary Western worldview. Enjoyment of life comes not in the quest for personal fulfillment, but in the recognition that everything comes from the hand of God.

Questions for Further Study and Discussion

1. Should the Christian seek fulfillment in life? Explain "fulfillment" in your answer.
2. What are the practical results of viewing adversity with attention to purpose rather than cause?
3. What advice would Qoheleth offer Job?
4. Compare Qoheleth's approach to experience with the similar approach offered by C. S. Lewis in *Mere Christianity* (New York: Macmillan, 1986).

For Further Reading

Eaton, Michael. *Ecclesiastes.* Downers Grove, Ill.: InterVarsity, 1983. The most helpful of the evangelical commentaries.

Fox, Michael. *Qoheleth and His Contradictions.* JSOTSS 71. Sheffield, England: Almond Press, 1989.

Gordis, Robert. *Koheleth: The Man and His World.* New York: Schocken, 1968.

Kaiser, Walter C. *Ecclesiastes: Total Life.* Chicago: Moody Press, 1979.

Loader, J. A. *Ecclesiastes: A Practical Commentary.* Grand Rapids: Eerdmans, 1986. Not evangelical, but very stimulating insight into the book.

Ogden, Graham. *Qoheleth.* Sheffield, England: JSOT Press, 1987.

Whybray, R. N. *Ecclesiastes.* Grand Rapids: Eerdmans, 1989.

Chapter 26

Song of Songs

The book takes its title from the opening verse (1:1) and is variously labeled "The Song," "Songs," "Song of Solomon," or even "Best Song." The alternative name "Canticles" is derived from the Latin Vulgate version, which renders the title *Canticum Canticorum* (Song of Songs).

The Song is placed among the books of wisdom and poetry in the Septuagint and most English versions. While not classified as wisdom literature in the strict sense, the Song shares some affinities with wisdom in that the book is associated with wise King Solomon (1 Kings 4:29–34), concerns itself with the mystery of humanity created male and female, and offers instruction (at least implicitly) on behavior concerning sexuality and marriage. The Song is grouped first among the five festival scrolls (Megilloth) in the Hebrew canon, and in later Judaism it was designated to be read as part of the Passover Feast, since it was understood to represent God's love for Israel.

The Writing of the Book

Traditional biblical scholarship has ascribed the Song of Songs to King Solomon and dated the poetry to the late tenth century B.C., largely on the strength of the book's title verse (1:1). Some ancient Jewish traditions credit the work to King Hezekiah, the king of Judah who is accorded a prominent place in the preservation of Israelite wisdom literature (Prov. 25:1; cf. 2 Chron. 32:27–29).

The problems of authorship and the date of the Song are closely entwined. The inconclusive nature of the book's title further complicates the matter. The phraseology of the title verse or superscription may be understood variously as "of/to/for/about Solomon" (cf. the notations in Psalms 3:1; 4:1; 5:1, etc.). Thus the title may imply that Solomon was the author of the poetry, that it was dedicated to him, or that it represents songs composed about him as a primary character in the action. Although Solomon's name occurs six times elsewhere in the book (1:5; 3:7, 9, 11; 8:11–12) and other Scripture attests his literary skill (1 Kings 4:29–34), these references assert nothing concerning his authorship. Instead, they merely confirm Solomon's role as a key figure in the love story.

Another factor influencing informed opinion on the authorship and date deserves mention. The interpretive stance adopted by the individual translator-commentator determines in large measure how one outlines the text, understands the poetry in respect to plot development and the number of characters in the story, and ultimately colors the way one arranges and evaluates the various strands of evidence bearing on the question of authorship and date.

For example, those who contend that the love story is a two-character drama are likely to focus attention on the exotic vocabulary, the abundance of references to flora and fauna, and the apparent unity of geography within the poems and therefore decide on a date in the Solomonic age, if not Solomonic authorship. By contrast, those who view the poetry as depicting a love triangle with King Solomon cast as "the villain" would suggest a setting in the northern kingdom early in the divided monarchies. A scholar using the typological or cultic approach would emphasize the linguistic features (e.g., Aramaic, Persian, and Greek influence) and the device of "literary fiction" in the poetry, in which Solomon represents "the great lover," and conclude that the book should be dated to the Persian period.

Given the uncertainties associated with understanding the title verse (1:1) and the unusual nature of the book's vocabulary and style, the Song of Songs is best regarded as an anonymous composition. The weight of literary, historical, and linguistic evidence currently assessed points to a northern kingdom provenance and an early preexilic date for the writing of the book. Attempts to be more precise than this are tenuous and return relatively little benefit for the overall comprehension of the message and meaning of the love songs.

Historical Background

Aside from the ambiguous references to King Solomon (1:1, 5; 3:7, 9, 11; 8:11–12), clear historical parallels or allusions are lacking in the Song. Other than citing the reign of Solomon in general (ca. 970–930 B.C.), little else can be said about the historical background of the book. It is very likely that the love poetry reflects actual events associated with the reign of Solomon, possibly those summarized by the Old Testament historians in 1 Kings 3–11 and 2 Chronicles 1–9. Solomon's domination by sensuality—a trait he shared with his father David and showed in the extravagance of his kingship and the size of his royal harem—proved to be his undoing (cf. 1 Kings 4:20–28; 10:14–29; 11:1–3). Ironically, the sage who counseled young men against the wiles of the "foreign" woman was entrapped in her snares (Prov. 5:1–23; 7:1–7; cf. 1 Kings 11:4–13).

Outline of the Book

One of the problems associated with the interpretation of the Song of Songs is identifying clearly who is speaking in the love poetry. Attempts to outline the Song are as numerous and varied as the interpretive approaches to the content of the book. The following outline assumes that the love poem depicts the interaction of three primary characters (the Shulammite maiden, the shepherd lover, and King Solomon) in a series of sequential events.[1] The major headings or sections of the outline are essentially adaptations of the book divisions as found in Calvin Seerveld and C. Hassell Bullock.[2]

---

[1]Note that although the authors of this survey appeal to the *New International Version* in Scripture quotations, they take a different approach from the NIV's presentation of the Song as a two-character love story.

[2]Calvin Seerveld, *The Greatest Song* (Amsterdam: Trinity Pennyasheet Press, 1967; C. Hassell Bullock, *An Introduction to the Old Testament Poetic Books*, 2d ed. (Chicago: Moody Press, 1988), 242–55.

Interpretation of the Book

No single book of the Old Testament has proved more perplexing for biblical interpreters than the Song of Songs. Centuries of careful study by scholars of various religious traditions and theological persuasions have produced little interpretive consensus. There are three primary reasons for the impasse.

First, the theme, the topic, and the frank language of the Song have confused, shocked, and embarrassed both Jewish and Christian readers—so much so that for generations the rabbis and early church fathers debated the value of the book and its place in the Old Testament.

Second, the nature and structure of the love poetry does not lend itself to easy analysis. Much of the language of the book is unusual, if not unique and obscure, making translation and interpretation difficult. By definition, lyrical poetry is brief in length, concentrated in meaning, and often lacking smooth transitions. This poses a dilemma for commentators seeking to divide the book into smaller logical units. It also means uncertainty for identifying the number of characters in the love story and assigning these smaller units of speech to specific persons.

Third, the book is unfocused sociologically in that its setting is ambiguous, historical backgrounds and characterizations are vague, and the text seems to assume the moral teaching of earlier Old Testament books.

Several major interpretive approaches have emerged for understanding the meaning of the Song.

1. Dramatic. The dramatic approach understands the Song as an ancient Hebrew play. This view, visible in church tradition since the third century A.D., is based largely on analogy to Greek tragic drama, which developed in the sixth century B.C. The poetry is considered a dramatic script intended for royal entertainment. The play, whether acted or sung, is usually outlined in six acts, each with two scenes. Speeches are assigned to the principal characters (two or three, depending on whether the shepherd is one and the same with the king), with "the daughters of Jerusalem" (or harem) represented by a female chorus.

2. Typological. The typological model recognizes the historicity of the book (whether it commemorates Solomon's marriage to the pharaoh's daughter or recounts the king's wooing of a Shulammite maiden), but subordinates the literal presentation of Old Testament history to a correspondent New Testament pattern or parallel. The traditional "type-antitype" fulfillment is read as God's covenant relationship to Israel by the Jewish interpreter or Christ's relationship to the church as his bride by the Christian interpreter.

3. Cultic. The cultic, or mythological, approach views the Song as a Hebrew adaptation of Mesopotamian fertility cult liturgy. Proponents argue that the word "beloved" is in fact a reference to the god Dod (at least in 5:9), the Syro-Palestinian equivalent of Tammuz in the Sumero-Akkadian Tammuz-Ishtar cult. The annual ritual was a reenactment of the ancient myth recounting the goddess Ishtar's search for her dead lover in the netherworld, finally restoring him to life through sexual union and thus ensuring the continued fertility of the creation. It is assumed that the cultic associations of the Song were forgotten or consciously changed to make the book acceptable to the Israelite faith.

4. Wedding Cycle. Understanding the book as a wedding cycle assumes the Song is an amalgam of nuptial poems similar to the *wasf* of Arabic wedding ceremonies. The series of songs honoring the bride and groom was eventually formalized into a cycle of recitations that were finally incorporated into the wedding celebration.

5. Didactic. While historical aspects of the book are not denied, the didactic view interprets the poem as a vehicle for instruction and simply discounts the circumstances surrounding the occasion of the book in favor of the moral and didactic purposes of the literature. The book is seen to present the purity and wonder of sexual love, promote ideals of simplicity, faithfulness, and chastity, and instruct on the virtues of human affection and the beauty and holiness of marriage.

6. Allegorical. The allegorical method is

the oldest and remains the most popular approach to the Song in the Jewish and Christian traditions—though the book nowhere claims to be an allegory. Allegory is defined as obvious symbolic representation in literature, or simply extended metaphor. Allegory says one thing but conveys a deeper or hidden meaning. The "allegorizing" of a text occurs when an interpreter understands a given passage as allegory even though it was not intended as such by the author. The allegorizing method as applied to the Song has yielded much the same interpretations as the typological approach. The chief distinction is that the typological view accepts a historical basis for the setting, while the allegorical does not.

7. *Literal.* The literal, or natural, view takes the Song at face value and interprets the love poetry for what it appears to be—a sensual, even erotic, expression of emotions and passion as two young lovers voice their desire for each other. The literal-historical variation on this seeks to balance the natural sense of the literary qualities of the poem with an appreciation for the historical setting or situation prompting its writing.

The reading supported in this textbook assumes a love story with three characters (King Solomon, the shepherd-lover, and the Shulammite maiden) and combines the literal-historical approach with elements of the didactic. The book is likely a northern kingdom satire on the reign of Solomon and his exploitation of women (ironically to his own demise) and a memorializing of the exemplary character of the Shulammite maiden who rejected the wooing of the king out of faithfulness to her commoner-lover.

Structure and Organization

Like Psalms, Proverbs, and Lamentations, the Song of Songs is entirely poetic in literary form, with the exception of the superscription, or title verse. As lyrical love poetry, the Song has an idyllic flavor and pastoral scenes that seem strange to modern Western readers living in a highly technological society. Thus the bucolic similes and metaphors make comparisons that we frequently find humorous or even uncomplimentary—e.g., "your belly is like a heap of wheat" (7:2, KJV) or "your nose is like the tower of Lebanon" (7:4)— not to mention difficult to understand. The bold and vivid imagery sometimes shocks and embarrasses us (e.g., 7:8).

Yet the Song conforms to literary conventions and a genre of love poetry that were prevalent in the second millennium B.C. For example, the Egyptian love songs of the New Kingdom (1570–1085 B.C.) contain similar themes and figures of speech. The garden motif as erotic symbol and lyrics in praise of the rapture and mystery of human sexual love are prominent. Simile and metaphor abound, including descriptive songs that compare the physical features of the lovers to exotic flora and fauna. The song of desire calling the partners to love, partaking of delicate foods and spiced wine to refresh "love-sickness," and even the attention to fine apparel and exquisite perfumes and ointments are commonplace in the literature. When viewed against this literary backdrop, the strangeness of the Song is diminished and appreciation of its simple beauty and sensitive treatment of the subject matter enhanced.[3]

---

[3]Cf. G. Lloyd Carr, *The Song of Solomon*, TOTC (Downers Grove, Ill.: InterVarsity Press, 1984), 55–67; see further W. K. Simpson, ed., *The Literature of Ancient Egypt*, 2d ed. (New Haven: Yale University Press, 1975), 296–326. Specific literary forms and formal features of love poetry such as descriptive songs, self-description, songs of admiration, search narratives, and oath formulas are catalogued in J. B. White, *A Study of the Language of Love in the Song of Songs and Ancient Egyptian Poetry*, SBL Dissertation Series 38 (Missoula, Mont.: Scholars Press, 1978), 91–159.

Attempts to discern structure in the book must base textual divisions on one's analysis of the content. In turn, this necessitates adopting an interpretive stance from which to examine the poetry. Obviously this means there will be as many outlines of the content as there are methods of interpretation. While the book contains repeated phrases and lines—

"How beautiful you are, my darling!"
(1:15; 4:1, 7)
"My lover is mine" (2:16; 6:3)
"Who is this?" (3:6; 6:10; 8:5)
"My sister, my bride" (4:9, 12; 5:1)
"Daughters of Jerusalem, I charge you"
(2:7; 3:5; 5:8; 8:4)

—only the charge to the daughters of Jerusalem appears to serve as a refrain perhaps marking separate poetic sections.

The speeches or direct discourse provide clues for dividing the text, yet the speaker remains largely unidentified. Speech content can aid in the identification of the speaker, but this is not conclusive. The terse language and cryptic nature of the poetry often make ascertaining the exact extent of a given speech difficult.

These efforts to assign the speeches to specific participants in the love story are complicated by the question of the number of characters. Useful here is Bullock's insightful suggestion that the Song was an ancient lyrical ballad, "the narrative of which was known by the original audience but has now been lost. Thus the effort to reweave the narrative or supply some missing links, however risky, must be undertaken."[4]

Hence our reading of the Song views the poetry as a unified composition and "reweaves" the narrative along the lines of a three-character love story in a series of sequential events (see outline above).

Purpose and Message

Viewed with a literal-historical interpretive stance, the import of the Song of Songs is essentially the same whether we see the story as having two characters or three. In either case the Song is viewed as instruction on and celebration of the physical nature of human beings created male and female by God (Gen. 1:27; 2:4–7, 18–24). The book extols the God-ordained goodness and virtue of sexual love between a man and a woman united in matrimony (Song 2:3–7, 16; 7:9–12; cf. Prov. 5:15–20; Eccl. 9:9; Mal. 2:14–16). In fact, the contention that to some extent this poetry reviews the heterosexual love relationship through "Edenic glasses"— almost an extended commentary on Genesis 1–2—has substantial merit.[5]

The meaning of the Song of Songs is a welcome antidote for the perversion of sexuality and decay of the institution of marriage. The Song praises the goodness of humanity created male and female and argues for the propriety and dignity of human affections and sexual expression within the divinely decreed bounds of a one-man-to-one-woman relationship (Gen. 2:23–24; cf. Rom. 1:24–32). Indeed, "marriage is honorable in all" (Heb. 13:4, KJV), and "he who finds a wife finds what is good" (Prov. 18:22).

While this union of male and female before God is important for the procreation of the human race (Gen. 1:28), the Song indicates that the sexual intimacies shared by a husband and wife are appropriate in themselves for mutual joy and pleasure and for growth and enrichment of the relationship (Song 6:2–3; 7:10–13; 8:1–3; cf. Prov. 5:19; 1 Cor. 7:1–5).

Understanding the Song as a three-character love story introduces further didactic elements to the purpose and message of the poetry. The contrast between two kinds of human affection is

---

[4]Bullock, *An Introduction to the Old Testament Poetic Books*, 238.
[5]Cf. F. Landy, "The Song of Songs and the Garden of Eden," *JBL* 98, no. 4 (1979): 53–58.

established by juxtaposing the coarse, sensual, and polygamous relationship of Solomon to the "daughters of Jerusalem," or harem (comprising more than 140 women; cf. 6:8) with the simple, pure, sincere, and erotic but faithful love of the Shulammite maiden and her shepherd-lover. The one incites jealousy and flashes of rage (8:6); it brings the wrath of God (cf. 1 Kings 11:1–9). The other is like a seal displayed boldly and guaranteeing private ownership and public faithfulness— love as strong as death (8:6–7).

Major Themes

The poet affirms the virtue of chastity in the young lovers (4:12; 6:3; 7:10–13; 8:10), which makes a striking contrast with the self-destructive bent of sexual mores in many societies historically. The Bible gives no place to premarital or extramarital behavior, whether heterosexual or homosexual (Exod. 20:14; Lev. 18:22; 20:13; Matt. 5:27–28; Rom. 1:24–27; 1 Cor. 6:13, 18; Eph. 5:3). Scriptural warnings are plain enough: God will judge all who are sexually immoral (1 Cor. 6:9, 18–20; Heb. 13:4b). Recent studies disclosing the harmful emotional, psychological, and lethal physical side effects of sexual license within and outside marriage only confirm the wisdom of biblical teaching.

The positive dimensions of human love portrayed in the Song are important as cues for molding strong male-female relationships. The Shulammite maiden and the shepherd-lover model genuine love that demonstrates its sincerity and fidelity by strength of character and by flame of passion. Their manner of love for each other exudes integrity, loyalty, commitment, and faithfulness (4:12–16; 7:11–14; 8:10–12). This brand of love is "as strong as death" (8:6), or better, in Seerveld's phrase, "as permanent as death."[6] It respects and nurtures the partner of the marriage covenant and doesn't break faith (Mal. 2:14–15). The apostle Paul encouraged this selfless, other-motivated, and directed kind of love because it reflects the relationship of Christ and his church (Eph. 5:21–33).

Finally, the Song affirms the goodness and righteousness of physical love within the confines of God-ordained marriage (Gen. 1:26–28; 2:20–25; Matt. 19:1–12). The Old Testament especially encourages married couples to "rejoice" in the partner of their youth (Prov. 5:18; Eccl. 9:9; Mal. 2:14) and to "drink" from their own cistern (i.e., find sexual satisfaction with one's own partner—Prov. 5:15; cf. 5:19–20). The sanctity of marriage and the appropriateness of physical intimacy within marriage (presented as erotic faithfulness in the Song) are vital truths for the church of God set in a society espousing sexual license and easy divorce.[7]

Questions for Further Study and Discussion

1. Why have both Jews and Christians preferred the allegorical interpretation of the Song of Songs?
2. How does the teaching of the book compare with the instruction in the rest of the Bible regarding human sexuality and marriage?
3. What role should the teachings of the Song of Songs play in the instruction of young people in the contemporary church?

[6]Seerveld, *The Greatest Song*, 60.
[7]On the sanctity of marriage and the idea of "intimacy with restraint" between lovers before marriage and the physical consummation of the marriage bond (like the Shulammite girl and her shepherd-lover in the Song), see Walter Trobisch, *I Married You* (New York: Harper & Row, 1971).

For Further Reading

Balchin, J. A. "The Song of Solomon." *The New Bible Commentary: Revised.* 3d ed. Donald Guthrie et al., eds. Grand Rapids: Eerdmans, 1970. 579–87.

Bullock, C. Hassell. *An Introduction to the Old Testament Poetic Books.* 2d ed. Chicago: Moody Press, 1988. 223–55.

Carr, G. Lloyd. *The Song of Solomon.* TOTC. Downers Grove, Ill.: InterVarsity Press, 1984.

Fox, M. V. *The Song of Songs and the Ancient Egyptian Love Songs.* Madison: Univ. of Wisconsin Press, 1985. A detailed comparison and literary analysis of the love song in the Old Testament and the ancient Near East.

Fuerst, W. J. *The Song of Songs.* CBC. Cambridge: Cambridge University Press, 1975.

Hill, Andrew E. "The Song of Solomon." *The Evangelical Commentary on the Bible.* Walter A. Elwell, ed. Grand Rapids: Baker, 1989. 452–66.

Murphy, R. E. *The Song of Songs.* HER. Philadelphia: Fortress, 1990.

Olhsen, W. *Perspectives on Old Testament Literature.* New York: Harcourt, Brace, 1978. 283–88. A concise essay espousing a three-character interpretation, with emphasis on the message and teaching of the Song of Songs.

Pope, M. *Song of Songs.* AB. Vol. 7. New York: Doubleday, 1977. Ponderous and technical analysis from the mythological or cultic perspective, including a comprehensive survey of the history of interpretation of the book and a thorough bibliography

Seerveld, Calvin. *The Greatest Song.* Amsterdam: Trinity Pennyasheet Press, 1967. A three-character adaptation of the book in critique of Solomon and arranged for oratorio performance.

PART V

THE PROPHETS

Chapter 27

Introduction to Prophetic Literature

What Is a Prophet?

A prophet is someone who speaks on behalf of someone else. Though in Scripture a prophet is usually a spokesman or mouthpiece for God, Exodus 7:1 speaks of Aaron as being a prophet for Moses (cf. Exod. 4:16). In modern politics this concept is well represented in the United States in the president's press secretary. He is the one who conveys the president's opinions, reactions, intentions, and his very words when necessary. The press secretary holding a news conference is never seen to be speaking for himself, but is believed to be expressing only the words that the president desires him to speak. Another example would be the function of ambassadors to foreign countries who convey the official reactions and opinions of the government. Thus it is also with prophets. They are the mouthpiece of God, conveying God's opinions, reactions, intentions, and very words. In short, God's agenda, or program, is announced through the words of the prophets.

The prophets are designated in the Old Testament by several different titles. The most frequent is *nabî*, which, though still somewhat controversial, appears to indicate that the prophet was "one who is called." A second title is "seer," which refers to the prophet's inclination to receive revelatory visions. Of course, the prophets did not always receive their messages through trances or visions; this was but one mode. Usually the text of Scripture does not specify how a message came.

The biblical prophets tended to be clustered around times of crisis. Whether it was the religious crisis posed by the official sponsorship of Baal worship during the time of Elijah, the political crises caused by the Assyrian and Babylonian threats, or the identity crisis with which the postexilic community struggled, God used the prophets to offer guidance to his people in troubled times.

Prophecy in the Ancient Near East

Evidence of the existence of a prophetic institution has been found throughout the ancient Near East. Among the Mari tablets from the eighteenth century, about fifty texts have been found in which local officials wrote to the king (Zimri-Lim) to inform him of prophecies that had been pronounced in their districts concerning him. Another group of prophecies came from the Neo-Assyrian Empire during the days of Esarhaddon and Ashurbanipal.

In these prophecies from the ancient Near East the king was the one addressed, rather than the people as a whole. The messages generally concerned ritual activity, military matters, or building projects. Sometimes the messages encouraged the king in particular activities (which is especially true of the Neo-Assyrian examples), while at other times they could be quite critical. Frequently the prophets of the ancient Near East received their messages through dreams, visions, or trances, though at other times the mode of revelation is not stated. A variety of deities was represented by these prophets in the extant literature.

Despite some general similarities, there are distinct differences between the prophetic traditions of Israel and those of the rest of the ancient Near East.

Prophecy in Israel

Pre-Classical Prophecy

We can observe several stages in the development of the prophetic institution in Israel (fig. 27.1). When Israelite history began, prophets often held the reins of leadership. Moses is the best example of this; he was qualified to lead the people by virtue of his prophetic office. Later on, Deborah provided prophetic leadership during the period of the judges. After Moses, the best example of a prophet prior to the monarchical era in Israel is Samuel. First Samuel 3 relates how Samuel's prophetic credentials were established. He provided essential leadership during the important transition to the monarchy.

Pre-monarchic prophecy was just one stage of what is called pre-classical prophecy in Israel. Once Samuel anointed Saul as king, the role of prophet became one of adviser (though sometimes unofficially) to the king. This type of prophecy was very much like the kind that was prevalent throughout the ancient Near East. We have no books collecting the prophecies of pre-classical prophets, though scattered oracles occur in the historical books. Samuel's service to Saul is documented in the book of 1 Samuel, and Nathan's official capacity in the administration of David is evident in 2 Samuel. Although we can hardly consider Elijah an employed counselor of King Ahab, he nevertheless served as the mouthpiece of the Lord in that time.

Because the intended audience of the pre-classical prophet was generally the king, the messages were specifically tailored to the circumstances of the royal court. As a result, the prophecies usually consisted of a word of encouragement or a warning to the king.

Classical Prophecy

The most familiar phase of Israelite prophecy is known as classical prophecy. The prophetic books of the Bible are all collections of the oracles of classical prophets. Classical prophecy began in the eighth century during the reign of Jeroboam II in the northern kingdom of Israel. Amos and Hosea were the earliest examples in the north, while Micah and Isaiah were the first known classical prophets in the southern kingdom of Judah. Though many of the classical prophets continued to address the king and had specific messages for the king, most of their oracles addressed the people. Just as the pre-classical prophets announced God's agenda for the king, the classical prophets announced God's agenda for the people. Consequently they became social-spiritual commentators to a degree the pre-classical prophets never did.

While the pre-classical prophets functioned in a similar way to other prophets of the ancient Near East, there was no counterpart for classical prophets. The distinction goes beyond the divine authority expressed in the "messenger for-

Figure 27.1. Function of the Prophets

Period	Function	Audience	Message	Examples
Pre-monarchy	Mouthpiece–leader	People	National guidance Maintenance of justice Spiritual overseer	Moses Deborah
Pre-classical	Mouthpiece–adviser	King and court	Military advice Pronouncement of rebuke or blessing	*Transition: Samuel* Nathan Elijah Elisha Micaiah
Classical	Mouthpiece–social/spiritual commentator	People	Rebuke concerning current condition of society; leads to warnings of captivity, destruction, exile, and promise of eventual restoration Call for justice and repentance	*Transition:* *North—Jonah* *South—Isaiah* Writing prophets Best example: Jeremiah

mula" that introduced the prophetic utterances—i.e., the phrase "thus says the Lord Almighty" and its variations ("Lord of hosts," KJV).

Classical prophecy was also distinguished by the content and range of the message. For example, the message given in the ancient Near East often concerned performing certain prescribed rituals. By contrast, Israel's classical prophets have often been accused of antiritualism because of their staunch opposition to the popular notion of appeasing God's anger through ritual. Also, there was nothing in the ancient Near East to parallel the far-reaching messages of exile and destruction that typified the preexilic classical prophets.

All these distinctions can be summed up in classical prophecy's having its basis in the covenant. Since no other people in the ancient Near East had anything like the concept of the covenant—namely, God's choosing a people as a means of revealing himself and carrying out his plan in history—prophecy took a different shape in Israel than anywhere else.

In range, the eschatological aspect of classical prophecy made it unique in the ancient world. This is to be expected, because it was only the Israelite concept of a totally sovereign God that allowed for the development of eschatology. Here eschatology should be understood as dealing with the final stage of the plan of God in history. If classical prophecy had its premise in the idea that God had a long-range plan to proclaim, we can find nothing similar to it in the ancient Near East because no other deity had such a plan to execute in history. In other ancient cultures there was no sovereign god and therefore no plan to be executed. By definition, then, there could be no eschatology. In fact, there was no concept of eschatology even by a broader definition. The possibility of a final stage of history was nowhere considered in Mesopotamian theology.

All this was precisely the point of the prophetic rhetoric of Isaiah 41–48, for example.

Remember the former things, those of
     long ago;
   I am God, and there is no other;
   I am God, and there is none like me.
I make known the end from the begin-
     ning,
   from ancient times, what is still to
     come.
I say: My purpose will stand,
   and I will do all that I please.
From the east I summon a bird of prey;
   from a far-off land, a man to fulfill my
     purpose.
What I have said, that will I bring about;
   what I have planned, that will I do
     (Isa. 46:9–11).[1]

This theology was the foundation of classical prophecy, and it was unique to Israel among the peoples of the ancient Near East.

Apocalyptic Literature

There are some recognizable variations of style within the category of classical prophecy. Most significant is the subgenre of apocalyptic literature, which made its debut as early as Isaiah (chaps. 24–27 are often so designated) and became prominent with Daniel and Zechariah.

It is difficult to define apocalyptic literature because it shares a number of features with prophetic literature. There has been little agreement regarding its distinctive features, but there appears to be a growing consensus for speaking in terms of a prophetic-apocalyptic continuum in which some works lean more to one side or the other, with all sharing a general set of characteristics. Elements that would position a section on the apocalyptic side of the continuum include rich symbolism (often mythological), visions, conversation with spiritual beings, and cosmic catastrophe leading to the establishment of the kingdom of God on earth. In general, apocalyptic literature can be characterized as simply using a slightly different medium for conveying the prophetic word of God.

The use of symbols in apocalyptic literature has often created confusion and uncertainty for interpreters. Many books offer incredible revelations of the symbolic meaning of this or that passage from the apocalyptic literature. Much confusion is caused, however, by one's mistakenly treating the *vision* of a prophet as the *message* of a prophet. The vision was not the message, but the occasion for the message. In Zechariah 1, for instance, the vision is of horses in a grove of myrtle trees (vv. 8–11). It would be a serious mistake to conclude that the Israelites listening to Zechariah were to keep their eyes on the myrtle trees and be alert for a group of horsemen and riders. The message was not that there would be horses among the myrtle trees, but that the Lord was still concerned about Jerusalem—as the text makes eminently clear (vv. 14–17).

Likewise, in Zechariah 5 the vision concerns carrying off to Babylon a measuring basket with a woman in it. Again, this was the vision, not the message. The message is not so explicitly stated in this text as in Zechariah 1, but verse 6 gives the information necessary to deduce that the message concerned a purging from the sin of idolatry.

Understanding the message does not require an interpretation of everything in the vision, or even an understanding of the chronological placement of the events of the vision. The features of the vision are incidental; they are not the message. Unfortunately, some interpreters place too much confidence in their ability to discern the meaning of symbols in prophetic literature and spend much time devising and defending such meaning. Yet it cannot be assumed that every

---

[1]See also Isaiah 41:21–24; 43:10–13; 44:6–8; 45:20–21; 48:3–7.

Figure 27.2. Interpreting Prophetic Literature

Message	*Fulfillment*
Authoritative word from God ◀	▶ Unfolding of God's plan
Understood by prophet, relevant to contemporary audience ◀	▶ May be vague or obscure or take unanticipated direction
Identified with author's intention as guiding criteria ◀	▶ Identified often only with aid of interpreter's hindsight
Uses objective evidence ◀	▶ Subjective perspective
One message ◀	▶ Possibly many fulfillments
Does not change ◀	▶ May shift directions
Aim of Old Testament interpreters ◀	▶ Elaborated by New Testament authors

object in a vision has symbolic value, and when the meaning of a symbol is not given in the text, the interpreter must be cautious in supplying such a meaning. It is possible that the symbolism is used to conceal rather than to reveal.

In the examples given, the myrtle trees and the basket may or may not have symbolic value. If they do, the text has not disclosed the meaning, and any speculation, no matter how thoughtful, would fall short of coming with the authority of God's prophetic word. Unrevealed symbolism cannot be considered the inspired message of the prophet.

In general, the prophet was given a message by God that he was supposed to communicate to his audience.[2] In apocalyptic prophecy, the seer was often given a vision of what was to come, and the message was predicated on the information received in the vision. To reiterate, the vision was not the message, but the occasion for the message.

The Message of the Prophet

Each prophet came with a message from God, and his job was to communicate that message. It should be assumed that the prophet had some understand-ing of the message, that is, it had relevance to him and to the people who heard it. This did not preclude the message's taking on a fuller meaning or additional meaning in the future as it found fulfillment.

It is important to distinguish between the message of the prophecy and the fulfillment of the prophecy (fig. 27.2). The message is found in the proclamation of God's word to the contemporary audience (at least initially). The fulfillment comes in the unfolding of history. Each prophecy had a message as soon as it was proclaimed, independent of its eventual (and assured) fulfillment. Too often the prophetic books are studied merely by seeking out potential fulfillments while overlooking the inspired message of God's words. This is a grave error.

The message of the prophets can be best understood by analyzing the types of oracles that were used. There were four major kinds:

— Indictment oracles (description of offense)

— Judgment oracles (punishment coming because of offense)

— Instruction oracles (how the recipients were to conduct themselves)

---

[2]The masculine pronoun is used in this chapter, even though some of the prophets of Israel were women, because the focus of this discussion is on the so-called writing prophets, all of whom in the canon of the Old Testament were men.

— Aftermath or Hope oracles (developments after the judgment or hope for deliverance and restoration)

Some of these can be further subdivided into political, spiritual, or socioeconomic types. Each prophet used some kinds of oracles more than others, and these are plainly identifiable (fig. 27.3).

The diversity of oracles demonstrates some key differences between the messages of the preexilic classical prophets and the postexilic ones. The indictment found in the preexilic prophets focused primarily on idolatry, ritualism, and social injustice (e.g., Isa. 1:10–15; Jer. 2:2–3:5; Mic. 3:1–3 respectively). In contrast, the indictment of the postexilic prophets often confronted the people's failure to give proper honor to the Lord (e.g., Zech. 7:5–6; Mal. 1:7–14).

Judgment (which constituted about half the oracles) in the preexilic prophets was usually political in nature and projected for the near future. The judgment oracles of postexilic prophets were more inclined to be interpretations of current crises than projections of future judgment (e.g., Hag. 1:6–11; Joel 1).

There were strikingly few instruction oracles among the prophets, probably because the law included all the instruction the people should have needed. In preexilic prophecy, the emphasis of the instruction was on returning to the Lord by ceasing wicked conduct (Jer. 3:12–13; Amos 5:14–15; Mic. 6:8). Postexilic prophecy had slightly more instruction, often more specifically addressed to a particular situation (e.g., Hag. 1:8; Mal. 3:10).

Finally, the aftermath oracles of the preexilic period generally offered hope, not for the deliverance of the generation that the prophet addressed, but for a future generation of Israel. This deliverance and restoration was usually projected after the judgment had come (with some exceptions—e.g., Mic. 5:5–6). The hope offered by the postexilic prophets did not have a set period of judgment intervening, but was presented as gradual restoration over a protracted period of time. Religious restoration was available for them immediately, with socioeconomic restoration coming gradually and political deliverance being an eventual outcome (e.g., Dan. 9).

Each of these messages has relevance to the prophet's audience and to us not so much for the information they offer of the present or the future, but for what they reveal about God. It must be remembered that prophecy is part of God's self-revelation. That self-revelation is to be found in the prophet's message, the proclamation of God's agenda. We come to know God by what he has done in the past (history) and by what his plans are for the future (prophecy). The fact that history and prophecy flow together in a single sovereignly devised and executed plan ought to produce a distinctive awe for the Creator of that plan.

Prediction and Fulfillment

"Prediction" and "fulfillment" are two of the terms most often connected to prophetic literature, but both can lead to harmful misperceptions about the nature of prophecy.

Prediction

If someone today were to predict that the stock market will take a plunge and then took some action that actually caused this to happen, he or she would not be praised for the ability to predict. The aspect of predictiveness is diminished by the direct link to causation.

In the same way, the predictive element in biblical prophecy must usually be kept distinct from causation, else it ceases to be prediction. On these terms it is obvious that "prediction" would not be the best word to describe biblical prophecy. Prophets themselves were not predicting anything, but merely giving the word of the Lord. The prophecy was God's message, not the prophet's. If pre-

Figure 27.3. Categories of Prophetic Oracle

Oracular categories	Description	Preexilic emphasis	Postexilic emphasis
Indictment	Statement of the offense	Focus primarily on idolatry, ritualism, and social justice	Focus on not giving proper honor to the Lord
Judgment	Punishment to be carried out	Primarily political and projected for near future	Interprets recent or current crises as punishment
Instruction	Expected response	Very little offered; generally return to God by ending wicked conduct	Slightly more offered; more specifically addressed to particular situation
Aftermath	Affirmation of future hope or deliverance	Presented and understood as coming after an intervening period of judgment	Presented and understood as spanning a protracted time period Religious: Now Socioeconomic: Potential Political: Eventual

dicting is understood to preclude causation, then God cannot predict, for he is the final cause of all. So in the end, it must be recognized that prophecy is more interested in causation than in prediction. It is true that biblical prophecy spoke of events before they happened, but the purpose was that God would be properly recognized as having caused those events as a part of his ongoing plan.

Rather than regarding prophecy as prediction, we find it more helpful to consider prophecy "God's syllabus." The syllabus for a course does not "predict" what will happen in each class period of the term, but presents the instructor's plans and intentions for each period. The significance of the document is that the instructor is in a position to carry it out. Likewise, when a judge passes a sentence on a criminal, he is not "predicting" what will happen to that person. Rather, he is decreeing what ought to be done and is in a position to see that it is done.

This is like the relationship between God and prophetic literature. God was declaring his intentions and decreeing his judgments. Though these were still future when spoken, they could be considered prediction only in the broadest terms. It would not be accurate to speak of the prophets as predicting, for they were just the spokesmen. When a student assistant gives out a professor's syllabus, he is not predicting what the professor will talk about each day. It is the professor's syllabus; the student is but a delivery boy. So it was with the prophets.

Fulfillment

"Fulfillment" can also be a misleading term. We have already noted that some people are inclined to neglect the message of the prophets in an often elusive search for fulfillments that inevitably leads to speculation that departs further and further from the text. It is often assumed that the prophets had specific events in mind, but that was not necessarily the case. It is not essential to be able to discern a prophet's intention in terms of fulfillment as long as the intended message is understood. The prophet was aware what the message was, yet he did not necessarily know what shape the fulfillment of the prophecy might take. It was the message that was inspired, and it was the message that was the medium of God's revelation. The fulfillment was almost incidental, though it was certainly important that it take place.

Whether or not the interpreter is able to identify the fulfillment with confidence is open to question. There are numerous passages in the Old Testament that, if read in the context of the time, would clearly suggest that certain things were going to happen in certain ways. As history unfolded, however, those things did not come to pass in the expected ways.

For example, if someone in the time of Isaiah had been able to read the text that we identify today as Isaiah 11:16, he or she would have supposed that the verse clearly and unambiguously suggested that the inhabitants of the northern kingdom would return from their exile in Assyria in a massive emigration comparable to the Exodus. That did not happen. That it did not happen is not a blot on God's reputation, for who knows how the word could yet be fulfilled? But it suggests that assurance about fulfillment cannot always be achieved. Consequently, one must not become so absorbed in figuring out when and how fulfillment will take place that the message is neglected.

What is fulfillment? The Greek term translated "fulfill" in the New Testament is quite broad. When the New Testament authors spoke of something from the Old Testament as being fulfilled, they were certainly drawing a correlation between that Old Testament passage and something that was being said or done in their own time. At times the correlation is close and implies that the Old Testament was speaking directly to the New Testament

event (e.g., Isa. 61:1 and Luke 4:18–19; Zech. 9:9 and Matt. 21:5). On other occasions the correlation is much looser and suggests only the vaguest relationship (e.g., Hos. 11:1 and Matt. 2:15).

To account for this wide range of possible connotations, fulfillment should be seen as indicating an *appropriate correlation* between the prophetic word and the event to which it is related. So when a New Testament author suggests that some event "fulfilled" an Old Testament passage, he is not suggesting that the Old Testament author was speaking or thinking of this event, but rather that an appropriate correlation can be drawn between the Old Testament and the event.

The Old Testament authors intended to communicate a message. Their writings show little interest in identifying the specific fulfillment of the message. In contrast, the New Testament authors specifically addressed fulfillment rather than trying to disclose the message of an Old Testament prophet. Since Old Testament and New Testament authors focus on different aspects of the prophetic pronouncement, we are not under obligation to try to bring them into conformity with one another.

The New Testament authors were not using the Old Testament inductively to prove that Jesus was the Messiah. They had already accepted the fact of his messiahship. Instead, the Old Testament was used deductively to give further evidence of and to support that belief. Inductive proof was found in Jesus' miracles and in his words and deeds.

If the cited fulfillments did not necessarily represent the intentions of the Old Testament authors, one might wonder how the doctrine of inspiration is maintained. Inspiration can be strongly affirmed as long as the perspective of the Old Testament about prophecy is understood. Prophecy as the word of God was expected to be appropriate to numerous situations as history unfolded. In other words, only time would tell how appropriate a prophetic statement might be. It had an obvious appropriateness to the contemporary audience, but there was no thought that its fitness was exhausted on the contemporary situation. Hindsight would come into play in order to identify other emerging appropriatenesses. Neither the prophet nor the audience had any confidence in being able to anticipate what form a future appropriateness might take. Such an insight could only come by revelation.

Therefore the various appropriate situations that would emerge from a prophetic statement could not be considered part of the prophet's intention, yet by the same token he would not have objected to its being used in this expanded way. Consequently, the prophets would not have considered the apparently subjective correlations drawn by the New Testament writers as bad method. Endowed with inspiration, the New Testament writers were able to make reliable, acceptable, and appropriate correlations that the prophets did not anticipate even though further developments were expected.[3]

Questions for Further Study and Discussion

1. Whence did false prophets and prophets of other gods get their messages?
2. What distinctive evidences are there in the Old Testament that God has a predetermined plan for history?
3. Of what significance for eschatology is the principle that the vision is not the message, but the occasion for the message?
4. How are the "message" and the "fulfillment" different? What are the implications of this difference?
5. How much did a prophet understand his message? Or, was the object of the revelation of prophecy ever not actually the prophet and his audience? If so, why was the revelation given?
6. What are the implications of the statement, "prophecy is more interested in causation than in prediction"?
7. Are fulfillments inspired? Explain your answer.

For Further Reading

Blenkinsopp, Joseph. *A History of Prophecy in Israel.* Philadelphia: Westminster, 1983.

Bright, John. *Covenant and Promise.* Philadelphia: Westminster, 1976.

Brueggeman, Walter. *The Prophetic Imagination.* Philadelphia: Fortress, 1978.

Bullock, C. Hassell. *An Introduction to the Old Testament Prophetic Books.* Chicago: Moody Press, 1986.

Green, Joel B. *How to Read Prophecy.* Downers Grove, Ill.: InterVarsity, 1984. A good introduction to some of the key issues regarding prophecy.

Heschel, Abraham J. *The Prophets.* New York: Harper & Row, 1962. Classic study of the Hebrew prophets by a renowed Jewish scholar.

Holladay, John. "Assyrian Statecraft and the Prophets of Israel." *HTR* 63 (1970). 29–51. A good presentation of the categories of Israelite prophecy.

Huffmon, Herbert B. "Prophecy in the Ancient Near East." *IDB.* Supplemental vol.

---

[3]This understanding is built on a model using the significance of names in the Old Testament. For a fuller treatment see John H. Walton, "Isaiah 7:14: What's in a Name?" *JETS* 30 (1987): 298–303.

Nashville: Abingdon, 1976. 697–700. Classic essay on historical backgrounds of Israelite prophecy.

Koch, Klaus. *The Prophets.* 2 vols. Philadelphia: Fortress, 1982.

Lindblom, J. *Prophecy in Ancient Israel.* Philadelphia: Fortress, 1973. The classic study of the prophetic institution.

Russell, D. S. *The Method and Message of Jewish Apocalyptic.* Philadelphia: Westminster, 1964.

Smith, Gary V. "Prophet" *ISBE.* Rev. ed. Grand Rapids: Eerdmans, 1986. 3:986–1004. An excellent introduction to the whole area of prophecy from a conservative perspective.

Walton, John H. *Ancient Israelite Literature in its Cultural Context.* Grand Rapids: Zondervan, 1989.

_____ . "Isaiah 7:14: What's in a Name?" *JETS* 30 (1987): 289–306.

Ward, James M. *The Prophets.* Nashville: Abingdon, 1982.

Westermann, Claus. *Basic Forms of Prophetic Speech.* Translated by H. C. White. London: SCM Press, 1967.

Wilson, Robert R. *Prophecy and Society in Ancient Israel.* Philadelphia: Fortress, 1980. An exploration of the sociological aspects of prophecy.

Wood, Leon J. *The Prophets of Israel.* Grand Rapids: Baker, 1979. An emphasis on the personalities of the prophets.

Chapter 28

Isaiah

The book of Isaiah is a collection of the prophetic sayings and oracles of the prophet Isaiah, who was the dominant prophetic voice in the tumultuous latter half of the eighth century B.C. (ca. 740–700). Some of the richest Hebrew literature known is found here as well as a bold and forthright presentation of the trustworthiness and sovereign power of the God of Israel.

The Writing of the Book

The unity of the book of Isaiah is a subject of no small controversy. The fact that the prophet lived in the eighth century B.C. makes it very difficult for some scholars to accept that he could have identified Cyrus the Persian by name (44:28; 45:1), since Cyrus did not arrive on the scene of history until nearly two hundred years later. Even for those who are willing to accept the supernatural phenomenon of predictive prophecy, this has sometimes seemed irregular when compared with other prophetic oracles. The only other instance in the Old Testament is the naming of Josiah in 1 Kings 13:2, and that passage is further complicated by the probability that it was written in the time of Josiah. Technically, then, predictive identification such as this is unparalleled.

Even in a casual reading of the book of Isaiah in English we can detect a major shift occurring at chapter 40. The style becomes more poetic and theoretical. The tone becomes conciliatory rather than condemning. Indictment and judgment oracles that make up a large part of the first thirty-nine chapters become much rarer. The historical situation seems to have changed dramatically. The people being addressed are in exile rather than in eighth-century Judah. In light of these observations, one can easily understand why some are uncomfortable attributing the entire book to a single author writing in the eighth century.

It is commonplace for scholars to insist that there are at least two different authors of the book, separated from one another by at least 150 years. Typically, reference is made to a hypothetical "deutero–Isaiah" and often an additional "trito–Isaiah" as the unidentified individuals credited with writing chapters 40–66 in the sixth and fifth centuries B.C. More recently, computer analysis of writing style has been used to substantiate multiple authors.

Nevertheless, some scholars have felt that their view of biblical authority demands that the book be viewed as a unity. Consequently they have responded by fashioning a defense of the unity of the book and corresponding rebuttal of the objections to its unity. While this defense depends heavily on New Testament passages that associate the prophet Isaiah with the second part of the book (e.g., Matt. 3:3; 12:17; Luke 3:4; John 12:38–41; Acts 8:28; Rom. 10:16), evidence from the Old Testament is also used.

The testimony of the book itself certainly insists on the reality of supernatural predictive prophecy. The whole case for the sovereignty of God in Isaiah 40–48 is built around the Lord's ability to say beforehand what he is going to do and the challenge to the idols to do the same. Therefore the predictive element that pervades this section cannot be easily neutralized. The naming of Cyrus comes at a crucial climax of a highly structured poetic composition (44:24–28) and cannot be easily eliminated as if it were incidental or superfluous. Furthermore, the evidence that the book of Kings, completed by the middle of the Exile, used the complete book of Isaiah as a source favors a preexilic date for the writing of the entire book.[1]

For those who do not view the statements of Christ as literary references, but as affirmations of authorship, the New Testament would require that Isaiah be considered the prophet who delivered these oracles to Israel, for he is identified at the least as their source. That does not necessarily mean that he wrote them down, but it does register that what was written represents faithfully what Isaiah said. If 2 Kings used the book of Isaiah as a source, the book must have been written down fairly soon after Isaiah died, and there is no reason to deny that it was put into written form during his lifetime,

though such cannot be proved. On the whole, we remain unconvinced that the book of Isaiah must be divided among several authors.

The Background

The book of Isaiah is set against the background of the second half of the eighth century B.C. It will be remembered that this is when the Neo-Assyrian empire was taking its place as the first world power known in history.

Two major events serve as the focus of chapters 1–39:

1. The invasion of Israel by the Assyrian king Tiglath-Pileser III serves as the backdrop to chapters 7–12. This came in response to the military action of Damascus (the capital of Aram) and the northern kingdom, Israel, against the southern kingdom, Judah. The reason for the aggression of Damascus and Israel against Judah (the Syro-Ephraimite War, 735–732 B.C.) is not given in the text. It is clear, however, that their action was considered a real threat against the survival of the Davidic monarchy. The response of Ahaz, king of Judah, was to summon Assyria to police the region, an invitation that Tiglath-Pileser gladly accepted. The result was that Damascus was conquered, her people were deported, and all of Aram was incorporated into the Assyrian empire (732 B.C.). Sections of the northern kingdom were annexed, and a new king was put on the throne. Several years later, Israel rebelled again and was totally assimilated into the Assyrian Empire, with the capital city of Samaria destroyed in 721; but this event is given very little coverage in the book of Isaiah.

2. The invasion of Judah by the Assyrian king Sennacherib in 701 resulted from Hezekiah's involvement in an anti-Assyrian coalition (fig. 28.1). It brought the destruction of many of the fortified cities

---

[1]For proof of this, see John H. Walton, "New Observations on the Date of Isaiah," *JETS* 28 (1985): 129–32.

of Judah, leading finally to the siege of Jerusalem. In contrast to his father, Ahaz, Hezekiah trusted the Lord for deliverance, and the Assyrian army was destroyed.

This was a time of fear and political uncertainty. The Assyrians terrorized the populace of the ancient Near East with an aggressive program of subjugation. A country could choose to be a submissive vassal paying annual tribute and supplying auxiliary troops to the Assyrians; any sign of disloyalty, however, would bring territorial reductions and increased Assyrian control of the government—not to mention increased tribute demands. Behind all this lay the threat of ultimate deportation, with all political independence revoked.

The deportation program was designed to destroy any sense of nationalism or political identity. The goal was assimilation of foreign peoples into a massive empire ethnically and politically generic. For the Israelites this was a theological issue. They were a people chosen and set apart by God and living in a land promised and delivered to them by God. The Assyrian policy was a threat to the covenant distinctiveness of Israel.

Outline of the Book

I. Introduction
A. Overture (1–5)
B. Commissioning (6)
II. Assyrian context
A. Oracles at the time of Syro-Ephraimite coalition (7–12)
B. Oracles against nations (13–23)
C. Apocalyptic conclusion to oracles against the nations (24–27)
D. "Woe" oracles at the time of the siege of Jerusalem (28–33)
E. Apocalyptic conclusion of "Woe" oracles (34–35)
F. Resolution of the Assyrian crisis (36–37)
G. Transition to Babylonian crisis (38–39)

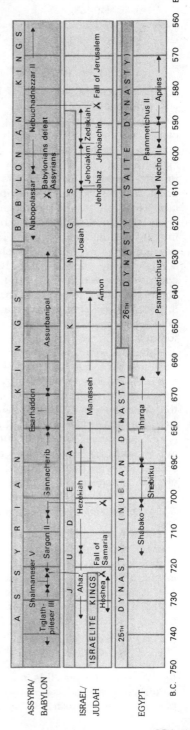

III. Projected oracles addressing
exiles (40–55)

IV. Projected oracles addressing
postexilic situation (56–66)

Purpose and Message

The material of the book of Isaiah is
arranged to highlight the trustworthiness
of Yahweh, the covenant God. This is
clearly seen in the contrast between the
actions of the two kings Ahaz and Hezekiah. Ahaz did not trust Yahweh, but sent
for the Assyrians to aid him in time of
political crisis (against the advice of Isaiah). This only resulted in replacing one
crisis with another. Hezekiah, though he
initially counted on Egyptian help, depended on Yahweh and was delivered in
a mighty way. Hezekiah thus became a
cogent example of how God in his sovereignty can bring deliverance. This was an
important lesson for the Israelites in exile,
who were thereby encouraged to respond
to their crisis with trust.

Although some oracles explicitly give
this emphasis (e.g., chaps. 30–31), it is
more discernible in the arrangement of
the oracles. The purpose of a prophet was
to deliver the words that God gave him to
say. The oracles of the first part of Isaiah
(1–39) are largely oracles of indictment
and judgment. Chapters 40–66 are more
concerned with God's forgiveness, deliverance, and restoration of Israel.

Organization and Structure

There has been considerable dispute
over the nature of chapters 1–5, since the
formal commissioning of Isaiah is related
in chapter 6. Some have contended that
1–5 contain oracles from before the time
of the vision that Isaiah had in the year
Uzziah died. Others believe that those five
chapters serve as an introduction to the
book by gathering selected oracles from
many different periods of Isaiah's ministry. Whether or not this material was
editorially gathered or chronologically
prior, it does serve as a suitable introduc-

Figure 28.1. The Sennacherib Prism, also
called the Taylor Prism, a hexagonal solid that
bears an account of Sennacherib's raid into
Judah in 701 B.C., another version of which is
given in Isaiah 36–37. (*Trustees of the British
Museum*)

tion to the book and its themes. Many of
the indictment oracles come in this section.

Chapter 6 could be seen as a conclusion to this introduction, for it suggests
that the people were not going to pay any
attention to the message of Isaiah. Isaiah's unheeded preaching would stand as
a confirmation of the guilt of Israel estab-

lished by the indictments in 1–5 and would lead to their eventual destruction.

The purpose of chapters 7–12 is to highlight the failure of Ahaz to trust Yahweh and the results of that failure. These are mostly oracles of judgment, but are interspersed with glimpses of future hope. The point of this is to show that, while Ahaz' failure was serious, it would not annul the covenant. God still intended to bring the promised kingdom after the period of judgment was over (e.g., chaps. 9 and 11).

The oracles against the nations (13–23) are properly placed here as demonstration of God's sovereign control over all the nations. The fact that Damascus and Israel were going to be unsuccessful in their attempted overthrow of the Davidic line, and the fact that Assyria successfully invaded the west are neither incidental nor isolated. Israel was to trust Yahweh because he was in control over all that transpired politically or in any other realm. These oracles were not given for the sake of the nations whom they concern. Rather, through these oracles Israel was given a sense of the transcendent power of God. Chapters 24–27 conclude this segment by speaking generally of the deliverance of Israel and the destruction of her enemies.

The "Woe" oracles of chapters 28–33 shift the focus to the time of Hezekiah in the last decade and a half of the eighth century b.c. Jerusalem was in potential distress (29), and Hezekiah was making alliances with Egypt (30–31). These oracles are filled with indictment for the nation's failure to trust Yahweh. Chapter 33 speaks of deliverance for the righteous ones in Zion, while chapters 34 and 35 speak of the wrath and judgment of Yahweh to fall on all his enemies.

The end of the Assyrian crisis (36–37) came when Hezekiah called on Yahweh to overthrow the armies of Sennacherib. It is interesting that the writer used the Assyrian officer to summarize the significant theological points. In his speech to Hezekiah's envoys, Rabshakeh insisted that the Egyptians would not be of any help to Israel. This parallels the idea that the Israelites were not to put their trust in Egypt. Rabshakeh made reference to Hezekiah's reforms (which he portrayed as making God angry, though the reader knows that they brought God's favor) and then presented the challenge that no other gods had been able to withstand the Assyrian armies. This heightened the irony of the situation, because the subsequent act of God's deliverance stands as testimony to the unique power of the God of Israel.

Chapters 38–39 function as a transition from the Assyrian crisis to the Babylonian crisis. Hezekiah's miraculous recovery from mortal illness came in response to his prayer and confirmed his standing as a godly king. But word of that recovery prompted Merodach-Baladan, the king of Babylon, to send envoys to Hezekiah with personal congratulations (see fig. 28.2). Hezekiah took the liberty to show them the royal treasury. All this provided the backdrop for the oracle of Isaiah 39:6–7, which indicated that the Babylonians would be the ones to carry Judah into exile. This oracle sets the scene for the major literary and thematic shift that occurs with chapter 40.

The crisis related in chapters 40–55 was the Babylonian exile spoken of in 39:6–7. If we accept this as the prophecy of Isaiah son of Amoz in the eighth century, we should note that he was not prophesying about the Exile; rather, he was assuming it and addressing his message to those who were part of it. Was this intended to have meaning for Isaiah's eighth-century audience? Yes, for two reasons: (1) its emphasis was to establish trust in the sovereignty of God. Exile did not come because of any divine inability to deliver; whether God delivered (as in the destruction of Sennacherib's army) or not (as in the fall of Jerusalem), his sovereign plan was being carried out and everything was under his control; and

Figure 28.2. A black marble relief that depicts Merodach-Baladan II (left), king of Babylon and contemporary to the Assyrian king Sennacherib, presenting an official with a grant of land. Above them is a carving of four major Babylonian deities. (*Bildarchiv Foto Marburg*)

(2) in keeping with the purpose of most "aftermath" oracles (see previous chapter), the people of Isaiah's time needed to be reassured that God would not fail to carry out his promises. After the period of judgment, God would bring restoration. This confidence and hope put the threat of punishment in a larger perspective.

The themes of chapters 40–55 are subjects such as the coming deliverance of the exiles, the worthlessness of idols, the coming judgment on the nations, and God's use of a particular "Servant" as an instrument to carry out his plan. All this was directed toward the political and spiritual restoration of Israel. Throughout this section of the book the recurrent challenge is issued for the idols and pagan gods to reveal a plan for history, to show how it was followed in the past, and how it would be carried forward in the

future. The extension of Yahweh's plan from the past into the future is presented as prima facie evidence of his sovereignty and uniqueness (41:21–29; 45:20–21; 46:7–11; 48:1–7).

Finally, chapters 56–66 project even further into the future to address those who have returned from exile. Upright living, the future glory of Jerusalem, and God's vengeance on his enemies are common topics. In all this, Yahweh laid out before Israel his agenda, so that the people might understand and affirm his holiness, sovereignty, and faithfulness.

Major Themes

Isaiah was among the first of the classical prophets to the southern kingdom of Judah. In a sense he could be considered both classical and pre-classical, for he served the king as adviser just as the pre-classical prophets had done. Much of his message, however, was comparable to the message of the classical prophets, including the indictment of the people, the promise of exile and destruction as God's punishment, and the hope of future fulfillment of covenant promises. The most prominent traits and themes of Isaiah's prophecy are the following:

Sons' Names as Signs

Chapters 7–9 feature four sons whose names were given prophetic significance. Isaiah's own children—Shear-Jashub ("a remnant will return," 7:3) and Maher-Shalal-Hash-Baz ("quick to the plunder, swift to the spoil," 8:1–3)—had such names, and so did Immanuel ("God with us," 7:14; 8:8, 10) and the child identified in 9:6. These highlighted God's short-term and long-range agendas for Israel.

The Servant

Four sections in the book of Isaiah have been designated "Servant Songs," for they speak of a Servant who would be instrumental in fulfilling God's plans for Israel.

These passages are 42:1–7; 49:1–9; 50:4–11; and 52:13–53:12; in addition, 61:1–3 shows some similarity to the Servant Songs, although the designation "servant" is not used. Israel is at times referred to as God's servant in the book (e.g., 41:8; 44:1) and Cyrus plays an instrumental role in God's program of deliverance; nevertheless, the description of the Servant in the songs goes far beyond what could be said of either of them. The function described for the Servant is strikingly parallel to the function ascribed to the future, ideal Davidic king elsewhere in the book (cf. chap. 11 and 55:3–5). The New Testament further confirms this as the preferred and common interpretation of these passages. Though the Servant is not called "Messiah" by Isaiah, the function and accomplishments attached to him lead many to that conclusion.

The Holy One of Israel

A title for God used almost exclusively by Isaiah in the Old Testament is "The Holy One of Israel." This title not only shows Isaiah's emphasis on the holiness of God, but also reflects the book's concern over the seriousness of Israel's offenses against that God. Reconciliation is God's ultimate goal. Punishment is used to effect reconciliation, and the Servant had a primary role in making it accessible to the people. Yet, in the end God brought the people back to himself for his name's sake (43:22–28).

Redeemer

Another attribute emphasized in Isaiah is that Yahweh is the Redeemer of Israel. This title for Yahweh is used only four times elsewhere, but more than a dozen times in the book of Isaiah. All the references lie within chapters 40–66 (namely, 41:14; 43:14; 44:6, 24; 47:4; 48:17; 49:7, 26; 54:5, 8; 59:20; 60:16; 63:16). The verb is used another nine times as an action carried out by Yahweh (likewise all in 40–66: 43:1; 44:22–23; 48:20; 51:10; 52:3, 9; 62:12; 63:9). Again the focus is on the sovereign grace of God.

Eschatology

The eschatology (the study of the conclusion of God's agenda) found in the book of Isaiah is a kingdom eschatology. By that we mean that the emphasis is on the future kingdom of Israel. It is depicted as a kingdom centered in Jerusalem. Peace and prosperity will abound, and all the world will come to Jerusalem and marvel and be taught. Proper worship and the centrality of the law are significant characteristics of this kingdom. A descendant of Jesse will be on the throne, but this aspect of the kingdom is not prominent in Isaiah. The emphasis is on the fact that Yahweh will reign (24:23; 33:22; 43:15; 44:6) and will be the pride of the remnant of Judah and the glory of Jerusalem.

Questions for Further Study and Discussion

1. How important is the unity of Isaiah as a current theological issue?
2. Of what significance is it that prophetic activity becomes more prominent in times of crisis?
3. In what ways is the theology of Isaiah distinctive in the Old Testament?
4. How is the kingdom eschatology in Isaiah different in emphasis from eschatological approaches that are common today?

For Further Reading

Alexander, Joseph Addison. *The Prophecies of Isaiah.* Grand Rapids: Zondervan, 1953. A reprint of a commentary that first appeared in the mid-nineteenth century; a classic, but quite outdated in historical and linguistic matters, offering no insight to the last hundred years of scholarship.

Hayes, John, and Stuart Irvine. *Isaiah.* Nashville: Abingdon, 1987. One of the more recent liberal treatments that argues for the unity of chapters 1–33 (where some scholars divide the book rather than after chapter 39) in the eighth century B.C.

Holladay, William. *Isaiah: Scroll of a Prophetic Heritage.* New York: Pilgrim, 1988.

Lindsey, F. Duane. *The Servant Songs.* Chicago: Moody Press, 1985. A thorough analysis of the Servant material from a conservative perspective.

MacRae, Allan A. *The Gospel of Isaiah.* Chicago: Moody Press, 1977. A conservative treatment of chapters 40–56.

Oswalt, John. *Isaiah 1–39.* Grand Rapids: Eerdmans, 1986. The best of the conservative commentaries.

Walton, John H. "Isaiah 7:14: What's in a Name?" *JETS* 30 (1987): 289–306. A treatment of the interpretation of Isaiah 7:14 and a discussion of the hermeneutical issues involved.

_____. "New Observations on the Date of Isaiah." *JETS* 28 (1985): 129–32.

Wolf, Herbert M. "A Solution to the Immanuel Problem in Isaiah 7:14–8:22." *JBL* 91 (1972): 449–56. Support for the identification of Immanuel as Maher-Shalal-Hash-Baz, Isaiah's son.

_____. *Interpreting Isaiah.* Grand Rapids: Zondervan, 1985. A conservative work with a textbook approach that provides a very useful summary of Isaiah.

Young, E. J. *The Book of Isaiah.* Grand Rapids: Eerdmans, 1972. A conservative classic in three volumes.

Chapter 29

Jeremiah

The book of Jeremiah occupies more space in the Bible than any other book, and the prophet Jeremiah's stature is comparable to anyone else's in the Old Testament. He was a man sent by God at Israel's darkest hour and proclaimed God's word at great personal cost for over forty years. More than any other, he provides us with glimpses of a prophet struggling with the God he served faithfully and with the message he was commissioned to deliver. His piety and integrity stood out as beacons in a generation that was to feel the scorching heat of the wrath of God. Jeremiah was their last chance, and he felt crushed under the weight of that responsibility.

Because of the great personal struggles of Jeremiah, we learn more about his personality than that of any other prophet. This information helps us to feel as though we know him as an individual.

The Writing of the Book

Jeremiah is one of the few books of the Old Testament to provide information about its writing. In 605 B.C., after Jeremiah had been prophesying for more than twenty years, God instructed him to record his prophecies in writing (36:1–3).

Jeremiah employed a scribe to do the actual writing as he dictated the words (36:4). This scroll was read before the king, who destroyed it, but a second copy was subsequently made (36:32). The scroll produced by Baruch was most likely very similar to what is preserved for us in chapters 1–25 of Jeremiah, usually designated Book 1. In this section Jeremiah is referred to in the first person. Two other collections of Jeremiah's sayings can be found in the book in chapters 30–31 (Book 2) and chapters 40–51 (Book 3).

Interspersed among these are biographical sections (26–29, 32–45) that refer to Jeremiah in the third person and focus mainly on the latter part of his career. These are commonly thought to have been added to the collections of Jeremiah's sayings by Baruch, his scribe, at a later time. That chapter 52 is also a later addition is indicated by the text, for Jeremiah 51:64 reports: "The words of Jeremiah end here."

The Background

Jeremiah's call came at a very strategic time. Josiah had ascended to the throne of Judah as a child of eight, but when he reached the age of twenty (628 B.C.), it is

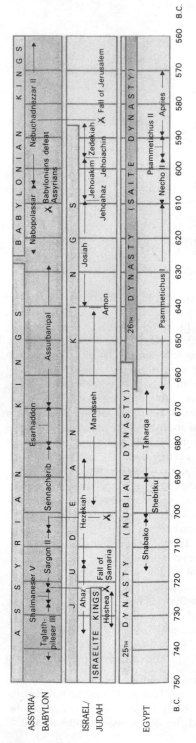

reported that he began to purge Judah and Jerusalem of pagan worship (2 Chron. 34:3–7). Jeremiah's call came shortly after, in 627 B.C., which was also the year of the death of the Assyrian king, Ashurbanipal, the last great ruler of the Assyrian Empire. That led to the establishment of an independent Babylonian state in the following year, 626. This Babylonian state was to grow into the empire that would eventually swallow Judah and Jerusalem, as declared in the word of the Lord through Jeremiah. As a result, the time of Jeremiah's call was both a time of hope, because of the spiritual reform in progress, and a time of danger, for a new enemy loomed on the horizon.

As it turned out, hope was short-lived, for the reform of Josiah died with him when he was killed in battle on the plain near Megiddo. During the remaining twenty-five years of the independent state of Judah, Josiah's sons presided over only the collapse of the kingdom. Once the Babylonians overthrew the Assyrians, Judah again came under the tight control of an eastern empire. Not content with being a vassal, Judah repeatedly became mired in conspiracies doomed to failure, leading in 586 B.C. to the final destruction of Jerusalem by Nebuchadrezzar, who deemed the city politically unreformable (see fig. 29.1). Judah had already proven itself unreformable spiritually. During this whole tragic period, Jeremiah was continuing to proclaim the word of the Lord. (More on the military and political struggles is given in chapter 31, "Ezekiel.")

Besides the destruction of the city and the temple, the state of Judah was dismantled by means of deportation of the populace. The first stage of deportation took place in 597 B.C., when Jehoiakim rebelled. Jehoiakim's son, Jehoiachin, was taken to Babylon at that time, as was the prophet Ezekiel. Despite the claims by some prophets in Judah that this was the full extent of the Lord's punishment and that thereafter the situation would improve, Jeremiah contended that the worst was yet to come. Sadly, this proved true when Zedekiah's rebellion in 589 brought the Babylonians back to Jerusalem with intent to destroy. Though deportation was used politically to obliterate national and ethnic identities, the Lord planned to use it to preserve a remnant for himself.

Outline of the Book

I. The call of Jeremiah (1)
II. Book 1 of the oracles of Jeremiah (2–25)
III. Biographical interlude 1 (26–29)
IV. Book 2: The book of consolation (30–31)
V. Biographical interlude 2 (32–45)
VI. Book 3: Oracles against the nations (46–51)
VII. Historical appendix: The fall of Jerusalem (52)

Purpose and Message

Jeremiah's purpose as a prophet was, of course, to deliver the message the Lord gave him. In doing so he desired to bring the people back to the Lord and to warn them of the consequences should they continue their present course of action. The purpose of the book is to record the prophecies of Jeremiah, but also to tell us something about the man Jeremiah and his lot as God's prophet, struggling both with the people and with the Lord.

While Jeremiah's struggles with the Lord concerning his mission ("the confessions of Jeremiah") reveal much about the prophet, they reveal even more about the Lord as we see how he responded to the man's complaints. Likewise, Jeremiah's problems with the people of Judah are presented to demonstrate the response of Judah and her kings to his message. Their rejection of the word of the Lord and their actions against Jeremiah served to increase their guilt before God.

The message of Jeremiah can be summarized by the content of the four oracular categories. Indictment oracles are all

Figure 29.1. A portion of the Lachish Letters, written on pottery, which represents military correspondence from the days when Nebuchadrezzar was closing in on Jerusalem. Several of the eighteen letters, which were found in the Israelite city of Lachish, give useful information that sheds light on the days of Jeremiah. (*Israel Antiquities Authority*)

in Book 1 and are most heavily concentrated in chapters 5–9. The most prominent indictment is that the people had forsaken the Lord and had worshiped idols (cf. 2:5–3:5). This was a covenant violation of the first degree. Also included are stubbornness and injustice (5:20–31) and improper use of temple and sacrifice (7:8–31).

Judgment oracles are more prevalent in the book than any of the other kinds of oracles. These are national in scope and mostly political in nature (e.g., exile, destruction, plunder). There is close correspondence between these and the curses listed in Deuteronomy 28:15–68 for failure to keep the covenant (cf. Jer. 11:8).

There are fewer than a dozen instruction oracles in the book. This near absence of instruction is typical, for the people had the covenant and knew what God required of them. Therefore the call

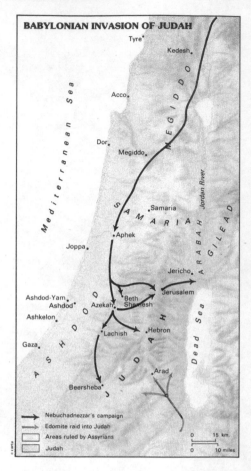

BABYLONIAN INVASION OF JUDAH

Tyre
Kedesh
Acco
Dor
Megiddo
Samaria
Aphek
Joppa
Jericho
Jerusalem
Ashdod-Yam
Ashdod
Azekah
Beth Shemesh
Ashkelon
Lachish
Hebron
Gaza
Arad
Beersheba
Mediterranean Sea
MEGIDDO
SAMARIA
Jordan River
ARABAH
GILEAD
Dead Sea
JUDAH
ASHDOD

Nebuchadnezzar's campaign
Edomite raid into Judah
Areas ruled by Assyrians
Judah

0   15 km.
0   10 miles

have for you,' declares the LORD, 'plans to prosper you and not to harm you, plans to give you hope and a future.' " The message they gave is that the Lord would bring the people of Israel back from exile (29:10) and would make a new covenant with them (31:31–34). The city would be rebuilt (30:18), the people would return to God (29:12–14), and a righteous Davidic king would sit on the throne (33:15–26).

The purpose and message of the book are summarized in one verse in the call of Jeremiah: "See, today I appoint you over the nations and kingdoms to uproot and tear down, to destroy and overthrow, to build and to plant" (1:10). These six verbs recur in key places throughout the book as Jeremiah proclaims the word of the Lord (cf. 18:7–10; 24:6; 31:28).

Structure and Organization

The literary features of Jeremiah become evident on even a cursory reading of the book. There are three major categories usually referred to as Types A, B, and C. Type A consists of prophetic oracles written in poetry. Type B comprises historical narratives about Jeremiah. Type C is the prose speeches of the book. Each of these is distributed widely throughout the book, so identifying them does not provide a system of organization.

In many of the prophetic books it is difficult to identify with confidence any meaningful organization of the oracular material, and Jeremiah is no exception. Many of the oracles are not dated, but from those that are it is clear that the ordering of the material is not chronological. Likewise, any attempts to uncover a topical arrangement have failed. That leaves rhetorical structuring as the most likely approach, and this is the direction that most recent studies have taken.[1]

Chapters 1–20 consist entirely of undated material. After the call, related in

was to return to the Lord (3:12–13) and to change their ways (7:3–7). Jeremiah also includes instruction about the supremacy of the Lord, by comparing him with the idols of the nations (10:2–16), and instruction about the Sabbath (17:19–23).

Aftermath oracles are found primarily in the Book of Consolation and the sections immediately preceding and succeeding it (29–33), with just a half-dozen other examples included (3:16–18; 16:14–15; 23:3–8; 24:5–7; 46:27–28; 50:4–5, 20). The purpose of these oracles is summarized in 29:11: " 'For I know the plans I

[1]See especially W. L. Holladay, *The Architecture of Jeremiah 1–20* (Cranbury, N.J.: Associated University Presses, 1976).

chapter 1, Holladay has identified a "harlotry cycle" woven through chapters 2–3 and a "foe cycle" as the basis of chapters 4–6. In the former, the allegory of a harlot is used to highlight Israel's faithlessness. In the latter, judgment is threatened at the hands of the irresistible foe from the north. The other major component of these early chapters is the famous Temple Sermon of Jeremiah (7:1–8:3). The foe cycle is resumed in chapters 8–10. These early chapters are built around themes that focus on the indictment and the approaching judgment of the people of Judah.

Chapters 11–20 contain the "confessions" of Jeremiah and most of the symbolic actions he performs. In the confessions, the prophet utters his laments and complaints to the Lord about the job he had to do and the way he was being treated by the people. They are somewhat similar to the psalms of lament found in the book of Psalms in their cry for justice and vindication, and occasionally they border on what sounds like blasphemy (esp. 20:7; to a lesser degree, cf. 12:1–2).

The confessions serve the important function of revealing God's compassion, justice, and sovereignty in a unique way. Symbolic actions in this section include burying a linen waistband (13:1–11) and the activities at the potter's workshop (18–19). These actions were used as occasions for oracles of judgment against the people. Book 1 is brought to a close by chapters 21–25, which contain some dated material and are largely addressed to the royal house and to the false prophets.

Nothing needs to be added to what has already been said about the two biographical interludes and Books 2 and 3.

Major Themes

God's Policy with Nations

In Jeremiah's sermon at the potter's house he expounds on the Lord's policy for handling nations (18:7–11). This policy is seen at work not only in the book of Jeremiah, but consistently through the Old Testament. We might picture it through the metaphor of a balance scale for the nation, with weights representing good deeds loaded on one side and weights representing wicked deeds piled on the other. Each generation's conduct added weights to the scale. On the wicked side we might further picture a button located under the pan. When the nation's wicked conduct was sufficiently greater than the righteous aspect, their weight would depress the button, setting off a warning bell that signaled the mandate for God's judgment. (This concept is a significant theme in the book of Habakkuk, so it will be discussed in more detail in chapter 40.)

The operation of this metaphor can be seen in a passage such as Genesis 15:16, in which Abraham is told that several centuries need to elapse before the land can be given to him because "the sin of the Amorite is not yet complete." It is also evident in the promises to Hezekiah and Josiah that the judgment on the nation would not come in their day (2 Kings 20:16–19; 22:20). It is significant for Jeremiah and Ezekiel, for it contradicts a parable being circulated at the time to the effect that this generation was suffering for the sins of previous generations (Jer. 31:29–30; Ezek. 18).

The metaphor demonstrates that only generations loading weights onto the side of the wicked deeds could create the mandate for judgment. Even the most superficial cessation of wickedness could induce God to delay his judgment, as was proved by the example of Nineveh (Jonah 3–4) and was stated explicitly by Jeremiah (18:7–11).

In conclusion, it must be noted that this system is operative for nations, not individuals, so it should not be confused with salvation by works. This scale of deeds is never conveyed as the way that God deals with individuals, and the differences must be well-noted. Nations are not "saved" from sin, nor do they exist eternally. Nations are therefore treated solely on physical and temporal terms, so the system can in no way be equated to the eternal destiny of individuals. Grace does exist in the system as evidenced by the long-suffering character of God, and it continues to manifest his grace, because there is nothing in Scripture to suggest that God has changed his policy for dealing with nations.

The New Covenant

The proclamation of the new covenant in Jeremiah 31 is generally considered to be the foremost of the prophet's contributions to theology. To understand its significance we must examine the terms of this new covenant and how it is related to other covenants.

In the chapter on Deuteronomy we noted the use of the treaty format in the covenant. This format included a preamble, historical prologue, stipulations, a document clause, a list of witnesses, and a list of curses and blessings. When we compare this format with Jeremiah's new covenant, we find that only the document clause is discussed. Rather than being etched in stone, it was to be written on the heart. As a result, people would not have to be taught the law, but would intrinsically know the law. It must be noticed that the terms of the covenant are not explained, but only where the document was recorded. We are thus left to infer that the terms of this covenant were no different from the covenant that was currently in force, that is, the Abrahamic covenant as expanded and elaborated at Sinai and to David. This is confirmed in the immediate context in that it was the

law that was written on the people's hearts (31:33) and in the near context by the confirmation of the promise of the land (32:36–44) and the promise of an established dynasty for David (33:15–26).

Consequently, the use of "new" here should not be thought of as indicating a totally separate covenant distinct from the previous ones, but an extension of them with new features and dimensions added. This new configuration was announced by Jeremiah, but was not actually ratified and put into operation until the means for its accomplishment were at hand. Hebrews 8–10 shows us that Jesus Christ makes those conditions achievable and that the indwelling of the Holy Spirit actually accomplishes the objective.

False Prophets

A very frustrating problem for Jeremiah arose in the fact that not only was his message one of doom and gloom, but there were many other prophets—claiming also to be spokesmen for Yahweh—who were prophesying deliverance, peace, and prosperity (14:11–16; 23:9–40; 28:1–17). Thus outnumbered, Jeremiah was the one accused of being a false prophet, and there were times when he appeared to suspect that the charge was correct (20:7–10). He contended that it could be construed as an act of deception for the Lord to allow false prophecy to be spoken in his name and not to punish the perpetrator, for the people had no other means of determining who was a true spokesman. In response, the Lord rebuked Jeremiah, calling him to repentance and faithful service and promising protection from his enemies (15:15–21).

Questions for Further Study and Discussion

1. How would the political and religious events occurring at the time of Jeremiah's call affect the response of the people to his message?
2. What would Jeremiah and his audience have expected with regard to the new covenant?

3. Why would God allow false prophets to speak in his name and mislead the people?

For Further Reading

Bright, John. *Jeremiah.* New York: Doubleday, 1965. Though superceded by some larger commentaries, still a readable introduction to the book from a moderate perspective.

Carroll, Robert. *Jeremiah.* Philadelphia: Westminster, 1986. Primarily concerned with literary reconstruction.

Dumbrell, W. J. *Covenant and Creation.* Nashville: Thomas Nelson, 1984.

Harrison, R. K. *Jeremiah and Lamentations.* TOTC. Downers Grove, Ill.: InterVarsity, 1973.

Holladay, William. *Jeremiah.* 2 vols. Philadelphia: Fortress, 1986–89. Superb treatment of every aspect of the text and interpretation of the book by the foremost Jeremiah scholar of this generation. Highly recommended, though often technical. By no means conservative, yet more moderate than many other commentators.

Janzen, Gerald. *Studies in the Text of Jeremiah.* Cambridge: Harvard University Press, 1973.

McComiskey, Thomas. *The Covenants of Promise.* Grand Rapids: Baker, 1985.

McKane, William. *A Critical and Exegetical Commentary on Jeremiah.* Edinburgh: T. & T. Clark, 1986. Primarily concerned with matters of textual and literary criticism and reconstruction.

Perdue, Leo, and Brian Kovacs. *A Prophet to the Nations: Essays in Jeremiah Studies.* Winona Lake, Ind.: Eisenbrauns, 1984. A collection of many of the classic journal articles on the book of Jeremiah.

Raitt, Thomas. *A Theology of Exile: Judgment and Deliverance in Jeremiah and Ezekiel.* Philadelphia: Fortress, 1977. A helpful analysis of the oracle types in these two prophetic books.

Thompson, J. A. *The Book of Jeremiah.* NICOT. Grand Rapids: Eerdmans, 1980. The best of the evangelical commentaries.

Chapter 30

Lamentations

"Lamentations" takes its title from the Latin Vulgate Bible. The book's placement after Jeremiah in the English canon reflects the influence of the Greek Old Testament, the Septuagint, which in the title verse ascribes the poetry to the prophet Jeremiah. The Hebrew title, *'êkāh,* is derived from the first word of chapters 1, 2, and 4. The interjection is usually translated "how" or "alas" and was commonly used in the opening line of Israelite funeral dirges. For example, there was David's lament over Jonathan's death, "How the mighty have fallen!" (2 Sam. 1:19), and Isaiah's taunting song against the king of Babylon, "How you have fallen from heaven!" (Isa. 14:12).

Lamentations is included in the third division of the Hebrew canon, "the Writings." The book is ordered third among the five books comprising the Megilloth, or "Festival Scrolls" (i.e., the Song of Songs, Ruth, Lamentations, Ecclesiastes, and Esther), which are used on specified Jewish feast days. Lamentations is assigned to be read annually on the ninth day of Ab, the day of mourning the destruction of the temple in Jerusalem (by the Babylonians in 587 B.C. and by the Romans in A.D. 70).

The book of Lamentations is entirely poetic in form. The five poems are coextensive with the five chapters of the book.

The Writing of the Book

The Septuagint and Jewish tradition both ascribe the writing of Lamentations to the prophet Jeremiah. This association was probably based on a misunderstanding of the statement in 2 Chronicles 35:25 that "Jeremiah composed laments for Josiah." The arguments for and against Jeremiah's authorship of the poetry approaches a stalemate. Evidence supporting the prophet, such as the similarities in tone and vocabulary between the books of Jeremiah and Lamentations, is countered by their differences of poetic style and theological perspective. It seems best to assign the composition to an unknown eyewitness of the fall of Jerusalem, since the text itself records nothing of authorship.

This collection of funeral songs for Jerusalem was probably composed sometime between the fall of the city in 587/586 B.C. and Jehoiachin's release from prison in Babylon (ca. 562 B.C.—cf. 2 Kings 25:27–30). The despairing tone of the petition for national renewal in the closing lines of the final poem (5:19–22) indicates that the writer apparently knew nothing of Jehoiachin's discharge from prison and its implications for the fulfillment of Jeremiah's prophecies for covenant restoration in Israel (Jer. 30–33).

The Background

The book is a response to the destruction of Jerusalem, and its aftermath, by the Babylonian armies of King Nebuchadrezzar in 587 B.C. The biblical accounts of the invasion of Judah and the fall of Jerusalem are recorded in 2 Kings 24–25 and 2 Chronicles 36.

The prophets had forewarned Judah of the impending catastrophe for two centuries (cf. 2 Kings 24:3; 21:12). Alas, the repetition of the threat of divine judgment dulled the ears of the people and insulated them against the idea of repentance. Moreover, the delay of Yahweh's visitation had lulled the nation into a false sense of security (e.g., Jer. 6:13–14; 7:1–4). Lamentations bewails the day, warned of by the prophets, in which Yahweh would become "like an enemy," destroying Israel "without pity" (Lam. 2:2, 5).

Outline of the Book

I. Lamentation for Jerusalem's misery and desertion (1)
II. Lamentation for the Daughter of Zion cut down in Yahweh's wrath (2)
III. The poet's grief and hope (3)
IV. The horror of the siege (4)
V. Zion's disgrace remembered; a petition for restoration (5)

Purpose and Message

In contrast with 2 Kings 24–25, which documents the historical data about the fall of Jerusalem, Lamentations captures the pathos of that tragic turn in Israel's covenant experience with Yahweh. The poems preserve the Hebrew response to the unthinkable and inexpressible—the utter destruction of David's Zion, the ruin of Yahweh's temple, and the divine abandonment of "the elect" of God. ("Zion" is a favorite expression for Jerusalem and especially the temple mount in the Psalms, Isaiah, and Lamentations. The origin of the term is uncertain, but the Hebrew *Ṣîyôn* may be understood as "fortified tower.") While the tragedy did confirm the prophetic message and vindicate prophetic interpretation of the relationship between covenant stipulations and curses, there was little comfort for the stunned survivors of the Babylonian onslaught.

Lamentations records "the day of the Lord" for Judah enacted in all its terrible fury. The threat of covenant curse became a grim reality and an unforgettable nightmare. Moses' admonition that covenant violations jeopardized Israel's presence in the land of Canaan was revealed to be more than hollow theologizing. Yahweh had finally exacted punishment for Judah's covenant transgressions. Israel had been "vomited" out of the land of Yahweh's covenant promise (Lev. 18:24–30). The only consolation for the "Daughter of Zion" was the knowledge that one day the nations would also drink from the cup of God's wrath (Lam. 4:21–22; cf. 3:55–66).

As funeral dirges, the poems of Lamentations were designed to offer a type of catharsis to the survivors of Judah's calamity. This expression of sorrow and venting of emotions could never fully answer the questions related to the "how" and "why" of God's sovereign rule over human history. But it did allow the suffering Hebrews to deal honestly with their grief and to mitigate the trauma of Yahweh's abandonment.

The poet bared the soul of the penitent nation, bowed in shame and admitting her many transgressions and great rebellion (e.g., 1:14, 22). The purging of sin and guilt permitted the "widow of Zion" to acknowledge that Yahweh was indeed

Figure 30.1. The Acrostic Structure of Lamentations

Poem 1 (22 three-line verses)	Poem 2 (22 three-line verses)	Poem 3 (66 three-line verses)	Poem 4 (22 two-line verses)
a	a	a	a . . . .
. . . . . .	. . . . . .	a	. . . . . .
. . . . . .	. . . . . .	a	b . . . .
b	b	b	. . . . . .
. . . . . .	. . . . . .	b	c . . . .
. . . . . .	. . . . . .	b	. . . . . .

just in his judgment of Jerusalem's covenant unfaithfulness (1:18).

Only this response of confession and repentance could give meaning and substance to the words of future hope uttered in the prayer of chapter 3. The very wrath of God signaled his covenant love for Israel. The loving father must mete out the deserved punishment to his wayward child. The call to wait upon the Lord and his unfailing mercy instilled hope for Israel's future restoration, because the nation's history had demonstrated that Yahweh would not cast her off forever (3:21–29).

Structure and Organization

Lamentations, as we have noted, comprises five poems. Three of the poems are funeral dirges, opening with the customary wail "how?" (chaps. 1, 2, and 4). The other two poems are cast in the form of the "lamentation," with chapter 3 being an individual lamentation and chapter 5 a community lamentation. The "lamentation" is distinguished from a "lament" in form and content. The former is an expression of grief over a catastrophe that is irreversible, while the latter is an appeal to a merciful God for divine intervention in a desperate situation.

Four of the five poems are alphabetic acrostics, that is, each line in succession introduces one of the twenty-two letters of the Hebrew alphabet. The structure of the acrostic poems in chapters 1 to 4 may be outlined as in figure 30.1.

The purpose of the alphabetic acrostics

in Lamentations is threefold: (1) the acrostic form has mnemonic value—the poet preserves the memory of Jerusalem's tragedy through the recitation of the alphabet; (2) the acrostic poems convey the full expression of lamentation over Zion's destruction—effectual catharsis "from A to Z"; and (3) in constricting the range of artistic expression, the rigid use of the acrostic form enables to the poet to devote full attention to the topic or theme at hand.

The concluding poem is not an acrostic, but it does follow the twenty-two-verse pattern of poems 1, 2, and 4. The deviation from the formula may have been simply a stylistic choice or an emphatic ploy by the poet.

Poem 1 is a funeral dirge personifying the city of Jerusalem as a once proud and dignified woman, now brutally raped and abandoned by treacherous friends. This image is intensified in the use of words and phrases like "widow" and "queen" (v. 1) and "Daughter of Zion" (v. 6). The poem emphasizes the desolation, loneliness, and sense of abandonment felt by survivors of the calamity (vv. 2, 9, 16, 17).

Poem 2 describes the vehemence of Yahweh's anger against Zion, and poem 4 records the grim aftermath of Yahweh's judgment. The Daughter of Zion's only comfort was the knowledge that the punishment for her sins had been accomplished (4:22). Some scholars suggest that the deliberate inversion of the sixteenth and seventeenth letters of the alphabet in chapters 2 and 4 serves to emphasize

Figure 30.2. The Problem of Human Suffering

1. Retributive—just punishment for sin (Job 4:7–9; 8:20)
2. Disciplinary—corrective affliction (Deut. 8:3; Prov. 3:11–12)
3. Probationary—God's testing of the heart (Deut. 8:2; Job 1:6–12; 2:10)
4. Temporary or apparent, in comparison with the good (or bad) fortune of others (Job 5:18; 8:20–21; Ps. 73)
5. Inevitable, as a result of the Fall (Job 5:6–7; Ps. 14:1–4)
6. Necessarily mysterious, since God's character and plan are inscrutable (Job 11:7; 42:3; Eccl. 3:11)
7. Haphazard and morally meaningless, in that time and chance happen to all (Job 21:23, 25–26; Eccl. 9:11–12)
8. Vicarious—one may suffer for another or for the many (Deut 4:21; Ps. 106:23; Isa 53: 3, 9, 12).

From R. B. Y. Scott, *The Way of Wisdom* (New York: Macmillan, 1971), 144–47.

Judah's shame before the nations and Yahweh's irrepressible purposes in history—since it was the Lord himself who scattered them.

The poem of chapter 3 is the longest and most-developed acrostic of the book. Only the seven-line acrostic stanzas of Psalm 119 surpass it for intricacy of construction. This poem functions as the literary and theological center of the composition. The poet's complaint contains his personal suffering (representative of the nation, 3:1–20), a prayer of consolation and hope (3:21–29), a plea for repentance and a return to Yahweh (3:40–54), and a cry for vengeance and vindication (3:55–66).

Major Themes

Human Suffering

There is a sense in which every manner of human suffering is inevitable and inexplicable. It is inevitable because in the fall of humanity recorded in Genesis 3, all have rejected God and practiced evil deeds (Ps. 14:1–4). All have turned away from God and have become corrupt. So God in his holiness and justice will not leave the guilty unpunished, despite his long-suffering nature (Nah. 1:3). The suffering is inexplicable in that the plans of God are unsearchable (Isa. 55:8–11). In-

deed, the ways of God are beyond finding out (Job 9:10). Yet the Old Testament does offer some tentative explanations for the question of human suffering, especially that of the innocent.

R. B. Y. Scott suggests eight solutions to the problem of human suffering, based on his analysis of Old Testament wisdom literature (fig. 30.2).

Lamentations clearly illustrates the retributive aspect of human suffering. Judah as a nation acknowledged that she deserved the punishment inflicted by Babylonia as Yahweh's instrument of justice (e.g., 1:5, 14, 22; 4:13). Indeed, Yahweh was right to judge the insubordination of those who rebelled against his commandments—even his elect (1:18).

Divine Abandonment

Amid the aftermath of Jerusalem's destruction, the poet lamented that Yahweh had spurned, rejected, and abandoned Judah—king, priest, and sanctuary (2:6–7). This so-called divine abandonment motif has been identified in the literature of ancient Mesopotamia as far back as Sumerian times. In the Mesopotamian texts the patron deity leaves his or her temple, either because the city has been destroyed or because it is under such severe distress that the deity is impotent to alter the situation.[1]

By contrast, Yahweh's abandonment of his temple and the city of Jerusalem (as witnessed and announced by Ezekiel) was due to Judah's covenant trespass, not Yahweh's impotence. God chose willfully to remove his glory from the temple in Jerusalem because of the idolatry and sin of Israel and Judah (Ezek. 9:9). Ironically, divine abandonment by the gods in Mesopotamian literature prompted confession of sin and pleading for the deity's return. In Judah the departure of Yahweh's glory from the temple should have induced prayer and repentance; instead, the people provoked God by using his absence as an excuse for their sin and rebellion.

With this in mind, the poet petitioned Yahweh at the end of his funeral dirge to look once again on his people and to return to them, coming to dwell in their midst and renewing them in his love.

Questions for Further Study and Discussion

1. How is the form of the poetry in Lamentations (i.e., the acrostic poems) important to the message of the poetry?
2. How might the book of Lamentations be used today as a resource for corporate or individual grief and suffering?
3. What portrait of God can be drawn from the book of Lamentations?
4. What does the book of Lamentations reveal about the conditions in Jerusalem during the siege by the Babylonians?
5. How does suffering as punishment for sin in Lamentations relate to the blessings and curses of covenant theology disclosed in Leviticus 26 and Deuteronomy 28?

For Further Reading

Ellison, H. L. "Lamentations." *EBC.* Vol. 6. Grand Rapids: Zondervan, 1986. 695–753.

Gordis, R. *The Song of Songs and Lamentations.* Rev. ed. New York: Ktav, 1947. Classic Jewish commentary, careful linguistic analysis combined with detailed attention to interpretive and theological problems.

Gottwald, N. K. *Studies in the Book of Lamentations.* SBT. Vol. 14. London: SCM Press, 1954. Valuable insights on the poetic and theological dimensions of Lamentations.

Harrison, R. K. *Jeremiah and Lamentations.* TOTC. Downers Grove, Ill.: InterVarsity, 1973.

Hillers, D. R. *Lamentations.* AB. Vol. 7A. Garden City, N.Y.: Doubleday, 1972. Thorough introduction and commentary, probably the best volume currently available.

Kaiser, Walter C. *A Biblical Approach to Personal Suffering.* Chicago: Moody Press, 1982. Contemporary application of Lamentations to personal suffering, but lacking any clear distinctions between the retributive suffering in Israel for covenant trespass and the kinds of deserved and undeserved suffering in the life of a Christian.

Provan, Iain. *Lamentations.* NCBC. Grand Rapids: Eerdmans, 1991.

Scott, R. B. Y. *The Way of Wisdom.* New York: Macmillan, 1971. Especially 142–47 on the problem of human suffering.

---

[1]On the motif of divine abandonment see D. I. Block, *The Gods of the Nations*, ETSMS 2 (Jackson, Miss.: Evangelical Theological Society, 1988), 129–61.

Chapter 31

Ezekiel

Ezekiel was a priest and the son of Buzi, a Zadokite priest (Ezek. 1:3). He was one of a company of 10,000 Hebrews taken captive by King Nebuchadrezzar of Babylon in 597 B.C. (2 Kings 24:10–17). Ezekiel and the captives who survived the trek to Mesopotamia settled near the Kebar River (or Canal) in Babylonia. Ezekiel was married (Ezek. 24:15–16), but nothing else is known of his life before he was called to his prophetic ministry. His name means "God strengthens," recalling to our minds his work of consolation and encouragement among the Hebrew exiles.

The book of Ezekiel comprises part of the section labeled the Major Prophets in the Hebrew canon, following Isaiah and Jeremiah. The English Bible adopts the order of the Septuagint in placing Ezekiel after Lamentations, which was at that time associated with the prophet Jeremiah. While Ezekiel was always included in the Hebrew canon, later Jewish scholars disputed the book's canonical value. At issue were seeming discrepancies between the prophet's understanding of temple ritual and the prescriptions of Mosaic law (e.g., a disagreement in the number and kinds of animals sacrificed at the New Moon festival—cf. Num. 28:11

and Ezek. 46:6). The rabbis eventually restricted the public and private use of Ezekiel, commenting that the ultimate harmonization of the difficulties must await "the coming of Elijah" (cf. Mal. 4:5).

The Writing of the Book

Few books of the Old Testament have withstood the literary dissection characteristic of critical biblical scholarship as well as Ezekiel's prophecies. Still, many modern scholars suggest that the book of Ezekiel was composed in four stages but that the cleverness of the scribes and editors makes it virtually impossible to distinguish these various literary strands. First, this theory goes, the prophet's original words were handed down orally by his disciples or the prophetic school. The literary stage (i.e., oral tradition put in writing) and editorial stage (i.e., the collection and arrangement of written materials) followed. Final shaping of the text occurred during the scribal period when (unknown) editors refined, polished, and embellished the story of Ezekiel's ministry. According to this hypothesis, the oral and literary stages of the book were completed before the Hebrew return from the Babylonian exile.

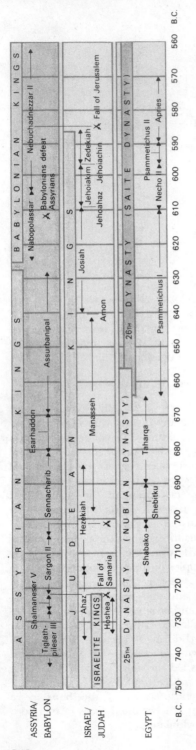

However, the autobiographical style of the book suggests that Ezekiel penned the prophecies himself. Personal and possessive pronouns like "I," "me," and "my" pervade every chapter of the book (cf. the first ten verses of chapter 2). The widely recognized uniformity of language and style and the consistency of theme and message also support the premise that Ezekiel narrated his own experiences as God's "watchman to Israel" (3:16–19; 33:1–9).

Later Jewish tradition attributes the compilation of Ezekiel's oracles to the men of the Great Synagogue (a council of scribes and other Hebrew leaders reputedly founded after the Babylonian exile to reorganize Jewish religious life and culture). The idea of a later disciple of the prophet or even his personal scribe collecting, organizing, and publishing the prophet's writings is not inconsistent with Old Testament practice. It is clear that a "school of the prophets" was established in Israel by Elijah and Elisha (cf. 2 Kings 2:3; 6:1–7).

Information regarding these "sons of the prophets" is scant, but they were servants under the charge of Elijah and Elisha and they apparently lived communally with the man of God as prophetic understudies of a sort. Part of the duties performed by these "prophetic interns" may have been the preservation and promulgation of the words and deeds of their mentors. The prophet Jeremiah had a companion named Baruch, who served as an amanuensis, or personal scribe, for the man of God (cf. Jer. 36:4). This practice carried into the New Testament, as both the apostles Paul and Peter dictated letters to personal scribes (Rom. 16:22; 1 Peter 5:12).

The actual date of writing for the book may be determined in part on the basis of internal evidence. Thirteen of Ezekiel's messages are dated precisely to the day, month, and year of King Jehoiachin's exile to Babylon. Ezekiel's first pronouncement is connected with his call to

Figure 31.1. A general view of the Ishtar Gate from the north in excavations at the walled city of Babylon. (*Staatliche Museen zu Berlin*)

be a prophet and is fixed in 593 B.C. The prophet's last dated oracle is his prophecy about Egypt delivered in 571 B.C. (29:17). Since Ezekiel communicates nothing of Jehoiachin's release from prison in Babylon in 562 B.C., it is likely that the account of his prophetic ministry was composed sometime between 571 and 562 B.C.

The provenance, or geographical location, of Ezekiel's ministry remains a topic of scholarly debate, largely due to the precision of the temple vision in chapters 8–11. Elaborate multiple residence theories have been constructed in an attempt to account for the prophet's eyewitness detail of events in Jerusalem and his captivity in Babylon. Internal evidence overwhelmingly supports a Babylonian locale for Ezekiel's ministry. Ezekiel's message to the Judeans, as in his oracles against the nations, should be understood as indirect communication. Likewise, his awareness of circumstances in Jerusalem was attributable to his ecstatic transport to the scene: "The Spirit lifted me up between earth and heaven and in visions of God he took me to Jerusalem" (8:3).

The Background

The ministry of Ezekiel was but a by-product of earlier political and religious policies implemented by Manasseh, king of Judah.[1] Manasseh sealed Judah's fate when he sanctioned the worship of the Canaanite god Baal as the official state religion. The southern kingdom had entered a "covenant of death" that was irrevocable. Disaster was thus decreed for Jerusalem (2 Kings 21:9–15; 24:3–4).

The reign of King Josiah, Manasseh's

---

[1]The biblical accounts of the historical events related here are found in 2 Kings 21–25 and 2 Chronicles 33–36.

grandson, marked Judah's "last gasp of righteousness" before God's judgment came in the form of a series of Babylonian invasions. The rediscovery of the Book of the Law (probably Deuteronomy) prompted spiritual revival and religious reform in Judah. Unfortunately, Josiah's reformation died with him in battle against the Egyptians and Pharaoh Neco on the plain of Megiddo in 609 B.C. The series of "puppet kings" who followed were all disobedient to the covenant stipulations of God and unrepentant in the face of prophetic rebuke—"until . . . there was no remedy" (2 Chron. 36:15–16).

Pharaoh Neco installed Jehoahaz and Eliakim, both sons of Josiah, on the Judean throne as Egyptian vassals. Jehoahaz was deposed within three months for insubordination, but his successor Eliakim (throne name: Jehoiakim) ruled for eleven years in Jerusalem. According to Jeremiah, Jehoiakim's tenure in office was a "reign of evil" characterized by idolatry, social injustice, robbery, murder, extortion, adultery, and rejection of the covenant of the Lord (Jer. 22:1–17).

Judah remained a vassal state to Egypt until the battle of Carchemish in 605 B.C., when Nebuchadrezzar and the Neo-Babylonians routed Neco and his army along with the Assyrians. Jehoiakim and Judah were then subjugated as a Babylonian tributary state by Nebuchadrezzar. However, Jehoiakim attempted to revolt and cast off the Babylonian yoke when Nebuchadrezzar failed to subdue Pharaoh Neco in a second clash in 601 B.C. The move proved foolhardy. The Babylonians again swept into Judah to punish the disloyalty of the vassal king. Jehoiakim subsequently died during the latter stages of the Babylonian siege of Jerusalem (598–597 B.C.). His son, Jehoiachin, ruled only three months in his place before the Babylonians overran and plundered the city.

King Jehoiachin and the royal family were deported to Babylon, along with another 10,000 people from the elite of Hebrew society (fig. 31.1). The prophet Ezekiel was among that number, and Jehoiachin's exile became the watershed by which Ezekiel dated both his divine commission to prophesy and also many of his messages to the Hebrew captives in Babylon (Ezek. 1:1–3; 8:1, etc.).

Outline of the Book

I. Prophecies against Jerusalem
   A. Ezekiel's vision and call (1–3)
   B. Object lessons and oracles (4–7)
   C. Ezekiel's vision of the temple (8–11)
   D. Object lessons and oracles (12–15)
   E. An allegory (16)
   F. A parable and a proverb (17–18)
   G. A lament (19)
   H. Rebellious Israel (20–22)
   I. Allegory of the two adulterous sisters (23)
   J. Parable of the cooking pot (24)
II. Prophecies against the nations
   A. Ammon (25:1–7)
   B. Moab (25:8–11)
   C. Edom (25:12–14)
   D. Philistia (25:15–17)
   E. Tyre and Sidon (26–28)
   F. Egypt (29–32)
III. Prophecies of restored Israel
   A. Object lessons and oracles (33–35)
   B. A new heart, dry bones, and two sticks (36–37)
   C. Gog and Magog (38–39)
   D. The new temple (40–43)
   E. The prince, Levites, and priests (44)
   F. The temple ritual (45–46)
   G. The boundaries of restored Israel (47)
   H. The division of the land (48)

Purpose and Message

The prophetic message and literary structure of Ezekiel are closely related.

The book's three-part message is really a theodicy (i.e., a defense or interpretation of God's judgment and the resultant destruction), and it corresponds to the three dimensions or phases of Ezekiel's ministry to the Hebrew exiles. Chapters 1–24 predate the fall of Jerusalem and are directed toward the rebellious house of Judah. The purpose of Ezekiel's divine commission as God's "watchman" was to warn a generation of obstinate and hardened Israelites of impending judgment (2:3–8), to underscore each generation's accountability for sin (18:20), and to call those willing to heed the counsel "repent and live" (18:21–23, 32).

After the destruction of Jerusalem in 587/586 B.C., Ezekiel turned his attention to the nations surrounding Israel that had been active participants in or gleeful onlookers to "the day of Jacob's trouble" (chaps. 25–32). Lest in their arrogance they assume an exemption from divine judgment, they too were warned that God had determined to visit them in wrath and vengeance for their misdeeds (e.g., 25:1–11).) Implicit in this phase of Ezekiel's ministry was a reminder to Israel that Yahweh is indeed righteous and just in his sovereign rule of the nations (cf. 28:24–26).

Finally, in chapters 33–48 Ezekiel instills hope among the captive Hebrew remnant by encouraging them with the promise of a new "covenant of peace" superintended by the "Davidic shepherd" (34:20–31). Yahweh, the covenant-keeping God of Abraham, would once again restore the fortunes of Israel and Judah by joining them into a single nation under one messianic king—the Davidic prince who will rule forever. The Lord would cleanse his people, establish faithfulness in the land, relocate his sanctuary in their

midst, and bless Israel through his "servant David" (37:15–28).

Structure and Organization

Thirteen of Ezekiel's messages are introduced by a date formula. The table below illustrates the general chronological arrangement of the prophecy, with three exceptions (29:1, 17; 32:1). All three are oracles against Egypt and have been placed together with the other Egyptian prophecies rather than in chronological sequence.

The prophet's revelations from God were delivered to the Hebrew people orally and presumably recorded at a later date, as evidenced in expressions like "speak . . . say" (14:4), "set forth an allegory" (17:2–3), "preach" (20:46), "declare" (22:2–3), etc. The lack of strict chronological ordering of the literature may argue in favor of Ezekiel as the compiler of the oracles, since it is very likely another editor would have been more concerned with the deliberate sequencing of the dated materials.[2]

Ezekiel's dated oracles:

Chariot vision	1:1–3	June 593 B.C.
Call to be a watchman	3:16	June 593
Temple vision	8:1	Aug/Sept 592
Discourse with elders	20:1	Aug 591
Second siege of Jerusalem	24:1	Jan 588
Judgment on Tyre	26:1	Mar/Apr 587/586
Judgment on Egypt	29:1	Jan 587
Judgment on Egypt	29:17	Apr 571
Judgment on Egypt	30:20	Apr 587

[2]The first year of Jehoiachin's captivity is dated to June 597 B.C. (2 Kings 24:12). The second siege of Jerusalem began in December-January 589/588 B.C. (2 Kings 25:1), and the destruction of Jerusalem came in September 586 B.C. (2 Kings 25:8). See K. S. Freedy and D. B. Redford, "The Dates of Ezekiel in Relation to Biblical, Babylonian and Egyptian Sources," *Journal of the American Oriental Society* 90, no. 3 (1970): 460–85.

Judgment on Egypt	31:1	June 587
Lament over pharaoh	32:1	Mar 585
Lament over Egypt	32:17	Apr 586
Fall of Jerusalem	33:21	Dec/Jan 586/585
New temple vision	40:1	Apr 573

This book is one of the richest anthologies or collections of Hebrew literary forms in the Old Testament. Several types of prophetic and poetic speech are incorporated in the prophet's message, as shown in figure 31.2.

As drama, Ezekiel's words and actions gave "shock treatment" to a nation made callous by sin against the Lord. His bold and provocative language (especially the imagery of harlotry in chapters 16 and 23) was designed to scandalize and convict a people desensitized to the truth by a life of spiritual adultery. Meanwhile, his symbolic pantomimes served to underscore the urgency of the hour as Yahweh's wrath was about to be unleashed on Judah (e.g., chaps. 4–5; 12:1–7; 24:1–14; 37:15–23). Few heard the call of God. In fact, Ezekiel was likened to a "bard" skillfully playing and singing beautiful love songs to people who loved to listen—but refused to heed the warning of his message (33:30–33).

Finally, the overall structure of Ezekiel's oracles contribute to the basic purpose of the prophet's message, indicated earlier—namely, the sovereignty of God. The oracles against Jerusalem (1–24) reinforced Ezekiel's teaching on the sovereignty of Yahweh over Israel by calling attention to the curse of judgment for covenant trespass. Yahweh's sovereignty was then extended to Israel's neighbors as well in the oracles against the nations (25–32). If Yahweh is sovereign over the nations, how much more is he the king over his elect people, Israel?

The concluding section of the book promises covenant renewal and the restoration of Davidic kingship in Israel (33–48). The new temple vision confirmed Yahweh's sovereignty over Israel in vindicating his holiness for the sake of his covenant name (36:22–32). The repetition of the phrase "and you will know that I am the LORD" (some ninety times in the book) stands as a not-so-subtle reminder of the certainty of God's judgment and the efficacy of the Sovereign Yahweh in doing what he had spoken (36:36).

Major Themes

"Son of Man"

The Lord addressed Ezekiel by the title "Son of man" some ninety times in the book. The phrase appears elsewhere in the Old Testament only in Daniel 8:17, and it is used to emphasize the humanity of the messenger in contrast to the divine origin and authority of the message.

The expression also connoted the symbolic nature of Ezekiel's life and ministry for both the Hebrew captives in Babylon and those who remained in Jerusalem. Ezekiel played the "fool for God" in that his life was a living object lesson to the rebellious house of Israel (e.g., the pantomimes prefiguring the Babylonian siege and sack of Jerusalem and the exile of the Hebrews—chaps. 4–5). His unorthodox ministry and unconventional lifestyle were sanctioned by Yahweh and energized by the Holy Spirit as the "antidote" for a patient in the last stages of a "terminal disease." Ultimately these conditions ensured that Israel would know that a prophet of God had been among them (2:5; 33:33).

Ezekiel's Chariot Vision

The ecstatic visions of Ezekiel were essential to the overall message of the book for two reasons. First, they reinforced the correctness of the prophet's understanding of God's role in the fall of Judah and the destruction of his holy city Jerusalem. The predominant eschatologi-

Figure 31.2. Speech Types in Ezekiel's Message

Judgment oracle	Usually introduced by formula, "I am against you"	21:1–5
Aftermath or restoration oracle	Reversing judgment formula, "I am for you"	34:11–15
Command formula	Especially "Son of man, set your face . . ."	6:2–3; 20:46–47
"Woe" oracle of indictment		13:3–7; 34:2–6
Demonstration oracle	Usually containing "because . . . therefore" clauses	13:8–9; 16:36–42
Disputation oracle	In which popular proverb is recited and then refuted by prophetic discourse (e.g., the "sour grapes" proverb)	18:1–20; cf. 12:22–25
Lament Over Tyre Over Pharaoh		26:15–18 32:1–16
Wailing lament	Introduced by "wail"	30:1–4; 32:17–21
Riddles, parables, allegories	E.g., parable of the vine Allegories of eagle and cedars, lion, boiling pot, etc.	15 Chaps. 17, 19, 23, 24, 27

cal (or end times) emphasis of Ezekiel's visionary experiences assured those Hebrews in exile that Yahweh's covenant promises were still valid—the dry bones would one day be revived and rejoined!

Second, and more important, Ezekiel's visions were unconventional vehicles for instructing the Hebrew captives in Babylon in the knowledge of God. His "chariot vision" is particularly significant because it appears three times in the text, in relation to Ezekiel's call (chaps. 1–3), Jerusalem's judgment (10), and Israel's restoration (43–46).

The details of this strange and complex vision, replete with bizarre creatures and fantastic mechanical contraptions, almost defy explanation. The basic intent of the vision, however, is unmistakable. The God of Ezekiel and the Hebrews lives and reigns in the heavens, majestic in his transcendent "otherness." He exercises full control over all his creation, even those Israelites held captive in Babylon. The very throne of Yahweh rests upon a magnificent carriage, enabling his movement to and signifying his presence in any location. More than this, his eyes see all, and because he sees he will certainly act on behalf of his people. This was joyful news indeed for the Hebrew captives exiled some six hundred miles away from Yahweh's temple in Jerusalem!

Individual Responsibility

Ezekiel's discourse on individual responsibility in chapter 18 refuted the "sour grapes" proverb that was popular among the Israelites as a fatalistic expression of the hopelessness of their plight in view of impending judgment and God's seemingly unjust decree of wrath. The people of Judah had displaced blame by attributing their dire predicament to the sinful behavior of previous generations.

The covenant people had rejected the idea of each generation's responsibility and impugned God's righteousness by this false understanding of Mosaic teaching on the concept of inherited guilt (cf. Exod. 20:5; 34:7).

True, children may be punished for the sins of their ancestors to the third and fourth generations. However, this teaching was abused in Judah by the erroneous application of the effects of one generation's sin upon the next, whether families of the wicked or families of the righteous. Ezekiel sought to correct this misinterpretation of corporate personality in the covenant community by reminding the people that each generation (and each person) would be held accountable for their own sin (cf. Deut. 24:16).

Ezekiel's stress on the doctrine of "individualism" in Old Testament covenant faith represented a distinct break from the philosophy current in his day. Yet this neither denied the reality of corporate solidarity among the Hebrews as Yahweh's covenant people (cf. chap. 22) nor constituted a new development in Hebrew thought and theology (cf. the personal experiences of King David in Psalm 51 or Jeremiah the prophet in chapter 20). Rather, Ezekiel sought to counterbalance the teaching of the Torah by integrating the principles of both corporate and individual responsibility. On this, J. B. Taylor aptly comments, "It was Ezekiel's genius to spell out the application of the principle of individual respon-

sibility in the face of the corporate judgment that was about to overtake Jerusalem. Destruction was coming, but [people] could repent and be saved. Ezekiel the watchman was also Ezekiel the evangelist."[3]

Old Testament Apocalyptic Literature

Ezekiel also contributed to the development of Old Testament apocalyptic literature. His ministry to Israel was a response to the crisis of Babylonian exile, and it marked a new stage in the Hebrew prophetic movement. By employing strange visions and unusual symbols in combination with eschatological themes of judgment, divine intervention in human history, and the ultimate victory of God over the enemies of Israel, Ezekiel pointed to later Jewish apocalyptic writings.

Among specific apocalyptic features identified in the prophecy are Ezekiel's ecstatic experiences, including journeys taken in the Spirit (e.g., 8:1–4; 40:1–4), visions (e.g., 37:1–6), judgment of the nations (chaps. 25–32), and the symbolic rehearsal of history accompanied by interpretation and prediction (e.g., 17:3–24).[4] Although it lacks the angelic messengers and the divine revelation of heavenly secrets characteristic of the apocalyptic sections of Daniel, the book of Ezekiel does function as a literary bridge between the preexilic "little apocalypse" of Isaiah (24–27) and the proto-apocalyptic writing in the exilic book of Daniel.

---

[3]J. B. Taylor, *Ezekiel: An Introduction and Commentary*, TOTC (London: Tyndale, 1969), 46.
[4]According to J. Lindblom, "ecstasy" is the intensification of the inspiration process characterized by "an abnormal state of consciousness in which the prophet is so intensely absorbed by one single idea or feeling, or a group of ideas or feelings, that the normal stream of physical life is more or less arrested" (*Prophecy in Ancient Israel* [Philadelphia: Fortress, 1965], 4). There are many degrees of religious ecstasy, including the extinction of personality and loss of consciousness (e.g., King Saul in 1 Sam. 19:18–24) and the frenzied, self-induced ecstasy of the Canaanite Baal prophets (1 Kings 18:20–29). Ezekiel's ecstatic experience was more normative among Old Testament prophets in that it was a Spirit-induced state of mind and body in which the man of God remained conscious and contemplative, physically and emotionally involved in his vision (cf. Dan. 8; Zech. 3).

Questions for Further Study and Discussion

1. How were the ministries of Jeremiah and Ezekiel similar? How were they different?
2. Does the title "son of man" used for Ezekiel have any theological significance for the Old Testament prophets in general or Jesus Christ as the Prophet in particular? Explain.
3. List the symbolic actions of Ezekiel the prophet and discuss their significance.
4. What was the divine purpose in commanding the symbolic actions of prophets like Ezekiel and Jeremiah? Does "playing the fool" for God on the part of the prophet enhance or detract from the divine message?
5. What does Ezekiel's teaching on the "sour grapes" parable in chapter 18 mean for the notion of corporate solidarity in the Israelite covenant community?
6. Identify the allegories used by Ezekiel. How do they contribute to the message and purpose of Ezekiel's prophecy?
7. What does the book of Ezekiel teach about the ministry of the divine Spirit in the life of the Israelite covenant community?
8. How does Ezekiel's temple vision in chapters 40–48 relate to the idea of messianic kingship and the ceremonial law of the Pentateuch?

For Further Reading

Alexander, R. H. "Ezekiel." *EBC.* Vol. 6. Grand Rapids: Zondervan, 1986. 737–996.

Allen, Leslie. *Ezekiel 20–48.* WBC. Vol. 29. Dallas: Word, 1990.

Brownlee, W. H. *Ezekiel 1–19.* WBC. Vol. 28. Waco, Tex.: Word, 1986.

Bullock, C. Hassell. "Ezekiel: Bridge Between the Testaments." *JETS* 25 (1982): 23–31.

Carley, K. W. *Book of the Prophet Ezekiel.* CBC. New York: Cambridge, 1974

———. *Ezekiel Among the Prophets.* SBT 31. Naperville, Ill.: A. R. Allenson, 1975.

Eichrodt, Walter. *Ezekiel: A Commentary.* OTL. Translated by C. Quin. Philadelphia: Westminster, 1970. A thorough and well researched commentary, reflecting considerable "tradition history" influence, hence having a tendency to emend the Hebrew text or dismiss sections of the book as "expansions." Special attention on ancient Near Eastern historical backgrounds and literary analysis.

Ellison, H. L. *Ezekiel: The Man and His Message.* London: Paternoster, 1956.

Greenberg, M. *Ezekiel 1–20.* AB. Vol. 22. New York: Doubleday, 1983. Holistic interpretation of Ezekiel rooted in the "structuralist" approach of literary criticism.

Hals, R. M. *Ezekiel.* FOTL 19. Grand Rapids: Eerdmans, 1989.

Howie, C. G. *Date and Composition of Ezekiel.* JBLMS 4. Philadelphia: Society of Biblical Literature, 1950. Classic work on the unity and integrity of Ezekiel's prophecy.

Levenson, J. D. *Theology of the Program of Restoration of Ezekiel 40–48.* HSM. Missoula, Mont.: Scholars Press, 1976.

Lindars, B. "Ezekiel and Individual Responsibility." *VT* 15 (1965): 452–67.

Newsome, J. D. *By the Waters of Babylon: An Introduction to the History and Theology of the Exile.* Atlanta: John Knox, 1979.

Raitt, T. M. *A Theology of Exile: Judgment and Deliverance in Jeremiah and Ezekiel.* Philadelphia: Fortress, 1977.

Taylor, J. B. *Ezekiel: An Introduction and Commentary.* TOTC. London: Tyndale, 1969.

Somewhat brief, but readable treatment of Ezekiel rooted in evangelical pre-convictions, attempting to integrate Ezekiel theologically with the rest of the Old Testament, with concern for contemporary application of the prophet's message.

Wevers, J. W. *Ezekiel*. NCB. London: T. Nelson, 1969. Useful introductory sections, especially on the literary features and structure of Ezekiel.

Zimmerli, W. *Ezekiel*. HER. Translated by R. E. Clements. Philadelphia: Fortress, 1979 (vol. 1), 1983 (vol. 2). A monumental commentary, exhaustive and technical. Extensive bibliographies. For the serious student only.

Chapter 32

Daniel

Daniel is one of the best known, yet most complex books of the Old Testament. It contains the story of a young Israelite taken forcibly from his homeland to be trained for diplomatic service in the great city of Babylon. He rose quickly through the ranks, becoming one of the most respected officials in the Babylonian government. His reputation remained even as the Babylonian Empire collapsed around him; though he was aged, his career reached its apex as he was appointed one of a triumvirate of officials second only to the king in the sprawling Medo-Persian Empire.

The Writing of the Book

The events of the book of Daniel are clearly set against the background of the sixth century B.C. Nevertheless, many present-day scholars concur in attributing the writing of the book to an author from the second century B.C., specifically between 168 and 164 B.C.

The reason for targeting this date and the precision of it are both derived from chapter 11 of the book. There Daniel discusses a number of kings whom he does not name, but refers to as "king of the North" and "king of the South." As it turns out, however, the details presented in this chapter coincide quite closely with the history of the Middle East from the time of Alexander the Great in the fourth century B.C. (see vv. 3–4) through the time of Antiochus IV (Epiphanes) in the second century B.C. (vv. 21ff.).

Scholars who support the second-century dating of the book contend that Daniel fits into the category of apocalyptic literature, which they view as having certain traits in common. Among them are pseudonymity (attributing a piece of writing to a well-known person of the past to give it credibility) and *vaticinium ex eventu* (Latin, meaning writing about events that have already happened as if the author were living before they took place). These traits are observable in some Akkadian literature dating back to the twelfth century B.C. and are quite common in extrabiblical Jewish apocalyptic literature from the second century B.C. to the second century A.D.

By including Daniel in this group, scholars imply that the book is thereby also pseudonymous (thus not written by Daniel or in the time of Daniel) and that the book contains *vaticinium ex eventu*. Since the book accurately reflects events that we know took place in the year 168 B.C. (vv. 31–39), it is supposed that the book was written soon after that date. It could not have been written long after that time, for these interpreters consider verses 40ff. to be an inaccurate prediction of how Antiochus IV (Epiphanes) would die. Since he died in 164 B.C., the book must have been written before that time.

An additional feature that causes some to question the historicity of the book is the series of sensational events recorded in the narrative, such as the deliverance of Daniel's friends from the fire (chap. 3), the handwriting on the wall at Belshazzar's feast (chap. 5), and Daniel's ordeal in the lion pit (chap. 6). Such sensationalism was characteristic of much noncanonical literature of the intertestamental period.

A final objection concerns people and occurrences in the book that remain unconfirmed from extrabiblical sources. Darius the Mede (chaps. 6, 9, 11) has yet to be identified, and the seven-year insanity of Nebuchadrezzar has been thought to be more easily attributable to the last Neo-Babylonian king, Nabonidus.

While acknowledging the similarities that exist between Daniel and some of the intertestamental literature, some scholars are still wary of thereby attributing to the book of Daniel all the same characteristics. The book is different in many aspects from both the so-called Akkadian apocalypses and the later Jewish apocalypses. Though it would not be denied that Daniel shares some features of apocalyptic literature, it is not easy to give a clear definition of apocalyptic, nor to differentiate it entirely from prophetic literature. More and more scholars choose to speak of a prophetic-apocalyptic continuum to accommodate all of the variables of the literature (see chap. 27). The further toward the apocalyptic side of the continuum a book leans, the more likely it is to have features such as pseudonymity or

vaticinium ex eventu. But one could not infer that books toward the middle of the continuum such as Daniel would of necessity be so characterized.

In fact, the scenario that would be required for Daniel to be considered *vaticinium ex eventu* appears to face considerable problems. The four-year time span (168–164) is far too short for a book of that time to be written, copied, circulated, and adopted as truth and then preserved as canon despite the apparent failure of its predictions.[1] On this count, it seems that the presuppositional rejection of supernaturalism is largely responsible for the rejection of a sixth-century date for the book.

The identity of Darius the Mede is still in question. Attempts have been made to identify him with Gobryas, the governor of Babylon during the early years of Cyrus the Great, or with Cyrus himself. Both of these views remain speculative, and neither is without problems. As more information becomes available, more positive identity may become possible.

Finally, while it is true that the insane king of chapter 4 would be more easily identifiable with Nabonidus, it is not impossible to fit seven years of insanity into the reign of Nebuchadrezzar. To date, there is no attested activity by Nebuchadrezzar between the years 581–573 B.C. except the ongoing, drawn-out siege of Tyre.

The result of all of this is that we see no evidence to preclude dating the book to the sixth century B.C. Furthermore, the linguistic evidence (in regard to both the Hebrew and the Aramaic of Daniel) points toward a time earlier than the second century, as does the appearance of Daniel in the Septuagint (usually dated as early as the third century B.C.) and the Dead Sea Scrolls (from the first and second centuries B.C.). The fact that Daniel speaks in first-person narrative from chapter 7 to

---

[1]For this argument in detail, see D. W. Gooding, "The Literary Structure of the Book of Daniel and Its Implications," *TB* 32 (1981): 73–74.

the end naturally suggests that he is the author, though the use of third person in the first part of the book may indicate that someone else laid out the framework and organized it.

The Background

In 626 B.C. Nabopolassar was enthroned as king of Babylon as the Babylonians declared their independence from the waning Assyrian Empire. Allying themselves with the Medes to the east, they began testing the strength of the Assyrians. By 612 the capital city of Nineveh fell, and with the collapse of the government after the fall of Carchemish in 605 the once mighty Assyrians became nothing more than a memory for the people of the Near East whom they had terrorized for almost a century and a half.

At the death of Nabopolassar, the throne was ably occupied by his son and field general, Nebuchadrezzar, in 605. At that time he assumed control of all the territories forfeited by the Assyrian capitulation, including Judah. The sons of Josiah occupying the throne of Judah proved themselves unable to accept a vassal role, as over the next two decades they became constantly embroiled in conspiracies against the Babylonians. This led not only to several deportations, but eventually to the destruction of Jerusalem and the temple in 586 B.C. by the armies of Nebuchadrezzar. During all this time, Daniel was serving in the Babylonian court, for he had been among the first group taken to Babylon in 605.

Nebuchadrezzar's long and prosperous reign came to an end in 562, and not long after, the Persians began to build their empire under the leadership of Cyrus the Great. Over the next two decades the successors of Nebuchadrezzar performed so poorly that, by 539, Cyrus was welcomed into the city of Babylon as deliverer rather than as conqueror.

Within a year after gaining control of the Babylonian Empire, Cyrus established

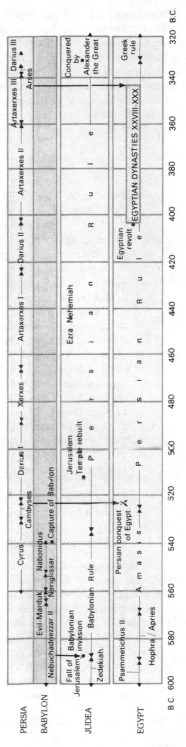

his policy of rule through benevolence by allowing many of the deported peoples to return and rebuild their homes and their sanctuaries (cf. Ezra 1:1–4). The people of Judah rightly viewed this as a fulfillment of the prophecies and a reestablishment of the covenant, and they looked forward to the formation of a worldwide theocracy with Jerusalem at its center.

Outline of the Book

I. Daniel's experiences
  A. Training in Babylon (1)
  B. Two images (2–3)
    1. Nebuchadrezzar's dream image (2)
    2. Nebuchadrezzar's golden image (3)
  C. Two kings disciplined (4–5)
    1. Nebuchadrezzar's pride and punishment (4)
    2. Belshazzar's presumption and punishment (5)
  D. Decree of Darius (6)
II. Daniel's visions
  A. Two visions of beasts-empires (7–8)
    1. Four beasts (7)
    2. Goat and ram (8)
  B. Two prophecies explained (9–12)
    1. Jeremiah's seventy years (9)
    2. Events leading to the end (10–12)[2]

Purpose and Message

The sovereignty of God is the core of this book and can be seen operating in both the spiritual and the political arenas. In the narratives of events in the lives of Daniel and his friends, the emphasis is on living a life of faith in an increasingly hostile world. God's sovereignty is seen in his ability to prosper or deliver those who are true to their faith convictions.

God's sovereignty in political affairs is addressed more directly in the visions of the book. The purpose was to deal with expectations of the exilic and postexilic communities. Based on their reading of the earlier prophets, the people of Israel were looking for the kingdom of God to be established upon their return from seventy years of exile. Daniel's visions informed them that four kingdoms were yet to come before the establishment of God's kingdom, and that while the return from exile would come within seventy years of Jeremiah's prophecy, this should not be confused with the full restoration. Rather than seventy years, the required span would be seventy weeks of years.

In the meantime the Israelites were to live out their faith in a gentile world under circumstances that would make it more and more difficult to do so. They had to count on the sovereignty of God to sustain them generation by generation, crisis by crisis, and also had to trust the power of God to control the flow of world empires as they rose and fell. God's agenda is never in jeopardy, but they were to be prepared for the long term.

Structure and Organization

The book can be seen to divide evenly between chapters 6 and 7, as shown in the outline, if the material is organized into events and visions. In this case, each half follows a chronological sequence, proceeding in chapters 1–6 from the first year of Nebuchadrezzar (1) through the last day of Belshazzar (5) and on into the reign of Darius (6). In chapters 7–12, the narrative begins in the first year of Belshazzar (7) and moves eventually to the third year of Cyrus (10).

When we consider some of the parallel structure of the book, however, another possible organization can be identified that places the major break between chapters 5 and 6. In this scheme, chapters 1–5 witness a steady deterioration in

---

[2]Outline adapted from D. W. Gooding, "Literary Structure of the Book of Daniel."

the attitude toward the Jewish religion. Highlights are the command to worship the statue (3) and the desecration of the sacred temple vessels (5). Chapters 6–12 show an increasing persecution of Jewish worship. Daniel is thrown to the lions when he refuses to alter his prayer habits (6). Pagan kings attempt to stop Israelite worship, and they desecrate the temple and altar (8–12).

Besides this progression of hostile attitudes toward the Israelite religion, there are parallels between the sections. Chapters 1 and 6 both see Daniel refuse to adjust his practices to conform to expectations. Chapters 2 and 7 both deal with four empires. Chapters 3 and 8 both deal with kings who set themselves up as God and so interfere with proper worship. Chapters 4 and 9 have in common a sevenfold scheme of punishment (4:23, 25; 9:24–25). Chapters 5 and 10–12 both deal with the coming of the end.[3]

The court stories of chapters 1–5, then, show that during the initial reign of gentile kingdoms over Jerusalem, only the first small indications of hostility toward Jewish religion were observable, and those were in isolated cases dealing with individuals. This small beginning already had at its core the pride of the kings involved. This bears an eerie resemblance to the account of the Tower of Babel in Genesis 11, in which pride was a factor in the first small steps of an escalating pattern of hostility toward God: "This is what they began to do, and now nothing which they purpose to do will be impossible for them" (v. 6, NASB).

Chapter 1 shows God honoring the act of faith of Daniel and his friends. In chapter 2 the sovereignty of God is evident in his providing Daniel with the interpretation of the dream and thereby sparing their lives. It is also evident in the contents of the dream, where we see a succession of kingdoms that conveyed to

the Israelites that it was not yet time for the kingdom for which they had been waiting. Certainly this would have been a disappointing message for the exiles to hear. The main significance, however, is the fact that in God's agenda, the mighty empires of the world come and go, and they will all be superseded by the kingdom of God that will never be destroyed (2:44). This would give reason for continued hope.

The placement of chapter 3 implies that it may have been the dream of chapter 2 that had a role in inspiring the presumption of Nebuchadrezzar in building the statue for everyone to worship. Again, as in chapter 1 we see God honoring an act of faith with deliverance. A key statement is in 3:17–18: God may choose to provide deliverance or he may not, but his sovereignty is in no way threatened if he should not choose to deliver in any single instance.

Chapters 4–5 both demonstrate God's power and control over the gentile kings and kingdoms. This goes beyond the assertion of chapter 2 that God has an overall agenda. Here we see the ability of God to intervene at any given point along the way to make his control evident.

In chapter 6 the insidious new development is that, unlike anything in chapters 1–5, we see a malicious conspiracy against Daniel specifically focused on his religious practice. Here it is the gentile king who affirms the sovereignty of Daniel's God (v. 16).

A significant difference from the discussion of the four kingdoms in Daniel 2 is that chapter 7 shows clearly the perversity, especially of the fourth kingdom, and the hostility toward the godly (vv. 7, 25). Again, however, the emphasis is on the fact that after these pagan kingdoms, the kingdom of God is coming and will endure forever (vv. 16–18, 27).

The orchestrated persecution of chap-

---

[3]Much more detail of this structure can be found in Gooding, "Literary Structure of the Book of Daniel."

ter 8 moves well beyond the isolated incident that was reported in chapter 6. Both the pride of the king and his program of persecution make the Babylonians pale in comparison. Chapter 9 addresses the way in which Israel and her prophesied restoration fit into the four-kingdom framework. The information is given that Israel's persistence in rebellion meant that full restoration would be slow in coming, but this in no way implied any lack of control on the part of God. This also shows that, contrary to the expectations of those returning from exile, things would get worse before they got better.

Finally, chapters 10–12 speak of the eventual end of gentile rule. Implicit in this, however, was the warning that there might be several periods of history that look like the end. It was not the task of the godly to know when the end was coming, but to persevere until the end that certainly would come in God's time. The assertion of Shadrach, Meshach, and Abednego in a very real sense stands as the central message of the book, namely, trust in the sovereignty of God sustains through crisis and persecution (3:16–18).

Major Themes

The Kingdom of God

That the kingdom of God is the climax of God's agenda for Israel and the world is communicated very clearly in the book of Daniel. The concept is introduced in chapter 2 as a kingdom that will never be destroyed (2:44), though in some senses God already rules an everlasting kingdom (cf. 4:3, 34–35). In 7:9–14, little additional information is given except in the introduction of one referred to as the "son of man" to whom the kingdom of God was given. From our vantage point we can surely identify this individual with Jesus, though that would not have been clear to the ancient readers. Yet there is no doubt that the "son of man" was recognized as a messianic figure, and this title became

one of the most common to be connected to Jesus during his earthly ministry. Chapters 9 and 11 are concerned primarily with the time of the end that is to precede the setting up of the kingdom of God, but there is no discussion about that kingdom.

In contrast, the kingdoms of the nations are seen as temporary and exercising limited dominion. The Babylonian kingdom is the object of discussion in chapters 4–5, the Medo-Persian and Greek kingdoms are explicitly discussed in chapter 8, and the Greek kingdom, especially the Seleucid branch, is clearly the object of discussion in chapter 11.

The four-kingdom scheme presented in chapters 2 and 7 is a common motif in the literature of the time and afterward. The identification of the four kingdoms is not made in the book, though Nebuchadrezzar is identified with the first kingdom (2:38) and we would expect that the other two kingdoms mentioned explicitly in other sections—Medo-Persia and Greece—are two of the remaining three. Such identification, however, has relatively little significance. The pertinent facts for the context of the book are (1) the contrast between human empires and the kingdom of God, and (2) the latter is coming and will be everlasting.

Pride and Rebellion

A highly visible theme is the pride of kings that leads to their eventual downfall. Nebuchadrezzar's golden image and his pride over his accomplishments in building the city of Babylon (3); Belshazzar's pride demonstrated in the desecration of the utensils from the temple and his rebuke by Daniel (5:18–23); even Darius the Mede's vulnerability to the decree suggested by his administrators—all provide specific examples of this characteristic. Pride is seen further in the actions of the fourth beast of chapter 7, the little horn of chapter 8, the prince who was to come in chapter 9, and the king of the South in chapter 11.

While pride led to the downfall of the kings of the nations, it was Israel's rebellion against God that led to her punishment. Daniel's confession on behalf of the people of Israel acknowledged transgressing the law of Moses and ignoring the warnings of the prophets. So the pride and presumption of the nations was paralleled by the rebellion and disobedience of Israel, bringing the wrath of God. The book of Daniel served to remind the people that their troubles would not be over when they returned from exile. Though judgment for the sins of the preexilic generations had been carried out in full, the people of Israel had still not reached the spiritual plateau that God wanted them to achieve. Expectations would therefore have to be put on hold, and times of distress endured. But God gave them the hope of resurrection (12:2) and encouraged them to persevere through this important time of purging (12:10–13).

Questions for Further Study and Discussion

1. How does a contextual understanding of the eschatology of the book of Daniel compare with its use in modern eschatologies?
2. Is the kingdom of God in Daniel presented as spiritual or political or both? What evidence from the book can be applied to the question?
3. Discuss the concept and scope of the sovereignty of God as disclosed by the major prophets (Isaiah, Jeremiah, Ezekiel, and Daniel), citing the specific emphases borne out in these books.

For Further Reading

Archer, Gleason L. "The Aramaic of the Genesis Apocryphon Compared with the Aramaic of Daniel." In *New Perspectives on the Old Testament*. Edited by J. Barton Payne. Waco, Tex.: Word, 1970. 160–69.

––––––. "Daniel." *EBC*. Vol. 7. Grand Rapids: Zondervan, 1985. Conservative and traditional.

Baldwin, Joyce G. *Daniel*. TOTC. Downers Grove, Ill.: InterVarsity, 1978. Though somewhat brief, a well-researched and fresh conservative treatment of the book.

Goldingay, John. *Daniel*. WBC. Vol. 30. Waco, Tex.: Word, 1989. Probably the most thorough and up-to-date treatment, though not necessarily conservative.

Gooding, D. W. "The Literary Structure of the Book of Daniel and Its Implications." *TB* 32 (1981): 43–79.

Hartmann, Louis, and Alexander DiLella. *The Book of Daniel*. New York: Doubleday Anchor, 1978.

McComiskey, Thomas. "The Seventy Weeks of Daniel Against the Background of Ancient Near Eastern Literature." *Westminster Theological Journal* 47 (1985): 18–45.

Montgomery, J. A. *The Book of Daniel*. Edinburgh: T. & T. Clark, 1927. One of the classics, very thorough, but by now considerably outdated.

Waltke, Bruce. "The Date of the Book of Daniel." *Bibliotheca Sacra* 133 (1976): 319–29.

Walton, John. "Daniel's Four Kingdoms." *JETS* 29 (1986): 25–36.

––––––. "The Decree of Darius the Mede in Daniel 6." *JETS* 31 (1988): 279–86.

Wiseman, Donald J. *Notes on Some Problems in the Book of Daniel*. London: Tyndale, 1965. Excellent treatment of some of the most complex issues of the book from an informed evangelical perspective.

Wood, Leon J. *A Commentary on Daniel*. Grand Rapids: Zondervan, 1973. Evangelical and dispensational.

Yamauchi, Edwin. "The Greek Words in Daniel in the Light of Greek Influence in the Near East." In *New Perspectives on the Old Testament*. Edited by J. Barton Payne. Waco, Tex.: Word, 1970. 170–200.

————— . "Hermeneutical Issues in the Book of Daniel." *JETS* 23 (1980): 13–21.

Young, Edward J. *The Prophecy of Daniel*. Grand Rapids: Eerdmans, 1949.

Chapter 33

Hosea

Hosea the prophet was the son of Beeri and a resident of Israel during the kingdom's "golden age" under King Jeroboam II. The name "Hosea," or "Hoshea," was common in Old Testament times and means "help" or "deliverance" (e.g., "Joshua" in Num. 13:16; Deut. 32:44). The name is derived from the Hebrew word meaning "salvation." "Jesus," or "Yeshua," is a form of this name (cf. Matt. 1:21). Hosea was a prophet to Israel during the eighth century B.C., and with the possible exception of Jonah, he was the only writing prophet to live in the northern kingdom.

God commanded Hosea to marry a prostitute named Gomer, the daughter of Diblaim. Hosea was a father to three children of Gomer's unfaithfulness—Jezreel, Lo-Ruhamah, and Lo-Ammi. The circumstances surrounding Hosea's marriage are integral to his prophetic ministry, since Gomer's behavior was analagous to Israel's spiritual adultery and breach of covenant with Yahweh.

The book of Hosea leads off the collection of briefer prophetic writings labeled "The Twelve" in the Hebrew Bible, although Amos actually predates Hosea. Today these twelve books are usually called "the Minor Prophets." These writings are roughly ordered chronologically, with Hosea, Amos, Jonah, and Micah belonging to the early Neo-Assyrian period (middle and late 700s B.C.), while Nahum, Habakkuk, Zephaniah, and Obadiah are ascribed to the Neo-Babylonian period (late 600s B.C.). The rest—Joel, Haggai, Zechariah, and Malachi—are considered prophets of the Persian period (ca. 500 B.C.).

The Writing of the Book

The superscription or introductory verse of the book attributes the work to Hosea, son of Beeri. In general this has been taken to mean that Hosea uttered the prophecies, although some scholars have questioned the authenticity of two types of texts in the book: the "Judah" references (1:1, 7; 2:2; 4:15; 5:5, 10, 12, 13, 14; 6:4, 11; 8:14; 10:11; 11:12; 12:2), and the "salvation" passages (11:8–12; 14:2–9).

The Judah references have been considered "intrusive" to the message of Hosea, because he was a prophet to the northern kingdom of Israel. Yet other preexilic prophets such as Amos and Isaiah also mention both Israel and Judah (e.g., Amos 2:4–8; Isa. 5:7; 48:1). Deletion of

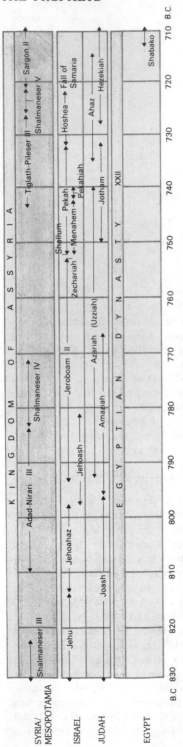

the "Judah" verses only serves to hamper the understanding of the passages in their larger context. It also damages the parallelism of the poetic couplet of Judah/Ephraim or Israel. Moreover, the majority of the citations portray Judah in an unfavorable manner. This is hardly consistent with the notion that these verses were the later additions of some "pro-Judahite" editor whose agenda included enhancing Judah's standing in relation to Israel.

The "salvation" passages of Hosea have been dismissed by some scholars as unauthentic because they are uncharacteristic of the prophet's gloom-and-doom message. However, the contrast between the overall tone of Hosea's book and the salvation oracles has been overstated. Specifically, the theme of salvation is introduced in the first three chapters of the prophecy (1:10–11; 2:14–23; 3:5). Generally the promise of deliverance for the righteous among Yahweh's covenant people was always a key component of the prophetic message (e.g., Isa. 10:20–27; Amos 9:11–15; Micah 4:1–7).

Israel's spiritual harlotry and breach of the "marriage" covenant with Yahweh, coupled with the menacing threat of Assyrian aggression, prompted Hosea to prophesy. Hosea probably began his prophetic ministry shortly before the death of Jeroboam II (ca. 753 B.C.). It is likely his mission to the northern kingdom ended when Shalmaneser V of Assyria invaded Israel, sacked Samaria, and deported more than 27,000 Israelites to Mesopotamia (ca. 722 B.C.; recorded in 2 Kings 17:1–34). Hosea's message was probably put in writing sometime between the date of King Menahem's payment of tribute to Tiglath-Pileser III of Assyria (ca. 739 B.C.; hinted at in 5:13; 8:9; 12:1) and the fall of Samaria in 722 B.C. (since Hosea does not mention that event). If Hosea is alluding to the Syro-Ephraimite conflict of 735–734 B.C. (5:8–6:6?), this may help to specify further the book's date of writing.

The Background

The reign of Jeroboam II is commonly deemed the northern kingdom's golden age. The ground for the nation's political and economic resurgence had been laid by Jeroboam's father, Jehoash. Previously he led three successful military campaigns against the Syrians or Arameans (2 Kings 13:25), freeing Israel from the humiliation and oppression of foreign bondage.

Jeroboam II continued his father's policy of military expansion, nearly reestablishing the territorial boundaries Israel secured to the east and north during the era of David and Solomon (2 Kings 14:25, 28). The military prowess and political stability achieved under Jeroboam's capable leadership produced a wealthy merchant class in Israel. The affluence of Jeroboam's monarchy was demonstrated by architectural splendor, material luxury, and agricultural abundance.

Yahweh, however, had evaluated Jeroboam's golden age by different criteria. Some years earlier, God had commissioned Amos to prophesy in Israel (ca. 760–750 B.C.). Hosea's older contemporary boldly warned the "cosmopolitan" nation, cursing the violent, oppressive, unjust, and self-indulgent policies of Jeroboam's regime (cf. Amos 2:6–16). Amos' warning went unheeded, and he was ordered out of the country and commanded never again to prophesy in Bethel (Amos 7:10–17).

In due time Yahweh prepared—to use an appropriate legal metaphor—a lawsuit against Israel. Hosea delivered the divine indictment and pronounced the certainty of God's verdict (4:1–6). The selfishness, pride, and greed often fueled by wealth and prosperity had corrupted the people of Israel (9:9). Complete social and moral decay soon followed (4:2, 18; 6:8–9; 7:1).

Even more damning evidence lay in Israel's religious apostasy. Forsaking the Lord God who had delivered them from Egypt, the nation pursued "the east wind" (a metaphor for her vacuous foreign policy) and multiplied lies (12:1) by turning to the Baals, idolatry, and "great wickedness" (10:15; cf. 4:17; 7:16; 11:2; 13:1–2).

The rapid decline of the northern kingdom after the death of Jeroboam II substantiated Hosea's words as more than idle threats. A series of royal assassinations followed by military usurpation of the throne quickly eroded internal political stability. During the last thirty years of Israelite autonomy, four of the six kings who occupied the throne were murdered. The last Israelite king, Hoshea, was deported to Assyria (2 Kings 17:6). As Hosea had predicted, Samaria's kings perished like "a twig on the surface of the waters" (10:7).

The external pressure exerted on the northern kingdom by the Assyrians, Egyptians, and Judeans prompted foolish and desperate Israelite diplomacy (7:11). A suicidal sequence of political missteps proved fatal to Israel:

1. Menahem's decision to make Israel a vassal state to Assyria by paying tribute to Tiglath-Pileser, thus averting imminent invasion (ca. 740 B.C.; cf. 2 Kings 15:19).

2. Pekah's subsequent raid into Judah as punishment for refusing to join the Israelite-Aramean coalition against Assyria (cf. 735 B.C.; cf. 2 Kings 16:5–9). Ahaz of Judah enlisted the aid of Tiglath-Pileser (by means of excessive tribute money), thus making Judah an Assyrian vassal state. The Assyrian campaign against the Israelite-Aramean coalition, called the Syro-Ephraimite war, crushed the opposition (2 Kings 15:29; 16:9). The Assyrians usurped all the Israelite territorial holdings in Galilee and the Transjordan, sacked numerous cities, and deported large portions of the population to Mesopotamia.

3. King Hoshea's unsuccessful attempt to ally Israel with Egypt against the Assyrians, sealing the nation's fate. By withholding the tribute payment due the

Assyrian overlord, the king was directly responsible for Israel's doom. The brutal Assyrian response to the vassal's disloyalty ended Israelite political history. Samaria was pillaged, thousands of Israelites were deported to areas of northern Mesopotamia, and Israel was carved up into Assyrian royal provinces (ca. 724–722 B.C.; cf. 2 Kings 17:1–6).

Outline of the Book

I. Superscription (1:1)
II. Hosea's marriage to Gomer the harlot
   A. Children of harlotry (1:2–2:1)
   B. Gomer's unfaithfulness (2:2–23)
   C. Hosea's faithfulness (3:1–5)
III. Hosea's message to Israel
   A. Israel's ignorance and unfaithfulness (4:1–6:3)
   B. Israel's judgment (6:4–10:15)
   C. Yahweh's faithfulness and love for Israel (11–14)

Purpose and Message

Hosea's relationship with his harlot wife, Gomer, typified Yahweh's covenant tie with faithless Israel (1:2). The poignant dramatization of love rejected and love restored in his marriage became the foundation for his preaching to a "harlot" nation. The prophet's exhortation to Israel to walk in "the ways of the LORD" (14:9) was rooted in the pathos of his own heart-wrenching experience.

Israel's past figured prominently in Hosea's prophecies to Ephraim. The recounting of Yahweh's covenant love to the Hebrew patriarchs (12:2–6) and the infant nation of Israel at the Exodus (11:1–4; 12:9; 13:4) served as strong reminders of God's constancy. This demonstration of steadfast love for Israel throughout the nation's history guaranteed that God would keep his pledge of restoration.

Mercy and judgment are also important themes in Hosea's message. He was a prophet of "eventual hope" (2:14–23) and "immediate doom" (5:8–9), given his understanding of covenant blessings and curses as outlined in the Torah (cf. Lev. 26:1–39). Hosea stood proudly in the tradition of God's prophets (6:5; 9:7–8; 12:10–13) and was bold in his rebuke of Israel's political and religious leadership (5:1; 6:9; 13:10). Yet he readily identified with the Yahweh whose heart "recoiled" within as he wrestled with the dilemma of punishing the child he loved so dearly (11:8).

Hosea has a reputation as "the deathbed prophet of Israel" because he was the last of the writing prophets to address the northern kingdom before the Assyrian onslaught. His was the task to "hew and slay" Israel with words of judgment (6:5, KJV) and to call a "straying people" back to the knowledge of God (2:5–8; 4:1, 6; 5:4; 6:3, 6) through repentance and covenant renewal (6:1; 14:1). Ultimately Hosea's personal experience with the "prostituting" Gomer was probably the most profound message the prophet could deliver about Yahweh's desire and ability to heal and freely love "adulterous" Israel (14:4).

Structure and Organization

The narrative of Hosea's marital relationship to the prostitute Gomer in chapters 1–3 contains both biography and autobiography. These chapters function as a preface to the prophecies of chapters 4–14. The marriage story is arranged in a literary pattern known technically as a palistrophe. This chiastic structure counterbalances key theological themes focused on one fundamental teaching or idea. Israel's lack of knowledge of God is the "hinge" for this literary construction:[1]

---

[1]Cf. C. Hassell Bullock, *An Introduction to the Old Testament Prophetic Books* (Chicago: Moody Press, 1986). For examples of more complex palistrophes, see Gordon J. Wenham, "The Coherence of the Flood Narrative," *VT* 28 (1977): 336–48.

The prophecies of chapters 4−14 are an extension of the biography of Hosea's marriage, in that his union with the unfaithful harlot Gomer mirrored the covenant relationship of Yahweh with faithless and treacherous Israel. This section of Hosea has been described as the most "poetic" of all the prophetic writings. The literary style is a hybrid of prose and poetry identified as "oracular prose," which was peculiar to the Hebrew prophets.[2]

The standard four-point outline characteristic of the preexilic writing prophets is embedded with the oracles and provides the basic structure for the book's message: (1) indictment, including specific charges of covenant violation (e.g., 4:1−11); (2) judgment, including destruction and exile (5:1−8, 14); (3) instruction, including the call to repentance (6:1−3), and (4) the aftermath, including the promise of restoration to the righteous (14:1−8).

The language of Hosea's message to Israel stems from the covenant violation motif as reflected in the "lawsuit" Yahweh has brought against Israel. Legal terminology abounds in the prophecies, as Yahweh brings his case against the land of Israel: for example, "controversy" (4:1), "contend" and "accuse" (4:4), "guilty" and "swear" (4:15), "judgment" (5:1), "testifies" (5:5), "break faith" (5:7, etc.). Other distinctive literary features of the book include the use of "Israel" and "Ephraim" as a synonymous poetic couplet or word pair for the northern kingdom (e.g., 4:16−17;

5:3), and the prophet's familiarity with "covenant" vocabulary: for example, "return" (6:1), "know" (6:3), "redeem" (7:13), "transgress" and "covenant" and "law" (8:1), "love" (11:1), and "indictment" (12:2).

Major Themes

Hosea's Marriage

Hosea's marriage to the prostitute Gomer at the command of God has prompted a variety of interpretive opinions among biblical scholars. The several views concerning the prophet's marriage can be summarized thus:

1. *Symbolic Marriage.* This approach understands the marriage hypothetically as an allegory or prophetic vision, not as a real event in Hebrew history.

2. *One Literal Marriage: Sequential Narrative.* This interpretation affirms the historicity of Hosea's marriage to Gomer and views chapters 1 and 3 as two separate events in the prophet's life. Alternative views are offered as to Gomer's virtue at the time of the union. Three distinct options have emerged from the discussion. Some argue that Gomer was unchaste, a practicing harlot, when Hosea married her. Others, finding such a command from God to Hosea ethically unthinkable (given the ranking of sexual sin in our Western hierarchy of taboos), contend Gomer was chaste at the time of her wedding and only later turned faithless to Hosea and become a prostitute. Still others have concluded that Gomer was a "harlot" spiritually speaking, in that she was a worshiper of pagan gods.

3. *One Literal Marriage: Parallel Narrative.* This somewhat strained rendering of Hosea's personal experience affirms the historicity of the marriage, but understands chapters 1 and 3 as parallel accounts of the same event or two versions of the same event written at different times in the prophet's career.

---

[2]For a discussion of "oracular prose" in the Hebrew prophets, see F. I. Andersen and David N. Freedman, *Hosea*, AB, vol. 24 (Garden City, N.Y.: Doubleday, 1980), 57−66.

4. Two Literal Marriages. According to this view, chapter 1 describes Hosea's first marriage to chaste Gomer and chapter 3 recounts a second marriage to a "prostituting" woman of unknown identity.

The best of the interpretive options in our opinion remains the view that holds to one literal marriage for Hosea to a "prostituting" woman named Gomer (with chapters 1 and 3 treating two separate events in the prophet's life). She was not only an unchaste bride, but also promiscuous as his wife. Later on, Hosea had to purchase her from a slave market, redeeming her from a life of indebtedness and prostitution and thus restoring her as his wife after a period of quarantine. Though none of the views is without problems, this is the most natural reading of the account of Hosea's marriage presented in chapters 1 and 3. More important, it provides the most complete analogy to the history of Israel's spiritual pilgrimage with her covenant God, Yahweh (see esp. Ezek. 16 and 23).

Although Hebrew priests were forbidden by law to marry harlots (Lev. 21:7, 14), no such prohibition applied to God's prophets. In fact, Hosea is not even called a "prophet" in the title verse of his book. His marriage to "prostituting" Gomer was most unusual, but certainly not unethical (cf. Isaiah's prophesying "naked and barefoot" for three years, Isa. 20:1–6). Neither should the character of God be questioned, given his singular directive to his spokesman Hosea. Desperate times demand radical actions! Israel was on the brink of oblivion—mere words were no longer enough. Elsewhere, Old Testament Scripture makes it clear that our evaluation of God's methods is sure to prove erroneous. As the heavens are higher than the earth, so are Yahweh's thoughts and ways higher than ours—and beyond finding out (Job 9:10–12; Isa. 55:8–9).

Baalism

God's controversy with Israel was rooted in the conflicting religious ideologies

Figure 33.1. A clay figurine of the fertility goddess Astarte (also known as Ishtar or Ashtoreth), discovered in Judea and dating from the late seventh century B.C. (*Israel Antiquities Authority. Photo Israel Museum*)

of Canaanite Baalism and Hebrew Yahwism (Hos. 4:4). According to the stipulations of Israel's covenant with Yahweh, the nation was bound by oath to worship him alone (Exod. 20:1–6; Deut. 4:15–31). This strict monotheism was jeopardized by the religious syncretism that resulted from the Hebrew compromise and coexistence with the Canaanite peoples after Joshua's incomplete conquest of Palestine (Josh. 13:1–7; Judg. 1:22–35). Inevitably, Hebrew coexistence with the Canaanites led to intermarriage and eventually to the worship of the Canaanite gods (Judg. 2:11–15; cf. Deut. 7:1–5).

The god Baal was but one of a pantheon of deities worshiped by the Canaanites (see fig. 33.1). As the son of El and Asherah, he was the rain-and-storm-god whose chief concerns were agricultural fertility and sexual reproduction among animals and humankind. Mot, the god of sterility and death, was Baal's eternal rival. According to Canaanite mythology, the seasons of rain and plenty and drought and famine were the consequence of the perpetual conflict between Baal and Mot.

To aid Baal in his struggle against the god Mot, Canaanite worship of the storm-god included human sacrifice and ritual prostitution (cf. Ps. 106:34–41; Deut. 23:17). These male and female prostitutes were employed by the local shrines and were considered "priests" and "priestesses" of the gods. The people of Canaan engaged in sacred sexual intercourse with the cult prostitutes as part of Baal worship to ensure fertility by reenacting sacramentally the god's marriage to the land as Baal (or "lord, husband") of the earth.

Hosea's experience with the faithless prostitute Gomer directly paralleled Yahweh's relationship with a people who had left their God to "play the harlot" with Baal (4:10, 12, 15, 17; 5:3–4, etc.). This figurative use of the terms "harlotry" and "prostitution" for religious apostasy is common in both the Pentateuch and the Prophets (e.g., Exod. 34:14–16; Num. 25:1; Jer. 3:2; Ezek. 16). Hosea's description of Baalism is consistent with that of other ancient sources. The drunkenness (4:11, 18), ritual prostitution (4:13b–14), false prophecy and pagan sacrifice (4:12; 8:11–13), idolatry (4:17–11:2), and the shrines in the high places (10:8) are all equally condemned.[3]

For Hosea, Israel's harlotry had a double meaning. The people were not only committing spiritual adultery against Yahweh by turning to Baal (7:16), but were also literally prostituting themselves in the sex acts associated with the rituals of the Canaanite fertility cults (4:13–15). Unsure if they could trust Yahweh for the rain necessary for life in Palestine, Israel chose to mix Yahwism and Baalism in a syncretistic religion. It failed. Ironically, God's sentence of judgment on faithless Israel was aimed at the very things most sacred to the Baal cult: agricultural abundance (8:7–10), material prosperity (9:1–4), sexual vitality and fertility (9:10–17), shrines, altars, and idols (10:1–6), and military might (10:9–15).

Questions for Further Study and Discussion

1. Discuss how the various interpretive options for Hosea's marriage to Gomer illustrate or fail to illustrate Israel's covenant relationship with Yahweh.
2. Discuss the ethical implications of God's charge to Hosea to marry a prostitute—specifically, the prophet's integrity and the risk of God's message being misunderstood or rejected.
3. What does Hosea mean by "acknowledging the Lord" (e.g., 4:1; 6:3)?
4. How were the religious, political, and social conditions of Israel similar as encountered by the prophets Amos and Hosea? How were they different?
5. What does Hosea have to say about religious syncretism? How do we avoid this mixing of pagan and orthodox religious traditions today?

[3]For example, H. Ringgren, *Religions of the Ancient Near East*, trans. J. Sturdy (Philadelphia: Westminster, 1973), 124–76; and J. Finegan, *Myth and Mystery: An Introduction to the Pagan Religions of the Biblical World* (Grand Rapids: Baker, 1989), 119–54.

6. Discuss Hosea's attitudes toward religious institutions, ritual, and liturgy. Can he correctly be called an "iconoclast"?

For Further Reading

Albright, William F. *Yahweh and the Gods of Canaan.* Reprint. Winona Lake, Ind.: Eisenbrauns, 1978. A standard work on Canaanite religion and its impact on Israelite religion.

Andersen, F. I., and David N. Freedman. *Hosea.* AB. Vol. 24. Garden City, N.Y.: Doubleday, 1980. Exhaustive and technical introduction and commentary. Fresh translation combined with appreciation for the poetic nature of prophecy and careful linguistic study of the Hebrew text. The best book in English on the topic.

Brueggemann, Walter. *Tradition for Crisis: A Study of Hosea.* Atlanta: John Knox, 1969. Penetrating "tradition-history" analysis of Hosea as an interpretation of Mosaic law, with constructive suggestions for prophetic ministry in the contemporary situation.

Bullock, C. Hassell. *An Introduction to the Old Testament Prophetic Books.* Chicago: Moody Press, 1986.

Emmerson, G. I. *Hosea: An Israelite Prophet in Judean Perspective.* JSOTSS 28. Sheffield, England: JSOT Press, 1984.

Kidner, Derek. *Love to the Loveless: The Message of Hosea.* Downers Grove, Ill.: InterVarsity, 1981. Readable, yet solid exposition of Hosea's message, with insightful contemporary application.

Mays, J. L. *Hosea.* OTL. Philadelphia: Westminster, 1969. Valuable theological treatment of the book's message.

Ostborn, G. *Yahweh and Baal: Studies in the Book of Hosea and Related Documents.* Lund, Sweden: Gleerup, 1956.

Stuart, D. *Hosea–Jonah.* WBC. Vol. 31. Waco, Tex.: Word, 1987. Concise introductory sections on the historical background, message, literary structure, and themes of Hosea.

Wolff, Hans Walter. *A Commentary on the Book of the Prophet Hosea.* HER. Translated by G. Stansell. Philadelphia: Fortress, 1974.

Chapter 34

Joel

—

Joel's vision of the locust plague is perhaps among the most familiar prophetic images of impending invasion and devastation. Since the prophet is mentioned nowhere else in the Old Testament, little is known about him personally, though his book shows him to be a powerful and effective preacher. He has at times been counted among the official "temple prophets" who, during Jeremiah's time, for instance, were not always accurate spokesmen for the Lord (e.g., Jer. 28). But the message of Joel rings true and has the added significance of serving as a catapult for the Christian church as Peter uses it at the core of his message on the Day of Pentecost.

The Writing of the Book

A difficult issue surrounding the book of Joel is its date. Theories have placed it from the ninth to the second centuries B.C. and many dates in between. While the overall message of the book is not hindered by not knowing the date, the historical context can often shed wel-

come light on the some of the details of the message. Therefore an interpreter needs to identify the date as precisely as the evidence allows. Since the superscription (1:1) contains no chronological data, determination must be made from whatever internal evidence the book might offer.

The first noteworthy piece of evidence is that the book is addressed to "elders" rather than to the king. Though some scholars attach no significance to this fact,[1] many others have assumed that Joel must therefore have prophesied at a time when there was no king in Israel. A most obvious option is the period after the fall of Jerusalem; another possibility that has a long tradition of support is the era (835–830 B.C.) of the minority of Joash, who came to the throne at the age of seven (2 Kings 11). The period of the Exile is ruled out in that the sacrificial system was in operation when Joel testified (1:9), which leaves the ninth century and the postexilic period the two primary candidates for consideration.

Supporters of the preexilic dating sug-

[1]See the plausible case built by Richard Patterson for a date in the first half of the eighth century, in his commentary in *EBC*, vol. 7 (Grand Rapids: Zondervan, 1985), 231–33.

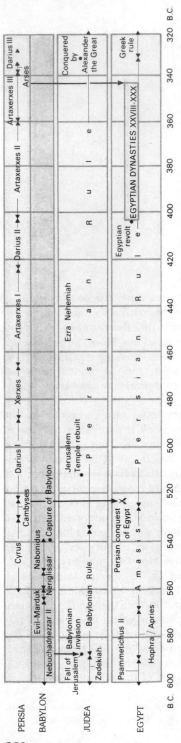

gest as evidence Joel's being placed second in the canonical arrangement of the Twelve, between the early books of Hosea and Amos. Additionally, the emphasis on "the Day of the Lord" is more characteristic of preexilic prophecy; even as early as Amos it was already a well-known theological concept (Amos 5:18). The fact that neither Assyria or Babylon is listed among the enemies of Israel is used to suggest that Joel predated the empire age.

Support for the postexilic period includes, prominently, reference to Joel 3:1–2, in which the scattering of the Israelites is treated as an event in the past. This cannot be an example of the "prophetic perfect" (the use of the past tense to convey that future events are certain to happen) because it occurs amid a future-tense sequence. Moreover, idolatry and Baal worship, the normal fare of preexilic prophets (and a fault of Queen Athaliah) are not mentioned even in passing. The failure to mention Assyria and Babylon is easily explainable in the postexilic period, when both empires had moved off the world scene, and the mention of the Greeks (3:6) is thought to make much more sense in the postexilic period than in the ninth century, when there would have been little knowledge of the Greeks in the Near East.

Perhaps the strongest evidence for the postexilic date is that Joel is clearly an example of classical prophecy, which did not get its start until the eighth century B.C. This would argue strongly for a date later than Amos. If Joel was later than Amos, the other evidence cited would make the postexilic period the most logical context for the book, and it is the one preferred here. The reference to the future destruction of Edom (3:19) and the general picture of the priesthood would favor an early postexilic date, perhaps the late sixth or early fifth century.

The Background

The literary background for the book of Joel can be seen in the prophetic literature of Israel. Joel was a well-versed student of preexilic prophecy, as his abundant use of words, phrases, and motifs from those writings demonstrates. Especially evident is his use of Amos, Isaiah, and Ezekiel.

Joel	Use of Other Prophets
1:15	Isa. 13:6
2:3	Isa. 51:3; Ezek. 36:35
2:10	Isa. 13:10
3:10	Isa. 2:4; Mic. 4:3
3:16	Amos 1:2; Isa. 13:13
3:17	Ezek. 36:11; Isa. 52:1
3:18	Amos 9:13

The historical background is more difficult to address because of the uncertainties as to the date of the book. If the postexilic dating is accepted, then, of course, the setting is the Persian period. But the question of whether the book should be seen in relation to Haggai and Zechariah during Zerubbabel's governership, or in relationship to Malachi and the period of Ezra and Nehemiah is still a matter of dispute. It is perhaps best to choose the time between these two periods in which the temple constructed by Zerubbabel had been in operation for a generation or two, but when Edom had not yet been destroyed. This would be closest to the time of Esther, during the reign of Xerxes, or perhaps a bit earlier in the latter days of Darius the Great. However, we know nearly nothing of what was taking place in Israel during this period, though the Persian activities, especially their incipient skirmishes with the Greeks, are documented in the histories of Herodotus.

Outline of the Book

I. The current crisis
   A. Description of current locust plague (1:1–12)
   B. Call to lament the lost sacrifices (1:13–14)
   C. "The Day of the Lord" is near: plague as judgment (1:15–20)

II. The coming escalation
   A. Description of escalation of locust plague (2:1–11)
   B. Call to repent so as to prevent escalation (2:12–17)
   C. The Day of the Lord postponed: renewed prosperity (2:18–27)

III. The future Day of the Lord
   A. Description of the Day of the Lord (2:28–32)
   B. Judgment on nations (3:1–17)
   C. Prosperity of Israel (3:18–20)

Purpose and Message

Joel's concern throughout the book was to address "the Day of the Lord." He began by correlating the current locust plague with the inception of the Day of the Lord in anticipation that the judgment would get worse. Consequently he called on the people to repent—though no indictment is mentioned, so the offense is unknown. When the people responded positively, the Lord's favor was proclaimed (2:18–19a uses past tense, contrary to NIV and NASB) and coming prosperity was announced. In the treatment of the future Day of the Lord, the nations were to be the focus of the Lord's judgment. For Israel, both judgment and restoration were socioeconomic in nature (i.e., prosperity).

Structure and Organization

Like Haggai, Joel's first oracle was occasioned by a crisis that he prophetically identified as God's judgment on the community. Thus he interpreted a current situation as judgment, rather than projecting a future situation of judgment, as the preexilic prophets were inclined to do. He spurred the people to action by suggesting that matters would get worse before they got better. This projection of worsening judgment was then used as the basis for his instruction to the people. It is noteworthy that this instruction was spiritual in nature and included the appropriate ritual. This was in stark contrast to the consistent appeals of the preexilic prophets to respond with just conduct rather than through the ritual approach that they had been inclined to abuse.

The Lord's favorable response serves as the climax to the portion of the book that is rooted in the contemporary context of Joel. As presented in the outline, the contemporary section contained two cycles of description of judgment, instruction, and identification of the Lord's role. The contrast is that in the first cycle the Lord was judging Israel, while in the second, he was prospering them.

The common denominator between the contemporary oracle (1:2–2:27) and the eschatological oracle (2:28–3:20) is the Day of the Lord. Though it is not specifically mentioned in the eschatological section, there is no doubt that it is the subject of the oracle. After a description of the Day of the Lord as a time of deliverance and endowment of the Spirit, Joel resumed the themes of judgment and prosperity. Here, however, the object of God's judgment was the nations rather than Israel.

Major Themes

The Locust Plague

Throughout the Old Testament period, Israel had a largely agricultural economy. Any natural disaster that destroyed crops was devastating to the people at nearly every level of society. The ability of a swarm of grasshoppers or locusts to devour everything green over dozens of square miles is well-documented, not only in the ancient Near East, but in modern times around the world. The economy would be ruined for at least two years, and hardship of every imaginable sort would ensue. It is no mystery, then, why such plagues would be popularly understood as the judgment of God.

Though the belief that the gods showed their anger by bringing about natural disaster was common throughout the ancient Near East, there was always the need to resolve which deity had sent it, what he or she was angry about, and how appeasement could be accomplished. For Israel the first question was easy enough, but the other two were rarely self-evident. In the book of Joel, instead of attaching the judgment to a specific community offense, the prophet identified the plague as the harbinger of the Day of the Lord when, in general, the just will be vindicated and the wicked will be punished. Thus it behooved the Israelites to throw themselves on the mercy of the Lord, lest they be the ones to instigate this divine action.

Excursus: Joel and Pentecost

The prophecy of Joel had an impact far beyond the audience that he personally addressed, because later interpreters applied it directly to their own generations. This is particularly evident in the apostle Peter's use of Joel's prophecy in the birth of the church at Pentecost.

When the Holy Spirit came on those in the upper room, the change that occurred in them caused quite a stir among the many visitors who were in Jerusalem for the Pentecost feast. Peter spoke up and immediately explained the phenomenon as a fulfillment of Joel's prophecy found in 2:28–32. He launched into a sermon explaining who Jesus was and calling on the people to repent and be baptized (Acts 2:1–41).

This citation has sometimes perplexed scholars, for it is difficult to see how the endowment of the Holy Spirit at Pentecost had much if anything to do with the Day of the Lord that was addressed in Joel. Peter's use of this passage, however, need not indicate that he considered the Day of the Lord to have arrived. The apostles' situation had two significant similarities with the prophecy of Joel— the endowment of the Spirit, and the need of the moment to call upon the Lord and be saved. These conditions would have been sufficient for Peter to draw the connection. As we discussed in the introduction to prophetic literature, Peter was free to identify the events of Pentecost as the fulfillment of Joel in the sense that there were certain ways that the events of Pentecost shed some appropriate light on what Joel had to say, and vice versa.

Questions for Further Study and Discussion

1. In what ways did Pentecost parallel the Day of the Lord as discussed in the book of Joel?
2. What would have been the significance of the Day of the Lord to those living in the time of the Persian Empire?

For Further Reading

Allen, Leslie. *The Books of Joel, Obadiah, Jonah and Micah.* NICOT. Grand Rapids: Eerdmans, 1976. A good, in-depth analysis.

Craigie, Peter C. *Twelve Prophets.* Vol. 1. Daily Study Bible: Old Testament Series. Philadelphia: Westminster, 1984.

Patterson, Richard. "Joel." *EBC.* Vol. 7. Grand Rapids: Zondervan, 1985.

Stuart, Douglas. *Hosea–Jonah.* WBC. Vol. 31. Waco, Tex.: Word, 1987. The best commentary on Joel. Evangelical in perspective.

Thompson, J. A. "Joel's Locusts in the Light of Near Eastern Parallels." *Journal of Near Eastern Studies* 14 (1955): 52–55.

———. "The Date of Joel." In *A Light Unto My Path.* Edited by Howard Bream, Ralph Heim, and Carey Moore. Philadelphia: Temple University Press, 1974. 453–64.

Wolff, Hans Walter. *Joel and Amos.* Philadelphia: Fortress, 1977. The most thorough treatment of the book from a liberal perspective.

Chapter 35

Amos

Amos is the third book of "the Twelve," or the Minor Prophets. Chronologically Amos stands first among the writing prophets, an older contemporary of Hosea and Micah. His name means "burden-bearer."

Amos was a shepherd and sycamore fig farmer from Tekoa, a village some ten miles south of Jerusalem. His disclaimer to be part of the "religious establishment" emphasized his detachment from formal institutions such as the royal court and the temple (7:14–15). Given his platform as an "independent layman" and "blue-collar" worker, Amos had freedom to proclaim God's message unencumbered by vested interests or public opinion.

God's willingness to use people without "formal" academic and religious training highlights the truth that he shows no partiality—a timely reminder for an age of professionalism like ours.

The Writing of the Book

The details of how the prophecies Amos delivered to Israel at Bethel came to be recorded remain unknown. It is impossible to ascertain whether he dictated his revelations to a scribe or composed them himself. It seems easier to assume

Amos committed his revelations to writing upon returning to Tekoa from his brief "preaching tour" in Israel. The first-person accounts of his messages and visions lend support to this assumption (e.g., 5:1; 7:1–9; 8:1; 9:1).

It has been suggested that the reference to the earthquake in the book's title verse is better understood as "during the two years before the earthquake" (NRSV margin). If this reading of the phrase is correct, it means Amos probably wrote down the messages within two years after his brief prophetic ministry in Bethel.

The earthquake may have been the event prompting Amos to publish his experience, since the citation in the book's introductory verse indicates that the prophet viewed the natural disaster as a partial fulfillment of his prophecy to Israel and as confirmation of his divine commission (9:1).

The book of Amos has traditionally been assigned to the middle or latter years of the reign of Jeroboam II (ca. 760 B.C.). More recent historical investigation and chronological calculations have pushed the date for the writing of Amos' prophecies nearer 750–748 B.C., just prior to the death of Jeroboam. This understanding is based on indications that the historical events alluded to in the book are reflections of a time when pro-Assyrian Israel was under assault by an anti-Assyrian Syro-Palestinian coalition.

The Background

Amos ambiguously dated the words "he saw" concerning Israel to the reigns of King Uzziah of Judah and King Jeroboam II of Israel. Both of these monarchs' reigns extended over a period of more than four decades. The exact dates for Uzziah and Jeroboam II vary some two to seven years, depending on the source consulted.[1]

The reference to "the earthquake" in the superscription provides little help in fixing the precise date of Amos' prophecy. Archaeological discoveries at sites like Samaria and Hazor attest such destruction by earthquake, and Zechariah's mention of the natural disaster indicates that the tremor was long remembered in Israel (14:5). Yet attempts to pinpoint the year in which the quake occurred are highly speculative. Consequently the time of Amos' prophetic activity is best assigned to the general time period ranging from 760–750 B.C.

The biblical accounts of the reigns of Uzziah (or Azariah) and Jeroboam II are found in 2 Kings 14:17–15:7 and 2 Chronicles 26. Politically and economically, both monarchs brought stability and prosperity to their respective kingdoms. Territorial borders were expanded through successful military conquest against foreign foes, Israel and Judah managed a peaceful coexistence, and commercial enterprise and agricultural production burgeoned.

However, the prophets of God looked past the facade of the so-called golden age to the dry rot of social and moral

Figure 35.1. Ivory object found at Samaria, one of many examples unearthed in the capital city that represent some of the finest artwork found in ancient Palestine. (*Israel Antiquities Authority. Photo Israel Museum*)

decay in both Israel and Judah. Amos and Isaiah paint similar pictures of "real life" in the divided kingdoms. Contrary to all appearances, these seers charged that the Hebrew nations were "loaded with guilt" (Isa. 1:4) and "ripe" for the judgment of God (Amos 8:1–2; cf. 3:9–15; Isa. 3:13–15; 5:8–30).

Outline of the Book

I. Introduction (1:1–2)
II. Oracles against the nations
   A. Damascus (1:3–5)
   B. Gaza (1:6–8)
   C. Tyre (1:9–10)
   D. Edom (1:11–12)
   E. Ammon (1:13–15)
   F. Moab (2:1–3)
   G. Judah (2:4–5)
   H. Israel (2:6–16)
III. Further oracles against Israel
   A. Hear this word, people of Israel (3)
   B. Hear this word, cows of Bashan (4)
   C. Hear this word, house of Israel (5:1–17)
   D. Woe to those anxious for the Day of the Lord (5:18–27)

---

[1]The higher chronology is based on Edwin R. Thiele, *The Mysterious Numbers of the Hebrew Kings*, rev. ed. (Grand Rapids: Zondervan, 1983); the lower chronology is based on John Bright, *A History of Israel*, 3d ed. (Philadelphia: Westminster, 1981).

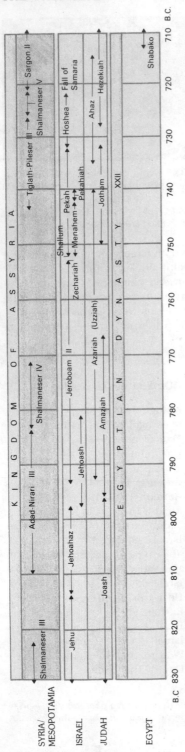

710 B.C.

720

730

740

750

760

770

780

790

800

810

820

B.C 830

SYRIA/
MESOPOTAMIA

ISRAEL

JUDAH

EGYPT

SYRIA / MESOPOTAMIA: Shalmaneser III, Jehu (Shalmaneser III), Adad-Nirari III, Shalmaneser IV, Tiglath-Plieser III, Shalmaneser V, Sargon II

ISRAEL: Joash, Jehoahaz, Jehu, Jehoash, Jeroboam II, Zechariah, Shallum, Menahem, Pekahiah, Pekah, Hoshea → Fall of Samaria

JUDAH: Joash, Amaziah, Azariah (Uzziah), Jotham, Ahaz, Hezekiah

EGYPT: XXII DYNASTY, EGYPTIAN DYNASTY, Shabako

KINGDOM OF ASSYRIA

E. Woe to those at ease in Zion (6)

IV. Visions of judgment
   A. Vision 1: The plague of locusts (7:1–3)
   B. Vision 2: The devouring fire (7:4–6)
   C. Vision 3: The Lord's plumbline (7:7–9)
   D. Historical interlude: Amaziah challenges Amos (7:10–17)
   E. Vision 4: The basket of summer fruit (8:1–3)
   F. Prophetic interjection: Oracles of judgment (8:4–14)
   G. Vision 5: The Lord standing beside the altar (9:1–4)
   H. Theological exposition: On the sovereignty of God and the restoration of Israel (9:5–15)

Purpose and Message

The religious apostasy, moral and social collapse, and political corruption of the northern kingdom prompted God to send the Judahite Amos across the border to prophesy in Bethel of Israel. The shepherd-preacher's basic message to Jeroboam II and Israel was that "the end has come for my people" (cf. 8:2). Amos' pronouncement against the false priest Amaziah represented a condensed version of the prophet's word of judgment to the whole nation (cf. 7:10–17):

> "This is what the LORD says:
> 'Your wife will become a prostitute in the city,
>   and your sons and daughters will fall by the sword.
> Your land will be measured and divided up,
>   and you yourself will die in a pagan country' " (v. 17).

Both message and purpose spring logically from the book's general outline and are closely connected with the prophet's prediction of judgment and exile for Israel:

First Message (2:6–16): The prophet

Figure 35.2. The Oracles of Amos Against the Nations

1. The introductory formula "This is what the Lord says"
2. A numerical expression, "for three sins . . . even for four," certifying that Yahweh's judgment was absolutely irrevocable. The $x : x + 1$ formula is a type of synonymous parallelism borrowed from Hebrew poetry (e.g., Prov. 30:15, 18, 21, 29) and connotes "repeated" or "continual" sin
3. The charge of specific sins committed by the individual nations (the indictment)
4. Announcement of judgment introduced by the formula "I will send fire" (except Ammon and Israel)
5. The closing formula "says the Lord" (except Tyre, Edom, Gaza, and Israel)

denounces Israel's sin and forecasts national disaster for the purpose of reminding the people of the consequences of covenant disobedience.

Second Message (3:1–6:14): Amos condemns specific acts of social injustice and religious hypocrisy. The several purposes of this message include calling some to repentance of personal sin, encouraging a return to the standards of behavior consistent with Yahweh's covenant stipulations, and repudiating the popular notion that the "Day of the Lord" was a day of national blessing only.

Third Message (7:1–9:4): Amos relates five visions he experienced, all dealing with God's wrath and judgment on Israel. The visions served to reinforce the prophet's oracles against the nation, emphasize the certainty of Israel's destruction and exile, and introduce the remnant theme.

Fourth Message (9:5–15): The prophet concludes his ministry to Israel with the promise of messianic restoration and blessing. Here his purpose is to encourage and instill hope in the righteous remnant among the people by assuring them that God's judgment is not final—he will remember his covenant with Israel and renew again his steadfast love.

Structure and Organization

Few scholars question the overall unity of Amos' prophecies, and there is a growing appreciation for his literary skill. His bold and arresting style bespeaks a man of integrity and conviction. The visionary elements of the book help account for the vivid language employed, as he actually "saw the words" God revealed to him. The pastoral imagery of his illustrations, metaphors, and rhetorical questions betray the prophet's rural roots (e.g., 3:3–8, 12; 6:11–14). Finally, the hymnic portions of the book (e.g., 5:1–2) along with the three doxologies (4:13; 5:8–9; 9:5–6) indicate Amos had some poetic and musical abilities or that he borrowed from existing well-known songs.

The larger structure of the book includes four basic sections:

1. Eight oracles against the nations (1:3–2:16)
2. Five prophetic words (3–6)
3. Counterbalance of five prophetic visions (7:1–9:10)
4. Epilogue promising blessing and renewal for Israel (9:11–15)

The oracles against the nations set the tone for the book in that all emphasize destruction and exile. The series of prophetic words and visions targeted Israel specifically as the object of God's wrath, advanced the theme of judgment from threat to reality, and reinforced the certainty of the nation's imminent and inescapable doom. The authenticity of the concluding oracle of restoration for Israel has been seriously challenged by modern

Figure 35.3. Social Concern in Amos' Teaching

Social Service	Social Action
Relieve human need (5:12)	Remove the causes of human need (8:4–6)
Philanthropic activity (4:5; 6:4–7)	Political and economic activity (5:10–11, 15)
Ministering to individuals/families (4:1; 5:6–7)	Transforming the structures of society (4:4–5; 7:7–9)
Works of mercy (4:1; 6:4–7)	Quest for justice (2:6–8; 5:7, 24; 6:12)

Adapted from John R. W. Stott, *Involvement: Being a Responsible Christian in a Non-Christian Society*, vol. 1 (Old Tappan, N.J.: Revell, 1984), 19–51.

scholars on the grounds that the interest in Edom (9:12) was a postexilic concern and that the salvation oracle seems out place with the earlier oracles of doom. Yet the word of hope and blessing was anticipated by Amos' call to repentance (5:8, 14–15). For the faithful remnant in Israel, the oracle stood as a logical complement to the message of exile and destruction. God would stay total destruction of Israel and would rebuild what he had torn down (cf. 7:1–6; 9:11–15).

The particular structure of the book includes extensive use of various prophetic speech forms, repeated words and phrases, and standardized literary constructions. For example, the book contains proclamation ("Hear," 4:1), revelation ("the LORD showed me," 7:1), and oath formulas ("the LORD has sworn," 4:2).

Several types of prophetic oracles may be found in the text, including judgment (2:6–8), instruction or admonition ("do" or "do not," 5:4–5), repentance ("return," 5:4–10), and "woe" or indictment oracles (5:18). In addition, rhetorical questions are scattered through every section of the prophecy (e.g., 3:3–8; 6:11–14).

The prophet used repetition to emphasize aspects of his message—e.g., "seek

. . . and live" (5:4, 6, 14); "yet you have not returned to me" (4:6, 8, 9, 10, 11). He marked out subsections within literary units—e.g., "the Lord/the lion roars from Zion" (1:2; 3:8); "Bethel and Gilgal" (4:4; 5:5); "the mansions/great houses will be demolished/smashed into bits" (3:15; 6:11); and "turn justice to bitterness/poison" (5:7; 6:12).

The eight oracles against the nations (1:3–2:16) sound the note of the entire book, namely, divine judgment and foreign exile. The cleverly arranged messages crisscross the northern kingdom and in effect reach a climax with the prophet's "target" nation, Israel. The oracles share a standard form (fig. 35.2).[2]

The rest of the book follows the pattern typical of the preexilic prophets: further oracles of indictment, instruction, or admonition; a call to repentance; and a promise of future restoration to the faithful remnant. In the case of Amos, the five visions of judgment simply reinforced the divine indictment of Israel.

Major Theme

Social Justice

Amos condemned Israel for an inability "to do right" (3:10). While the prophet

[2]Shalom P. Paul has noted that these oracles are linked by the literary device of concateny, or the stringing together of a series of items (here oracles) into a chain by the repetition of a word or a phrase shared only by those literary units in sequence ("Amos 1:3–2:3: A Concatenous Literary Pattern," *JBL* 90 [1971]: 397–403).

affirmed the "internal" aspects of covenant relationship with Yahweh (including loving God with a whole heart and obeying his statutes), he clearly understood the ethical implications of covenant relationship with Yahweh for individual and corporate behavior. His impassioned pleas for the socially disadvantaged (the poor, needy, and afflicted—cf. 2:6–7; 4:1; 5:11–12; 8:4, 6) and his castigation of their affluent oppressors (rich women, dishonest merchants, corrupt rulers, opportunistic lawyers and judges, and false priests—cf. 4:1; 6:1, 4; 7:8–9) have earned Amos a reputation as God's spokesman for social justice (cf. 5:7, 15, 24; 6:12).

The letter of James in the New Testament echoes the importance of faith in Christ Jesus (2:1), but the book goes on to describe "pure religion" as discipline in speech, aiding orphans and widows in distress, and avoiding "pollution" from the world (1:26–27). True biblical faith manifests itself in sound speech, genuine and practical social concern, and sound doctrine, prompting godly behavior that permits the believer to remain "unstained" from the world.

Amos' teaching provides a useful Old Testament illustration embracing the concepts of both social service and social action, the essential components of a genuine Christian social concern (fig. 35.3).

According to John Stott, the key to proper development of Christian social concern is sound biblical doctrine. He identifies five specific areas of Christian teaching that help foster meaningful involvement in society. Here again, Amos presents an Old Testament demonstration of this important association between Bible doctrine and social concern. One model follows:[3]

1. A doctrine of God as the Creator and sustainer of creation, deliverer of his people, merciful God of all nations, a God who hates evil and loves justice, because he is concerned for the whole of humanity (2:10; 4:13; 5:8, 15; 9:7).

2. A doctrine of humanity that understands that all persons are God's creatures, and the reality of cause and effect in human social experience due to sin, because as one values all human beings as created in the image of God, the desire to serve them increases (1:9; 2:1; 9:7).

3. A doctrine of Jesus Christ as Messiah that understands the renewal and restoration associated with true redemption, because the historical, biblical Christ was truly the "Son of Man" (9:13–15).

4. A doctrine of salvation that admits human fallenness and sin, looks beyond itself to God for the solutions to the problems of sin and evil in the world, and truly "does justice," because God's salvation is for the whole person, not just the "soul" (2:4; 3:2; 5:4–6, 14–15).

5. A doctrine of the church as a covenant community that sees its responsibility to be an agent of reconciliation and restoration in our fallen world, because the church is distinct from the world as "salt and light," yet it is called to penetrate the world for Christ (3:1; 9:11–15).

Questions for Further Study and Discussion

1. What kinds of social and religious conditions in Israel prompted Amos' ministry?
2. Why did God bring a Judahite like Amos to prophesy against the northern kingdom of Israel?

---

[3]On the book of Amos as an Old Testament paradigm for social concern, see B. Thorogood, *A Guide to the Book of Amos* (London: Theological Education Fund, 1971), esp. 47–54.

3. What do Amos' oracles against the nations reveal about Amos' understanding of God?
4. In light of Amos 3:7–8, how did Amos understand the nature of prophetic ministry?
5. What did Amos mean by "the Day of the Lord"? Compare this with Joel's teaching.
6. In what ways is the message of Amos relevant for the church today? For so-called secular society?

For Further Reading

Andersen, F. I., and David N. Freedman. *Amos.* AB. Vol. 24A. Garden City, N.Y.: Doubleday, 1989.

Barton, J. *Amos' Oracles Against the Nations.* Cambridge: Cambridge University Press, 1980.

Coote, Robert B. *Amos Among the Prophets: Composition and Theology.* Philadelphia: Fortress, 1981.

Harper, W. R. *A Critical and Exegetical Study on Amos and Hosea.* ICC. Edinburgh: T. & T. Clark, 1955.

Hayes, J. H. *Amos: His Times and His Preaching.* Nashville: Abingdon, 1988. A response and challenge to older historical-critical assumptions about Amos as literature. Insightful historical analysis of Amos' times. Extensive bibliographies.

Howie, C. G. "Expressly for Our Times: The Theology of Amos." *Interpretation* 13 (1959): 273–85.

Mays, J. L. *Amos: A Commentary.* OTL. Philadelphia: Westminster, 1969. Thoroughly researched exposition, not always rooted in evangelical pre-convictions.

McComiskey, Thomas E. "Amos." *EBC.* Vol. 7. Grand Rapids: Zondervan, 1985. 269–331.

Motyer, J. A. *The Day of the Lion: The Message of Amos.* Downers Grove, Ill.: InterVarsity, 1974. Easy-to-read approach that appreciates Amos as literature with practical, contemporary application.

Smith, Gary V. *Amos: A Commentary.* Grand Rapids: Zondervan, 1988.

Smith, George Adam. *The Book of the Twelve Prophets.* Expositor's Bible. Vol. 4. Rev. ed. Grand Rapids: Eerdmans, 1956. 456–549. Classic Old Testament commentary, with the exposition of Hosea and Amos deserving special attention.

Stuart, D. *Hosea–Jonah.* WBC. Vol. 31. Waco, Tex.: Word, 1987. Useful introductory sections on the book of Amos, with extensive bibliography.

Thorogood, B. *A Guide to the Book of Amos.* London: Theological Education Fund, 1971. Special emphasis on the interpretation and application of Amos' message in a non-Western context. Theme discussions on judgment, social justice, priest, and prophet.

Vawter, Bruce. *Amos, Hosea, Micah: With an Introduction to Classical Prophecy.* Wilmington, Del.: Michael Glazier, 1981.

Ward, J. M. *Amos and Isaiah: Prophets of the Word of God.* Nashville: Abingdon, 1969.

Wolff, Hans Walter. *Amos the Prophet: The Man and His Background.* Translated by F. McCurley. Philadelphia: Fortress, 1973.

——— . *A Commentary on the Books of the Prophets Joel and Amos.* HER. Translated by W. Janzen, S. D. McBride, and C. A. Muenchow. Philadelphia: Fortress, 1977.

Chapter 36

Obadiah

The shortest book of the Old Testament—one chapter with twenty-one verses—is ascribed to the prophet Obadiah. His name means "servant (or worshiper) of Yahweh," and it is a common biblical name, borne by at least a dozen other persons in the Old Testament. The identification of Obadiah as King Ahab's God-fearing steward according to later Jewish tradition remains unsubstantiated (Babylonian Talmud: *Sanhedrin* 39b; cf. 1 Kings 18:3–16).

The Writing of the Book

Unlike other prophetic books, the title of Obadiah's oracle contains no information about the time or place of its origin, nor does it include any autobiographical data about the prophet and author. Obadiah was probably a Judahite. His prophecy was a response to the role Edom played in the fall of Jerusalem to the Babylonian hordes of King Nebuchadrezzar (2 Kings 24–25).

The word translated "vision" (v. 1), describing Obadiah's prophecy, is a technical term having to do with receiving a revelatory word from God. More than mere human insight, this visionary experience is the result of divine inspiration and implies that the prophet really saw and heard the divine communication. This gave him the perception necessary to understand this unveiling of future events. The same expression occurs in Isaiah 1:1 and Nahum 1:1.

Obadiah's oracle has been dated to various time periods ranging from 850 to 400 B.C. The date can be ascertained only by assuming that verses 11–14 refer to a specific episode in the history of Israelite interaction with the nation of Edom. The two most likely events are (1) the attack on Jerusalem by the Philistines and Arabs about 844 B.C. during the reign of Jehoram (cf. 2 Chron. 21:16–17; 2 Kings 8:16–20), or (2) the destruction of Jerusalem by the Babylonians in 587 B.C. (2 Kings 25:1–12; cf. Ps. 137:7–9; Ezek. 25:1–3, 12–14). Dating Obadiah shortly after the fall of Jerusalem seems to be the most favorable option, since the total conquest of the city described in verse 11 is best accounted for by Nebuchadrezzar's invasion, siege, and sacking of the Judean capital.

The Background

Edom—also called "Hor" (Num. 20:23), "Seir" (Gen. 36:8–9), and "Esau" (Deut. 2:4–5)—and Israel were kin, according to

Figure 36.1. The land of Edom, a wilderness of rugged mountains and plateaus south of the Dead Sea, whose inhabitants were conquered by King David and figure prominently in the writings of the prophets. (*Studium Biblicum Franciscanum, Jerusalem*)

the ancestral traditions recorded in the Old Testament. The patriarchs of Edom and Israel were Esau and Jacob respectively, who were sons of Isaac.

The country of Edom was located in the highlands and sandstone cliffs on the southeastern edge of the Dead Sea, from the Brook Zered in the north to the Gulf of Aqaba in the south (fig. 36.1). A strong tribal organization existed in Edom from patriarchal times (Gen. 36:1–30). The Edomites gravitated toward a form of monarchy before Israel's exodus from Egypt, at which time they denied the Israelites passage to the east and threatened them with a show of force (Num. 20:14–21; 21:4).

Edom and Israel coexisted peacefully until the reigns of Saul and David (1 Sam. 14:47; 2 Sam. 8:13–14). Judah controlled Edom as a satellite state through Jehoram's rule (ca. 853–841 B.C.), when the Edomites successfully revolted and reestablished autonomy (2 Kings 8:20–22; cf. 1 Kings 11:14–25; 22:47). Subsequent incursions by the Judean kings Amaziah

(2 Kings 14:7) and Uzziah (2 Kings 14:22) were evidently localized and temporary.

As early as 597 B.C., control of the Negev was wrested from Judah by the Babylonians (cf. 2 Kings 24:8–17), and the Edomites moved into the area to fill the vacuum. Edom not only assisted Babylon in the sack of Jerusalem in 587, but also occupied Judean villages well into the Persian period (cf. 1 Esdras 4:50).

The exact date of Edom's collapse is still unknown, and the specific circumstances giving rise to its demise are uncertain. By the time of Malachi's prophecy (ca. 500–450 B.C.) the Edomite kingdom was in ruins (Mal. 1:2–4). Edom apparently remained largely independent of Babylonian influence until 550 B.C. or so (cf. Jer. 40:11). According to scholarly consensus, a coalition of Arab tribes gradually infiltrated, overpowered, and displaced the Edomites sometime during the fifth century B.C. By 312 B.C., inscriptional evidence indicates the Nabatean Arabs had overrun the region of Edom, making Petra their capital city. Surviving

Edomites either moved to Idumea or were absorbed by the Nabateans.

Outline of the Book

I. Superscription (1a)
II. Yahweh's message against Edom
   A. Judgment pronounced and reaffirmed (1b–9)
   B. Indictments (10–14)
III. The Day of the Lord
   A. Universal judgment (15–16)
   B. Zion delivered (17–18)
   C. Yahweh's kingdom established (19–21)

Purpose and Message

Obadiah, as Yahweh's envoy, proclaimed a three-part message to the nations (v. 1). First, he condemned the pride and cruelty of the Edomites in their mistreatment of Judah as an ally of Babylon during the sack of Jerusalem. This gross misconduct would not go unpunished, and the future but certain doom of Edom was forecast (vv. 2–9).

Second, the prophet addressed the godly remnant of Israel and assured them of the ultimate triumph of Yahweh and righteousness over the wickedness of all the nations in the Day of the Lord (vv. 15–16). That day held the promise of deliverance and restoration for the people of God and Zion in the kingdom of the Lord—a theme common to the Twelve Prophets (vv. 17–21, cf. Joel 3:4–8, 17–21; Zeph. 3:9–20).

Finally, implicit throughout this brief prophecy and virtually all prophetic literature in the Old Testament is Yahweh's universal dominion over the nations. He is the Sovereign Lord (v. 1, NIV) who logs the iniquities of the peoples (vv. 10–14), administers divine justice in his creation (vv. 4, 8, 15; cf. Pss. 40:7; 69:27–28; Amos 1:3, 5, 9, etc.; Mic. 3:3–5; Nah. 1:9), and practically speaking, controls the destinies of human governments (Isa. 14:24–28; Dan. 2:19–24).

Obadiah's oracle of divine retribution against Edom for assisting in and gloating over Judah's day of misfortune clearly teaches God's sovereignty over the nations of the earth and his justice in respect to punishing the guilty (cf. Nah. 1:2–3). It also serves as a warning to the nations, since they, too, are in jeopardy of having their deeds returned upon them as the day of God's wrath approaches (Obad. 15–16).

More important for Israel, this prophetic statement of God's activity in history was designed to call to mind his covenant love for his people and thus intended to bring a word of encouragement for the present and a promise of hope for the future to the remnant of Jacob in the face of the recent disaster (cf. Ps. 111:2–9; Lam. 3:21–28).

Structure and Organization

Obadiah is one of several Old Testament oracles against Edom (Isa. 21:11–12; 34:5–17; Jer. 49:7–22; Ezek. 25:12–14; 35:1–15; Amos 1:11–12). Its literary form is generally construed as a national oracle, much like Nahum's prophecy against Assyria (cf. the national oracles in Isaiah 13–23; Jeremiah 46–51; Ezekiel 25–32; Amos 1:3–2:16; and Zephaniah 2:4–15). This anti-Edomite theme can be traced through the Old Testament from the mixed blessing Isaac pronounced on Esau (Gen. 27:39–40) to the psalmic imprecations hurled at Edom for her part in the overthrow of Jerusalem (Ps. 137:7) and finally to Malachi's affirmation of Edom's obliteration (Mal. 1:2–4).

Obadiah's oracle—like the prophecies of Isaiah (1:1), Daniel (8:1), and Nahum (1:1)—is a "vision," or revelation. In the broader sense the word "vision" signifies a divine communication to God's prophet or spokesman and connotes the authority and authenticity of the prophetic message. More specifically, the word is a technical term associated with a visible conveying, largely confined to the preexilic prophets. It often has a context of

Timeline Chart (600–320 B.C.)

Top axis (B.C.): 320 · 340 · 360 · 380 · 400 · 420 · 440 · 460 · 480 · 500 · 520 · 540 · 560 · 580 · 600

PERSIA: Darius III · Arses · Artaxerxes III · Artaxerxes II · Darius II · Artaxerxes I · Xerxes · Darius I · Cambyses · Cyrus · Nabonidus

Conquered by Alexander the Great

BABYLON: Evil-Marduk · Neriglissar · Nebuchadnezzar II · Capture of Babylon

Babylonian Rule · Fall of Babylonian Jerusalem invasion

JUDEA: Greek rule · EGYPTIAN DYNASTIES XXVIII–XXX · Ezra Nehemiah · Jerusalem Temple rebuilt · Zedekiah

Egyptian revolt · Persian conquest of Egypt · Persian Rule

EGYPT: Amasis · Psammetichus II · Hophra / Apries

---

impending judgment. That Obadiah's oracle is a "vision" can greatly account for its terse language, its vivid imagery, and the sure realization of the event seen in advance.

Obadiah 1b–4 and 5–6 are nearly verbatim with Jeremiah 49:14–16 and 49:9–10. Naturally this has raised the question of which text came first, and there are three views among scholars on this: (1) Obadiah's priority, (2) Jeremiah as the original source, with Obadiah drawing from it, and (3) a source, now lost, common to both prophets. This common anti-Edomite source is the most likely explanation for the similarities between the two prophecies, with Jeremiah drawing more loosely from it and Obadiah adhering more carefully to the received tradition.

Although the literary unity of Obadiah has been challenged by some scholars, there are distinct divisions or stanzas in the prophecy, giving evidence of an overarching design. The repetition of "Yahweh" at the beginning and end of verses 1–4 and 15–21 mark out clear literary units. While less striking, verses 8–10 and 11–14 are marked by repetition of the phrase "in that/on the day," with the refrain "day of misfortune/trouble" occurring in verses 12 and 14. Finally, the formula "declares the LORD" (vv. 4, 8) and "the LORD has spoken" (v. 18) are also indicators of a deliberate structure.

Theological structure and theme in Obadiah further corroborate the premise of literary unity. The classic four-point outline standard in Hebrew prophetic literature surfaces in this brief work. The charges leveled against specific sins (indictment), the pronouncement of divine judgment, and the promise of restoration (aftermath) are easily identified. The call to repentance is omitted, but this is characteristic of all the anti-Edomite prophecies. This basic theological continuity is underscored by the recurrent themes of the Day of the Lord, Esau/Edom, Edom's sin in relation to Judah, and the eventual reversal of the roles divinely appointed for each nation in the major sections of the prophecy.

The catalog of criminal behavior on the part of the Edomites (vv. 10–14) calls to mind the "lawsuit" oracle or judicial speech (e.g., Hos. 4:1–3; Mic. 6:1–2). Usually this prophetic speech form had three parts: the summons, the trial (with speeches by the prosecution and the defense), and the sentence.[1] In this case, the treachery and faithlessness of Edom's callous and ruthless conduct toward Judah were so heinous that the sentence (Edom's humiliation and dissolution, vv. 2–9, 10, 15) immediately follows the summons (v. 1b). The trial contains only the speech by the prosecution (i.e., the indictments), and this merely to underscore Edom's guilt and the justice of the verdict—Edom's death warrant.

Major Themes

Pride

Obadiah condemned Edom's trust in her own sages because of their inability to detect the plotting of false friends to pilfer and overpower the nation (vv. 7–8). Pride distorts reality and blinds people to the truth. Edom's pride (v. 3) carried the seeds of its own destruction in that God has purposed to bring low all who boast in conceit and insolence (Prov. 11:2; 16:16–18; Isa. 16:6; 25:11). Edom's reputation as a storehouse of wisdom tradition in the ancient world was widespread (cf. Jer. 49:7). Babylon, too, was vaunted for her wisdom, yet it proved impotent in the face of divine judgment (Isa. 47:8–15). So it was with Edom, and so it will be with all who oppose God in the strength of human wisdom (cf. 1 Cor. 1:18–31).

Lex Talionis

The notion that crime punishes itself— "your deeds will return upon your own head" (v. 15)—is well founded in biblical teaching. (See discussions of the principle of retribution in part IV, "The Poetic Books.") The legislation of the Torah is rooted in the concept of lex talionis, or "an eye for an eye" (Exod. 21:23; Lev. 24:19; Deut. 19:21), meaning that punishment for criminal acts will be exacted in a fashion commensurate with the misdeed. Israelite wisdom tradition echoed this belief (Prov. 26:27; cf. Ps. 7:15–16), and the apostle Paul also acknowledged that one reaps what one sows (Gal. 6:7–10). Judah became quite aware of this precept earlier, when the Sovereign Lord removed Samaria into Assyria (2 Kings 17:21–23), crushed the Assyrian Empire by the hand of Nebuchadrezzar (Isa. 14:24–27), and by that same hand made Judah a desolation because of her guilt (Jer. 25:8–14).

Universal Judgment

The beginning of the second principle section of Obadiah's prophecy (vv. 15–16) marks the shift from the specific indictment of Edom to a more general statement of the universal judgment that characterizes the Day of the Lord. This attention to the broader themes of judgment on the nations and the restoration of Israel served two purposes. First, it was a response to the immediate concern for divine justice in view of Edom's role in the fall of Jerusalem. Second, by it Obadiah bolstered future hope among the remnant of Jacob in affirming the final triumph of Yahweh in the world order (e.g., Isa. 24–27, 32; Jer. 29–33; Ezek. 33–35; Hos. 13–14; Amos 9).

[1]Cf. Claus Westermann, *Basic Forms of Prophetic Speech*, trans. H. C. White (Philadelphia: Westminster, 1967), 127.

Restoration

Like other prophetic literature, Obadiah's oracle concluded with the promise of restoration for the remnant of Israel (e.g., Joel 3:17–21; Amos 9:11–15; Mic. 7:8–20). No doubt the prophet intended to stir up memories of distant promises made to the Israelite forefathers concerning the land of Canaan as an inheritance and everlasting possession. The purpose of Obadiah's appeal to past history was to instill hope in the Babylonian exiles (and those who remained in Jerusalem as vassals to Nebuchadrezzar) by reinforcing their faith in Yahweh as a covenant-keeping God (Pss. 115:5–8; Mic. 7:20).

Israel's ultimate restoration, like the final outcome of human history, will be consummated with the Lord's kingdom or sovereign rule in the created order (v. 21). This theme of Yahweh's ultimate dominion over the world through Israel as his signet occurs frequently in the Old Testament as part of the messianic expectation of the Day of the Lord (e.g., Ezek. 37:24–28; Dan. 2:44–45; Zech. 12:3–13:6).

Questions for Further Study and Discussion

1. In what ways does Obadiah's prophecy, while addressed to a nation, pertain to individuals?
2. How does Obadiah understand God's role in human history? What does the prophet offer as the goal of human history?
3. Discuss the principle of *lex talionis* and its significance and value for society today.

For Further Reading

Allen, L. C. *The Books of Joel, Obadiah, Jonah and Micah.* NICOT. Grand Rapids: Eerdmans, 1976.

Bullock, C. Hassell. *An Introduction to the Old Testament Prophetic Books.* Chicago: Moody Press, 1986.

Craigie, Peter C. *Twelve Prophets.* Vol. 1. Daily Study Bible: Old Testament Series. Philadelphia: Westminster, 1984. Penetrating discussion of God's justice and human sin, with insightful application of Obadiah's message to the contemporary scene.

Laetsch, T. *The Minor Prophets.* St. Louis: Concordia, 1956.

Stuart, Douglas. *Hosea–Jonah.* WBC. Vol. 31. Waco, Tex.: Word, 1987.

Walton, John H., and Bryan E. Beyer. *Obadiah, Jonah.* Bible Study Commentary series. Grand Rapids: Zondervan, 1988.

Watts, J. D. W. *Obadiah: A Critical and Exegetical Commentary.* Grand Rapids: Eerdmans, 1969. A thorough, scholarly, and readable analysis of Obadiah's times and message; the standard commentary on the book.

————. *The Books of Joel, Obadiah, Jonah, Nahum, Habakkuk, and Zephaniah.* CBC. London: Cambridge University Press, 1975.

Wolff, Hans Walter. *Obadiah and Jonah: A Commentary.* Minneapolis: Augsburg, 1986.

Chapter 37

Jonah

The book of Jonah is unique among the prophetic books of the Old Testament. Rather than being a collection of the oracles of the prophet, it relates an episode in his life. In the Old Testament, the prophet Jonah is mentioned outside the book only in 2 Kings 14:25, in reference to the reign of Jeroboam II in the northern kingdom of Israel in the first half of the eighth century B.C.

The Writing of the Book

Although the prophet lived in the eighth century B.C., there is some dispute about the dating of the book because there is no certainty about who was its author. It is written in the third person, and no author is identified anywhere in the Bible. Nevertheless, if the book is factual, we would expect that either Jonah or someone getting information from Jonah would have to have written the book—e.g., someone from the "sons of the prophets" (cf. 2 Kings 2:3).

Much discussion has focused on the nature of the book. The incredibility of some of the events related there (e.g., Jonah surviving inside the fish, the fantastic rate of growth of the plant) has prompted many scholars to identify the book as allegory (in which the characters and events are symbolic), as parable (a story with a moral behind it), or as midrash (a story intended to convey religious truth by elaborating and embellishing an event in a historical setting). Thus it would be claimed that the events did not really happen, but that the story is obviously contrived with some type of moral in view. At times, an unwillingness to accept the possibility of miraculous occurrences may be at the root of the issue, though for others it is solely a question of literary genre.

Other interpreters remain more inclined to affirm the historical, though sensational, nature of the book. Objections raised against a historical interpretation such as the unbelievable size of Nineveh (3:3) and reference to a "king of Nineveh" (3:6), rather than to the king of Assyria, have been met with suitable explanations.[1] It is also argued that Jesus'

[1] See Donald J. Wiseman, "Jonah's Nineveh," *TB* 30 (1979): 29–51. For instance, the title "king" could be used for a governor, or this could be the king of Assyria. The use of "king" with a city

Figure 37.1. A drawing of the seal of Shema found at Megiddo, a carving in jasper that bears the inscription "belonging to Shema, servant of Jeroboam," which is probably a reference to Jeroboam II, a contemporary of Jonah. (*Carta, Jerusalem*)

reference to the events of the book in Matthew 12:40–41 suggest his belief in its historicity. Furthermore, although the Assyrian king is not identified by name, the account has not been convincingly identified with any of the known nonhistorical genres.[2] Therefore, in view of present information, we feel it is best to accept the factuality and authenticity of the narrative, though other positions concerning the book's genre are not indefensible.

Affirming the factual nature of the book does not require one to attempt to identify what species of fish was involved (not necessarily a whale) on the basis of gullet size and having the Mediterranean as a natural habitat, etc., as many conservative interpreters have felt obliged to do. The fish's action was ordained by God, and if the possibility of the miraculous is accepted philosophically, further identification is irrelevant and may be impossible.

The Background

Set in the first half of the eighth century B.C., the events of this book came at a time of great optimism for the northern kingdom of Israel. The Assyrian Empire that had flexed its muscles in the ninth century had entered into decline, leaving Jeroboam II free to regain much of the territory that had belonged to Israel during the times of David and Solomon. Territorial expansion brought greater economic prosperity than at any previous time in Israel's history. While the Assyrians were not forgotten, they were not a threat to Israel during this time period. Little did the Israelites know that by the close of the century the Assyrian Empire would be the strongest political force the world had known, and the northern kingdom would be overtaken and its people deported.

Scholars still have not determined who was the king of Assyria when the events of the book transpired. Some have tried to look for evidence of a mass conversion to Judaism, or at least monotheism, in the records of the Assyrians, but no such evidence has been found; yet the merit of this line of investigation is questionable. Others have suggested that Jonah's message be correlated with great disasters such as earthquakes or eclipses in order to explain the momentous response of the Assyrians. There is really no need for such a correlation, however, since much less significant occurrences could also portend catastrophic destruction to the Assyrians (e.g., something as simple as a fox in the city square was thought to be an omen of the impending fall of the city). As a result, the precise placement of these events chronologically is impossible.

name is not impossible (cf. "king of Samaria" in 1 Kings 21:1). As for the size of Nineveh, it is more likely that Jonah 3:3 relates to the size of the task or the length of stay rather than the actual circumference or diameter of the city (cf. the same terminology in Nehemiah 2:6).

[2] An excellent presentation of the issues surrounding the sensational nature of the book and its genre and historicity can be found in the commentary by Douglas Stuart, *Hosea–Jonah*, WBC, vol. 31 (Waco, Tex.: Word, 1987), 435–42.

Outline of the Book

Purpose and Message

The purpose of the book of Jonah is often misunderstood. Interpreters have been inclined to seek in it a message to Israel. In so doing, it has seemed most natural to equate Jonah, the Israelite, with an Israel set in contrast to Nineveh and to see a lesson directed to Israel in the lesson that Jonah learns.

Consequently some have construed Jonah as a missionary book. Through it they see God urging Israel to move beyond its theological exclusiveness and evangelize other nations. Others have suggested that the book instructs Israel that as God has compassion on the heathen, they too ought to love and forgive even their worst enemies.

While all these are noble ideas—and even good theology—the book points us in a different direction.

The equation that the book offers to us is not Jonah = Israel, but Jonah = Nineveh. Two key observations dictate this equation. The first is the use of the compound divine name "the LORD God" (Yahweh Elohim) in 4:6. Until this point in the narrative, "the LORD" (Yahweh) was the name used by Jonah, while "God" (Elohim) had been used when the Ninevites were involved. This is to be expected, since "Yahweh" was the personal name of the God of Israel and "Elohim" was a more generic term for deity. That the compound name occurs only once in the book signals an important change, for after its use, the object lesson consistently uses the name "Elohim" even though Jonah is the one involved.

The second observation concerns Hebrew terminology in the prophecy. The word translated "destruction" by the New International Version in 3:10 is the same word translated "discomfort" in 4:6. Both Nineveh and Jonah had a "calamity" from which they needed relief. These observations suggest that Jonah, in the object lesson of 4:6–8, was being treated like Nineveh.

Once this equation is accepted, the correlation takes shape, and the message becomes clear. Both Jonah and Nineveh faced an impending calamity: Jonah, the climate; Nineveh, destruction. Both sought to avert the calamity by taking what action they could—Jonah building his hut, Nineveh repenting. Neither action was sufficient to bring relief, but each was aided by an act of divine grace—God's sending a plant to Jonah and relenting toward Nineveh. So Jonah was put in a situation that paralleled Nineveh's.

At this point, however, a change took place. There was no parallel in Nineveh's experience to the parasite's destroying the plant that shaded Jonah. We find that Jonah was not spared his calamity after all, for God sovereignly removed his instrument of grace—thus the parasite devoured the plant. Jonah then received the very treatment he desired God to show Nineveh. Jonah wanted to negate the compassionate act of God's grace toward Nineveh, so that is how God treated him.

The lesson is brought home in the two discussions concerning Jonah's anger (4:3–4, 8–9). In both cases, Jonah's anger was focused on the mechanism of God's grace. In 4:3–4 Jonah was angry that God's grace was applied, because, he would have insisted, Nineveh did not deserve any more chances. In 4:8–9, Jonah was angry that he lost the benefit of God's gracious protection, although, as

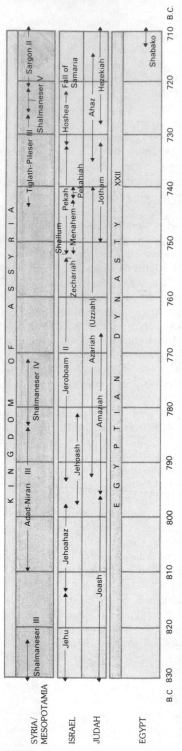

God pointed out, he had done nothing to earn such protection.

It becomes evident that the message of the book concerns God's sovereign right to bestow gracious acts of compassion on whomever he will. Although Nineveh's attempted act of self-preservation was insufficient by God's standards to warrant their deliverance, God honored a small step in the right direction by postponing the announced judgment. The Ninevites were still under the threat of doom, but it was no longer imminent, thanks only to the grace of God.

This equation not only helps us to understand the significance of the object lesson and to see the message of the book clearly, but also gives an indication of the nature of the repentance of the Ninevites: it was most likely quite shallow. This is suggested, first, by the parallel in the object lesson. Jonah's hut was evidently quite incapable of serving its function; it was the plant that provided shade. When the plant was gone, the hut did nothing to protect Jonah from the climate. Nineveh's repentance could be described in similar terms.

Second, in their zeal to promote evangelism, interpreters have at times depicted the response of the Ninevites as a grand and glorious conversion to faith in the one true God, Yahweh. While we would rejoice in such an enthusiastic response on the part of these Assyrians, a careful examination of the text produces no support for such a view. It is clear that the Ninevites repented, but that is not the same as conversion. Nothing in the text suggests that they were introduced to Yahweh or convinced of the philosophical superiority of a monotheistic faith. The message of the prophet to them was a simple oracle of judgment. While it is possible that the oracle has been abridged in the text, there is no reason to suppose that any sort of instruction or exhortation was included in it. (Compare the book of Nahum, which is an extended judgment oracle against the Ninevites of a later generation). Jonah 3:5 affirms that they "believed God" (NIV), but this need indicate nothing more than believing that what Jonah (i.e., God) threatened would actually come to pass. Furthermore, 3:10 makes it clear that Yahweh relented on the basis of their deeds rather than on the basis of their faith. Even the fact that the Ninevites would be present at the judgment (Matt. 12:41) gives no evidence concerning their supposed conversion, for the Queen of Sheba is mentioned along with them (12:42).

The significance of all this is that it helps us to see that the response of the Ninevites is not in any sense the key to understanding the message or purpose of the book. Their repentance was very controversial in Jonah's estimation, and he was frankly skeptical that it was even worth noting. It was a rather typical Assyrian response, counting on ritual to appease an angry deity.

The book is not configuring Israel as Jonah and thereby urging action (e.g., evangelize, forgive, be compassionate, etc.). Rather it is identifying all three (Jonah, Nineveh, and Israel) as the object of God's activity. God reserves the sovereign right to be compassionate, and he delights in performing acts of compassion—even when those acts controvert an already issued prophetic warning.

It cannot be accidental that this incident occurred in the early part of the eighth century just prior to the dawning of the classical period of prophecy. The classical prophets had a new message that they began to expound to the Israelites: The Lord is angry at Israel's disobedience and rebellion, and he is going to punish them with destruction and exile. It is evident that in the message of the classical prophets, Israel was treated as Nineveh was in the book of Jonah. God's punishment was imminent, and the Israelites had no hope of protecting themselves from the impending calamity. What did God expect of them? This is the message of the book of Jonah. God de-

lights in responding to small steps in the right direction with gracious acts of compassion. The resulting postponement of punishment is evident in a narrative such as 2 Kings 22, where Josiah's return to the Lord was an occasion for God's grace. Certainly if God responded that way to Nineveh, the epitome of pagan wickedness, he would respond compassionately to his chosen people, Israel.

It is the object lesson of Jonah 4, then, that conveys the purpose of the book. Without the object lesson, the equation would be unrecognizable. Some interpreters have worried that the narrative is somehow incomplete, because the reader never finds out what Jonah's response was or whether the Ninevite repentance had long-term effects. But we can now see that both Jonah and the Ninevites are secondary characters. We are being taught about God, so the narrative ends exactly where it should—speaking of his compassion.

Organization and Structure

The book of Jonah is a highly structured composition. It is organized in two parallel halves, with chapters 1–2 roughly parallel to chapters 3–4. Each starts out with a call from God and a response from Jonah (1:1–3/3:1–3). Then Jonah encounters pagans who are forced to consider the influence of Jonah's God (1:4–11/3:4–10). Jonah is in each case forced into a confrontation with God because of his attitudes (1:12–17/4:1–9). God's compassionate deliverance highlights the end of each section (2:1–9/4:10–12).

In the first part of the book (chaps. 1–2) God demonstrates his compassion for both the sailors and Jonah, as they are both delivered. Jonah's prayer in chapter 2 is integral to the book because it sets the scene for discussing the compassionate grace of God. The psalm is a thanksgiving hymn rather than the lament that some have expected. Jonah was not complaining about his predicament inside the fish; rather, he was thanking God for delivering him from death. The psalm uses generic language that could have made it applicable to any number of situations. It may have been a common hymn or may have drawn lines from several different hymns.[3] The prayer serves an important function of showing the reader that Jonah fully recognized himself as an undeserving recipient of God's grace. This in turn gives us much less patience with Jonah's position in chapter 4 and prepares us to see the truth in the book's teaching.

Chapter 3 provides the main event of the book, with chapter 4 bringing the lesson of the book into focus.

Major Themes

Compassion

It has already been mentioned that the compassion of God and his sovereign right to perform acts of compassion is the major focus of the book. Even the introduction of Jonah in the book of Kings is a fitting preparation for the discussion of God's compassion, for there God showed undeserved compassion on the northern kingdom of Israel by prospering a wicked king (Jeroboam II). Just as Jonah 1–2 provides an example by which Jonah as an individual was prepared to comprehend and accept God's sovereign right to act compassionately, so 2 Kings 14:25–27 provides a national context by which Israel could understand God's sovereign compassion.

Anger

The anger of God is assumed to have begun the whole sequence of events in the book of Jonah. The wickedness of Nineveh inspired the wrath of God to move into action. By contrast, Jonah affirmed that God was slow to anger (4:2), though he himself certainly was not. Jonah's anger appeared to rebuke God, who, in Jonah's estimation, was not angry enough about the right things. Righteous anger is balanced by compassion, and God must be granted the freedom to exercise either. Thus God's sovereignty must be viewed in relation to his compassion.

Theodicy

Justifying the ways of God (theodicy) is a common theme in the Old Testament, but rarely does it take the form that we see in the book of Jonah. Typically, the Israelite concerned about theodicy asked the question that was posed by God to Jonah: "Do you have a right to be angry" (4:4, 9), because the Israelites were often puzzled by the suffering of the righteous. In the story of Jonah, however, the question was reversed, for it concerns God's leniency toward the wicked—a charge that was just as serious.[4] The book resolves the question by affirming God's right not to be angry or, better, to be "slow to anger." His justice is not negated by the offering of extensions by grace. This was the same answer given in Habakkuk and is reflected in New Testament theology as well in places such as Romans 3:25 and Matthew 20:15. Yet God is not obligated to offer extensions endlessly. His just punishment will eventually be carried out (cf. Jer. 13:14; Ezek. 7:1–9). God must be free to act as he sees fit.

---

[3]Psalms such as 18, 31, and 69 show some interesting parallels.

[4]See T. Fretheim, "Jonah and Theodicy," *Zeitschrift für die alttestamentliche Wissenschaft* 90 (1978): 227. This article is full of good observations, many of which have influenced this chapter.

Questions for Further Study and Discussion

1. What aspects of the book of Jonah commend it as a pattern for missions? What aspects do not so commend it?
2. What are some implications and applications of this "second-chance" theology for Israel? For us?
3. What evidence in the book suggests that Nineveh's repentance was shallow? What are the implications of such a conclusion?
4. Is there a difference between expressing gratitude and asking forgiveness? Which was Jonah's intent in chapter 2?
5. Did Jonah have a right to be angry over God's grace being bestowed on a wicked ignorant people? What aspects of this reaction by Jonah show "good" theology?

For Further Reading

Alexander, Desmond. "Jonah." In *Obadiah, Jonah, Micah.* TOTC. Downers Grove, Ill.: InterVarsity, 1988. An evangelical treatment less technical than many others.

Allen, Leslie. *The Books of Joel, Obadiah, Jonah and Micah.* NICOT. Grand Rapids: Eerdmans, 1976. Broadly evangelical, though does not take the book as a record of actual events.

Burrows, Millar. "The Literary Category of the Book of Jonah." In *Translating and Understanding the Old Testament.* Edited by Harry Frank and William Reed. Nashville: Abingdon, 1970. 80–107.

Clements, Ronald E. "The Purpose of the Book of Jonah." VT Supplement 28 (1974): 16–28.

Fretheim, T. "Jonah and Theodicy." *Zeitschrift für die alttestamentliche Wissenschaft* 90 (1978). 227–37.

Landes, George M. "The Kerygma of the Book of Jonah." *Interpretation* 21 (1967): 3–31.

Sasson, Jack. *Jonah.* AB. Vol. 24B. Garden City, N.Y.: Doubleday, 1990. The most comprehensive treatment from a critical perspective.

Stuart, Douglas. *Hosea–Jonah.* WBC. Vol. 31. Waco, Tex.: Word, 1987. 424–510. An excellent commentary, evangelical and thorough in its treatment of the text.

Walton, John H., and Bryan E. Beyer. *Obadiah, Jonah.* Bible Study Commentary series. Grand Rapids: Zondervan, 1988.

Wiseman, Donald J. "Jonah's Nineveh." *TB* 30 (1979): 29–51.

Wolff, Hans Walter. *Obadiah and Jonah.* Minneapolis: Augsburg, 1986.

Chapter 38

Micah

A contemporary of the well-known prophet Isaiah, Micah was a prophet from the small town of Moresheth located in the hilly region of Judah between Jerusalem and the Mediterranean Sea. He is one of the few prophets who is referred to specifically in another prophetic book. When Jeremiah was threatened with death for his prophecies of doom against Jerusalem, he was spared by elders who reminded the people that Micah had prophesied the same more than one hundred years earlier (Jer. 26:18–19). This gives some indication of the prominence of Micah as a spokesman for the Lord.

The Writing of the Book

The superscription of the book gives plain information about the time of Micah's prophetic activity. He is said to have prophesied during the days of kings Jotham, Ahaz, and Hezekiah. These three kings reigned during the last half of the eighth century B.C., and it is a safe assumption that the prophecies would have been recorded at that time. The fact that the prophecies were remembered over a century later also suggests that they had been preserved.

The only sections of the book of Micah that some scholars identify as later additions are the oracles of hope (2:12–13; 4:1–5:9; 7:8–20). This is consistent with their belief that oracles of hope were not given by preexilic prophets, for that would have weakened the power of their oracles of judgment. But such an assumption is unwarranted, because the hope oracles represent a significant theological response to questions about the Lord's faithfulness to his covenant promises. Prophetic affirmations of eventual restoration generally did not offer hope to the generation hearing them, but rather confirmed that the judgments of God coming on that generation did not mean an end to the covenant. There is therefore no reason to excise the oracles of hope from collections of preexilic oracles.

The Background

Micah ministered during the great Assyrian crisis. He was a witness to the events that brought about the destruction and deportation of the northern kingdom of Israel. (The Assyrian rise to power is described in chapter 3.) It was a time of fear and anxiety among the small nations of the west.

Micah's oracles are not dated, so it is

difficult to assign them precisely to one incident or another. There were several major invasions of Judah by the Assyrians during Micah's lifetime, and any of them could have served as the backdrop for some of his prophetic pronouncements. The most threatening of these, and the one that is typically thought to provide the historical setting for many of Micah's prophecies, was the campaign of Sennacherib that culminated in a siege of Jerusalem in 701 B.C. In this campaign many cities of Judah were besieged and destroyed—most notably, Lachish (cf. 1:13). This not only fulfilled some of the judgment oracles of Micah, but also provided an opportunity for the Lord's deliverance. Though Sennacherib's armies had surrounded Jerusalem and were prepared to overthrow her, the Assyrian annals offer no conclusion to the campaign. That is understandable, because 2 Kings 19:35 records that the Assyrian army, 185,000 strong, was slain in the night by "the angel of the LORD."

In these critical times the Lord sent Micah with a message for the people. It was a time of both political upheaval and social unrest. The great military success of King Uzziah in the first half of the eighth century had blossomed into a period of economic prosperity—for some. With the economic growth came the development of a merchant class in Israel and divisions in society that had not previously existed. Now the agrarian segment of society often found itself at the mercy of the merchants, who seemed to enjoy monarchical support. Equity in the marketplace had fast become the exception rather than the rule. It was against this social backdrop that Micah denounced injustice and false religiosity.

Outline of the Book

I. Prologue (1:1)
II. The people
   A. Indictment and judgment against the people (1:2–2:11)

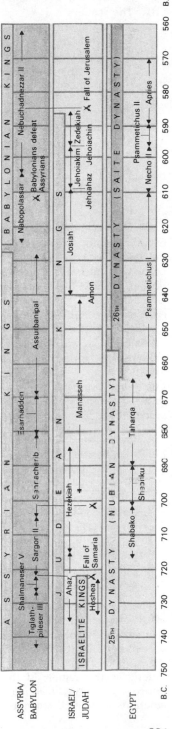

B. Hope for the people (2:12–13)
III. The leaders
  A. Indictment and judgment against the leaders (3)
  B. Hope for the Lord's leadership and restoration (4:1–8)
  C. Current crisis and deliverance (4:9–5:9)
  D. Future purging (5:10–15)
IV. The nation
  A. Indictment and judgment against the nation (6:1–7:7)
  B. Hope for the nation (7:8–20)

Purpose and Message

Micah is one of the few prophets who explicitly stated his purpose: "But as for me, I am filled with power, with the Spirit of the LORD, and with justice and might, to declare to Jacob his transgression, to Israel his sin" (3:8). This purpose is reflected in the preponderance of indictment and judgment oracles in the book.

His message was that the people, particularly the upper class, were guilty of injustice (2:1–2; 3:1–3, 9–11; 6:10–11). The result was that they would suffer destruction and exile. The five judgment oracles took five different directions:

1. Destruction of cult places and objects, using cosmic terms (1:3–7; 3:12)
2. Political devastation, including overthrow of cities and sending their inhabitants into exile (1:10–16)
3. Personal judgment against specific offenders (2:3–5)
4. Spiritual judgment, depriving the prophets of revelation (3:6–7)
5. Socioeconomic judgment, affecting the fertility of the land (6:13–16)

There are also a number of sections offering hope and deliverance to at least a remnant of the people. These appear to project both short-term deliverance from the Assyrians (2:12–13; 5:2–9) and restoration for the nation in the indefinite future (4:1–5; 7:8–20), although time designations, as usual, are not clear.

Structure and Organization

Each of the three divisions opens with a call to "listen" to the word of the Lord. As the outline shows, each division also contains an initial section focusing on the sin of the people and its consequences, then proceeds to a note of hope. In the first and last divisions, the language of legal proceedings is used, first depicting God as witness (1:2), then indicating that he has a lawsuit to bring against Israel (6:1–2). The middle division differs from the first and last by not using legal terminology and by including a few additional sections. After the oracles introduced by the phrase "in that day" (cf. 4:1, 6) that delineate the hope section, the middle division continues with three sections introduced by "now" (4:9, 11; 5:1, KJV) that address the current crisis. Deliverance from the crisis is prophesied (5:2–9), leading into a final "in that day" section that speaks of a future purging of Israel from all those elements that caused them to stray from the Lord (5:10–15).

Major Themes

The Deliverer

Two places in the book of Micah speak of royal deliverers who would serve as the Lord's instruments for saving Israel from her enemies. In 2:13 the king is depicted as leading the people as they "break out of" the enclosure. The fact that the king is paralleled by the Lord has led some interpreters to insist that the king pictured here is the Lord (cf. 4:7), while others contend that the parallel merely shows that the king was acting in the power of the Lord. Since verse 12 speaks of a remnant (survivors) being gathered in an enclosed place, and chapter 1 had referred to the destruction of towns in Judah, it is likely that 2:12 is a reference to the refugees from all the towns of Judah gathering for safety in Jerusalem in the wake of the Assyrian onslaught of 701 B.C. If this was the incident referred to, it was the Lord who brought deliverance in response to King Hezekiah's request.

In 5:2–9, the deliverer is not referred to as "king" but as "ruler." The term "Messiah" was not used in the preexilic prophets to refer to the future, ideal Davidic king, so such a person must be recognized by function rather than title. His emergence from Bethlehem signifies that he was to be a new David and indicates some discontinuity from the reigning administration, whose heirs would have been born in Jerusalem. He is depicted as the one who would eventually bring deliverance for the remnant. There is no question that Micah was discussing the ideal Davidic king whom we are accustomed to referring to as the Messiah. Yet there is little to indicate that Micah received any revelation as to when this person might come on the scene or how he might carry out his function. It must again be stressed that the interpreter's primary task is to understand the message of the prophet. Identifying when or how fulfillment took place is not unimportant, but it is secondary.

Micah's message about a deliverer was clear. The Lord intended to provide one after the necessary judgment was complete (5:3). However, his identity and the timing of his appearance remain obscure in the text. As history progressed, the New Testament authors offered new insight into the significance of Micah's prophecy. They did not hesitate to see Jesus, born in Bethlehem, as "the new David" who was anticipated by Micah and the other prophets. This insight offered fresh understanding of the Lord as a God of deliverance.

What Does the Lord Require?

Perhaps the best-known verse in the book is Micah 6:8:

> He has showed you, O man, what is
> good.
> And what does the LORD require of
> you?
> To act justly and to love mercy
> and to walk humbly with your God.

This verse has often been understood as a comprehensive statement of God's demands on humanity, but such an interpretation fails to see the statement in its context. Verse 8 needs to be read as a contrast to verses 6–7. There the Israelites were questioning how the Lord could be appeased from the anger aroused by their offenses. In considering the answer, they were inclined to try to appease the Lord through ritual. But here again the Israelites showed the extent to which they had been influenced by the religious beliefs of their neighbors. Micah had to explain to them that rituals themselves do not appease. Appeasement was not the issue. It was proper conduct that would put an end to God's anger. They acted unjustly, they violated their agreements with God and with others, and they were a proud people. This behavior must stop.

Micah 6:8, therefore, is not a comprehensive statement of human responsibility before God, but an indication of what Micah's audience needed to do to get back on the right track in their relationship to the Lord. The message is that obedience is more important than sacrifice (cf. 1 Sam. 15:22). A more suitable comprehensive statement can be found in Deuteronomy 10:12–13: "And now, O Israel, what does the LORD your God ask of you but to fear the LORD your God, to walk in all his ways, to love him, to serve the LORD your God with all your heart and with all your soul, and to observe the LORD's commands and decrees that I am giving you today for your own good?"

Questions for Further Study and Discussion

1. How would Micah's audience have understood the announcement of a coming ruler in the historical context of Assyrian oppression?
2. How should the constant tension in the prophets between responding to God by just conduct and responding by ritual be understood in relation to the need to respond by faith?

For Further Reading

Allen, Leslie. *The Books of Joel, Obadiah, Jonah and Micah.* NICOT. Grand Rapids: Eerdmans, 1976. Thorough analysis of the text.

Hillers, Delbert R. *Micah.* Philadelphia: Fortress, 1984. A good critical study.

Mays, James L. *Micah.* Philadelphia: Westminster, 1976. One of the best treatments from a critical scholar.

McComiskey, Thomas E. "Micah." *EBC.* Vol. 7. Grand Rapids: Zondervan, 1985. Helpful evangelical analysis.

Smith, Ralph L. *Micah–Malachi.* WBC. Vol. 32. Waco, Tex.: Word, 1984.

Waltke, Bruce. "Micah." In *Obadiah, Jonah, Micah.* TOTC. Downers Grove, Ill.: InterVarsity, 1988. Brief but well-done analysis.

Wolff, Hans Walter. *Micah the Prophet.* Philadelphia: Fortress, 1981. A rare homiletical and expositional treatment from a critical scholar.

Chapter 39

Nahum

In the eighth century B.C. the prophet Jonah went to the city of Nineveh to proclaim a judgment oracle against her. The Ninevites responded with repentance, and God spared them. More than a century later, Nahum also declared the judgment of God upon the wicked city of Nineveh. This time there was no fasting or sackcloth, and Nineveh was not spared.

The Writing of the Book

The most disputed section of the book of Nahum is the psalm found in 1:2–8. Since it is unusual for the oracular material in the book to be introduced by a psalm, it has been questioned whether or not it was originally connected to the oracle or appended at a later date. The latter option has been favored by those who consider the psalm to be a fragment of what was once an alphabetic acrostic (a composition in which each letter of the alphabet follows in succession as the lead letter of successive lines of text). There is no evidence, however, that would preclude Nahum from having introduced his

oracle with this psalm, and on the whole, the unity of the book has been accepted.

It has been suggested that the book of Nahum owes a great literary debt to Isaiah, and indeed many parallels can be identified in vocabulary, phrasing, theme, and motif. Particularly noticeable is the phrase unique to these two books, "On the mountains, the feet of one who brings good news, who proclaims peace" (Nah. 1:15; cf. Isa. 52:7).[1] This shows that Nahum was following in the tradition of the great classical prophets who preceded him.

The book contains no chronological information in its superscription, so it must be dated on the basis of internal evidence. Because the oracle projects the downfall of Nineveh, it is logical to place it prior to 612 B.C., when Nineveh fell. Of course, some scholars who discount the possibility of prophesying about something before it happens have been content to view the book as postexilic, but that is often only a reflection of anti-supernatural presuppositions.

Another piece of information is gleaned from 3:8, where it is made clear that the

---

[1]For a full treatment of the parallels, see Carl E. Armerding, "Nahum," in *EBC*, vol. 7 (Grand Rapids: Zondervan, 1985), 453–56.

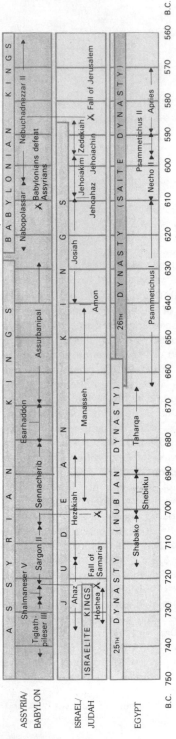

city of Thebes (Heb., No Amon; "No," KJV) had already fallen. This event took place in 663 B.C., when the Assyrian king Ashurbanipal achieved the maximum penetration into Egypt. It may be of significance, however, that by 650 the Assyrians had been driven out of Egypt again, and certainly by the time of Jeremiah Thebes had been rebuilt (Jer. 46:25). While the point of the analogy is probably the apparent invulnerability of Thebes and Nineveh, the prophecy would lose some of its force if Thebes had meanwhile been rebuilt and was again thriving.

The kings of Judah during most of the period under discussion were Manasseh (695–642) and Josiah (640–609). Since the oracle against Nineveh was favorable to Judah, who had long endured subjugation to the Assyrians, some interpreters have been inclined to connect Nahum to the time of Josiah. Manasseh had been the most apostate of Judean kings (2 Kings 21:1–18) and thus not a likely candidate to receive a favorable oracle. However, Manasseh did repent of his wickedness toward the end of his reign (2 Chron. 33:12–16). This occurred after he had been taken captive to Assyria, which may have been the result of his joining a conspiracy against Ashurbanipal. The most likely occasion for Manasseh's insubordination would have been in conjunction with the Babylonian revolt in 652 B.C. It might even be imagined that a prophecy like Nahum's constituted a critique of Manasseh's vassal relationship to Assyria that inspired him to sever ties. This chronology also best fits the data on Thebes, and accordingly the book of Nahum may tentatively be dated to 655–650 B.C.

The Background

Although the Assyrian Empire did not actually expire until the last decade of the seventh century, its breaking point came mid-century. At that time the revolts in the empire began to take their toll, and by

Figure 39.1. A stele depicting King Esarhaddon of Assyria (the son of Sennacherib and the father of Ashurbanipal) holding two captives. (*Staatliche Museen zu Berlin*)

the 640s and 630s Assyrian control was first lagging and then crumbling as the empire disintegrated. Within a few years of Ashurbanipal's death (627), the Babylonians had achieved their independence; over the next two decades they, along with the Medes, dismantled the mighty Assyrian state. The centerpiece of the Assyrian collapse was the fall of Nineveh in 612, as prophesied by Nahum.

Nineveh had been fashioned into the gem of the Assyrian Empire by Sennacherib (704–681). He had nearly tripled the size of the city and made it his capital, constructing a magnificent palace there and beautifying the city with parks, a botanical garden, and a zoo. Its splendor was probably surpassed in the ancient world only by Nebuchadrezzar's Babylon. Yet, despite its splendor, Nineveh represented the brutal wickedness of the Assyrians that the Lord had determined to punish—prophesied, for example, in Isaiah 14:24–25 and Zephaniah 2:13–15.

Outline of the Book

I. Introductory psalm (1:1–8)
II. The doom of Nineveh and the deliverance of Judah (1:9–2:2)
III. The siege of Nineveh (2:3–3:19)

Purpose and Message

The purpose of the book was to pronounce the doom of Nineveh. This is an oracle of judgment similar to the oracles of judgment spoken against the nations as found most prominently in the major prophets. It is unlikely, though not impossible, that Nineveh was the audience for this prophecy. Rather, it was probably given as an encouragement to the people of Judah, who had long suffered under Assyrian domination.

The message was that the days of Assyrian rule were coming to an end at the hands of the Lord. This was not just a case of the ebb and flow of history, but the action of the Lord's punishment against Nineveh. The sovereignty of Yahweh was an essential ingredient to the intended message. He announced Nineveh's doom, and he would accomplish it.

Structure and Organization

The book begins with a graphic psalm that is intended to put the vision in its proper perspective. Some researchers have concluded that the psalm was at one time an acrostic that has now been either partially lost in transmission or was adapted by Nahum. The idea that Nahum would have adapted a well-known psalm as an introduction does not pose a problem, and it could even be considered probable. Whether the psalm was an acrostic or not remains a matter of speculation and does not contribute one way or another to its interpretation. The emphasis of the psalm on the attributes of God and his mastery of the cosmos affirms both his inclination and ability to bring judgment on Nineveh.

The second section of the book comprises alternating addresses to Nineveh and Judah. This makes it clear that the message ostensibly given to Nineveh was actually addressed to Judah. The promises announced to Judah were that she would no longer be under the yoke of Assyria (1:12–13) and that she would have peace and freedom to celebrate her festivals (1:15). This latter promise was fulfilled when King Josiah reinstituted the Passover celebration in 622 B.C. in connection with his reform (2 Chron. 35).

The final section details the siege and sack of Nineveh, with 2:3–12 being narrated in the third person and 2:13–3:19 in the second person. The dirge of 3:1 suggests the reasons for God's actions against them, though there is no formal indictment. None was needed, for the whole audience would have realized that Nineveh was merely being treated the same way she had treated others. If any question had been raised, it would have been to ask why the Lord had waited so long to say, "I am against you" (3:5).

Major Theme

Assyria and the Old Testament

Assyria holds pride of place (even over the Philistines) as the archvillain of the Old Testament. Though the Babylonians were responsible for the destruction of Jerusalem and the temple, they cannot compare with the Assyrians in their reputation for brutality. The barbaric military policies and practices of the Assyrians terrorized the ancient Near East for more than two centuries. The Assyrians cultivated their ability to intimidate the victims of their imperialistic expansion by developing propaganda intended to establish an image of invulnerability. The fear they generated is attested throughout the Near East. Failure to submit had its consequences, and the Assyrians had always appreciated the value of making public examples of those who rebelled.

All this psychological warfare had the desired effect of reducing the need for actual military engagement. Abject surrender was much easier. Enemies and prisoners were publicly subjected to torture that included flaying, burning alive, amputation of various body parts—including parts of the face—and various other atrocities. Though they may have limited this treatment to punitive measures for the most flagrant offenders, one can be certain that the extent of the destruction prophesied for Nineveh stirred little pity among her victims.[2]

Nahum was the herald of God's intention to call Assyria to account for its unbridled brutality. He thereby vindicated God's justice and proclaimed his sovereignty. Empires rise and fall only at his bidding, and through the orchestrations of history, each nation receives its just due. This is a sterling example of Israel's theology of history. The proclamation preceded the event so that none should mistake sovereign intervention for the "natural" ebb and flow of history. In Israel's theology, the latter did not exist.

---

[2]For a treatment of the Assyrian military, see H. W. F. Saggs, *The Might That Was Assyria* (London: Sidgwick and Jackson, 1984), 243–68.

Questions for Further Study and Discussion

1. What relevance does the message of Nahum have today?
2. Compare the books of Jonah and Nahum in regard to the judgments they pronounced against Nineveh.

For Further Reading

Armerding, Carl E. "Nahum." *EBC*. Vol. 7. Grand Rapids: Zondervan, 1985.

Baker, David W. *Nahum, Habakkuk, Zephaniah*. TOTC. Downers Grove, Ill.: InterVarsity, 1988.

Maier, Walter. *The Book of Nahum*. Grand Rapids: Baker, 1959. The most thorough of the evangelical treatments.

Robertson, O. Palmer. *The Books of Nahum, Habakkuk, and Zephaniah*. NICOT. Grand Rapids: Eerdmans, 1990.

Smith, Ralph L. *Micah–Malachi*. WBC. Vol. 32. Waco, Tex.: Word, 1984.

Chapter 40

Habakkuk

Little is known of the prophet Habak-kuk, for no genealogical or historical information about him is given in the book. Unlike most of the other prophetic books, this one places a higher priority on addressing a particular topic rather than simply serving as a literary vehicle to preserve the oracles of the prophet (see chap. 27, esp. pp. 313–14). In this sense it is more like Jonah than like Jeremiah, for example. Furthermore, the "wisdom" tone of the prophecy and its organization around the inquiries of the prophet distinguish it from the rest of the prophetic literature (see chap. 21, esp. p. 248). The wisdom tone is evident in its focus on the justice of God.

The Writing of the Book

There is little dispute concerning the unity or integrity of the book. There is more room for discussion, however, about the date of the prophecy. Parameters may be established from information within the book. In 1:5–6 the raising up of the Chaldeans (so KJV; "Babylonians," NIV) is identified as something astonishing and unexpected. The Chaldeans took control of the throne of Babylon, declaring independence from Assyria in 626 B.C.

By 612 Nineveh, the Assyrian capital, had fallen, but as early as 614, the alliance between the Medes and the Babylonians portended their eventual success against Assyria. The statements of 1:5–6 would be most understandable if they were made prior to 626. Though they could possibly come as late as 615, any time beyond that would seem to trivialize the claim of these verses.

It should also be noted that this judgment on Judah at the hands of the Chaldeans was coming "in your days" (1:5). The judgment referred to could hardly apply to anything earlier than 597 B.C., when Judah had its first major confrontation with Babylon. Calculating a generation prior to this suggests about 640 as the earliest likely date for the prophecy.

Josiah came to the throne of Judah in 640, and some interpreters have felt that the negative conditions in Judah described in Habakkuk 1:2–4 would not be likely during the reign of a good king such as he. Yet it seems to stretch the chronological limits too far to extend the prophecy back into the reign of Josiah's wicked grandfather, Manasseh. It should also be remembered that Josiah was a child when he came to the throne, and he did not begin his reforms until twelve years into his reign. Even then, the reform focused more on matters of cultic practice than on a social agenda. As a result, the complaints of injustice by Habakkuk were not necessarily contradictory to the nature of the early years of Josiah's reign. The injustice fostered by the fifty-year rule of Manasseh would not have dissipated quickly.

The boundaries thus established for the prophecies of Habakkuk suggest that they should be dated somewhere between 640 and 626 B.C., with 630 perhaps being the best estimate. This would make Habakkuk a contemporary of Jeremiah.

The Background

Ashurbanipal had come to the Assyrian throne in 668 and had inherited an empire that was at its height of glory. By the end of his reign, however, deterioration was evident and the tumultuous fall was to come within a score of years. Trouble arose as early as the mid-650s, when Psammetichus I, the Egyptian pharaoh, began to clear the Assyrians out of Egypt. Ashurbanipal was unable to prevent this, for he was largely preoccupied with the civil war taking place in the southeastern part of the empire. There his brother, Shamash-shum-ukin, backed by the Elamites and Chaldeans, was attempting to wrest control of Babylon from Ashurbanipal and establish it as an independent kingdom. Though this attempt was unsuccessful, the hope of independence did not die with Shamash-shum-ukin; this region remained unstable until the collapse of Assyria. Unrest persisted throughout the empire during Ashurbanipal's reign, though Assyria continued to succeed in suppressing any serious challenges to its power.

By 630, Ashurbanipal yielded the reigns of the faltering empire to his son, Ashur-etil-ilani—though whether he did so voluntarily is not known. After Ashurbani-

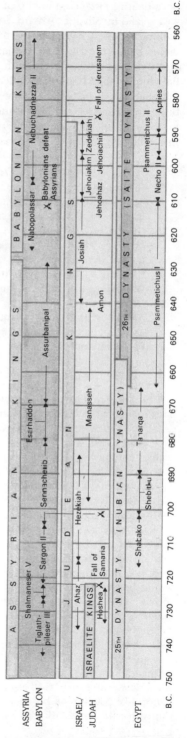

401

pal's death in 627 B.C., the city of Babylon was seized by Sin-shar-ishkun, brother of Ashur-etil-ilani. A year later, the Chaldeans in turn drove out Sin-shar-ishkun and thereby established the independent Babylonian state under the rule of Nabopolassar. It was he who would eventually bring the ancient Near East under Babylonian control and deliver the new empire into the hands of his capable son, Nebuchadrezzar. These days of the waning power of Assyria form the backdrop for the prophecy of Habakkuk.

As Assyrian power continued to disintegrate, the reforms of the young king Josiah began to take hold in Judah. No longer menaced by the threat of Assyrian recriminations, Josiah freely laid a visionary foundation for the people's return to the ideals of the covenant.

Outline of the Book

I. Discourse 1
   A. Prayer: Habakkuk's complaint concerning Judah (1:1–4)
   B. Answer: Oracle of judgment—Babylon to invade Judah (1:5–11)
II. Discourse 2
   A. Prayer: Habakkuk's questions concerning God's justice (1:12–17)
   B. Instruction from God (2:1–3)
   C. Answer 1: Responsibility of the righteous (2:4–5)
   D. Answer 2: Oracle of judgment against Babylon (2:6–20)
III. Discourse 3
   A. Prayer: Habakkuk's request for mercy (3:1–2)
   B. Reflection: The sovereign power of God to deliver (3:3–15)
   C. Acceptance: Habakkuk's trust in God's sovereignty (3:16–19)

Purpose and Message

The Assyrian Empire had been dominant for more than a century, and by 630 B.C. it seemed apparent that decline was irreversible and would lead to a major realignment of world political power. One of the problems that faced the prophets was reconciling the fact that Assyria, the rod of God, was passing from the scene, yet Judah remained unpunished for her obvious offenses against God and the covenant. Habakkuk's complaint about this dismal state of affairs brought the response from God that the Babylonians would be the divine means of punishing Judah. This revelation introduces the major topic for discussion in the book.

The book's purpose is to examine the issue of God's justice on a national plane. The question at hand in the theodicy (the justification of God's ways with humanity) was, How can a just God use a wicked nation like Babylon as his instrument for punishment? Habakkuk did not suggest that the people of Judah were not deserving of punishment. Rather, if God gave the Babylonians victory over Judah, would that not show God's approval of the Babylonians? In many ways the book of Habakkuk deals with the same basic issue as the book of Job. Job was concerned about the justice of God when a righteous individual was suffering; Habakkuk was concerned about the justice of God when a wicked nation was prospering.

As in the book of Job, the message of the book is found in God's response. Job is answered by being confronted with the awesomeness of God. The theophany (visible appearance of God) was intended on the one hand to inspire trust in God's wisdom and on the other hand to demonstrate that mortal finiteness restricts human ability to find answers to some of the questions of life. In Habakkuk, the theophany of chapter 3 accomplishes the same thing. The display of God's presence should be in one sense sufficient in and of itself to promote trust even when answers are not forthcoming.

Unlike the book of Job, however, God did give Habakkuk a few answers as well. These actually serve as the core to the message of the book. The twofold answer to Habakkuk's question concerning God's use of the Babylonians helps to put things in their proper perspective. The first part of the answer is given in 2:4–5, where individual responsibility is addressed. Even when the world is in confusion and God's purposes and plans are obscured, the righteous person has a responsibility to conduct himself with integrity. It is in those situations that faithfulness to God and trust in him are most difficult and so most significant. In the shadow of trying circumstances, the integrity and faith of a righteous person shine like a beacon.

The second part of the answer offers some assurances with regard to God's justice. The message of 2:6–20 was that God would punish the Babylonians for their wickedness, but that the time had not yet come. His use of the Babylonians as an instrument to punish Judah did not imply approval of them. Until their time of punishment arrived, God could use them as he would.

Structure and Organization

The book of Habakkuk is organized around the prayers of the prophet and the responses by the Lord. The dialogue begins with a complaint to the Lord about the injustice that the prophet saw all around him. This serves to introduce the main question of the book, Why do the wicked go unpunished? God's response in 1:5–11 asserts that this situation would not last for long, because that generation was going to come under divine judgment at the hands of the Babylonians. This sets the scene for the book's message: The wicked will not go unpunished.

The second prayer of Habakkuk advances the discussion to the next point of logic. Here the argument arose that the Babylonian involvement, far from solving the dilemma about God's justice, only raised more serious questions. Now a people even more wicked than the Israelites not only was going unpunished, but also was enjoying victory.

Habakkuk did not pose these questions brashly or presumptuously. His attitude appeared to be one of sincere inquiry rather than self-righteous challenge. Nevertheless, God affirmed that what he promised would happen (2:2–3), and then went on to address Habakkuk concerning the questions that had been raised. It should be noticed that God did not seek to defend his justice. Instead of answering the "why" sort of question, he began by suggesting that human responsibility lay not in having all the answers, but in responding to God in the proper way.

The key to this is found in 2:4b: "But the righteous will live by his faith." Though the apostle Paul later quoted this verse in the context of his emphasis on faith over works (Rom. 1:17; Gal. 3:11), here it serves the function of suggesting that the upright person will maintain his lifestyle of integrity and faithfulness even when he does not understand God's ways. This offers a simple reaffirmation of the principle portrayed in the oracle of judgment against Judah (1:5–11). This in turn leads to the next section, in which the oracle of judgment against Babylon (2:6–20) confirms God's justice: The wicked will be punished.

Recognizing his obligation to live in a right relationship with God and to trust that God, in his justice, will punish the wicked, Habakkuk's third prayer (3:1–2) requested that God be merciful in the exercise of his wrath. This led to the hymn of 3:3–15 that depicts an appearance of God in judgment but also in deliverance (v. 13), thus reflecting the two answers previously given. The end result of this (3:16–19) was the acceptance of God's justice, not because a full explanation was given, but because God is God and people are but dust. Acceptance was not an act of philosophical nihilism, but simply an act of trust.

Major Theme

God's Policy for Handling Nations

The theology of the book concerns God's policies in dealing with nations. From Habakkuk and other books of the Old Testament, we can draw the inference (introduced in the study of Jeremiah) that God's dealing with nations can be understood by using the analogy of a scale balancing good and bad conduct. Each successive generation of a nation can be pictured as loading weights into the dish on the good side or the dish on the evil side. Under the evil side we can imagine a button that sounds a bell. When the evil side sufficiently outweighs the good side, the dish will press against the button, signaling that judgment is now required. This analogy can explain various statements in the Old Testament that indicate that a city or people were wicked enough to mandate God's judgment (e.g., Gen. 18:20–21; 15:16; cf. Lev. 18:25; Jonah 1:2).

At times the mandated judgment can be postponed by a sudden repentance that in effect begins putting weights on the good side and lifts the dish off the button (Jonah 3:10; 2 Kings 22:19–20). Then it is only when wicked behavior resumes that the nation endangers itself. This is the meaning of a passage like Jeremiah 18:7–10, in which we see successive generations treated according to their deeds.

Beyond this basic scheme, a few caveats can also be inferred from passages of Scripture. The first is that good conduct apparently carries more weight than evil conduct. Deuteronomy 5:9–10 relates that the effects of a wicked generation become evident to the third or fourth generation, while the impact of a righteous generation carries influence to thousands of generations.

A second caveat is that the scale is only emptied when God judges the wickedness that has been accumulated. In Exodus 32:34 Moses had made an impassioned plea for God's mercy toward the Israelites in the aftermath of their worshiping the golden calf. God agreed to spare them from judgment at that time, but insisted that when the time for punishment came (again), they would be punished for this sin as well. To complete the analogy, God's mercy is like a thumb pressed down on the good side of the scale so that the bell stops ringing; but the "weight" of their sin is not removed from the dish—they will still be punished for that sin at some future time when God removes his thumb and punishment is again mandated.

The final caveat can easily be inferred from the Old Testament, but is stated explicitly in the New: To whom much is given shall much be required (cf. Luke 12:48). Using the analogy of the scale, this means that revelation has the effect of raising the button closer to the dish. As a result, those like the Israelites who have benefited from having the law of the Lord revealed to them will be judged by God for less offense than those who have not so benefited. God will tolerate a lot more from the pagans than he will from his chosen people before judgment is sanctioned.

This last principle provides further explanation for the dilemma faced by Habakkuk. Even though the Babylonians were more wicked than the Israelites, Israel should have known better. They had not only the law, but also the warnings sent by God through the prophets. Therefore the time for their judgment had already come, while the judgment for the Babylonians had not yet been mandated.

It must be remembered that this scheme is only applicable as a whole to nations. There need be no fear here of a doctrine of salvation by works, for these principles concern nations, not individuals. Furthermore, there is no reason to think that God's way of dealing with nations has changed since Old Testament times. The book of Habakkuk gives us confidence in God's sovereign and just control in a world today that often ap- pears on the brink of self-destruction. We cannot expect to be privy to the inner workings of God's day-by-day operations, but we can rest assured that his purposes are being accomplished.

Questions for Further Study and Discussion

1. What is the significance of chapter 3 for the message and purpose of the book of Habakkuk?
2. How should the theology of nations presented here affect our understanding of current events?

For Further Reading

Armerding, Carl E. "Habakkuk." *EBC*. Vol. 7. Grand Rapids: Zondervan, 1985. 493–534.

Baker, David W. *Nahum, Habakkuk, Zephaniah*. TOTC. Downers Grove, Ill.: InterVarsity, 1988.

Gowan, Donald E. *The Triumph of Faith in Habakkuk*. Atlanta: John Knox, 1974.

Robertson, O. Palmer. *The Books of Nahum, Habakkuk, and Zephaniah*. NICOT. Grand Rapids: Eerdmans, 1990.

Smith, Ralph L. *Micah–Malachi*. WBC. Vol. 32. Waco, Tex.: Word, 1984.

Each of these commentaries is broadly evangelical and offers helpful treatment of the text.

Chapter 41

Zephaniah

Zephaniah, who was possibly a member of the royal household (if the person mentioned in 1:1 was King Hezekiah), was a contemporary of Jeremiah. These two prophets signaled the beginning of God's witness to Judah during the turbulent Babylonian period that would eventually bring the destruction of Jerusalem and the temple. Their ministries were the parallel of those of Micah and Isaiah a century earlier. In the interim the only prophets whose writings were preserved were Habakkuk and Nahum, and their oracles were directed primarily against foreign nations. There may have been prophets pronouncing judgment earlier in the seventh century, but the religious conditions in Manasseh's regime discouraged dissent and criticism and would have hampered prophetic activity. With Zephaniah, then, came a resurgence of prophetic witness, announcing the coming judgment on Judah.

The Writing of the Book

In the superscription to the book (1:1), the prophecies of Zephaniah are dated to the reign of Josiah (640–609 B.C.). Of greater interest, however, is the question of whether the prophecies came before or after the reforms of Josiah (628 and 622 B.C.; see 2 Chron. 34:3, 8). In Zephaniah 1:4–6 the list of the people who were to be cut off is very similar to those targeted by Josiah's reform (2 Kings 23:4–7). Unless Zephaniah was suggesting that Josiah's reforms had not accomplished in practice what they set out to do in theory, this similarity would support a date prior to the reform of 622. It is possible that because 1:4 refers to the remnant of Baal, the prophecy is best placed between the two reforms and was meant to encourage Josiah to finish the good work he had begun.

A date about 627 or 626 B.C. would also fit well with events that were taking place in the political arena. Ashurbanipal, the last of the great Assyrian kings, died in 627, and the Babylonians declared their independence from Assyria the next year. These would serve as a fine setting for the pronouncement of the doom of Nineveh in 2:13–15. Tentatively, then, the date that seems most fitting for the prophecy of Zephaniah is 627/626, which is also when the prophetic career of Jeremiah was inaugurated.

The Background

The five decades of Manasseh's apostasy (697–642 B.C.) exacted a heavy spiritual toll on Judah from which she never totally recovered. A whole generation knew no other king but Manasseh. His official sponsorship of religious syncretism saw Baalism and other Canaanite practices reinstituted that had always been at least on the fringes of Israelite religion since the exodus from Egypt a millennium earlier.

Josiah's reform measures were the most austere ever attempted. They succeeded in changing the Israelite religious practices and ridding Israelite worship of foreign elements, but they apparently failed to change the hearts of the people. As a result, freedom from bondage to the Assyrians did not usher in the heralded ideal Davidic king who would restore the boundaries of Israel and the prominence of Jerusalem. Instead, it merely marked a transition from Assyrian control of Israel to Babylonian control.

Outline of the Book

I. Judgment
  A. Warning of universal judgment (1:1–3)
  B. Judgment against Judah and Jerusalem (1:4–13)
  C. The Day of the Lord (1:14–2:3)
    1. Judgment against Philistia (2:4–7)
    2. Judgment against Moab and Ammon (2:8–11)
    3. Judgment against Cush (2:12)
    4. Judgment against Assyria (2:13–15)
  D. Indictment against Judah and Jerusalem (3:1–7)
  E. Warning of universal judgment (3:8)
II. Restoration (3:9–20)

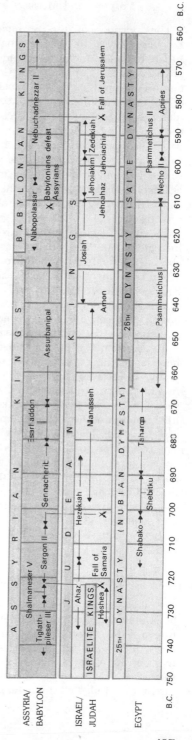

Purpose and Message

The purpose of the prophecies of Zephaniah was to initiate change in Judah by pronouncing God's judgment on wickedness. Coupled with God's intention to punish came the proclamation of his intention to restore Judah. The message of Zephaniah was focused on the Day of the Lord which, he contended, was fast approaching. His indictment of Judah included denunciation of her corrupt officials and her continuing rebellion against the Lord. (This fits into the religio-spiritual category of oracle; see chap. 27, esp. pp. 313–14.)

Judgment against Judah was clearly indicated, but Zephaniah was vague about the form that judgment would take. There is no mention of siege, exile, or a Babylonian threat. The universal nature of the judgment is a significant part of the book's perspective and suggested to the audience that the political upheaval they were experiencing at that time would have far-reaching effects. The instruction given (2:1–3) was directed toward the humble of the land and urged them to seek the Lord so that in his mercy they might be spared from the judgment that was to come on the rest of the people. The restoration that is projected in 3:9–20, like the indictment, was for the most part religio-spiritual in nature. The purified remnant would enjoy peace and the favor of the Lord, who was their king and deliverer (3:15). The reference to gathering (3:20) is the only intimation of exile.

Structure and Organization

Besides Amos, Zephaniah is the only book among the minor prophets to feature a series of oracles against the nations. In Amos they pronounced judgment on Israel and Judah; in Zephaniah they served as examples of the Lord's intention to judge all the nations. In this way the judgment that was declared against Judah was not viewed in isolation, but as part of Yahweh's overall agenda articulated in the concept of the Day of the Lord.

Major Theme

The Day of the Lord

The expression "the Day of the Lord" was used by the prophets to indicate the time when the current state of affairs will be replaced by the Lord's intended order of things. Most of the oracles in the prophetic literature represent movement toward this ideal condition. What becomes plain as prophecy unfolds is that the new state is to be achieved, not through one immense intervention of God (though such an intervention may be involved in the last step), but through a process of dealing with inequities that have become a great threat to the desired end.

The result of this is that there may be numerous "days of the Lord" before *the* Day of the Lord that will inaugurate a new order that will never again be at risk or destabilized. In this way the overthrow of the Assyrian Empire can rightfully be considered the Day of the Lord; likewise the Fall of Babylon. The destruction of Jerusalem and the temple surely qualified as the Day of the Lord, as did Josiah's campaign to reform the priesthood.

In the Day of the Lord, justice is done. This is a positive time for those who have been victims, but a day of reckoning for those who have been oppressors. It has political, social, spiritual, and cosmic ramifications and can include reversal or restructuring of any number of conditions. For example, overlords will serve those who were formerly their vassals; the poor will be elevated over the rich who had exploited them; people will again call on the name of the Lord; and there will be darkness even at midday. This reversal is a common motif in prophetic literature dealing with the Day of the Lord and is called a "world upside down."[1]

The people of Judah and Israel had always anticipated that the Day of the Lord would be a time of rejoicing for them. They expected that their enemies would be destroyed and their nation would be exalted to become the chief of the nations, with a Davidic king ruling over a vast empire. Early on, prophets like Amos doused such optimism by insisting that the Israelites would be counted among God's enemies who were ripe for punishment (Amos 5:18–20). Only after punishment and purging would the hoped-for benefits be realized. Thus the Day of the Lord became widely proclaimed by the prophets to convey God's approaching judgment on Israel and Judah, though the related aftermath oracles conveyed that God's eventual new order was to feature a politically restored and theologically purified people.

Questions for Further Study and Discussion

1. Compare and contrast the contemporaneous prophets Zephaniah and Jeremiah.
2. What is the significance of the "world upside down" concept for understanding prophetic literature? In what other places in the Bible is "world upside down" identifiable?
3. Discuss whether God's eventual world order is pictured in the Old Testament as coming within a historical framework or as a final condition when history has ended.
4. What do you see as the spiritual aspects of this final order of things? The political aspects?

For Further Reading

Baker, David W. *Nahum, Habakkuk, Zephaniah.* TOTC. Downers Grove, Ill.: InterVarsity, 1988.

Craigie, Peter C. *Twelve Prophets.* Vol. 2. Daily Study Bible: Old Testament Series. Philadelphia: Westminster, 1985.

Robertson, O. Palmer. *The Books of Nahum, Habakkuk, and Zephaniah.* NICOT. Grand Rapids: Eerdmans, 1990.

Smith, Ralph L. *Micah–Malachi.* WBC. Vol. 32. Waco, Tex.: Word, 1984.

Walker, Larry. "Zephaniah." *EBC.* Vol. 7. Grand Rapids: Zondervan, 1985.

Each of these commentaries gives helpful evangelical analysis of the book.

[1]See R. van Leeuwen, "Proverbs 30:21–23 and the Biblical World Upside Down," *JBL* 105 (1986): 599–610.

Chapter 42

Haggai

Haggai and Zechariah are complementary books of prophecy of the postexilic period. Along with Daniel, Joel, and Malachi, they comprise the corpus of Old Testament prophetic literature dating to the Persian period of Hebrew history (ca. 550–330 B.C.). Haggai exhorted the Hebrew restoration community in Jerusalem to rebuild the temple and to reinstitute the liturgical calendar, including proper Levitical sacrifice, worship, and observation of the feast days. The prophet Zechariah complemented Haggai's call to erect the temple in his summons for an accompanying spiritual renewal among the people of God.

The Writing of the Book

Two expressions identify Haggai as a "spokesman" for God. He is called "the prophet" (1:1; 2:1, 10; Ezra 6:14) and he is labeled "the Lord's messenger" (1:13). Both titles attest the prophet's divine commission. Haggai was a contemporary of Zechariah, and through their combined ministry the temple was rebuilt in Jerusalem. Additional biographical information is scant. According to a tradition preserved by Epiphanius (an ascetic monk and the bishop of Salamis, ca. A.D. 315–403), Haggai was among those who came to Jerusalem from Babylonia under the leadership of Sheshbazzar. However, he is not numbered in the catalog of returnees recorded in Ezra 1–2. Attempts to identify Haggai as a priest on the basis of his teaching about ritual purity in 2:11–14 remain unconvincing.

Haggai's four messages were delivered to the restoration community in Jerusalem during a four-month period and were dated precisely to the second year of the Persian king Darius. The specific dates for his pronouncements may be converted as shown in figure 42.1.

It is assumed that Haggai penned his own prophecy, although the individual oracles are little more than résumés in the third person, and the book itself is silent on the issue of authorship. Even though the date of 520 B.C. for Haggai's prophetic activity is universally acknowledged, the interval between public address and written compilation is open to question. It seems likely that the book was completed sometime between Haggai's challenge to rebuild the temple in 520 B.C. and the completion of its reconstruction in 516/515 B.C.

Figure 42.1. Dating Haggai's Oracles

		520 B.C.
1:1	Year 2, month 6, day 1	= 29 August
2:1	Year 2, month 7, day 21	= 17 October
2:10	Year 2, month 9, day 24	= 18 December
2:20	Year 2, month 9, day 24	= 18 December

The Background

The backdrop for Haggai's prophecy was the reign of Darius I, king of Persia from 521 to 486 B.C. Cyrus had consolidated his power base by defeating the Medes in 549 B.C. and was welcomed into Babylon as king of Persia in 539. According to the Cyrus Cylinder, a decree issued in 538 B.C. permitted conquered peoples who had been deported by the Babylonians to return to their homelands. This naturally included the Jews, although they are not named on the cylinder (see illustration, chap. 19).

The first wave of emigrants to Jerusalem numbered 42,360 along with 7,337 servants (cf. Ezra 2:64–65), and they were led by Sheshbazzar (Ezra 1:5–11). He was a prince of Judah and became the first governor of the restoration community. The foundation for a new temple was laid during the early stages of his administration (Ezra 5:16). The meager project was soon abandoned, however, as the vision of a temple-state described by Ezekiel quickly faded amid the stark reality of Persian domination and the problems of survival in a city surrounded by hostile foreigners and plagued by drought and crop failure.

Zerubbabel, the new governor, and Joshua, a priest, were inspired by the ministry of the prophets Haggai and Zechariah to mobilize the community for a second reconstruction project in 520 B.C. (Ezra 5:11–12). The rebuilding of the temple was finally completed in 515 B.C. (Hag. 1:15; Ezra 6:15; cf. 3:8–13), some seventeen years after the initial attempt was made under the guidance of Sheshbazzar.

The story of Haggai and Zerubbabel ends abruptly, and only Zerubbabel is mentioned again in the Old Testament (in the book of Zechariah). We can understand this silence for Haggai, since he had fulfilled his divine commission as a prophet. As for Zerubbabel, it is probable (although the documentation is sketchy) that he was either executed or deposed by order of King Darius, who was attempting to control social turmoil in his newly acquired empire by subduing anyone in Persia or outlying provinces who was deemed a political liability (see fig. 42.2).

Outline of the Book

I. Message 1: Haggai's challenge to covenant renewal
   A. The call to rebuild the temple (1:1–11)
   B. The remnant responds (1:12–15)
II. Message 2: The promise of restoration (2:1–9)
III. Message 3: The call to holiness (2:10–19)
IV. Message 4: Zerubbabel: Davidic servant and "signet ring" (2:20–23)

Purpose and Message

Haggai was a prophet on a solitary mission. His divinely assigned task was to instigate the reconstruction of the temple of God, which had been plundered and left in ruins by the Babylonians nearly seventy years earlier. The prophet's four interrelated messages were designed to fulfill that commission by awakening the

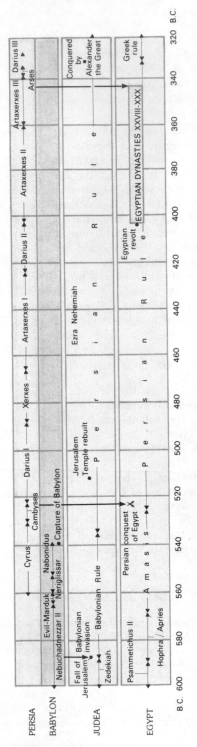

people of Jerusalem to the responsibilities, obligations, privileges, and promises of their covenant heritage.

In the first address, Haggai upbraided the community of former exiles for their preoccupation with personal comforts (e.g., "living in your paneled houses," 1:3) while the temple precinct remained a heap of rubble (or at best a bare foundation from the abandoned reconstruction project). Haggai's unflagging zeal and single-mindedness served effectively as a foil to the complacency and truancy of the people.

On the second occasion, the man of God called the people to repentance and challenged them to honor the Lord by rebuilding his temple. The repeated expression "give careful thought to your ways" (1:5, 7) actually connotes bringing about a change or establishing a new relationship. Essentially Haggai called the people to make covenant renewal with Yahweh, as the divine oath of affirmation in 1:13 indicates. The people responded immediately, their actions recorded tersely in 1:12, 14: they "obeyed," "feared the Lord," and "began to work."

Haggai's third declaration revealed God's intention to overthrow the nations and restore the fortunes of Israel. It served to encourage and unify the community in their initiative. The reminder that divine justice was still operative in human history both fortified the people in spirit and awakened dormant faith. The long-deferred hope of Zion's "shame changed into praise" was finally becoming a reality (cf. Zeph. 3:14–20, esp. v. 19).

In the fourth address, the promise to establish Zerubbabel as a "signet ring" in Zion rekindled the messianic expectation among the Israelites. The terms "my servant" and "chosen" (2:23) have direct association with the Messiah concept presented elsewhere in the Old Testament (e.g., Isa. 41:8; 42:1; 50:10; 52:13; 53:11). More important, the signet was a symbol of royal authority, much like a scepter or crown. Zerubbabel's designation as the "signet of the Lord" indicated God had canceled the curse pronounced by Jeremiah on King Jehoiachin and his descendants (cf. Jer. 22:24–30). The restoration of royal authority to the Davidic family as referred by Haggai to Zerubbabel represented a resumption of the Judahite messianic lineage (cf. Matt. 1:11–12). As such, Haggai's prophecy constituted a divine pledge vindicating Israel as God's elect and guaranteeing his fulfillment of all covenant vows.

Structure and Organization

Each of Haggai's four messages is dated exactly to a day and month in Darius' second year of rule over Persia. The practice has its precedent in the prophecies of Jeremiah and Ezekiel (cf. Jer. 1:2–3; Ezek. 1:1). Unlike their preexilic predecessors, the exilic prophets such as Jeremiah and Ezekiel could not date their revelations by the reigns of Judean or Israelite kings. Instead they keyed their words from God to the year of Babylonian exile, which served as a "covenant time clock" marking the duration of the curse of captivity and counting down with anticipation and hope toward the blessing of release and renewal (cf. Jer. 52:31; Ezek. 20:1).

The postexilic prophets Haggai and Zechariah dated their prophecies so precisely during the days of Persian rule because Isaiah foresaw the importance of Cyrus and the Persians to the fortunes of elect Israel (Isa. 45:1–13). It is very likely that both Haggai and Zechariah—in light of Ezekiel's temple vision (chaps. 40–48)—understood the rebuilding of the temple as the cornerstone of the long-awaited messianic age. Thus the chronological precision attached to their oracles may have served as reminders of Yahweh's intentions to restore unified kingship under the prince of David (cf. Ezek. 37:15–28).

The repetition of the messenger formula ("thus says the LORD" and its variations) some twenty-nine times in two short chapters underscored the gravity of the message and the urgency of the hour for the people of God.

Further investigation of the language and themes in Haggai reveal chiastic patterns, or the deliberate inversion of word order and ideas. The first and third messages both begin with the formula "this is what the LORD Almighty says" (1:2; 2:11), treat the topic of current agricultural blight, and conclude on a note of curse or warning. The second and fourth messages both close with the expression "declares the Lord Almighty" (2:9, 23), promise the seismic shaking of creation, and predict blessing and restoration for Israel.

The book of Haggai also gives evidence of considerable literary skill in multiple ways:

— Its use of varied phraseology (e.g., nine different constructions of the messenger formula)

— The use of chiasmus for emphasis (e.g., 1:4, 9, 10; 2:23)

— The word play on "ruin" (Heb., *hārēb*, 1:4) and "drought" (Heb., *hōreb*, 1:11)

— The repetition of the imperative mood (e.g., "give careful thought to" in 1:5, 7; 2:15, 18)

— The use of the rhetorical question in three of the four messages (e.g., 1:4; 2:3, 19).

Major Theme

The Temple

Moses had intimated that eventually there would be one place where the Lord God would establish his name (Deut. 14:23–25; 16:2, 11). Shiloh was the interim site for Yahweh's name as the tabernacle was stationed there during the era of the tribal league (Josh. 18:1). Ultimately David obtained the permanent site for Yahweh's name when he purchased the threshing floor of Araunah near Jerusalem with the intention of building a temple for God (2 Sam. 24:18–25; 1 Chron. 21:18–30).

Figure 42.2. Limestone relief uncovered at Persepolis in Persia, showing King Darius seated on the throne with Crown Prince Xerxes, attendants, and guards behind him. (*The Oriental Institute, Univ. of Chicago*)

Although he was denied the privilege of building the temple by decree of the prophet Nathan (2 Sam. 7:1–17), King David collected the raw materials necessary for its construction and made ample preparation to ensure that the project would succeed (1 Chron. 22:1–16). David's son, King Solomon, actually confirmed the blueprint for the temple's design and organized the labor for its construction (1 Kings 5–6).

It took seven years to complete the erection of the temple (1 Kings 6:37–38). The glory of Yahweh in the form of a cloud entered the sanctuary upon Solomon's prayer of dedication (ca. 953 B.C.; 1 Kings 8). The temple symbolized God's presence among his people and served as a tangible reminder of Yahweh's covenant with Israel. Its physical existence in the Jewish community was designed to prompt obedience to covenant stipulations and inspire true worship of the Lord.

By the time of Jeremiah (ca. 627–582 B.C.), the temple had become a fetish or talisman. The people of Judah assumed that the mere association of Yahweh's temple with Jerusalem and the people of God ensured protection and security. Jeremiah indignantly condemned this misplaced trust in the physical structure and predicted its eventual destruction (Jer. 7–10; esp. 7:1–11). Later Ezekiel saw the cloud of glory depart from the temple, signifying God's disaffection for the Judahites because of their idolatry and great abominations committed in the temple precincts (ca. 591 B.C.; cf. Ezek. 8, 10). Jeremiah's pronouncement of doom was fulfilled in 587 B.C., when King Nebuchadrezzar and the Babylonians looted the temple and the city of Jerusalem (2 Kings 25:8–17).

The message of Haggai to rebuild the temple and thus revive the flow of God's covenantal blessings to Israel should not be viewed as a contradiction to the words of Jeremiah. Haggai called the people to proper worship of Yahweh in contrast to blind faith in a building. He also assumed that the appropriate attitudes of reverence and humility and unfeigned behavior demonstrating obedience to the law of God would naturally accompany the initiative to reconstruct the temple edifice. Then this second temple would again symbolize the covenant presence of Yahweh among his people and stamp the Hebrew repatriates as the elect of God among the nations.

Questions for Further Study and Discussion

1. What does Haggai contribute to our understanding of the temple of God in the Old Testament?
2. What was the significance of Haggai's fourth message for the Davidic dynasty and the messianic expectation in postexilic times?
3. How is the task facing the Christian church today similar to the situation that Haggai encountered?

For Further Reading

Alden, Robert L. "Haggai." *EBC*. Vol. 7. Grand Rapids: Zondervan, 1985. 569–94.

Baldwin, Joyce G. *Haggai, Zechariah, Malachi*. TOTC. Downers Grove, Ill.: InterVarsity, 1972.

Craigie, Peter C. *The Twelve Prophets*. Vol. 2. Daily Study Bible: Old Testament series. Philadelphia: Westminster, 1984. Interesting and thoughtful application of Haggai's message to the Christian church, especially in regard to theory versus practice and "voluntarism."

Meyers, Carol, and Eric Meyers. *Haggai and Zechariah 1–8*. AB. Vol. 25B. New York: Doubleday, 1987.

Petersen, D. L. *Haggai and Zechariah 1–8*. OTL. Philadelphia: Westminster, 1984.

Smith, Ralph L. *Micah–Malachi*. WBC. Vol. 32. Waco, Tex.: Word, 1984.

Verhoef, P. A. *The Books of Haggai and Malachi*. NICOT. Grand Rapids: Eerdmans, 1987. Thorough research, careful exegesis, reverent exposition, and practical application. The most detailed evangelical commentary available on Haggai.

Wolf, Herbert M. *Haggai and Malachi*. EvBC. Chicago: Moody Press, 1976. Solidly evangelical, brief and easy to read, yet thorough and well-researched.

Wolff, Hans Walter. *Haggai: A Commentary*. Translated by M. Kohl. Minneapolis: Augsburg, 1988.

Chapter 43

Zechariah

Haggai and Zechariah were complementary postexilic prophets. Zechariah was the younger and began prophesying about two months after Haggai's brief, ministry. While Haggai called on the people to erect the temple of God, Zechariah summoned the community to repentance and spiritual renewal. His task was to prepare the people for proper worship and temple service once the building project was completed.

"Zechariah" means "Yah(weh) has remembered," which is the essence of his message to Jerusalem after the Exile. The book's superscription identifies him as the son of Berekiah and the grandson of Iddo (1:1). Ezra records Zechariah as the son of Iddo (5:1; 6:14); here the word "son" was used simply to designate "any descendant." The frequency with which the name "Zechariah" appears in the Old Testament—some thirty-two people are called by it—invites misidentification. For example, Zechariah, son of Berekiah, is not to be confused with Zechariah, son of Jeberekiah (Isa. 8:2).

According to Nehemiah, Zechariah's grandfather, Iddo, returned to Jerusalem from the Babylonian captivity with Zerubbabel and Joshua (12:4). Elsewhere Nehemiah lists Zechariah as the head of the priestly family of Iddo (12:16). This means Zechariah was a member of the tribe of Levi and served in Jerusalem as both a priest and a prophet.

The Writing of the Book

The date and history of the book of Zechariah are directly linked to one's view of the literary unity of the composition. Conservative biblical scholars have traditionally upheld the literary integrity of Zechariah, while scholars inclined toward more critical viewpoints have divided the book into two or three distinct literary segments. Those holding to a Second or even a Third Zechariah do so on the basis of perceived differences in style, vocabulary, theme, and genre (i.e., apocalyptic) between the sections.

Both scholarly camps readily assign the materials of chapters 1–8 to Zechariah the prophet of 520–518 B.C. The chronology of Zechariah's ministry is keyed to the reign of the Persian king Darius (ca. 521–486 B.C.). Based on the three date formulas in the book, the specific dates for Zechariah's pronouncements may be converted as follows.

The time lag between these utterances

1:1–6	Year 2, month 8	= Oct./Nov. 520 B.C.
1:7–6:8	Year 2, month 11, day 24	= 15 February 519 B.C.
7–8	Year 4, month 9, day 4	= 7 December 518 B.C.

of Zechariah and the actual composition of the prophecies is difficult to determine. Because chapters 1–8 fail to mention a rebuilt temple in Jerusalem, it seems likely that this portion of the book was compiled before the temple's reconstruction and dedication (ca. 520–515 B.C.; cf. Ezra 6:13–22).

Scholarly opinion is sharply divided over the remaining chapters of Zechariah. Conservative scholars ascribe them to Zechariah, son of Berekiah, and it is usually suggested that he wrote these oracles later in his life. They often cite the failure of the Persian expedition against Greece under King Xerxes as the event prompting the prophecies of chapters 9–14. They also emphasize the similarities in style, theme, vocabulary, and theology of the two parts of the book while attributing the differences to Zechariah's age, the peculiar nature of apocalyptic literature, and the changing historical and political circumstances of the later Persian Empire. The final draft of the book of Zechariah was probably completed sometime between 500 and 470 B.C.[1]

Many biblical scholars assign chapters 9–11 to a "Second" Zechariah and chapters 12–14 to a "Third." These alleged and unknown writers are supposed to have lived in Jerusalem sometime during the fourth to the second centuries B.C. It is argued that these anonymous oracles, along with Malachi, were appended to Zechariah 1–8 to complete the sacred number of the Twelve Prophets. According to this view, Zechariah may not have taken its final written form until the

Maccabean period (ca. 160 B.C.). Evidence offered in support of the multiple-author hypothesis includes the differences of style, tone, theology, and historical situation between the two parts of the book—most notably the reference to Greece in 9:13 (which is viewed as an allusion to the Hellenistic period)—and the distinctively apocalyptic flavor of chapters 12–14.

Like Haggai's prophecy, Zechariah's messages originated in Jerusalem and were intended for the people of postexilic Jerusalem and its environs. The spiritual apathy, despair, and sense of hopelessness pervading the early postexilic period of Hebrew history were the motivation behind Zechariah's exhortations and predictions.

The Background

The setting for Zechariah's prophecy, like Haggai's, was the reign of Darius I, King of Persia (521–486 B.C.). Despite the Hebrews' return from Babylonian exile, there was little evidence of the program of covenant restoration Yahweh had promised Jerusalem (e.g., Jer. 30–33; Ezek. 36–39). Selfishness crippled community spirit, and the general mood of the period was gloomy and dismal. In fact, only a small percentage of the Hebrew captives had actually returned to Judah, the city walls still lay in ruins, the temple of God was a rubble heap, and drought and blight ravaged the land. Judah remained a Persian vassal state, and the surrounding nations continued to harass the leaders in Jerusalem and thwart their timid efforts to improve the bleak situation.

[1]Recent computer-assisted linguistic and grammatical analysis of Zechariah corroborates a date of the early fifth century B.C. for Zechariah 9–14 and indicates that the literary break between chapters 1–8 and 9–14 is not nearly so pronounced as some scholars contend. Cf. Andrew E. Hill, "Dating 'Second Zechariah': A Linguistic Reexamination," *Hebrew Annual Review* 6 (1982): 105–34; and Y. T. Radday and D. Wickmann, "The Unity of Zechariah Examined in the Light of Statistical Linguistics," *Zeitschrift für die alttestamentliche Wissenschaft* 87 (1975): 30–55.

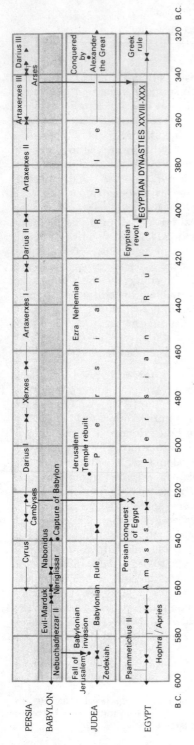

In response to this distress, God raised up two prophetic voices to initiate programs for the physical rebuilding and spiritual renewal of Jerusalem. Haggai was called to exhort and challenge the Hebrew community to rebuild the temple (see fig. 43.1). He prophesied for only four months in the year 520 B.C. Yet the people of God responded to his message and began the reconstruction of the temple (cf. Hag. 1:12–15).

The prophet Zechariah complemented Haggai's message in calling for a spiritual revival among the people (1:3–6; 7:8–14). His ministry began just two months after Haggai's, and his last dated message was delivered in 518 B.C. So Zechariah's ministry in Jerusalem probably lasted more than two years. The reference to Haggai and Zechariah in Ezra 5:2 suggests that they continued to support and encourage the people until the temple was completed and rededicated to the worship of Yahweh with the celebration of the Passover Feast in 515 B.C. (Ezra 6:13–22)—(see further in chap. 42).

Outline of the Book

I. Prelude: Call to national repentance (1:1–6)
II. Zechariah's visions
  A. Vision 1: Patrol report of world at rest (1:7–17)
  B. Vision 2: Horns and craftsmen (1:18–21)
  C. Vision 3: Measuring Jerusalem (2:1–5)
  D. Postscript 1: Investiture of Joshua (2:6–3:10)
  E. Vision 4: Lampstand and olive trees (4)
  F. Vision 5: Flying scroll (5:1–4)
  G. Vision 6: Woman in ephah basket (5:5–11)
  H. Vision 7: Four chariots of judgment (6:1–8)
  I. Postscript 2: Crowning of Joshua (6:9–15)
III. Zechariah's messages

Figure 43.1. The Behistun Rock, depicting a king confronting captured rebels, with the Persian god Ahura Mazda above them, and hewn by order of Darius I, under whose authority the temple at Jerusalem was reconstructed after the Babylonian exile. (*B. Brandl*)

Purpose and Message

Zechariah's message was one of rebuke, exhortation, and encouragement—a tract for troubled times. First, the prophet upbraided the postexilic community because they had perpetuated the evil ways and deeds of their ancestors (1:3–5). The people were guilty of the very same covenant violations that sent a previous generation into exile (7:8–14).

The solution Zechariah offered to the problem of sin and rebellion among the people included genuine repentance and a return to God (1:3–5). Only spiritual renewal could engender true worship and meaningful service in the temple, which was now under construction at the prompting of the prophet Haggai. Only obedience to the voice of the Lord would usher in the long-awaited blessing, prosperity and righteousness of the messianic age (6:9–15; 8:13).

Yahweh's intention to "do good" to Jerusalem was contingent on the community's adherence to the stipulations of the covenant code, especially those governing behavior (7:8–12; 8:14–17). Unlike later Jewish apocalyptic literature, with its heavy emphasis on the futuristic aspects of the restoration of Israel in the Day of the Lord, Zechariah's message was laced with concern for social justice in the present. Before the nations of the world came to seek the Lord in Jerusalem, Israel had to entreat the favor of Yahweh, render justice, and show kindness and mercy to Hebrew widows and orphans and to foreigners (7:9–10; cf. 14:16–21).

Zechariah explicitly stated that part of his duty as God's spokesman was to "comfort" and "strengthen" the people of Judah and Jerusalem (1:13; 8:9). His word of encouragement took several forms. For example, his series of visions (1:7–6:8) reminded Israel that God still cared for his people and continued to rule the destinies of the nations for the ultimate benefit of his elect Zion (cf. esp. 2:6–13). The ordination of Joshua as the priest and Zerubbabel as the governor marked the resumption of divinely appointed leadership in Israel. This in turn rekindled messianic hopes and confirmed the divine blessing of the efforts to rebuild the temple and reform the people (cf. 4:6).

Finally, Zechariah's repeated reference to the words of the "former prophets" authenticated his own ministry and assured the Hebrew community that they had not misinterpreted Yahweh's earlier prophetic revelations (1:4; 7:7, 12). Despite their current distress, the people were not to despair. Zechariah certified the continued validity of Yahweh's covenant program for Israel. Their hope was not misplaced!

Structure and Organization

The book of Zechariah conveniently divides into two major parts. The first includes the introductory verse (or superscription) and the call to repentance (1:1–6), the seven night visions (1:7–6:15), and the two oracles addressing the topic of fasting (7–8). The second part consists of eschatological oracles, subdivided into sections: the word of the Lord concerning Hadrach (9–11), and the word of the Lord concerning Israel (12–14).

Building on the literary analysis of P. Lamarche, Joyce G. Baldwin has identified chiastic structure underlying both parts of Zechariah's prophecy. This pattern of inversion gives evidence of deliberate structuring of themes and argues for the unity of the entire work. It also supports the idea that Zechariah not only composed, but also arranged and edited his own visions and oracles.[2]

The chiastic arrangement of parts 1 and 2 is illustrated in figure 43.2.

The prelude of Zechariah exhorts the nation to repentance and thus complements Haggai's charge to rebuild the temple. The physical rebuilding of Jerusalem and the temple were to be accompanied by a corresponding spiritual renewal. The night visions of the prophet substantiated his claim that "God will return to Israel" (cf. 1:3, 16; 2:10). The visions graphically outlined God's plan to bring peace to Israel, retribution to the nations who scattered her, restoration to the city of Jerusalem, divinely appointed leadership, a purging of evil from among the people of God, and the establishment of covenant righteousness in Zion.

The two sermons related to fasting connected the pursuit of social justice in the current age with the eventual reversal of Judah's fortunes among the nations in the age to come (e.g., 8:9–13). As Judah sought the favor of the Lord, so too the nations would one day seek the Lord in Jerusalem (cf. 7:2; 8:22). Finally, the two eschatological oracles bolstered hope and encouraged the community by depicting the promised, coming kingdom of God.

The book is cast in "oracular prose," or combination of prose and poetry, which is typical of prophetic literature (except for the poetic materials in chapters 9–10). The composition contains a variety of literary forms, among them:

---

[2]Joyce G. Baldwin, *Haggai, Zechariah, Malachi*, TOTC (Downers Grove, Ill.: InterVarsity, 1972), 75–81, 85–86. Cf. P. Lamarche, *Zacharie i–xiv: Structure, Litteraire, et Messianisme* (Paris: Gabalda, 1961).

Figure 43.2. The Structure of the Book of Zechariah

Part 1:

I.	Prelude: Call to national repentance	1:1–6
II.	Visions and postscripts	
	a Vision 1: Patrol report of world at rest	1:7–17
	b Vision 2: Horns and craftsmen (retribution for the nations)	1:18–21
	b¹ Vision 3: Measuring Jerusalem (the city protected by God)	2:1–5
	c Postscript 1: Investiture of Joshua	2:6–3:10
	d Vision 4: Lampstand and olive trees	4
	b² Vision 5: Flying scroll (retribution for evil)	5:1–4
	b³ Vision 6: Woman in ephah basket (Jerusalem purified by God)	5:5–11
	a¹ Vision 7: God's chariots patrol the earth	6:1–8
	c¹ Postscript 2: The crowning of Joshua	6:9–15
III.	Messages on fasting	
	a The inquiry	7:1–3
	b First sermon	7:4–14
	c Covenant sayings	8:1–8
	b¹ Second sermon	8:9–17
	a¹ The response	8:18–19
IV.	Postlude: Entreat and seek the Lord	

Part 2:

I.	Triumphant intervention of the Lord: His shepherd rejected	
	a The Lord triumphs from the north	9:1–8
	b Arrival of the king	9:9–10
	c Jubilation and prosperity	9:11–10:1
	d Rebuke for sham Leaders	10:2–3
	c¹ Jubilation and restoration	10:4–11:3
	b¹ The fate of the good shepherd	11:4–17
II.	Final intervention of the Lord: The suffering involved	
	c² Jubilation in Jerusalem	12:1–9
	b² Mourning for the pierced one	12:10–13:1
	d¹ Rejection of sham leaders	13:2–6
	b³ The shepherd slaughtered, the people scattered	13:7–9
	c³ Cataclysm in Jerusalem	14:1–15
	a¹ The Lord worshiped as King over all	14:16–21

—Exhortation with repentance oracle (1:1–6)

—Narrative in the form of a vision (1:7–6:8)

—Prediction with revelation and interpretation formulas (e.g., 5:1–4)

—Inquiry with instructional response (e.g., 6:1–8).

—Symbolic actions (6:9–15)

—Admonition with messenger and date formulas (7:1–7)

—Divine oracles of judgment and salvation (e.g., chap. 10)

Zechariah is often classified as proto-apocalyptic in contrast to the apocalyptic literature that appears in later Jewish writings of the intertestamental period (e.g., 1 Esdras and 1 Enoch). True, the

Figure 43.3. Zechariah's Predictions About Messiah

Come in a low and humble station of life	9:9; 13:7 (cf. Matt. 21:5; 26:31, 56)
Restore Israel by the blood of his covenant	9:11 (cf. Mark 14:24)
Serve as shepherd to a people scattered and wandering like sheep	10:2 (cf. Matt. 9:36; 26:15)
Be rejected and betrayed	11:12–13 (cf. Matt. 26:15; 27:9–10)
Be pierced and struck down	12:10; 13:7 (cf. Matt. 24:30; 26:31, 56; John 19:37)
Return in glory and deliver Israel from her enemies	14:1–6 (cf. Matt. 25:31)
Rule as king in peace and righteousness in Jerusalem	9:9–10; 14:9, 16 (cf. Rev. 11:15; 19:6)
Establish a new world order	14:6–19 (cf. Rev. 21:25; 22:1, 5)

book exhibits some features of apocalyptic writing: revelation in the form of visions, the presence of a divine messenger who also interprets the visions, the use of symbolism, and the themes of judgment for the nations and the ultimate triumph of God in human history. But many others are absent, such as rigid determinism and pervasive pessimism, a rewriting of earlier history, and pseudonymity (writing under a false name).

Major Themes

Messiah

Zechariah has more to say about the messianic shepherd-king than any other Old Testament book except Isaiah. This foreshadowing of the Son of Man as Messiah is explained to the disciples by Jesus himself as a method of Old Testament interpretation (cf. Luke 24:44). Our approach (fig. 43.3) identifies as "messianic" only those Old Testament passages that New Testament writers explicitly cited in reference or application to the life and ministry of Jesus of Nazareth as the Christ (while recognizing that some of these citations are not that explicit in the context of Zechariah).

Old Testament Eschatology

Eschatology is the doctrine of end-time events, or the study of last things. Al-though Zechariah did not use the phrases "the Day of the Lord" and "the kingdom of God," the book contributes greatly to our knowledge of Hebrew understanding of end-time events.

Central to Old Testament teaching about the last days is the salvation of Israel, for "the LORD their God will save them on that day" (9:16). The teaching is that this deliverance will be accomplished by a shepherd-king who is first rejected and smitten (11:4–17). Yet his ministry will be one of peace and reconciliation and cleansing by the Holy Spirit (9:9–10).

A second concept associated with the Day of the Lord in Zechariah is the regathering and restoration of Israel (10:9–12). Through the agency of his servant Messiah, God will again unify Judah and Israel and restore the fortunes of his elect. All this will come to pass after the nations have waged war against Jerusalem, only to be vanquished by the Lord (12:1–9; 14:1–5). Then Israel will mourn over "the one they have pierced," their repentance leading to cleansing and covenant renewal with Yahweh (12:10–13:9).

Yahweh's restoration of Israel is to culminate in the establishment of a new created order, the Lord himself ruling over all the earth. There will be a new Jerusalem, and the wealth of the nations will flow into Zion (14:6–15). Prominent in this restored city of David is the temple of Yahweh—the very temple Haggai and Zechariah had encouraged the postexilic community to build. The temple will stand as a symbol of the peace, righteousness, and holiness that will characterize the kingdom of God (14:16–21). Even the peoples of the nations will make regular pilgrimages to worship the God of Israel there (14:16).

This sequence of events comprising the Day of the Lord was so compressed and condensed, historically speaking, that the distinctions made by later interpreters between the first and second advents of Messiah became blurred in the prophets' minds into one coming. In fact, whole

interpretive and theological systems have been constructed in an attempt to understand Old Testament prophecies (i.e., dispensationalism and covenant theology).

However, Zechariah's perspectives on "that day" are consistent with the rest of Old Testament teaching in that they conform to the general pattern, which falls out as apostasy in Israel followed by oppression and scattering as judgment for sin, with Israel's subsequent repentance prompting God to regather the elect and restore the covenant blessings and judge the sin of the oppressive nations so that Israel might enjoy the presence of God in a kingdom experience (e.g., Ezek. 36–39; cf. Matt. 24).

Questions for Further Study and Discussion

1. Discuss how the messianic passages in Zechariah illustrate the relationship between the Old and New Testament writings.
2. What does Zechariah teach about God's relationship to human history, in terms of both Israel and the nations?
3. Explain Zechariah's understanding of the "eschatological day." How does the book of Zechariah enlarge our understanding of eschatology as presented in the New Testament?
4. What similarities between the conditions of the world of the Persian Empire and the current international political scene make apocalyptic literature useful today?
5. What does Zechariah reveal about postexilic Judaism, specifically, its customs, culture, and problems?
6. How did the prophet reconcile his ideas about a day of doom, a remnant of the Hebrew people, and a new world order ruled by Messiah?

For Further Reading

Baldwin, Joyce G. *Haggai, Zechariah, Malachi.* TOTC. Downers Grove, Ill.: InterVarsity, 1972. Thorough exegesis from an evangelical perspective, with useful introductory sections on the authorship and literary character of Zechariah.

Barker, Kenneth L. "Zechariah." *EBC.* Vol. 7. Grand Rapids: Zondervan, 1985. 595–697. Helpful analysis and discussion of the language of Zechariah's prophecies, with emphasis on the book's theological value.

Laney, J. C. *Zechariah.* EvBC. Chicago: Moody Press, 1984.

Mason, R. *The Books of Haggai, Zechariah, and Malachi.* CBC. Cambridge: Cambridge University Press, 1973.

Meyers, Carol, and Eric Meyers. *Haggai and Zechariah 1–8.* AB. Vol. 25B. Garden City, N.Y.: Doubleday, 1987. A superior but technical commentary, with extensive bibliographies, excellent historical and linguistic analysis of Zechariah's time and message.

Petersen, D. L. *Haggai and Zechariah 1–8*. OTL. Philadelphia: Westminster, 1984.

Smith, Ralph L. *Micah–Malachi*. WBC. Vol. 32. Waco, Tex.: Word, 1984.

Unger, Merrill F. *Zechariah: Prophet of Messiah's Glory*. Grand Rapids: Zondervan, 1963.

Chapter 44

Malachi

The name "Malachi" occurs in the Old Testament only in the title verse of the book (1:1). As a proper name, Malachi may be translated "my messenger" or "my angel" (cf. Zech. 1:9, 11). Some biblical scholars contend that the name is merely an editorial heading for the book borrowed from the phraseology of 3:1 ("See, I will send my messenger . . ."), and assume the work to be an anonymous prophecy. Granted that there is no attestation elsewhere, Malachi is nevertheless similar to other Old Testament names ending in "i," such as Beeri (Gen. 26:34) and Zichri (1 Chron. 8.19). Moreover, both Jonah and Habakkuk are solitary names among the prophets. So this single occurrence of the name "Malachi" should not count as evidence against its use as a proper name (see below).

Little is known about the prophet Malachi. As with Obadiah, the opening verse of the prophecy traces no genealogical heritage. Jewish tradition has regarded Malachi along with Haggai and Zechariah as a personage of the Great Synagogue. This synagogue was a council of scribes and other Hebrew leaders who helped to reorganize religious life and culture after the Babylonian exile; these

men played a key role in formulating the Twelve Prophets as a part of the Hebrew canon.

Malachi's staunch convictions against idolatry (2:10–12), easy divorce (2:13–16), and social injustice (3:5) bespeak a man of commitment and integrity—a throwback to the days of the preexilic prophets. He was also a man of some courage, seen in his bold upbraiding of the influential priestly class and the social elite (cf. 1:1– 14; 2:1–4; 3:2–4).

The Writing of the Book

The obscurity of Malachi's title verse has spawned a range of opinion as to the book's author and its date of writing.

In addition, the similarity of the introductory formulas of Zechariah 9:1 and 12:1 and Malachi 1:1 has led many modern scholars to conclude that Zechariah 9–11 and 12–14 and Malachi 1–4 were originally a series of anonymous prophetic oracles appended to Zechariah 1– 8. Eventually the two longer documents coalesced with Zechariah 1–8 to become chapters 9–14. The introduction of the expression "my messenger" (Mal. 3:1) as a title for the book of Malachi ultimately permitted its detachment from Zechariah

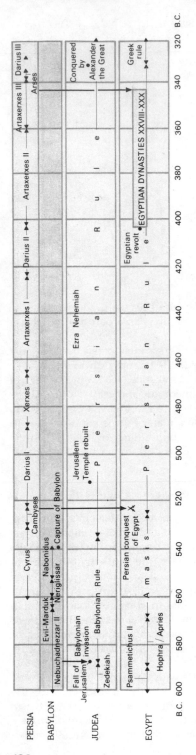

and completed the sacred number of Twelve Prophets.

By contrast, more traditional biblical scholars have regarded the title "Malachi" as a proper name identifying a prophetic figure rooted in postexilic Hebrew history. Instead of viewing the book as a convenient offshoot of Zechariah, they acknowledge the integrity and independent status of the work.

Like many other prophetic books of the Old Testament, it is unclear whether Malachi penned his own message or whether the prophecies were compiled and edited in writing by a disciple or someone else. The terse sentences and forthright style of the book attest that the prophecies were originally delivered orally and suggest that there was little time between the pronouncement and the recording of the oracles.

It is important to recognize that Malachi's position at the end of the Old Testament in the English Bible (based on Luther's rearrangement of both canonical and noncanonical books during the Reformation) has little bearing on the chronological placement of the book in Hebrew history. Malachi predates other Old Testament books such as Esther, Ezra–Nehemiah, and Chronicles, with the date of its writing usually assigned to a time coinciding with the work of Ezra and Nehemiah in Jerusalem (ca. 450–430 B.C.). This view is based largely on the parallel descriptions of religious and social decay in the postexilic community recorded in Malachi and the books of Ezra and Nehemiah. For example, all three confront the problems of intermarriage with foreigners, divorce, abuses associated with the priesthood, temple services, the tithe, the Sabbath, and the oppression of the poor (1:6–13; 2:1–16; 3:5–10; cf. Ezra 9–10; Neh. 5:1–5; 10:32–39; 13:1–30).

However, careful study of the Hebrew language of Malachi reveals that the book has considerable associations linguistically with Old Testament writings dated to the sixth century B.C. rather than the fifth century. Based on the detailed information gleaned from this kind of technical linguistic analysis of the postexilic prophets, we conclude that Malachi was most likely composed in Jerusalem during the very early years of pre-Ezra decline (roughly 500 to 475 B.C.).[1]

Persian influence on the thought and language of Malachi can be seen in the prophet's references to "a scroll of remembrance" (3:16; cf. Esth. 6:1; Dan. 7:10; 12:1) and "the sun of righteousness" (4:2). The book of remembrance, in which are recorded the names of the righteous, points to the continued theological development of the Hebrew belief in afterlife in the Old Testament. The unique expression "sun of righteousness" is reminiscent of the winged solar disk that represents the sun god in Mesopotamian and Egyptian iconography and symbolizes protection for the king and assures victory in battle. The imagery suggests that in the same way, Yahweh would grant protection and restoration to those who feared his name when the fiery consummation of the Day of the Lord should come.

The Background

The message of Malachi reflected conditions associated with the period of pre-Ezra decline (ca. 515–458 B.C., or from the completion of the second temple to the ministry of Ezra in Jerusalem, assuming the traditional date for Ezra's journey to Jerusalem is correct). The second temple had been completed at the urging of Haggai and Zechariah (Hag. 1:1–6; Ezra 3:10–13; 5:1–2; 6:13–15), but the achievement ushered in no hoped-for messianic age (Mal. 3:6–12; cf. Zech. 8:9–23). Instead, the apathy and disillusionment that had forestalled the temple's construction for nearly twenty years persisted within the restoration community. The expectations of a renewed Davidic state under Zerubbabel went unfulfilled (cf. Hag. 2:20–23). The material prosperity predicted by Haggai (2:6–9) was only partially realized, and the streaming migrations of former Hebrew captives foreseen by Zechariah (8:1–8) proved to be as yet a mere trickle. Zechariah's call to a deeper spiritual life went unheeded and was even mocked by God's apparent failure to restore covenant blessings to Jerusalem (Zech. 8:4–13; cf. 10:1–2; Mal. 3:13–15).

If the records of Ezra and Nehemiah are any indication, the messianic oracles of Zechariah and Malachi had little impact on postexilic morale (cf. Ezra 9:1–4; Neh. 5:1–8; 11:1–3). Given the testimony of scanty written documents to the contrary, even the prophetic voice soon ceased to be a factor in the Hebrew restoration community (Mal. 4:5; cf. 1 Maccabees 4:46; 9:27; 14:41).

Jerusalem, which was likely a satrapy (or province) under the rule of a Persian governor, remained small, struggling, and insignificant in the vast Persian Empire— a social and political backwater. The ongoing petty hostilities with the Samaritans and the burdensome vassal status to Persia contributed to the skepticism and doubt that characterized popular response to Yahweh as God (Mal. 1:2). The Persians themselves were engaged in a titanic contest for control of the West against the Greeks. It was in this dismal setting that Malachi prophesied in Jerusalem as God's "divine messenger."

[1]Cf. Andrew E. Hill, "Dating the Book of Malachi: A Linguistic Reexamination," in *The Word of the Lord Shall Go Forth: Essays in Honor of D. N. Freedman*, ed. C. Meyers and M. O'Connor (Winona Lake, Ind.: Eisenbrauns, 1983), 84–86.

Outline of the Book

Purpose and Message

The predominant theme of Malachi's prophecy is Israel's covenant relationship with Yahweh and its ramifications. The prophet specifically cited the covenant of Levi (1:6–2:9), the covenant of the fathers and the covenant of marriage (2:10–16), and the messenger of the covenant (3:1).

The teaching of the six disputations in Malachi may be conveniently summarized as follows: (1) Yahweh loves Jacob (1:2–5); (2) he is Israel's father and desires honest worship (1:6–9); (3) he is father of all Israelites and expects true faithfulness (2:10–16); (4) God wants honesty, not words, because he is just (2:17–3:5); (5) God is faithful to his word and desires genuine worship (3:6–12); (6) again, God desires honesty (3:13–4:3).[2]

In his first disputation Malachi had to remind the people of Yahweh's sovereign station as father and suzerain (overlord) and as covenant maker (cf. Deut. 32:6–12). As such, he was deserving of conduct appropriate to that bond of covenant relationship (Exod. 20:12; Deut. 31:1–10).

As covenant maker, Yahweh was also a covenant keeper (Exod. 34:6–7; Ps. 111:9), unchanging and faithful to his word (Mal. 3:6; Deut. 7:6–11).

Malachi's five remaining disputations contrasted Israel's faithlessness with Yahweh's faithfulness by reciting specific violations of covenant stipulations.

The desired responses to Malachi's call to repentance and covenant renewal for elect Israel were practical and specific: (1) the purification of a corrupt and complacent priesthood, (2) the transformation of insincere and boring worship into the joyful sacrifice of praise in which God delights, (3) the correction of abuses associated with the tithe and temple sacrifices, (4) the restoration of broken family relationships, and (5) the initiation of a program of social justice rooted in the covenant ethic.

Structure and Organization

The literary genre of Malachi remains a subject of debate. Past and present German scholars have considered the proph-

[2]J. A. Fischer, "Notes on the Literary Form and Message of Malachi," *CBQ* 34 (1972): 317.

ecy a type of poetry, assuming an oral poetic tradition lying behind the written oracles of Malachi (hence the numerous alterations of the Hebrew text suggested by those adhering to this position). Most English-speaking scholars have generally understood Malachi as a prose composition. Recent studies analyzing the Hebrew language of the postexilic prophets have corroborated this second view. This language may be designated "prophetic prose" or "oracular prose" to distinguish it as a literary genre from narrative prose.[3]

Malachi's prophecy is simple, direct, and forceful. Forty-seven of the fifty-five verses in the book are addressed to Israel in the first person, presenting a vivid encounter between God and his people. Unlike the pattern of the messenger formula (e.g., "thus says the LORD") followed by an oracle that was predominant in the earlier prophets, Malachi punctuates his message of six oracles with a series of ten rhetorical questions and answers.

This disputational, or catechetical, format can be characterized by a four-point outline: (1) The statement of a truth, (2) a hypothetical audience rebuttal in the form of a question, (3) the prophet's answer to the rebuttal by restating his initial premise, and (4) the presentation of additional supporting evidence. This disputational pattern is not unique to Malachi in the Old Testament (cf. Isa. 40:27–28; Jer. 2:23–25, 29–32; 29:24–32; Ezek. 12:21–28; Mic. 2:6–11), but it is distinctive in that it becomes the linchpin of the book's literary structure.

The form and arrangement of Malachi's oracles also contribute to the development of his message on the theme of covenant. The last five disputations reinforce the teaching about God's covenant love for Israel offered in the first disputation. In the second, Malachi indicted the priesthood for its failure as guardian of the covenant relationship, but then, in the next disputation, he rebuked the people for breach of covenant, lest the priests be made scapegoats. As the priests had transgressed the covenant of Levi, so too the people had broken the covenant of their fathers. The fourth disputation reminded Israel of the reality of God's judgment for covenant trespass. The fifth called Israel to repentance and covenant renewal. The final disputation warned Israel about the Day of the Lord, which would verify God's covenant love for Israel and vindicate his justice in dealing with the wicked.

This rhetorical-question-and-disputation format became the precursor of the expositional method peculiar to the later rabbinic schools of Judaism.

Major Themes

Marriage and Divorce

The prophet's lofty teaching on the institution of marriage as companionship with the wife of one's youth (2:14) and the shared responsibility of child rearing (2:15) is reminiscent of Old Testament wisdom literature (e.g., Prov. 5:18; 10:1; 15:20; 31:26). Marriage is a sacred covenant blessed by God and an honorable union between male and female for the purpose of fellowship and establishing family life (Gen. 2:24; Ezek. 16:8, Hos. 2:19). For Malachi, the connections between covenant keeping with Yahweh and covenant keeping with a mate are obvious and based on the familial nature of covenant relationships presented elsewhere in the Old Testament. (Note, for example, the imagery of husband and wife used for God and Israel in Jeremiah 2:1–3; 31:32; Ezekiel 16:6–34; Hosea 2:1–19.)

The divorce provisions of the Mosaic law were instituted because of man's sin generally (Gen. 3:1–19) and Israel's sin specifically (Matt. 19:8). Divorce shatters the covenant bond between the marriage

---

[3]On the prose-poetry issue, see further P. A. Verhoef, *The Books of Haggai and Malachi*, NICOT (Grand Rapids: Eerdmans, 1987), 166–67.

partners. The prophet's choice of vocabulary graphically illustrates this truth, as he uses a unique Old Testament word for "partner" in 2:14. The term is related to the Hebrew root meaning "to be joined," as in the nailing together of pieces of wood in a construction project (Exod. 26:6).

Malachi also condemned those among God's people who, having divorced, intermarried with foreign people, consequently contaminating the Hebrew religion (cf. Num. 25:1–9; 1 Kings 11:1–4). Malachi's censure of easy divorce anticipated the more rigid instruction of Jesus and Paul in the New Testament (Matt. 5:31–32; 19:1–10; Mark 10:1–10; Rom. 7:1–3; 1 Cor. 7:10–16, 39).

Elijah the Prophet

The second appendix (Mal. 4:5–6) connects the messenger of the covenant (3:1) with Elijah reincarnate. Elijah was deemed the archetype or role model for the prophetic enterprise associated with the "forerunner" for several reasons. First, he boldly confronted religious and political leaders on the issues of religious orthodoxy, moral purity, and social justice. Second, he preached a message of repentance from sin in the face of God's impending judgment. Third, his divine commission and message was authenticated by accompanying miraculous signs. Fourth, he was truly "the voice of one crying in the wilderness" in that his ministry stood outside the recognized structures and traditional institutions of Israelite society.

Elijah's role as a herald proclaiming the appointed time of Yahweh's wrath and the inauguration of the messianic age was an important part of later Jewish tradition regarding the prophet (e.g., Sirach 48:10–11; cf. Matt. 17:3, 10; 27:47, 49; John 1:21). His appearance on the Mount of Transfiguration with Moses and Jesus lends support to this eschatological dimension of the prophetic ministry. Jesus of Nazareth clearly understood the prophecy of Malachi as prefiguring the ministry of John the Baptist (Matt. 11:7–15), and the New Testament record testifies to the unconventional, Elijah-like life and ministry of John (e.g., Matt 3:1–12; Luke 1:14–17). The early church also accepted Malachi's prediction about the "forerunner" as being fully realized in John's heralding the initiation of the messianic kingdom of heaven accomplished by the advent of Jesus as the Christ (Mark 1:2–8; Luke 1:16–17; cf. Matt. 1:1–6).

Questions for Further Study and Discussion

1. Discuss the meaning of the statement "Esau I have hated" (Mal. 1:3) and what it reveals about God. Include in the discussion any other references in Scripture to things God is said to "hate."
2. How does Malachi describe the religious practices of the Hebrews during his day? What does we learn in the book about individual and corporate worship experience?
3. Why does Malachi censure divorce (2:10–16)? How do we appropriate this teaching today?
4. Discuss Malachi's passage on giving and tithing (3:8–12) and its implications regarding material prosperity.
5. What is the meaning of Malachi's prophecy about "Elijah" (4:5–6)?

For Further Reading

Ackroyd, P. R. *Exile and Restoration*. OTL. Philadelphia: Westminster, 1968.

Baldwin, Joyce G. *Haggai, Zechariah, Malachi*. TOTC. Downers Grove, Ill.: InterVarsity, 1972.

Fischer, J. A. "Notes on the Literary Form and Message of Malachi." *CBQ* 34 (1972): 315–20.

Glazier-McDonald, B. *Malachi: The Divine Messenger*. SBLDS 98. Atlanta: Scholars Press, 1987.

Hill, Andrew E. "Dating the Book of Malachi: A Linguistic Reexamination." In *The Word of the Lord Shall Go Forth: Essays in Honor of D. N. Freedman*. Edited by C. Meyers and M. O'Connor. Winona Lake, Ind.: Eisenbrauns, 1983. 77–89.

Kaiser, Walter C. *Malachi: God's Unchanging Love*. Grand Rapids: Baker, 1984. Detailed and readable study of Malachi's message and its application to our day. A "prototype" commentary based on the author's "exegetical theology" methodology.

Mallone, G. *Furnace of Renewal*. Downers Grove, Ill.: InterVarsity, 1981. Insightful and penetrating contemporary application of Malachi's message to the life of the church, including tithing and prayer, social service and evangelism, worship, leadership, and sacrament.

McKenzie, S. L., and H. W. Wallace. "Covenant Themes in Malachi." *CBQ* 45 (1983): 549–63.

O'Brien, Julia M. *Priest and Levite in Malachi*. SBLDS 121. Atlanta: Scholars Press, 1990.

Petersen, D. L. *Late Israelite Prophecy: Studies in Deutero-Prophetic Literature and in Chronicles*. SBLMS 23. Missoula: Scholars Press, 1977.

Smith, Ralph L. *Micah–Malachi*. WBC. Vol. 32. Waco, Tex.: Word, 1984.

Verhoef, P. A. *The Books of Haggai and Malachi*. NICOT. Grand Rapids: Eerdmans, 1987. Very good introductory discussions of author, date, historical background, style, and text.

Wolf, Herbert M. *Haggai and Malachi*. EvBC. Chicago: Moody Press, 1976. Brief, easy to read, and well-researched. Accessible and usable, especially for the nonspecialist.

PART VI

EPILOGUE

Chapter 45

Toward the New Testament

The Old Testament in the New

The Holy Scriptures of the Christian church contain two Testaments, but they comprise one Bible. The Old Testament, or Old Covenant, remains an essential part of the Christian Bible because the two covenants form one record of God's progressive and redemptive revelation to humankind. The promise of the "former" covenant finds its fulfillment in what the writer to the Hebrews called the "superior" covenant (Heb. 8:6). The study of either covenant in isolation not only leads to an imbalanced and inadequate picture of God's self-disclosure and his purposes for creation, but also robs the Word of God of its full force as God-breathed truth and distorts its unified and unique "salvation history" message.

The apostle Paul said that the Christ child was born at exactly the proper moment in human history (Gal. 4:4). God the History Maker arranged the optimum historical, cultural, political, and theological environment for the birth of Jesus Christ and his church (cf. Isa. 14:24–27;

Dan. 2:20–23). This made the Old Testament an integral part of God's "preparation history" for the coming Messiah.

The New Testament writers clearly understood the importance of this continuity between the covenants, because the Hebrew Old Testament was the Bible for the early church. The Old Testament served as the source book for preaching (cf. Acts 2:14–36 and 3:12–26) and public reading in those apostolic days (cf. 1 Tim. 4:13). The apologetic of the early church was essentially to defend Jesus as the Christ by appealing to his fulfillment of Old Testament prophecy (e.g., Acts 4:5–12; 7:2–53; cf. Matt. 11:2–6, a method used by Jesus himself).

Finally, the New Testament made extensive use of the Old Testament in the form of direct quotation and indirect allusion. In fact, according to careful calculation, approximately 32 percent— nearly one-third—of the New Testament is composed of Old Testament quotations and allusions.[1] An analysis of these Old Testament quotations and allusions yields several major themes or emphases

[1]For the details on this remarkable statistic, see Andrew E. Hill, *Baker's Handbook of Bible Lists* (Grand Rapids: Baker, 1981), 102–4.

and shows us how the disciples of Christ broadly understood his statement about his "presence" in the Law, the Prophets, and the Psalms (cf. Luke 24:44).[2]

Figure 45.1 offers a representative sampling of the Old Testament verses most frequently cited in the New Testament.

The themes and emphases of these New Testament references to the Old Testament may be grouped under three major headings: those related to God Almighty, those related to Jesus as the Christ, and those related to humankind.

1. The New Testament writers highlighted several important aspects of God's nature and character as portrayed in the Old Testament, including the enthroned Sovereign of creation and the nations (e.g., Rev. 4:2ff.), the God of awesome deeds and power (e.g., Acts 26:8), and a God who is generous in extending his steadfast love without partiality (e.g., Acts 10:34). These themes were no doubt especially significant for the early Christian church, given the iron rule of the Romans within the vast empire.

2. Jesus Christ was foreshadowed in the Old Testament and recognized in the New Testament as Lord and King (Col. 1:15–20), as son of David (e.g., Matt. 9:27), as son of God (e.g., Matt. 3:17), as suffering servant and savior (e.g., Matt. 16:21) announced by the messenger of God (e.g., Luke 3:1–17), as the Lamb of God whose blood of the covenant purchased redemption for humanity (e.g., Matt. 26:28), and as the prophet greater than Moses and the eternal priest greater than Melchizedek (e.g., Heb. 3:1–6; 7:15–28). These Christological themes constituted the basic message of salvation in Christ Jesus as the son of God preached to the Gentiles, and they formed the chief apologetic of the early church demonstrating Jesus of Nazareth as Messiah to the Jews.

3. The New Testament identifies several areas of continuity with the Old Testament in regard to the need and destiny of humanity, including an impending day of distress and trouble as judgment for sin (e.g., Matt. 24:15–28), the need for deliverance and redemption by a blood covenant better than that of bulls and goats (e.g., Heb. 9:23–10:18), the priority of faith for relationship to God (Heb. 11:6), the need for holiness (e.g., 1 Peter 1:16), and the demands of obedience to the decrees of God, issuing in "life" to the believer (e.g., Heb. 5:9). These emphases prove foundational for basic aspects of New Testament theology like eschatology (the doctrine of last things), soteriology (the doctrine of salvation), and sanctification (the pursuit of holiness by the believer).

Bridging the Two Covenants

A second model for bridging the Old and the New is the theme of the covenant, the Old Testament conception of faith. Elmer A. Martens identifies four basic purposes or designs of Yahweh for Israel, including salvation or deliverance, the covenant community, the knowledge of God, and the land of covenant promise.[3] These designs not only capture the central message of Old Testament revelation, but also anticipate the person and work of Messiah in the New. Thus they serve as a grid by which key Old Covenant theological themes may be transposed and developed in the New Covenant.

1. God's design for salvation in the Old Testament demanded a faith commitment to God Almighty by acts of obedience to his word (e.g., Abraham's trek to Canaan and his offering of Isaac, cf. Heb. 11:8–22). Deliverance was accomplished by mighty deeds performed by Yahweh on behalf of his people Israel (e.g., the

[2]Based on the Index of Quotations in *The Greek New Testament*, ed. K. Aland et al. 2d ed. (New York: United Bible Societies, 1969), 897–920.

[3]Elmer A. Martens, *God's Design: A Focus on Old Testament Theology* (Grand Rapids: Baker, 1981), 25–36.

Figure 45.1. Use of the Old Testament in the New

OT Verse		Number of NT Occurrences
Psalm 110:1	The LORD says to my Lord: "Sit at my right hand until I make your enemies a footstool for your feet."	18
Daniel 12:1	At that time Michael, the great prince who protects your people, will arise. There will be a time of distress such as has not happened from the beginning of nations until then. But at that time your people—everyone whose name is found written in the book—will be delivered.	13
Isaiah 6:1	In the year that King Uzziah died, I saw the Lord seated on a throne, high and exalted, and the train of his robe filled the temple. (Cf. 2 Chron. 18:18; Ps. 47:8; Ezek. 1:26–28.)	12
Psalm 2:7	I will proclaim the decree of the LORD: He said to me, "You are my Son; today I have become your Father."	10
Isaiah 53:7	He was oppressed and afflicted, yet he did not open his mouth; he was led like a lamb to the slaughter, and as a sheep before her shearers is silent, so he did not open his mouth. (Cf. Ps. 44:22.)	10*
Leviticus 19:18	"Do not seek revenge or bear a grudge against one of your people, but love your neighbor as yourself. I am the LORD."	10
Deuteronomy 10:17	For the LORD your God is God of gods and Lord of lords, the great God, mighty and awesome, who shows no partiality and accepts no bribes.	8
Malachi 3:1	"See, I will send my messenger, who will prepare the way before me. Then suddenly the LORD you are seeking will come to his temple; the messenger of the covenant, whom you desire, will come," says the LORD Almighty.	8
Exodus 24:8	Moses then took the blood, sprinkled it on the people and said, "This is the blood of the covenant that the LORD has made with you in accordance with all these words."	7
Psalm 62:12	. . . you, O LORD, are loving. Surely you will reward each person according to what he has done.	7
Psalm 110:4	The LORD has sworn and will not change his mind: "You are a priest forever in the order of Melchizedek."	7
Deuteronomy 18:15	The LORD your God will raise up for you a prophet like me among your own brothers. You must listen to him.	6
Genesis 15:6	Abram believed the LORD , and he credited it to him as righteousness.	5
Exodus 19:6	" 'You will be for me a kingdom of priests and a holy nation.' These are the words you are to speak to the Israelites."	5
Leviticus 18:5	"Keep my decrees and laws, for the man who obeys them will live by them. I am the LORD ."	5

*The New Testament contains thirty-eight references to Isaiah 53 and twenty-four references to Psalm 22.

---

exodus from Egypt, Exod. 12–13), while worship of Yahweh was established on the principle of substitutionary sacrifice for sin (cf. Lev. 1–7). Likewise, Jesus demanded a faith commitment shown in acts of obedience (e.g., the radical call to discipleship in Luke 14:25–33), and through his substitutionary and atoning sacrifice he defeated the final enemy— death itself (cf. 1 Cor. 15:20–28, 51–58).

2. God's design for a new relationship with humankind was enacted by treaty

formula (e.g., Exod. 20–24), emphasized legislative holiness (e.g., Exod. 20:20), and was conditioned by the promise of blessing and the threat of curse (e.g., Lev. 26). In the same way, the New Testament constituted a new covenant relationship with God (i.e., "friends" of God, John 15:14–15, and "heirs" with Christ, Eph. 3:6) and spawned a new community in which "all the believers were together and had everything in common" (Acts 2:44; cf. vv. 42–47). This new covenant was also legitimized by treaty formula (cf. Luke 22:7–30) and conditioned by the promise of blessing and the threat of curse (cf. 1 Peter 2:4–10). But this new covenant implemented an operative holiness through the dynamic power of the Holy Spirit (cf. Rom. 7:7–8:17).

3. Yahweh's design for a new relationship with humanity was based on the knowledge of God (Hos. 6:3). For the Hebrews this knowledge was disclosed in the revealed word spoken by Yahweh's servants (e.g., Isa. 6:8–13), divine acts of "salvation history" (e.g., Exod. 14:30–31), the divinely ordained offices of prophet, priest, king, judge, and sage (cf. Jer. 18:18), and the sacrificial system of the Hebrew religion (cf. Lev. 1–7).

This knowledge of God is a primary concern of the New Testament as well (cf. John 17:3; Phil. 3:10). Jesus Christ came to reveal or make known the Father (John 1:18), and he commissioned the church to make the word of God fully known to all people (not just the Hebrews, Col. 1:25). Elsewhere Paul described Christ Jesus as the believer's wisdom, righteousness, sanctification, and redemption (1 Cor. 1:30) and affirmed the "office" gifts of apostle, prophet, evangelist, and pastor-teacher so that all may attain the unity of faith and the knowledge of the Son of God (Eph. 4:11–13).

4. God's design for Israel included a land of covenant promise for the Hebrews (Gen. 12:1–3). The "covenant land" was a gift from a loving and gracious God and a reward for obedience to the stipulations of Yahweh's covenant (Deut. 30:11–31:8). The presence of the Hebrews in the land of Canaan served as a reminder of God's faithfulness to his covenant promises to the patriarchs (cf. Pss. 106:45–46; 111:4–6).

More important, the land was symbolic of a way of life that included God's dwelling in the midst of his people and the restoration of order and balance in nature, human relationships (both within the community of Israel and extending to the "foreigner" and the socially disadvantaged), work and worship, space and time, and material possessions (cf. Exod. 25:8; Lev. 18–27).

The new covenant also focuses on God dwelling with his people, first by means of his indwelling Holy Spirit (cf. 1 Cor. 3:16–17; 6:19–20) and eventually with the very throne of God established among humanity (Rev. 21:1–4). Likewise, the redemptive ministry of Jesus Christ initiated a new order of righteous behavior in the world (cf. Matt. 5–7) that ultimately gives way to complete and perfect recreation of heaven and earth where "the old order of things has passed away" and "I am making everything new!" (Rev 21:4–5).

The New Testament opens with the joyful response to God's fulfillment of long-awaited prophetic expectations. God's Messiah and Israel's salvation had arrived in the person of Jesus, the son of Mary (Luke 2). The timetable for the Lord's new covenant with Israel as predicted by Jeremiah was finally realized (cf. Jer. 31:30–33). Yes, the "promise" of the old covenant had given way to "fulfillment" in this new covenant, ushered in by Christ Jesus, but like Israel, the church of Christ was charged to wait—even prayerfully long—for his triumphant return (cf. 1 Thess. 1:9–10; Titus 2:11–14; Rev. 22:20).

During this interim period of tension between "the now and the not yet," the church of Jesus Christ anticipates the culmination of her salvation (cf. Matt. 24:13; 1 Thess. 3:12–13; 5:23), a completely restored and perfect relationship with God through Christ (cf. Phil. 3:17–21; Rev. 19:1–10; 21:1–8), full of knowledge of God in Christ (cf. 1 Cor. 13:8–13), and the blessing and rest of the new creation and the heavenly city (cf. Rev. 21:9–22:5).

Questions for Further Study and Discussion

1. What made the Roman occupation of Palestine during the first century A.D. the "fullness of time," according to historians?
2. What is the relationship of Israel in the Old Testament to the Christian church in the New Testament?
3. According to William Dyrness, the Old Testament is often useful in evangelistic situations because there is a natural bridge between it and the common people, especially in non-Western cultures. Discuss this concept. (Cf. William Dyrness, *Themes in Old Testament Theology* [Downers Grove, Ill.: InterVarsity, 1979], 15–19.)
4. How are the Old Testament and New Testament "continuous" and "discontinuous"?
5. The two Testaments correspond to each other "typologically." What is typology? What are the strengths and weaknesses of using typology to unify the Old and New Testaments? (Cf. Walter C. Kaiser, *The Uses of the Old Testament in the New* [Chicago: Moody Press, 1985], 103–44.)
6. How do we account for those occasions when the New Testament writers take liberties in quoting the Old Testament text? What does this mean for the biblical doctrine of the inspiration of Scripture?

For Further Reading

Baker, D. L. *Two Testaments; One Bible.* Downers Grove, Ill.: InterVarsity, 1977 Standard work on the theological problem of the relationship between the Old and New Testaments.

Baylis, A. H. *On the Way to Jesus.* Portland, Oreg.: Multnomah, 1986. Fresh, personal, and practical survey of the Old Testament, with great appreciation for the concept of two-covenants-one-Bible.

Bruce, F. F. *New Testament Development of Old Testament Themes.* Grand Rapids: Eerdmans, 1968.

Brueggemann, Walter. *Living Toward a Vision: Biblical Reflections on Shalom.* Reprint. New York: United Church Press, 1982. Synthetic analysis of the Old Testament *shalom* and its implications for the church in light of New Testament teaching.

Dyrness, William. *Themes in Old Testament Theology.* Downers Grove, Ill.: InterVarsity, 1979.

France, R. T. *Jesus and the Old Testament.* Reprint. Grand Rapids: Baker, 1982. Detailed examination of Jesus' use of the Old Testament, with emphasis on how his interpretation shaped his understanding of his central role in salvation history.

Fuller, D. P. *Gospel and Law: Contrast or Continuum?* Grand Rapids: Eerdmans, 1980.

Kaiser, Walter C. *The Uses of the Old Testament in the New.* Chicago: Moody Press, 1985. Discussion of the hermeneutical uses of the earlier Testament in the later.

Kuske, M. *The Old Testament as the Book of Christ.* Translated by S. T. Kimbrough. Philadelphia: Westminster, 1976.

Longenecker, Richard N. *Biblical Exegesis in the Apostolic Period.* Grand Rapids: Eerdmans, 1975.

Martens, E. A. *God's Design: A Focus on Old Testament Theology.* Grand Rapids: Baker, 1981. A lucid, comprehensive, and readable description of Old Testament faith and its implications for New Testament faith.

Scott, J. B. *God's Plan Unfolded.* Revised. Wheaton, Ill.: Tyndale House, 1978.

Shires, H. M. *Finding the Old Testament in the New.* Philadelphia: Westminster, 1974.

Walton, John H. "Isaiah—What's in a Name?" *JETS* 30 (1987): 289–306.

Youngblood, Ronald. *The Heart of the Old Testament.* Grand Rapids: Baker, 1971.

Chapter 46

What We Have Learned

Major Teachings About God

Outlines fade away and kings' names often take their place only in the darkest recesses of the memory, but if nothing else is retained, the person studying the Old Testament should come away with an expanded view of God. In Exodus 3:14, as God is speaking to Moses from the burning bush, he offers "I AM" as his name, and it is from this that the name "Yahweh" is derived. The verbal form stresses the nature of Yahweh as "One who causes to be." While this has implications concerning creation and sovereignty, it can possibly be applied also to his election of Israel and his nature as the covenant-making God. His name is the introduction to his attributes. The key attributes of God emphasized in the Old Testament are summarized here by means of some of the clearest passages addressing them. These are among the greatest theological affirmations of the Old Testament.

Creator

From the hymnic verses of Amos comes one of the many characterizations of Yahweh as the almighty Creator:

He who forms the mountains,
    creates the wind,
    and reveals his thoughts to man,
he who turns dawn to darkness,
    and treads the high places of the
      earth—
the LORD God Almighty is his name.
                (Amos 4:13)

There is nothing that God did not create. As discussed in the chapter on Genesis, the point of establishing God as Creator is to establish him as the sovereign. There is a straight line of logic from Creation to Covenant to History to Eschatology.

Since God created everything, he is sovereign over everything. Nothing is beyond his power or knowledge; he is accountable or subordinate to no one; he shares his position with no other being. This is affirmed in the testimony of Job: "I know that you can do all things; no plan of yours can be thwarted" (Job 42:2). It is also foremost in God's own presentation of his credentials.

Remember the former things, those of
    long ago;
  I am God, and there is no other;
  I am God, and there is none like me.
I make known the end from the begin-
    ning,

from ancient times, what is still to
come.
I say: My purpose will stand,
and I will do all that I please. . . .

What I have said, that will I bring about;
what I have planned, that will I do.
(Isaiah 46:9–11)

Wise

Creation was not accomplished in a haphazard or arbitrary way. The Old Testament affirms on numerous occasions that God's wisdom is evident throughout creation. Wisdom personified speaks in Proverbs:

The LORD brought me forth as the first of his works, before his deeds of old; I was appointed from eternity, from the beginning, before the world began.

When there were no oceans, I was given birth, when there were no springs abounding with water; before the mountains were settled in place, before the hills, I was given birth, before he made the earth or its fields or any of the dust of the world.

I was there when he set the heavens in place, when he marked out the horizon on the face of the deep, when he established the clouds above and fixed securely the fountains of the deep, when he gave the sea its boundary so the waters would not overstep his command, and when he marked out the foundations of the earth.

Then I was the craftsman at his side. I was filled with delight day after day, rejoicing always in his presence, rejoicing in his whole world and delighting in mankind (Prov. 8:22–31).

Further expression of this is found in the great hymn to wisdom in Job:

Where then does wisdom come from? . . .

God understands the way to it and he alone knows where it dwells, for he views the ends of the earth and sees everything under the heavens.

When he established the force of the wind and measured out the waters, when he made a decree for the rain and a path for the thunderstorm, then he looked at wis-

dom and appraised it; he confirmed and tested it (Job 28:20, 23–27).

Sole God

The fact that Yahweh alone created and that he is sovereign leads inevitably to the conclusion that there is no God but Yahweh. Generally speaking, Isaiah 41–48 contain the most eloquent statements of this fact, a summary brief and to the point: "I am the LORD; that is my name! I will not give my glory to another or my praise to idols. See, the former things have taken place, and new things I declare; before they spring into being I announce them to you" (Isa. 42:8–9).

Holy

As sole God, Yahweh is distinct and separate from every other being. He is creator, not creature. This separateness is expressed in his attribute of holiness. The holiness of God is much emphasized in the Pentateuch as laws are given concerning how God is to be approached. His holiness is the standard that is to be considered the normative basis for human conduct: "Be holy because I, the LORD your God, am holy" (Lev. 19:2). His holiness is evident in situations in which it is violated (Lev. 10:1–2; 1 Sam. 6:19; 2 Sam. 6:6–10) and is proclaimed continually by the seraphim in Isaiah's vision (Isa. 6:3).

Transcendence

An attribute similar to God's holiness is his transcendence. This focuses not so much on his distinctiveness as on the fact that he is beyond us. One might say that transcendence defines the direction of his holiness. This means that we cannot always expect to understand his purposes:

"For my thoughts are not your thoughts, neither are your ways my ways," declares the LORD. "As the heavens are higher than the earth, so are my ways higher than your ways and my thoughts than your thoughts" (Isa. 55:8–9).

God warns against underestimating him:

"Am I only a God nearby," declares the Lord, "and not a God far away? Can anyone hide in secret places so that I cannot see him?" declares the Lord. "Do not I fill heaven and earth?' declares the Lord (Jer. 23:23–24).

Righteous and Just

The fact that God is holy and transcendent does not mean that he has made himself unaccountable. It is God's nature to be righteous and just, and therefore he reflects those attributes consistently. When at times it may appear that he is not being righteous or just, we cannot assume that he defines those terms arbitrarily to suit his own whims. Rather, such instances reflect our inability to see the larger picture. Righteousness and justice can only be absolute in the company of sovereignty. Our only boast is in the firsthand experience and knowledge of this God:

"Let not the wise man boast of his wisdom or the strong man boast of his strength or the rich man boast of his riches, but let him who boasts boast about this: that he understands and knows me, that I am the Lord, who exercises kindness, justice and righteousness on earth, for in these I delight" (Jer. 9:23–24).

Compassionate and Gracious

God's righteousness and justice have at times been viewed as negative attributes because they lead to the judgment of the wicked. Since no one but God can claim absolute righteousness, that puts all of humanity in jeopardy. It is therefore essential to balance God's righteousness and justice with his attributes of compassion and grace. It is these attributes that lead him to act on behalf of humanity by forgiving and by giving second chances, rather than exacting immediate punishment. They are evident in Nehemiah's prayer of confession on behalf of his forefathers.

But they were disobedient and rebelled against you; they put your law behind their backs. They killed your prophets, who had admonished them in order to turn them back to you; they committed awful blasphemies. So you handed them over to their enemies, who oppressed them. But when they were oppressed they cried out to you. From heaven you heard them, and in your great compassion you gave them deliverers, who rescued them from the hand of their enemies.

But as soon as they were at rest, they again did what was evil in your sight. Then you abandoned them to the hand of their enemies so that they ruled over them. And when they cried out to you again, you heard from heaven, and in your compassion you delivered them time after time.

You warned them to return to your law, but they became arrogant and disobeyed your commands. They sinned against your ordinances, by which a man will live if he obeys them. Stubbornly they turned their backs on you, became stiff-necked and refused to listen. For many years you were patient with them. By your Spirit you admonished them through your prophets. Yet they paid no attention, so you handed them over to neighboring peoples. But in your great mercy you did not put an end to them, or abandon them, for you are a gracious and merciful God (Neh. 9:26–31).

Covenant-Making God

The election of Israel as God's chosen people was an act of grace, not of justice. God was under no obligation to choose anyone, and there was nothing Abraham or Israel did to deserve being chosen. Once they accepted their elect status (signified by circumcision), however, they also accepted God's expectations for them.

And now, O Israel, what does the Lord your God ask of you but to fear the Lord your God, to walk in all his ways, to love him, to serve the Lord your God with all your heart and with all your soul, and to observe the

LORD's commands and decrees that I am giving you today for your own good?

To the LORD your God belong the heavens, even the highest heavens, the earth and everything in it. Yet the LORD set his affection on your forefathers and loved them, and he chose you, their descendants, above all the nations, as it is today (Deut. 10:12–15).

Loyal

Once Yahweh entered into the covenant with Israel, he was characterized by steadfast loyalty to that covenant. His loyalty in reference to both the created order and the covenant with Israel is praised in Psalm 136. The term was translated "mercy" in the King James Version and rendered "lovingkindness" by the New American Standard Bible. The NIV renders the word "love." While it is true that love, kindness, and mercy all result from Yahweh's covenant with Israel (among other things; see Deut. 7), it should be recognized that the driving force behind all these qualities was his loyalty to his elect people and the agreement that he made with them.

Redeemer

Finally, one of the most significant attributes to surface as a result of Yahweh's election of Israel is his deliverance of them. As his revelatory people, they witnessed his salvation.

> "You are my witnesses," declares the LORD, "and my servant whom I have chosen, so that you may know and believe me and understand that I am he. Before me no god was formed, nor will there be one after me. I, even I, am the LORD and apart from me there is no savior. I have revealed and saved and proclaimed—I, and not some foreign god among you.
>
> "You are my witnesses," declares the LORD, "that I am God" (Isa. 43:10–12).

One of the best Old Testament summary statements serves as a fitting conclusion: "For the LORD your God is God of gods and Lord of lords, the great God, mighty and awesome. . . . Fear the LORD your God and serve him. Hold fast to him and take your oaths in his name. He is your praise; he is your God" (Deut. 10:17, 20–21).

False Dichotomies

Once the picture of God in the Old Testament is brought into focus, it is possible to conclude that perhaps the contrasts between the nature of God in the Old Testament and in the New Testament have been too facile.

Judge vs. Savior

One often hears that in the Old Testament God can be seen as a God of judgment and punishment, while in the New Testament he is personified as a God of love and salvation. This is an inappropriate dichotomy. When we consider the span of history covered in the Old Testament and witness God's patience with Israel over centuries at a time in the face of deep-seated and obvious violation of the most basic terms of the covenant, it would be truly begging the question to complain of God's judgment. His grace is evident in acts of revelation, election, deliverance, and restoration, and these fill the pages of the Old Testament. Only the most superficial, short-sighted reading of Scripture could obscure these major aspects of Old Testament theology in the shadow of the handful of extraordinary acts of divine judgment such as the tenth plague or the obliteration of the Canaanites.

Law vs. Grace

Another frequently mentioned contrast between two Testaments is that the Old is Law and the New is Grace. It is common to hear preachers refer to the "age of law" or the "age of grace." Again, however, there are objections to be raised. Law and grace are not two ends of a spectrum. Law was what God offered to help the

Israelites to understand that who he was should affect who they were and how they acted. Law is grace in the sense that the provision of the law was an act of grace; though it is different from the grace that offered salvation to individuals in the writings of the New Testament.

"Law" applies to revelation and came through the "revelatory" people of God. "Grace" as applied to individual salvation comes to the "soteriological" people of God. To contrast law and grace, therefore, creates a misleading dichotomy. The law told Israel how God expected them to live as his covenant people—the revelatory people of God. Though it was specifically pertinent to Israelite society, it is not immaterial for the soteriological people of God from any age or place, for the holiness of God should still be the standard by which our conduct is measured. Deuteronomy shows that even the Israelites understood that the law was God's instrument for revealing his character and nature as the basis for conduct. Morality is rooted in God and does not change, though different cultures may represent morality through various approaches to the legal structuring of society.

Likewise, the grace concerning individual salvation that is offered to the soteriological people of God in the New Testament is not a totally new development in the apostolic period. The faith relationship of an individual with God is important throughout the Old Testament, but since the focus of the Old Testament is on the revelatory people of God, there is little said about personal faith or salvation. The true dichotomy is not Law vs. Grace, but Revelatory People of God vs. Soteriological People of God.

Central Theme

A pressing issue of Old Testament theology has always been the question of whether there is a central theme that brings the books of the Old Testament together. The exploration goes beyond searching out major motifs to ask whether there was a writing plan to which each author knowingly contributed. Failure to find such a center would not imply lack of coherence or even lack of unity, but if such a center exists, it would certainly help to establish the Bible as a single book rather than a collection of books. It is essential, however, that such a theme be given inductively by the text itself rather than being forced on the text.

Though many theologians today maintain that there is no distinguishable center, others have championed themes such as "covenant," "plan," or "promise" as presenting viable options. While all these should be considered central motifs, it remains difficult to substantiate that any of them was consciously addressed by each and every author of the Old Testament. Books such as Esther, Job, Ecclesiastes, Song of Songs, Nahum, and Obadiah present seemingly insuperable challenges to those who seek to defend a central agenda. Until more success is achieved in discovering a center that is inductively derived from a careful exegesis of the text, it is preferable to be content with the coherent integration that can be found by identifying the major motifs that recur with some frequency even though some books may not address them.

Having said this, we consider it appropriate to discuss the issue of the Christ, or Messiah, as the center. One cannot ignore the perspective of Jesus himself, who insisted that many of the Old Testament authors were writing of him (Luke 24:27, 44; John 5:39, 46; 12:41). It must be understood, however, what Jesus meant by this sort of statement. Surely he did not mean that every phrase referred to him. Yet, in the statements made in those contexts, he seemed to have in mind more than the obvious messianic prophecies. The most plausible suggestion is that Christ was speaking of the way that his ministry—and especially his atoning death—played a central role in the plan of God (Matt. 5:17; Mark 10:45) that had been initiated at Creation and was traced throughout the Old Testament.

This idea is supportable in general by Christ's teaching about the kingdom, but it is specifically evident in verses such as Luke 19:10. The fact that the work of Christ is central to the plan of God and that the plan of God is the most prominent motif in the Old Testament justifies the broad terminology Jesus used in referring to his relationship to the Old Testament. The Old Testament speaks of him on many different levels.

The Old Testament as a Basis for Social Action

The Old Testament promotes a worldview in which morality plays a central role. God's holiness is to be the model for our own conduct. God's justice and righteousness are to be reflected in society. The prophets frequently insisted that any return to God needs to begin by conforming one's behavior to godly standards of ethics (Amos 5:14; Isa. 58:6ff.; Mic. 6:8; Mal. 3:7). The treatment of Deuteronomy suggests that a full half of the Ten Commandments are concerned with preserving the dignity, rights, and privileges of others and honoring both explicit and implicit commitments we have to others.

It must be said, then, that in the Old Testament, faith is much more than ritual and its effects on a person's life cannot be confined to the shadow of the temple. The person of faith must exercise and promote justice in every corner of life and society. The Old Testament depicts Yahweh as provider for the needy, defender of the vulnerable, protector for the oppressed. As his people we can be no less.

Nevertheless, it must also be admitted that the Old Testament does not always offer specifics regarding a "biblical" social agenda. Many sincere people of faith find themselves on different sides of issues such as welfare, the homeless, immigration laws, abortion, ecology, and national defense. These matters are multifaceted, and their complexity often prohibits the issuing of a "biblical" position. The Old Testament, however, does not intend to answer all our questions and give conclusive advice regarding anything that happens to perplex us. By offering us a way to know God it asks only that we take that knowledge and use it to be God's people in a fallen world. That is not an excuse for inactivity where the Bible does not speak clearly, but is a clarion call to active godliness in a world of desperate needs.

Eschatological Hope

The Old Testament leaves us with hope. God is not done. Everything is under his sovereign control. His plan has not been and can never be thwarted. Our faith is an Old Testament faith that God will keep his promises no matter how bleak the circumstances may look. The New Testament contribution to that faith is that Jesus Christ made this hope incarnate and revealed in his ministry, death, and resurrection a major new component of that hope. We wait for his return and the accomplishment of God's plan as history is guided to its grand finale.

Questions for Further Study and Discussion

1. Are there ways in which the portrayal of God in the Old Testament is different from that in the New Testament? Does the New Testament place more emphasis on certain attributes than the Old? If so, which ones, and why?
2. What evidence would have to be presented to prove that there was a "center" to Old Testament theology?

3. What are the implications of the dichotomy between the terms "revelatory people of God" and "soteriological people of God" for our understanding of the continuing role of Israel in God's plan?

For Further Reading

Hasel, Gerhard. *Old Testament Theology: Basic Issues in the Current Debate.* Grand Rapids: Eerdmans, 1972.

Packer, J. I. *Knowing God.* Downers Grove, Ill.: InterVarsity, 1973.

Schmidt, Werner H. *The Faith of the Old Testament.* Philadelphia: Westminster, 1983.

Snaith, Norman H. *The Distinctive Ideas of the Old Testament.* New York: Schocken, 1964.

VanGemeren, Willem. *The Progress of Redemption.* Grand Rapids: Zondervan, 1988.

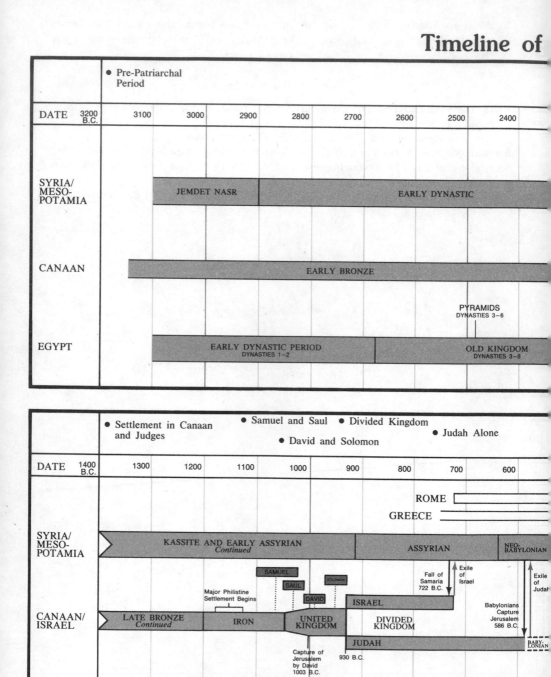

- Pre-Patriarchal Period

DATE	3200 B.C.	3100	3000	2900	2800	2700	2600	2500	2400
SYRIA/ MESO- POTAMIA			JEMDET NASR				EARLY DYNASTIC		
CANAAN					EARLY BRONZE				
EGYPT			EARLY DYNASTIC PERIOD DYNASTIES 1–2				OLD KINGDOM DYNASTIES 3–8	PYRAMIDS DYNASTIES 3–6	

- Settlement in Canaan and Judges
- Samuel and Saul
- Divided Kingdom
- David and Solomon
- Judah Alone

DATE	1400 B.C.	1300	1200	1100	1000	900	800	700	600
							ROME		
							GREECE		
SYRIA/ MESO- POTAMIA		KASSITE AND EARLY ASSYRIAN Continued				ASSYRIAN			NEO- BABYLONIAN
CANAAN/ ISRAEL	LATE BRONZE Continued	IRON		SAMUEL SAUL DAVID Major Philistine Settlement Begins	UNITED KINGDOM Capture of Jerusalem by David 1003 B.C.	SOLOMON ISRAEL DIVIDED KINGDOM JUDAH 930 B.C.		Fall of Samaria 722 B.C. Exile of Israel Babylonians Capture Jerusalem 586 B.C.	Exile of Judah BABY- LONIAN
EGYPT	NEW KINGDOM Continued			THIRD INTERMEDIATE PERIOD DYNASTIES 21–25				SAITE RENAISSANCE DYNASTY 26	

Biblical History

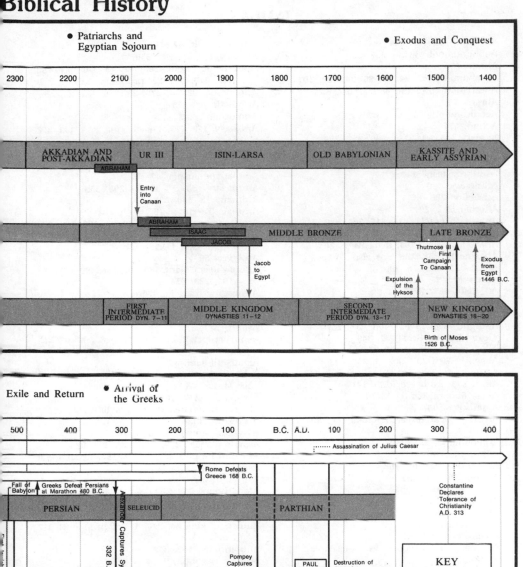

- Patriarchs and Egyptian Sojourn
- Exodus and Conquest

| 2300 | 2200 | 2100 | 2000 | 1900 | 1800 | 1700 | 1600 | 1500 | 1400 |

AKKADIAN AND POST-AKKADIAN | UR III | ISIN-LARSA | OLD BABYLONIAN | KASSITE AND EARLY ASSYRIAN

ABRAHAM

Entry into Canaan

ABRAHAM
ISAAC
JACOB
MIDDLE BRONZE
LATE BRONZE

Jacob to Egypt

Thutmose III First Campaign To Canaan

Expulsion of the Hyksos

Exodus from Egypt 1446 B.C.

FIRST INTERMEDIATE PERIOD DYN. 7–11 | MIDDLE KINGDOM DYNASTIES 11–12 | SECOND INTERMEDIATE PERIOD DYN. 13–17 | NEW KINGDOM DYNASTIES 18–20

Birth of Moses 1526 B.C.

Exile and Return

- Arrival of the Greeks

| 500 | 400 | 300 | 200 | 100 | B.C. | A.D. | 100 | 200 | 300 | 400 |

········ Assassination of Julius Caesar

Rome Defeats Greece 168 B.C.

Fall of Babylon | Greeks Defeat Persians at Marathon 480 B.C.

Constantine Declares Tolerance of Christianity A.D. 313

PERSIAN | Alexander Captures Syria, Palestine, Egypt | SELEUCID | PARTHIAN

332 B.C.

Pompey Captures Jerusalem 63 B.C.

PAUL

JESUS

Destruction of Jerusalem A.D. 70

PERSIAN | PTOLEMAIC | SELEUCID | MACCABEAN/HASMONEAN | ROMAN

Cambyses Conquers Egypt 525 B.C.

Rome Defeats Egypt 30 B.C.

LATE DYNASTIC DYNASTIES 27–31 | PTOLEMAIC DYNASTY

KEY

→ Invasion

⟶ Movement of People

INDEX